MACHINE LEARNING

An Artificial Intelligence Approach
Volume III

MACHINE LEARNING
An Artificial Intelligence Approach
Volume III

Contributors:

E. Ray Bareiss
Francesco Bergadano
Pavel B. Brazdil
Jaime G. Carbonell
Gerald F. DeJong
Kenneth A. De Jong
Brian C. Falkenhainer
Jean-Gabriel Ganascia
Yolanda Gil
Attilio Giordana
Stephen J. Hanson
David Haussler
Geoffrey I. Hinton
Haym Hirsh
Robert C. Holte
Alex Kass
Yves Kodratoff
Michael Lebowitz
Sridhar Mahadevan
Ryszard S. Michalski

Tom M. Mitchell
Michael J. Pazzani
Bruce W. Porter
Armand E. Prieditis
J. Ross Quinlan
Larry A. Rendell
Ronald L. Rivest
Roger Schank
Robert E. Schapire
Jude W. Shavlik
Pawel A. Stefanski
Louis I. Stenberg
Robert E. Stepp
Gheorghe Tecuci
Christel Vrain
Craig C. Wier
David C. Wilkins
Janusz Wnek
Zianping Zhang

Editors:

Yves Kodratoff
*French National Research Center
and George Mason University*

Ryszard S. Michalski
George Mason University

MORGAN KAUFMANN PUBLISHERS, INC.
SAN MATEO, CALIFORNIA

Editor and Publisher: *Michael B. Morgan*
Production Manager: *Shirley Jowell*
Project Management: *Jennifer Ballentine*
Cover Design: *Andrea Hendricks*
Electronic Composition: *Ocean View Technical Publications*

The publisher gratefully acknowledges permission to reproduce the following figures: 20–4, 20–5, 20–6 reprinted with permission from "Learning Internal Representations by Error Propagation," *Nature*, Vol. 323, pp. 533–536. Copyright © 1986, MacMillan Magazines, Ltd.; Figure 23–3, adapted from *The Little Prince*, by Antoine de Saint-Exupéry, © 1943 and renewed 1971, by Harcourt, Brace, Jovanovich, Inc., reprinted with permission of the publisher.

Library of Congress Cataloging-in-Publication Data
(Revised for vol. 3)

Machine learning.

    Vol. [1] previously published: Palo Alto, Calif. : Tioga Pub. Co., c1983.
    Vol. 3-   edited by Yves Kodratoff and Ryszard Michalski.
    Includes bibliographies and indexes.
    1. Machine learning. 2. Artificial intelligence.
1. Anderson, John R. (John Robert), 1947–
II. Michalski, Ryszard Stanislaw, 1937–
III. Carbonell, Jaime G. (Jaime Guillermo)
IV. Mitchell, Tom M. (Tom Mitchell), 1951–
Q325.M32 1983b   006.3'1   86-2953
ISBN 0-934613-09-5 (v. 1)
Vol. 3 ISBN 1-55860-119-8

Printed in the United States of America

10 9 8 7 6 5 4 3 2 1

MORGAN KAUFMANN PUBLISHERS, INC.
Editorial Office
2929 Campus Drive, Suite 260
San Mateo, CA 94403
415-578-9911

Order From
P.O. Box 50490
Palo Alto, CA 94303-9953
415-965-4081

CONTENTS

PREFACE

As the field of machine learning enjoys unprecedented growth and attracts many new researchers, there is a need for regular summaries and comprehensive reviews of its progress. This volume is a sequel to the previous volumes of the same title: Volume I appeared in 1983, Volume II in 1986. Volume III presents a sample of machine learning research representative of the period between 1986 and 1989.

One noteworthy characteristic of that period is that a much larger portion of research has been done outside of the United States, particularly in Europe. To reflect his, Volume III contains a significant number of non-U.S.A contributions. In addition, this volume covers topics not covered at all or covered only sparsely by the previous volumes, such as connectionist learning methods, genetic algorithms, and computational learning theory.

To provide a comprehensive representation of research, this volume has drawn on several sources. Most of the chapters are directly invited contributions by leading researchers in the field. Several chapters are updated and extended versions of invited presentations at the International Meeting on Advances in Learning (IMAL) held in Les Arcs, France in July 1986. These chapters are accompanied by commentaries prepared by the discussants at the meeting. Finally, few chapters are based on papers selected from among those presented at the 4th and 5th International Machine Learning conferences, held at the University of California at Irvine in June 1987 and the University of Michigan at Ann Arbor in June 1988, respectively.

The bibliography at the end of the book provides a comprehensive guide to these and related publications. It contains over 1000 entries and refers to publications in all major ML subareas for the period 1985–1989. All the entries are indexed, using a classification of ML publications into 17 categories.

For more complete coverage of the progress of the field, the reader is referred to relevant journals, in particular, *Machine Learning*, *Artificial Intelligence*, and *AI Magazine*, and to the proceedings of various conferences. Among the most relevant conferences are international machine learning conferences [T87, T88, T89], the meetings of the American Association for Artificial Intelligence [AAAI T86, T87 and T88], workshops on computational learning theory [COLT T88 and T89], the workshop on explanation-based learning [T88], international conferences on genetic algorithms [T87 and T89], conferences on neural nets, the European Working Sessions on Learning [EWSL T87, T88 and T89], the European congresses on artificial intelligence [ECAI T86 and T88], the International Joint Conferences on Artificial Intelligence [IJCAI T87 and T89], and International Workshop on Tools for Artificial Intelligence (1989).

It is the editors pleasant duty to thank all those who helped in the preparation of this book. Our deep gratitude goes to all the contributors for their efforts to write the chapters in a highly comprehensive and easy-to-read manner. We are very grateful to the reviewers, whose help was indispensible. We wish to thank Shirley Jowell, Production Manager for Morgan Kaufmann, for her contribution to this book.

Special thanks go to DIGITAL-EUROPE and the London office of the U.S. Army. These organizations sponsored IMAL, which gave the first impetus this volume. The editors also acknowledge the help and technical support extended to them by the faculty, staff, and research assistants of the Center for Artificial Intelligence and the Department of Computer Science at George Mason University and by the French National Research Center (CNRS).

Ryszard S. Michalski
George Mason University

Yves Kodratoff
French National Research Center (CNRS)
and George Mason University

PART
ONE

GENERAL ISSUES

1

RESEARCH IN MACHINE LEARNING:

Recent Progress, Classification of Methods, and Future Directions

Ryszard S. Michalski
(George Mason University)

Yves Kodratoff
*(CNRS, Université de Paris-Sud and
George Mason University)*

Abstract

The last few years have produced a remarkable expansion of research in machine learning. The field has gained an unprecedented popularity, several new areas have developed, and some previously established areas have gained new momentum. While symbolic methods, both empirical and knowledge intensive (in particular, inductive concept learning and explanation-based methods), continued to be exceedingly active (see Parts Two and Three of the book, respectively), subsymbolic approaches, especially neural networks, have experienced tremendous growth (Part Five). Unlike past efforts that concentrated on single learning strategies, the new trends have been to integrate different strategies and to develop cognitive learning architectures (Part Four). There has been an increasing interest in experimental comparisons of various methods, and in theoretical analyses of learning algorithms. Researchers have been sharing the same data sets and have applied their techniques to the same problems in order to understand the relative merits of different methods. Theoretical investigations have brought new insights into the complexity of learning processes (Part Six).

This chapter gives a brief account of the recent progress and prospective research directions in the field, attempts to clarify some basic concepts, proposes a multicriteria classification of learning methods, and concludes with a brief description of each chapter.

1.1 INTRODUCTION

One of the most striking differences between how people and computers work is that humans, while performing any kind of activity, usually simultaneously expend efforts to improve the way they perform it. This is to say that human performance of any task is inseparably intertwined with a learning process, while current computers are typically only executors of procedures supplied to them. They may execute very efficiently, but they do not self-improve with experience.

Research in machine learning has been concerned with building computer programs able to construct new knowledge or to improve already possessed knowledge by using input information. So far, this input information (examples, facts, descriptions, etc.) has been typically typed in by a human instructor. Future machine learning programs will undoubtedly be able to receive inputs directly from the environment through a variety of sensory devices.

The great appeal of this field to its practitioners is that machine learning offers an immense diversity of research tasks and testing grounds. This diversity is due to the fact that learning can accompany any kind of problem solving or process, and thus it can be studied in many different contexts, such as decision making, classification, sensory signal recognition, problem solving, task execution, control, or planning.

This continual appeal of the field has been enhanced recently by the fact that progress in machine learning has become central to the development of the field of artificial intelligence (AI) as a whole and affects almost all of its subareas. In particular, the work in machine learning has importance for expert systems development, problem solving, computer vision, speech understanding, autonomous robotics, conceptual analysis of databases, and intelligent tutoring systems. Consequently, the development of powerful learning systems may ultimately open an unprecedented range of new applications (e.g., [Michalski, 1986]).

Research on building learning programs goes back almost to the beginning of the computer area. After the first significant burst of research on perceptrons and self-organizing systems in the 1950s and the first few years of the 1960s, the field has been growing slowly but steadily. Some early successes include, for example, the Samuel's checkers program [Samuel, 1959], Winston's program for learning structural descriptions [Winston, 1970; 1975], the Meta-DENDRAL program for heuristic rule formation [Buchanan, Feigenbaum, and Sridharan, 1972], the AM and EURISKO discovery programs [Lenat, 1977; 1983], AQ11 for diagnostic rule learning [Michalski and Chilausky, 1980], LEX for learning symbolic integration [Mitchell, Utgoff, and Banerji, 1983], and CLUSTER for conceptual clustering [Michalski and Stepp, 1983].

These successes and the ever-present challenge to build powerful learning systems, have exerted strong pressure to expand the activities in this field. The first machine learning workshop was held at Carnegie Mellon University (CMU) in 1980. This workshop and the publication in 1983 of the first volume of *Machine Learning* [Michalski, Carbonell, and Mitchell, 1983] marked a breaking point. These two events gave the field a clear identity and a sense of direction, which in turn stimulated the rapid growth that has continued unabated since then.

There have been subsequent workshops and conferences: at the University of Illinois at Urbana-Champaign in 1983, at Rutgers University in 1985, at the University of California at Irvine in 1987, at the University of Michigan in 1988, and at Cornell University in 1989. In 1986, *Machine Learning, Volume II* appeared [Michalski, Carbonell, and Mitchell, 1986]. In response to the growing need for an adequate forum for presenting research progress, *Machine Learning* journal was established in 1986.

There have also been numerous workshops and meetings on special topics, such as computational learning theory (COLT 88 and 89), explanation-based learning (AAAI workshop at Stanford University, 1988), connectionist models of learning (e.g., summer schools at CMU in 1986 and 1988 and a number of international conferences), and knowledge discovery in databases (IJCAI-89 workshop in Detroit).

In parallel, there has been a rapid increase of interest in machine learning in Europe, as signified by many activities, meetings, and conferences. Among the most noteworthy were the European Working Sessions on Learning (Orsay 1986, Bled 1987, Glasgow 1988, and Montpellier 1989), the International Meeting on Advances in Learning in Les Arcs in 1986, the workshop on Knowledge Representation and Organization in Machine Learning (KROML 1987), Workshop on Machine Learning, Metareasoning and Logic (Sesimbra 1988), and Summer Schools in Machine Learning (Les Arcs 1988 and Urbino 1989), International Schools for the Synthesis of Knowledge (ISSEK 1987 and 1989). To reflect these activities, this volume includes a significant number of non-U.S. contributions.

1.2 RECENT DEVELOPMENTS

The last few years have witnessed both a continuation of the major traditional research approaches and a rapid increase of interest in several new methodologies. The most active research area in recent years has continued to be symbolic empirical learning (SEL). This area is concerned with creating and/or modifying general symbolic descriptions, whose structure is unknown *a priori*. This type of learning can be contrasted with, e.g., learning weights assigned to connections in a given neural net, or coefficients of equations in a predefined form. The descriptions are created on the basis of examples or specific facts. The word "empirical" signifies the fact that the learning process does not require much prior knowledge of the learner (if the process relies on a large amount of explicitly stated prior knowledge, then we have knowledge-intensive symbolic learning).

An important criterion underlying SEL methods is that knowledge created by a learning program is supposed to be easy for humans to interpret and comprehend. This means that there is a concern to make knowledge representations simple in terms of the structures used and the number of operators involved. It also means that the concepts employed in the descriptions should directly correspond to those used by human experts. This criterion is sometimes called the *comprehensibility principle* [Michalski, 1983]. Typical knowledge structures employed in the SEL systems include commonly used symbolic representations, such as logic-based descriptions, rules, decision trees, semantic networks, equations, frames, and grammars. Due to the comprehensibily criterion, the SEL systems can be particularly useful in applications in which people need to fully comprehend the results of learning—for example, in technical, medical, or agricultural diagnosis; decision making, planning, economic or political analysis; discovery of knowledge in databases, prediction, etc.

The most common topic in SEL is developing concept descriptions from concept examples. The machine learning bibliography (MLB; the last chapter of this book), which contains 1050 entries covering the period 1985—89, lists about 190 publications on this topic. Other major topics in SEL include qualitative discovery, conceptual clustering, and empirical sequence prediction. The MLB lists another 130 publications on these topics; thus together, there are about 320 papers listed in the MLB on symbolic empirical learning.

As mentioned above, empirical methods typically use relatively little background knowledge, by which we mean the relevant domain-dependent knowledge, such as facts or rules characterizing the application domain, and domain-independent knowledge, such as general definitional knowledge, commonsense knowledge, and explicit rules of inference, which the learner can bring to bear in the process of learning. In SEL systems, the background knowledge may include merely information about the value sets and types of attributes or terms (descriptors) used, the constraints on the attributes, preference criteria or biases for judging candidate solutions, etc. The domain-dependent information can be introduced to a program when it is applied to a particular problem, and therefore it is relatively easy to develop a general-purpose empirical learning program. The AQ family of rule learning programs (e.g., [Michalski, 1973; and Chapter 3, this volume], and the ID3-type decision tree learning programs [Quinlan, 1979; and Chapter 5, this volume] are examples of such general-purpose SEL systems. The AQ programs generate rules by manipulating knowledge structures according to rules of inference and knowledge transformation. The ID3-type systems create a decision tree by a recursive selection of attributes from a given set. The attribute selection is based on statistical considerations (e.g., the *minimum entropy rule*), rather than on explicit rules of inference.

The primary inference type used by SEL methods is *empirical induction*. This form of induction (as other forms, such as constructive induction and abduction, see the next section) is a falsity-preserving, rather than truth-preserving inference. Therefore, the results of SEL methods are generally hypotheses, which need to be validated by further experiments. This is often viewed as an important weakness of the empirical methods. It reflects the intrinsic uncertainty of any process of creating new knowledge about the world, and therefore is unavoidable in principle. The only way to circumvent it is to restrict the learning process either to copying existing knowledge or to strict deductions from knowledge that has been tested and assumed to be true. Such an *a priori* knowledge has to be encoded into the system before any learning can occur (see analytic methods in the next section).

Another weakness of the SEL methods is that the knowledge learned by them represents relations expressed merely in terms of attributes or concepts either directly specified in the input data, or closely related to them (an empirical program may include procedures for transforming the initial description space). Because the methods rely primarily on the input information, rather than on background knowledge, they cannot discover complex relationships or causal dependencies, which require high-level terms or concepts, not provided by the input.

The fact that symbolic empirical methods do not use/require much background knowledge is appealing to many researchers. Examples or observations are often easily available from existing databases or can be measured by sensors. There is no need for debugging and handcrafting large amounts of knowledge into the system. Consequently, empirical learning systems are readily applicable to a wide spectrum of practical problems. In addition, because the results are usually easy to interpret (in contrast to subsymbolic systems; see below), the methods are particularly attractive in application areas where understandability of the results is an important factor. A selection of research in symbolic empirical learning is presented in Part Two, Chapters 3 through 9.

In recent years, there have been various efforts to extend the capabilities of conventional SEL systems. A considerable amount of work has been done on learning concepts from imperfect inputs, e.g., learning from examples with noise (see Chapter 5). Related efforts have been concerned with learning concepts that lack precise definition and/or are context dependent (see Chapter 3).

Another major extension of empirical methods addresses the problem of employing more background knowledge in the process of inductively creating concept descriptions. The motivation is that people, due to their prior knowledge, can often create plausible inductive hypotheses from a few, or just one, instances. For example, if one sees a single window of a particular style in a tall skyscraper, then one does not need to look at other windows to hypothesize that all the windows in that building are of this style. The reason is that we know that windows in a building are typically made in the same style. As another example, consider a person who deceptively misinforms others about something really important. Usually, it would not take more than one such instance to cause others to never trust that person in the future. Again, this is because of a common belief, that if a person lied once, it is likely that this person may continue such behavior, and trusting such a person would carry a very high risk. Thus, by involving prior knowledge, one can create plausible inductive hypotheses from very little input information, contrary to some beliefs about inductive learning.

Also, in many applications, it is important to discover relationships that go beyond associations between inputs and outputs. In such applications, it is important to search for relationships that involve higher level concepts than those defined in the inputs, to generate and employ abstract attributes and relations, and/or to determine causal explanations of the observations. Any process of theory formation requires much background knowledge in addition to observational data.

To this end, some researchers started to work on *constructive induction*, which is a term for characterizing inductive processes that engage significant amount of background knowledge ([Michalski, 1983]; see also [Muggleton and Buntine, 1988; Rouveirol and Puget, 1989]). Such background knowledge may be in the form of expert-given domain knowledge rules, logical implications and equivalences, abstract concept definitions, heuristic procedures for generating new concepts, goal-oriented criteria for evaluating the importance of created knowledge, and others. This knowledge may be used in the conventional, deductive manner, thus, constructive induction typically includes a large component of deductive inference. Equipped with appropriate background knowledge, constructive inductive systems can change the representation of the problem or invent new attributes or concepts. As described in ([Michalski, 1990]; see also Section 1.3), constructive induction involves "reverse reasoning" or "tracing backward" of certain implicative rules, which are either *domain-independent* (tautological implications) or *domain-dependent* (representing domain knowledge). When domain-independent rules are primarily involved (specifically, the falsity-preserving generalization rules), then constructive induction reduces to empirical induction. When certain domain-dependent implicative relationships are "traced backward," then such induction becomes abduction (see next section). There are over 50 publications listed in the MLB in the area of constructive induction, abduction, and representation change.

Other classes of empirical learning systems include parametric and heterogeneous systems. In parametric systems, the learning process involves a modification of certain parameters or weights associated with predefined structures (networks, equations, production rules, etc.). Learning in heterogeneous systems involves both a direct modification of knowledge structures and a modification of the parameters associated with these structures. The most popular and important representative of parametric systems are neural nets and connectionist systems. In those systems, the learning process typically involves a modification of the strength of the connections between units in a statically or dynamically defined network. All units often perform the same general transformation, and therefore it is easy to build very large networks of that kind. It is important to note that a modification of the strengths of connections in a neural network can lead to a change in the knowledge structure. This structural change, however, is indirect and implicit, rather than direct and explicit, like in symbolic systems. The most explored subsets of heterogeneous systems are genetic algorithms and classifier systems. In those systems, the modification of the structures is done either by random changes (mutation), or semirandom changes (crossover), rather than by explicit rules of inference, like in typical symbolic systems. The weights assigned to individual production rules represent their importance or effectiveness in performing the assigned task.

Recent years have witnessed a remarkable renaissance of research on learning in neural networks. There is rapidly growing interest in exploring their properties and potential applications. Since these systems employ a general and uniform knowledge representation, and typically use little background knowledge, it is easy to implement them and apply them experimentally to a wide spectrum of problems. As they require very little guidance from a teacher, they are very appealing to many researchers.

A major limitation of neural networks and genetic algorithms is the difficulty of introducing large amounts of domain specific knowledge to them, and explicitly exploiting that knowledge or any feedback information in the learning process. To explain the latter, suppose that a neural network or genetic algorithm gets feedback that some example was incorrectly classified. To take care of the mistake, the system modifies its knowledge representation by stepwise corrections, rather than by an explicit analysis of the reasons for the mistake. This seems to explain why such systems tend to exhibit relatively slow rates of learning. Another weakness is the lack of transparency of the results of learning. The knowledge acquired by neural networks or conventional genetic algorithms is not in the form that people can easily understand. The comprehensibility principle has not been viewed as a major issue in implementing such systems. For that reason, they are sometimes called *subsymbolic learning systems*.

The lack of transparency is not necessarily always a problem. There are many application domains that do not require that the knowledge learned be easy to understand. For example, it is not important to understand the control algorithm of a robot, as long as it can move its hand to the given destination and within a defined space. This weakness is only a problem in areas where people need to understand the knowledge underlying the system's behavior; e.g., in diagnostic, advisory, or planning systems. It can be pointed out that a genetic algorithm could potentially be applied with a high-level symbolic knowledge representation (such a method would not be classified as subsymbolic any more). So far, relatively little has been done in this direction, and therefore it is difficult to predict how successful such methods will be. Some recent experimental studies seem to suggest that in tasks involving learning "human-type" concepts from noise-free examples, symbolic empirical methods might be better than subsymbolic ones both in terms of the error rate and the complexity of the descriptions learned [Wnek, *et al.*, 1990].

The MLB lists a selection of about 50 papers on learning in connectionist systems (neural networks) and about 60 papers on learning using genetic algorithms. This book includes review chapters on subsymbolic learning systems (Chapters 20 and 21).

The primary goal of the symbolic and subsymbolic empirical learning methods, as well as the knowledge-intensive constructive induction systems, is to create a "fundamentally new" knowledge from the given input information. "Fundamentally new" means knowledge that cannot be deduced from the knowledge already known. Therefore, such systems can be classified as *synthetic learning systems.*

Synthetic systems can be contrasted with analytic learning systems, whose primary goal is to analyze and transform the knowledge already possessed into more effective or "operational" form. Analytic systems rely on large amounts of prior knowledge and use deduction as the primary inference. Because such inference is truth-preserving, the results of analytic learning are as valid as the background knowledge and the input information supplied to them. Thus, if one can assume that the background knowledge and the input facts are correct, the results of learning need not be validated. This feature makes analytic systems very appealing to many researchers.

The last several years have seen a major and rapid growth of research in the area of analytic learning. In this area, the most active research was on explanation-based learning (EBL), which is concerned with explaining an observed example in terms of the learner's background knowledge, and then using this explanation for creating a more effective or "operational" concept description. In "pure" EBL, the background knowledge must be complete, consistent, and tractable, so that the program can deduce a consistent explanation of the input example from it.

Determining such a consistent, complete, and tractable background knowledge and handcrafting it to the program may require a substantial effort, and thus it is often not easy to apply EBL in a practical setting. Also, domain knowledge is frequently incomplete or not totally correct, and one needs to apply an inductive method to improve it or to fill in the holes. A recent trend has been to combine EBL methods with inductive techniques in order to cope with such situations.

The above effort on extending analytic methods by adding to them inductive learning capabilities seems to be a mirror image of research on constructive induction that extends empirical methods by introducing to them more domain knowledge and more powerful deductive capabilities. One may also note that EBL or other analytic methods do not address the problem of learning abstract concept descriptions or specifications, as these are assumed to be given to the system. For such problems, inductive methods are necessary. The MLB lists about 170 publications on explanation-based learning and related methods. A selection of research in this area is presented in Part Three, Chapters 10 through 14.

There has been a growing understanding that future learning systems should not be centered around a single learning strategy in acquiring knowledge but should combine several strategies in a goal-oriented fashion. In this context, there is an interest in moving from single-strategy-oriented systems to multistrategy systems [Michalski, 1990]. Most work in this direction has so far been concentrated on developing learning systems that integrate empirical and explanation-based learning methods and building large-scale cognitive architectures. The MLB lists about 65 publications in this area. A selection of research is described in Chapters 15 through 19.

In view of the proliferation of different learning methods and paradigms, there has been growing interest in experimental investigation and comparison of various learning methods. The MLB lists about 60 publications in this area. Several chapters of this volume report results of various experimental comparisons of learning methods.

A significant amount of activity and major progress has also occurred in the area of computational theory of machine learning algorithms. A large portion of this work has been concerned with *probably approximately correct* (PAC) *concept learning methods*, originally introduced by Valiant (see Chapter 22). There is a considerable and growing interest in this area, as evidenced by 120 papers listed in the MLB. A selection of research in this area is in Chapters 22 and 23.

Concluding, one might ask about the expected future role of the symbolic versus subsymbolic approaches in machine learning. It appears that both these approaches will be useful for various classes of applications. Ultimately, however, machine learning systems must be able to acquire and use vast amounts of diverse human knowledge, perform all kinds of inference, and to explain their knowledge to people. These qualities and functions seem to be easier to implement in symbolic systems. Therefore, some authors believe that symbolic systems will likely continue to play a "preeminent" role in the field of machine learning [Michalski and Littman, 1989].

1.3 SYNTHETIC VERSUS ANALYTIC LEARNING

As mentioned above, learning processes can be classified into *synthetic* and *analytic* on the basis of their main goal. Synthetic learning aims primarily at creating new or better knowledge, and analytic learning aims primarily at reformulating given knowledge into a better form. Synthetic learning employs induction as the primary inference, and analytic learning employs deduction as the primary inference. To explain the difference between these two classes of learning processes, one needs to clarify the meaning of these two types of inference.

Inductive inference has been often misunderstood, and different authors have defined it in different ways. One view is that induction is merely an empirical generalization of examples without using much prior knowledge. Another view is that induction includes every inference process under uncertainty, i.e., any inference that is not strictly deductive (e.g., [Holland, *et al.*, 1986]. Both views are somewhat extreme. The first one is clearly inconsistent with mainstream scientific thoughts on this subject, which go back to Aristotle [1987]), while the second seems to be overly general. Our view is that induction is simply a process opposite of deduction. While deduction is a derivation of consequents from given premises, induction is a process of hypothesizing premises that entail given consequents.

The above is a very simplified characterization of these inference types, and it does not explain the role of the reasoner's background knowledge and other important issues involved in these processes. Let us then analyze these processes in a more detailed way.

Consider a relationship stating that P and BK entails C:

$$P \And BK \vdash C \tag{1}$$

where P is a premise, BK stands for the relevant reasoner's background knowledge, and C is a consequent. If the reasoner observes P (e.g., it is a newly perceived fact), then using its prior knowledge the reasoner can conclude by deduction that C must be true. A weak form of deduction is when the entailment does not always hold, an observation matches P only partially, or BK is not totally certain. On the other hand, if the reasoner observes C, then it may hypothesize P, because it would entail (explain or generalize) the observation. This is an inductive inference. Its type depends on the nature and the role of background knowledge, particularly, on whether the background knowledge includes only domain-independent knowledge (e.g., tautological implications), domain-dependent knowledge (reflecting the properties observed in the world), or both.

Based on these distinctions, inductive processes can be classified into three categories:

- *Empirical induction*, in which the system creates an inductive hypothesis on the basis of the given facts, using primarily domain-independent background knowledge (tautological implications or valid logical statements). A particularly important instance of empirical induction is empirical reasoning from particulars to universals, i.e., empirical inductive generalization. It can be viewed as a special form of reasoning from effects to premises, which is guided by "generalization rules" [Michalski, 1983]. These are domain-independent, falsity-preserving rules, which reverse certain tautological implications. Domain-dependent knowledge plays only a supportive role—for example, providing the constraints on the set of possible attribute values, specifying relations that hold among these attribute values, and influencing the preference criterion.

Consider, for example, a tautological implication (a domain-independent rule): ($\forall$ x $\in$ S, P(x)) $\Rightarrow$ (P(e), e $\in$ S), which states that if a property holds for all instances then it must hold for some particular instance. Tracing such a rule backward—that is, concluding that P holds for all x from the set by observing that it holds for one or more elements of this set—is an empirical induction. The plausibility of such induction depends on how *typical* event e is in the set S [Collins and Michalski, 1989], and on the general knowledge about the property P. For example, if one is very happy with a car made by a particular company, then one may conclude that all cars made by this company are good and recommend the company to a friend. The strength of this conclusion will depend on the degree to which the car can be viewed as typical of this company, and on the degree of belief that the quality of a product is preserved across all products of a company. If the latter belief is nonexistent or weak, then the conclusion is highly empirical. If the belief represents a relatively strong background knowledge, then the inference becomes a form of constructive induction (see below). Finally, if the belief represents proven knowledge, then the inference becomes an ordinary deduction.

- *Abduction*, a form of reasoning introduced by Peirce in his classic and influential treatise *Elements of Logic* [Peirce, 1965]. Abduction, as defined by Peirce (also referred to by him as *retroduction*), is "the operation of adopting an explanatory hypothesis that would account for all the facts or some of them." In Peirce's abduction such a hypothesis can be obtained by tracing backward rules that express relationships among facts about the domain, i.e., domain-dependent rules. For example, consider a (domain-dependent) rule: $\forall$ x $\in$ {locations} [fire(x) $\Rightarrow$ smoke(x)]. Tracing such a rule backward—hypothesizing that there may be fire—if one observes smoke is abduction.

  Usually, domain knowledge does not include many rules that point to the same consequent. For that reason Peirce and other workers on abduction usually ignore the issue of the preference criterion for choosing an explanatory hypothesis. This issue would arise, however, when more than one candidate hypothesis can be generated abductively. Therefore, the general formulation of induction (see equation (2), below) includes the preference criterion as an important component.

- *Constructive induction* (knowledge-based induction), in which creating a hypothesis may involve both the domain-dependent and the domain-independent background knowledge. In this formulation, constructive induction includes both constructive inductive generalization, which uses background knowledge rules to create higher level generalizations, and abduction that produces explanations. The domain knowledge can be used both deductively and inductively, i.e., for forward and backward tracing of implicative relationships. For example, suppose that the background knowledge of a learner includes a rule that a high degree of automation in a company leads to high reliability of the product. If one learns that a particular company has completely automated automobile production, and observes a car of that company that is highly reliable, then one may hypothesize that all cars of this company are very reliable (this would be a forward tracing of the background knowledge rule; the example is not actually needed, but it helps remove the possibility that the automation was not implemented properly). On the other hand, if one sees a highly reliable car, one may create a hypothetical explanation that the company that produced it may be highly automated (this would be a backward tracing of the background knowledge rule).

As another example of combining empirical generalization with deduction, suppose one notices several students working late into the night in the AI Laboratory. A conclusion that all students in the laboratory are hard-working is a constructive induction. It involves a step of empirical generalization (from several students to all) and a weak deduction (from working late into the night to being hard-working). As an example of combining empirical generalization and abduction, suppose that someone observed smoke coming out from different parts of a building. By constructive induction one may conclude that the whole building is on fire (reasoning from different parts of the building to the whole building is empirical generalization; reasoning from smoke to fire is abduction).

It should be mentioned, that the original formulation of constructive induction [Michalski, 1983] emphasized using background knowledge for developing new concepts or attributes, beyond those supplied in the input. However, depending on the type and the way background knowledge is used, the new concepts so created can serve both for creating generalizations or explanatory hypotheses. Therefore, the idea of constructive induction can be viewed generally as an inference that includes constructive generalization, abduction, or a combination of the two.

Finally, one needs to mention that induction is usually an underconstrained problem, and there may be many possible hypotheses generalizing or explaining given facts. Thus, a general formulation of induction is that, given a consequent C (an observational statement, partial knowledge, etc.) and background knowledge BK, the reasoner searches for a premise P (a hypothesis) such that P & BK strongly or weakly entails C, which we write:

$$P \& BK \mid > C \qquad\qquad (2)$$

and which satisfies a preference criterion. This criterion (also called *bias*) specifies extra-logical conditions for selecting a hypothesis among other candidate hypotheses, i.e, the ones that satisfy equation (2). These conditions may include, e.g., a preference for a simpler hypothesis, a more plausible one (based on the learner's back-ground knowledge), the least costly to use, a hypothesis that is expressed in a certain form, or a combination of such criteria.

1.4 A MULTICRITERIA CLASSIFICATION OF LEARNING PROCESSES

Learning processes can be classified from many different viewpoints, for ex-ample, the type of strategy used, the research orientation, the type of knowledge rep-resentation, the application areas, etc. These classifications have been described and discussed in [Michalski, Carbonell, and Mitchell, 1983 and 1986]. Here, we will pro-pose a classification that is based on a few interrelated criteria and intended to help the reader get a general view of the whole field. As with any classification, its valid-ity can be judged by the degree it illustrates important distinctions among various categories.

The categories presented in Figure 1–1 should not be viewed as having pre-cisely delineated, sharp borderlines, but rather as labels for central tendencies that can be continuously transformed from one to another. The criteria for classification include the primary purpose of the learning method, the type of input information, the type of primary inference employed, and finally, the role of the learner's prior knowledge in the learning process. This classification is based on [Michalski, 1990].

As mentioned above, from the viewpoint of the primary purpose, learning methods can be classified into synthetic and analytic. The primary purpose of syn-thetic methods is to create new or better knowledge, while the primary purpose of the analytic methods is to transform or organize the prior knowledge into a better form according to some goal.

If the input to a synthetic learning method are examples classified by an inde-pendent source of knowledge—for example, a teacher, an expert, a simulation model, etc.—then we have learning from examples (e.g., see Chapter 3). When the input are facts that need to be classified or organized into a knowledge structure by the learner itself, then we have learning from observation. An example of the latter is conceptual clustering (e.g., [Stepp and Michalski, 1986]). Connectionist methods, genetic algorithms, and qualitative discovery have been classified into empirical in-ductive methods. This is because they rely on relatively small amounts of back-ground knowledge, and their primary inference type is inductive. This inference, however, can be executed in an explicit way, as in typical symbolic methods, or in an implicit way, as in subsymbolic methods.

As described in Section 1.2, inductive learning can be empirical (BK-poor) or constructive (BK-intensive). Empirical induction can be viewed conceptually as "tracing backward" tautological implications, e.g., domain-independent generaliza-tion rules. The most common work in this area deals with empirical generalization, which creates general descriptions from specific examples using basically concepts

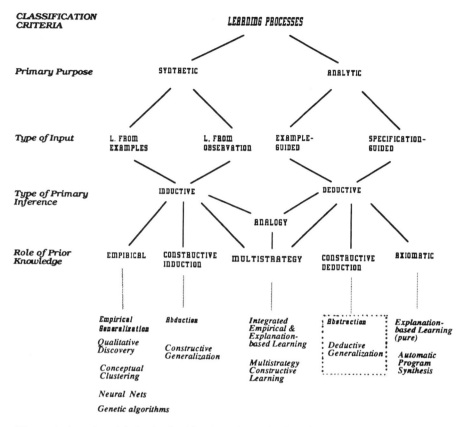

Figure 1–1:   A multicriteria classification of machine learning methods

(attributes) that are present in the descriptions of the examples. In contrast, constructive induction is a knowledge-intensive induction that uses background knowledge to create new concepts, explanations, or high-level characterizations of the input information. The input information can be in the form of low-level specific facts or descriptions at higher levels of abstraction.

There is an additional classification within inductive methods, which is not shown Figure 1–1, but represents some existing research. A concept description can be matched with examples in a simple and direct way, or can employ a substantial amount of background knowledge and inference. Case-based or exemplar-based methods use past facts as concept characterizations and employ relatively sophisticated matching procedures that allow the system to recognize new examples that do not directly match any past example (Chapter 4). Such a process can be characterized as a "dynamic" induction that is performed during the matching process (or the recognition process). The method based on the two-tiered concept representation (Chapter 3), uses a general concept description and employs a matching procedure that can potentially include any kind of inference.

As mentioned earlier, abduction can be conceptually classified as a form of induction, which "traces backward" certain domain-dependent knowledge rules. Such a characterization can be illustrated, for example, by an abductive recovery of failed proofs [Cox and Pietrzykowski, 1986; Duval and Kodratoff, 1990]. A trivial way to recover from a failure would be to add the needed theorem into the knowledge base. The technique described determines the place where the proof encounters an impasse, and then proposes a minimal hypothesis necessary to achieve the missing step. The minimal hypothesis is determined by analyzing the obtained partial proof and "tracing backward" certain domain-dependent knowledge.

To reformulate its knowledge, an analytic method can be guided by an example or by a knowledge specification. The example-guided methods include explanation-based learning [DeJong, 1981; DeJong and Mooney, 1986], explanation-based-generalization [Mitchell, et al., 1986], and explanation-based specialization [Minton, 1988; Minton, et al., 1989]. The specification-guided methods include automatic program synthesis, operationalization, and advice taking (e.g., [Biermann, Guiho, and Kodratoff, 1984]).

Explanation-based learning is classified as an example of an axiomatic method, because it is based on a pure deductive process utilizing complete and consistent background knowledge. This knowledge plays a role analogous to axioms in formal theories. The automatic program synthesis is a process of transforming a program specification into an executable algorithm. While specification tells the system what relations should hold between the inputs and outputs, an algorithm specifies how these relations can be achieved. This process of automatic program synthesis uses truth-preserving deductive techniques to ensure the logical equivalence between the program and its specification [Biermann, et al., 1984].

In synthetic methods, the primary inference type is inductive; and in analytic methods, the primary inference type is deductive. *Learning by analogy* has been placed between inductive and deductive learning, because it can be viewed as a combination of both. Learning by analogy involves transferring certain properties of the base knowledge (a concept, a procedure, etc.) into the target knowledge. Such a transfer includes elements of both inductive and deductive learning. To recognize (or discover) an analogy, one needs to detect a similarity or common relations between the base and the target knowledge and hypothesize that it might extend beyond the compared relations. This is primarily an inductive process. Once these common relations have been determined, then the transfer of properties from the base to the target knowledge is deductive.

For instance, consider an example of a ruthless dictator, say, Ceausescu of Romania, who governed by intimidation and deceit and eventually was ousted in a brutal way. Suppose that there is a person, say, Patrick, a "small-time" dictator, who imposes his will on others by scheming and manipulation. The first phase of the analogy is to detect a certain similarity in the attitude and general behavior between the two individuals, although the specifics are very different, and then to hypothesize that the detected similarity may extend to other correlated aspects of the comparison. This is an inductive phase of analogy. The second, deductive phase, is to develop a prediction that Patrick may also end up badly, though on a correspondingly smaller scale.

In machine learning, analogy has been usually used either to learn concepts or to learn problem-solving algorithms. Illustrative examples of analogical concept learning are described in [Winston, 1982] and [Burstein, 1986]. A theoretical framework and a method for analogical problem solving is presented in [Carbonell, 1986]. Because analogical learning combines two fundamental inference types, it has a widespread presence and is interwoven into many learning processes.

By *multistrategy learning systems* are meant systems that combine several basic strategies and/or paradigms. Many current systems are concerned primarily with integrating empirical generalization and explanation-based learning. Part Four presents several examples of recent research in this area. Future multistrategy systems will undoubtedly integrate other strategies and paradigms, including possibly combinations of symbolic and subsymbolic learning methods [Michalski, 1990]. Such multistrategy systems will be capable of adapting the learning strategy to the task at hand, and cope with learning problems involving various kinds of imperfection of background knowledge and/or the input data and by that will be applicable to a wide range of learning situations.

As the famous precedent of the Mendeleev classification of elements has shown, a possible effect of a taxonomy is helping to identify or introduce a new field even before its actual appearance. Such a field may be suggested by trying to balance a taxonomy. The concept of *constructive deduction* and its subdivision to abstraction and deductive generalization (the dotted rectangle in Figure 1–1) seems to play such a role, as it identifies a general research area and relates it to other areas.

By *constructive deduction* is meant a knowledge-based process of transforming descriptions from one representation space or language to another, which preserves information important for an assumed goal. Abstraction is classified as a constructive deduction, which transforms a description at a high level of detail to a description at a low level of detail while preserving the truth of the relations and/or properties relevant to the assumed goal. In other words, while reducing the total information content of the original description, abstraction preserves the information important to performing an implicitly or explicity defined goal. Depending on the goal, a given description can be abstracted in many different ways. Each such process is essentially deductive, as it is not supposed to introduce or hypothesize any information that is not contained in the initial description or information source, or which cannot be deductively inferred from it using the learner's background knowledge. The difference between constructive deduction and what we call *axiomatic deduction* is that the former emphasizes a change in the representation space or language and may use a variety of knowledge transformations, rather than strictly logic-based formal methods. Although constructive deduction is essentially truth-preserving, it may also include elements of inductive inference and approximate reasoning.

Abstraction is sometimes confused with generalization. To see the difference, note that generalization transforms descriptions along the set-superset dimension and may be falsity-preserving, as in the case of inductive generalization, or truth-preserving, as in the case of deductive generalization ([Michalski and Zemankowa, 1990]; see Section 1.5). In contrast, abstraction transforms descriptions along the level-of-detail dimension and is truth-preserving with regard to the characteristics of the entity or entities important for the assumed goal. While generalization often uses the same description space (or language), abstraction often involves a change in the representation space (or language). The reason generalization and abstraction are frequently confused may be the fact that many processes include both of them.

Deductive generalization is concerned with making generalizations that are logical deductions from the base knowledge. It differs from abstraction as it moves from considering a set to considering a superset and typically uses the same representation formalism. For example, transforming a statement "George Mason University is in Fairfax" to "George Mason University is in Virginia" is a deductive generalization. In contrast, changing a high-resolution digitized satellite image of Fairfax into a low-resolution image is a simple form of abstraction. A more sophisticated abstraction would be to use the high-resolution image and appropriate background knowledge to create a map of Fairfax, which emphasizes important (according to the goal) aspects of the area. Research on problem representation, transformation of problem representation spaces, determination of a representative set of attributes, deductive transformation of a knowledge base, and related topics can be classified under the rubric of constructive deduction.

The above discussion suggests that in parallel to multistrategy learning systems, a potentially important research area in machine learning is multirepresentation learning systems (not shown in the classification). Such systems would employ various forms of constructive deduction or induction to create and use representations at different levels of abstraction, and/or apply different description languages in the process of learning. The use of these descriptions and languages would depend on the task at hand and on the application domain. The importance of this area has been acknowledged very early by pattern recognition researchers [Bongard, 1970], as well as by AI researchers [Newell, 1969; Amarel, 1970]. Nevertheless, it has received relatively little attention during recent years. Among notable exceptions are [Amarel, 1986] and [Mozetic, 1989].

Summarizing, we have distinguished three pairs of overlapping but different reasoning and learning mechanisms. Each pair contains two opposing processes, which are concerned with different aspects of reasoning and knowledge transformation. Two of these pairs have been relatively well explored in machine learning: deduction/induction and generalization/specialization. The third pair, which has been relatively less studied, consists of abstraction and its reverse, which we propose to call *concretion* (after Webster's dictionary, which defines it as being a process of concretizing something). These three types of mechanisms can be combined in different ways, giving some classical, well-known reasoning mechanisms and some less known. The classical ones include inductive generalization and deductive specialization. Less investigated are inductive specialization, abstraction, deductive generalization, inductive concretion, and others.

The above "grand" classification appears to be the first attempt to characterize and relate all major methods and subareas of machine learning within one general scheme. As such, this attempt may suffer from various weaknesses and imprecision and can be criticized on various grounds. Its primary purpose is to try to help the reader, especially a novice in this field, to view different learning mechanisms and paradigms as parts of a one general structure, rather than as a collection of unclearly related components and research efforts. By analyzing this classification, the reader may be stimulated to improve it or to develop a new, more adequate one.

1.5 A BRIEF REVIEW OF THE CHAPTERS

The book is organized into six parts. Part One gives an introduction and a discussion of some general issues in the field of machine learning. After the overview presented here, in Chapter 2, Schank and Kass discuss various aspects of creativity. They view the creativity as an essential part of human (or machine) intelligence and propose an algorithm for implementing it. The algorithm relies on *explanation patterns* (XPs), that are a form of scripts for creating explanations. In their view, the creativity lies in the use of XPs in unexpected situations, where new analogies can be drawn. This chapter is followed by Ganascia's commentary, which elaborates several topics and presents some critical views. This commentary, as every subsequent commentary, discusses the preceding chapter and gives some flavor of the discussion that followed its original presentation at the International Meeting on Advances in Learning (IMAL).

Part Two presents some new developments in the area of empirical learning methods. Chapter 3 presents a new approach to learning concepts that lack precise definition and are context-dependent. Such concepts are called *flexible*. The method employs the idea of two-tiered representation, in which the meaning of a concept depends on two components: an explicit part, defined by the base concept representation (BCR); and an implicit part, characterized by the inferential concept interpretation (ICI). The BCR (the first tier) expresses the general, typical, and easy-to-define concept meaning, and the ICI (the second tier) defines allowable modifications of the typical meaning, the matching procedures, context-dependency, and describes special cases. In matching an instance with a concept, the ICI may employ, in general, deductive, analogical, or inductive inference. Early experiments with this methodology have shown that by shifting a large part of the concept description from the BCR to the ICI, the amount of memory needed for concept representation can be greatly reduced, without decreasing its performance accuracy on new examples. This chapter is followed by Stepp's commentary.

Bareiss, Porter, and Wier, in Chapter 4, define exemplars of a concept whose features are presented together with their functional explanation. Providing such explanations becomes one of the main tasks of the teacher, in contrast to approaches in which the role of the teacher is to provide examples and/or required relevant domain knowledge. The concepts are described in a form that represents a blend of an extensional definition, that defines the concept by all its instances, and an intentional definition that gives a general recognition rule for the concept. The method stores all concepts examples together with their prototypicality. This chapter is followed by Holte's commentary.

Next, in Chapter 5, Quinlan describes certain improvements to the well-known ID3 learning method. One is a mechanism for exploring the probability that a case belongs to more than one class. Another involves taking into account the noise in the attribute values and an introduction of "soft" thresholds for cases in which the attribute values are continuous. Each learning cycle consists of building a decision tree, followed by a pruning of the obtained tree. The pruned tree contains only subtrees that cannot be replaced by leaves without significantly increasing the predicted error rate of the tree. Each tree growing and pruning cycle is repeated several times on randomly chosen subsets of the training set. The most promising pruned tree is chosen as the final outcome of learning.

Next, in Chapter 6, Falkenheiner and Michalski describe a method for integrating quantitative and qualitative discovery in the system ABACUS. This system formulates a set of equations characterizing data and determines descriptions stating the applicability conditions for these equations. The performance of ABACUS is illustrated by applying it to some classical discovery problems, such as the discovery of the law of ideal gases. It was also applied to the analysis of chemical compounds in order to predict the distance between the atoms of bimetallic compounds, given the values of other attributes. The relations generated this way are beyond the present explanatory abilities of chemistry.

In Chapter 7, Carbonell and Gil describe how a planning system can learn by experimenting on the external environment when detecting divergence between internal expectations and external observations. The main issues addressed are acquiring and refining control knowledge, augmenting an incomplete domain theory, and refining an incorrect domain theory. Three types of failures are discussed. The first failure happens when achieving a goal violates a precondition, the second when an operator fails to apply, and the third when a postcondition is not satisfied. Depending on the kind of failure, different recovery strategies are applied.

In Chapter 8, Pazzani describes a failure-driven learning system that integrates explanation-based learning with empirical learning. The goal of the system is to create heuristics for fault diagnosis that capture the information implicit in the device models. The method explains why a heuristic does not apply in a certain case and corrects the heuristic to avoid proposing an erroneous fault hypothesis. This work is applied to a spacecraft failure correction.

Part Two ends with Chapter 9, in which Hanson presents a system called WITT, which implements a form of conceptual clustering. The system has three components. The first selects the seeds, around which initial clusters are created. The second component applies three operators: object selection, new seed selection, and seed merging. The third component is an information metric by which the system evaluates the cohesion and distinctiveness of a cluster. WITT uses the most representative instance of a cluster as a prototype and allows clusters to share some of their instances (polymorphy).

Part Three gives an account of various analytical learning methods. In Chapter 10, Mitchell, Mahadevan, and Steinberg describe a learning apprentice system called LEAP. The authors define a learning apprentice as an interactive, knowledge-based consultant, which improves its knowledge by observing and analyzing the activities of the users during their normal interaction with the system. When a user provides an unexpected (to the system) solution, at first, the system tries to prove the validity of this solution. When the user's solution is proven to be valid, then the system generalizes the trace of its proof and creates a new rule justified by the proof. This rule is introduced into the system for future use. This chapter is followed by Brazdil's commentary.

Next, in Chapter 11, Shavlik and DeJong (Gerald) study the problem of detecting recursion in explanations. This requires an analysis of the explanation structures and the detection of repeated, interdependent applications of the rules. The detection of such recursive structural patterns is implemented in their system, BAGGER. The system is illustrated by applying it to a blocks-world problem.

The remaining three chapters of this part show how analytic learning can be applied to various specific problems. Chapter 12, by Prieditis, describes an application of explanation-based methods to program generation, generally referred to as *automatic programming*. In this case, the training example is a "weak" algorithm that is used to solve a problem. The method first generates a trace of its solution. Then it generalizes the trace by including iterative macro-operators in the places where the trace repeats several times the same kind of actions. The novelty of this approach lies in generalizing trace structures, rather than generalizing instantiated operators.

In Chapter 13, Vrain describes how a domain theory, expressed in the form of first-order logic theorems, can be used to improve the reliability of generated generalizations. It amounts to the addition of a theorem prover to an induction system. The paper concentrates on the way the theorem prover is used as a feature finder during the detection of the similarities among examples. The author also discusses a method for reducing the number of possible generalizations by using negative examples and a method for incremental learning.

In Chapter 14, the last chapter of this part, Hirsh describes a method, called ROE (Reasoning about Operationality in EBL), which is concerned with operationality of descriptions generated by explanation-based generalization. The method, in addition to generalizing proofs that some property holds for a given training instance, determines the general conditions of operationality for the results. The user is required to provide general knowledge about operationality in the domain of interest, and, from some examples of operationality criteria, the system will find operational rules of operationality.

Part Four describes several efforts on integrating different learning strategies. In Chapter 15, Lebowitz describes the system UNIMEM, which empirically discovers similarities among examples. These empirical generalizations may represent purely coincidental effects. The author proposes to use background knowledge to explain the obtained generalizations and choose on that basis the most appropriate one. This chapter is followed by Rendell's commentary.

In Chapter 16, Kodratoff describes how to construct explanations from a trace of the proof that a training example is an instance of some concept. The notion of "explanation" is generalized so that it includes also processes of detecting similarities among concept examples, i.e., empirical concept learning. In the latter case, a generalization is viewed as a form of an "explanation" why an example is a concept instance. It is then shown how to learn from past successes to explain new instances, and how to learn from failures to explain. These processes include recovering from error in proof, learning from unrecognized positive examples and from incorrectly recognized negative examples. An account of how to use human experts' explanations is also given. This chapter is followed by Stepp's commentary.

Next, in Chapter 17, Bergadano and Giordana propose a methodology for integrating empirical and analytical methods for learning concept descriptions. The method involves a search for concept descriptions in a tree of logic descriptions, ranking from the most general to the most specific. The tree is tested on a set of positive and negative examples. This search is guided by several domain-independent criteria, such as consistency and completeness, limiting the size of the obtained expressions, and an understandability criterion. This chapter also suggests methods to use background knowledge as a major domain-dependent search heuristic in order to expand the specialization tree toward a promising description or, conversely, to prune the branches that are not in agreement with domain theory.

In Chapter 18, Wilkins presents an apprentice system, ODYSSEUS, which, in contrast with LEAP (Chapter 11), can handle situations in which the domain theory is incapable of producing an explanation of a given training instance. It is assumed that the domain knowledge is incomplete or erroneous, and the learning process involves making improvements to this knowledge. The improvements are made by completing failed explanations using general-purpose metarules.

In Chapter 19, Tecuci and Kodratoff describe DISCIPLE, a multistrategy system capable of learning with imperfect background knowledge. If the background knowledge is complete and consistent, the system executes standard explanation-based learing to improve its performance. Otherwise, the system compensates for its imperfect knowledge by interacting with the user, and employing a combination of explanation-based learning, analogical learning, and empirical learning. Depending on the degree of background knowledge imperfection, such a process may lead to the improvement of the system's competence, or to the improvement of both the competence and performance.

Part Five gives an overview of research in the area of subsymbolic learning methods. Hinton, in Chapter 20, provides a comprehensive characterization of the work on connectionist approaches, and explains how to construct internal representations for difficult learning problems. The chapter describes the advantages and disadvantages of various connectionist methods, such as the least mean square procedure, the back-propagation method, Boltzman machines, competitive learning, and others. The description of what is a generalization in a neural network is also presented.

In Chapter 21, De Jong (Kenneth) describes basic aspects of genetic algorithms and presents them as a means for achieving robust learning systems. In a learning mode, a genetic algorithm searches the space of legal structural changes to determine situations that achieve a desired behavioral change. The search is done using certain operators, such as crossover, mutation, and inversion. The chapter discusses the relevance of various features of adaptive systems to machine learning.

Part Six presents two types of formal approaches to machine learning. In Chapter 22, Haussler, in the spirit of the Valiant's approach, presents an improvement over Mitchell's version space method. Instead of being concerned only with hypotheses that are consistent with examples, the method also looks for hypotheses that are sufficiently "close" to the target concept. Such an approach allows the author to define the notion of convergence of the learning method. The compexity of the method is analyzed.

Finally, in Chapter 23, Rivest and Schapire explore the learning problem faced by a robot in an unfamiliar, deterministic, finite-state environment. With little built-in knowledge about its environment, the robot's goal is to infer the hidden "structure" of the environment through systematic experimentation. The authors describe a new technique, based on the notion of a "test," that the robot can use to build up such a model of the unknown environment. They illustrate their technique by applying it to several simple problems, and they show that it can be used effectively to infer the structure of some very large, but well-structured, environments, such as one based on Rubik's Cube.

1.5 FRONTIER PROBLEMS

In the conclusion, we would like to discuss several areas of machine learning that seem to be of particular challenge and importance in future research. One such area is concerned with the development of methods that can utilize different learning strategies depending on the task at hand, i.e., building integrated multistrategy learning systems. The importance of this area is that real-world situations rarely present problems that can be handled by a neat, single-strategy approach. There have been several learning systems developed that combine two or more strategies. Typically they combine simple empirical learning and explanation-based learning. Most of these systems integrate different strategies in a rather inflexible and *a priori* defined way. A natural development of this research could be in the direction of a goal-based integration of a spectrum of machine learning strategies. An attempt in this direction is presented in [Michalski, 1990].

With the growing sophistication of learning programs, there is an interest in increasing the transfer of machine learning programs from university laboratories to the real world, where they can be applied to problems of practical significance. This trend is of great consequence, as it challenges researchers to test their research in the context of real-life problems, and it may lead to economically important applications. Such applications may, in turn, generate new interesting research problems, not to mention the needed support for further research. An exposure of a learning system to real-world problems will require further advancement of learning systems in many areas, such as handling erroneous or missing data, learning imprecise and context-dependent concepts, employing sophisticated methods for plausible inference, and causal reasoning, drawing complex analogies, and using quantitative and/or qualitative models in a learning process. Some applications will require systems that are capable of analyzing and understanding past behavior of a complex system, and then using this understanding to predict future behavior. Thus, there is a need for developing advanced prediction systems.

In view of the above applications, there will also likely be a need for developing multirepresentational learning systems. Such systems employ knowledge representations in different goal-oriented forms, expressed in different structures, and at different levels of abstraction. At present, most empirical learning methods, both symbolic and subsymbolic, tend to be oriented toward only single attribute-based representations. Concept instances are described in terms of attribute-value pairs, and concept descriptions as simple structures (rules, trees, etc.) that utilize these attributes. The strong interest in such systems has been probably due to the fact that such representations are sufficient in many simple, practical applications, and because many methods do not use much background knowledge. As application problems become more complex, there will be an increased need to use much richer, structural, and multiform knowledge representations. In fact, if a learning program needs to use an extensive amount of background knowledge, it will undoubtedly need to employ a structural rather than attributional representation.

To exhibit advanced learning capabilities, a learning program—synthetic or analytic—needs to draw on a substantial amount of both factual and general knowledge. Future learning systems will then require a connection to large databases and knowledge bases. The CYC project [Lenat, 1989] is an example of a long-term effort to develop such a computer-manipulable, large-scale knowledge base. In this context, an important research area is an application of machine learning to the analysis and extraction of knowledge from large databases. This application will involve a construction of "intelligent" interfaces between existing large databases and machine learning systems.

In view of the proliferation of machine learning projects, there is also a strong interest in experimental and analytical comparative studies of different methods and paradigms. At present, basic paradigms and areas of research concentration include: symbolic inductive learning, analytic methods, integrated systems, neural networks, and genetic algorithms. Each of these paradigms can be subdivided into various subareas. For example, symbolic inductive learning includes empirical concept learning from examples, discovery systems, exemplar-based learning, conceptual clustering, and constructive induction. Different paradigms and methods seem to be primarily oriented toward different areas of applicability, and their relative merits and limitations are not clearly understood.

In the context of building large-scale learning systems that utilize significant background knowledge, it is important to assure high instructability of the learning systems. This means that they should be combined with advanced knowledge acquisition systems. This way, the knowledge can be economically introduced to a learning system without always involving a learning process. This direction of research calls for an increased collaboration between the machine learning and knowledge acquisition communities.

Finally, future machine learning systems should exhibit high-level capabilities for interacting with humans and employing for that purpose multimedia representations. They should be capable of explaining what they have learned, and what they still need to learn. This implies that learning systems should have the ability to perform metaknowledge reasoning, generate learning tasks by themselves, ask questions, and know how to utilize different answers, exhibit advanced explanatory facilities, and perform causal and model-based reasoning. In perfoming such processes, the systems might employ visual or auditory representations.

ACKNOWLEDGMENTS

The authors thank Kejitan Dontas, David Littman, Eugene Norris, Gheorghe Tecuci, Gail Thornburg, and Jianping Zhang for useful comments and suggestions. This research was supported in part by the Office of Naval Research under grants No. N00014-88-K-0397 and No. N00014-88-K-0226, and in part by the Defense Advanced Research Projects Agency under the grant administered by the Office of Naval Research No. N00014-K-85-0878.

References

Amarel S. 1970. "On the Representation of Problems and Goal-Directed Procedures for Computers," in *Theoretical Approaches to Non-Numerical Problem Solving*, R.B. Banerji and M. Mesarovic (Eds.), Springer Verlag, Heidelberg.

———— , 1986. "Program Synthesis as a Theory Formation Task: Problem Representations and Solution Methods," in *Machine Learning: An Artificial Intelligence Approach, Volume II*, R.S. Michalski, J.G. Carbonell, T.M. Mitchell (Eds.), pp. 499–569, Morgan Kaufmann.

Aristotle. 1987. *Posterior Analytics, in Great Books of the Western World*, vol. 8, R.M. Hutchins (Ed.), Encyclopedia Britannica, Inc.

Biermann, A.W., Guiho, G., and Kodratoff, Y. 1984. *Automatic Program Construction Techniques*, MacMillan Publishing Company, New York.

Bongard, M. 1970. *Pattern Recognition*, Spartan Books, Washington D.C.

Buchanan, B.G., Feigenbaum, E.A., and Sridharan, N.S. 1972. "Heuristic Theory Formation: Data Interpretation and Rule Formation," *Machine Intelligence*, Vol. 7, pp. 267–290, Halsted Press, Wiley.

Burstein, M.H. 1986. "Concept Formation by Incremental Analogical Reasoning and Debugging," in *Machine Learning: An Artificial Intelligence Approach, Volume II*, R.S. Michalski, J.G. Carbonell, T.M. Mitchell (Eds.), pp. 351–369, Morgan Kaufmann.

Carbonell, J.G. 1986. "Derivational Analogy: A Theory of Reconstructive Problem Solving and Expertise Acquisition," in *Machine Learning: An Artificial Intelli-*

gence Approach, Volume II, R.S. Michalski, J.G. Carbonell, T.M. Mitchell (Eds.), pp. 371–392, Morgan Kaufmann.

Collins, A. and Michalski, R.S. 1989. "The Logic of Plausible Reasoning: A Core Theory," *Cognitive Science*, Vol. 13, pp. 1–49.

Cox, P.T. and Pietrzykowski, T. 1986. "Causes for Events: Their Computation and Applications, " in *Proceedings of the Eighth International Conference on Automated Deduction*, Oxford.

DeJong, G. 1981. "Generalizations Based on Explanations," in *Proceedings of the Seventh International Conference on Artificial Intelligence*, pp. 67–69, Vancouver, August 1981.

DeJong, G. and Mooney, R. 1986. "Explanation-based Learning: An Alternative View," *Machine Learning*, Vol. 1, No. 2, pp. 145–175.

Duval, B. and Kodratoff, Y. 1990. "A Tool for the Management of Incomplete Theories: Reasoning about Explanations" in *Machine Learning, Metareasoning and Logics*, P. Brazdil and K. Konolige (Eds.), Kluwer Academic Press, pp. 135–158.

Holland, J.H., Holyoke, K.J., Nisbett, R.E., and Thagard P.R. 1986. *Induction: Processes of Inference, Learning and Discovery*, The MIT Press, Cambridge MA.

Lenat, D.B. 1977. "Automated Theory Formation in Mathematics," in *Proceedings of the Fifth International Joint Conference on Artificial Intelligence*, pp. 833–842.

————— , 1983. "The Role of Heuristics in Learning by Discovery: Three Case Studies," in *Machine Learning: An Artificial Intelligence Approach*, R.S. Michalski, J.G. Carbonell, and T.M. Mitchell (Eds.), pp. 243–306, Morgan Kaufmann.

————— , 1989. "When will Machines Learn?," *Machine Learning*, Vol. 4, No 3/4.

Michalski, R.S. 1973. "Discovering Classification Rules Using Variable-valued Logic System VL1," in *Proceedings of the Third International Conference on Artificial Intelligence*, pp. 162–172, Stanford University.

————— , 1983. "A Theory and Methodology of Inductive Learning," in *Machine Learning: An Artificial Intelligence Approach*, R.S. Michalski, J.G. Carbonell, T.M. Mitchell, (Eds.), pp. 83–134, Morgan Kaufmann.

————— , 1986. "Understanding the Nature of Learning: Issues and Research Directions," in *Machine Learning: An Artificial Intelligence Approach, Volume II*, R.S. Michalski, J.G. Carbonell, T.M. Mitchell (Eds.), pp. 3–25, Morgan Kaufmann.

———— , 1990. "Integrated Multistrategy Learning: Toward a Unified Theory of Learning," *Reports of Machine Learning and Inference Laboratory, MLI90–1, Center for Artificial Intelligence*, George Mason University, 1990 (an earlier version of this paper appeared in the *Proceedings of the ONR Workshop on Knowledge Acquisition*, Arlington, VA, November 6–7, 1989).

Michalski, R.S. and Chilausky, R. 1980. "Learning by Being Told and Learning from Examples: An Experimental Comparison of the Two Methods of Knowledge Acquisition in the Context of Developing an Expert System for Soybean Disease Diagnosis," in *Policy Analysis and Information Systems*, vol. 4, No. 2, (Special Issue on Knowledge Acquisition and Induction), June 1980.

Michalski, R.S. and Littman, D.C. 1989. "Future Directions of AI in a Resource-Limited Environment," in *Proceedings of IJCAI-89 Workshop on Knowledge Discovery in Databases*, Detroit, August 1989.

Michalski, R.S. and Stepp R.E. 1983. "Learning from Observation: Conceptual Clustering," in *Machine Learning: An Artificial Intelligence Approach*, Michalski, R.S., Carbonell, J.G., Mitchell, T.M. (Eds.), pp. 331–363, Morgan Kaufmann.

Michalski, R.S. and Zemankova, M. 1990. "What is Generalization? An Inquiry into the Concept of Generalization and its Types," *Reports of Machine Learning and Inference Laboratory*, George Mason University, MLI90–7.

Michalski, R.S., Carbonell, J.G., and Mitchell, T.M. (Eds.). 1983. *Machine Learning: An Artificial Intelligence Approach*, Morgan Kaufmann.

———— , 1986. *Machine Learning: An Artificial Intelligence Approach, Volume II*, Morgan Kaufmann.

Minton, S. 1986. "Improving the Effectiveness of Explanation-based Learning," in *Proceedings of the Workshop on Knowledge Compilation*, Oregon State University, Corvallis, OR.

Minton, S., Carbonell, J.G., Etzioni, O., Knoblock, C.A., and Kuokka, D.R. 1987. "Acquiring Effective Search Control Rules: Explanation-based Learning in the PRODIGY System," in *Proceedings of the Fourth International Machine Learning Workshop*, pp. 122–133, Univ. California, Irvine.

Mitchell, T.M., Keller, R.M., Kedar-Cabelli, S.T. 1986. "Explanation-based Generalization: A Unifying View," in *Machine Learning*, Vol. 1, No. 1, pp. 47–80.

Mitchell, T., Utgoff, P., and Banerji, R. 1983. "Learning by Experimentation, Acquiring and Refining Problem-solving Heuristics," in *Machine Learning: An Artifi-*

cial Intelligence Approach, R.S. Michalski, J.G. Carbonell, T.M. Mitchell (Eds.), pp. 163–190, Morgan Kaufmann.

Mozetic, I. 1989. "Hierarchichal Model-based Diagnosis," *Reports of Machine Learning and Inference Laboratory*, MLI 90–2, George Mason University.

Muggleton, S. and Buntine, R. 1988. "Machine Invention of First Order Predicates by Inverting Resolution," in *Proceedings of Fifth International Machine Learning Workshop*, pp 339–352, Morgan Kaufmann.

Newell, A. 1969. "Heuristic Programming III: Structured Problems," in *Progress in Operation Research*, Vol. 3, Aronofsky J.S. (Ed.), John Wiley, New York.

Peirce, C.S. 1965. "Elements of Logic," in *Collected Papers of Charles Sanders Peirce (1839–1914)*, C.H. Hartshone and P. Weiss (Eds), The Belknap Press Harvard University Press, Cambridge, MA.

Quinlan, J.R. 1979. "Discovering Rules from Large Collections of Examples: A Case Study," in *Expert Systems in Microelectronic Age*, D. Michie, (Ed.), Edinburgh University Press, Edinburgh.

Rouveirol, C. and Puget, J.F. 1989. "A Simple Solution for Inverting Resolution," in *Proceedings of the Fourth European Working Session on Learning*, pp 201–211, Pitman.

Samuel, A.L. 1959. "Some Studies in Machine Learning Using the Game of Checkers," in *IBM Journal of Research and Development*, No. 3, pp.211–229.

Winston, P.H. 1970. *Learning Structural Descriptions from Examples*, PhD thesis, MAC TR-76, Massachusetts Institute of Technology, September.

———— , 1975. "Learning Structural Descriptions from Examples", in *The Psychology of Computer Vision*, P.H. Winston, (Ed.), McGraw-Hill, New York, ch. 5.

———— , 1982. "Learning New Principles from Precedents and Exercises," in *Artificial Intelligence* 19, pp. 321–350.

Wnek, J., Sarma, J., Wahab, A.A., and Michalski, R.S. 1990. "An Experimental Case Study in Concept Learning Comparing Symbolic, Neural Net and Genetic Algorithm Methods," *Reports of Machine Learning and Inference Laboratory*, MLI 90–2, George Mason University.

2

EXPLANATIONS, MACHINE LEARNING, AND CREATIVITY

Roger Schank
Alex Kass
(Northwestern University)

Abstract

Creativity is obviously a crucial aspect of human intelligence, and yet it has not been explored much by AI researchers. A principal reason for this lack of attention is the mystical aura that the word "creativity" has about it. Creativity is thought to be something so mysterious that AI researchers have been intimidated by it. We claim that creativity is a much simpler, more algorithmic process than many have thought and that AI is ready to start designing creative computers.

2.1 INTRODUCTION—WHAT IS INTELLIGENCE?

If one tries to define what it means for a machine to be intelligent, it becomes clear that learning is a key issue. Stuffing a lot of knowledge into a machine is simply not enough to make it intelligent. One would never say that a person was intelligent simply because he had memorized an encyclopedia and was able to spit portions out at appropriate occasions. There is more to intelligence than just that.

The ability to perform an intelligent act is not enough to qualify as intelligent either. For example, playing chess is an intelligent task, but the chess computers that can be purchased in almost any supermarket are not intelligent machines. One of the reasons is that they cannot learn from their mistakes; they do not develop the way human chess players do. After a chess machine has been beaten by the same move sequence a hundred times it will still respond the same way. It never explains its failures, and it never takes corrective action. A human who did this would be considered quite dumb.

We claim that in order to be considered intelligent a machine must be able to exhibit the following:

- Explanation
- Learning
- Creativity

Intelligent beings explain events to themselves and thereby learn from them. They explain so that they can adapt their model of the world to account for the new experience, and thereby be better prepared to deal with similar events in the future. This ability to refine understanding of the world by explaining individual experiences is an absolutely central feature of human cognition. Humans do not just accumulate more facts, they evolve into better explainers. The difference between a 6-year-old and a 30-year-old is not just that the 30-year-old knows more facts; the 30-year-old has also evolved a more powerful explanation ability.

Creativity comes into the picture when we try to explain something for which we have no explanation in memory. People can do this. In fact, we can hypothesize new explanations on demand so well that we have come to take this ability for granted. But we shouldn't because this ability is at the heart of the creative process!

In this chapter, we do not intend to discuss the technical details of how a computer program can develop creative explanations. We refer readers interested in that sort of discussion to the papers we and our colleagues have published elswhere (e.g., [Kass, *et al.*, 1986; Leake and Owens, 1986; Leake, 1986; 1990; Kass, 1989; 1990]). Instead, we intend to use this chapter to make some more general points about the direction that we think research in machine learning ought to take. We will try to show how creativity is closely related to the learning process. In this important sense everybody is creative. It follows from this that it will probably not be possible to produce an intelligent computer that is not also a creative computer. Of course, we don't mean by this that intelligent computers will have to be painters or poets, but simply that they will have to be able to develop creative hypotheses—to creatively adapt their knowledge structures to cope with new experiences.

2.2 EXPLANATION AND THE UNDERSTANDING PROCESS

Although this chapter isn't about natural language processing *per se*, it is about understanding. And since some of the most common understanding tasks, such as listening to others and reading newspaper stories, involve natural language processing, language will creep into our discussion.

Consider the problem of processing a sentence. AI work on text understanding has generally claimed that to understand a sentence is to fit the representation of the sentence into an appropriate memory structure. Memory structures that have been proposed for use in AI systems include scripts [Schank, 1975; Schank and Abelson, 1977], frames [Minsky, 1975; Charniak, 1978], and others. For example, the SAM system [Cullingford, 1978] understood sentences like, "Can I have some coffee?" by matching them against a line in its restaurant script.

The important question raised by systems such as SAM is, what happens when an understander doesn't have a script in which to put the sentence? These are the sentences that people find anomalous—the ones that require explanation. SAM would ignore such a sentence, but people are more clever than that. When an input sentence does not readily hook up to a memory structure, people will build an explanation that hooks it up (in effect, they are building new memory structures). We must get our computers to do this.

2.3 EXPLANATION GOALS

The direct purpose of an explanation is always to render an anomaly "non-anomalous" by connecting it to a memory structure. Beyond this, there are many different kinds of explanations serving different goals. The goal served by an explanation will depend partially on the type of anomaly being explained and partially on the interests of the explainer. Seven of the most common goals are:

1. *Establish that an actor has something coherent in mind (when all signs are to the contrary).* For instance, if we hear that someone has gone jogging across Death Valley for several days in the middle of the summer we are likely to be baffled about his behavior (perhaps falling back to the default explanation that he is just crazy). However, if we conjecture that he is a medical doctor who is taking part in a scientific experiment about how the human body can adapt to temperature extremes, we then have an explanation, since we can now fit his behavior into the "scientists devoted to their work" memory structure.

2. *Find the context for an action in the belief–action chain.* People do things for reasons. Therefore our representation of why actions are performed is often a chain of beliefs leading to those actions, and an action can be anomalous because we aren't aware of one of those beliefs. For example, suppose you hear about someone who refuses a blood transfusion even though she will probably die if doesn't get one. This is likely to strike you as totally anomalous, but suppose you learn that she is a member of some religious sect which refuses most medical treatment because it believes that medical treatment interferes with God's plan. The behavior is still likely to seem bizarre to you if you don't share the belief, but you will feel that you have some sort of explanation.

3. *Find new predictive rules that hold for an individual.* One kind of explanation says merely that person X performed action Y because person X always per-

forms action Y. The main. purpose of such an explanation isn't really to shed new light on the particular event, but rather to learn rules that will predict X's behavior. For example, some people are always late. If you explain a late arrival by realizing that the person is always late, you will be better prepared the next time you have an appointment with that person.

4. *Find new predictive rules that hold for a group.* Instead of referring to rules about an individual, an explanation can operate by connecting an actor's actions to group behavior. These explanations say that X is a member of group Y and members of group Y always perform action Z. These explanations develop rules that allow you to predict behavior of future actors when you discover that they're members of group Y. If you learn that X is a Moslem, and you have the rule that all Moslems go to Mecca once in their lives, then you can predict that X will go to Mecca.

5. *Get new rules by copying successful behavior.* When you see someone else being successful in a way that you are not, you may want to copy the behavior that brings about positive results. In order to do so, you have to develop an explanation about what aspect of his behavior is leading to those results. This is also called *credit assignment* or *causal attribution*.

6. *Add new facts to your personal database.* Of course, our point about it not being intelligent to simply memorize an encyclopedia was meant to imply that raw information isn't sufficient, not that it isn't necessary. One kind of learning is simply gathering more facts. Explanations typically imply facts you didn't know about before; these facts are sometimes useful in their own right.

7. *Discover universal truths that hold over a wide range of phenomena.* By asking the right questions and developing explanations that answer those questions at a high enough level of generality, you can learn things not directly related to the anomaly that initiated the explanation process in the first place.

2.4 EXPLANATION IN ACTION

Much of the explanation process occurs so easily and naturally that it is hard to catch yourself doing it. The trick in studying explanation is to catch people in the act, to collect lots of examples of yourself and others engaged in explanation.

One of our means of doing this over the last few years has been to listen to a radio station in Connecticut that has a program called "60 Seconds," during which they do brief "man in the street" interviews. They walk up to someone, ask them the question of the day, and record the answers. Here is an example:

Q1: If you could live anywhere, where would it be?

A1.2: Boulder Colorado. That's where my man is.

A1.3: I want to live in a sand trap at the third hole of Golf Acres.

A1.4: I'd live in New England because it has everything in it. It has all the culture, tradition, and history.

A1.5: A tropical island with a mountain for skiing and a beach for swimming.

A1.6: I'd like to live in an enchanted castle with goblets of wine, joints of beef and wenches at hand.

A1.7: Essex, Connecticut. I could dock my yacht there.

A1.8: Hawaii. It's still in the U.S., and I would not want to go out of the U.S. I would like to stay here.

A1.9: Bristol, Connecticut. That's where I live now, and I love it.

A1.10: New York City. It's got a lot of class.

A1.11: Estonia, but I can't because it got taken over by the Russians.

A1.12: I think I'd like to live in Disneyland so I would never have to face reality.

Notice that although the question did not call for explanations explicitly, many of the answers included explanations. More importantly, you will find yourself searching for explanations as you read them. Try to pay attention to what is going on in your mind while you process each answer. What questions do you ask yourself?

When we read answer A1.2 we are led to ask ourselves why isn't the interviewee living in Boulder now if that's where her man is? We start to develop an explanation that says something like, "This person must believe that X is more important than living with her boyfriend." We start searching for what the X might be. We are trying to find a missing link in the belief–action chain. We begin to think of possibilities—maybe her job is more important, or maybe the expectations of her parents. We can't be sure what the answer is, but we feel like we have some pretty good guesses.

Notice two points. First, notice how effortlessly the explanation process gets rolling and comes up with explanations. Second, notice how much it relies on stereotypes. We don't know anything about the woman, but we still feel we can construct a few reasons why she lives in Connecticut rather than in Boulder, Colorado.

Answer A1.11 is also pretty interesting. You could launch off into all kinds of speculation about this person and his motivations. It is quite likely that he is someone who once lived in Estonia or whose parents lived in Estonia, and who identifies himself with being an Estonian much more than being an American. Clearly the political situation in Estonia has forced him to construct the belief that "it is better to live in the U.S., where I don't like it too much than to live in my homeland while the Soviets are occupying it." It is quite surprising that we can dream up such a story about someone we know virtually nothing about. Of course, the reason we can do so is that we know other people who fit the same pattern. We might not know anyone from Estonia, but that's not vital because all the details do not have to match—we can adapt an existing pattern to fit new situations.

Let's look at another "60 Seconds" question:

Q2: Why do you think that bank robberies are occurring more frequently?

A2.1: Society's posing a challenge for the robbers to deal with all the publicity and all the guards.

A2.2: The punishment isn't great enough for bank robbery.

A2.3: It's a good way to find sustenance.

A2.4: The state of the economy.

A2.5: It's probably because people aren't receiving long enough sentences.

A2.6: People need the money, now more than ever. They have no other way of getting it, and a bank is the best opportunity because it's the largest return for the least effort.

A2.7: The court system is all backed up. The prison systems are all backed up too. Chances are they'll get off with a very light prison sentence if they get caught at all. There's a big risk involved, but they have a good chance of just getting away with it and getting the money.

One interesting thing to note about this question is that its premise wasn't even true; at the time the question was asked, the robbery rate in Connecticut was *not* higher than usual at all. Therefore, none of the answers given could have been prepared in advance; they were developed on the spot. Once again, this emphasizes how easy people find this task.

Why would this be? Surely people are not practiced at giving quick explanations to interviewers. But they do have to produce explanations for their own use—when something is experienced but isn't well understood, it is necessary to form hypotheses about what it might be. We do this constantly, without even thinking about it. It isn't very important that we get our snap explanations correct (if they're wrong, they simply won't be confirmed by future experiences), but is important that we form the explanations quickly.

2.5 INDEXING MEMORY: A KEY ISSUE

Remindings offer an important window into the world of mental processes. In [Schank, 1982] we dealt at length with the role of reminding, and especially the connection between reminding and learning. We will talk a little bit about reminding here as well because reminding and explanation are closely related.

One of the things we learned in the course of studying remindings is that they almost always result from expectation failures. People understand the world by making and confirming expectations. These expectations guide our processing, telling us what to look for. We have noticed that reminding usually results when one of these expectations is not confirmed. When we make an incorrect prediction, our natural inclination is to search memory for a similar expectation failure. We collect failures in our mind because failures are the key to learning.

AI researchers are doing a lot of good work on learning from success. For example, the work on generalizing successful proofs by [Mitchell, 1986] or acquiring new schemata via explanation-based learning [DeJong, 1981]. This is certainly important work, but we believe that learning from failures is an even more crucial issue, because the need to learn is rooted in our need not to make the same failures over and over again. When we fail, we seek an explanation for our failure so that we can improve our reasoning. Making predictions inevitably leads to making mistakes, but the good part of this is that making mistakes is what leads to learning. A successful explanation of why a particular prediction is in error helps us to be more effective in coping with the world.

At the core of a failure-based learning algorithm is the ability to retrieve similar failures from memory. Thus, indexing memory is the most crucial problem in AI. If you have thousands of items in memory indexed intelligently, you will be able to learn—otherwise you won't. If you've ever understood something like what you're experiencing now, chances are good that the old experience will have something to teach you about the new and that considering the two experiences together will allow you to make useful generalizations. But if you can't find the old experience in memory—if your memory isn't indexed in such a way that you are reminded of the experience—then you can't do anything with it.

Earlier we spoke about memorizing an encyclopedia, and how this wasn't intelligence. The only interesting problem related to this task is indexing memory so that the right information can be accessed at the right times. The principal method by which the encyclopedia is indexed is alphabetical. Letters are the indices. The human mind clearly is not indexed this way. (If you have any doubts about this, try naming the 50 American states in alphabetical order.) It *is* clear that human memories are very richly indexed; any item can be accessed in a large number of ways. But just what these indices are (or ought to be in our programs) is still an open research question. We think that explanations are important indices for human memories.

Consider the following conversation:

Person1: I can never get my wife to cook my steaks rare enough for me.

Person2: That reminds me of when I was in England. I could never get my hair cut as short as I wanted it.

How could Person2 have been reminded of his experience in England? On the surface the episodes have nothing in common. Person2 must have constructed an explanation along the following lines: Person1's wife does not really believe that Person1 could possibly want things as extreme as he says. She therefore applies her own standard and cooks the steak less rare than he requests. It is this explanation that served as an index into Person2's memory and retrieved the England experience, where the barbers didn't believe that he wanted as extreme a haircut as he said.

2.6 CREATIVITY: AN ALGORITHMIC PROCESS

Our view of creativity is essentially a case-based one (see [Kolodner, 1988; Hammond, 1988] and [Riesbeck and Schank, 1988], for discussions of many of the issues involved in case-based reasoning). In a nutshell the process works as follows: Something goes wrong (an expectation fails); you get reminded of a similar problem; you recall the solution to the previous problem (assuming there is one); you apply the old solution to the new problem, "tweaking" the solution (if necessary) to make it fit the new situation.

By the term "tweaking," we mean making successive small changes to the old solution until it fits the needs of the new situation. When the problem is, specifically, developing a new explanation, this means taking an old, generalized explanation and applying modification rules that reduce the differences between the explanation and the requirements of a new situation, until it is only a matter of supplying the correct variable bindings to make the explanation match the new situation.

So computers don't have to be brilliant in order to be creative, they simply have to be good at adapting old explanations. In order to explain something new, they have to find a standard explanation pattern and tweak it to make it fit the new situation. There are two important research problems involved with getting computers to do this: The first is the indexing problem, which we have already mentioned. It is crucial to be able to find other similar problems, which provide the input to tweaking. This problem is made trickier and more interesting by the fact that "similar" must be interpreted loosely when looking for input to the tweaker. What you're looking for isn't necessarily an exact match; you're looking for some structure that might be close enough to be tweakable, and it's hard to know in advance what differences will go away when tweaked and what won't. It's better to be liberal when searching memory (and come up with lots of junk) than to be conservative and thereby miss the opportunity to have a really exciting idea.

The second hard question is how to do the tweaking itself. Computers need to have a battery of tweaking rules if they are to use their stored knowledge structures creatively. Tweaking rules can say things like the following:

Search for someone other than the standard actor for a given action;

Search for nonstandard plan that may have been used to achieve a known goal;

Substitute other objects that share a given class membership with the standard object;

Transpose the actor and the object in a given action.

[Hammond, 1989] and [Kass, 1990] present two rather different corpuses of tweaking rules. Hammond's are tweaking plans; Kass's for tweaking explanations. Of course, since not all tweaking rules are applicable in any given situation, each system must also include a set of heuristics for choosing which tweaking rule to try for each kind of mismatch between a knowledge structure and a given situation.

With this view of creativity in mind let's look at some additional explanations from "60 Seconds."

Q3: What do you think of our increased assistance to El Salvador?

A3.1: I am against it. I don't want to see us get involved anymore. I think we have to start taking care of things at home first.

A3.2: It makes me fairly nervous. I look at it as a sort of Vietnam. I think it's great for the U.S. when a country does indeed need our help, but I also think we should be very careful about how we spend our money, the way the economy is here in the States.

A3.3: What happened in Vietnam should have taught the American people a lesson.

A3.4: I'm fearful that it might lead to a situation similar to what we faced in Vietnam 15 years ago, and therefore I would examine carefully anything we did before we get ourselves stuck in a situation we can't get out of.

At least three out of the four responses involve Vietnam remindings! When deciding how to deal with a new situation we get reminded of old situations and adapt our understanding of them to the current problem. In Vietnam we attempted to send troops a long distance to defend a friendly regime, and it did not work, so let's not do it again. A very mechanical, but powerful way to think about things. A computer could do this.

The creative explanation algorithm we are suggesting looks roughly like the following:

2.6.1 Explanation Algorithm

1. Detect an anomaly.

2. Establish the kind of explanation that will make it less anomalous.

3. Find some explanation in memory that may suffice.

4. If none suffices, find some that might be tweakable.

5. Tweak.

6. If tweaked explanations are better but still don't suffice, tweak some more.

7. Determine if the final explanation can be generalized.

8. If generalization is called for, then find the items for generalization, find the breadth of the generalization, and formulate the new explanation.

9. Verify the new explanation (often by reminding).

10. Reorganize memory to include the new, more general version of the explanation pattern.

2.7 EXPLAINING SWALE'S DEATH

Swale was the best three-year-old thoroughbred racehorse in the U.S. in 1984. Three days after winning one of the biggest races of the year Swale was found dead in his stall. Racing fans, veterinarians, and other curious people everywhere tried to figure out what had happened. Everyone was wondering how a horse, which had such fantastic qualities, could have died so young without warning. We tried running our own version of "60 Seconds" in which we asked random graduate students (most of whom had no interested in Swale or any other racehorse), "Why did Swale die?" Most of them had no trouble coming up with fairly plausible explanations. Some of the most popular answers were:

- Swale was killed for the insurance money.
- Swale was killed by the owner of a rival horse to eliminate him from some big, upcoming race.
- Swale died because his owners were pushing him too hard.

Although it is quite unlikely that any of these explanations are actually true, they are pretty good first guesses. Our claim is that people come up with explanations like this by drawing on standard *Explanation Patterns* (henceforth XPs), and adapting them, along the lines of the algorithm enumerated in the previous section. XPs are memory structures that store explanations the person has learned. We will have some more to say about explanation patterns later, but first we want to talk about how relevant XPs are retrieved from the huge library of such structures that a real-world explainer would need to have.

2.7.1 Explanation Questions

The best way to understand searching for XPS is to think of it as asking yourself a series of *Explanation Questions* (abbreviated EQs). We have collected a series of EQs that are appropriate in a wide range of situations, such as, "How will this event benefit others?," "What did the victim do to cause this bad event?," "How does this behavior fit in with a group of behaviors?," and "How is this apparently ineffective plan in reality a good plan for some unseen goal?" The idea is that these questions, combined with features drawn from the specific anomaly, help index down to a set of XPs that propose answers for the EQs, and thus explain the anomaly. For a much lengthier explication of EQS and a more complete list of the common EQs that we have observed, see [Schank, 1986]. In this paper we'll just try to give a flavor of EQs by looking at specific questions applied to Swale's death.

Before an EQ can be used to index an XP, it must be instantiated, or applied to the current problem. This is not a trivial operation, and we won't have much to say about how to do it here; this is an important open question. What we do want to do here is to show that the library of standard EQs does, in fact, translate into a set of interesting questions about a specific case (such as Swale's death). Of course, not all EQs apply equally well to all anomalies, so that some of the questions generated are humorous, and some are downright nonsense. This is not a bad thing though. Humorous questions have their place, and enough of the questions generated are quite reasonable, so that the silly questions are not a cause for alarm.

Below we detail some of the questions the system would derive about Swale when instantiating EQs like the ones described in [Schank, 1986].

- **How will Swale's death benefit others?** Derived from EQ1.1: How will an unexpected event benefit others? Thinking about how deaths in general can benefit others can remind one of insurance-related and inheritance-related killings. Thinking about the benefits stemming from the death of competitive athletes can lead to the explanation that a competitor knocked Swale off. Other benefits of death would probably generate other, less relevant explanations too. For example, the racehorse cemetery probably made money on Swale's death, so maybe they killed Swale. Other horses in Swale's barn might have coveted his stall, etc.

- **What were the medical causes of Swale's death?** Derived from EQ3.1: What were the underlying physical causes of Swale's death? This would focus attention on Swale's known physical ailments. This is an excellent question about death in general, but since Swale seemed to have no ailments, it doesn't generate any explanations in this case.

- **How did Swale contribute to his own death?** Derived from EQ4: How did the victim enable this bad event? Swale's outstanding actions were running incredibly fast and winning races. Could any of these things contribute to early death? Driving fast certainly can. Perhaps Swale crashed. This doesn't seem very reasonable, since we know he died in his stall, but in other circumstances this question might lead to something interesting.

- **What circumstances under Swale's control led to his death?** Derived from EQ6: What circumstances led to this event? Since we don't know what caused the death yet this question doesn't get us anywhere, but once we started to have such an explanation, this question might help us elaborate it.

- **Why did this institution act this way?** EQ7: This can be instantiated several ways, depending on which institution we focus on. If we think of the racing establishment as an institution, we could focus on how the ills of gambling or competition might have killed Swale. We could also look at Swale as a pawn in the capitalist game, thinking about big capitalism as the institution. This can lead to explanations involving the capitalist exploitation of Swale. After all, Swale was treated very poorly for a millionaire—he was kept in a barn and fed oats all the time! This is not a genuine explanation, of course, but it is a fun one. A comedian might well be able to build a good joke out of it, and enough playing with it might lead to something more serious.

- **Is early death a policy for racehorses?** Derived from EQ8: What are the policies of this institution?
- **Is early death a goal for racehorses?** Derived from EQ9: What are the goals of this institution?
- **Is early death a plan for racehorses?** Derived from EQ10: What plan was this institution carrying out?
- **Was something else more important for racehorses than avoiding early death?** Derived from EQ11: What did this institution decide was more important?

At first glance none of the questions that deal with the goals and plans of racehorses seems reasonable since racehorses aren't planners. In many circumstances these questions wouldn't be appropriate. But to be creative we must resist the temptation to dismiss ideas that seem odd too soon. Instead, we must ask what conjecture we might use to *make* the question relevant. What if Swale were a super-intelligent horse? In that case questions relating to his planning ability would be very helpful.

- **What made Swale decide to die?** Derived from EQ13: What caused the actor to behave this way? This would get us to thinking about why Swale might have killed himself, but is not a reasonable question for the same reason as above; we don't believe that Swale was a decider.
- **Is Swale a member of some group for whom early death is normal?** Derived from EQ14: Is the actor a member of any group that is known to perform this anomalous behavior? This question is a rich source of remindings and can lead to different kinds of groups to focus on.

  Thinking about Swale as an athlete who died despite top conditioning can remind us of the famous jogger, Jim Fixx, who also died unexpectedly. Jim Fixx had a heart defect that interacted badly with his jogging and caused him to have a heart attack. Perhaps this is what killed Swale?

  You can also think of Swale as an incredibly successful performer and get reminded of other performers who died young, like Janis Joplin and John Belushi. Perhaps the pressure of being on top got to Swale, and he started taking recreational drugs. This sounds dumb because horses don't do recreational drugs. But once you start thinking about drugs you can be led to lots of interesting explanations. Perhaps Swale's owner was giving him drugs to make him run faster, and he accidentally gave the horse too much. Perhaps Swale was poisoned.

The point is that thinking about these standard questions can get you started toward an explanation. Sometimes the obvious answer makes no sense but can be turned into something that makes sense. Creativity depends on taking standard questions and not accepting the standard answers.

2.7.2 Explanation Patterns

An XP is a fossilized explanation in much the same way that a script is a fossilized plan. Both are memory structures that encode some knowledge in memory so that it does not have to be rederived every time it is needed. The function of an XP is very specific: It connects a "to be explained" event to things that have been understood in the past by applying an explanation that has worked in previous situations. We have tons of XPs in memory, and the purpose of asking ourselves EQs is to access some appropriate ones.

An explanation pattern consists of several parts, each of which is used by some portion of the explanation process. The components of an XP are as follows:

2.7.3 Components of an Explanation Pattern

1. A pattern representing the kinds of anomalies that the XP will explain.
2. A set of indices under which the XP can be retrieved.
3. A set of states of the world in which the pattern is likely to apply.
4. A set of states of the world in which the pattern is likely to be relevant even if it doesn't apply directly. (It may still supply some useful input to the tweaker.)
5. A network of states and actions, with the causal relationships among them, that show how the premises of the explanation could lead to explaining the event.
6. Specific remindings associated with the explanation.

One of the death-related XPs many of the subjects in our informal poll about Swale seemed to have is the one that we call, "KILLED FOR INSURANCE MONEY." This XP looks something like the following:

2.7.4 Killed for the Insurance Money XP

1. **Anomaly:** untimely death
2. **Indices:** unexpected death; death of heavily insured person
3. **When likely to apply:** Unsavory character is beneficiary of a policy that is worth more to him than the person is worth alive. Person has been killed.

4. **When likely to be relevant:** Deceased was rich; relatives of deceased didn't like him; beneficiary of policy is greedy.

5. **Causal Network:**
    - Beneficiary dislikes policyholder.
    - Dislike makes beneficiary want to harm policyholder.
    - Beneficiary has goal to get lots of money.
    - One plan for getting lots of money is to get it from an insurance company.
    - Insurance plan requires death of policyholder without company knowing that beneficiary killed him.
    - Beneficiary kills the insured to satisfy desire to harm him and to get the money.

Of course there are many, many XPs that you might retrieve when thinking about Swale. Some of the proverbial explanations that come to mind about death in general include:

- Early death comes from being malnourished as a youth.
- High living brings early death.
- An inactive mind can cause the body to suffer.
- High pressure jobs cause heart attacks.
- Only the good die young.
  And so on...

It is easy to get overloaded with XPs. The tricky research question is how to organize memory so that just the right number of XPs pop out when an anomaly arises. We don't want to get so few that we miss interesting explanations, but at the same time, we don't want to have every death we've ever heard of come to mind and suggest a new explanation.

2.8 CREATIVE PROBLEM SOLVING

Why is it that you want to come up with creative explanations? Creative explanations lead to creative solutions. When we are faced with a problem, the solutions we can come up with are a function of how we understand the problem. If we are stuck with the standard explanations, we'll be stuck with the standard solutions. If we can develop new, creative explanations, they will suggest new solutions.

Let's take a look at applying the methods discussed throughout this chapter to the problem of terrorism. Now, we don't of course claim to have solved the problem of world terrorism, that's not the point. The point is to show how, by thinking about a problem using the creative explanation methods we've talked about, we could develop some unusual solutions to a problem, some of which just might have value.

We start by describing some of the standard EQs as applied to terrorism, along with some XPs associated with each EQ. The XPs are all in the form of proverbs, since that is a nice way to think about many XPs and to express them concisely. We gathered them simply by searching through a book of proverbs [Fergusson, 1983] and picking out some that seemed relevant to terrorism.

- **EQ1.1: How does terrorism benefit people?** Adversity makes a man wise not rich. He that is down need fear no fall. Adversity is the touchstone of virtue.
- **EQ2: What motivates the terrorists?** Covetousness is the root of all evil. No mischief but that woman or a priest is behind it. Poverty is the mother of crime. He that has suffered more than is fitting will do more than is lawful.
- **EQ7: What are the motives of the institutions that back terrorism?** Pouring oil on the fire is not the way to prevent it. The stick is the surest peacemaker. If you want to see blackhearted people, look among those who never miss their prayers.
- **EQ8: What are the policies of those institutions?** Ask and it shall be given unto you. He that demands misses not, unless his demands are foolish. It is better to be the hammer than the anvil. Cities are taken by their ears.
- **EQ9: What are the goals of those institutions?** No penny, no paternoster. Keep not ill men company lest you increase their number.
- **EQ10: What plans are those institutions carrying out?** There is no cure for fear but to cut off the head. For a flying enemy make a golden bridge.
- **EQ11: What will this institution do next?** You may play with the bull till his horn gets in your eye. Danger makes men devout. Out of the frying pan into the fire.
- **EQ14: What other groups behave in a similar manner?** Show me a liar, and I'll show you a thief. Some have been thought brave because they were afraid to run away.

Let's now look at the some of these explanatory proverbs and see what kind of solution we might build out of these XPs.

Adversity makes a man wise, not rich. This is a reference to the effects of terrorist acts on the victims. It suggests that people who suffer from terrorism become wiser, but this isn't too helpful when trying to stop terrorism. However, one might get the idea of reversing the actor and objects in this XP, generating the idea of subjecting the terrorists to adversity to make them wiser.

Covetousness is the root of all evil. The reason terrorists do what they do is that they want something, say money or power. Two plans that might be associated with covetousness are to give them what they want, or to convince them that they can't get what they want. This instantiates into two ideas: giving large grants to terrorist groups in exchange for stopping terrorism, or arming antiterrorist groups so well that the terrorists will have no hope.

No mischief but that a woman or a priest is at the bottom of it.   At first this doesn't seem like it applies, unless we think of generalizing one of the actors from priests to other religious leaders such as Khomeini. We might get the idea that getting rid of Khomeini would be a way to end terrorism.

He that has suffered more than is fitting will do more than is lawful.   This is a fairly realistic explanation and suggests relieving the suffering experienced by downtrodden peoples in order to eliminate the cause of terrorism.

Pouring oil on the fire is not the way to prevent it.   This suggests different interesting explanations depending on who is pouring oil on the fire. If the terrorist leaders are pouring oil on the fire, you might think of reasons they want the troubles to continue. One is faced with a new explanation problem that suggests new XPs, such as *"Little man benefits from war between two big men."* By adopting this view you could try to find some way to keep terrorism from being a method for terrorist leaders to gain power. You might also think that it is the attention paid to terrorism that is pouring oil on the fire. Encouraging the news media to pay less attention to terrorism is a counterplan suggested in this case.

2.9 CONCLUSION

In this chapter we have argued that the roots of creativity lie in a very simple, mechanical process: Notice a problem, get reminded of a similar problem, tweak the solution that worked for the old problem into a solution for the new problem. We have shown that it should not be impossibly hard to inject some creativity into our computer programs if we can start them off with a large enough library of Explanation Patterns and enough knowledge about how to modify them to fit new situations as they arise. Of course, the algorithms for getting reminded and for tweaking are not by any means trivial. In part, this chapter represents a call to action, to work on solving these problems. Some work on these issues has been ongoing in our lab at Yale (see [Kass, Leake, and Owens, 1986; Kass, 1986; Leake and Owens, 1986; Kass, 1989; 1990; Leake, 1990]).

The main problem that we didn't touch on at all is the evaluation of explanations. A good explainer has to be able to rank competing explanations and to reject bad explanations in favor of better ones. The explainer has to know when to be satisfied with the explanations it has developed and when to go on explaining because everything so far has been junk. Lenat ran into some similar problems with evaluating new ideas in the EURISKO experiment [Lenat, 1984] and had to rely partly on manual rejection of uninteresting concepts. Evaluation is a difficult process to make mechanical because so many different kinds of knowledge could conceivably come into play.

On the other hand, evaluation isn't so critical to creative thinking. If our goal is to produce creative computers, we ought to design machines that can come up with exciting ideas before we worry about being able to weed out bad or uninteresting ideas. In fact, if someone is too good at throwing out "uninteresting" ideas, it will actually hurt his creativity. Creativity relies on taking a hypothesis that may seem absurd at first and keeping it around long enough to change it into something interesting. This is why we expect that computers will eventually become even more creative than human beings because, unlike most humans, they won't get bored spending long periods playing with seemingly absurd ideas.

References

Charniak, E. 1978. On the use of framed knowledge in language comprehension, *Artificial Intelligence,* 11/3 (1978), pp. 225–265.

Cullingford, R. 1978. *Script Application: Computer Understanding of Newspaper Stories,* PhD Thesis, Yale University, Research Report #116.

DeJong, G. 1981. Generalizations based on explanations, *Proceedings of the Seventh International Joint Conference on Artificial Intelligence,* Vancouver, B.C., Canada, August 1981.

Fergusson, R. 1983. *The Penguin Dictionary of Proverbs,* Market House Books, LTD., Middlesex, England.

Hammond, K., ed. 1989. *Proceedings of the 1989 Workshop on Case-Based Reasoning.* Morgan Kaufmann, San Mateo, CA.

Hammond, K. 1989. *Case-Based Planning as a Memory Task.* Academic Press.

Kass, A. 1986. Modifying explanations to understand stories, *Proceedings of the Eighth Annual Conference of the Cognitive Science Society,* Cognitive Science Society, Amherst, MA, August 1986.

——— , 1989. Adaptation-based explanation: Extending script/frame theory to handle novel input, *Proceedings of the Eleventh International Joint Conference on Artificial Intelligence.* Morgan Kaufmann, San Mateo, CA.

——— , 1990. *Developing Creative Hypotheses by Adapting Explanations,* PhD Thesis, Yale University.

Kass, A.M. and Leake, D.B. and Owens, C.C. 1986. *SWALE: A Program that Explains*. In [Schank 1986].

Kolodner, J., ed. 1989. *Proceedings of the 1988 Workshop on Case-Based Reasoning*. Morgan Kaufmann, San Mateo, CA.

Leake, D.B. 1990. *Evaluating Explanations*, PhD Thesis, Yale University.

Leake, D.B. and Owens, C.C. 1986. Organizing memory for explanation, *Proceedings of the Eighth Annual Conference of the Cognitive Science Society*, Cognitive Science Society, Lawrence Erlbaum Associates, NJ.

Lenat, D.B. and Brown, J.S. 1984. Why AM and EURISKO appear to work, *Artificial Intelligence*, /23 .

Minsky, M. 1975. A framework for representing knowledge, *The Psychology of Computer Vision*, P. Winston ed., McGraw-Hill, NY, Chapter 6, pages 211–277.

Mitchell, T.M., Keller, R.M., and Kedar-Cabelli, S.T. 1986. Explanation-based generalization: A unifying view, *Machine Learning*, 1/1, pp. 47–80.

Riesbeck, C.K. and Schank, R.C. 1989. *Inside Case-Based Reasoning*. Lawrence Erlbaum Associates, Hillsdale, NJ.

Schank, R.C. and Abelson, R. 1977. *Scripts, Plans, Goals and Understanding*, Lawrence Erlbaum Associates, Hillsdale, NJ.

Schank, R.C. 1975. *Fundamental Studies in Computer Science*, Volume 3: *Conceptual Information Processing*, North-Holland, Amsterdam.

——— , 1982. *Dynamic Memory: A Theory of Learning in Computers and People*, Cambridge University Press.

——— , 1986. *Explanation Patterns: Understanding Mechanically and Creatively*, Lawrence Erlbaum Associates, Hillsdale, NJ.

COMMENTARY

Jean-Gabriel Ganascia
(Laforia, Paris, France)

It is obvious that Schank's contribution to artificial intelligence is very original. But, beyond his personal style of presentation, which is very illustrative, Schank presents such a different approach to AI that it raises many questions not only on technical topics, but also on the basis of AI. In fact, his approach is not limited to technical answers to machine learning problems, but it also deals with the incorporation of learning into AI techniques. Moreover, Schank himself uses philosophical words, like "creativity," and he asks fundamental questions, as in the introductory title "What is Intelligence?" Those questions are so important that people working in AI cannot ignore them, but at the same time, they are so general that they could be understood from a philosophical, psychological, logical, or technical point of view. According to which point of view is chosen, the answers may be different. Schank seems to criticize the traditional AI point of view which is, according to his view, too close to logic, so he proposes a point of view more oriented towards psychology. The purpose of this commentary is to highlight and discuss some of the questions that underlie Schank's chapter in order to show both the consistency and the limitations of Schank's approach to machine learning.

Before going into more detail, we can note that, as is often the case in Schank's work, the presentation is accompanied by many examples. It may be only for the sake of clarity, with a pedagogical aim. However, since the substance of the paper is precisely to demonstrate the central role of examples in the process of understanding, it is then natural to think that the predominant role of examples in the presentation cannot be reduced to illustration. Studying the text more carefully, we can note that the examples are redundant: Where one example would illustrate a notion, Schank uses many examples to show the generality of the purpose. Moreover, Schank's text seems to be, *per se*, an illustration of the understanding process it describes: By using many common life experiences, Schank forces us to ask questions and remember personal experiences.

Later we shall study this question in more detail, but, in parallel, let us also note that there is neither formalism nor proof in the mathematical sense of the word.

Schank establishes the validity and generality of his ideas by illustrating them in particular cases without having to exhibit logical proofs. Therefore, the examples, being demonstrative, would constitute a proof by themselves. The difference between a mathematical proof and an "examples proof" lies both in the problems that can be handled and in the nature of the conviction which follows from the proof. However, they are all proofs and the "examples proof" is obviously easier to understand. According to his presentation, Schank himself explicitly supports the elimination of logic and mathematics from AI to the benefit of the psychological likelihood of elementary mental acts. The following comment by Shank illustrates this point clearly:

> Schank: *Mathematical reasoning is a very interesting kind of mechanistic thought that some people are capable of doing. But it is a very small part of the general reasoning process. The more interesting question to me is: "Why is AI obsessed with logical reasoning?" Mathematicians are going to AI just as if things were going to be easier in AI. This fascination with PROLOG is a good example of the same phenomenon. They want things to be easy. There is this desire to have AI be a simpler problem than it is. But I always say that AI is so much more difficult than any of us has ever conceived, that the idea that it is going to be solved by adapting predicate calculus is bizarre somehow. It is more complicated than that. I have only one thing to say for the sake of simplicity: When you see human behaviors that are fascinating in their complexity, there are often simple underlying mechanisms and, in a way, this is the point of my talk. How can you get machines to create explanations* ex nihilo *seems very hard. Since even very stupid people seem to do it all the time, they must be simpler mechanisms.*

At first sight, such a claim could be surprising for at least two "candid" reasons—a technical reason and a philosophical one. On the one hand, from a technical point of view, it seems inconsistent to avoid the logical decomposition of thought operators since, eventually, the ultimate goal of AI is to reproduce these operators in a logical machine. On the other hand, from a philosophical point of view, AI, as every scientific activity, requires some rational foundations which, up to now, were mainly established by logic and mathematics. Therefore, rejecting them leads to the removal of the backbone of AI. Although these two criticisms are severe, it is interesting to refute them because it will help us go deeper into the study of Schank's chapter.

As regards the technical aspect, it is obvious that Schank does not want to exclude programming thought operators by coding them in a formal language. He only wants to delay the formalization by studying, beforehand, the thought processes themselves—learning, explaining, etc.—and the objects they handle—explanations, memory structures etc. More precisely Schank says that logic and mathematics are not appropriate to study thought activities, which does not mean that mental processes cannot be described by formal languages once they have been isolated. However, of all the processes isolated, some such as indexing or tweaking, seem combinatoric. Moreover, to be introduced in AI programs, they must be broken down into elementary processes which Schank does not describe. Therefore, according to Schank, a systematic study of intelligent acts ought to lead to discovering and then describing such elementary processes. But, although this study could constitute the main part of AI, it is far from being complete. This is why Schank's chapter is closer to a research program than to an achievement description. That is also why our commentary is simply oriented towards the possible implications of this work.

In addition to that, those elementary thought processes, once discovered, may correspond to processes already studied such as analogy, generalization, explanation-based generalizations (EBG), or subgoaling. In this case, it would be possible to compare Schank's work with previous ones which would enable us to measure its originality, to establish its formal bases and maybe to enrich it. The first part of this commentary will be devoted to this comparison, so we shall partially answer the first objection, the technical one. However, this technical study of cognitive modeling does not answer Schank's claim that basic mental processes need to be elucidated by AI before any formalization. Of course, it seems obvious that it is wiser to understand phenomena clearly before formalizing them than to formalize without understanding. But Schank proposes a particular way of understanding those phenomena. What could prove the relevance of mental processes isolated in such a way? With this question we come back to the second objection to Schank's chapter we addressed, the philosophical one. It concerns the lack of a rational foundation of AI without logic and mathematics. Without attempting to define the foundations of rationality, it is possible to give some strong evidence that could help us understand and justify Schank's work. We shall see below that Schank's work is mainly based on the observation of what humans actually do and do not do. So, it relies on a natural psychology collecting facts about daily life. Having said that, it is interesting to note that the model of thought proposed by Schank is also based on the organization of large collections of data. Thus, there is a parallel between the method used to discover how humans act and the model of thought that Schank proposes.

While rejecting formal logic, Schank proposes a perfectly consistent theory of intelligence. This is what we shall demonstrate in this paragraph, then we shall see that learning and creativity play a central role in that theory. Before, to understand better, let us note that the word "truth" is absent from Schank's text. This absence is surprising as one would naturally imagine that thought has to discriminate between the true and the false. In fact, this classical view certainly explains the traditional approach of AI based on logic that Schank opposes. However, although absolute truth is not common in everyday life and establishing formal proofs constitutes a very small proportion of intellectual activity, it is amazing to speak about intelligence without mentioning truth. Does it only mean that Schank wants to substitute the absolute truth used in classical logic for a weak truth? or, do we need to reconsider all the thought-analysis categories which, having been inherited from logic, have been used as a basis for problem solving? Considering this point, there is no doubt that Schank criticizes the traditional approach of AI:

> Schank: *Problem solving is probably one of the worst paradigms you could study, if you want to study intelligence. I realize that attacking Newell and Simon is considered a heresy in AI. But, I have listened to Simon's lecture too many times to accept it any longer, and maybe the time has come to do that. I think that, when you are dealing with problem solving, you have a fairly artificial situation not necessarily related to the kind of things that intelligent people do easily. What I mean is: at school, many people are poor problem solvers. They do poorly in mathematics, in physics, they do poorly in a whole range of subjects, and yet the same people speak English, and read stories, and can write good literature. They are poor problem solvers, but they may be very brilliant. One of the things that got me into this kind of work was that I realized that one of the reasons why they did not do that well is that problem solving as it is approached in mathematics and, therefore, in AI tends to be very abstract.*

Without any ambiguity this text shows how severe Schank's attitude is against classical AI. His criticisms are mainly oriented against problem solving, which is considered as limited to artificial situations. But, the main point is that Schank opposes the ability to deal with an abstract situation with the ability to speak English, understand and write books, etc. Therefore one of the main characteristics of intelligent behavior could be to master natural language and the goal of AI ought to be shifted from problem solving to understanding. Considering this shift of objective, it is easy to understand that logical categories like proposition, proof, or truth tend to disappear: They are adapted to represent and manipulate formal descriptions but not to describe understanding processes. As an illustration, let us read Schank's criticism against one fundamental concept inherited from logic, the concept of provability:

> Schank: *This concept of provability is wrong from the point of view of AI. You cannot argue about anything being provable. What you can argue is that, if you have a, b, and c, and if they always occur together, you can say therefore that they occur together. That is human reasoning. Humans often do not know what they are doing. They like to delude themselves and think they know. How many people here really know how an electric light works? Not too many, I am quite sure.*

In order to exclude fundamental concepts inherited from logic, Schank introduces new thought-analysis categories like explanations, memory structures, expectations, and consistency. Consequently the role that learning has to play in AI is slightly different from what it is in a more traditional view. But, to understand this role better, let us summarize schematically the objectives of theorem proving and understanding.

A theorem-proving process has to establish the truth value of a proposition. Usually it builds up a proof by chaining axioms. In this framework, learning is a complementary process which has to build up new axioms, or correct old ones, or modify the theorem prover itself by improving its efficiency. It is then possible to consider learning as a process separated from theorem proving even though learning requires theorem-proving techniques.

On the other hand, considering the understanding process, learning is so intricate that it is impossible to separate its role from other processes. That is what we are going to show, but, in order to do that it is important to see that, for Schank, the understanding process is not limited to rendering a text meaningful. There is a gradation in understanding that comes from a simple meaning attribution: Something makes sense, to a full understanding when you are in a complete empathy with something. More precisely the understanding act could be seen as an iterative process whose basic cycle could be broken down into two steps: First, ask expectation-generating questions and then, if expectations are not confirmed, build up an explanation for this failure. In that sense, explanations are defined as connections to memory structures that render an anomaly; i.e., an expectation failure, nonanomalous. We can note that in that way the meaning of explanations is completely different from that in explanation-based generalization [Mitchell, *et al.*, 1986] where explanations mean proof tree. In this framework, two complementary processes play a central role: anomaly discovery and explanation construction.

The search for questions that make anomaly detection possible is certainly a central part of intelligence, but it is not conceived by Schank as a creative process. It is only the pretext to creativity; it simulates wondering, which provokes creativity. As to creativity, it is the ability to construct new explanations from older ones stored in the memory. Once created, these new explanations are generalized and introduced into the memory. Thus, learning could be classified here as explanation and failure based. However, what distinguishes Schank's learning from most of the symbolic learning techniques usually represented in AI is neither the learning strategy using failure, nor the use of explanations. Instead it is the central role learning plays since it is totally enmeshed with the creation of explanations. Hence, learning is completely integrated into the understanding process: Learning means to understand a situation in such a way that this understanding can be reused when a similar situation occurs. Therefore, once it is stored in the memory, an explanation must be retrieved whenever necessary and adapted to deal with the new anomaly.

It is then easy to understand why Schank introduces an indexed memory and a tweaking mechanism. The memory is indexed with anomalies in order to retrieve explanations when necessary, i.e., when a similar anomaly appears, without having to scan all the possible explanations stored in the memory, while the tweaking mechanism is intended to adapt the old explanation to the new anomaly.

So indexed memory and tweaking have well-defined objectives and the examples shown by Schank turn out their psychological likelihood. However, as Schank himself admits, full descriptions of indexing and tweaking are still an open area. That is both an unfortunate and fruitful consequence: Instead of starting from known and experienced abstract mechanisms to reproduce intelligent behavior, Schank begins by studying intelligence and then derives the nature of fundamental mechanisms that have to be simulated, even if those mechanisms are not yet totally elucidated. This approach is certainly fruitful because it reveals new problems and new questions, but it is also unfortunate since some of those mechanisms would turn out to be uncomputable. In addition to that first unfortunate consequence, nothing except a small set of examples proves the relevancy of those mechanisms. Therefore they could be relevant only for the examples that help us to induce them. We can always argue about the psychological validity of those mechanisms; but, even though the modalities of demonstration may differ in psychology and in "hard sciences" like mathematics or physics, psychology has to make its assumptions clear.

We shall not discuss, here, the rational bases of psychology that go beyond the purpose of this commentary, but, we would like to prevent creating a circle in which AI programs would be validated by their psychological consistency and psychological concepts by their successful use in AI programs. Schank argues that people do not use logic when thinking. This may be true, but psychological introspection is not sufficient to prove how people index their memory or how they tweak their old explanations. That requires some psychological study that cannot be reduced to the exhibition of 10 or 20 well-chosen examples. It is necessary to make an experimental study, the protocol of which is not described at all. More precisely, if we read in detail Schank's arguments in favor of psychology, they do not rely on a real scientific method. Institutional psychology is an experimental science in the sense that it has to validate assumptions with experiments. This means a real protocol and a relevant, statistical analysis of resulting data. With his examples, Schank relates experiences that are closer to an illustration of what he advanced than to a scientific experiment. They convince because they make reference to everybody's daily life. Therefore, the psychology to which Schank refers is not an experimental science. Nevertheless, that does not mean that it could not be considered as a scientific activity; but, it is more similar to the natural sciences, such as geology or zoology, which rely on a large number of observations that they have to classify in order to make analogies and, if possible, predictions. In conclusion, whatever the scientific validity of the natural sciences, it seems that the point of Schank's references to psychology is not to look for a scientific validation, but to make a lot of observation in order to understand what humans actually do and what they never do when they think. However, the scientific validation of this work remains a real problem.

It is interesting to compare new mechanisms introduced by Schank with more classical mechanisms used in AI, even though they are not oriented toward the same perspective. These classical mechanisms could be used either directly or by marriage with the ones proposed by Schank. So it is for discovery and analogy. Without going into a detailed parallel between these works and Schank's work, it could be fruitful, as proposed by L. Rendell at IMAL, to match up Gentner's structural mapping [Gentner, 1983] and Schank's indexed memory. In the same way, Kodratoff's theoretical work on generalization uses a mechanism called structural matching, which seems very similar to tweaking. More precisely structural matching applies syntactical transformations to formulae until they match, while particular details are represented by bound variables. With semantics, heuristics channel these tranformations in order to limit alternatives (for more details see [Kodratoff and Ganascia, 1986]). With structural matching it should be easy to choose heuristics by translating Schank's in order to realize the tweaking. For instance "transpose the actor and object in a given situation" could be translated as constraining the variabilization of a constant or "substitute other objects that share a given class membership with the standard object" can be understood as climbing a generalization taxonomy. Then it is sufficient to structurally match two anomalies, the first to be explained and the second to be stored in the memory associated to an explanation. When the two anomalies structurally match, it is sufficient to reuse the old explanation corresponding to the second anomaly and, then, to add its variable bindings corresponding to the new anomaly. In addition to that, once validated, the explanation could be easily generalized by simply dropping useless variable bindings.

Reusing structural matching for tweaking is only an example showing how classical AI techniques could be applied to simulate processes isolated by Schank. However it is interesting to see that structural matching has been completely integrated into a logical framework, which does not exclude the introduction of heuristics. More generally, it seems quite impossible to implement or validate powerful mechanisms without using logic and mathematics. If psychological elucidation of elementary thought processes is necessary, it is also important to take into account the logical dimension of programming that plays a central role in AI. Failing this, there is a risk that isolated mechanisms could not be reproducible or, if they were, that such a reproduction would be limited to a small set of examples.

In the same way, Schank makes many references to the notion of indexed memory. This memory stores past experiences, which are indexed so that it would be possible to retrieve an old experience when a similar experience occurs. Schank admits that the nature of indices is not well defined—anomalies, explanations, explanation patterns, explanation questions, etc.—but he insists on the fact that memory is episodic and that it stores real cases; i.e., little stories. The following discussion illustrates this point:

> Michalski: *I think we have to raise the issue of what you mean by case, because I agree that, whatever we see of experience, we relate it to our past experience, to our own past knowledge. That is not the same as relating to cases, as a case may be*

understood as something very specific, as the one you mentioned where people re-late the situation in El Salvador to what happened in Vietnam. The case you men-tioned is not actually what happened in Vietnam, but rather a personal interpretation of what happened. If you asked Vietnamese or Russians or Poles or Americans what the Vietnam episode means to them you will get very different an-swers. So a case is not the real thing, but an interpretation.

Schank: *No, they are real things, but your argument is that cases are not shared by everybody. They are cultural. All Americans share certain cases, by virtue of being Americans, but individual experience cases act in the same way. I can recall how often I heard you say, "When I was in Poland, X" or "In Poland they do X." Those are your cases. Your cases are the little stories that you choose to tell to illustrate a situation. A case is a story. The stories that you tell over and over again are the cases. Afterwards, there are thousands of cases. We have the case of staying in this hotel. It has nothing unusual about it. It will never come up again. But, when there is something unusual, as the only time you ever stayed in mountains like these, then it becomes a case. A case does not have to be defined very critically. It is definitely a question of person. It is definitely one of the reasons why somebody recalls with a story and somebody else does not. The question of knowing why one remembers a case comes from the fact that he has had a personal experience that was indexed that way.*

Michalski: *It is important to relate what you are saying to what in our community we call examples. Your cases are not examples. Your cases are a sort of generalized interpreted example. They are some kind of abstraction.*

Schank: *My cases are not abstractions. We reason from particulars and not from abstractions. The society at large—this is not only an attack on AI—teaches ab-stractions and not particular cases. There is a fascination with abstractions in our society that, I think, happens to go against the natural process of learning. We should try to teach things that are much more concrete. Human beings do not say, "I had this abstract experience, and I try to remember particulars." They tell you the particulars. They have no problem remembering the particulars. The details of the particulars that they can reconstruct: "I was in a restaurant, and I ate with a fork." That they did not remember but they reconstructed it from the prototype. The interesting details of the case get remembered just in that way, not in terms of any abstraction.*

But we can also argue against Schank's claims that we memorize formal laws, for instance every scientist knows Ohm's law $V = RI$. Formal laws are part of a back-ground knowledge that has to be used in parallel with particulars. The rest of Schank's and Michalski's discussion illustrates this point:

Michalski: *What I am arguing, is that cases alone are not enough. You need both cases, which are very useful, because they can modify, improve, and refine your knowledge, but you also need knowledge.*

Schank: *Let me rephrase your question. I am not arguing against knowledge, and please, do not think I am. What I am arguing against is abstract rules. Knowledge is also cases. Do not put me on the side of being anti-knowledge. That having been said, my argument about abstract rules is that they are cases that people can do. Let us talk about an engineer that can figure out computers, and he has learned to do like that. After a while, he does not have to think about what he is doing, does he? Same thing with a doctor "Take an aspirin and call me in the morning!" That works... He does not have to remember what the words mean because he can get away with it. My argument is that there have to be cases, beneath those rules, that you can refer to and that you can get away with, when something goes wrong. Then abstract, rule-based systems, which do not have those cases underneath, are not intelligent. That is the claim.*

However, Schank's claim that cases are particular, can be countered in two ways—a psychological way and a formal way. Schank refutes this objection by saying that human memory is only based on particulars even if people can memorize abstract rules, since, eventually these are based on particulars. What is interesting in this discussion is that Schank refutes the objection only in a psychological way. In fact, he does not fully answer Michalski's question. More precisely, in AI, each experience has to be represented in a machine, so that whatever the data structure used—frames, schemas, scripts—this representation uses descriptors as, for instance, slot identifiers, which are abstractions. Even though they can evolve, these identifiers bias the knowledge representation, thus it seems impossible to have a knowledge representation for cases independent from the descriptors used for that representation. Consequently, it may be possible that humans can memorize cases without reference to any interpretation, but in the practice of AI we need to interpret cases before memorizing them.

On the other hand, it is amazing that Schank does not mention any more work on concept discovery in his chapter on creativity. Actually, it seems obvious that creativity has to do not only with adapting old experiences to new situations, but also with modifying, refining, and creating concepts. Moreover work on genetic psychology, like Piaget's, tend to show that the progressive acquisition of abstract concepts plays a central part in knowledge acquisition. Even if abstractions are not memorized, concepts are necessary to represent and interpret cases. Thus, it would be very important to acquire new concepts from experience and then change automatically the representation of examples as the conceptual background evolves. But Schank says nothing about concepts. Are they explanations, indices, or descriptors that make the explanations possible? How do they evolve? So many questions with no answers.

This absence of reference to work on concept discovery seems because Schank considers cases and their representation independently. But, in so doing he ignores one of the main aspects of creativity.

As an illustration, let us recall the following example given by Schank:

Schank: *Would you go to a doctor who memorizes a textbook or one who has treated 10,000 cases?*

Michalski: *I have a question. Would you rather be treated by a doctor who did not have much experience, but went to the best medical schools, or let's say some kind of witchcraft bushman doctor who had seen 10,000 cases (most of these people died afterwards of course).*

Schank: *In fact that is rarely the choice!... It tends not to be choices that we would have to deal with. I think the real choice in our life is a doctor who has been out of school for 10 years and one who just has gotten out of school. You always choose the one who has been out of school for 10 years. Why? Not because of the rules, because of the cases. We are not interested in rules.*

It seems obvious that, in that case, there is no real choice. Nevertheless, let us rephrase the question: would you rather be treated by a nurse who has worked for 15 years or by a young doctor who has just finished school?

Knowing that, in the course of medical studies, there are not only theoretical courses but also case studies, I would undoubtedly rather go to the young doctor. Even if the nurse has seen more cases, the young doctor has the theoretical knowledge that makes him able to envisage all the risks and to understand how drugs or therapies act. Although textbooks cannot replace years of experience, they structure the knowledge and enable us to have a better organization of memory. So, abstract knowledge plays an important role in observation based subjects like medicine. This does not mean that medicine could be reduced to abstractions or to logic but that the way a doctor makes a diagnosis and the way she treats a patient depend on knowledge she has acquired at university in textbooks. Therefore, we can say that the representation and organization of cases are influenced by years of education and that nothing could replace textbooks, even experience, which doesn't contradict Schank's claim that there are cases underlying everything we memorize.

In conclusion, the style of Schank's paper makes it appear as a manifesto, in the sense that it opens many new perspectives and puts forwards many new ideas without showing actual programs implementing all those ideas. Indeed, he could be accused of wanting to study only the hard problems in AI. Schank's answer is obviously that these are the only problems that really matter. But what are those problems? Wouldn't it be better to leave the conclusion to Schank himself?

Porter: *A long time ago, Allan Turing made three suggestions on major areas to work on, such as natural language and chess. Since you are right there on top of the mountain, what would you recommand the AI community work on for the next 20 years?*

Schank: *Memory! Memory! That keeps being left out by all these great thinkers.*

Porter: *But memory is too big a thing.*

Schank: *Yes, I know. It can do for 100 years.*

Porter: *Would you have a suggestion of something which would give it a chance to perform and make quick progress?*

Schank: *I think that the history of AI tends to show that such statements are impossible. In terms of understanding, to aim farther than a few years ahead is difficult. My guess is that the issue is really memory organization, representation inside the memory.*

Porter: *Do you have any specific suggestions as what kinds of memory organization issues are critical in the long term for the survival of AI?*

Schank: *I have some heuristics. Things I would do and things I would not do. One I made is stay away from mathematics, which is not the issue. The other is get into domains which seem very close, so that you can really explore them in depth. One of those reasons why cooking, which is really a horrible domain to try to sell to people, actually is a great domain to do work on, is that it is a very close domain. The heuristic I would suggest is, "towards the massive within the particular." Instead of looking at programs that can play with block worlds—which are microworlds, are not rich and did not do it with a large number of things—we have to work on micro-worlds which are rich, which remain microworlds and rich at the same time. I am arguing that the rich microworld of cooking is probably still too grand. The rich microworld of Swale is probably narrower.*

References

Kodratoff, Y. and Ganascia, J.G. 1986. "Improving the generalization Step in Learning," *Machine Learning: An Artificial Intelligence Approach, Volume II*, Michalski, R.S., Carbonell, J.G., Mitchell, T.M., (eds.) Morgan Kaufmann, pp. 215–244.

Genter, D. 1983. "Structure Mapping: A Theoretical Framework for Analogy," *Cognitive Science*, Vol. 7, No. 2, pp. 155–70, April–June 1983.

Mitchell, T.M., Keller, R.M., and Kedar-Cabelli, S.T., 1986. "Explanation-Based Generalizations: A Unifying View," *Machine Learning*, Vol. 1. No. 1, pp. 47–80.

PART
TWO

EMPIRICAL LEARNING
METHODS

3

LEARNING FLEXIBLE CONCEPTS:

Fundamental Ideas and a Method Based on Two-Tiered Representation

Ryszard S. Michalski
(George Mason University)

Abstract

Most human concepts elude precise definition—they have fluid boundaries and context-dependent meaning. We call such concepts *flexible*, in contrast to *crisp* concepts, which are well defined and context independent. As machine learning research has concentrated primarily on learning crisp concepts, learning flexible concepts emerges as a new challenge to the field and an important research direction.

This chapter describes an approach to learning flexible concepts based on a *two-tiered* concept representation. In such a representation, the concept meaning is defined by two components: the *base concept representation* (BCR), and the *inferential concept interpretation* (ICI). The BCR (the first tier) is an *explicit* description of basic concept properties, while the ICI (the second tier) characterizes allowed modifications of the concept meaning and its possible variations in different contexts. Thus, the ICI defines concept boundaries *implicitly*, by the results of matching procedures and inference processes. The latter can be deductive, analogical or inductive.

In the method described, the initial BCR is a complete and consistent concept description, induced from concept examples by a conventional AQ inductive learning program (AQ15). This description is then simplified by the so-called TRUNC procedure, to maximize a *description quality measure*. The so-obtained BCR is usually much simpler than the initial description, but in a strict, logical sense is incomplete with regard to the training examples. The ICI is implemented in the form of a procedure for *flexible matching*, which determines a degree to which instance matches different candidate concepts and chooses the concept that makes the best match. Due to this procedure, training examples that have been "uncovered" during the description-reduction process may still be classified correctly.

The method has been implemented in the learning system AQTT-15, and experimentally applied to learning diagnostic rules in a sample of medical domains. Experiments have shown that the method may produce more significantly reduced concept representations than the traditional approach and that these representations may also perform better in recognizing new concept examples. This surprising and potentially significant result calls for further research and new experiments. In particular, the method should be tested on other problems and in different domains. Other interesting topics for future work include the development of a "direct" method for learning two-tiered representations, an extension of the form of such representations, acquiring the second tier of descriptions through examples, and the development of techniques for learning hierarchically organized two-tiered representations.

We have no sound notions either in logic or physics; substance, quality, action, passion, and existence are not clear notions...

Sir Francis Bacon
Novum Organum, First Book, Chapter 15, 1620

3.1 INTRODUCTION

Most machine learning research done so far has focused primarily on learning *crisp* concepts, by which we mean concepts that have precise and context-independent meaning. Such concepts are usually represented by explicit descriptions, which are either satisfied or not satisfied by any given instance. Popular representations of crisp concepts include logical expressions, production rules, semantic networks, decision trees, and frames. For relevant references see, for example, Volumes I and II of *Machine Learning* [Michalski, Carbonell, and Mitchell, 1983 and 1986]. The tendency to use crisp concepts is characteristic of not only machine learning research but every scientific activity. The clarity and precision of concepts and of their interrelationships has traditionally been, and remains, a mark of quality of scientific theories. Crisp concepts enable us to reason precisely and derive strong conclusions.

Yet, most human concepts used for characterizing real-world objects and employed in communication are *flexible*—as they have fluid and modifiable boundaries, and their meaning often depends on the context of discourse. Note how difficult it is to define precisely and in a context-independent fashion such concepts as "chair," "music," "key," "space," "game," "freedom," or "mechanism," which are frequently used in conversations. To make machine learning programs more applicable to real-world problems, it is crucial to make them able to learn flexible concepts. The key problem in learning such concepts lies in the difficulty of accounting, for all their possible forms, permissible modifications and context dependence. Developing methods for representing and learning flexible concepts thus represents a fundamental new challenge to the field.

Some researchers view the imprecision and flexibility of human concepts as some fault of our language or an imperfection of our mind. In our view, these properties are a consequence of the necessity to cope efficiently with the complexity of our world. As discussed in [Michalski, 1988b], flexible concepts are a powerful means of increasing cognitive economy of our descriptions.

One evidence of this is that in an abstract, simplified world created by our imagination, concepts typically have a precise, well-defined meaning. But once they leave this abstract world and are applied to the real world, these concepts acquire a flexible and context-dependent meaning. Consider, for example, the concept of a triangle. It has a well-defined meaning in geometry. But outside of geometry, the concept "triangle" becomes imprecise and highly context dependent. For example, it can be used to characterize a configuration of streets, a relationship among people, or the shape of a musical instrument. In all these usages certain core properties of the ideal, geometrical concept are preserved, but the specific meaning depends on the context in which it is used.

Moreover, even in the context of geometry, one can distinguish between more or less *typical* triangles. This means that there is a perceived distinction in the *representativeness* of different instances of a given concept. Consider, for example, the concept of a bird. A cardinal is viewed in the U.S. as a more typical bird than, say, an ostrich or a kiwi. In most machine learning programs, however, the distinction between degrees of typicality of different concept examples has been largely ignored. Among the few early exceptions from this general rule is, for example, the idea of *near miss* [Winston, 1975] or the method of *outstanding representatives* for selecting "best" learning examples [Michalski and Larson, 1978].

A related and also relatively unexplored issue involves the degree of precision and accuracy with which individual examples are presented to a learning system. For example, a triangle can be drawn in many different ways: with dotted lines, lines made of other shapes, or to appear as a shadow on an uneven surface. In all these cases, the form may still be recognizable as a triangle. Thus, concept examples may vary greatly in the ways they are presented and may be strongly distorted or modified. Nevertheless, they represent the same concept.

Finally, the complete concept meaning perceived by a person depends on the amount of knowledge this person possesses about it. Clearly, the conceptualization of a triangle by a layperson is different from that of a mathematician specializing in geometry. The difference lies in the number of facts they know about and in the depth of their understanding of the concept and its properties. Such background knowledge-dependency in understanding a concept indicates that human concepts are personalized, living and growing constructs, rather than fixed and stable entities that mean exactly the same thing to all those using them. As the meaning of concepts may change from individual to individual and evolve in time, such concepts cannot be defined precisely as objective impersonal entities with a context-independent meaning. Note, that even fundamental scientific concepts, such as energy, force, light, gravitation, atom and electricity, have been changing and evolving over time. Nonscientific concepts are almost universally flexible, rather than crisp. Thus, in general, human concepts are very different entities than the well-defined and context-independent structures we use to represent concepts in today's computer systems. Determining representations of human concepts that would account for all their possible manifestations, allowable modifications and a change of meaning in different contexts is a fundamentally difficult and unresolved problem.

This problem is not new, however, and there have been many attempts to solve it. One of the most widely known is the work on fuzzy sets by Zadeh and his collaborators and many followers (e.g., [Zadeh, 1965; 1976; 1978; Mumdani and Gaines, 1981]). This approach has concentrated primarily on representing the imprecision of concept boundaries and has proposed to associate with an imprecise concept a *set membership function* that defines the degree to which an instance represents the concept. This is usually a continuous numeric function, which expresses a subjective view of a person about the concept variability. One way to interpret the set membership function is to view it as a representation of the typicality of instances. It has been shown that such a function is useful for computationally representing the influence of linguistic modifiers, such as "very," "more or less," "slightly" on the meaning of concepts. The fuzzy set approach has been widely studied and has found a number of applications, in particular, in the control of complex systems.

This approach does not address, however, several issues relevant to representing flexible concepts. The membership function must be defined by a person and for every context; the approach does not offer methods for automatically deriving such a function. The membership function is usually defined as one argument function; it is difficult to characterize in this way concepts whose boundaries depend on many arguments. For example, it is relatively easy to define the membership function for the concept "tall," whose meaning depends on one argument, the numerical height (and on the context). It is much more difficult to define the membership function for *multiargument* concepts, such as "chair," or "heart condition." The fuzzy set approach does not seem to provide adequate mechanisms for capturing concept extensions, representing multiple but interrelated meanings of a concept, reasoning about the context dependence, or employing background knowledge for interpreting a concept. A set membership function is not sufficient for handling such problems.

In the cognitive science literature, the inadequacy of representing human concepts by context-independent, logic-style definitions (the *classical* view), has been widely recognized (e.g., [Wittgenstein, 1922; McCloskey and Glucksberg, 1978; Barsalou and Medin, 1986; and Lakoff, 1987]). There have been other views advanced, such as the *probabilistic view* and the *exemplar view* (e.g., [Smith and Medin, 1981; Medin and Smith, 1984; Nosofsky, 1987; Allen, *et al.*, 1988]).

The probabilistic view represents concepts by prototypes and uses the so-called *family resemblance principle* (e.g, [Rosch and Mervis, 1975]), while the exemplar view claims that concepts are represented by means of examples (e.g., [Smith and Medin, 1981; Bareiss, Porter, and Craig, 1990—Chapter 4, this volume]). Both views can be criticized on various grounds. The prototype view, which formally is based on the idea of linear separability, disregards the existence of correlations between the attributes, the context dependence, and other information that has been shown to be relevant to human concept understanding (e.g., surprisingly, [Kempler-Nelson, 1984; Estes, 1986; Flannagan, Fried, and Holyoke, 1986]).

The exemplar view promotes the idea of using similarity-based and context-sensitive matching; a view that has received support in the cognitive science literature. It ignores, however, the importance of general concept descriptions, that clearly play a role in human concept formation. Such general descriptions are useful, for example, for comparing different concepts, for recognizing them from partial information, for identifying exceptions, handling context dependence, recording concept changes or for efficiently storing invariant information about concepts. The above operations are difficult to perform, if concepts are represented only by examples. In some work using the exemplar view, general aspects of concepts are captured under the idea of *category structure*, which is a network of domain knowledge that specifies the relevance of exemplars to the concept they define [Bareiss, Porter, and Craig, 1990—Chapter 4, this volume]. Some recent work has advocated a *knowledge-based view*, which emphasizes the need to define concepts through their role in theories in which they exist as interelated components [Carey, 1985; Hofstadter, 1985; Schank, Collins, and Hunter, 1986; Medin, 1989].

The *two-tiered representation* (TT), employed in this chapter, constitutes a significant departure from the existing approaches, although it has a relationship to most of them. The TT approach assumes that concepts have a certain central tendency and proposes to describe this tendency explicitly, as the "first approximation" of the concept. On the other hand, it assumes that concepts' variability and context dependence are best represented implicitly, by appropriate matching methods and context- and background knowledge-dependent rules of inference.

Thus, in the sense that it recognizes that concepts have a central tendency, and that there are typical and less typical concept examples, the TT approach is similar to the probabilistic view and the fuzzy set representation. It has also a relationship to the exemplar view, as it postulates the use of sophisticated matching procedures and inference rules in classifying new instances, and recognizes the usefulness of storing individual examples (by advocating a full or partial memory learning [Reinke and Michalski, 1988]). The TT approach is also closely related to the knowledge-based view, as it stresses the role of background knowledge (and inference) in matching concept with instances, especially, nontypical or borderline instances.

The TT approach was originally proposed by the author in [Michalski, 1986] and was motivated by an observation that although a given individual human concepts may lack precise definition when used alone in a context-independent sense, it acquires precise meaning when used in a combination with other concepts and in a specific context. Consider, for example, the statement: "This tall man in the group in the corner of the room." If there is only one man visibly taller than other people in the indicated group, the statement above precisely specifies the man of interest. The concept "tall," although by itself and/or without context is imprecise (as are the concepts "group," "corner," or "room"), in the given context it conveys a precise meaning—the height of the man pointed out in the group.

Thus, the TT approach views flexible concepts as inherently and intentionally imprecise when they are considered alone and outside of a specific context. Consequently, it does not try to give them a complete and precise meaning in an explicit and context-independent sense. Instead, this approach attempts to describe precisely only the central tendency and to use inference rules and matching procedures to implicitly characterize the complete concept meaning and context dependence.

As mentioned in [Michalski, 1986], the underlying supposition for the TT approach is that the imprecision of human concepts stems not from an undesirable vagueness of our concept definitions, but rather from the universal need for cognitive economy. By allowing concepts to have a context-modifiable meaning, and making them precise only to the extent to which a given situation and/or context requires them to be precise, the expressive power of concepts is greatly enhanced. This means that one can employ fewer concepts for expressing more meanings and helps us simplify our descriptions of our immensely complex universe. The experiments reported here seem to confirm this idea in a microworld to which it was applied.

The following sections describe various aspects of the proposed approach to learning flexible concepts using TT representation, present a simple computational method, and report early experimental results. The learning method employs the inductive learning program AQ15, which is also briefly described. For more details about AQ15, see [Michalski, et al., 1986]. Various improvements to the method and a number of new experimental results with two-tiered representations are reported in [Bergadano, et al., 1988b; 1988c; 1990].

3.2 TWO-TIERED CONCEPT REPRESENTATION

In order to develop a computational method for learning concepts one needs to make assumptions about the meaning of "concepts" in the method. We assume that concepts are named representations of classes of entities, whose borderlines can be imprecise and context dependent. The entities are assumed to have central tendencies within the concept classes, and therefore different concept instances may be characterized by different *typicality*. A concept representation can take a wide range of forms: an explicit description of observable properties of the entities in the class, an abstract description of the function of the entities and their relation to other concepts, a complete or partial listing of the entities, an implied concept characterization by the concept usage, or as a combination of the above. There can be an enormous variation in the specific instantiation of some concepts. Consider, for example, the concepts such as "object" or "set." Because of the assumed central tendencies, context dependence and other previously mentioned properties, a concept representation should allow a varying degree match with concept instances, and use of context-dependent inference rules in performing such matches (examples below illustrate this point in more detail). The problem then is how a concept with such central tendencies and context-dependent meaning can be efficiently represented and learned?

As mentioned earlier, the proposed approach to this problem is based on the idea of two-tiered (TT) concept representation. In the TT representation, a concept is defined by two components: the *base concept representation* (BCR) and the *inferential concept interpretation* (ICI). The BCR (the first tier) is an explicit characterization of a concept, stored directly in the learner's memory. The ICI (the second tier) is a set of matching procedures and inference rules that characterize the allowed modifications and possible variations of the concept meaning in different contexts. Thus, the ICI determines the meaning of a concept by executing these matching procedures and inference rules in the given context, and thus only *implicitly* defines concept boundaries.

In the general theory, the "distribution" of the meaning between the BCR and the ICI is not assumed to be fixed, but is modifiable based on a *criterion of description quality*. One extreme of such a distribution is when the BCR represents explicitly all possible concept variations in different contexts, and the ICI is just direct match. Another extreme is when the BCR is empty, and all concept meaning resides in context-dependent inference rules. The description quality criterion reflects computational properties of the learner and requirements of the problem domain. The former ones include, e.g., the relative costs of remembering concept properties versus deriving them through inference.

In an important, cognitively oriented special case of the TT representation, the BCR is assumed to express the general unifying idea, the typical function of the concept, and/or common measurable properties implied by or correlated with this idea or function. Such a BCR can be viewed as representing the "first approximation of the concept." The ICI, in this case, defines the matching procedures and inference rules for handling less typical instances and context dependence. This type of distribution of the concept meaning between the two tiers facilitates an efficient concept recognition and is related to the idea of censored production rules [Michalski and Winston, 1986].

In matching an instance with the BCR of a concept, the ICI may employ deductive, analogical, or inductive inference. A deductive inference is involved when the instance is a logical consequence of the BCR. An analogical inference is employed when the instance is similar to the BCR in a context-dependent sense. Finally, an inductive inference is employed when in order to match the instance with the BCR the latter needs to be generalized. Illustrative examples of such inference processes are given in Section 3.3. Performing these inferences may involve concept metaknowledge, e.g., the *importance* of concept attributes and frequencies of concept occurrence, the relation to other concepts and other relevant domain knowledge.

An advantage of distributing the concept meaning between the BCR and the ICI is that it permits a learner to flexibly modify or extend the concept meaning by varying matching procedures and inference rules and/or by changing the context of discourse. The concept meaning can thus be changed without having to alter the base concept representation. By evaluating the type and the amount of inference involved in matching a concept with an instance, one may produce a qualitative or quantitative estimation of the strength of such a match. The ability to produce a measure of the strength of match indicates one principal difference between this approach and the fuzzy set approach (e.g., [Zadeh, 1978]). In the fuzzy set approach, a set defining a concept is associated with a membership function, which needs to be *defined* to the learner by a person. The influence of the context is hidden in the definition of this membership function. In the proposed approach, a concept is associated with interpretation procedures and context-dependent inference rules, which implicitly define the membership of an instance in a concept. These rules and procedures can be used to *compute* the membership function in different contexts.

Figure 3–1 illustrates the relationship between the BCR and the ICI in a TT concept representation. It shows that the ICI can, in general, extend the concept meaning beyond the BCR in one area of the description space and reduce the meaning in another area.

The concept explicitly defined by BCR   The concept modified by applying ICI

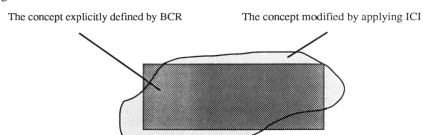

Figure 3–1:   An illustration of the relationship between the Base Concept Representation (BCR) and the Inferential Concept Interpretation (ICI)

Learning a two-tiered representation of a concept consists thus of two parts:

1. acquiring the base representation, and

2. acquiring the inferential concept interpretation (i.e., matching procedures and inference rules for various contexts).

The ICI can be completely or partially shared by concepts in the same class or inherited from a superclass. By sharing ICI, a significant economy of the concept representation can be achieved. As mentioned earlier, the distribution of the concept meaning between BCR and ICI can vary, in order to optimize the obtained description according to an assumed criterion of *description quality*. Such a criterion depends on the use of the concept and the properties of the learner. This implies that the BCR may be in several forms. For example, it can be in the form of an abstract definition, capturing the general principle and the central function of the concept. Such a description can be short, but inefficient for concept recognition. Alternatively, it can be in the form of a specification of easy-to-measure properties of concept instances. The latter description facilitates an efficient concept recognition, but it may be complex and too restrictive. In general, a BCR can be a combination of such forms.

3.3 EXAMPLES ILLUSTRATING TWO-TIERED REPRESENTATION

Let us consider a few examples illustrating the idea of two-tiered representation.

Example 1. Concept of Sugar Maple   Our prototypical image of a sugar maple is that it is a tree with three- to five-lobed leaves that have V-shaped clefts. Some of us may also remember that the teeth on the leaves are coarser than those of red maple, that slender twigs turn brown, and the buds are brown and sharp pointed. As a tree, of course, a maple has roots, a trunk, and branches.

Suppose that while strolling on a nice winter day someone tells you that a particular tree is a sugar maple. A simple introspection tells you that the fact that the tree does not have leaves would not strike you as a contradiction of what you know about sugar maples. Yet, clearly, the presence of leaves of a particular type is deeply embedded in your typical image of a maple tree. The two-tiered theory explains this phenomenon simply: The inferential concept interpretation associated with the general concept of deciduous trees evokes a rule, "In winter deciduous trees lose leaves." Since a maple is deciduous tree, the rule would apply to the maple tree. The result of this inference would override the stored standard information about maple trees, and the inconsistency would be resolved. In this case, matching an instance with the concept requires deductive reasoning from the knowledge associated with a more general concept.

Example 2. Concept of an Abstract Tree Structure   Suppose that a student is reading his first book on computer data structures and encounters a drawing of a graph
structure, which the author calls a "tree." Calling such a structure a tree will likely
not evoke any objection in the student, because he can see in this structure some
abstracted and modified features (e.g., upside-down direction) of a biological tree. In
this case, matching the graph structure with the concept of a tree involves a generalization operation on the base representation.

Example 3. Concept of a Triangle   Let us go back to the concept of a triangle. Formally, a triangle can be described as a geometrical figure consisting of three non-
colinear points connected by straight lines. Using the notation of annotated predicate
calculus (APC), which is equivalent to predicate calculus but permits one to write
logical expressions in a more compact form [Michalski, 1983], one can write:

$$Triangle(T, P1, P2, P3) <= Consists(T, P1 \& P2 \& P3) \& Type(P1 \& P2 \& P3)$$
$$= point \& Connected\_by$$
$$(P1,P2 \& P1,P3 \& P2,P3) = straight\_line \&$$
$$RelationAmong(P1, P2, P3) = noncolinear \qquad (1)$$

In (1), the symbol "&" is used in two related meanings: one, to denote an ordinary (external) conjunction connecting predicates; and second, to denote an *internal
conjunction*, i.e., conjunction of terms, treated as a *compound* argument of a predicate. For example, the predicate "Consists(T, P1 & P2 & P3)" states that the triangle
T consists of points P1 and P2 and P3.

Suppose that someone tells us that the towers in his hometown form a big triangle. Obviously, the meaning of the triangle in this statement differs from that in the
formal geometrical description. To match the two, one needs to make the following
assumptions and transformations:

a. In the context of describing a configuration of physical objects such as towers,
    the individual objects play the role of nodes. Thus, the statement implies that
    there are three towers in the town. The matching operation involves drawing an
    analogy between the abstract nodes and the towers, which can be characterized
    as consisting of one step of generalization (GEN):

Point —GEN → Object

and one step of specialization (SPEC):

Object —SPEC → Tower

b. In the context of towers, the presence of a "straight line" is imaginary, i.e.,
    there is no physical connection, but one could imagine a straight line between
    the objects (towers). The condition "Connected By" is satisfied in such an ab-
    stract sense. This is an operation of generalization. Thus, matching the state-

ment about a triangular arrangement of towers with the formal definition of a triangle involves here both generalization and specialization.

The examples above show that relating a concept instance to a concept representation is not just a straightforward comparison of attribute values in an instance with those in the concept representation, as done in various mechanized decision processes. They show that such a process may involve different forms of inference.

3.4 TRADING BCR FOR ICI

As mentioned earlier, the TT representation does not assume that the distribution of the concept meaning between BCR and ICI is fixed, but that it can change to reflect the goals or the properties of the learning agent. To illustrate the interrelationship between the BCR and the ICI, let us consider an imaginary concept, which we call the "R-ball." Suppose that the complete meaning of this concept is defined by the diagram in Figure 3–2.

Each "1" in the diagram describes an instance of the R-ball by specifying values of attributes for this instance. The set of all instances of the R-ball depicted in the diagram defines precisely the concept of an R-ball. A complete and consistent (CC) description of the concept (i.e., one that covers all "1"s, and does not cover any empty cells) is:

SHAPE = round & BOUNCES = yes
or
SHAPE = round & SIZE = medium or large
or
BOUNCES = yes & SIZE = medium or large   (2)

Any instance that strictly matches any of the above rules is recognized as an R-ball (It is assumed that "&" is interpreted as a logical conjunction, the "or" linking conjuncts as a logical disjunction; and the "or" linking attribute values as an internal disjunction [Michalski, 1983]). Assuming that satisfied conditions give the degree of match equal 1, and unsatisfied conditions give the degree of match 0, such an interpretation is equivalent to treating a conjunction as the minimum function (MIN), and a disjunction as the maximum function (MAX) of the degrees of match.

Let us now consider the diagram in Figure 3–3, which presents only four examples of the R-ball (the four "1"s). A CC description of these examples is:

SHAPE = round & BOUNCES = yes & SIZE = medium or large   (3)

If interpreted the same way as above, this description covers only the indicated four R-balls, and thus is an incomplete concept description. Suppose, however, that we interpret "&" not as the minimum function but as the *average* function. Suppose

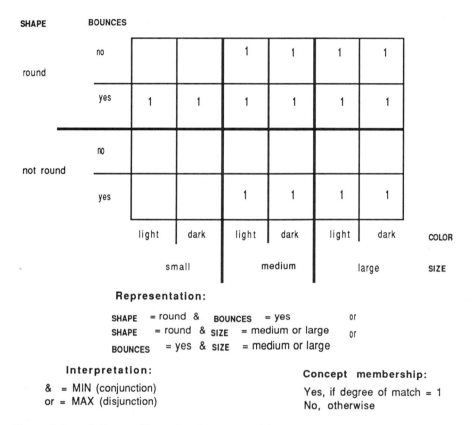

Figure 3–2:   A diagram illustrating the concept of R-ball

also that we assume that an instance is classified as an R-ball, if it gives a degree of match with the description equal to or greater than ⅔.

The above interpretation, as it can be easily verified, gives a classification of instances into R-balls and not-R-balls exactly the same as the description in equation (2). Thus, we have two logically equivalent representations of R-balls: one, that explicitly describes all concept instances; and the second, that describes explicitly only a subset of the instances, and takes care of the remaining examples implicitly, by the matching procedure. Table 3–1 summarizes information about the two representations, denoted as CR1 and CR2.

In Table 3–1, "rules" are single conjunctions of conditions associated with a given concept. Although representations CR1 and CR2 are logically equivalent, they are pragmatically different. The first representation, CR1, is significantly more com-

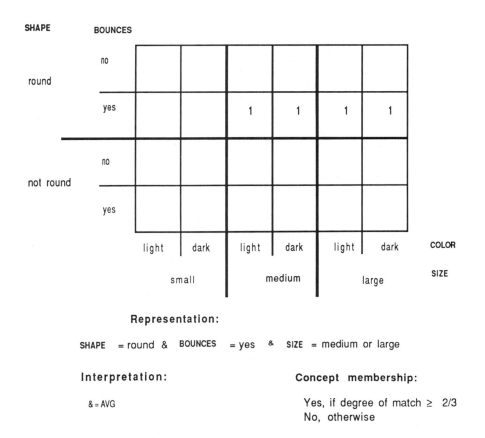

Figure 3–3:   A subset of examples of the R-ball

plex than CR2. The BCR of the first representation consists of three rules, while the BCR of the second representation consists of only one rule. To compute the degree of match (DM), the ICI of the first representation uses a conventional interpretation of logical connectives (applicable also to multiple-valued conditions); while the ICI of the second representation uses a less conventional interpretation.

The above two concept representations illustrate two different "distributions" of the concept meaning between the BCR and the ICI. In general, there can be a range of logically equivalent concept descriptions that differ in the distribution of the meaning between the BCR and the ICI. The ICIs presented here are just an illustration. A more elaborate interpretation method, called *flexible matching*, is discussed in Section 3.6.

Table 3–1:   A comparison between two representations of the concept of R-ball

CR1		CR2	
BCR	**ICI**	**BCR**	**ICI**
3 rules 6 conditions	& = MIN V = MAX DM = 1	1 rule 3 conditions	& = AVG V = MAX DM ≥ 2/3

3.5 LEARNING TWO-TIERED REPRESENTATIONS

The method of learning two-tiered concept representations from examples proposed below utilizes our previous work on inductive concept learning. In the method, learning the BCR of a concept consists of two phases. In the first phase, a complete and consistent (CC) concept description is induced from a set of positive and negative examples of the concept. This phase is performed by using a standard AQ inductive learning methodology, such as implemented in the program AQ15 (see below).

The second phase reduces the so-obtained CC description to a simpler description that maximizes a criterion of description quality. Such a criterion evaluates various properties of the description from the viewpoint of the goals of learning (Section 3.5.2). The description reduction is done using the so-called TRUNC method, which iteratively removes components of the description, from the least "important" to the most "important" (Section 3.5.2). A reduced description that scores best on the assumed quality measure is taken as the base concept representation (BCR).

To determine the ICI, one needs to develop a matching procedure that would handle all positive examples of the concept that do not match BCR, and all negative examples that match BCR. In general, such a procedure needs to involve various context-dependent inference rules. In the method described here, we limit ourselves only to a very simple ICI, based on a *flexible matching* procedure (Section 3.6).

The above method of learning TT descriptions has been implemented in the learning system AQTT-15. The system integrates the AQ15 learning program with the TRUNC procedure and flexible matching. The next two sections give a brief description of the AQ15 module and the TRUNC procedure, respectively.

3.5.1 An Overview of the AQ15 Module

AQ15 is a descendant of the AQ family of inductive learning programs (e.g., [Michalski, 1972; Michalski and Larson, 1975; Mozetic and Hong, 1984]). From the viewpoint of its capabilities, AQ15 is a highly advanced program for learning attributional descriptions from examples, which can serve as a mini-laboratory for exploring various aspects of inductive learning.

Different versions of the AQ family were experimentally applied to a variety of practical tasks, such as learning criteria for discriminating between cancer of the pancreas and cancer of the liver [Michalski, 1973], defining provably correct general characterizations of the "win" and "draw" positions in a chess endgame [Negri and Michalski, 1977], determining rules for plant disease diagnosis [Michalski and Chilausky, 1980], and automatically creating a knowledge base for diagnosing cardiac arrhythmias from electrocardiograms [Mozetic, 1986; Bratko, Mozetic, and Lavrac, 1989]. The latter work is one of the most advanced and most interesting applications of machine learning to a practical problem.

The AQ programs are based on the AQ algorithm for a quasi-optimal solution of the general covering problem, originally developed by the author [Michalski, 1969]. (For a more tutorial presentation, see [Michalski and McCormick, 1971].) The algorithm generates the near-minimum or minimum number of general rules distinguishing between a set of positive examples and a set of negative examples. The complete version of the algorithm also produces an upper bound on the maximal difference in the number of the rules between the obtained solution and the minimal one. This upper bound allows the algorithm to produce a provably minimal solution for some classes of covering problems (which are NP-complete) in the polynomial time. While the complete version of the algorithm is more interesting from a theoretical viewpoint, for machine learning problems a simplified version seems to be more useful. The simplified version does not produce the upper bound on the complexity of the solution, but it is easier to implement and faster to run. Here is the basic structure of a simplified version of the AQ algorithm:

1. A single positive example, called a *seed*, is selected (randomly or by design) from the available positive examples, and a set of alternative, most general rules (conjunctive descriptions) characterizing this example is computed. The limits to which the rules are generalized are defined by negative examples. The obtained set is called a *star* for the seed.

2. The most preferred rule is selected from the star according to a *rule preference criterion* (see below). If this rule, jointly with any previously generated rules, covers all positive examples, the algorithm stops.

3. Otherwise, a new seed is selected among the examples uncovered so far, and steps 1 and 2 are repeated until all examples are covered.

The ruleset assembled from rules selected in each step constitutes a complete and consistent concept description and optimizes the assumed *description preference criterion*.

Typically, supplied examples are insufficient for uniquely defining a concept description. Therefore, one needs a criterion that would enable one to choose among alternatives, which represent different generalizations of positive examples. In the AQ approach, such a criterion is not viewed as a "bias," which might imply that the choice is arbitrary, but is supposed to reflect the requirements of the problem domain. For example, if costs of measuring attributes vary significantly in the given problem domain, it may be desirable to choose a description that is more complex (e.g., has more components), but which involves "inexpensive" attributes, and thus is less costly overall. If input examples are "noisy" and/or the overall efficiency and accuracy of concept recognition is the primary goal, then it may be desirable to chose a description that is incomplete and/or inconsistent with regard to the training examples (see Section 3.5.2, and [Bergadano, *et al.*, 1990]).

The *rule preference criterion* used in selecting a rule from a star is assumed to produce a concept description that will score high on a *description quality criterion*. That is, the rule preference criterion should reflect the desirable properties of the goal concept description, according to the requirements of the problem domain. For example, if the description quality criterion requires descriptions to have the minimum number of rules, then the rule preference criterion might rank high the rules that individually cover the maximum number of examples. If each rule covers many examples, then it is likely that fewer rules will be needed to cover all examples.

The rule preference criterion is defined by a list of elementary criteria assembled by a user from a set of predefined criteria. In AQ15, the predefined criteria relate to various measurable properties of a rule, such as the coverage (the number of positive examples covered by a rule), the simplicity (measured by the number of attributes involved in the rule), the cost (the sum of the measurement costs of individual variables), an estimate of generality (such as the ratio of the number of possible examples to the number of actually observed examples covered by the rule), and others.

To determine the "best" rule, the elementary criteria on the list are applied one by one to individual rules in the star, and the rule that best satisfies all criteria within a certain tolerance range is selected. Such a multicriterion measure for selecting the best alternative from a set of alternatives is called a *lexicographic evaluation functional* or LEF [Michalski, 1973; 1983].

AQ programs express concept descriptions using the *variable-valued logic system 1* (VL_1), which is a multiple-valued logic extension of the proposition calculus with typed variables [Michalski, 1974]. It is an easy-to-interpret, highly concise and powerful language for expressing any relationship among multivalued and multitype attributes.

The simplest expression in VL_1 is an elementary condition, called *selector*, which relates a variable or an attribute to a value or an *internal disjunction* of values, for example, [color = blue or red] or [height = 3 inches]. A conjunction of such conditions forms a *complex*, which can be viewed as a rule for partially or completely defining a concept. For example, suppose that the complex [weight = high] & [length = 2..5 meters] describes (some or all) examples of the class "big objects." Such a complex can be viewed as a rule [weight = high] & [length = 2..5 meters] $\Rightarrow$

[class = big objects]. A set of complexes (rules) can be expressed as a disjunctive normal expression, in which individual complexes are linked by disjunction.

From now on, by *rules* we will mean VL_1 complexes associated with an appropriate decision class, and by *conditions* (briefly, conds) we will mean VL_1 selectors. By a *concept (class) description* we will mean a set of rules (a ruleset) whose right-hand side points to that concept. A ruleset that describes all positive examples and none of the negative examples is a *complete and consistent* (CC) concept description (such a ruleset is also called a *cover*).

The AQ15 module is capable of *incremental learning with full memory* of past examples. In this type of incremental learning, the process of modifying the current hypothesis to accommodate new facts takes into consideration all past examples [Reinke and Michalski, 1988]. This way, it can be guaranteed that any so-modified concept description (hypothesis) is always complete and consistent with regard to all examples. Such a method can therefore produce higher quality concept descriptions than incremental methods *with no memory* of past examples (e.g., [Winston, 1970; Michalski and Larson, 1976; Gross, 1988; Iba, Woogulis, and Langley, 1988]). Because the costs of computer memories are decreasing, the need for storing past examples is not considered a strong disadvantage of such incremental learning.

In the sense that this method keeps past concept examples, it is related to exemplar-based learning, in which concepts are represented by positive examples (e.g., [Bareiss, Porter, and Craig, 1990—Chapter 4, this volume]). The principal difference between the two approaches is, however, that the method represents concepts by "optimized" general descriptions rather than by examples. As mentioned earlier, keeping a general concept description facilitates a number of operations, such as determining the relationship between the concept and other concepts, incrementally modifying the concept, etc.

The program also has a "generality parameter," which enables it to generate descriptions of different generality from the same input examples. Depending on the setting of this parameter, the generated concept description may be maximally general, maximally specific or intermediate. The default value of the parameter produces a maximally general description, which covers the maximum number of instances, observed or hypothetical, without covering any negative examples. By specializing such a description, one can produce another extreme; i.e., a maximally specific description, which cannot be more specialized without "uncovering" some positive examples.

Because the program can learn incrementally, it allows a user to supply some initial, partially correct decision rules, which are then improved in the process of applying them to new examples. The program can also perform *constructive induction*, in which domain background knowledge is used to generate new concepts (e.g., attributes) that are not initially specified, but may produce a better final description. Such domain knowledge can be expressed using two types of rules: *L-rules*, which are in the form of logical assertions or if–then rules, and *A-rules*, which are in the form of arithmetic functions or term-rewriting rules. A more detailed description of AQ15 can be found in [Michalski, *et al.*, 1989b].

3.5.2 The TRUNC Procedure

The purpose of the TRUNC procedure is to determine the "best distribution" of the concept description between the explicit base concept representation (BCR) and the inferential concept interpretation (ICI) [Michalski, 1986a; 1986b]. The procedure starts with a complete and consistent concept description, whose rules have been ordered on the basis of their "importance" from the most important to the least important. This description is then reduced, by truncating one rule at each step, starting with the least important rules. After each step, a "quality" of the reduced description is measured. The description that has the highest quality is chosen as the base concept representation (BCR). To measure the description quality, the method takes into consideration the description complexity and its performance on testing examples. In general, a number of other factors can be taken into consideration in evaluating a description (e.g., [Zhang and Michalski, 1989]).

To determine the importance of a rule, each rule in the description is associated with a pair of weights, t and u, representing the *total* number of training examples covered by the rule, and the number of training examples covered *uniquely* by that rule, respectively. Obviously, the t-weight is always greater or equal to the u-weight of a rule, and the difference between the two indicates the degree of overlap between the rule and other rules in the description. The t-weight of a rule can be interpreted as a measure of its representativeness as a concept description, and the u-weight as a measure of its interrelationship with other rules. The rule with the highest t-weight may be viewed as characterizing the most typical concept properties, and thus serve as its prototypical description. The rules with the low t-weight describe rare, exceptional cases. If training examples are noisy, such "light" rules are indicative of errors in the data. A rule with a large u-weight (and consequently large t-weight) is a highly representative and irreplaceable component of the concept description. A rule with zero u-weight is redundant. A rule with a large t-weight and a small u-weight is a good candidate for a merger with another rule.

Let us now describe the TRUNC procedure in more detail and illustrate it with an example. The procedure starts with a complete and consistent (CC) description obtained from the AQ15 module. The rules in the CC description are linearly ordered from those with the highest t-weight to those with the lowest t-weight. (If two rules have the same t-weight, the one with the higher u-weight has precedence; if they also have the same u-weight, the order is arbitrary.)

Figure 3–4 illustrates such an ordering. A consistent and complete description consists of four rules, depicted as rectangles. The rectangles overlap because rules may logically intersect; i.e., some training examples may be covered by more than

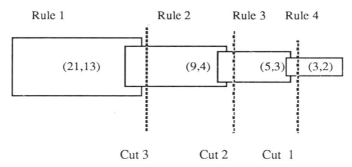

Figure 3–4:   An illustration of a t-ordered concept description

one rule. In each pair (x,y), x denotes the t-weight, and y denotes the u-weight of the corresponding rule.

The procedure proceeds by removing at each step a rule that in the currently considered description has the smallest t-weight. In Figure 3–4, first rule 4 is removed, then rule 3, etc., until only one, rule 1, is left. The description consisting of the last remaining rule, i.e., the rule with the highest t-weight, is called the "top rule" description.

In Figure 3–4, cuts 1, 2 and 3 mark consecutive truncations, producing descriptions with the number of rules equal to 3, 2, and 1, respectively.

Removing a rule from a description is equivalent to removing a disjunctively linked condition from a description. Such a process *specializes* the knowledge representation [Michalski, 1983] and produces an *incomplete* concept description (one that does not cover some positive training examples).

All so-reduced descriptions are evaluated according to a *description quality criterion*. A simple form of such a criterion is to require the description to perform well on testing examples and to have low complexity. Indicators of complexity are the number of rules in the description and the total number of conditions in these rules. The description that best satisfies the assumed description quality criterion is taken as the BCR.

The criterion of description quality should reflect the needs of the problem at hand and can depend on many factors. For more details about this topic, see [Bergadano, *et al.*, 1988a; Zhang and Michalski, 1989].

Intuitively, one might expect a trade-off between the simplicity of a description (a reciprocal of complexity) and its performance. Such an expectation is justified because simplifying the description (by removing a rule) uncovers some training examples. To test this hypothesis, we have performed a series of experiments with data from the area of medical diagnosis. Results of these experiments have been quite surprising. They are described in Section 3.7. The problems of other potential trade-offs characterizing concept descriptions are studied in *variable precision logic* [Michalski and Winston, 1986].

In summary, the TRUNC method reduces the initial CC concept description to the "best" description, which is used as the BCR of the concept.

3.6 RELATING INSTANCES TO CONCEPTS: FLEXIBLE MATCHING

We now turn to the topic of inferential concept interpretation (ICI) of a concept description. In order to determine the identity of an unknown instance, the instance needs to be matched against a set of candidate concept descriptions. One can distinguish between two basic methods for matching an instance with a set of descriptions: the *sufficient* match and the *best* match.

In the sufficient match method, the properties of the instance are matched against conditions in the candidate descriptions to determine which description is satisfied. An instance may satisfy a description either completely (a *crisp match*) or "sufficiently" (a *satisficing match*). Assuming that an instance can belong to only one candidate concept and that the descriptions are logically disjoint, then any description that is found to be satisfied determines the instance identity. In such a situation, there is no need to test other candidate descriptions. This property has been explored in *dynamic recognition*, which tries to achieve an instance recognition with the minimum number of operations and without actually matching individual rules [Michalski, 1989].

In the best match approach, one determines a degree of "fit" or "similarity" between the instance and candidate descriptions, and selects the description that provides the closest match. Determining a "similarity" between a description and an instance can be accomplished in a variety of ways, ranging from an approximate matching of feature values to "conceptual cohesiveness" [Michalski and Stepp, 1983].

In the two-tiered approach, an instance is matched against the BCR (base concept representation) of candidate concepts, using the ICI (inferential concept interpretation). In the method described here, the ICI consists of a *flexible matching* procedure, which applies the best match approach and does not involve any explicit rules of inference. If there is no crisp match with the BCR of just one description, the procedure measures the fit between an instance and the candidate BCRs, and chooses the concept that provides the best fit. A more advanced ICI is considered in [Bergadano, *et al.*, 1990].

As described before, the BCR of a concept is a logic-style description consisting of one or more rules (a ruleset). When matching a new example against such a ruleset, three outcomes are possible: There may be only one match (one ruleset is satisfied), more than one, or there is no match. These three types of outcomes are called *single-match, multiple-match,* and *no-match,* respectively (Figure 3–5).

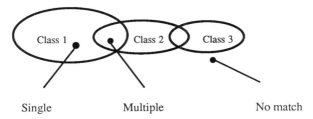

Single   Multiple   No match

Figure 3–5: An illustration of single-match, multiple-match, and no-match

In the implemented flexible matching procedure, each type of match involves a different decision assignment procedure. When there is a single-match case, the instance is immediately assigned the concept associated with the matched BCR. The decision is counted as correct, if it is equal to the expert-given classification of the testing example, and as incorrect otherwise. If there is multiple match or no-match, the system makes the decision on the basis of the best match. This decision is compared with an expert decision and evaluated as correct or incorrect.

There are potentially many ways to define a measure of fit between an instance and a description. Below are simple heuristic measures, one for the multiple-match case, and the other for the no-match case.

Let $C_1,...,C_m$ denote concepts (decision classes) and e denote an event (instance) to be recognized. For each concept C_i, we have a BCR consisting of one or more rules. Each rule is a conjunction of conditions (Conds). For generality, it is not assumed that BCRs of different concepts are logically disjoint.

The Multiple-Match Case When an event matches the BCR of more than one concept, the system selects the concept whose BCR provides the highest *degree of fit* with the event. To determine such a degree, we first define the degree of fit, $F(e, \text{Rule}_j)$, between an instance e and a Rule_j. If the instance satisfies the Rule_j, then $F(e, \text{Rule}_j)$ is equal to the *significance* of the rule, otherwise 0. The rule significance is defined as the ratio of the t-weight(Rule_j); i.e., the number of training examples covered by the Rule_j, by the total number of training examples (#examples). Thus, we have:

$$F(e, \text{Rule}_j) = \begin{cases} \text{t-weight}(\text{Rule}_j)/\text{\#examples, if } e \text{ satisfies Rule}_j \\ 0, \text{ otherwise.} \end{cases} \tag{4}$$

A justification for this measure is that if an event satisfies a rule that describes a large proportion of training examples, then it is likely that this event belongs to the class implied by the rule.

The degree of fit, $F(e, C_i)$, between the instance e and the concept description C_i, is the *probabilistic sum* of the degrees of fit between e and rules in C_i. If C_i consists of just two rules, $Rule_1$ and $Rule_2$, we have:

$$F(e, C_i) = F(e, Rule_1) + F(e, Rule_2) - F(e, Rule_1) \times F(e, Rule_2) \tag{5}$$

If C_i consists of more than two rules, equation (5) is iteratively applied. The reason for using the probabilistic sum is that individual rules may logically intersect. The most plausible concept is defined as the one with the largest degree of fit.

The No-Match Case   If an event does not satisfy the BCR of any concept (ruleset) under consideration, but it is assumed that it belongs to one of the candidate concepts, the degree of fit between the event and a ruleset depends on the degree of "closeness" between attribute values in the event and those in the ruleset, and on the prior probability of the concept.

For illustration, we will use here a measure of fit described in the study by [Michalski, *et al.*, 1986]. First, we define the degree of fit, $F(e, Cond_k)$, between event e and condition $Cond_k$. This measure takes value 1, if the condition is satisfied; otherwise, it is proportional to the relative size of the attribute's domain covered by the condition:

$$F(e, Cond_k) = \begin{cases} 1 & \text{if condition } Cond_k \text{ is satisfied by e} \\ \#values/DomainSize, & \text{otherwise.} \end{cases} \tag{6}$$

In (6), #values is the number of alternative attribute values in the condition, and DomainSize is the total number of attribute's possible values. For example, if $Cond_k$ is [attribute = 2..5], the #values is 4.

A justification for this measure is that conditions in which an attribute can take many values are viewed as weaker than conditions in which it can take only one or few values. For example, if an event does not satisfy condition [blood type = A v O], than this should cause a lower loss in confidence than if it does not satisfy condition [blood type = A].

The degree of fit, $F(e, Rule_j)$, between an event e and the $Rule_j$ is the product of degrees of fit between e and conditions in the rule, weighted by the ratio of t-weight($Rule_j$) over the total number of training examples:

$$F(e, Rule_j) = \prod_k F(e, Cond_k) \times (\text{t-weight}(Rule_j)\#examples) \tag{7}$$

The above measure is based on the assumption that individual conditions in a rule are independent, which is justified, because the induction algorithm tends to form rules with independent conditions. This measure can be viewed as a combination of a "closeness" of the event to a rule and an estimate of the prior probability of the rule in the description. This measure could be further refined by replacing a discrete degree of satisfaction of a condition by a continuous degree, such as described in [Michalski and Chilausky, 1980].

The measure of fit, $F(e, C_i)$, between the event e and a concept C_i is defined as the probabilistic sum of the Fs of rules in the concept description, the same way as in the multiple match case (equation (5)).

3.7 EXPERIMENTS WITH AQTT-15

The presented method of learning concept descriptions from examples combines a conventional inductive learning approach with ideas of TT representation. It has been implemented in the system AQTT-15, whose major components include the AQ15 inductive learning program, the TRUNC method of description reduction and a procedure for flexible matching.

To illustrate the performance of the system, this section presents results from its experimental application to learning diagnostic rules in three medical domains: lymphatic cancer, prognosis of breast cancer recurrence, and location of primary tumor. All the data were obtained from the Institute of Oncology of the University Medical Center in Ljubljana, Yugoslavia [Kononenko, Bratko, and Roskar, 1984].

Lymphatic Cancer In this domain there were four possible diagnoses; i.e., decision classes. The available data consisted of descriptions of about 148 patients and their diagnosis. Each patient was described in terms of 18 multivalued attributes. The diagnoses were not verified independently. A specialist's estimation is that internists diagnose this kind of disease correctly in about 60% of the cases, and specialists in about 85% of the cases.

Prognosis of Breast Cancer Recurrence There were two decision classes. The available data described 286 patients with known diagnostic status five years after the operation. Each patient was characterized by nine multivalued attributes. The set of attributes was incomplete; i.e., the measured attributes were insufficient to always completely discriminate between patients with different diseases. Diagnosing on the basis of these attributes therefore has to produce a certain amount of error. Five oncologists of the Institute of Oncology in Ljubljana were tested, and they gave correct prognoses in 64% of the cases. There is no estimate of the performance of internists in this domain.

Location of Primary Tumor Physicians distinguish between 22 locations of a primary tumor. The available data characterized 339 patients with known locations of primary tumors. Each patient was described in terms of 17 attributes. As in the prognosis of breast cancer recurrence, the set of attributes was also incomplete. Four internists (who were tested) determined the correct location of the primary tumor in 32% of the cases, and four oncologists in 42% of the cases.

All the data used in the experiments are summarized in Table 3–2. Individual columns represent respectively: the disease type; the number of available examples for this disease type; the number of different diseases of the given type (decision classes); the number of attributes used to characterize a patient, and the average number of values per attribute for each of the disease types.

Table 3–2:   A characterization of three problem domains

Disease type	#Examples	#Classes	#Attrs	#Vals/Attr
Lymphatic cancer	148	4	18	3.3
Breast cancer	286	2	9	5.8
Primary tumor	339	22	17	2.2

For all three domains (disease types), 70% of the examples were selected for learning diagnostic descriptions of diseases, and the remaining 30% were used for testing the learned descriptions.

The first phase of the experiment was to induce complete and consistent (CC) descriptions from training examples for all decision classes (diseases) in each domain. The results are summarized in Table 3–3.

Table 3–3:   The average complexity of complete and consistent descriptions(i.e., before truncation)

Disease type	#Rules/Class	#Conds/Rule	#Values/Attr	#Examples/Rule
Lymphatic cancer	3.0	3.1	1.8	8.0
Breast cancer	20.0	3.9	1.7	5.0
Primary tumor	5.2	5.3	1.0	2.3

Individual columns list, respectively: the disease type, the average number of rules in the description of each decision class, the average number of conditions per rule, the average number of attribute values in a condition (i.e., values linked by the internal disjunction), and finally, the average number of training examples covered by one rule. One can see that in the domain of lymphatic cancer, rules cover on the average eight examples, which indicates the presence of relatively strong patterns.

On the other hand, in the domain of primary tumor, the rules cover on the average only slightly more than two examples, which suggests an absence of strong patterns.

The second part of the experiment was to apply the TRUNC method to reduce the above CC descriptions and to determine the best candidate for a BCR of each decision class. The quality of initial and reduced descriptions was evaluated in terms of their complexity and their performance on testing examples. The description complexity was measured by the number of rules in the description and the total number of conditions in it.

Results reported here compare three types of descriptions. The first type were the initial CC descriptions induced from training examples of each decision class. The second type descriptions consisted of only those rules in CC descriptions that covered uniquely more than one training example (the "unique>1" case); all other rules were removed. (Notice, that the removed rules could cover several training examples, because the removal condition relates only to uniquely covered examples). The third type descriptions consisted of only "top rules" for each class; i.e., rules that cover the largest number of training examples in each class. Such descriptions can be viewed as covering only the most "typical" examples.

The experiment was performed four times, using randomly chosen training and testing examples. The results describing the average of the four experiments are presented in Table 3–4. A more detailed description of the experiments is in [Michalski, *et al.*, 1986].

Table 3–4: Results of testing three types of diagnostic rules generated by AQTT-15

Disease type	Description type	Complexity		Diagnostic accuracy	Experts/ internists	Random decision
		#Rules	#Conds			
Lymphatic cancer	Complete	12	37	81%	85/60%	25%
	Unique>1	10	34	80%		
	Top rule	**4**	10	82%		
Breast cancer	Complete	41	160	66%	64%	50%
	Unique>1	32	128	68%		
	Top rule	**2**	7	68%		
Primary tumor	Complete	104	551	39%	42/32%	5%
	Unique>1	42	257	41%		
	Top rule	22	112	29%		

The column "Description Type" indicates the type of the description used in testing. The types are:

"Complete"   Original CC description of the each decision class

"Unique>1"   Description with rules that cover uniquely more than one training example

"Top rule"   Description with only one rule covering the largest number of examples.

The bold description represents a suggested candidate for the BCR of each decision class, assuming that the diagnostic accuracy takes precedence over the simplicity.

The column "Complexity" gives a characterization of the complexity of a concept description in terms of the number of rules in it and the total number of conditions in all rules. The column "Diagnostic Accuracy" specifies the percentage of correct diagnoses made by the descriptions for testing cases (where the "correctness" is defined as the agreement of the rule-based diagnosis with the diagnosis stated in the data). The column "Experts/Internists" gives an estimate of the percentage of correct diagnoses made by specialists in the given domain and internists, respectively [Kononenko, Bratko, and Roskar, 1986]. The column "Random Decision" indicates the probability that a decision taken at random is correct.

Some results shown in Table 3–4 seem to be rather surprising. One striking case concerns the diagnosis in the domain of lymphatic cancer. The "top rule" description gave the highest diagnostic accuracy (82%) among all descriptions, although it was the simplest (it had three times fewer rules than the CC description). A similar phenomenon occurred in the breast cancer domain, where the diagnostic accuracy of the "top rule" description was 68% versus 66% of the "complete" description; while it had about 20 times fewer rules (two rules versus 41). Thus, in both cases, the "top rule" description is the clear candidate for the BCR of the concepts, as it gives both the highest diagnostic accuracy and the simplest concept representation.

In the domain of the location of primary tumor, the diagnostic accuracy of all learned descriptions was significantly lower than in the previous two cases, ranging from 29% to 41%. The best performance was achieved by the "Unique>1" description (41%), which has on the average about two rules per disease (42/22). Although this is a low performance, it is comparable with that of specialists (42%). The performance of the "top rule" description (29%) was significantly lower than both, the "Unique>1" and the "Complete" descriptions. This indicates that truncating the description below two rules per class goes too far. As the "top rule" description is, of course, the simplest (22 rules; one rule per class), there is a trade-off between the diagnostic accuracy and the complexity. Assuming the precedence of the diagnostic accuracy over the simplicity, the "Unique>1" description is chosen as the BCR.

Why did the "top rule" descriptions give a better diagnostic accuracy than the CC descriptions in the first two domains? Clearly, these descriptions do not cover examples that were uniquely covered by the truncated rules (the total eight rules were removed from CC descriptions in the domain of lymphatic cancer, and 82 rules in the domain of breast cancer).

One reason for this behavior seems to be the use of flexible matching. Due to such matching, events that are not covered by a description are still correctly classified, if they have the "best fit" with the description of the correct class (recall the example with the R-ball). Since the "top rule" can be viewed as representing the "central tendency" of examples from the given class, then even examples not covered by it are likely to fit better to it than to the "top rule" of other classes. Another reason may be the well-known phenomenon of "overfitting" [Watanabe, 1969]. It has been observed, that in the presence of noise in the data, a simpler description, although giving a greater error rate on the observed data, may be a better representation of the true relationship than a complicated one with a lower error rate on the observed data.

In diagnosing the location of primary tumor, the results were generally poor, which may be attributed to several factors. This domain has significantly more decision classes than the other two domains (22 versus four in lymphatic cancer and two in breast cancer), and relatively few examples per class were available (about 15 versus 37 in lymphatic cancer and 143 in breast cancer). The set of available attributes was relatively small (17) for such a large number of classes, and incomplete (i.e., the attributes were insufficient to discriminate completely between different classes). The attributes were mostly binary, and thus less informative than those in the other two domains (the average number of possible attribute values was over three in the domain of lymphatic cancer, and about six in breast cancer). The available data can then be classified as being of a substantially lower quality than the data in the other two domains. Individual rules in the CC description covered only few examples (2.3 on the average), in contrast to rules in the other two domains (in lymphatic cancer, eight examples per rule, and in breast cancer, five examples per rule). Thus, the rules have covered only small portions of the examples in the description space.

The above indicates an absence of a single, strong pattern in this domain, which explains why the "top rule" description gave a poor diagnostic accuracy. The relatively high performance of the "Unique>1" descriptions (with two rules per class) indicates that there were on the average two relatively important patterns in this domain.

3.8 A COMPARISON WITH THE ASSISTANT PROGRAM

A popular approach to empirical learning from examples is based on building a decision-tree representation of a group of related concepts (e.g., [Quinlan, 1983; Chapter 5, this volume]). This section discusses representational issues of the rule-based method implemented in AQTT-15, and the decision-tree-based method, implemented in ASSISTANT [Cestnik, *et al.*, 1986], a descendant of ID3 (e.g., [Quinlan, 1983]). It also presents results from applying ASSISTANT to the same medical problems as above [Kononenko, Bratko, and Roskar, 1986].

In the decision-tree representation, individual nodes correspond to single attributes, the branches from the nodes to the values of the attributes, and the leaves to individual concepts (decision classes). The process of creating a decision tree involves an iterative application of an attribute-selection technique. At each step, the "best" attribute (e.g., the most predictive as to the identity of examples) is selected from a given set of attributes and assigned to a node of the generated tree, until the leaves of the tree give a unique classification of the training examples. Such a process is simple to implement, since it does not involve any complex reasoning or taking into consideration an explicitly defined domain knowledge.

Like AQTT-15, ASSISTANT creates first a description (here, a decision tree) that gives a complete and consistent classification of training examples for all concepts (decision classes). This tree is then reduced by a *tree-pruning* technique, in order to maximize the classification accuracy on testing examples (see also Chapter 5 of this book).

The tree-pruning technique removes certain subtrees from the given decision tree, and replaces them with leaves. Each leaf so created is assigned the most dominant concept among the concepts associated with the leaves of the removed subtree. For this dominant concept, such pruning is equivalent to removing conjunctively linked conditions from a concept description, and thus represents a generalization operation [Michalski, 1983].

For other concepts associated with leaves of the pruned subtree, the pruning is equivalent to removing disjointly linked conditions from a description, and thus represents a specialization operation. Notice, that the training examples of these other concepts have no longer any representation in the tree. Therefore, the so-pruned tree will necessarily misclassify some of the training examples. From the standpoint of the TT representation, a pruned tree can be viewed as a special case of the BCR of a class of concepts represented by the tree.

As indicated above, the tree-pruning technique performs an *interdependent* generalization and specialization of the initial knowledge representation. It moves the boundaries of a partition of the whole description space, but it cannot independently modify the boundaries of individual concepts; i.e., to independently generalize or specialize individual concepts. Therefore, pruning a subtree may improve performance for one decision class, but may decrease it for other classes.

In the rule-based representation used in AQTT-15, concept descriptions can be independently modified. The TRUNC procedure removes individual rules from a description, which is a specialization operation. This operation is done independently for each decision class. The union of the conditions of the rules does not have to cover the whole description space. Instances that do not match any rule to a sufficient degree can be assigned the "undecided" decision. In contract, a decision tree always partitions the whole description space. Thus, if there are undecided instances, one needs to introduce an explicit "undecided" class, which will be associated with some leaves. Therefore, the decision tree representation may be overly complex in decision problems where there are many undecided cases. Also, for a similar reason, it is usually not possible to add a new concept to a decision tree without building a new tree from scratch. Adding new concepts using a rule representation, may be done by adding new rules.

When there are many concepts differing only slightly from each other, a decision tree may produce a very compact and efficient representation, because classes will share many of the same nodes. On the other hand, if there are few concepts, but each described by somewhat different sets of attributes, the decision tree may be very complex. The complexity of rule representation depends directly on the number of concepts (unless rules are organized into a hierarchy).

In a decision tree, a classification decision is determined by a sequential testing of attributes assigned to the nodes from the root to the leaves. Each node represents a clear-cut test, which results in the selection of one specific branch to follow. Such a process can be quite efficient, if the values of all relevant attributes are known. If some attribute value is unknown, however (e.g., the value of the attribute corresponding to the root), it is difficult to derive a classification decision. In the rule-based representation, the evaluation order of attributes is unimportant. Because rules are independent units of knowledge, a decision can often be reached without knowing the values of many attributes.

From the logical viewpoint, rulesets and trees are equivalent representations. A ruleset can be represented as a logically equivalent decision tree, and vice versa. (This is true, of course, only in the case of *attributional* rules; i.e., rules that involve only attributes, as opposed to multiargument predicates or relations. *Structural rules*, which involve predicates and quantifiers, cannot be represented as a decision tree.)

Given a decision tree, by tracing paths from the root to individual leaves, one can determine an equivalent set of rules. Each path generates one rule. Given a set of rules, one can also determine a logically equivalent decision tree. The latter process can be done simply by using *decision diagrams* (e.g., [Michalski, 1978a; 1978b]).

From the pragmatic viewpoint, however, the rule representation has greater expressive power than the decision tree representation. This means, that a ruleset may be significantly simpler than a logically equivalent decision tree. As a simple illustration of this, consider representing the following ruleset as a decision tree:

$$
\begin{array}{ll}
a \ \& \ b & \Rightarrow \text{Class 1} \\
c \ \& \ d & \Rightarrow \text{Class 1} \\
{\sim}a \ \& \ {\sim}c \ \& \ d & \Rightarrow \text{Class 2;} \\
\end{array}
$$

Otherwise, the class is U. \hfill (8)

The simplest decision tree (i.e., with the smallest number of nodes; there are few equivalent such trees), which is logically equivalent to this ruleset is shown in Figure 3–6. The left branch stemming from a node denotes the "false" value, and the right branch, the "true" value of the attribute assigned to this node.

Reexpressing this tree as a ruleset by tracing different paths from the root to the leaves gives the following rules:

a & b   => Class 1
a & ~b & c & d => Class 1
~a & d & c   => Class 1
~a & d & ~c   => Class 2
Otherwise, the class is U.   (9)

Comparing (8) with (9), one can see that the ruleset produced from the tree has more rules than the original ruleset, and that some rules in it have more conditions than corresponding rules in (8). For example, the second rule for Class 1 in (9) involves four conditions. Out of these four conditions, two are redundant (a and ~b). This means, the Class 1 decision can be assigned in some cases without knowing values of attributes a and b, contrary to what is stated by the second rule in (9). Thus, a tree representation may be misleading as to the logical dependence of a decision class on some attributes.

As mentioned above, using a tree for decision making requires a sequential testing of attributes. Because of this, the decision-tree approach makes it difficult to determine a fit (or similarity) between an instance and the whole concept description

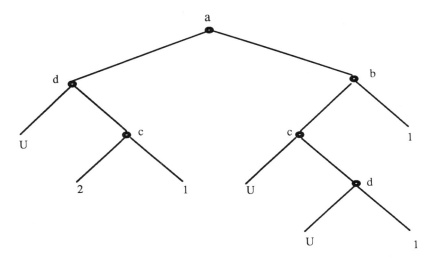

Figure 3–6:   A decision tree logically equivalent to the ruleset in equation (8)

(a path through the tree). Therefore, it seems difficult to use a flexible matching technique (like the one described here) with a decision-tree representation (unless one transfers the tree to a ruleset).

To decrease the inflexibility of "clear-cut" tests of decision trees, Quinlan (Chapter 5 of this book) describes a method of "soft thresholds," which is somewhat similar to the method of determining a "degree of consonance" between an attribute value and a test [Michalski and Chilausky, 1980]. In a decision tree, the evaluation considers only one attribute at a time, and therefore the decision-tree approach is inherently more sensitive to small variations of the attribute values than a rule-based approach.

The technique used in ASSISTANT nevertheless often leads to an improvement of accuracy in classifying testing examples, which can be attributed to the previously mentioned phenomenon of "overfitting." More general descriptions (due to pruning) may avoid misclassifications produced by overly specific descriptions.

Table 3–5 presents the complexity and diagnostic accuracy of decision trees generated by ASSISTANT, with and without the tree-pruning mechanism, from the same data as used in the experiments with AQTT-15 [Kononenko, Bratko, and Roskar, 1986]. It should be noted, however, that although the training and testing examples were drawn from the same data, the specific examples used for training and testing by AQTT-15 and ASSISTANT were different, and therefore the results listed in Table 3–5 are not totally comparable with those in Table 3–4.

Table 3–5: Results from the ASSISTANT program

Disease type	Tree type	Complexity		Diagnostic accuracy
		#Leaves	#Nodes	
Lymphatic cancer	Complete	22	38	76%
	Pruned	14	25	77%
Breast cancer	Complete	63	120	67%
	Pruned	9	16	72%
Primary tumor	Complete	90	188	41%
	Pruned	18	35	46%

To compare the relative complexity of rulesets generated by AQTT-15 with that of the corresponding decision tree, one may compare the total number of rules with the number of leaves in the tree. (As mentioned before, a decision tree can be turned into a ruleset by tracing paths from the root to individual leaves, and each such path corresponds to one rule. Notice, however, that comparing the number of conditions in a collection of rulesets with the number of nodes in a tree is not very meaningful, because an attribute assigned to a node in the tree will be repeated several times in the corresponding ruleset).

Comparing results in Table 3–5 with those in Table 3–4, in the first two domains the diagnostic accuracy of the selected rule representation ("top rule") and the pruned decision tree is roughly similar (82% versus 77% for lymphatic cancer, and 68% versus 72% for breast cancer). The striking difference is in terms of complexity. In both domains, the complexity of the rule representation is substantially lower than that of the pruned decision tree (four rules versus 14 leaves for lymphatic cancer; two rules versus nine leaves for breast cancer). In the domain of primary tumor, the pruned decision tree and the chosen rule representation (unique>1) were relatively close in terms of accuracy (46% versus 41%), and comparable to the performance of specialists (42%), but in terms of complexity, the pruned decision tree was considerably simpler (18 leaves versus 42 rules). Notice, however, that the pruned tree has only 18 leaves, while the number of decision classes is 22. This means, that for four diagnostic classes there are no corresponding leaves; i.e., these diagnostic classes have no representation, and instances from these classes cannot be recognized by the decision tree.

The discussion above explored some of the aspects of the rule-based and decision-tree-based approaches. A number of other issues were not considered, such as learning and testing efficiency, the extensibility and modifiability of representations, their cognitive comprehensibility, or the use of background knowledge in learning. While the analysis of representational aspects of the two approaches does not depend on the specific application domain, and represents a valid finding, experimental results should be viewed only as a few datapoints. Further experiments are needed for making a more conclusive evaluation.

3.9 CONCLUSION AND TOPICS FOR FUTURE RESEARCH

Unlike conventional representations, which try to describe all concept instances in one explicit structure, the proposed two-tiered (TT) representation describes explicitly only the "first approximation" of a concept. Finer aspects, less typical instances and context dependence are defined implicitly, through a matching procedure and inference rules. The explicit part of a concept description is called the base concept representation (BCR); and the implicit part is called the inferential concept interpretation (ICI).

The learning method described is the first and limited implementation of the idea of TT representation. To determine a concept's BCR, it first employs a conventional program to learn a consistent and complete (CC) concept description. This CC description is then reduced by removing from it rules in the increasing order of their importance (the TRUNC procedure). The truncated description that scores best on a description quality measure is selected as the BCR.

The rule truncation is a specialization operation, and therefore all truncated descriptions are incomplete (with regard to training instances). An opposite method would be to remove individual conditions from the rules and merge identical or closely related rules, which is a generalization operation. Such a process would produce inconsistent concept descriptions. One might expect that an application of both, the specialization and generalization operations, may lead to a better concept representation than when only one type of operation is used. To test this hypothesis, such a method has recently been developed. The experimental results have demonstrated that the resulting descriptions are indeed simpler and give better performance [Bergadano, *et al.*, 1988b; 1988c; 1990]. Future research might explore different methods of applying specialization and generalization operators to a CC description, and also address the problem of directly determining the BCR from examples. There is also a need for applying more advanced description quality measures (e.g., [Zhang and Michalski, 1989]).

In the method, the ICI consists of a procedure for flexible matching, which measures a "fit" between an instance and candidate descriptions. Due to this procedure, an incomplete concept description may still classify correctly training examples. The current method, however, does not address the issue of employing inference rules for reasoning about concept boundaries and handling context dependence. These problems are important tasks for future research. Further work may employ more advanced procedures for flexible matching and may investigate the problem of automatically determining the "best" interpretation method.

The system AQTT-15, implementing the current method, was experimentally applied to learning diagnostic rules in three medical domains. Concept descriptions obtained by the method were substantially simpler than the original CC descriptions, and at the same time performed better in diagnosing new cases. In all three domains, the diagnostic accuracy was comparable with that of specialists in these domains.

The rule-based method employed in AQTT-15 was compared with the decision-tree-based method used in ASSISTANT, a descendant of ID3. Although a ruleset can be converted to a logically equivalent decision tree, and vice versa, it has been shown that the rule representation has pragmatically greater representational power than decision trees. For some problems, a ruleset can be significantly simpler than the equivalent decision tree. It has been also shown that a decision tree may suggest a nonexisting dependence of the concept description on some attributes.

The flexible matching procedure may allow an incomplete rule representation to classify correctly training examples that were "uncovered" by the truncation process. Such a procedure does not apply to the decision tree representation, because it is difficult to measure a fit between an instance and the whole concept description in a decision tree (unless the tree is transformed to a ruleset). Consequently, truncated trees cannot avoid producing errors on some training examples.

Both programs have been experimentally applied to the same problems in three medical domains. In domains, in which training examples had relatively high quality and concept descriptions had strong patterns (lymphatic cancer and breast cancer), the diagnostic accuracy of both representations was high, but the AQTT-15's rules were significantly simpler than the ASSISTANT's decision tree. In the domain where data were of poor quality and there were no strong patterns (location of primary tumor), the diagnostic accuracy of rules and decision trees was quite low (trees performed somewhat better than rules), although comparable with that of humans specialists. The pruned decision tree was considerably simpler than the rule representation. It did not provide, however, any representation for four out of 22 diagnostic classes.

One general conclusion from experimental results seems to be that the proposed method offers significant advantages over conventional methods that use complete and consistent concept representations. Concept descriptions that it produces may be much simpler, while their performance on classifying new examples may also be higher. More research is needed to test these conclusions in other domains and across different application areas.

Knowledge representation used in AQTT-15 is limited to attributional descriptions. To extend the proposed method to learning structural descriptions, one could replace the AQ15 module by the INDUCE 3 learning program [Hoff, Michalski, and Stepp, 1983], or its incremental learning version, INDUCE 4 [Mehler, Bentrup, and Riedesel, 1986]. There would also be a need to develop a flexible matching procedure for structural descriptions and to implement a corresponding TRUNC procedure. The current method has concentrated on problems of learning TT representations of a relatively small class of concepts. Future work might address the problem of learning TT representations of a large system of concepts, and the related issue of the inheritance and sharing parts of the BCR and the ICI among different concepts.

Concluding, we would like to emphasize the importance to artificial intelligence and cognitive science of the problem of learning flexible concepts. As most human concepts are flexible, the issues of their representation, learning, and use in reasoning constitute a major part of the agenda for future research in these fields.

ACKNOWLEDGMENTS

The author thanks members of the Advanced Machine Learning Seminar and the Center for Artificial Intelligence at George Mason University for the discussion and criticism of ideas presented here. Special thanks go to Jianping Zhang, Gheorghe Tecuci, and Pawel Stefanski for their careful reading of the manuscript and many insightful comments, and Dr. Elizabeth Marchut-Michalski for important stylistic suggestions that improved the final version of this chapter.

The work described was done partially in the Laboratory for Artificial Intelligence at the University of Illinois at Urbana-Champaign, and partially in the Center for Artificial Intelligence at George Mason University. Various aspects of research were supported by the National Science Foundation under grant No. DCR 084-06801, the Office of Naval Research under grants N00014-88-K-0226 and N00014-88-K-0397, and the Defense Advanced Research Projects Agency under the grant administered by the Office of Naval Research No. N00014-87-K-0874.

References

Alen, S.W., Brooks, L.R., and Norman, G.R. 1988. "Effect of Prior Examples on Rule-based Diagnostic Performance," *Proceedings of the 29th Annual Meeting of the Psychologic Society*, November, 1988.

Bareiss, E.R., Porter, B.W., and Craig, C.W. 1990. "Protos: An Exemplar-based Learning Apprentice," in *Machine Learning: An Artificial Intelligence Approach, Volume III*, Y. Kodratoff and R.S. Michalski (eds.), Morgan Kaufmann Publishers.

Barsalou, L.W. and Medin, D.L. 1986. "Concepts: Fixed Definitions or Dynamic Context-dependent Representations," *Cahiers de Psychologie Cognitive*, 6, pp. 187–202.

Bergadano, F., Matwin, S., Michalski, R.S., and Zhang, J. 1988a. "Measuring Quality of Concept Descriptions," *Proceedings of the Third European Working Session on Learning*, D. Sleeman, pp. 1–14, Pitman, London, (an extended version was published under the title "A Measure of Quality of Descriptions," *Reports of the Machine Learning and Inference Laboratory*, No. 88–3, Artificial Intelligence Center, George Mason University, 1988.)

———, 1988b. "Learning Flexible Concept Descriptions Using a Two-tiered Knowledge Representation: Ideas and a Method," *Reports of the Machine Learning and Inference Laboratory*, No. 88–4, Artificial Intelligence Center, George Mason University.

———, 1988c. "Learning Flexible Concept Descriptions Using a Two-tiered Knowledge Representation: Implementation and Experiments," *Reports of the Machine Learning and Inference Laboratory*, No. 88–35, Artificial Intelligence Center, George Mason University.

———, 1990. "Learning Two-tiered Descriptions of Flexible Concepts," submitted to *Machine Learning*.

Bratko, I., Mozetic, I., and Nada, L. 1989. *Kardio: A Study in Deep and Qualitative Knowledge for Expert Systems*, MIT Press, Cambridge, MA.

Carey, S. 1985. *Conceptual Change in Childhood*, MIT Press, Cambridge, MA.

Cestnik, B., Kononenko, I., and Bratko, I. 1987. "ASSISTANT 86: A Knowledge Elicitation Tool for Sophisticated Users," *Proceedings of the second European Working Session on Learning*, I. Bratko and N. Lavrac (ed.), Bled, Yugoslavia, May 1987.

Estes, W.K. 1986. "Memory Storage and retrieval Processes in Category Learning," *Journal of Experimental Psychology: General*, 115, pp. 155–175.

Flannagan, M.J., Fried, L.S., and Holyoke, K.J. 1986. "Distributional Expectations and the Induction of Category Structure," *Journal of Experimental Psychology: Learning, Memory and Cognition*, No. 12, pp. 241–256.

Gentner, D. and Landers, R. 1985. *Analogical Reminding: A Good Match is Hard to Find*, paper prepared for the Panel on Commonsense Reasoning at the International Conference on Systems, Man and Cybernetics, Tucson, Arizona.

Gross, P.K. 1988. "Incremental Multiple Concept Learning Using Experiments," *Proceedings of the Fifth International Conference on Machine Learning*, Ann Arbor, June 12–14.

Hoff, W., Michalski, R.S., and Stepp, R.E. 1983. "INDUCE. 3: A Program for Learning Structural Descriptions from Examples," Report ISG 83-4, UIUCDCS-F-83–904, Dept. of Computer Science, University of Illinois, Urbana.

Hofstadter, D.R. 1985. "Analogies and Roles in Human and Machine Thinking," in *Metamagical Themas: Questing for the Essence of Mind and Pattern*, Basic Books, Inc.

Holyoke, K.J. 1985. "The Pragmatics of Analogical Transfer," *The Psychology of Learning and Motivation*, 19.

Hong, J., Mozetic, I., and Michalski, R.S. 1986. "AQ15: Incremental Learning of Attribute-based Descriptions from Examples, The Method and User's Guide," Report ISG 86–5, UIUCDCS-F-86-949, Dept. of Computer Science, University of Illinois, Urbana.

Iba, W., Woogulis, J., and Langley, P. 1988. "Trading Simplicity and Coverage in Incremental Concept Learning," *Proceedings of the Fifth Intern. Conference on Machine Learning*, Ann Arbor, June 12–14, 1988.

Kempler-Nelson, D.G. 1984. "The Effect of Intention on What Concepts are Acquired," *Journal of Verbal Learning and Verbal Behavior*, No. 23, pp. 734–759.

Lakoff, G. 1987. *Women, Fire and Dangerous Things: What Categories Tell Us About the Nature of Thought*, Chicago University Press.

Lenat, D.B., Hayes-Roth, F., and Klahr, P. 1979. "Cognitive Economy in Artificial Intelligence Systems," *Proc. IJCAI*, Tokyo, Japan.

McCloskey, M. and Glucksberg, S. 1978. "Natural Categories: Well-defined or Fuzzy Sets?," *Memory and Cognition*, No. 6, pp. 462–472.

Medin, D.L. 1989. "Concepts and Conceptual Structure," *American Psychologist*, vol. 44, pp. 1469–1481.

Medin, D.L. and Smith, E.E. 1984. "Concepts and Concept Formation," in *Annual Review of Psychology*, M.R. Rosenzweig and L.W. Porter (Eds.), No. 35, pp. 113–118.

Mehler, G., Bentrup, J., and Riedesel, J. 1986. "INDUCE. 4: A Program for Incrementally Learning Structural Descriptions from Examples," *Reports of Intelligent Systems Group 86*, Department of Computer Science, University of Illinois, Urbana.

Michalski, R.S. 1969. "On the Quasi-Minimal Solution of the General Covering Problem," *Proceedings of the V International Symposium on Information Processing* (FCIP 69), Vol. A3 (Switching Circuits), Bled, Yugoslavia, pp. 125–128.

———— , 1973. "AQVAL/1—Computer Implementation of a Variable-valued Logic System VL1 and Examples of its Application to Pattern Recognition," *Proceedings of the First International Joint Conference on Pattern Recognition*, Washington, DC, pp. 3–17, October 30–November 1, 1973.

———— , 1974. "Variable-valued Logic: System VL1," *Proceedings of the 1974 International Symposium on Multiple-Valued Logic*, West Virginia University, Morgantown, pp. 323–346, May 29–31.

———— , 1978a. "A Planar Geometrical Model for Representing Multidimensional Discrete Spaces and Multiple-Valued Logic Functions," Report No. 897, Department of Computer Science, University of Illinois, Urbana, January.

———— , 1978b. "Designing Extended Entry Decision Tables and Optimal Decision Trees Using Decision Diagrams," Report No. 898, Department of Computer Science, University of Illinois, Urbana, March 1978.

————— , 1983. "Theory and Methodology of Inductive Learning." In R.S. Michalski, J.G. Carbonell, T.M. Mitchell (Eds.), *Machine Learning: An Artificial Intelligence Approach*, Morgan Kaufmann, San Mateo.

————— , 1986. "Concept Learning," *Encyclopedia of Artificial Intelligence*, John Wiley & Sons.

————— , 1986. "Two-tiered Concept Representation, Analogical Matching and Conceptual Cohesiveness," Invited paper for the Workshop on Similarity and Analogy, Allerton House, University of Illinois, June 12–14, 1986. [An extended and improved version is in *Analogy and Similarity*, S. Vosniadou and A. Ortony (eds.), Cambridge University Press, 1989.]

————— , 1987. "How to Learning Imprecise Concepts: A Method for Employing a Two-tiered Knowledge Representation in Learning," *Proceedings of the Fourth International Workshop on Machine Learning*, University of California at Irvine, June 22–25, 1987.

————— , 1989. "Dynamic Recognition: An Outline of a Theory on How to Recognize Concepts without Matching Rules," *Reports of Machine Learning and Inference Laboratory*, Center for Artificial Intelligence, George Mason University, June 1989.

Michalski, R.S. and Chilausky, R.L. 1980. "Learning by Being Told and Learning from Examples: An Experimental Comparison of the Two Methods of Knowledge Acquisition in the Context of Developing an Expert System for Soybean Disease Diagnosis," *International Journal of Policy Analysis and Information Systems*, Vol. 4, No. 2, pp. 125–160.

Michalski, R.S. and Larson, J. 1975. "AQVAL/1 (AQ7) User's Guide and Program Description," Report No. 731, Dept. of Computer Science, University of Illinois, Urbana.

————— , 1978. "Selection of Most Representative Training Examples and Incremental Generation of VL1 Hypotheses: The Underlying Methodology and the Description of Programs ESEL and AQ11," *Reports of the Department of Computer Science*, University of Illinois, No. 867, Urbana, May 1978.

Michalski, R.S. and McCormick, B.H. 1971. "Interval Generalization of Switching Theory," *Reports of the Department of Computer Science*, No. 442, University of Illinois, Urbana.

Michalski, R.S. and Negri, P. 1977. "An Experiment on Inductive Learning in Chess End Games," *Machine Representation of Knowledge, Machine Intelligence 8*, E.W. Elcock and D. Michie (eds.), Ellis Horwood Ltd., New York, pp. 175–192.

Michalski, R.S. and Stepp, R.E. 1983. "Learning from Observations: Conceptual Clustering," in *Machine Learning: An Artificial Intelligence Approach*, R.S. Michalski, J.G. Carbonell, T.M. Mitchell (eds.), San Mateo, Morgan Kaufmann, 1983.

Michalski, R.S. and Winston, P.H. 1986. "Variable Precision Logic." *Artificial Intelligence Journal*, No. 29.

Michalski, R.S., Mozetic, I., Hong, J., and Lavrac, N. 1986. "The AQ15 Inductive Learning System: An Overview and Experiments," *Proceedings of the American Association for Artificial intelligence Conference (AAAI)*.

Mitchell, T.M. 1982. "Generalization as a Search," *Artificial Intelligence*, 1, 203–226.

Mozetic, I. 1986. "Knowledge Extraction through Learning from Examples" In T.M. Mitchell, J.G. Carbonell, R.S. Michalski (eds.), *Machine Learning: A Guide to Current Research*, Kluwer Academic Publishers.

Mumdani, E.H. and Gaines, B.R. (eds.). 1981. *Fuzzy Reasoning and its Applications*, Academic Press.

Murphy, G.L. and Medin, D.L. 1985. "The Role of Theories in Conceptual Coherence," *Psychological Review*, No. 92.

Nosofsky, R.M. 1988. "Exemplar-based Accounts of Relations between Classification, Recognition and Typicality," *Journal of Experimental Psychology: Learning, Memory and Cognition*.

Popper, K.R. 1979. *Objective Knowledge: An Evolutionary Approach*, Oxford at the Clarendon Press.

Quinlan, R.J. 1983. "Learning Efficient Classification Procedures and their Application to Chess End Games," in *Machine Learning: An Artificial Intelligence Approach*, R.S. Michalski, J.G. Carbonell, T.M. Mitchell (eds.), Morgan Kaufmann, San Mateo.

———, 1990. "Probabilistic Decision Trees," in *Machine Learning: An Artificial Intelligence Approach, Volume III*, Y. Kodratoff and R.S. Michalski (eds.), Morgan Kaufmann Publishers.

Reinke, R.E. and Michalski, R.S. 1988. "Incremental Learning of Decision Rules: A Method and Experimental Results," in J.E. Hayes, D. Michie, J. Richards (eds.), *Machine Intelligence*, Oxford University Press.

Rosch, E. and Mervis, C.B. 1975. "Family Resemblances: Studies in the Structure of Categories," *Cognitive Psychology*, No. 7.

Schank, R.C., Collins, G.C., and Hunter, L.E. 1986. "Transcending Induction Category Formation in Learning," *The Behavioral and Brain Sciences*.

Smith, E.E. and Medin, D.L. 1981. *Categories and Concepts*, Harvard University Press, Cambridge, MA.

Sowa, J.F. 1984. *Conceptual Structures: Information Processing in Mind and Machine*. Addison-Wesley Publishing Company.

Watanbe, S. 1969. *Knowing and Guessing: A Formal and Quantitative Study*, Wiley Pub. Co.

Wittgenstein, L. 1922. *Tractatus Logico-Philosophicus*, London: Routledge and Kegan.

Winston. P.H. 1975. "Learning Structural Descriptions from Examples," *The Psychology of Computer Vision*, Winston P.H. (Ed.), McGraw Hill, New York, chapter 5.

Zhang, J. and Michalski, R.S. 1989. "A Description Preference Criterion in Constructive Learning," *Proceedings of the Sixth International Workshop on Machine Learning*, Cornell University, Ithaca, New York, June 26–27, 1989.

Zadeh, L.A. 1965. "Fuzzy Sets," *Information and Control*, 8.

——— , 1976. "A Fuzzy-Algorithmic Approach to the Definition of Complex or Imprecise Concepts," *International Journal of Man-Machine Studies*, 8.

——— , 1978. "Fuzzy Sets as a Basis for a Theory of Possibility," *Fuzzy Sets and Systems 1*.

COMMENTARY

Robert E. Stepp
(University of Illinois)

Abstract

This chapter presents a commentary on Chapter 3 by Ryszard S. Michalski. Included in the commentary are excerpts from the discussion of Michalski's paper at the IMAL conference, July 30, 1986 at Les Arcs, France. The commentary consists of a distillation of the preceding chapter, along with a critique of the strengths and weaknesses of the two-tiered methodology and how it ties into other learning paradigms.

1 OVERVIEW OF THE PAPER

Michalski views learning as an inference process that builds or modifies knowledge structures. From an initial set of facts (specific examples), operators, inference rules, and goals, it transforms the given concepts into a more useful form.

Michalski defines two styles of concepts: *flexible* and *crisp*. He characterizes the crisp concepts as those whose interpretation is context independent; flexible concepts are those whose interpretation is context sensitive. Flexible concepts are said to have fluid and imprecisely defined boundaries. There seems to be a mixing here of both context sensitivity and escaping into an augmented representation language, as grounds for viewing concept boundaries as being "fluid."

Although not described as sets of crisp concepts, one could view flexible concepts that way: A flexible concept is the intentional representation of a set of crisp concept and context pairs. For example, a "triangle" could be the set of concepts {"geometrical triangle," "triangle of three streets," "musical triangle," "love triangle," etc.}. The choice of the exact concept is determined from the context in which it is used.

Traditional machine learning paradigms have made extensive use of crisp concepts in the form of Cartesian covers. The range of shapes of the cover is directly connected to the concept description language. For example, an extended language such as Michalski's APC provides for interval-valued descriptors and hence, describes interval covers with boundaries that would be awkwardly expressed using only Cartesian covers. One might then say that a concept described in a higher order language would have a boundary that undulates in ways hard to describe by a simpler language.

Michalski's flexible concept sets are represented intentionally by two parts: the base concept representation (a crisp but incomplete concept nucleus) and the inferential concept interpretation (some way to reinterpret the base concept according to its context). Although concept interpretation schemes involving inference are mentioned, Michalski's experiments so far have involved only simple partial matching techniques, which he calls *flexible* matching. Because the "context" of a partial matcher is determined *a priori* (from the training examples), it behaves like a representation language augmentation: Using partial match there is a precise concept boundary that does not vary from one testing example to the next, but it is a boundary that would be awkwardly described using only Cartesian covers.

Previously, learning systems simply produced concepts that were generated according to the preferences (biases) of the system, a preference that normally favors concepts that are consistent and complete with respect to the training events, and maximally general. A *base* concept need not be consistent and complete. It consists of typical ideal properties of the examples in the class. Note that there are predictability and utility issues that seem to operate to determine what in humans constitutes a typical or base concept [Fisher, 1988; Smith and Medin, 1981]. Michalski's idea of a base concept follows a syntactic view of typicality: A typical entity can be described by a rule with fewer terms. If one were to look for semantic typicality (as humans do), the issues of predictability and utility would have to become biasing components to the (AQ15) concept formulating algorithm.

In the conventional single-tier approach, the base concept is all there is, and it is expected to cover the examples in the class (positive examples) while avoiding any negative examples. In flexible matching, there is a two-tier approach composed of a base concept and a method of interpretation. One method of interpretation can be to specify a function that computes the degree of match between an event and a base concept. This can be thought of as some function $f(B,E,C,K)$ where E is an event to be matched to base concept B, and C and K give the context (e.g., other competing base concepts) and background knowledge, respectively. The idea is that the specification of function f allows for a variety of fuzzy match interpretations under which the base concept plays the role of an idealized prototype. Unlike a covering description, a prototype concept does not have to miss all negative events, and it can still perform well so long as the degree of match between the prototype and each negative event is below some threshold or below the degree of match of the negative event to some other base concept. In either case, interpretation will show the negative event as not belonging with the prototype, and a consistent conclusion can be reached.

1.1 Sample Learning Program: AQ15

Michalski illustrates the above points by describing the learning program AQ15 that generates new hypotheses from examples, prior hypotheses, and background knowledge. In the two-tier approach, learning requires generating both the base concepts and the method of interpretation. This provides a new range of possible preferences (biases) to the algorithm. There are possibilities for probabilistic learning and a more compact concept description (because prototypes can be generalized to a greater degree than covering descriptions and yet perform just as well). As it turns out, the AQ15 program presently automates relatively little of the new approach.

The improvement in the compactness of concept descriptions can be offset by increased computational difficulties in generating a concept interpretation method, especially if one wants an optimized one. Overall, this approach provides a new idea for trading off learning cost against decision cost and concept size. It is faster to learn only single-tier concepts because no interpretation method generation is required. But on the other hand, because many methods of interpretation appear to have approximately the same algorithmic cost, it may be profitable to suffer a higher learning cost for a greatly optimized two-tiered recognition rule that is reduced both in size (because less storage is needed for the more general prototype) and in decision time (because fewer variable/value relationships must be checked during rule evaluation).

The presented experimental evidence supports this analysis: When flexible match is adopted, the base concept complexity goes down and performance tends to improve slightly. On the surface it is surprising to find that simplified, less complete rules can give better recognition accuracy. The procedure used is to first generate crisp concepts using AQ15, then the TRUNC algorithm is used to discard the disjuncts covering the fewest examples. TRUNC is applied iteratively so long as accuracy does not fall much.

The TRUNC method works by removing disjuncts; i.e., pretending that certain positive events were not seen as input examples. Let $E_1 \cup E_2$ be the set of positive examples, partitioned such that the examples in E_2 are the ones whose cover is removed by applying TRUNC; i.e., the events in E_2 are *minority* events not well representing the core of the concept. Let $N_1 \cup N_2$ be the corresponding negative examples, again with N_2 being the ones removed by TRUNC. Let P(E) denote the decision performance of rules learned from considering all examples in set E (without doing TRUNC). What is surprising is that

$$P(E_1) > P(E_1 \cup E_2),$$

that is, learning from effectively more examples resulted in lower performance. But note that *all* negative events are used: when generating a consistent cover for E_1, negative events $N_1 \cup N_2$ are used, and vice versa. Experiments so far do not show that the performance with fewer *negative* events is greater than with more negative events; i.e., under the TRUNC method the simplified base concepts are not more general, they are in fact more specific; they are no less consistent, they are in fact less complete.

Rather than indicate how tailored interpretation schemes permit more generalization of the base concept (for the sake of concept simplicity), the presented evidence tends to show that the natural concept boundaries are not Cartesian: $P(E_1)$ is greater than $P(E_1 \cup E_2)$ because the events in E_2 are the less typical minority events (near the concept border), and given that the border is not easily described by Cartesian covers, the inductive leap to Cartesian covers needed to cover E_2 also covers a significant portion of the opposing concept space. Hence the performance goes down. It appears that some concepts (perhaps especially in medical domains) have borders that are better described by flexible match. Such concepts would thus have relatively simple base descriptions when interpretd via flexible matching. If the description can only be a crisp Cartesian complex, more disjuncts *and* more training examples are needed to achieve the same recognition accuracy. The additional training examples are required because the crisp cartesian generalization bias poorly fits the underlying concept shape in the event space.

2 ANOTHER VIEW OF MULTITIER LEARNING

Consider the simple problem illustrated in Figure 1. There are two attributes that take discrete values in the range 0 to 4. Training events in class 1 occupy the points labeled C1. Those from class 2 occupy the points labeled C2. The base concepts for this set of points are:

$$C1 \Leftarrow [x_1 = 2][x_2 = 1..3]$$
$$C2 \Leftarrow [x_1 = 3..4][x_2 = 0..1]$$

The numbers in the upper left corner of each square give the measure of fit (MF) of that event with base concept C1. The numbers at the lower right give the fit of the event with base concept C2. If one decides the class membership by taking the class with the greater measure of fit, a certain classification scheme results. In this problem, each square represents a possible event point that must either be in class 1 or in class 2. Those in class 1 according to the measure of fit are marked with a dot in the lower left corner. The unmarked squares are in class 2.

The top diagram in Figure 2 shows measure of fit scores that are unweighted by t-score: The scores are simply the product of the selector measures of fit. In the bottom diagram in Figure 2, the measure of fit of each complex is weighted by the factor

(t-score / total number of examples)

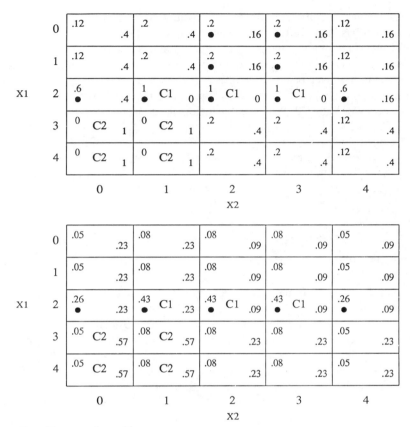

Figure 1:   Two sample problem spaces

as described in Michalski's experiments. This weights the MF for C1 and C2 by 3/7 and 4/7, respectively. Thus, C2 is weighted one-third more than C1. This alone changes the effective boundary of the concept, resulting in four fewer points belonging to concept C1 in the weighted (lower diagram) version. Neither weighting can be considered right or wrong. The observation is that subtle decisions on weighting have potentially significant influences on the problem-solving decisions the two-tiered rule will make.

There are two ways to interpret such two-tiered covers. One way is to say that the flexible match results in a shorthand for a more complicated cover. Here the interval cover of the top diagram for concept C1 (shown by the dots) is actually

$$C1' \Leftarrow [x_1 = 2] \ v \ [x_1 = 0..1][x_2 = 2..3]$$
$$C2' \Leftarrow [x_1 = 3..4] \ v \ [x_1 0..1][x_2 = 0v1v4]$$

which is a cover that one could but would not normally get by generalizing the base covers. What has happened is that a new bias has been introduced. For some problems this bias may improve the performance. For others it may make it worse.

Another way to look at the resulting cover is as an extension in the representation/explanation power of the system. Before using flexible match, statements like those above for C1′ and C2′ were more complex and required more effort to evaluate than the covers C1 and C2. With flexible match, the concepts are written exactly like C1 and C2, and the non-Cartesian shape of the cover is achieved by computing the measure of fit. Suddenly, it is easy and economical to express C1′ and C2′ in a language that interprets the base concepts using flexible match.

Letting MF denote the measure of fit, the intentional description of a decision rule for testing event e for class 1 has thus changed from

Class 1 if $[x_1(e) = 2][x_2(e) = 1..3]$ is true.

to

Class 1 if MF(e,C1) MF(e,Cj) for all j other than 1.

In APC, the "of e" annotation of the top statement is always implied; it is included here to make the point that facts describing some event are needed in either intentional description. In the second description, the function MF has become part of the semantics of the concept.

Given that partial matching is a numerical scoring function, it is not obvious how partial matching and inference should be combined into an all-encompassing concept interpretation. The unanswered question is how to generalize when the interpretation is not crisp but flexible. In the experiments reported by Michalski, the TRUNC algorithm did not generalize the base descriptions—it specialized them! The descriptions are constructed using AQ so that they are consistent with all training events, then TRUNC acts as though the positive events covered by the smaller disjuncts were forgotten. But their effect as negative events on the opposing concepts remain.

This is a lost opportunity. Take for example the Figure 3–2 depiction of the concept of R-ball. This can be simplified to a single complex as shown in Figure 3–3. This is worth comment for two reasons: First, the illustrated simplification cannot be done by the TRUNC algorithm; and second, a far simpler two-tiered concept is readily constructed from merely two events, as shown in Figure 2.

In Figure 2, each square contains two match scores: The one in the upper left is the number of unmatched selector values between its square and event E1; the score in the lower left applies to event E2. Dots mark those squares in which the sum of the two differences is four or less. The marked pattern is identical to the concept in Figure 3–2. The AQ15-based algorithm could not generate this two-prototype base concept because its concept language and generalization strategies cannot generate descriptions in terms of match-distance effects in the event space.

SHAPE BOUNCES

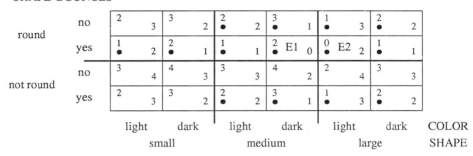

Figure 2: A generalized two-tiered solution

This use of flexible matching is akin to a simple case-based reasoning strategy. This view points out the trade-offs between approaches: The crisp concept is articulate in its relationships, i.e., when told a crisp concept, a picture often comes to mind of an entity with the proscribed characteristics; the flexible concept is mushy in its relationships, only an approximate prototype can be described often without much detail, and it is difficult to describe the interpretation criterion by which a categorical decision is to be made. Thus, the pattern in Figure 3–2 can be described either by a crisp concept involving disjunction but no special interpretation or it can be described by a pair of prototype cases and a partial-match threshold function to judge category decisions.

Ultimately, in some other implementation, the decision reached by applying a flexible concept will depend on the goal of the system and the application of background knowledge. For example, consider Michalski's concept of a "fish." Suppose you are told "it is a fish." What inferences or decision would you make? Probably you would expect "it" to exhibit typical fish properties; i.e., you would make use of a fish prototype and the predictability of fish properties from the prototype. On the other hand, if you are told of a person, "he is a fish," you would not expect many fish properties but only one or two (perhaps the person is a strong swimmer; perhaps it is Halloween, and the person is wearing a fish costume). One could view the interpretation as an analogy that provides a mapping between the base concept and the current context, a mapping that could be a literal one or one that is loose and highly selective. Thus the interpretation of the "fish concept" changes. The goal of the two-tiered approach is to facilitate this change without the need to process any additional training examples.

But what about learning the "fish concept"? Suppose the learner is shown a wide variety of fish. The learner should develop some concept that will later enable the recognition of other fish examples. Suppose several examples are members of the varsity swimming team. Are these examples noise? Are they metaphorical allusions to fishlike properties of humans? What concept should an intelligent learner derive from these examples? Are metaphorical concepts learnable in parallel with the base concept, or must the base concept be learned first in order to provide the analogical mapping of descriptors? The application of a two-tiered learning paradigm for learning analogies is not obvious in such cases.

There is a linguistic curiosity too: Is there but one concept of "a fish"? Or are there a family of concepts, each fairly crisp and distinct, all mapped onto the same linguistic term "fish"? Should one try to provide a machine learning scheme to learn the one-and-only "fish" concept? Or should one pursue a strategy for learning several "fish" concepts as well as the structure that connects them by way of the applicable context?

It appears that the issues can be separated and that there is profit to do so:

1. Representation language

   Not all concepts lie in the concept space shaped as simple Cartesian covers. It is more parsimonious to use higher order conceptual primitives to represent concepts. For Michalski's medical domains, medical decision processes appear to better fit a flexible match representation space than a Cartesian cover space.

2. Learning time versus decision-time trade-offs

   Many decision spaces can be well mapped by deciding the outcome on the basis of closest proximity to categorized prototypes. Michalski's R-ball concept can be handled well this way, using generalization techniques beyond the scope of AQ15 and TRUNC. At the same time, it appears that not all problems would do so well. It would truly be a surprise if Michalski's particular flexible match scoring formula proved to be universally applicable. The trade-off is there: One can put more or less effort into choosing the interpretation; it would seem worthwhile to determine when it is proper to use easy-to-learn standard interpretations (e.g., regular crisp concepts or simple case-based decisions) and when is it proper to find a problem-specific optimized interpretation. This issue is closely coupled to the topic of constructive induction.

3. Context sensitivity

   What is still unknown is whether it is better to try to represent (via a two-tiered approach or some other approach) universal linguistic concepts (e.g., "a fish") in all their possible contexts, or whether is it better to learn sets of "crisper" concepts and the context web that links them.

The two-tiered approach provides a valuable contrast and comparison between crisp rules and those that are not so crisp. This certainly points to the potential power of nondisjunctive non-Cartesian concepts for better fitting concept boundaries (providing better generalizations). There are as yet no learning algorithms for this type of concept representation, such algorithms would need extended techniques for controlling generalization in ways unique to flexible concepts (e.g., by understanding the effects of a selected measure of fit scoring function). Even more exotic would be learning mechanisms that incorporate analogical models. Analysis of learning bias shares some of these goals [Utgoff, 1986; Rendell, Seshu, and Tcheng, 1987].

How to address these issues is still a challenge. As machine learning addresses the structure of sets of concepts and how a base concept might be interpreted differently under different circumstances, the neural network model of inference and learning becomes more and more interesting. Some of this horizon has been opened by the two-tiered model and the experiments that have been performed.

References

Fisher, D.H. 1988. "A Computational Account of Basic Level and Typicality Effects," *Proc. Seventh Nat. Conf. on Artificial Intelligence*, August 21–26, St. Paul, MN, pp. 233–238.

Rendell, L.A., Seshu, R., and Tcheng, D. 1987. "Layered Concept-learning and Dynamically Variable Bias Management," *IJCAI-87*, pp. 308–314.

Smith, E. and Medin, D. 1981. *Categories and Concepts*, Harvard University Press, Cambridge, MA.

Utgoff, P.E. 1986. "Shift of Bias for Inductive Concept Learning," *Machine Learning: An Artificial Intelligence Approach, Volume II*, R.S. Michalski, J.G. Carbonell, T.M. Mitchell (eds.), Morgan Kaufmann, San Mateo, CA., pp. 107–148.

4

PROTOS:

AN EXEMPLAR-BASED LEARNING APPRENTICE[1]

E. Ray Bareiss
(Vanderbilt University)

Bruce W. Porter
(University of Texas, Austin)

Craig C. Wier
(Mentor Graphics Corporation)

Abstract

Building Protos, a learning apprentice system for heuristic classification, has forced us to scrutinize the usefulness of inductive learning and deductive problem solving. While these inference methods have been widely studied in machine learning, their seductive elegance in artificial domains (*e.g.,* mathematics) does not carry over to natural domains (*e.g.,* medicine). This paper briefly describes our rationale in the Protos system for relegating inductive learning and deductive problem solving to minor roles in support of retaining, indexing, and matching exemplars. The problems that arise from "lazy generalization" are described along with their solutions in

---

[1] Based on a paper presented at the Second AAAI Workshop on Knowledge Acquisition for Knowledge-based Systems, Banff, October 1987. Reprinted with permission from Academic Press, Ltd. from Bareiss, *et al., International Journal of Man-Machine Studies* 29(5) pp. 549–561, 1988.

Protos. Finally, an example of Protos in the domain of clinical audiology is discussed.

4.1 INTRODUCTION

Learning and reasoning from exemplars is a promising alternative to inductive learning and deductive reasoning. Exemplar-based learning involves remembering and indexing specific training cases. Reasoning from learned exemplars involves interpreting a new case by recalling a similar exemplar for guidance. In contrast, inductive learning generalizes specific training cases to form an abstract description. Reasoning involves deducing that a new case is subsumed by the abstract description. While this distinction might appear inconsequential, it has far-reaching implications, ranging from psychological validity to the feasibility of machine learning programs for diagnostic expert systems.

Our development of Protos, a learning apprentice system for heuristic classification tasks, provides impetus and context for the study of exemplar-based systems. The primary goal of our Protos research is to develop a general mechanism for acquiring classification knowledge while providing interactive assistance to users. The requirements for such a system forced us to reconsider the popular wisdom in machine learning that training should be compiled and compressed into generalizations. Before turning to our solution, we briefly review the major requirements of the Protos system.

First, the polymorphy of natural concepts must be centrally addressed in both the knowledge representation and the algorithms for learning and problem solving. Artificial domains, which have been the primary focus for machine learning researchers, permit simpler representations and algorithms. Concepts in artificial domains can be "classically defined" [Smith and Medin, 1981] using a set of necessary and sufficient conditions. Examples of such concepts are "a forked position in chess" [Minton, 1984], "a prime in number theory" [Lenat, 1976], and "a good problem state for applying substitution in symbolic integration" [Mitchell, *et al.*, 1983; Porter and Kibler, 1986c]. However, the significant variability among instances of natural concepts prevents inductive learning of a uniform set of necessary and sufficient conditions. For example, consider inductive learning of the concepts "science," "friend, " or "pollutant." If general descriptions for such concepts *can* be formed, they will be so vague as to be useless for classification of new cases. Abstract definitions also preclude other uses of concepts such as exclusion of near misses, generation of examples of concepts, explanation, guiding the interpretation of new cases, etc. [Schank *et al.*, 1986; Porter and Bareiss, 1986a]. Protos satisfies the requirement to address concept polymorphy by focusing on learning and indexing exemplars of each concept.

Second, classification of new cases has two interrelated requirements. The first requirement is that Protos must learn and apply concept models. The identity of new cases is frequently unclear due to concept polymorphy and incomplete or noisy case descriptions. Models can be effectively employed to guide the interpretation of individual cases [Weiss, et al., 1978; Nii, et al., 1982]. Related to this is the requirement for efficient generation of explanations. An explanation relating a new case to a generalized concept is commonly constructed by deducing that the general concept entails the specific case [Buchanan and Shortliffe, 1984; Mitchell, et al., 1986a; De-Jong and Mooney, 1986]. This can involve considerable deductive inference. The amount of inference required is a function of the "distance" between the new case, described in the instance language, and the concept description, described in the generalization language. These two requirements are satisfied in Protos by using learned exemplars, instead of general concepts, as the targets for matches with new cases. An exemplar can provide specific guidance in interpreting an unclear case and can be efficiently matched because of proximity.

The primary lesson of Protos is that learning apprentice systems for heuristic-classification tasks should be "lazy generalizers." Inductive learning is "eager" generalization, which assumes that (1) generalizations *can* be formed, (2) problem solving is primarily deductive inference from generalizations, and (3) classification is the primary application of learned knowledge. There have been numerous efforts to relax these assumptions, ranging from transformational matching systems [Kedar-Cabelli, 1985; McCarty and Sridharan, 1981] to probabilistic systems [Buchanan and Shortliffe, 1984; Zadeh, 1965]. We concluded that inductive learning and deductive classification should play only a minor role in Protos [Porter and Bareiss, 1986a]. Exemplar-based learning and problem solving have considerable psychological support [Bareiss and Porter, 1987; Medin, et al., 1983; Smith and Medin, 1981; Brooks, 1978] and together provide a unified solution to the problems faced by a learning apprentice system: learning and representing polymorphic concepts, classifying unclear cases, and efficiently generating explanations.

The next section describes the problems that are inherent in exemplar-based systems and discusses their solutions in Protos. We have applied Protos to the domain of clinical audiology. Section 4.3 details how Protos processed a typical case. Section 4.4 describes our preliminary evaluation of the performance of Protos as a learning apprentice.

4.2 ISSUES IN EXEMPLAR-BASED SYSTEMS AND THEIR SOLUTIONS IN PROTOS

Exemplar-based systems raise a number of questions. This section answers these questions in the context of the Protos algorithm shown in Figure 4–1. Examples are drawn from the Protos knowledge structure shown in Figure 4–2.

```
REPEAT
1 Input a case to be classified
2 Retrieve remindings based on the features of the case and
  heuristically combine them
 REPEAT
 REPEAT
3 Use the strongest combined reminding to select an exemplar
  from the category structure
4 Evaluate the similarity of the new case to the exemplar by
   constructing an explanation of their equivalence
   UNTIL an aedequately explained match is found
5 Use difference links to improve the classification by
   considering neighboring exemplars as alternates
6 Present the match and explanation to the teacher
  IF the teacher disapproves
7    THEN Request new domain knowledge from the teacher
8          Reassess the remindings which suggested the exemplar
 UNTIL the teacher approves
 IF the match is very strong
9  THEN Merge the case with the exemplar
10 ELSE Add the case to the category structure as a new
    exemplar
   IF the case was initially misclassified
11 THEN Install difference links to the exemplars involved
UNTIL training is complete
```

Figure 4–1: The Protos algorithm

4.2.1 What Unites the Exemplars of a Category?

Category cohesiveness requires that the underlying commonality of the category members be explicit in the representation. In Protos, each exemplar of a category is represented by features and explanations of each feature's relevance to the category. For example, Figure 4–2 shows two exemplars of the category **chairs** and the explanations of their features. The network of domain knowledge with the embedded exemplars is called a *category structure* in Protos. Each node in the category structure is either an exemplar-containing category or a domain primitive. For example, the node labeled *armrests* might contain exemplary armrests, each described with armrest features and explanations of their relevance.

4.2.2 How Are the Exemplars Indexed for Efficient Retrieval?

The first step in processing a new case is to efficiently identify a matching exemplar. This section describes the three primary indexing mechanisms that Protos

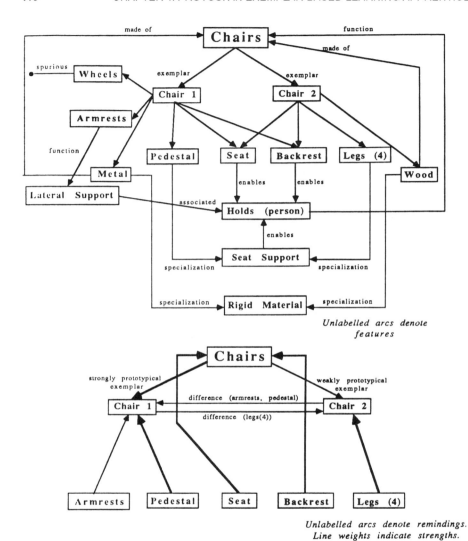

Figure 4–2:   A simple category structure. Top: Domain knowledge; bottom: indices for exemplar retrieval.

uses to retrieve exemplars. The methods for learning indices are described in Section 4.2.5.

The first indexing mechanism relies on cues gleaned from features of the new case (see line 2 of the Protos algorithm, Figure 4–1). Each cue, called a *reminding* (compare, [Schank, 1982; Kolondner, 1983]) is a link in the category structure from a feature to an exemplar or category (compare "cue validity of features" in [Rosch, 1978; Medin, 1983]). For example, the feature *backrest* in Figure 4–2 provides a reminding to the category of **chairs** while the feature *pedestal* is idiosyncratic to the exemplar *chair 1*. The features of a new case typically provide numerous remindings that are heuristically combined into a few candidate classifications for the new case. For example, if the features of a new case include *backrest* and *pedestal*, Protos is reminded of the category **chairs** and the exemplar *chair 1*. These two remindings are combined, yielding a strong reminding to *chair 1*.

The second form of indexing relies on the prototypicality of exemplars with respect to their containing categories. Prototypicality provides a partial ordering on the exemplars of a category. The prototypicality of an exemplar is determined by *family resemblance*: the extent to which its features overlap those of other category members [Rosch and Mervis, 1975]. Protos may use prototypicality (see line 3 of the Protos algorithm, Figure 4–1) to select an exemplar from a category in the set of candidate classifications. If there are remindings to a particular exemplar in the category, it is selected. Otherwise, an exemplar is selected from the category based on prototypicality. For example, given a new case that evokes remindings to **chairs** but no remindings to particular exemplars, Protos prefers *chair 1* based on prototypicality.

The third indexing mechanism is based on the differences between pairs of "neighboring" exemplars in the category structure (compare, [Kolodner, 1983]). This mechanism is used in line 5 of the algorithm after Protos constructs a match with a retrieved exemplar (the subject of the next section) and notes featural mismatches. Protos attempts to improve the match by considering neighbors of the retrieved exemplar. Those *difference links* from the exemplar, which are labeled with one or more of the noted mismatches are traversed to hill climb to an improved match. For example, if a new case partially matches *chair 2* but has the additional feature of *armrests*, then the difference link to *chair 1* is traversed.

4.2.3 How Are Exemplars Used During Problem Solving?

Each exemplar in the category structure is a model for interpretation of new cases. However, only those exemplars that are similar to the new case are useful. Initially, the remindings are used to retrieve an exemplar based on expectation of similarity. The true similarity is then determined by *knowledge-based pattern matching* (see line 4 of the Protos algorithm). Knowledge-based pattern matching uses the domain knowledge in the category structure to construct an explanation of the equivalence of the exemplar and the new case. The explanation is the justification for concluding the presence of criterial features of the exemplar based on the observed features of the new case. For example, Protos might match the feature *legs*(4) in a new case to *pedestal* in the exemplar *chair 1* based on the knowledge:

$$legs\ (4) \xrightarrow{\text{specialization}} seat\ support \xleftarrow{\text{specialization}} pedestal$$

This suggests that the features are equivalent because each provides evidence for the functional feature, *seat support*.

Protos gauges the amount of effort to expend on knowledge-based pattern matching between a new case and a retrieved exemplar. Effort is determined by multiple factors, including the combined strength of the remindings from the features of the case to the exemplar, the prototypicality of the exemplar, and the degree of direct match between the case and the exemplar. In summary, knowledge-based pattern matching (deductive inference) is used in Protos to confirm expectations about a new case. The amount of effort expended in the process is restricted, lest Protos "see mirages."

4.2.4 How Is the Category Structure Learned?

The category structure is learned from training provided by the teacher. The teacher provides cases for Protos to classify. When Protos fails, the teacher explains the correct answer (see line 7 of the Protos algorithm). The cases described to Protos become exemplars and the accompanying explanations become domain knowledge in the category structure. Past research has ignored the role of explanations in training and assumed that a teacher could compensate for a narrow communication channel by either providing numerous training examples (e.g., [Quinlan, 1986]) or relying on the learner's *a priori* knowledge (e.g., [Mitchell, *et al.*, 1986a]).

Protos expects an explanation of the relevance of each feature of a new case to the category to which the case is assigned. If Protos is unable to generate an explanation for a feature, then the teacher assists. The teacher provides domain knowledge in the form of terms and predefined relations, which Protos integrates into the category structure. For example, consider the case of a *hanging* chair suspended from the ceiling by ropes, with neither legs nor pedestal. Protos cannot form a close match with either *chair 1* or *chair 2* until the teacher provides the information in the form of an explanation that:

$$chair\ ropes \xrightarrow{\text{specialization}} seat\ support$$

4.2.5 How Are the Indices for Exemplars Learned?

As described in Section 4.2.2, there are three types of indices for exemplars in the category structure: remindings, prototypicality, and differences. Protos learns and adjusts these indices during the course of training. This section describes the learning process.

Remindings are heuristic estimates of the likelihood that particular exemplars or categories will be relevant to the processing of a new case. Initially these remindings are learned analytically. A teacher-supplied explanation that strongly relates a feature to a category or an exemplar is compiled into a reminding link. For example, the explanation:

$$seat \xrightarrow{\textit{enables}} holds\ (person) \xrightarrow{\textit{function}} chairs$$

suggests that *seat* should remind Protos of the category **chairs**.

When a reminding associated with a feature does not contribute to finding a successful classification, Protos reassesses its validity. Since remindings are compiled by analyzing explanations, Protos attempts to reassess a reminding by checking the consistency of the reminding with both the current state of its domain knowledge and the competing remindings. If analysis does not indicate that the reminding should be adjusted, Protos weakens the reminding to reflect diminished confidence; a reminding that continues to be weakened over time is eventually removed.

Protos estimates prototypicality by noting an exemplar's successful use in problem solving. When an exemplar closely matches a new case, the exemplar exhibits family resemblance within its category. The more new cases successfully matched by the exemplar, the more prototypical it becomes.

If Protos misclassifies a case, it installs difference links in the category structure to avoid similar near misses in the future. As discussed above, difference links allow Protos to improve a tentative match by identifying neighbors of the matched exemplar that may provide better matches.

4.2.6 When Are Exemplars Generalized?

As described in Section 4.2.4, each new case presented by the teacher is integrated into the category structure. This integration may involve merging the new case with an existing exemplar. Protos attempts to merge the descriptions if knowledge-based pattern matching determines they are highly similar and the teacher concurs. Specifically, all the important features of the exemplar must be accounted for by explanations to features of the new case. This means that Protos considers the exemplar and the new case to be equivalent with respect to its goals and training.

As a result of a merge, the features of the exemplar might be generalized. For example, consider the new case, *chair 2'*, which is the same as exemplar *chair 2* in Figure 4–2 except it is made of metal instead of wood. Protos would merge the new case with the exemplar after constructing the following explanation for the mismatched features:

$$metal \xrightarrow{\textit{specialization}} rigid\ material \xleftarrow{\textit{specialization}} wood$$

This explanation suggests that the exemplar feature *wood* can be generalized to *rigid material* in the resulting merged exemplar.

Another important source of exemplar generality is knowledge-based pattern matching. An exemplar implicitly represents all of the cases (seen or unseen) that are reachable by transforming the exemplar's features using domain knowledge. Therefore, the generality of an exemplar can increase with the amount of domain knowledge in the category structure.

4.3 AN EXAMPLE OF CLASSIFYING AND LEARNING

This section demonstrates how Protos learns while providing interactive assistance to the user/teacher. Our example is from the domain of clinical audiology, which involves evaluation and diagnosis of hearing disorders. We trained Protos with 200 sequential cases from Baylor College of Medicine. Each case presented to Protos consisted of patient-reported symptoms, patient history information, and the results of routine tests. This is the data that a clinician considers when diagnosing a patient. We believe that clinical audiology is representative of a large set of heuristic-classification tasks for which Protos is appropriate.

We now describe the 24th case of hearing disorder processed by Protos. For clarity, this case is called NewCase. Protos is presented with the features of New-Case, which represent the results of tests of the patient's hearing and the biomechanical and physiological status of the patient's ear. These features are:

air(moderate)   ipsi-AR(absent)
bone(normal)   contra-AR(absent)
speech-intell(normal) other-i-AR(normal)
tymp-pr(negative)   other-c-AR(absent)
tymp-peak(flat)

As shown in Figure 4–3, Protos is reminded of multiple diagnostic categories by the features of NewCase. Line weights indicate the strengths of the remindings. These "raw" remindings are heuristically combined to determine the most likely

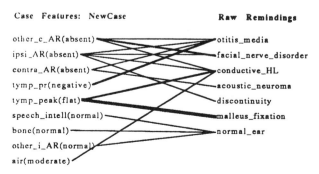

Figure 4–3:   The features of NewCase and the remindings to diagnostic categories

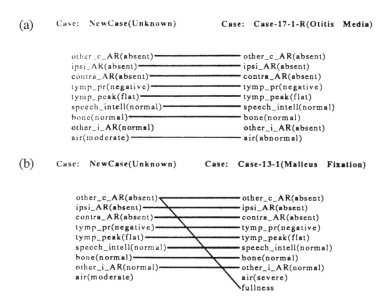

Figure 4–4: Featural matches from Protos's attempts to classify NewCase; (a) the first attempt, (b) the second attempt.

classifications for this case. As a result of this process, **otitis media** and **malleus fixation** emerge as the most likely categories.

The next step is to select an exemplar to serve as a model for NewCase. The reminding to **otitis media** is strongest, so Protos tries it first. Exemplar selection is based on prototypicality since Protos has no remindings to specific exemplars. Protos retrieves Case-17-1-R which is currently the most prototypical exemplar of **otitis media** in the category structure. The results of matching the two cases are illustrated in Figure 4–4(a). All of the featural matches are direct except for the match between *air(moderate)* and *air(abnormal)*. This match is justified by the explanation *air(moderate) has generalization air(abnormal)*. Protos presents this evidence, but the teacher rejects the diagnosis. The teacher approves of the explanation of the match but insists on considering the alternatives.

As a consequence of the teacher's rejection of the diagnosis, Protos weakens the remindings in the category structure that led to the misclassification. Protos then tries to match an exemplar of the category **malleus fixation**. Case-13-1 is selected as the most prototypical of this category. The result of using this case as a model for NewCase is illustrated in Figure 4–4(b). All featural matches are direct except for the match between *other-contra-AR(absent)* and *fullness*. This match is explained by:

other-c-AR(absent) co-occurs with conductive-HL which requires fullness

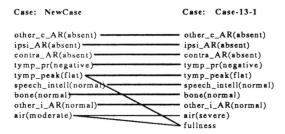

Figure 4–5:   Revised match following the teacher's correction of Protos's explanation

Presented with all of the evidence, the teacher accepts the diagnosis of **malleus fixation**. In an effort to improve the overall match, Protos asks about the unmatched exemplar feature *air(severe)*. The teacher tells Protos that

> *air(moderate) has generalization air(abnormal) which has specialization air(severe)*

Next Protos complains that the explanation linking *other-c-AR(absent)* to *fullness* is weak. Actually, the explanation is wrong, and the teacher corrects Protos by telling it that *conductive-HL only occasionally requires fullness*. The teacher then provides the correct explanation:

> *(tymp-peak(flat) AND air(moderate)) is usually sufficient for fullness*

Since the teacher has provided new information, Protos retries the match. Figure 4–5 shows the result, which is accepted by the teacher without further revision.

Because all of the features of Case-13-1 are matched, Protos suggests that NewCase and Case-13-1 be merged. The teacher agrees. As a result of this decision, Protos increases the prototypicality of Case-13-1, and NewCase is not added to the category structure. During the merging operation, Protos notes the explanation:

> *air(moderate) has generalization air(abnormal) which has specialization air(severe)*

and suggests that the feature *air(severe)* of Case-13-1 be generalized to *air(abnormal)*; the teacher concurs.

Since Protos found a mismatch to Case-17-1-R of **otitis media** before successfully matching Case-13-1 of **malleus fixation**, it suggests installing a difference link between the two exemplars to note how they differ. The teacher agrees and accepts this disposition of the case.

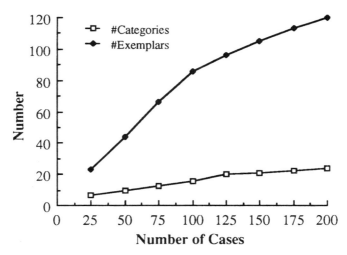

Figure 4–6:   The growth of the Protos category structure

4.4 EXPERIMENTAL EVALUATION OF PROTOS

During the application of Protos in the domain of clinical audiology, data was collected to assess the system's learning and classification performance. This section summarizes our empirical evaluation of Protos.

Professional training for clinical audiology typically requires two years of graduate school culminating in a Masters degree. Before becoming practicing clinicians, students must pass a national examination and serve a clinical-fellowship year following graduation. In the course of their graduate training, students see between 150–200 cases and then an additional 900–1200 cases in their clinical-fellowship year. To be consistent with this amount of training, we decided that Protos should learn to perform demonstrably well given a training set of 200 cases. A database of 200 consecutive cases was obtained from the Audiology Clinic at Baylor College of Medicine in Houston, Texas. This training set was presented to Protos by the domain expert without the direct intervention of a knowledge engineer.

The overall growth of the category structure as a function of the number of cases presented is shown in Figure 4–6. Protos learned 24 diagnostic categories, which were represented with 120 exemplars. We were surprised that so many exemplars were retained in the category structure. Protos made little use of exemplar merging and generalization for two reasons. First, many of the categories are highly polymorphic and good generalizations (which are complete, consistent, and can be operationalized) do not exist. Second, a shortcoming in the explanation language prevented the domain expert from giving *conditional* explanations of featural equivalence during presentation of the first hundred cases. Using this form of explanation, an earlier explanation could be more correctly expressed as:

IF the category is **malleus fixation** THEN
air(moderate) has generalization air(abnormal) which has specialization air(severe)

which equates the two values of *air* only in the context of this particular diagnosis. The expert estimated that this language facility would have allowed additional explanations enabling Protos to discard 30–40 of the retained exemplars. (Accordingly, a conditional explanation capability was incorporated into Protos after presentation of the first hundred cases.)

The primary measure of the performance of Protos is its accuracy in classifying new cases. Table 4–1 summarizes this performance.[2] After relatively little training, Protos' performance far exceeded the performance that the expert estimated would be typical of a human student with similar experience. Throughout the learning process, Protos correctly classified more than 80% of the cases. Much to our satisfaction, this performance was unaffected by continued growth of the category structure. After the 200 training cases, Protos was presented with a normal mix of 26 test cases and demonstrated similar performance.

The problem solving efficiency of Protos can be measured by the amount of effort expended during classification. There was a gradual increase in the average number of diagnostic hypotheses pursued and the number of matches attempted during the training process (Table 4–2). However, this increase was not apparent to the teacher. The average number of matches per case, which Protos determined to be strong enough to discuss with the teacher, was constant through the training and test sets; most of the effort in the classification process was independent of the teacher.

Table 4–1: Protos's classification performance

Cases	First match correct (%)	Strongest match correct (%)
Training	58%	82%
Test	92%	100%

---

[2] Since Protos is designed to perform heuristic classification (classifying cases into known categories) the first occurrence of each new category is excluded from this data.

Table 4–2:   Classification effort expended

Cases	Hypotheses pursued	Matches attempted	Matches discussed
1–50	2.7	not available	1.7
51–100	2.8	not available	1.6
101–150	2.5	4.6	1.5
151–200	4.0	7.4	1.9
average	3.0	6.0	1.6
Test	3.7	5.3	1.1

4.5 SUMMARY

Protos is a learning apprentice system for heuristic classification tasks. During the early design of Protos we concluded that inductive learning and deductive problem solving were unsuitable. The polymorphy of natural concepts coupled with the requirements for efficient classification and explanation precluded such simple solutions. We adopted an exemplar-based approach to learning and problem solving which was supported by considerable psychological evidence. We addressed the problems that arose from exemplar-based, "lazy generalization" and built the Protos system. While expert performance is not our primary concern, it is essential to our research paradigm to evaluate our methods by constructing and testing an expert system. This allows us to explore the "scaled-up" behavior of the methods. We have taught Protos about clinical audiology and have found that it quickly evolved into an expert system with a modest training set.

ACKNOWLEDGMENTS

The construction of Protos could not have succeeded without the generous assistance of Claudia Porter, Joe Ross, and Todd Stock. Adam Farquhar and Ken Murray also provided useful comments. Professor James Jerger, of the Baylor College of Medicine in Houston, Texas, graciously allowed access to the audiology clinic records which provided the database used to evaluate Protos's performance. Support for this research was provided by the Army Research Office under grant number ARO DAAG29-84-K-0060 and the National Science Foundation under grant number IRI-8620052.

References

Bareiss, E.R. and Porter, B.W. 1987. A survey of psychological models of concept representation. *Technical Report*, AI TR-87-50, Austin, TX: Department of Computer Sciences, University of Texas.

Brooks, L. 1978. Non-analytic concept formation and the memory for instances. In E. Rosch and B.B. Lloyd, Eds. *Cognition and Categorization*. Hillsdale, NJ: Erlbaum, pp. 169–211.

Buchanan, B.G. and Shortliffe, E.H. 1984. *Rule-based Expert Systems (The MYCIN Experiments of the Stanford Heuristic Programming Project*. Addison-Wesley.

DeJong, G. and Mooney, R. 1986. Explanation-based learning: An alternate view. *Machine Learning*, 1(2), 145–176.

Kedar-Cabelli, S. 1985. Purpose-directed analogy. *Proceedings of the Seventh Annual Conference of the Cognitive Science Society*, pp. 150–159.

Kolodner, J.L. 1983. Maintaining organization in a dynamic long-term memory. *Cognitive Science*, 7(4), 243–280.

Lenat, D.B. 1976. *AM: An Artificial Intelligence Approach to Discovery in Mathematics as Heuristic Search*. PhD Dissertation, Computer Science Department, Stanford University.

McCarty, L.T. and Sridharan, N.S. 1981. The representation of an evolving system of legal concepts. *Proceedings of the International Joint Conference on Artificial Intelligence*, pp. 246–253.

Medin, D.L. 1983. Structural principles of categorization. In B. Shepp and T. Tighe, eds. *Interaction: Perception, Development, and Cognition*. Hillsdale, NJ: Erlbaum, pp. 203–230.

Medin, D.L., Dewey, G.I., and Murphy, T.D. 1983. Relationships between item and category learning: Evidence that abstraction is not automatic. *Journal of Experimental Psychology: Learning, Memory and Cognition*, 9(4), 607–625.

Minton, S. 1984. Constraint-based generalization: Learning game-playing plans from single examples. *Proceedings of the National Conference on Artificial Intelligence*, pp. 251–254.

Mitchell, T.M., Keller, R.M., and Kedar-Cabelli, S.T. 1986. Explanation-based generalization: A unifying view. *Machine Learning*, 1(1), 47–80.

Mitchell, T.M., Utgoff, P.E., Nudel, B., and Banerji, R. 1983. Learning by experimentation: Acquiring and refining problem solving heuristics. In R.S. Michalski, J.G. Carbonell, and T.M. Mitchell, Eds. *Machine Learning*, Morgan Kaufmann.

Nii, H.P., Feigenbaum, E.A., Anton, J.J., and Rockmore, A.J. 1982. Signal-to-symbol transformation: HASP/SIAP case study. *AI Magazine*, 3(2), 23–35.

Porter, B. and Bareiss, E.R. 1986. Protos: An experiment in knowledge acquisition for heuristic classification tasks. *Proceedings of the First International Meeting on Advances in Learning*, 28 July–1 August 1986. Les Arcs, France, pp. 159–174. (Also available as *Technical Report* AI-86-32 from the Computer Sciences Department, University of Texas, Austin.

Porter, B. and Kibler, D. 1986. Experimental goal regression: A technique for learning problem solving heuristics. *Machine Learning*, 1(3), 249–285.

Quinlan, J.R. 1986. Induction of decision trees. *Machine Learning*, 1(1), 81–106.

Rosch, E. 1978. Principles of categorization. In E. Rosch and B.B. Lloyd, Eds. *Cognition and Categorization*. Hillsdale, NJ: Erlbaum.

Rosch, E. and Mervis, C.B. 1975. Family resemblance studies in the internal structure of categories. *Cognitive Psychology*, 7, 573–605.

Schank, R.C. 1982. *Dynamic Memory: A Theory of Reminding and Learning in Computers and People*. Cambridge: Cambridge University Press.

Schank, R.C., Collins, G.C., and Hunter, L.E. 1986. Transcending inductive category formation in learning. *The Behavioural and Brain Sciences*, 9, 639–686.

Smith, E. and Medin, D. 1981. *Categories and Concepts*. Cambridge: Harvard University Press.

Weiss, S.M., Casmir, A.K., and Amarel, S. 1978. A model-based method for computer-aided medical decision-making. *Artificial Intelligence*, 11, 145–172.

Zadeh, L.A. 1965. Fuzzy sets. *Information and Control*, 8, 338–353.

COMMENTARY

Robert C. Holte
(University of Ottawa)

1 KNOWLEDGE COMPILATION

The term "knowledge compilation" [Anderson, 1986; Dietterich, 1986] refers to the process of compressing and reformulating information. Knowledge compilation has several important effects. As the degree of compilation increases, the conciseness of representation increases and the information content decreases. The reformulation aspect of compilation has an equally important consequence. By carefully selecting the way information is represented, one can drastically reduce the amount of computation required to perform a task. If one knows ahead of time exactly how the training data will be used (the "performance task"), one can choose a representation ideally suited to the task and compile the training data into that representation. If the training data is not compiled, and its original representation is not well suited to the performance task, it often happens that processing resembling compilation occurs every time the training data is accessed. It is this phenomenon that is referred to below as "recompiling the data every time it is used."

Now follow excerpts of the discussion that took place between Larry Rendell, Robert Holte, Bruce Porter, R.S. Michalski, and Tom Mitchell during the presentation.

Rendell:

Figure 1 is an example of three knowledge structures that could be used to represent a set of training data; the exemplar, the probabilistic, and the classical.

As we move from an exemplar representation toward a classical representation, the concept can be expressed more concisely. However, we are making a commitment to the form of the concept, and as part of that commitment we are losing information. One of the central questions raised by Bruce is, when should compilation take place? Should it take place once and for all, or should the training data be recompiled every time it is used?

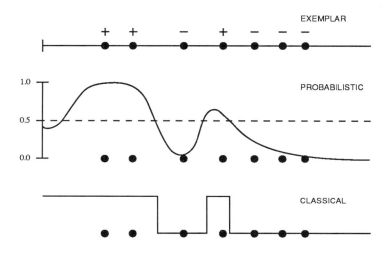

Figure 1

Bruce's answer is that compilation should not take place ahead of time. His reason is that there need not be just one performance task—there may be many. That is, the training examples may have to be used to satisfy a number of purposes; for example, to classify other examples, to generate examples, to remind one of features, etc. The typical approach is to try to make a single representation work for every task. Bruce rightly criticizes this approach: It won't work because there is no one compiled form that can support all these different tasks. But there are problems with Bruce's approach of storing the training data and recompiling each time it is used. What happens if there are a lot of examples? What happens if compilation is expensive? Certainly storage is going to be expensive in some cases. In some cases these factors are not important, but in general they must be considered. So it won't work to use the typical approach and, in some cases at least, the exemplar approach won't work either.

There are two possible answers to the question of when to compile [Holte, 1986; Rendell, 1985]. One is: Do not have just one target structure to which to compile. Compile once and for all into several different structures. It may be that a single target structure can be used for more than one performance task. But in general, one would have a different target structure for each performance task. For example, one could use one representation for classifying new examples and another representation for feature remindings. In this way each performance task can efficiently access the information it requires.

The other possibility—and the two can be used together—is to use intermediate structures. Instead of compiling the training examples directly into the task-oriented knowledge structures, we could go indirectly through a structure that compresses the exemplar (training) information somewhat, but not entirely. Such a structure is called an *intermediate structure*.

Porter:

I think the idea of overly compiling knowledge or compiling it prematurely is wrong. Human experts are able to use their knowledge in many ways and frequently they cannot even anticipate ahead of time what uses the knowledge will be put to. So it seems useful to keep it as close to its source form as we can, for as long as we can. Then we run into the problem of getting 100,000 exemplars. What do we do then?

Well, in some domains, it just does not occur. You do not get 100,000 examples of failures of the space shuttle. You may get 100,000 examples of dogs and cats. What do we do with such domains that are relatively dense? What we propose is similar to what Larry called intermediate structures. We do some minimal generalization. The questions then are: What do you generalize, when do you generalize, and what do you retain as the trace of where you have been so that you can get back there when you have to?

Our answer to when you generalize is: You generalize when you are given exemplars that can be shown to be similar. Similar means that you coerce a match between their feature sets, and you do the coercion by knowledge-based pattern matching. Knowledge-based pattern matching is computationally a very expensive process. We do not want to do it to consider all pairwise generalizations of the exemplars. So how can we restrict what we generalize, so that we do not consider generalizing over the whole cluster of exemplars, the whole category?

Our answer to that is: You only generalize when you are reminded of multiple exemplars based on some subset of their features. Remindings in Protos occur during problem solving. Then you ask: "What do these exemplars have in common? Are there other common features besides the remindings that led me to be curious about this in the first place?" Then you consider generalizing using the paths constructed by knowledge-based pattern matching for guidance.

What do you retain from a generalization? You retain, first a new prototype, which is more general than the exemplars that formed it. And you also maintain focal instances. So, if I generalize over a set of (say) golden retrievers, I am going to remember my own dog Biscuit who is a golden retriever and can be a focal instance for me. And when I am trying to identify a new dog or a new golden retriever, that is one that I want to have come to mind. So I won't throw away instances that, for one reason or another, are important.

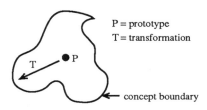

Figure 2

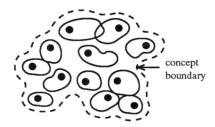

Figure 3

The last thing that I want to discuss is: Why have an exemplar representation at all? Why not consolidate the exemplars into a prototype? Prototype representations have been investigated by psychologists and used in the TAXMAN system at Rutgers [McCarty and Sridharan, 1981].

A prototype representation of a concept can be formed in a variety of ways, typically involving generalizing instances. In order to use a prototype to identify a new object, transformations are applied to the prototype to construct a variation that matches the object. As suggested by Figure 2, the prototype is the "center of the concept" and the transformations map out the concept boundary.

The problem with this method of representation is the transformations required for defining the boundary of the concept. The prototype representation relies on large deductive steps. The transformations move from the central idea to distant points. How are these transformations learned? How can the transformations be defined so that they are powerful enough to reach the boundary and accurate enough to include positive instances of the concept and exclude negative instances?

In contrast, our exemplar representation looks like Figure 3. That is, it uses a collection of "mini-prototypes" which it learns by the generalization process that I talked about. Knowledge-based pattern matching is considerably weaker than the transformations in the prototype representation: It can move from the central exemplar only to nearby examples.

2 KNOWLEDGE-BASED PATTERN MATCHING

Holte:

I was trying to understand what the roles were of the two different types of information that your system receives dynamically. It receives the exemplars themselves, together with their classifications, and it receives explanations. I drew a figure (Figure 4) in which points represent exemplars and a closed curve around a point encloses all the exemplars that would be regarded as similar to the central point by the knowledge-based pattern matching process. Let me call the region inside each closed curve a "sphere of influence."

For example, point J is inside the sphere of influence of point Y, and so if shown to your system, would match point Y; and the system would use Y's classification for J. Point K is inside the spheres of influence of both Y and Z, and so matches both. I do not require that Y matches Z—the "matches" relation is probably neither perfectly transitive nor perfectly symmetric.

What happens to this figure if a new explanation is given to the system? The spheres of influence are expanded as shown in Figure 5. Thus more exemplars would

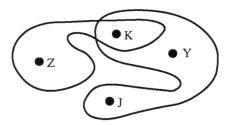

Figure 4

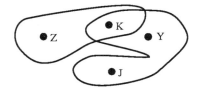

Figure 5

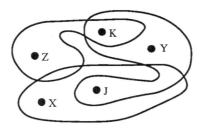

Figure 6

match any particular exemplar, and exemplars that matched previously would now match more strongly. These are the two effects I could see.

That is what happens if you add a new explanation. It we start again with the first diagram (Figure 4), what happens if new exemplar information is added? The spheres of influence stay the same size, but there is a new exemplar, X, with its own sphere of influence that can overlap with existing ones—Figure 6.

There might now be more paths from Y to J than there were before because the matching process can pass freely through the region covered by the new sphere of influence; previously this region contained gaps that the matching process could not get through. Now there is at least a possibility for the matching process to get through or around these gaps.

So what is happening in both cases, at least in a metaphorical sense, is this: If we think of the matching process as covering a certain part of the space of exemplars, it will have gaps in it. As new exemplars are added, and as explanation information is added, these gaps get filled in, although the mechanism is different. Adding explanation information is very much like improving the "domain model" in an explanation-based learning system. Within the present metaphor, however, it looks as if the same effect can be achieved either by adding exemplars or by improving the domain model. To relate this to several other chapters in this volume, it seems that this general view—and Bruce's framework in particular—in which domain model and training examples play the same role is a good way to approach the problem of integrating explanation-based learning and similarity-based learning (although knowledge-based pattern matching and dynamically acquired explanation information do not exactly coincide with what is commonly called EBL).

If it is truly the case that the same effect can be achieved by adding more exemplars and by adding more explanation information, the question arises: Why bother adding new exemplars at all? Why not eliminate exemplars altogether and just pump in more and more explanation information? Taking this approach, one would be doing pure knowledge engineering, with no machine learning. And so the next question that arises is: Is the Protos method of interaction an effective way to elicit a domain model from an expert?

Porter:

I agree that similar effects on the classification behaviour of Protos can be achieved by adding either exemplars or explanations. For what kind of domains is it appropriate to add only explanation information and no exemplar information? This is appropriate for domains in which you have so much confidence in your inferences that it is okay to have long inference paths. Most domains are not that way. In MYCIN, for example, the average inference path from raw data to a classification was short, and this was regarded as critical to its success [Adams, 1984; Buchanan and Shortliffe, 1984]. We have to be careful about over-reliance on inference because frequently we do not have domain "axioms" in which we have much confidence.

So it is useful to keep adding new examples. But how do we get these examples? More generally, is Protos an effective way of acquiring information from experts?

In addition to focusing the expert's attention on explaining individual examples, Protos should be able to examine the topology of its knowledge base. This should allow observations like: "I do not have many exemplars of this category"; "There is a big gap between two categories"; or "These categories are so overlapping that I have trouble distinguishing among them." Observations like these might be made from examining the topology of the space during knowledge-based pattern matching. So, analysis of the topology is one form of introspection that we anticipate using. It is possible, because we are not compiling the knowledge very far.

A major concern in Protos is asking good questions of the expert. Since we've been talking about a variety of learning techniques, let me add a new one: "Rambo learning." Rambo learning characterizes independent, stand-alone learning programs. Rambo learning is fine if you can do it. But, if you can't, then you have to look at: "What good questions can I ask?" Protos generates an example, constructs an explanation of its classification, and engages the expert in discussing the explanation.

Holte:

Because of all the inferencing during knowledge-based pattern matching, it seems to me it is a distinct possibility that the space of examples will be very well covered and so every example will turn out to match every other example through some chain of inference, perhaps a very long one. Even if things are not as bad as that, of all the examples that do match, we have to decide which of these resemblances is the strongest. Doesn't this mean we are forced to resort to precisely the kind of semantics-independent lexical-evaluation function that knowledge-based pattern matching was supposed to replace?

Porter:

There is always a question of how much energy (search time) should be spent in knowledge-based pattern matching. Protos uses a few heuristics based on psychology research. First, the strength of the overall reminding influences confidence in the match. Individual featural remindings can overlap and bolster one another, a featural reminding can be strong due to high cue validity of the feature (such as a reminding of the exemplar "my-car" from the feature "leaky trunk").

Second, confidence in the match is influenced by the prototypicality of the exemplar that has been selected as the model for the match. The prototypicality of an exemplar is increased when it is generalized with other exemplars. Third, a search path is terminated when the explanation it defines becomes too weak.

But the main point is that very little search effort should be required. This gets back to our discussion of the differences between prototype and exemplar representations. Protos covers the "space" of a concept with numerous exemplars and relies relatively little on knowledge-based pattern matching to transform them.

Holte:

You have mentioned that knowledge-based pattern matching is expensive, and there could be a considerable number of exemplars even if there is not a 100,000. And so there is an efficiency problem, which you have obviously recognized. You propose to solve this problem by using a sophisticated and dynamically evolving indexing scheme.

Ideally, the classification and explanation behaviour of the system should not be affected by replacing exhaustive knowledge-based pattern matching (with no indexing) by an indexing scheme. That is, you want the indexing scheme to be as faithful as possible to the original knowledge-based matching process—in some sense it should be a compilation of the matching process. I suspect that no indexing scheme can be a very good approximation of a process that is knowledge intensive and inferential in nature.

Porter:

You are right, we want the remindings to shadow the longer inference paths used by knowledge-based pattern matching. The remindings can be thought of as compilations of the inference paths. The remindings must change dynamically as new inference paths are created, exemplars are added, and Protos succeeds and fails at problem solving. We believe that our dynamic adjustments in reminding links will keep them substantially consistent with the inference paths. When a reminding link is incorrect, knowledge-based pattern matching fails to verify the path, and the reminding link is reevaluated.

3 THE LANGUAGE FOR EXPRESSING JUSTIFICATION

Holte:

With each exemplar the expert explains the relevance of the individual features of the exemplar to its classification. Must this explanation be about individual features or is it possible to say that certain combinations of features are relevant, for example that the classification depends on features Fl and F2 both being present? Second, is there any way of indicating relative importance—of saying that feature Fl is usually unimportant but feature F2 is absolutely necessary?

Porter:

The explanation language permits the expert/teacher to say that a combination of features is relevant to the classification. It also allows him to qualify the relationship between a feature and a classification. Currently, our language includes six adverbs or modifiers.

Michalski:

It is not possible to represent in any formal system all the properties of physical objects. It is always necessary to abstract the physical object by measuring only some of its properties and ignoring many others. So your exemplars are already generalizations of a low degree. Your position is to favor a lower degree of generalization over a higher degree, and it seems to me the advantage of lower degree generalizations is that we can have great confidence in them, assuming that the examples are correct in the first place. My approach is to keep both exemplars and hypotheses (which are a higher degree of generalization). A new example can be quickly classified using the hypotheses—only a few of its properties need be checked. Your approach suggests a new twist—confidence in classifications produced by the hypotheses can be increased by checking the example against the exemplars on which the hypotheses are based.

Porter:

Are the exemplars in Protos low-generalization things? In some sense they are, it you look at their featural descriptions. But, it you keep in mind the transformational power offered by knowledge-based pattern matching, then what is a fairly specific object, like the description of this table, can be matched with a wider collection of things. We should have more confidence in a match with an exemplar than a match with a highly generalized description. But, more fundamentally, our conjecture is that highly generalized descriptions rarely work for natural categories.

Also, not all the concepts learned by Protos are represented with exemplar-based categories. In the terminology of psychologists, our exemplar-based categories are "basic-level" categories. This is the level at which discourse is conducted and the level at which Protos receives training. "Superordinate" categories are more general than basic-level categories. For example, "table" might be a basic-level category and "furniture" might be a superordinate.

Now the representation of superordinates really needs to be looked at. In general, superordinates cannot be described in the instance language. They rely on inferred features that are typically functional. So, on the one hand, I really think it is useful to keep the hypothesis-base separate from the instance-base, as you suggest. But it is important to look at the requirements of the language for the hypothesis-base and to represent the relationship between the two levels. Explanations in Protos do this for us.

Mitchell:

Could you say more about the vocabulary and semantics of the language in which the expert expresses his explanations.

Porter:

I consider the semantics of the explanation language the weakest link in the current design.

The goal of disambiguating the "right arrow" seems to be OK, and we have rule-based systems that are able to move from very low-level perceptual data to final classification using nothing more than the right arrow relationship. We should not lose anything using relations of finer granularity. I think we are on the right track, although we have not proven anything yet.

What might be the advantages of our explanation language? Even if we do not understand the semantics of the relations well, we have a better way of talking with the expert to acquire information. He gives us explanations of classified examples in his language, we give him back explanation of objects that Protos classifies, using the same terms. So it extends the vocabulary.

But that is still not really getting at the semantics. It just means that Protos has more terms to throw around. How are we going to get at the semantics in this language? One way is to put into Protos information about properties of relations such as their transitivity, symmetry, and invertibility. This information might be used to evaluate the paths generated by knowledge-based pattern matching. You can think of it as an expert system sitting on the side just evaluating paths and criticizing them, suggesting ways that they might be strengthened, suggesting holes that they might have.

One source of information is Paul Cohen's work [Cohen, 1985], which can be viewed as this expert system that sits on the side and critiques inference paths. Cohen defines a collection of heuristics and, before we map our relations in the explanation language down to 6-digit numbers, we want to first employ this body of knowledge that Cohen captured.

Mitchell:

The reason I asked was because this is a source of difficulty in our learning apprentice for geology [Smith, *et al.*, 1985]. We tried to solve these difficulties by providing the system with explicit definitions of the relations and terms in this language. But it occurred to me that if your system uses exemplar-based definitions for classes, it might be possible to provide your system with exemplar-based definitions of the relations and other terms in your explanation language.

Porter:

Yes, this is an exciting possibility, but we have not investigated it.

References

Adams, J.B. 1984. "Probabilistic Reasoning and Certainty Factors," in *Rule-based Expert Systems*, edited by B.G. Buchanan and E. Shortliffe, Addison-Wesley.

Dietterich, T.G. (ed.). 1986. *Proceedings of the Workshop on Knowledge Compilation*, Computer Science Department, Oregon State University.

Anderson, John R. 1986. "Knowledge Compilation: The General Learning Mechanism," in *Machine Learning: An Artificial Intelligence Approach*, vol. 2, edited by R.S. Michalski, J.G. Carbonell, and T.M. Mitchell, pp. 289–310, Morgan Kaufmann.

Buchanan, B.G. and Shortliffe, E. 1984. "Uncertainty and Evidential Support," in *Rule-based Expert Systems*, edited by B.G. Buchanan and E. Shortliffe, Addison-Wesley.

Cohen, P.R. 1985. *Heuristic Reasoning About Uncertanity: An Artificial Intelligence Approach*, Pitman, London and Morgan Kaufmann.

Dietterich, T.G. (ed.). 1986. *Proceedings of the Workshop on Knowledge Compilation*, Computer Science Department, Oregon State University.

Holte, R.C. 1986. "Alternative Information Structures in Incremental Learning Systems," in *Proceedings of the European Working Session on Learning*, Rapport de Recherche No. 258, Lab. de Universite de Paris-Sud, Orsay, France.

McCarty, L.T. and Sridharan, N.S. 1981. "The Representation of an Evolving System of Legal Concepts," in *Proceedings of the International Joint Conference on Artificial Intelligence*, pp. 246–253.

Rendell, L.A. 1985. "Genetic Plans and the Probabilistic Learning System: Synthesis and Results," in *Proceedings of the International Conference on Genetic Algorithms and Their Applications*, pp. 60–73, Carnegie Mellon University, July 1985.

Smith, R.G., Mitchell, T.M., Winston, H.A., and Buchanan, B. 1985. "Representation and Use of Explicit Justifications for Knowledge Base Refinement," in *Proceedings of the Ninth International Joint Conference on Artificial Intelligence*, pp. 673–680.

5

PROBABILISTIC DECISION TREES

J.R. Quinlan
(University of Sydney)

Abstract

Decision trees are a widely known formalism for expressing classification knowledge and yet their straightforward use can be criticized on several grounds. Because results are categorical, they do not convey potential uncertainties in classification. Small changes in the attribute values of a case being classified may result in sudden and inappropriate changes to the assigned class. Missing or imprecise information may apparently prevent a case from being classified at all. This chapter suggests methods of overcoming these deficiencies through extensions to the way a case is classified by a decision tree.

5.1 INTRODUCTION

The traditional approach to constructing a decision tree from a training set of cases described in terms of a collection of attributes is based on successive refinement. Tests on the attributes are constructed to partition the training set into smaller and smaller subsets until each subset contains cases belonging to a single class. These tests form the interior nodes of the decision tree and each subset is associated with one of its leaves. An unseen case is classified by tracing a path from the root of the tree to the appropriate leaf and asserting that the case belongs to the same class as the set of training cases associated with that leaf.

The use of decision trees for real-world classification problems has highlighted deficiencies in this simple cut-and-dried approach. For example,

- Inadequate discriminating power of the given attributes or noise in the training set can rule out the division of that set into single-class subsets. Even when this ideal division is possible, inconclusiveness of the training set may make it inadvisable: "Fitting the noise" may lead to overly complex decision trees and higher error rates when classifying unseen cases. As a result, the subset of the training set associated with a leaf of the decision tree may contain cases from more than one class.

- Another problem arises when we must classify a case with unknown values of one or more attributes. If a test of such an attribute is encountered in the tree, the correct branch to take from that test cannot be determined. One way around this impasse is to investigate *all* branches emanating from the test and to combine the conclusions so reached in some reasonable way. This procedure may cause the case to be assigned to more than one leaf of the decision tree.

- In real-world problems, attributes often have continuous values. A test on a continuous attribute A is usually constructed by finding some threshold T and dividing the training cases into subsets having values of A above and below T respectively. If this test is encountered when classifying a case whose value of A is very close to T, it may be inappropriate to take a knife-edge decision and follow one or the other branch. Instead, as with unknown values, both branches may be considered relevant to the classification.

In short, then, a case may give rise to several paths from the root of the decision tree to different leaves, and each leaf may be associated with a subset of the training cases containing representatives of more than one class.

This chapter summarizes one method for constructing decision trees, then presents an extension of the categorical classification scheme. Rather than assigning an unseen case to a single class, the modified scheme uses the relative probability of branches in the tree and the composition of the subsets of training cases at the leaves to arrive at a distribution over one or more of the classes. For each such class, the membership of the unseen case is characterized by three parameters: an upper, central, and lower estimate of the probability that the case belongs to that class.

5.2 GROWING DECISION TREES

In this section we outline C4, an induction procedure that descends from ID3 [Quinlan, 1979; 1983] which is based in turn on Hunt's *Concept Learning System* [Hunt, Marin, and Stone, 1966]. The same basic approach is shared by other well-known systems such as CART [Breiman, *et al.*, 1984].

We begin with the collection of attributes used to describe examples. These are of two kinds: those whose possible values form a small, discrete set, and those whose values are real numbers. The attributes collectively establish a description space, and we treat a case as being synonymous with the description of a particular example object in terms of its value for each attribute. Such a case may have unknown values for one or more attributes of either type.

Each case belongs to one of a small collection of classes. The tree-building task can be stated briefly as: Given a training set of cases, each of whose class is known, find a rule that expresses a case's class as a function of its values of the attributes. This rule should perform correctly for the cases in the training set and, in addition, should accurately classify unseen cases.

The illustration used in this chapter concerns the diagnosis of hyperthyroid conditions, one aspect of thyroid assay interpretation [Horn, *et al.*, 1985]. Figure 5–1 shows the 23 attributes used to describe a case and the five classes to which it can be assigned, together with one sample case. Some attributes such as *sex* take values from a small set while others such as TSH take any (positive) real value. A case can have an unknown value for any attribute, as exemplified by the unknown value of TBG for the case in Figure 5–1.

C4's core algorithm, denoted FORM TREE in Figure 5–2, builds a decision tree using a divide-and-conquer strategy. Let S be any collection of cases. When all members of S are of the same class, the decision tree for S is just a leaf consisting of that class. Otherwise, let R be a test based on the value of one attribute. A test is specified completely by the mutually exclusive and exhaustive set of possible outcomes $\{R_1, R_2, \ldots, R_n\}$ that it might have. For a continuous attribute A we consider only tests of the form $\{$"$A \leq T$," "$A > T$"$\}$ for some real threshold T; for an attribute A with discrete possible values $V_1, V_2, \ldots, V_m$ we consider tests of the form $\{$"$A = V_i$," i $= 1,2, \ldots, m\}$. Whatever the form of the test, each case in S can have only one of the possible outcomes, so R partitions S into subsets $\{S_1, S_2, \ldots, S_n\}$, where S_i consists of those cases that have outcome R_i. The same process is then invoked recursively to replace each subset S_i with a decision tree for that subset. The resulting structure is a decision tree for the original set S.

The procedure as described above is too simplistic for use on anything other than toy tasks. In practice, if the data contains noise, it may be futile to continue subdividing until all members of S are of the same class, so a *stopping criterion* is sometimes used [Kononenko, Bratko, and Roškar, 1984]. If some cases have missing values for the attribute on which the test is based, the partitioning of S is more complex [Quinlan, 1989]. Finally, the choice of the test R is crucial if the decision tree is to have any predictive validity. C4 uses a *selection criterion* called the *Gain Ratio criterion* [Quinlan, 1988] that calculates for each possible test R the gain in classification information (based on the residual information needed to classify a case in S and the subsets $\{S_i\}$) and the information yielded by the test (based on the relative frequencies of the possible outcomes). C4 then chooses a test that maximises the ratio subject to some further minor constraints.

The middle layer of C4, labelled GROW in Figure 5–2, applies this tree-growing procedure iteratively. Although FORM TREE could be used directly on the whole training set, a more indirect approach sometimes produces simpler trees and, when the training set is extremely large, can require less computation. First, a subset

Attribute	Possible Values	Value for this case
age	continuous	19
sex	M, F	F
on thyroxine	f, t	f
query on thyroxine	f, t	f
on antithyroid medication	f, t	f
sick	f, t	f
pregnant	f, t	t
thyroid surgery	f, t	f
I131 treatment	f, t	f
query hypothyroid	f, t	f
query hyperthyroid	f, t	f
lithium	f, t	f
goitre noted	f, t	t
tumor	f, t	f
hypopituitary	f, t	f
psych	f, t	f
TSH	continuous	0.45
T3	continuous	3.4
TT4	continuous	130
T4U	continuous	1.83
FTI	continuous	71
TBG	continuous	*unknown*
referral source	WEST, STMW, SVHC, SVI, SVHD, other	STMW
Class	hyperthyroid, T3 toxic, goitre, secondary toxic, negative	goitre

Figure 5–1: Attributes, classes, and a case

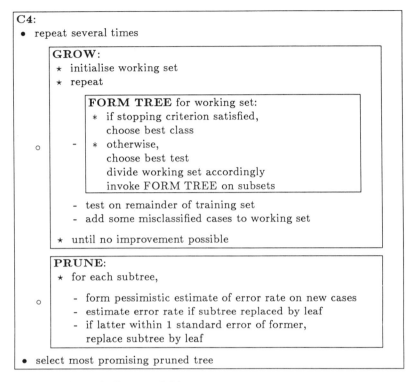

Figure 5–2:   Schematic diagram of C4

of about 10% of the training set is chosen randomly. A decision tree is constructed as above for this *working set* and used to classify the remaining cases in the training set. If they are all correctly classified, the decision tree is satisfactory and the process terminates. Otherwise, a small number of cases misclassified by the decision tree is added to the working set, the old tree discarded, a new tree constructed for the expanded working set, and so on. This iterative process incrementally assembles in the working set an interesting subset of the training set that contains key special cases along with examples of more common cases. The working set thus comes to resemble a tutorial set of examples such as might be prepared by a domain expert [Michie, 1987].

Again, shortcomings of the set of attributes as a description language and/or inconsistencies in the training set may mean that no decision tree can correctly explain all cases in the training set. Instead of continuing until the tree correctly classifies all training cases not included in the working set, the process is halted when no overall improvement has been observed over a few iterations.

Decision trees produced by any top-down approach are often more complex than can be justified by the data. This excessive complexity is typically due to noise in the attribute values and class information present in the training set; the tree-building machinery will produce subtrees that attempt to fit the noise. If complexity were the only cost this would be merely an annoyance, but unwarranted complexity causes an increased error rate when classifying unseen cases [Breiman, et al., 1984; Quinlan, 1986]. The remedy that suggests itself is to allow the tree-building machinery its head, then *prune* the resulting tree by replacing subtrees with leaves.

In contrast to approaches such as *cost-complexity pruning* [Breiman, et al., 1984], C4 prunes the decision tree using only the information in the training set. The process, called *pessimistic pruning*, is described in detail in [Quinlan, 1987] but can be sketched as follows: Suppose that some number n of cases in the training set end up at one leaf of the decision tree derived from that set, and that e of them belong to some class other than that nominated by the leaf. The ratio e/n apparently gives the error rate for this leaf, but is this a realistic estimate when unseen cases are classified by the tree? For instance, if $n = 1$ and $e = 0$, it is unreasonable to expect that *all* unseen cases classified by this leaf will belong to the nominated class—there is just not enough empirical support in the training set. Instead, a more hard-nosed estimate of the reliability of this leaf is given by

$$\frac{e + \frac{1}{2}}{n}$$

using Yates's correction [Snedecor and Cochran, 1980], or alternatively by the Laplace ratio

$$\frac{e + 1}{n + 2}$$

[Niblett and Bratko, 1986]. The pessimistic error rate of a subtree is then the average of the error rates of its leaves weighted by the relative frequency of cases from the training set they cover.

Consider a subtree X of the decision tree with predicted error rate E_X. If X were replaced by the most sensible leaf, this would generally cause the decision tree to misclassify more cases in the given training set; let the predicted error rate of this new leaf be E_L. Pessimistic pruning replaces X by the above leaf if E_L lies within one standard error of E_X. Each subtree of the given decision tree is evaluated under this criterion and the final, pruned tree contains only subtrees that cannot be replaced by leaves without significantly increasing the predicted error of the tree.

The outermost shell of C4 consists of a small number (default 10) of repetitions of the tree growing and pruning cycle. Because the initial working set is chosen at random from the training set, the same training set can give rise to different final trees. C4 constructs several decision trees, prunes them, then selects the most prom-

```
FTI ≤ 155:
  │  goitre noted = f:
  │    │  T3 ≤ 3.2: negative (1809)
  │    │  T3 > 3.2:
  │    │    │  age ≤ 53: negative (62)
  │    │    │  age > 53:
  │    │    │    │  age ≤ 66: T3 toxic (12/4)
  │    │    │    │  age > 66: negative (9)
  │  goitre noted = t:
  │    │  T3 ≤ 2.8: negative (37)
  │    │  T3 > 2.8: goitre (9/2)
FTI > 155:
  │  on thyroxine = t: negative (54)
  │  on thyroxine = f:
  │    │  TT4 ≤ 153: negative (49/2)
  │    │  TT4 > 153:
  │    │    │  age ≤ 11: negative (2)
  │    │    │  age > 11:
  │    │    │    │  query hypothyroid = t: negative (3)
  │    │    │    │  query hypothyroid = f:
  │    │    │    │    │  psych = t: negative (1)
  │    │    │    │    │  psych = f:
  │    │    │    │    │    │  TSH ≤ 0.21: hyperthyroid (55/5)
  │    │    │    │    │    │  TSH > 0.21: negative (13/2)
```

Figure 5–3:   Decision tree for hyperthyroidism

ising pruned tree based on its size and the number of cases in the training set that it misclassifies. Again, this selection process uses only information available in the training set.

The decision tree of Figure 5–3 shows the result when C4 was given a training set of 2800 hyperthyroidism cases from the archives of the Garvan Institute of Medical Research, Sydney. This training set had all the blemishes associated with real-world data; some attribute values were incorrect, many of them (20% of the values for T3, for example) were unknown, and some conditions such as secondary hypothyroidism were represented by very few cases. Despite these handicaps, the decision tree proved to be quite accurate, correctly classifying nearly 99% of unseen cases, compared with about 97% for the simple default rule *negative*.

In summary, C4 is a powerful inductive inference system for constructing decision trees from examples described in terms of a fixed set of attributes. It is capable of dealing with continuous or discrete attributes, noisy data, and missing attribute values.

5.3 IMPERFECT LEAVES

When the stopping criterion is invoked or a leaf results from pruning a subtree, that leaf will generally misclassify some cases in the training set. If each leaf is identified with the subset of training cases that it covers, some of these subsets will contain representatives from more than one class. In the decision tree of Figure 5–3, this is indicated by the annotation (n) or (n/e) following each leaf; n is the number of training cases in the subset for that leaf and e, if it appears, is the number of these cases that do not belong to the class nominated by the leaf.[1]

The accuracy of a leaf over the cases in the training set can be used to estimate the reliability of a classification arising from that leaf. Consider, for example, a case with FTI = 71, goitre noted = t, and T3 = 3.4. The decision tree will classify this case as *goitre* using the leaf annotated (9/2). Of the nine case in the training set that are identified with this leaf, seven belong to class *goitre* and two belong to some other class, so a *central estimate* of the probability that this new case is a member of class *goitre* is given by

$$\frac{n-e}{n}$$

or 0.78. For leaves with a very small value of n, as noted before, this simple ratio may not give a reliable estimate of the probability of error on unseen cases. A *lower estimate* can be obtained by applying either of the corrections discussed earlier, Yates's correction giving the ratio

$$\frac{n-e-0.5}{n}$$

or 0.72 for this leaf. In general, the composition of the training cases at a leaf L give a probability $P(C \mid L)$ that a case at L belongs to class C, and this probability can be either a central or lower estimate.

5.4 UNKNOWN AND IMPRECISE ATTRIBUTE VALUES

Real-world classifiers must be able to reach a conclusion even when some of the information needed for the classification is not available or is known only approximately.

In the previous case, suppose that the value of FTI was unknown. Since the test at the root of the decision tree is based on FTI, the outcome of this test cannot be determined, and so it would seem that the tree cannot be used to classify the case.

---

[1] The values of n do not sum to 2800 because some cases have unknown values of one or more attributes and so cannot be associated with a single leaf.

However, the test at the root of the decision tree has two outcomes, FTI ≤ 155 and FTI > 155, and the probability of each outcome can be estimated from the cases in the training set. A reasonable approach would be to determine the class of the case under the assumption that FTI ≤ 155, repeat the process under the assumption that FTI > 155, and combine the results in the light of the relative probabilities of these assumptions.

One method for doing this, described in [Quinlan, 1986], can be restated as follows: A path from the root of the tree to a leaf L passes through branches $B_1, B_2, \ldots$ say, where each branch corresponds to the outcome of a particular test. The probability that case Z will reach leaf L can be written as

$$P_Z(L) = P_Z(B_1) . P_Z(B_2 | B_1) . P_Z(B_3 | B_1 \& B_2) \ldots$$

If the outcomes of all tests are known, each of these probabilities will be either 0 or 1. If the outcome of the ith test cannot be determined, however, the corresponding probability can be estimated as the probability $P(B_i | B_1 \& B_2 \& .. \& B_{i-1})$ computed over cases in the training set; i.e., the proportion of those cases reaching the ith test that would take branch B_i. These probabilities for each test can conveniently be computed at the time the decision tree is constructed and stored with each branch.

When there are unknown attribute values and the outcomes of some tests cannot be determined, the probability $P_Z(L)$ that case Z will reach leaf L may be nonzero for more than one leaf. The probability that case Z belongs to class C is then given by

$$\sum_L P_Z(L) . P(C | L)$$

which may be taken either as a central or a lower estimate according as $P(C | L)$ is central or lower. Once this probability is computed for each class C, an upper estimate for any class is given by the complement of the sum of the lower estimates for all other classes.

As a simple example, consider a case with FTI = 71 and goitre noted = t as before, but whose value of T3 is unknown. Of the cases in the training set with FTI < 155 and goitre noted = t, 37 have T3 ≤ 2.8 and nine have T3 > 2.8. This case would be described as belonging either to class *negative* or to class *goitre* with probability

negative   [0.79, 0.80, 0.86]
goitre   [0.14, 0.15, 0.21]

where the three values are lower, central, and upper estimates respectively.

The same sort of approach can be used when there is partial information regarding an attribute value. For a discrete-valued attribute such as goitre noted, this might take the form of probabilities for one or more of its possible values, giving corresponding probabilities for outcomes of tests on this attribute. The value of a continuous attribute might be specified as a range [X,Y]. If it is reasonable to assume that the value of the attribute is uniformly distributed in this interval, the probability that the attribute has a value less than, or equal to, some threshold T can be estimated as

if $T < X$:   0
if $T > Y$:   1
otherwise: $(T - X)/(Y - X)$.

These estimated probabilities of outcomes for tests on attributes with (partially) known values can be used in place of the probabilities $P_X(B_i \mid B_1 \& \ldots)$ above.

5.5 SOFT THRESHOLDS

The decision tree of Figure 5–3 contains eight tests on continuous attributes. Each test compares the value of a continuous attribute against a threshold and invokes one or other subtree accordingly. For attribute values that lie clearly to one side or the other of the threshold, this causes no problem, but for values near the threshold, small changes might produce radically different classifications. In some areas this might be entirely appropriate—thresholds on critical mass or saturation of a queue exhibit this sort of behavior—but in many domains it would be unwarranted. In the example above, a case with FTI = 71, goitre noted = t, and T3 = 2.8 would be classified as *negative* with a high degree of certainty, but increasing the value of T3 to the next possible value in this domain (2.9) would cause the case to be classified as *goitre* with fair certainty.

The same kind of weighting presented in the previous sections can be used to "soften" absolute thresholds. A simple scheme proposed by Carter [1986] defines subsidiary cutpoints T^- and T^+ below and above each threshold T. If a test on continuous attribute A is encountered while classifying a case whose value of A is V, the outcome "$A \leq T$" is assigned probability $P(V \leq T)$ shown by the graph in Figure 5–4 while the outcome "$A > T$" receives the complementary probability. These probabilities of the respective outcomes are then used in the same manner as previously to give probability distributions at leaves.

This begs the question of how T^- and T^+ are to be determined. Carter has investigated a number of schemes which are apparently applicable only when there are exactly two classes. These attempt to find T^- and T^+ so that the probability of the outcome "$A < T$" defined above most closely approximates the probability that a training case is in one of the classes.

A more direct approach can be defined as follows: If the threshold T were to be changed to a new value T', the decision tree would classify some cases of the training set differently. The number of training cases misclassified by the tree can be determined for values of T' in the neighborhood of T. If the training set contains n cases associated with the node at which this test appears, and if e of them are mis-

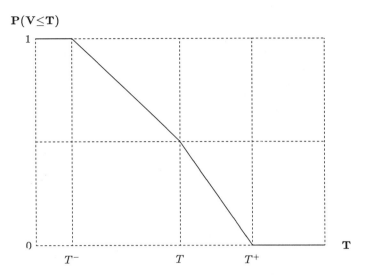

Figure 5–4:   Graph of $P(V \leq T)$ against T

classified when the threshold has its original value, the standard deviation of the number of errors can be estimated as

$$\sqrt{\frac{(e + 0.5)(n - e - 0.5)}{n}}$$

T^- and T^+ are then chosen so that, if the threshold were set to either of them, the number of misclassified training cases associated with this test would be one standard deviation above e.

The method is illustrated with reference to the threshold "FTI $\leq$ 170" at the root of the decision tree of Figure 5–3. In Figure 5–5, the number of training cases misclassified is plotted against possible values of the threshold between 100 and 300. The figure also indicates the central value T (170) and the ancillary values T^- (154) and T^+ (174) whose corresponding error rates are one standard deviation above the minimum.

This approach allows for either sharp or vague threshold effects. In the former situation, errors increase rapidly as T is changed so T^- and T^+ are close to T. In the latter situation, cases with values near the threshold might be expected to be classified equally well by the subtree associated with either outcome, so errors increase relatively slowly and the interval $[T^-, T^+]$ is broad.

The decision tree of Figure 5–3 contains thresholds of various types. For example, the test "T3 $\leq$ 3.2" has a small interval [3.1,3.3], "age $\leq$ 11" is relatively fuzzy as indicated by the interval [0,22], and "TSH $\leq$ 0.21" has the skewed interval [0.2, 1.2].

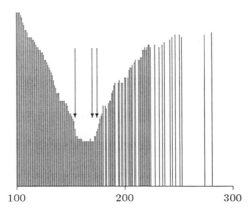

Figure 5–5: Misclassification rates versus threshold for FTI

Using this interpretation scheme, a case with FTI = 71 and goitre noted = t now changes from marginally *negative* when T3 = 2.8 to marginally *goitre* when T3 = 2.9.

5.6 CONCLUSION

This chapter has discussed some small extensions to the standard method of classifying cases with a decision tree. These extensions depend on the once-off calculation and retention of additional statistics derivable from the training set from which the decision tree was produced. The modified classification procedure can provide valuable information on the probability that a case belongs to one or more of the classes, and is less brittle with respect to unknown or imprecise attribute values and inexact thresholds.

ACKNOWLEDGMENTS

This chapter is based on a paper given at the Fourth International Machine Learning Workshop held at the University of California, Irvine in June 1987. Some work described in this paper was carried out at the Artificial Intelligence Laboratory of the Massachusetts Institute of Technology. Support for the Laboratory's artificial intelligence research is provided in part by the Advanced Research Projects Agency of the Department of Defense under Office of Naval Research contract N00014-85-K-0124. This research was also supported by grants from the Westinghouse Corporation and the Australian Research Grants Scheme.

References

Breiman, L., Friedman, J.H., Olshen, R.A., and Stone, C.J. 1984. *Classification and Regression Trees*, Belmont: Wadsworth.

Carter, C. 1986. Machine learning experiments in credit assessment, unpublished Honors thesis, Basser Department of Computer Science, University of Sydney.

Horn, K.A., Compton, P., Lazarus, L., and Quinlan, J.R. 1985. An expert system for the interpretation of thyroid assays in a clinical laboratory, *Australian Computer Journal* 17, 1, 7–11.

Hunt, E.B., Marin, J., and Stone, P.J. 1966. *Experiments in Induction,* New York: Academic Press.

Kononenko, I., Bratko, I., and Roškar, E. 1984. Experiments in automatic learning of medical diagnostic rules, technical report, Jozef Stefan Institute, Ljubljana, Yugoslavia.

Michie, D. 1987. Current developments in expert systems, in *Applications of Expert Systems,* (J.R. Quinlan, Ed.), Maidenhead: Addison-Wesley.

Niblett, T. and Bratko, I. 1986. Learning decision rules in noisy domains, technical report, Turing Institute, Glasgow.

Quinlan, J.R. 1979. Discovering rules by induction from large collections of examples, in *Expert Systems in the Micro Electronic Age,* (D. Michie, Ed.), Edinburgh University Press.

———— , 1983. Learning efficient classification procedures and their application to chess endgames, in *Machine Learning: An Artificial Intelligence Approach,* (R.S. Michalski, J.G. Carbonell and T.M. Mitchell, Eds.), San Mateo, CA: Morgan Kaufmann.

———— , 1986. Induction of decision trees, *Machine Learning* 1, 1, 81–106.

———— , 1987. Simplifying decision trees, *International Journal of Man-Machine Studies* 27, 4, 221–234.

———— , 1988. Decision trees and multivalued attributes, in *Machine Intelligence* 11, (J.E. Hayes, D. Michie and J. Richards, Eds.), Oxford University Press.

———— , 1989. Unknown attribute values in induction, in *Proceedings 6th International Machine Learning Workshop*, (A.M. Segre, ed.), San Mateo, CA: Morgan Kaufmann.

Snedecor, G.W. and Cochran, W.G. 1980. *Statistical Methods* (seventh edition), Iowa State University Press.

6

INTEGRATING QUANTITATIVE AND QUALITATIVE DISCOVERY IN THE ABACUS SYSTEM

Brian C. Falkenhainer
(Xerox Palo Alto Research Center)

Ryszard S. Michalski
(George Mason University)

Abstract

Most research on inductive learning has been concerned with qualitative learning that creates conceptual, logic-style descriptions from the given facts. In contrast, quantitative learning deals with discovering numerical laws characterizing empirical data. This research attempts to integrate both types of learning by combining newly developed heuristics for formulating equations with the previously developed concept learning method embodied in the inductive learning program AQ11. The resulting system, ABACUS, formulates equations characterizing observed data, and derives explicit, logic-style descriptions stating the applicability conditions for these equations. Several new techniques for quantitative learning are introduced. *Units analysis* reduces the search space of equations by examining the compatibility of variables' units. *Proportionality graph search* addresses the problem of identifying relevant variables that should enter equations. *Suspension search* focuses the search space through heuristic evaluation. The capabilities of ABACUS are demonstrated by several examples from physics and chemistry.

6.1 INTRODUCTION

Research on inductive learning investigates the principles that govern the process of constructing knowledge from observed data. Significant progress has been achieved in developing methods for inducing symbolic, logic-style descriptions that characterize classes of examples or observations. Reviews of some such methods can be found in Dietterich and Michalski [1981] and Mitchell [1982]. However, with the rapid expansion of expert systems applications, it is becoming clear that there is a need for utilizing in them not only qualitative knowledge, as has been the main thrust so far, but also quantitative, numerical knowledge [Kowalik, 1986]. This suggests that research in machine learning should develop methods for quantitative discovery, capable of automatically constructing numerical descriptions of the given phenomena. Such numerical knowledge would be a part of a deep model of the knowledge of an expert system.

There are also other reasons for research on quantitative discovery. For example, in many fields of science (especially in the life sciences), researchers gather empirical data as a prerequisite for building models and developing principles that explain the phenomena under study. Their tool box for analyzing the data has traditionally contained various statistical techniques, including regression analysis, numerical taxonomy, dimensional analysis, and the like. These methods manipulate numbers, equations, and similar structures without explicitly involving symbolic knowledge that represents domain constraints, control heuristics, underlying assumptions, etc. Symbolic knowledge, if it ever enters the process, must be supplied by a data analyst. A given statistical procedure can only cope with specially prepared and interpreted numbers. Therefore, it seems very desirable to develop AI methods for data analysis, which can reduce the amount of expert analysis currently required.

Some pioneering work in this direction has been done by Langley, Bradshaw, and Simon [1983a] with their BACON systems. Even earlier work has been done by Hajek [1978] on the GUHA method of data analysis and by Zagoruiko and Lbov [1976, 1985] on the SPAR [1968] and PINCH [1978] systems. The SPAR system predicts a value of a variable, and the PINCH system selects the most informative attributes from the set of initial attributes.

This chapter provides a comprehensive review of the issues in quantitative empirical learning and presents a methodology of such learning implemented in the program ABACUS. The ABACUS system is novel in two important ways. First, it is able to discover multiple mathematical equations for numeric data and derives explicit, logic-style descriptions stating preconditions for the application of the equations. Previous programs have typically worked under the assumption that a single equation will completely describe an observed set of events. Second, ABACUS was developed with a motivation to improve methods for exploring the space of possible equations. As a result, several new search techniques particularly suited to quantitative learning were developed. *Units analysis* enables the system to greatly reduce the size of the search space by examining the compatibility of variables' units. Two new search algorithms, *proportionality graph search* and *suspension search* address some of the unique search problems associated with quantitative learning. Section 6.2 outlines the issues that arise in quantitative discovery. Section 6.3 discusses related work in the field, and Section 6.4 introduces the new approach taken in the ABACUS system. Sections 6.5 and 6.6 discuss the way in which ABACUS discovers equations and formulates preconditions for these equations. Several examples illustrating the performance of ABACUS are presented in Section 6.7. Finally, Section 6.8 summarizes the ABACUS methodology and suggests directions for future research.

6.2 GOALS FOR QUANTITATIVE DISCOVERY

At the heart of quantitative discovery is the desire to induce mathematical descriptions that characterize the behavior of numerical observations. Independent of the technique used, there are a number of issues that any work in this area must address. Established disciplines, such as regression analysis, require the data analyst to resolve many of these issues. AI techniques attempt to automate this phase of the analysis. We therefore outline the following criteria for evaluating research on quantitative discovery.

1. *Coping with irrelevant variables.* In many discovery tasks, it is difficult to know which available variables are relevant to describing the observed events and which are not. A discovery program should be able to decide for itself what is relevant.

2. *Coping with incorrect and irrelevant observations.* In empirical data, it is often the case that some of the data is not representative of the process being observed. There are two common situations that give rise to this. First, some observations may simply be erroneous. Second, the process may not be defined outside a given range of values, such as the pressure being too high or the substance being in the wrong state.

3. *Discovering multiple equations characterizing a collection of data and stating the conditions under which the equations apply.* It may often be the case that more than one equation is required to adequately describe a given set of observations. In these situations, the observations should be clustered around the various equations to form subsets of the original events. Conditions should be placed on each equation to describe when it is applicable.

4. *Handling different types of variables.* Often, the observable variables in a given situation are both numeric and symbolic. When a discipline is young, for example, it may not be known that a given symbolic value has a one-to-one correspondence with an as-yet-undiscovered physical constant. A quantitative discovery system should take into account the symbolic information available.

5. *Imprecision and errors in the data.* The inaccuracy of experimental observations has always been a problem in science, and the discovery system should not be crippled because of it.

6. *Integrating with other learning systems.* While quantitative knowledge is quite valuable, it is only a part of the total knowledge available. Other types of knowledge might include knowledge of qualitative dependencies among variables, including causal dependencies. A quantitative discovery system should be able to interact with discovery programs for acquiring different types of knowledge.

7. *Robustness and efficiency.* Discovery is inherently prone to combinatorial explosion. This, combined with the difficulties introduced by the criteria defined above, make efficiency considerations particularly important for quantitative discovery. We want to be able to discover complicated equations and yet accomplish this in a reasonable amount of time.

6.3 RELATED WORK

Numerical data analysis and equation formation has traditionally used such standard techniques as regression analysis, numerical taxonomy, and dimensional analysis (e.g., [Chatterjee and Price, 1977; Daniel and Wood, 1971; Huntley, 1952; Langhaar, 1951]). These methods are very useful when the domain is well understood and when the observations correspond closely to the process being analyzed. For many situations, however, these methods are either difficult to use, requiring a great deal of human analysis, or they are simply inadequate. First, we are interested in discovering multiple equations in data when no single equation exists. Stepwise regression analysis is based on the implicit assumption that there is one best equation [Daniel and Wood, 1971]. It will attempt to fit a single equation to the set of observed data, no matter how complicated the resulting equation. This leads to our second concern, comprehensibility. It is important that the results of a learning program be easy to understand. This is especially important in situations where a set of data may be described by two or more succinct equations or approximated by one complicated one. Third, regression analysis assumes that the data are a representative sample of the process being observed. Techniques are described in the standard texts to remove, by hand, nontypical data points, called *outliners* [Daniel and Wood, 1971; Chatterjee and Price, 1977]. We are interested in the automatic removal of these data points. Fourth, we are interested in minimizing the amount of analysis required by the user. For the standard techniques, numbers and equations must be specially prepared and interpreted by the data analyst. Finally, we are interested in the smooth integration of quantitative and qualitative knowledge. Regression analysis uses *indicator variables*, which take on values of 0 or 1 to represent different qualitative categories. We would like to see qualitative variables explicitly included in the discovery program's hypotheses.

The equation formation part of our research is related to the BACON project at CMU [Langley, 1979, 1981; Langley, *et al.*, 1981; 1983; 1986; 1987], the COPER system [Kokar, 1981; 1986], the Hotep system [EI-Shafei, 1986], and the FAHRENHEIT system [Zytkow, 1987]. The precondition formation part is based on the methods of inductive learning developed by Michalski and his collaborators (e.g., [Michalski and Larson, 1978; Michalski, 1983]).

The BACON project began in 1978 with the construction of BACON.1; the most recent system is BACON.6. The basic approach taken in the early versions was to formulate empirical laws through the repeated application of hypothesis generation rules. Thus the ideal gas law ($PV/NT = 8.32$) would be formed in a layered fashion by creating the term PV, using this and the directly observed attribute T to form a more general term PV/T, and finally using this to formulate PV/NT, which summarizes all of the given data. A variety of additions were subsequently made to this basic methodology. BACON.4 was able to postulate intrinsic properties for symbolic entities and could detect when common divisors existed for a variable's values. BACON.5 included a simple method for learning by symmetry. BACON.6 [Langley, *et al.*, 1983b; 1986] deviated from the methodology of the previous systems. The major difference was that forms of the law must be provided by the user, allowing the system to formulate more complex laws including trigonometric and algebraic functions.

While BACON compares well with the above criteria for quantitative discovery, several weaknesses can be pointed out. One limitation is that it cannot derive multiple equations to describe different subsets of the data. The issues of data clustering and the formulation of preconditions are not addressed. The data is assumed to be correct and relevant to a single process and the user must state which variables are dependent and which are independent. The equation formation techniques used in BACON.6 appear to be quite powerful, enabling the system to derive rather complicated laws in a straightforward manner. However, much of this power is achieved by requiring the user to provide a form of the answer.

A different approach to quantitative discovery is taken by Kokar [1981; 1986] and EI-Shafei [1986]. Central to this approach is the application of dimensional analysis [Langhaar, 1951; Huntley, 1952]. Considering units of measurements, this analysis creates the set of all possible dimensionless products of variables provided in the data. These products are then used to form equations explaining the data. Traditional dimensional analysis requires that the relevant variables are known prior to application of the procedure, thus requiring extensive domain knowledge. Kokar solves the irrelevant variables problem by first trying to determine the completeness of the set of variables characterizing the given physical process. This step precedes the equation formation step and is able to discard irrelevant variables as well as detect when a needed relevant variable is missing. EI-Shafei effectively ignores the need for determining variable relevancy prior to dimensional analysis by using regression analysis to form the desired equation from the set of dimensionless terms. He assumes that terms involving irrelevant variables will automatically dropout during the regression analysis. This may be an oversimplification of the problem since great care is given to variable selection using classical regression analysis techniques [Daniel and Wood, 1971; Chatterjee and Price, 1977].

These systems are quite robust in that they will find an equation to fit the data, no matter how complex that equation may be. Therein lies one of the problems with these techniques. Because only a single equation is fit to the data, these systems cannot detect cases where the data could be better described piecewise by two or more equations. In addition, these systems fail to take into account the symbolic information available as well as having problems with situations requiring dimensional constants. In the following sections, we describe an approach to quantitative discovery that contains aspects of BACON, dimensional analysis, and symbolic approaches to inductive learning.

6.4 THE ABACUS APPROACH TO QUANTITATIVE DISCOVERY

There are many strategies for deriving an equation or set of equations summarizing the behavior of some physical process. In choosing a particular strategy, one must weigh the gains from the use of that strategy against the losses. The approach taken in ABACUS has been to satisfy as many criteria from our list for quantitative discovery as possible, and to reduce the user-supplied information to a minimum. ABACUS can handle irrelevant variables, symbolic variables of different types, and a certain degree of noise. Its great advantage is that it is able to discover multiple equations and ignore irrelevant observations. The only information required from the user besides the actual observations is a list of the attributes, their type (numeric or symbolic), and optionally their units (e.g., meters/second). The program is never told which variables to treat as dependent and which to treat as independent. In achieving these abilities, some sacrifices have had to be made in robustness and efficiency. The experimental results described in Section 6.7 indicate that the system is both general and powerful.

The ABACUS method of quantitative discovery consists of two steps. First, the *equation discovery module* analyzes the original empirical data and attempts to derive equations summarizing the observed behavior. If more than one equation is required to describe the observations, the data are divided into disjoint subsets, and equations are determined for each subset. The second step passes the resulting subsets to the *precondition generation module*. This module derives a logic-style description for each subset. Such a description is used as a precondition for each equation. The result is a series of if-then rules in which the "if part" states the precondition for applying the rule specified in the "then part."

The equation learning module searches for the best equation to describe the given empirical data.[1] If the discovered equation holds for all events, the learning task is completed, and no preconditions need to be generated. However, if the equation describes only a subset of the events then the subset described is removed from the list of events and associated with the equation describing it. Sometimes several classes of events can be described by one expression that evaluates to different values. When this occurs, a number of classes are formed, one for each value of the expression. Remaining events are passed to the equation learning procedure again in order to determine a separate equation for them. This iterative process repeats until all events are accounted for. When no equation can be determined for some events, they are placed in a "miscellaneous" class.

Once the data have been divided into classes, the precondition generation algorithm is used to create discriminant descriptions for these classes. The resulting logical expressions can be used to predict which equation should apply to a newly observed event. The following example is used to illustrate the general algorithm used in ABACUS.

Suppose the system is given the data depicted in Figure 6–1(a). Observed values for x and y, are read in and the equation discovery module is invoked. As there are only two variables, the space of possible equations is small. The best equation found, which describes 70% of the data, is $x^2 = y$ (a discussion of the equation formation technique is in Section 6.5). Events covered by the equation are put in a class associated with this equation. The equation discovery module is invoked again to analyze the remaining events. This time, $x + y = 30$ is found to hold for all events, and a class set is created for these events. Because all observations are accounted for, the equation discovery step is completed, and the precondition module is called. This module searches for properties of the data that distinguish between the two classes. The results are presented in Figure 6–1(b). They state that when x is below 5, the equation is $y = x^2$, and when x is between 5 and 30, the equation $x + y = 30$ holds.

6.5 DISCOVERING EQUATIONS

The technique used in ABACUS depicts quantitative discovery as a search through the space of equations that could possibly describe the behavior of the observed data. This search process mathematically combines variables representing terms to form new terms. For example, x and y might be combined to form $x + y$. Search in this domain is different than in many other domains because new nodes are

---

[1] There are many ways to determine the best equation. Here we refer to the equation describing the largest subset of the data (i.e., the most general). It is also important to consider syntactic and domain-dependent criteria, such as the equation's simplicity or its relation to known physical phenomena, but the current work has not yet addressed these methods.

(a)

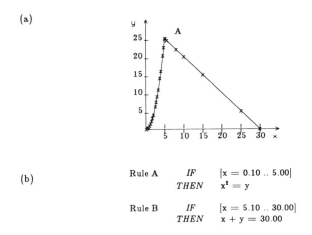

(b)

Rule A   *IF*   [x = 0.10 .. 5.00]
            THEN x^2 = y

Rule B   *IF*   [x = 5.10 .. 30.00]
            THEN   x + y = 30.00

Figure 6–1:   ABACUS analysis of graph example

formed by the combination of existing nodes rather than by node expansion. In addition, we have not been able to derive a good heuristic evaluation function which can accurately indicate the possibility that a given node lies on a promising path. Before describing the search algorithms used in ABACUS, we first discuss how nodes in the search tree are formed, how search through a potentially exponential search space is constrained, and how the goal node is recognized once it is found.

6.5.1 Variable Dependencies and Proportionality Graphs

At the heart of quantitative discovery is the concept that one variable's values may be dependent in some way upon the values of another variable. The early BACON systems look for monotonic relationships in the data to create new hypotheses [Langley, 1981a; 1983a]. Michalski [1983] defines the M-descriptor stating that if two variables exhibit a monotonic relationship, one should investigate the properties of their product. In the strict sense, variable x monotonically increases with y if the values of x always rise when the values of y rise while holding all other variables constant. There are two problems with such a strict definition. First, for a given set of data, it is not always possible to observe changing values for x and y while holding all other variables constant. Second, we must allow for inaccuracies and errors in experimental data. As a result, we are interested in the degree with which x is proportional to y rather than detecting if x exhibits a monotonic relationship to y for all of the data. With this in mind, we say that x is *qualitatively proportional* to y if, for a given percentage of the events (user specifiable), the values of x rise when the values of y rise while certain specified variables are held constant. Similarly, x and y are *inversely qualitatively proportional* if x decreases as y rises for a majority of the events under the same conditions.[2] There are then four assertions possible as the result of a qualitative proportionality measurement:

$Prop^+$ (x,y) x and y are qualitatively proportional to a user-specifiable degree

$Prop^-$ (x,y) x and y are inversely qualitatively proportional to a user-specifiable degree

$Prop^?$ (x,y) insufficient data to determine if x and y are related

Norel (x,y) x and y are not related

To make a qualitative proportionality assertion about variables x and y, ABACUS looks for general trends in the data. Since it is not always possible to hold all other variables constant, an *exclusion set* is defined to be the set of attributes that does not need to be held constant and is constructed by the program and the user. On rare occasions, the user must recognize which variables simply cannot or should not be held constant. Similarly, when measuring the proportionality between variables x and y, the program recognizes that if x is a program-generated variable composed of user-defined variables v and w, then v and w should be removed from the set of variables that must be held constant. Since they are necessarily dependent upon x, it would be impossible to hold v and w constant while changing x. The trend detection algorithm determines whether y rises or decreases as x rises when all user-defined variables not in the exclusion set are held constant. It never tries to hold program-generated variables constant. If no groups can be found where all of these variables remain constant, then $Prop^?$ must be asserted. For each of the groups found, a measurement is made of the monotonic relationship between x and y from which an average is obtained and used as the degree of proportionality between x and y. This measure is then used to assert $Prop^+$, $Prop^-$, or Norel. The proportionality criterion has a margin of tolerance, allowing a moderate degree of noise and a limited amount of *conflicting proportionalities*. Conflicting proportionalities occur when some of the data indicates $Prop^+$ (x,y) and some indicates $Prop^-$ (x,y). In Figure 6–1(a), there were 16 points given for the curve ($Prop^+$ (x,y)) and seven given for the line ($Prop^-$ (x,y)) causing the program to initially assert $Prop^+$ (x,y). We are developing an algorithm to handle the conflicting proportionalities problem in a more general manner, based on determining *breakpoints* in the monotonic relationship between variables. For the data in Figure 6–1(a), it would first determine the breakpoint A, and then process points to the left and right of A independently.

From these proportionality assertions we may construct an undirected graph, called a proportionality group, where the nodes represent variables, and edges indi-

---

[2]Notice that no dependency ordering is implied here and thus no causual relation in the strict sense. Forbus [1984] defines the qualitative proportionality, Prop(x, y) to read "y *causes* the value of x to change." His more restricted interpretation is not required for our use.

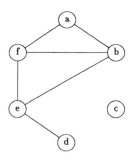

Figure 6–2:   Proportionality graph

cate the presence of a qualitative proportionality relation between their incident vertices (Figure 6–2). For our purposes, edges shall only be constructed for `Prop`$^+$ and `Prop`$^-$ relationships, and `Prop`$^?$ will effectively be treated as `Norel`. In Figure 6–2, a is proportional (+ or –) to b but not proportional to c. Notice that proportionality is not necessarily transitive, as one might expect. For example, d is proportional to e, but not proportional to f or b. As described, proportionality assertions are based on a rather loose, average degree of proportionality. Thus some edges may be incorrectly missing from the graph (e.g., between a and e) or incorrectly present (e.g., between d and e) due to noise or conflicting proportionalities.

As explained in Section 6.5.5, we are interested in nodes that form cycles in such a graph. In this context, the term cycle refers to any biconnected components [Aho, 1974] that may exist. A biconnected component refers only to the maximal cycles in the graph, or in other words, only those cycles that are not a subset of some other cycle. In Figure 6–2, the single maximal cycle (or biconnected component) consists of the set of nodes {a b e f}.

6.5.2 Equation Formation—A Search for Constancy

The existence of qualitative proportionalities between variables suggests the possibility of causal or other relationships between them. For example, if we knew that the value of x always goes down when the value of y goes up, then the relation xy = `constant` might be binding these variables. This may be generalized to a rule:

If `Prop`$^-$`(x,y)` then create a variable equal to xy

Such a variable is more likely to take on a constant value than x or y independently. Expanding on this concept, the following heuristics are formulated:

If `Prop`$^+$`(x,y)` then
Generate a variable equal to a quotient relation between x and y   (5.1)
Generate variables equal to difference relations between x and y

If $Prop^-(x, y)$ then

Generate a variable equal to a product relation between x and y (5.2)

Generate variables equal to sum relations between x and y

With these heuristics in mind, search in quantitative discovery involves the continual combination of qualitatively proportional variables to form new variables in the hope of finding one that takes on a constant value. Notice that application of the above heuristics tends to create variables with the same or higher degrees of constancy than the original variables.

The variables created from product and quotient relations are what one would expect. A variety of sum and difference relations may be formed, however, including $x + y$, $x^2 = y^2$, and $x^n + y^m$. Those actually generated will depend upon the units involved as well as other domain-independent constraints discussed below. Using these rules, the system can generate many new variables when qualitative relationships are detected among the current variables. In addition, ABACUS provides a facility for the user to predefine arbitrary functions or transformations on input variables that operate before the equation discovery module is called. For example, the user may instruct the program to replace all values of x with $\log(x)$ or to create a new input variable whose values are determined from a supplied function of existing variables.

6.5.3 Domain-Independent Constraints

Several domain-independent constraints are used to limit the large search space associated with quantitative learning. These constraints involve eliminating mathematically redundant expressions and physically impossible relationships. The constraints are divided into three categories:

- Units compatibility rule
- Redundancy detection
- Tautology detection

Below we discuss each of these in turn.

6.5.3.1 Units Compatibility Rule

When the system decides to create new variables by firing the rules presented in the previous section, the additive relation rules will attempt to create a variety of new variables. Were all of these variables created every time one of the rules fired, the number of variables would explode, and the search space would become unmanageably large. However, a simple physical constraint drastically limits the possible choices. For two entities to be added or subtracted they must be of the same type; that is, they should have the same physical units. One may divide meters by seconds, but one may not subtract seconds from meters. Therefore, any action that violates this *units compatibility* rule is blocked. This is similar in intent to the dimensional cohesiveness requirement of dimensional analysis [Langhaar, 1951; Huntley, 1952]. All equations generated by ABACUS are guaranteed to be dimensionally cohesive if units are specified for each variable.

When attempting to generate sum relations between two variables x and y, if the units of x and y are equal, then terms such as $x + y$ and $x^2 + y^2$ will be created. If, on the other hand, the units of x and y are not the same, but differ only in exponent such that the units of x^n is compatible with the units of y^m, then the term $x^n + y^n$ (where $n \neq m$), would be created and terms like $x + y$ would be blocked.[3] Finally, if the units are not equal and cannot be made compatible by exponentiation, then no sum relations will be created, effectively blocking all instantiations of the sum generation rule. In practice, this is the usual case. It should be pointed out that these constraints only test the identity of units and provide no semantic interpretation to guide the search. In the future we would also like to use constraints stemming from the physical properties of entities involved, such as trying to add the velocity of two unrelated entities.

6.5.3.2 Formula Redundancy

A common side effect of combining existing variables to form new ones is the possibility that for any new variable, a mathematically equivalent yet syntactically different expression defining a variable may have already been created. This is especially likely since variables created at one level in the search may be combined with existing variables from any other level. For example, say variable x represents the relation:

$$x = \frac{(ab)}{(cd)}$$

where the parentheses show that x was created by dividing a variable ab by another cd. Further, suppose during the course of the search the variable $b/(cd)$ had been created. At some point, the system will then try to create a new variable y:

$$y = a \left(\frac{b}{(cd)} \right)$$

As we can see, x and y represent the same variable, so creating y is redundant. From a purely syntactic examination, however, x and y are not equal. The solution to this problem is to use a canonical form for expressions so that equivalent formulas will always be syntactically equal. The form we use expresses all equations as a sum-of-products [Falkenhainer, 1985b]. Thus

---

[3] A further constraint requires that the exponents n and m be less than 4. This is a heuristic limitation, but seems reasonable given that higher powers are rare in the natural sciences.

$$\frac{x}{y}(a - b)$$

would be expressed as

$$\frac{ax}{y} - \frac{bx}{y}.$$

A canonical sum-of-products representation has also been used in the BACON systems to detect redundancy [Langley, 1981].

6.5.3.3 Numerical Tautologies

Another problem with combining mathematical formulas is the possibility that a mathematical cancellation may result, causing the program to effectively take a step backwards. Suppose, for example, the program discovers `Prop⁻ (a/b, bc)`. Creating a new variable

$$\frac{a}{b}bc$$

would result in `b` canceling out. Were such operations allowed to go unchecked, the system may soon discover that

$$\frac{abc}{abc}$$

always equals 1 for any data given.

ABACUS allows no action that would result in a mathematical cancellation. Using the canonical form for formulas mentioned in the previous section, a check for tautologies is reducible to a set of simple logical conditions. If the tautology condition for a given operation holds, the proposed action is blocked.

6.5.4 Recognizing the Goal

Because a valid equation may describe only a subset of the events, recognizing when a good equation has been found and when to terminate search is not as easy as it would be otherwise. There are three types of goal nodes recognized by the system. The first type corresponds to a term that describes all events; i.e., one that evaluates to the same value for every event (within a percentage range of uncertainty modifiable by the user). Such a goal is easily recognized and search terminates when one is discovered.

The second type of goal node is based on the notion of a nominal (symbolic) subgroup of events and also causes immediate cessation of the search process. A *nominal subgroup* is defined to be a set of events that are equal on all nominal attributes. If a term is found that evaluates to a single value for a nominal subgroup, search terminates on the assumption that an equation of significance has been found.

Table 6–1:   Sample goal node recognition

(a)

object	x	y	x/y
circle	2	2	1
circle	4 .	3	1.3
circle	6	4	1.5
box	2	1	2
box	4	2	2
box	5	2.5	2
box	6	3	2
triangle	3	2	1.5
triangle	5	3	1.6

100% Constancy in a Nominal Subgroup

(b)

object	x	y	x/y
circle	2	2	1
circle	4	2	2
circle	6	3	2
box	2	2	1
box	4	2	2
box	5	2.5	2
box	6	3	2
triangle	3	2	1.5
triangle	5	2.5	2

67% Constancy for Entire Event Space

For example, in Table 6–1(a), x/y has the same value for all events in the nominal subgroup corresponding to the object "box."

The third type of goal node does not halt the search algorithm. As each new variable is created, its *degree of constancy* is measured, and the variable having the largest degree of constancy is stored. The degree of constancy is defined to be the percentage of the data for which the function evaluates to a single value within a percentage range of uncertainty modifiable by the user. In Table 6–1(b), x/y has a 67% constancy because six out of the nine events are equal to 2. If two variables have the same constancy value, only the first discovered is remembered, since it is more likely to be of a simpler, and thus more desirable form. A more thorough approach would examine the equations according to various syntactic criteria and keep those that are both general and appealing. If search exceeds the allowed limit, the term having the highest degree of constancy is returned. If its constancy is greater than a user-modifiable threshold, the resulting equation is reported. Otherwise, the program states that no formula could be found.

6.5.5 Search

ABACUS discovers equations by searching through the space of possible terms that relate the user-supplied variables. These terms are formed by applying the variable generation rules to the current set of proportionality assertions. Even with domain-independent constraints, a search space generated in this manner can become quite large. In an effort to counter this problem, ABACUS uses a combination of two search algorithms that have been designed with quantitative learning in mind. The first algorithm, *proportionality graph search,* uses the graphical nature of the proportionality assertions to guide the search path and discriminate against irrelevant variables. The second algorithm, *suspension search,* enables the program to reduce the number of terms being examined by deferring those that do not look promising until all other possibilities have been exhausted.

In this section we will examine only the search process itself, ignoring operations done once a final term has been selected. For illustration, two examples will be used. The first example deals with discovering the ideal gas law:

$$\frac{PV}{nT} = 8.32$$

where P is the pressure of the gas, V is the volume, T is the temperature in degrees Kelvin, and n is the number of moles. The ideal gas law equation belongs to the class of relations consisting solely of multiplication and division, and whose variables are all of degree 1. It is a law that has been discovered in a variety of ways by the BACON programs [Langley, 1981; 1986].

The other example is the non-vector form of the conservation of momentum law:

$$m_1 v_1 + m_2 v_2 = m_1' v_1' + m_2' v_2'$$

This relation represents those equations that include addition and subtraction. It states that when two particles collide while traveling along the same line, their total momentum is the same before and after the collision. To complicate the example, the masses m_1' and m_2' will be allowed to change after impact producing m_1' and m_2'. When the masses do not change, reducing the number of variables to 6, ABACUS discovers the equation in much less time.

6.5.5.1 Proportionality Graph Search

Experience has shown that in terms of difficulty, the types of equations ABACUS is able to discover may be divided into two categories. Equations composed solely of multiplication and division tend to be easiest to discover, while those including other operators, such as addition and subtraction, tend to be more difficult [Falkenhainer, 1984; 1985b]. Proportionality graph search is designed to handle equations falling in the first category. They correspond to a large percentage of the physical laws round in elementary physics and chemistry texts. Proportionality graph search is based on the observation that these equations will form a cycle in the corresponding proportionality graph, barring the presence of an exorbitant number of `Prop`$^?$ assertions. As an example, equation (5.3) below represents a general equation of this type.

$$\frac{uvw^2}{xyz} = \text{Constant} \tag{5.3}$$

Holding the four variables u, v, w, and x in (5.3) constant and varying y will necessarily cause z to vary as well, in a direction that is completely predictable given the direction of change of y. This is true for equation (5.3) no matter which four variables are held constant and which two are allowed to vary. In the absence of `Prop`$^?$ assertions, each variable is therefore qualitatively proportional (+ or –) to the other five. For the given problem, which may have more observables than the six appearing in (5.3), the subgraph for vertices (u, v, w, x, y, z) must therefore be strongly connected, and these nodes will thus form a cycle. This introduces another observation about the proportionality graph for such an equation. Irrelevant variables are more likely to be excluded from the above cycle and may often be incident on only one edge.

The proportionality graph search technique directs its search to the interrelations of variables forming a cycle and avoids variables that are not contained in a cycle. The algorithm consists of the repeated application of the following steps:

1. Form a proportionality graph for the current set of variables, both those provided by the user and those generated by the program. Exclude all edges that occurred in previously generated graphs.

2. Extract the cycles (biconnected components) and represent each cycle by the set of nodes it contains.

3. Search each cycle in a depth-first manner for a depth given by the cardinality of the set.

This process repeats until a suitable relation is found up to a maximum of K times.[4] For each graph, the cycle sets are sorted in decreasing order under the assumption that the largest cycles will prove to be the most promising. A cycle (e.g., {V, N, P, T}) is searched in a depth-first manner by first removing two nodes that are proportional and combining them according to the equation formation heuristics to form new terms (e.g., V/N). The remaining nodes (e.g., {P, T}) are then tested one at a time against these terms to form new terms. For the set {P, T} and the

---

[4] The default search depth, K, is 4 since powers greater than 4 are seldom seen in the natural sciences.

(a)

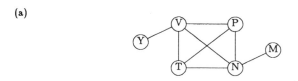

(b)

Cycle Sets:
{ (P V) (P N) (P T) (V N) (V T) (N T) }
{ (Y V) }
{ (N M) }

Figure 6–3: Proportionality graph for ideal gas law (PV/NT = 8.32)

current node V/N, P would be tested against V/N to possibly create new terms such as PV/N. If backtracking occurred, then T would be tested against V/N. This process repeats until either a solution has been found or until all combinations have been exhausted. Because nodes are removed from the cycle set as search progresses, powers of variables are not possible after the first round of search.

As an example of the heuristic power of this search technique, a sample proportionality graph is shown in Figure 6–3(a) for the ideal gas law, where a total of six attributes were initially provided by the user. As can be seen, the irrelevant variable Y is independent of pressure, volume, and temperature, but is estimated to be proportional to the number of moles of gas present. Furthermore, the variable z is found to be independent of the other five. The 2 cycles of the graph are given in Figure 6–3(b), where solitary edges are simply treated as "cycles" having only one edge. Figure 6–4 shows the search tree result from the above strategy applied to this example. The nodes shown were the only ones examined by ABACUS. For the ideal gas law, the program generated the minimum number of nodes possible to arrive at the correct solution.

While the proportionality graph search is quite adept at locating relations like the ideal gas law, this example happens to be ideally suited to such a search technique. Other types of relations, even those composed solely of multiplication and division but with higher powers, are not so well suited to proportionality graph search. For each iteration of the search algorithm, a new proportionality graph is constructed. The difficulty begins with the second graph constructed, and becomes increasingly worse with successive graphs. After completion of the first search pass, a large number of terms may exist in the system, many of which differ only slightly. Consequently, the second proportionality graph constructed has a much larger number of nodes than the first and, due to the similarity of the nodes, the graph tends to be highly interconnected. Therefore, the extracted cycles are quite large, sometimes encompassing the entire graph. As the depth of each search cycle is given by the

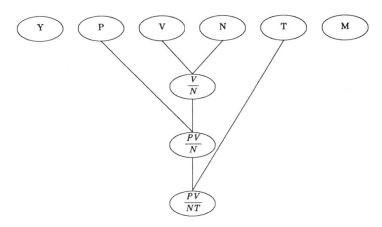

Figure 6–4:   Proportionality graph search path for ideal gas law example

number of nodes in the cycle and backtracking must be allowed, a great deal of time is wasted exploring very deep levels of the search tree.

6.5.5.2 Adding Suspension Search

To avoid the problems caused by repeated applications of proportionality graph search, ABACUS uses only one iteration of the algorithm. If no law is found, then the program employs a technique called suspension search. This algorithm is able to remove nodes from consideration, yet allows their return should they be needed. It combines the benefits of a beam approach with the allowances for faulty heuristics provided by backtracking. Suspension search begins as a normal breadth-first search. At each level, however, the values for each node are examined. As the ultimate goal is to find a variable whose values are constant or nearly constant, nodes possessing some degree of constancy are more likely to lie on a terminating path than are nodes that lack any degree on constancy. To this end, when each level is created, all nodes on that level are divided into *active nodes* and *suspended nodes*. Suspended nodes are those whose constancy is less than a low threshold, which is roughly 5% of the events. Search then proceeds on to the next level, where only the active nodes of previous levels are visible to the search algorithm. The next level is created by testing the proportionality between the new active nodes of the current level and all active nodes of the current and previous earlier levels. If no relation has been found by the time the depth limit (user specifiable) is reached, the best relation found so far is returned if its level of constancy is above a user-supplied threshold. If not, search backtracks to the previous level where its suspended nodes are now activated and related to each other, its old set of active nodes, and those active nodes of earlier

Table 6–2:   Suspension search algorithm

FUNCTION **Suspension** (active_ancestor_nodes, active-nodes, suspended_
nodes, environment) : boolean;
- If the *search-depth limit* has been reached
    then return true if the best constancy found is greater than a threshold
    else return false
- If new active or suspended nodes can be created from the current list of
active nodes
    then return true if one of these has a constancy of 100%
    or return true if a call to Suspension using the new nodes returns true
- If the *filter depth* has been reached
    then save the environment and return false
- If new active or suspended nodes and be created from the current list of
suspended nodes
    then return true if one of these has a constancy of 100%
    otherwise save the environment
        and return true if a call to Suspension using the new nodes returns true
- Save the environment and return false

---

levels. Search then returns to the next level with a new set of active nodes. If still no relation is found, backtracking will go back farther, and the process will repeat as before. An environment of each level is maintained to enable the program to remember which nodes were previously active and suspended when search returns. The suspension search algorithm is presented in Table 6–2. When invoked initially, nodes created during proportionality graph search join the user defined variables in level 1 to form the initial set of active and suspended nodes.

Because suspended nodes are ignored, fewer nodes are involved in the search at any one time. Therefore, search may be allowed to explore deeper than it could otherwise. A second search-depth limit is defined, called the *filter depth*, which cites a limit shallower than that of the absolute depth limit. Search may proceed beyond the filter-depth limit, but only active nodes are allowed for levels beyond this limit. Suspended nodes created at these levels are permanently discarded.

A partial suspension search tree for the example is given in Figure 6–5, involving the discovery of the law of conservation of momentum. The dashed horizontal line represents the filter-depth limit which has been set to three. A number of nodes may be eliminated as a result of this technique, considerably reducing the search cost.

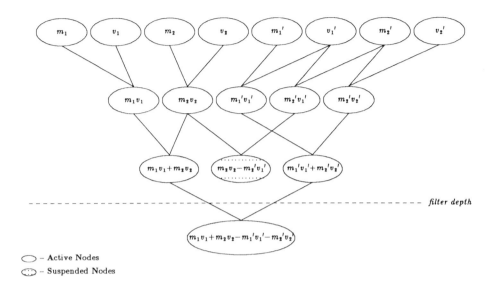

○ – Active Nodes
⬭ – Suspended Nodes

Figure 6–5:   Partial suspension search tree for conservation of momentum

Combining the proportionality graph search algorithm with the suspension search algorithm favors quick discovery of laws that are composed solely of multiplication and division while still being adept at discovering more complicated equations in a reasonable amount of time. As cycles in the first pass can never be larger than the number of given attributes, the depth-first search of the first phase is not deep for most problems, thus creating variables that would normally be created for more complicated examples anyway.

6.5.5.3 Analysis

Search algorithms representing all the possible combinations of proportionality graph search, breadth-first search, and suspension search have been constructed and directly tested in the ABACUS system. Empirical evidence has shown that among these, the most powerful strategy is the combination of algorithms presented above [Falkenhainer, 1985b]. Search strategies not including the proportionality graph search algorithm tended to be slower for examples such as the ideal gas law, while the algorithm by itself was slower on most other examples. Suspension search proved to be equivalent to breadth-first search on small examples and superior on large examples.

The method shown is quite flexible. Where it falls short is in robustness. The only equations that can be discovered are those composed of variables raised to some integer power and combined through the use of multiplication, division, addition, and subtraction. While this is usually sufficient for introductory treatments of the physical sciences, we would like to strengthen this aspect of the current implementation in future research.

6.6 FORMULATION OF QUALITATIVE PRECONDITIONS

When multiple equations are discovered for a given set of data, ABACUS generates a logical procondition for each equation that describes when the formula is applicable. Deriving preconditions for disjoint sets of events is an example of the general covering problem described by Michalski [1969] and Michalski and Larson [1978]: Given a list of observed events divided into classes, form a general description of each class in terms of the given concepts such that it covers every event in the class and distinguishes this class from the events in other classes. These results are called *discriminant descriptions* and can be used to predict the class membership of any new event. For example, suppose we are presented with examples of two classes as in Figure 6–6(a). An algorithm known as A^q would generate the descriptions in Figure 6–6(b) [Michalski, 1969; 1983; Becker, 1985a]. The description for class A spcifies that objects in this group consist solely of clear circles or any kind of triangle. Similarly, class B contains either striped circles or any squares or pentagons. These sets of conditions uniquely determine whether an object belongs to class A or class B.

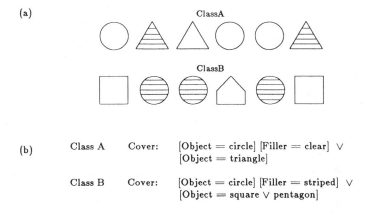

Figure 6–6:   A simple classification problem

6.6.1 The A^q Algorithm

The knowledge representation language used in our implementation of A^q is a variable-valued logic system known as VL_1 [Michalski and Larson, 1978]. Simple descriptions in this language are shown in Figure 6–6(b). Each term in square brackets specifying the value or values of an individual variable is called a selector (e.g., [Object = circle]). A conjunction of selectors, represented by writing them together on a single line, is called a *complex* and forms a partial description of a given class set. The entire description of the class is given by a disjunction of such complexes and is called its *cover*. Thus, VL_1 class descriptions are represented in disjunctive normal form (DNF).

The main generalization operator in A^q is *ExtendAgainst* at [Michalski, 1983]. To extend selector A against selector B, where A and B represent different selectors for the same attribute, generalize the list of possible values for A without including any values B currently possesses. The result of each selector operation is one or more generalized, single selector complexes. Variables may have nominal, linear, or structured domains and the operation is defined differently for each.

The A^q method consists primarily of two high-level algorithms. The first is *Cover*, which takes each event set representing a class in turn and generates a discriminant cover for the set (Table 6–3). When a cover is being generated for a class, its events are designated the positive examples, and the events from all the other classes are collectively considered as the negative examples. Cover first selects a single positive event, the *seed,* and passes this to the *Star* algorithm along with the list of negative events. The Star algorithm returns a list of complexes that represent maximally general descriptions of the seed that do not cover any of the negative

Table 6–3:   Cover algorithm

FUNCTION **Cover** (positive_events, negative_events : events) : cover;
While there are still uncovered positive events

- choose a seed event from the uncovered positive events
- generate a star from the seed against the negative events, using the lexical evaluation function (LEF) to limit the size of the star.
- use the LEF to choose the best complex from the star and add it disjunctively to the cover.
- modify the list of uncovered positive events to reflect the addition of the new complex.

Return the cover.

---

events. The Cover algorithm then selects the best complex according to a user-specified, lexicographic evaluation function (LEF), adds this disjunctively to the current cover, and removes from the list of positive events those described by the new complex. If any events remain uncovered, a new seed is chosen, and the process repeats. A modified version of A^q (called A^q/RU), used in the current ABACUS implementation, was borrowed from Becker's [1985] ExceL system. This system was designed to learn rules with exceptions. For a more detailed discussion of these algorithms see [Michalski, 1983; Becker, 1985; Falkenhainer, 1985b].

6.6.2 A^q in ABACUS

The covers generated by A^q have two possible uses in the ABACUS system. First, the combination of logical conditions with mathematical equations gives the results predictive power. Suppose one were able to only obtain values for $n - 1$ variables of an n variable equation. By knowing which equation should apply prior to evaluating it, one could determine the nth attribute from the other $n - 1$ attributes. Second, stating logical conditions for applying an equation often provide additional conceptual meaning for the user. For example, Coulomb's law relating the force of attraction, F, of two particles with charges q_1 and q_2, respectively, separated by a distance r may be stated as

$$\frac{F r^2}{q_1 q_2} = 4\pi\varepsilon$$

where ε is defined to be the permittivity of the surrounding medium. The corresponding law obtained by ABACUS is shown in Table 6–4.[5] The results show that all of the data obey the same general equation, but the constant in each case is dependent on the surrounding medium. The value of the constant was determined by the program for each medium. The changes in the value suggest that there may be some property associated with each substance that affects the electrical attraction of two charged particles.

6.7 EXPERIMENTS

Some example experiments will now be discussed to show what types of problems ABACUS is able to solve. These experiments investigate:

---

[5] The current implementation of ABACUS actually outputs an equation for each substance, as in the example shown in Figure 6–1. The summarized results given here represent what would be displayed by a postprocessor we have designed for the program.

Table 6–4:   ABACUS analysis of Coulomb's Law.

$F \times r^2 / q_1 \times q_2 = C_1$

If [substance = water]	Then C_1 = 8897.352
If [substance = air]	Then C_1 = 111.280
If [substance = silicon]	Then C_1 = 1312.363
If [substance = germanium]	Then C_1 = 1779.015

- Gravitational attraction and Stoke's Law for viscous fluids
- The law of conservation of kinetic energy
- Analysis of chemical compound data

The first two are experiments designed to illustrate the capabilities of the program. The data used for these were generated by hand with a knowledge of the correct answer. The final chemistry example represents an experiment run on data provided by members of the University of Illinois chemistry department.

6.7.1 Galilean Experiment on Free-Falling Bodies

When Galileo was studying the motion of projectiles, he concluded that the flight of all projectiles could be viewed as two completely separate motions, one in a horizontal direction, which is unaffected by the pull of the Earth, and the other up and down, controlled by the Earth's attraction. His dilemma then was how to describe this vertical component of motion, which is so firmly tied to the downward pull of the earth. By dropping various objects through different fluids, he noticed that objects of different weights fell at more nearly the same rate when fluids of lower density were used. From this he deduced that in a vacuum all objects fall at the same rate. Stoke later expanded on this by formulating a law that related the retarding force of a liquid to its viscosity. We presented ABACUS with a set of data to simulate these experiments. The dropped balls came in three sizes, for which there was a rubber ball and a clay ball in each size. The six balls were dropped from rest through three different media—namely glycerol, castor oil, and a vacuum—once each for two different size containers. The experiment was conducted in Death Valley and in Denver, and the temperature was maintained at 20° C at both locations. The measured attributes consist of the height of the container, the mass of the ball, its radius, the duration of the fall, and the velocity with which it strikes the bottom of the container (Figure 6–7). In addition, the substance through which the ball fell has been measured attributes consist of the height of the container, the mass of the ball, its radius, the duration of the fall, and the velocity with which it strikes the bottom of the container (Figure 6–7). In addition, the substance through which the ball fell has

Event $_i$:

velocity: 18.064 m/s
radius: 0.05 m
mass: 0.94 kg
time: 0.055 s
height: 1.0 m
substance: Glycerol
location: DeathValley

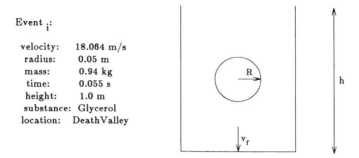

Figure 6–7:   Results of one experiment with a falling body

been noted along with the location of the experiment. Samples of the measurements taken are given in Figure 6–7.[6] Each ball was dropped once through each medium for both containers at each location for a total of 72 experiments.

ABACUS was run twice on the obtained data. First, the default ±2% margin of error was used, resulting in the following rules:

Rule A   IF   [substance = Vacuum]
            THEN   v = 9.8175 × t

Rule B   IF   [substance = Glycerol]
            THEN   v × r = 0.9556 × m

Rule C   IF   [substance = CastorOil]
            THEN   v × r = 0.7336 × m

The rules indicate that the equations are dependent on the medium through which the balls fall. ABACUS was then run a second time using a margin of error of ±0.2% and the following results were reported:

Rule A   IF   [location = Death Valley][substance = Vacuum]
            THEN   v = 9.8453 × t

Rule B   IF   [location = Denver][substance = Vacuum]
            THEN   v = 9.7898 × t

---

[6] Of course, the correct measurements were calculated by hand for this experiment. The mass of each ball was derived from the chosen radius and the standard densities for rubber and clay. Likewise. the standard viscosity for each substance was used. Gravitational acceleration was chosen to be 9.845 $^m/s^2$ in Death Valley and 9.79 $^m/s^2$ in Denver to reflect the fact that the force of gravity decreases at higher altitudes.

Rule C	IF	[location = Death Valley][substance = Glycerol]
	THEN	$v \times r = 0.9583 \times m$
Rule D	IF	[location = Denver][substance = Glycerol]
	THEN	$v \times r = 0.9530 \times m$
Rule E	IF	[location = Death Valley][substance = CastorOil]
	THEN	$v \times r = 0.7356 \times m$
Rule F	IF	[location = Denver][substance = CastorOil]
	THEN	$v \times r = 0.7315 \times m$

This time each equation is dependent upon both the medium through which the balls fall and the location of the experiment. In cases represented by rules A and B, it would appear that the behavior is independent of the characteristics of the balls used. Interpreting these findings, we observe that an object undergoes a constant acceleration due to earth's gravity and that an object under constant acceleration will change speed proportional to the length of time it undergoes this acceleration. This may be stated as $\Delta v = a\Delta t$ and corresponds to the cases of the balls falling in a vacuum. The constants for these cases simply represent the earth's gravitational acceleration at the two different locations. When we take the resistance of the medium into account, however, as we must do for glycerol and castor oil, the retarding force of the medium becomes involved and is stated by Stoke's Law as:

$$F_r = -6\pi\eta\, r\, v$$

where η is the viscosity coefficient of the fluid. Because of this added force, the object will reach a constant terminal velocity given by

$$v_T r = \frac{g}{6\pi\eta r}\, m$$

where g is the gravitational acceleration. This corresponds to the equation reported by ABACUS ($v \times r = $ Constant $\times$ m) for the glycerol and castor oil cases. In these cases, the constant combined values for η and g, and this explains why the values reported for rules C through F in the second example were dependent on both the type of liquid (η) and the location (g). If the location and substance variables had been replaced by the numeric variables g and η respectively, those variables would have shown up explicitly in the equations. This would reduce rules C through F to a single rule with the constant equaling 6π. Knowing when to explicitly represent conceptual constants such as π would be an interesting topic for future research.

    This experiment points out a number of properties of ABACUS. First, two different equation forms were discovered, each having only the velocity attribute in common. This demonstrates the program's ability to discover multiple equations for different groups of events, even when variables pertinent to one are irrelevant to another. Secondly, the necessity and power of the logical preconditions can be seen here. Finally, it points out the problems encountered when working with real numbers, noise, and uncertainties. The results obtained for the ±0.2% case were more interesting and correct than for the ±2% experiment. However, common sense and the presence of noisy data would generally rule out using ±0.2%.

6.7.2 Conservation of Kinetic Energy

The law of conservation of energy states that energy can neither be created nor destroyed. Therefore, when two bodies collide, the total energy of the system before the time of collision will be the same as the total energy after the collision. For inelastic collisions, some of this energy is converted to heat during the collision and so, at a macroscopic level, an apparent energy loss is observed. For perfectly elastic collisions, however, the sum of the balls' individual energies, namely their kinetic energies, will remain constant before and after their collisions:

$$\frac{1}{2}m_1v_1^2 + \frac{1}{2}m_2v_2^2 = \frac{1}{2}m_1v_1'^2 + \frac{1}{2}m_2v_2'^2 \tag{7.1}$$

Converting these concepts into an experiment for ABACUS to examine, data was constructed for a series of observations of various objects colliding. The data consisted of seven attributes and 12 events, where the seven attributes consisted of the masses of the two balls, their four corresponding velocities (magnitudes), and a nominal variable which described the observed collision as either elastic or inelastic.[7] For this data set, ABACUS produced the following results:

Rule A	IF	[collision – type = elastic]
	THEN	$m_1(v_1^2 - v_1'^2) = m_2(v_2'^2 - v_2^2)$
Rule B	IF	[collision – type = inelastic]
	THEN	No formula was found

An equation equivalent to (7.1) was found to hold for those events corresponding to an elastic collision. No equation could be found for the remaining "inelastic" events. ABACUS was not only able to discover the desired equation, but was also able to specify that the equation only held for elastic collisions. As we show later, ABACUS found this law rather difficult to discover because it contains subtraction.

6.7.3 Analysis of Chemical Compounds

Figure 6–8 shows the structure of a typical bimetallic coordination compound. The distance between the central metal atoms in such compounds is important to

---

[7] We recognize that indicating the collision type with a symbolic variable simplifies the data clustering task. The example is still very interesting as it stands, but we would like to develop more powerful clustering techniques, as discussed in the section on future research.

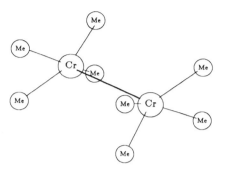

Figure 6–8:   Bimetallic coordination compound in eclipsed conformation

chemists, but it is difficult and expensive to measure. At present, there is no known way to predict this distance given the values of other attributes, providing a unique challenge for testing the usefulness of ABACUS and thus revealing its strengths and weaknesses.

The compounds are symmetric around the central covalent bond, each side consisting of a primary metal atom and up to five ligand molecules joined by ionic bond to the primary atom. Data for the experiment consisted of the values of 13 attributes for 30 different observed compounds as garnered from various chemical research articles.[8] The full collection of data is reproduced in Table 6–5, where the compound formula has been added for thoroughness. "Metal" is the name of the two central metal atoms, "Ox" is the oxidation state of the metals, "Rad" is the radius of one metal atom in angstroms, and "eM" represents the number of electrons per metal. The formal bond order of the covalent bond is given by "BO," "MMdist" gives the distance between the metals in angstroms, "Q" is the total charge of the molecule in units of electron charge, and the conformation (indicating the molecule's alignment) is shown by "Conf." In Figure 6–8, the molecule is in the eclipsed conformation because the ligand molecules of each side line up when viewed from on end. Finally, "L1" through "L5" are the names of the ligand molecules.

The experiment began by running ABACUS using all default parameter values. The response was that no relation could be found. A further examination of the output revealed that no nodes were created, thus indicating that either there were no relations in the data or that all proportionality tests returned $Prop^?$ and thus no examples could be obtained. The latter situation would occur if the presence of a large

---

[8]Data were collected by J.M. Hanckel and Theodore L. Brown of the University of Illinois Chemistry Department.

Table 6-5: Experimental data for bimetallic coordination compounds

Compound	Metal	Ox	MMdist	Rad	Q	eM	Conf	BO	L1	L2	L3	L4	L5
[Cr(CH3)8]4–	Cr	II	1.980	1.29	–4	12	eclip	4	Me	Me	Me	Me	None
[Mo2Cl8]4–	Mo	II	2.139	1.40	–4	12	eclip	4	Cl	Cl	Cl	Cl	None
[Mo(CH3)8]4–	Mo	II	2.148	1.40	–4	12	eclip	4	Me	Me	Me	Me	None
Mo2Br4(p-MeC5H4N)4	Mo	II	2.150	1.40	0	12	eclip	4	Br	NR3	Br	NR3	None
Mo2Cl4(p-MeC5H4N)4	Mo	II	2.153	1.40	0	12	eclip	4	Cl	NR3	Cl	NR3	None
Mo2(CH2SiMe3)6	Mo	III	2.167	1.40	0	9	stag	3	CH2SiR3	CH2SiR3	CH2SiR3	None	None
Mo2(NMe2)4Cl2	Mo	III	2.200	1.40	0	9	stag	3	NMe2	NMe2	Cl	None	None
Mo2(NMe2)4Me2	Mo	III	2.201	1.40	0	9	stag	3	NMe2	NMe2	Me	None	None
Mo2(NMe2)6	Mo	III	2.211	1.40	0	9	stag	3	NMe2	NMe2	NMe2	None	None
Re2Cl6[PEt3]2	Re	III	2.222	1.37	0	12	eclip	4	PEt3	Cl	Cl	Cl	None
Mo2(OCH2CMe3)6	Mo	III	2.222	1.40	0	9	stag	3	OCR3	OCR3	OCR3	None	None
Re2Cl4[P(Et)3]4	Re	II	2.232	1.37	0	14	eclip	4	Cl	PEt3	Cl	PEt3	None
[Re2Cl8]2–	Re	III	2.241	1.37	–2	12	eclip	4	Cl	Cl	Cl	Cl	None
Mo2(OSiMe3)6HNMe2	Mo	III	2.242	1.40	0	11	stag	3	OSiR3	OSiR3	OSiR3	NR3	None
W2[CH2Si(CH3)3]6	W	III	2.255	1.41	0	9	stag	3	CH2SiR3	CH2SiR3	CH2SiR3	None	None
[Re2Br8]2–	Re	III	2.270	1.37	–2	12	eclip	4	Br	Br	Br	Br	None
W2(NMe2)4Cl2	W	III	2.283	1.41	0	9	stag	3	NMe2	NMe2	Cl	None	None
W2(NEt2)4Me2	W	III	2.291	1.41	0	9	stag	3	NEt2	NEt2	Me	None	None
W2(NMe2)6	W	III	2.294	1.41	0	9	stag	3	NMe2	NMe2	NMe2	None	None
W2(NEt2)4I2	W	III	2.296	1.41	0	9	stag	3	NEt2	NEt2	I	None	None
W2Cl2(NEt2)4	W	III	2.301	1.41	0	9	stag	3	Cl	NEt2	NEt2	None	None
W2(NEt2)4Br2	W	III	2.303	1.41	0	9	stag	3	NEt2	NEt2	Br	None	None
W2(OCHMe2)6(pyr)2	W	III	2.332	1.41	0	11	stag	3	OCR3	OCR3	OCR3	NR3	None
Co2(CO)6[P(n-Bn)3]2	Co	O	2.665	1.25	0	17	stag	1	CO	CO	CO	None	PEt3
Mn(CO)8[PEt3]2	Mn	O	2.913	1.37	0	17	stag	1	CO	CO	CO	CO	PEt3
Mn2(CO)10	Mn	O	2.923	1.37	0	17	stag	1	CO	CO	CO	CO	CO
Cr2(CO)10	Cr	–1	2.970	1.29	–2	17	stag	1	CO	CO	CO	CO	CO
Re2(CO)10	Re	O	3.020	1.37	0	17	stag	1	CO	CO	CO	CO	CO
Tc2(CO)10	Tc	O	3.036	1.35	0	17	stag	1	CO	CO	CO	CO	CO
Mo2(CO)10	Mo	–1	3.123	1.40	–2	17	stag	1	CO	CO	CO	CO	CO

Table 6–6:   Initial results with margin of error at 8%

Rule A	IF	[L2 = CH2SiR3 v NEt2 v NMe2]
		[L1 = OCR3][L4 = None]
	THEN	MMdist = 0.2502 × eM
Rule B	IF	[L1 = OSiR3 v PEt3]
		[L2 = Br]
		[L2 = Cl v OCR3][Metal = Re v W]
	THEN	MMdist = 0.1954 × eM
Rule C	IF	[L2 = CO v Me v NR3 v PEt3]
		[OX = II]
	THEN	MMdist = 0.1735 × eM

number of nominal variables was interfering with the numerical relation-finding process. As a result, the program was instructed to ignore all nominal variables when trying to hold variables constant for the proportionality test. This time, nodes were created but still no relation was found to hold for the 40% default constancy criterion. A 40% constancy criterion coupled with a 2% margin of error appears too strict. Since actual measured data might contain a reasonable amount of noise, the decision was made to loosen the default margin of error of 2% to 5% and then again to 8%. Results now began to be reported (shown in Table 6–6). What is most promising about them is that the same equation was found to hold for all of the data, with only the constant differing. This suggests the discovery of some type of physical phenomenon more strongly than if different equations were uncovered.

After conducting numerous experiments in this manner, the most promising results were shown to the members of the chemistry department for their opinion. While the results looked promising, the conclusion was that these relations did not coincide conceptually with any known physical phenomenon and the margin of error used was far too high for these data. However, the chemists suggested trying the logarithm of the bond order as this type of term appears often in empirical bond order—bond-length correlations. Continuing with the experimentation, the program was instructed to replace Bond Order by log(Bond Order), a variety of parameter settings were tried, and the conclusions of Table 6–7 were obtained. As before, these results looked promising, but the margin of error was still too high.

After further analysis of the data by hand, it was reasoned that perhaps there was too much redundancy in the original data. For example, each metal atom has a unique radius associated with it. Therefore, our chemistry expert suggested that we

Table 6–7:   Results using log(BondOrder)

Rule A	IF	[OX = III][L4 = BR v Cl v Me v PEt3 v None]
	THEN	MMidst × log(BO) = 0.1180 × eM
Rule B	IF	[L4 = Me v NR3 v PEt3]
		[Q = –4.0000]
	THEN	MMdist × log(BO) = 0.1031 × eM

Table 6–8:   Results using reduced data set with margin of error at 2%

Rule A	IF	[L1 = CO][RAD = 1.29 .. 1.35]
		[L1 = CO][Rad = 1.4)
	THEN	MMdist = 2.2606 × Rad
Rule B	IF	[eM* = 18.0]
	THEN	MMdist = 2.149 × Rad
Rule C	IF	L2 = Br v OSiR3 v PEt3]
		[L4 = Cl][Rad = 1.37]
		[Rad = 1.41]
	THEN	MMdist = 1.6279 × Rad
Rule D	IF	[L2 = Me v NR3]
		[Rad = 1.4][L4 = Cl v None]
	THEN	MMdist = 1.5528 × Rad

reduce the number of attributes to nine, consisting of the radius, the metal to metal distance, the bond order, the five ligand names, and a new electrons-per-metal value (eM*) calculated by adding the bond order to the old value. Since a somewhat new data set was being used, the margin of error was returned to its default value of 2%, and no variables were to be ignored. On the first run, the equations of Table 6–8 were obtained. Our chemistry expert, Professor Ted Brown from the University of Illinois Department of Chemistry, has judged these equations to be quite interesting, since they hold with only a 2%, margin of error. However, he still considers them inconclusive because they need physical explanation. He suggested further analysis to uncover an underlying commonality between the compounds of each class that could explain these findings. Nevertheless, this experiment demonstrates that ABACUS is a useful new tool for analyzing real-world data and searching for unknown laws.

6.8 DISCUSSION OF METHODOLOGY

The experiments presented in Section 6.7 suggest that ABACUS could be used for discovering empirical laws in a variety of domains. This section summarizes its performance on different examples, and outlines several problems for future research.

6.8.1 Analysis of Experimental Results

ABACUS runs on a Sun Microsystems workstation running Franz LISP under a UNIX environment. A variety of examples have been presented, representing different complexities of equations and preconditions. Table 6–9 shows a comparison of how complex all of our examples turned out to be. Equations composed solely of multiplication and division have been shown to be quite simple discovery tasks. This is exhibited by the small number of nodes required for all of the examples except the ones for conservation of momentum and kinetic energy. The Coulomb example was more difficult than the ideal gas law because it contained a squared term, forcing the proportionality graph search algorithm to exhaustively search the initial, highly interconnected graph. Equations containing addition or subtraction are significantly more difficult using the methods presented here but are still quite manageable. From the times, given in CPU seconds, it can be seen that the program was relatively efficient for every example.

Performance is lessened somewhat by large numbers of events. This can be seen by comparing the time required to generate five nodes for the large set of Stoke's Law data against the time required to generate five nodes for the smaller chemistry example. Other factors, such as the number of proportionality tests performed, should be considered when comparing these times.

Table 6–9:   Relevant statistics of the quantitative learning experiments

Example	Number of Events	Number of Classes	Total Nodes	Equation Discovery Time	Precondition Generation Time	Total Time
Ideal Gas	15	1	3	3	0	3
Momentum	22	3	62	56	12	68
Coulomb	36	5	32	47	27	74
Stoke's Law	72	6	5	18	31	49
Kinetic Energy	12	2	987	850	5	855
Chemistry	30	4	5	3	28	31

NOTE: All times are given in CPU seconds.

6.8.2 Limitations

Equations that the current ABACUS can discover are limited to those involving multiplication, division, addition, and subtraction operators. The equations are of the form

$f(x) = Constant$

where $f(x)$ is composed solely of user defined variables and operations between them. General polynominals with coefficients cannot be discovered, preventing the discovery of a variety of physical laws. In addition, terms such as sin and log cannot be used unless the user explicitly tells the program to create them.

There are classes of equation forms that cannot be discovered by the methods used in ABACUS. For example, data corresponding to certain parabolas and oscillations often appear to be void of qualitative proportionalities due to the problem of conflicting proportionalities. In addition, the user is not required to supply carefully prepared data in which some attributes are held constant while others are allowed to change. This may cause many $Prop^2$ assertions, making the problem more difficult than it would be otherwise.

6.8.3 Current and Future Research

The most challenging assumption in our research was that the system should be able to discover multiple laws for a collection of data. This single decision prevented the use of curve-fitting techniques, since they would attempt to fit a single equation to the entire data set. This in turn eliminated the possibility of discovering a more general class of equations and made many very interesting relationships more difficult to discover. The search strategy employed and the trend detection algorithm used were forced to be quite loose. As a result, the potential search space was increased, irrelevant variables became harder to locate, and conflicting proportionalities became an issue. A possible solution may be to cluster the events prior to invoking the equation discovery module in some manner such that in each set of events, the events all hold the same set of proportionality assertions. Given this, the more precise approaches such as regression analysis could be taken once again. The method would be based on some form of clustering algorithm, much like the conceptual clustering described by Michalski [1980] and Stepp [1984], and might be quite simple, merely forming clustered groups so that all events support the same proportionality assertion. This task has been undertaken by Greg Greene, who at this time has reported some preliminary success with his numeric clustering algorithm. As mentioned earlier, the problem of conflicting proportionalities, such as shown in Figure 6–1, can be solved for most cases by determining the points where the proportionality between variables changes sign. This may introduce a new problem, that of merging two or more equations into one, as in the case of parabolic or sinusoidal functions.

Of major importance is recognizing the usefulness of a term once it is created. When a term is invariant across all events, the task is easy. When only a percentage of events are covered, when should the search algorithm stop? The problem lies in the basic ignorance of the program. What is needed is some form of conceptual knowledge that would enable the program to distinguish between conceptually good terms and conceptually useless terms. This became quite evident during testing of the program when occasionally an unexpected answer would be returned, which in fact covered more events than the desired equation but which was mathematically far more complicated. We need to develop a method for the program to consider syntactically desirable equations even when they may not be the most general.

In this work, we investigated what could be accomplished when only minimal information is provided by the user. Previous quantitative discovery systems have required that the user specify which variables are dependent and which are independent. They have also required that all permutations of variable values be given so that $Prop^?$ assertions will never exist [Langley, 1985]. The later condition means that the user must generate a great many more events than needed by ABACUS. In regression analysis, the form of the equation is predefined. In our experiments, however, it soon became evident that the value of ABACUS as a researcher's assistant tool would be enhanced if we allowed additional knowledge to be optional and didn't prevent the user from supplying available knowledge. A simple but useful addition would provide an option for a user to include or exclude specified variables from the equation discovery or precondition generation processes.

6.9 SUMMARY

The methodology of equation discovery and precondition generation used in ABACUS has been presented, analyzed, and illustrated through examples. ABACUS has proved useful for a number of problems in chemistry and physics, and the results show that it has also been quite efficient for each learning task.

ABACUS measures well against the criteria we proposed for a quantitative discovery system. It handles irrelevant variables, is capable of formulating multiple equations for characterizing the data and of determining qualitative or logical preconditions for each equation. The techniques of variable combination through search, as used in the early BACON programs, has been considerably improved by analyzing the specific search characteristics of the domain. The current version of ABACUS falls short on two points: It is relatively limited in the kinds of equations that can be discovered, and it occasionally suffers from the computational cost of search.

The work presented here is unique in several ways. First, no prior work has addressed the real-world issue of discovering multiple equations to describe different aspects of a physical situation. Even for cases where it appears that a single physical phenomenon is being observed, as in the falling bodies example, different physical situations may exist requiring different equation forms to describe them.

Previous programs have been unable to discover different equations for different subsets of the given events. Second, the explicit generation of logic-style preconditions for the discovered equations is novel. When different physical situations exist for what appears to be the same phenomenon, preconditions determine when each equation applies. Finally, new search techniques for equation discovery have been created. In conclusion, the ABACUS system seems to be a useful new tool for analyzing experimental data.

ACKNOWLEDGMENTS

This chapter is based on an earlier article of the authors published in *Machine Learning* [Vol. 1, No. 4, 1986]. The authors thank Theodore L. Brown and J. M. Hanckel from the University of Illinois chemistry department for providing the data used in the chemical compound analysis experiments, interpreting the results, and supplying very valuable comments about the observed methodology. Pat Langley, John Collins, and Greg Greene provided many useful comments and criticisms on earlier versions of this chapter.

This work was supported in part by the Defense Advanced Research Project Agency under grant N00014-K-85-0878, the National Science Foundation under grant DCR 84-06801, and the Office of Naval Research under grant N00014-82-K-0186.

References

Aho, A.V., Hopcroft, J.E., and Ullman, J.D. 1974. *The Design and Analysis of Computer Algorithms,* Addison-Wesley, Menlo Park, CA.

Becker, J.M. 1985. *Inductive Learning of Decision Rules with Exceptions: Methodology and Experimentation.* MS Thesis, Department of Computer Science, University of Illinois, Urbana-Champaign, IL.

Chatterjee, S. and Price, B. 1977. *Regression Analysis by Example,* John Wiley and Sons, NY.

Condon, E.U. and Odishaw, H. (Eds.), 1967. *Handbook of Physics,* Second Edition. McGraw-Hill, NY.

Daniel, C. and Wood, F.S. 1971. *Fitting Equations to Data,* Wiley-Interscience, John Wiley and Sons, NY.

de Kleer, J. 1975. *Qualitative and Quantitative Knowledge in Classical Mechanics.* MS Thesis (TR-352), Massachusetts Institute of Technology, Cambridge, MA.

Dietterich, T. and Michalski, R.S. 1981. "Inductive Learning of Structural Descriptions: Evaluation Criteria and Comparative Review of Selected Methods," *Artificial Intelligence,* Vol 16, No. 3, pp. 257–294.

EI-Shafei, N. 1986. *Quantitative Discovery and Reasoning about Failure Mechanisms in Pavement.* MIT Artificial Intelligence Laboratory, unpublished manuscript.

Falkenhainer, B.C. 1984. *ABACUS: Adding Domain Constraints to Quantitative Scientific Discovery* (Technical Report UIUCDCS-F-84-927, ISG 84-7). Department of Computer Science, University of Illinois, Urbana-Champaign, IL.

———— , 1985a. "Proportionality Graphs, Units Analysis, and Domain Constraints: Improving the power and Efficiency of the Scientific Discovery Process," *Proceedings of the Ninth International Joint Conference on Artificial Intelligence.* Morgan Kaufmann, San Mateo, CA.

———— , 1985b. *Quantitative Empirical Learning: An Analysis and Methodology.* MS Thesis (UIUCDCS-F-85-947, ISG 85-16), Department of Computer Science, University of Illinois, Champaign-Urbana, Illinois.

Forbus, K.D. 1984. "Qualitative Process Theory," *Artificial Intelligence* 24.

Hajek, P. and Havranek, T. 1978. "The GLTHA Method—Its Aims and Techniques," *International Journal on Man Machine Studies,* No. 10, pp. 3–22.

Huntley, H.E. 1952. *Dimensional Analysis*, MacDonald and Co, London.

Kokar, M. 1981. "A Procedure of Identification of Laws in Empirical Sciences," *Systems Science,* Vol. 7, No. 1 (pp. 32–41).

———— , 1986a. "Determining arguments of in variant functional descriptions," *Machine Learning* 1 (4).

———— , 1986b. "Discovering functional formulas through changing representation base," *Proceedings of the Sixth National Conference on Artificial Intelligence,* Morgan Kaufmann, San Mateo, CA.

Kowalik, J.S. 1986. *Coupling Symbolic and Numerical Computing in Expert Systems,* North-Holland, Amsterdam, The Netherlands.

Langhaar, H.L. 1951. *Dimensional Analysis and Theory of Models.* John Wiley and Sons.

Langley, P. 1979. "Rediscovering Physics with BACON.3," *Proceedings of the Sixth International Joint Conference on Artificial Intelligence,* pp. 505–507, Morgan Kaufmann, San Mateo, CA.

————— , 1981. "Data-Driven Discovery of Physical Laws," *Cognitive Science,* 5, pp. 31–54.

Langley, P., Bradshaw, G.L., and Simon, H.A. 1981. "BACON:5 The Discovery of Conservation Laws," *Proceedings of the Seventh International Joint Conference on Artificial Intelligence,* pp. 121–126.

————— , 1983. "Rediscovering Chemistry with the Bacon System," in *Machine Learning: An Artificial Intelligence Approach,* R.S. Michalski, J.G. Carbonell, and T.M. Mitchell (Eds.), Morgan Kaufmann, San Mateo, CA.

Langley, P., Bradshaw, G.L., Simon, H.A., and Zytkow, J. 1983. "Mechanisms for Qualitative and Quantitative Discovery," *Proceedings of the International Machine Learning Workshop,* Monticello, IL.

Langley, P., Simon, H.A., Bradshaw, G.L., and Zytkow, J.M. 1987. *Scientific discovery: Computational explorations of the creative processes,* MIT Press, Cambridge, MA.

Langley, P., Zytkow, J., Simon, H.A., and Bradshaw, G.L. 1986. "The Search for Regularity: Four Aspects of Scientific Discovery," in *Machine Learning: An Artificial Intelligence Approach, Volume II,* R.S. Michalski, J.G. Carbonell, and T.M. Mitchell (Eds.), Morgan Kaufmann, San Mateo, CA.

Michalski, R.S. 1980. "Knowledge Acquisition through Conceptual Clustering: A Theoretical Framework and an Algorithm for Partitioning Data into Conjunctive Concepts," *Policy Analysis and Information Systems,* Vol. 4, No. 3.

————— , 1983. "A Theory and Methodology of Inductive Learning," in *Machine Learning: An Artificial Intelligence Approach,* R.S. Michalski, J.G. Carbonell, and T.M. Mitchell (Eds.), Morgan Kaufmann, San Mateo, CA.

Michalski, R.S. and Larson, J.B. 1978. *Selection of Most Representative Training Examples and Incremental Generation of VL1 Hypotheses: The Underlying Methodology and the Description of Programs ESEL and AQ11* (Technical Report UIUCDCS-R-78-867). Department of Computer Science, University of Illinois, Urbana-Champaign, IL.

Mitchell, T.M. 1982. "Generalization as Search," *Artificial Intelligence,* Vol. 18, No. 2, March 1982, pp. 203–226.

Roller, D.E. and Blum, R. 1981. *Physics: Volume One. Mechanics, Waves, and Thermodynamica,* Holden-Day, San Francisco, CA.

Stepp, R.E. 1984. *Conjunctive Conceptual Clustering: A Methodology and Experimentation.* Doctoral Dissertation (UIUCDCS-R-84-1189), Department of Computer Science, University of Illinois, Urbana-Champaign, IL.

Weast, R.C. (Ed.). 1984. *CRC Handbook of Chemistry and Physics, 65th Edition.* CRC Press, Inc.

Zagoruiko, N.G. 1976. "Empirical Prediction Algorithms," in *Computer Oriented Learning Process,* J.C. Simon (Ed.), Noordhoff, Leyden, pp. 581–595.

Zagoruiko, N.G., Elkina, V.N., and Lbov, G.S. 1985. *Algorithms for Revealing Empirical Laws.* Nauka Publishing House, Siberian Division of the Soviet Union Academy of Sciences.

Zytkow, J.M. 1987. "Combining Many Searches in the FAHRENHEIT Discovery System," *Proceedings of the Fourth International Machine Learning Workshop,* Irvine, CA.

7

LEARNING BY EXPERIMENTATION:

THE OPERATOR REFINEMENT METHOD

Jaime G. Carbonell and Yolanda Gil
(Carnegie Mellon University)

Abstract

Autonomous systems require the ability to plan effective courses of action under potentially uncertain or unpredictable contingencies. Planning requires knowledge of the environment that is accurate enough to allow reasoning about actions. If the environment is too complex or very dynamic, goal-driven learning with reactive feedback becomes a necessity. This chapter addresses the issue of learning by experimentation as an integral component of PRODIGY.

PRODIGY is a flexible planning system that encodes its domain knowledge as declarative operators and applies the operator refinement method to acquire additional preconditions or postconditions when observed consequences diverge from internal expectations. When multiple explanations for the observed divergence are consistent with the existing domain knowledge, experiments to discriminate among these explanations are generated. The experimentation process isolates the deficient operator and inserts the discriminant condition or unforeseen side effect to avoid similar impasses in future planning. Thus, experimentation is demand-driven and exploits both the internal state of the planner and any external feedback received. A detailed example of integrated experiment formulation is presented as the basis for a systematic approach to extending an incomplete domain theory or correcting a potentially inaccurate one.

7.1 INTRODUCTION: THE NEED FOR REACTIVE EXPERIMENTATION

Learning in the context of problem solving can occur in multiple ways, ranging from macro-operator formation [Fikes and Nilsson, 1971; Cheng and Carbonell,

1986] and generalized chunking [Laird, *et al.*, 1986], to analogical transfer of problem solving strategies [Carbonell, 1983; 1986] and pure analytical or explanation-driven techniques [Mitchell, *et al.*, 1986; DeJong and Mooney, 1986; Minton and Carbonell, 1987]. All of these techniques, however, focus on the acquisition of control knowledge to solve problems faster, more effectively, and to avoid pitfalls encountered in similar situations. Newly acquired control knowledge may be encoded as preferred operator sequences (chunks and macro-operators), improved heuristic left-hand sides on problem-solving operators (as in LEX [Mitchell, *et al.*, 1983]), or explicit search-control rules (as in PRODIGY [Minton, *et al.*, 1987; 1989a]).

However important the acquisition of search control knowledge may be, the problem of acquiring factual domain knowledge and representing it effectively for problem solving is of at least equal significance. Most systems that acquire new factual knowledge do so by some form of inductive generalization,[1] but they operate independently of a goal-driven problem solver and have no means of proactive interaction with an external environment.

When one observes real-world learners, ranging from children at play to scientists at work, it appears that active experimentation plays a crucial role in formulating and extending domain theories, whether everyday "naive" ones, or formal scientific ones. Many actions are taken in order to gather information and learn whether or not predicted results come to pass or unforeseen consequences occur. Experimentation is a powerful tool to gather knowledge about the environment, about properties of objects and about actions.

In general, experimentation may be targeted at the acquisition of different kinds of knowledge:

- *Experimentation to augment an incomplete domain theory.* Experiments may be formulated to synthesize new operators, learn new consequences of existing operators, refine the applicability conditions of existing operators, or determine previously unknown interactions among different operators. Also, performing known actions on new objects in the task domain in a systematic manner, and observing their consequences, serves to acquire properties of these new objects and classify them according to pragmatic criteria determined by the task domain. Thus, experimentation may be guided toward acquiring new domain knowledge from the external environment.

---

[1] The reader is referred to the two previous machine learning books [Michalski, *et al.*, 1983; 1986] and other chapters of this book for several good examples of inductive methodologies and systems built upon them.

- *Experimentation to refine an incorrect domain theory.* No comprehensive theory is ever perfect, as the history of science informs us, whether it be Newton's laws of motion or more ill-structured domain theories embedded in the knowledge bases of expert systems. However, partially correct theories often prove useful and are gradually improved to match external reality (although they may be totally replaced on occasion by a newer conceptual structure). Here we deal only with minor errors of commission in the domain theory, which when locally corrected improve global performance. We believe automated knowledge refinement is a very important aspect of autonomous learning, and one where success is potentially much closer at hand than the far more difficult and seldomly encountered phenomenon of formulating radically new theories from ground zero. Thus, experimentation may be guided at incremental correction of a domain theory.

- *Experimentation to acquire control knowledge in an otherwise intractable domain theory.* When multiple sequences of actions appear to achieve the same goal, experimentation and analysis are required to determine which actions to take in formulating the most cost-effective or robust plan, and to generalize and compile the appropriate conditions so as to formulate the preferred plan directly in future problem-solving instances where the same goal and relevant initial conditions are present. Thus, experimentation may be guided toward making more effective use of existing domain knowledge.

- *Experimentation to acquire or correct knowledge about the external state of the world.* Given a partial description of the external world,[2] it often proves necessary to acquire a missing piece of knowledge in order to synthesize or elaborate a plan—regardless of the accuracy, tractability, or completeness of the domain theory itself. This kind of observation (or "exploration" or "experimentation") is a common data-seeking behavior prototyped in systems such as MAX [Knokka, 1990], but missing from most idealized work on planning, including all theoretical treatments of nonlinear, constraint-based planning.

We have investigated a series of methods for learning by experimentation in the context of planning that can yield factual knowledge as well as search control preferences. The work described here is a method for refining the specifications of operators, and it has been implemented in a version of the PRODIGY system augmented with capabilities for execution monitoring and dynamic replanning.

---

[2] All descriptions of a real robotic environment, for instance, are necessarily partial—as are all computational models of a complex external reality.

7.2 THE ROLE OF EXPERIMENTATION IN PRODIGY

The PRODIGY system [Minton, *et al.*, 1989a; 1989b; Carbonell, *et al.*, 1990] is a general purpose problem solver designed to provide an underlying basis for machine learning research. The appendix presents an overview of the basic architecture and the different learning mechanisms in the system. PRODIGY can improve its performance, by learning search control rules [Minton, 1988; Etzioni, 1990], by storing and replaying derivational traces in an analogy/case-based reasoning mode [Veloso and Carbonell, 1989], by learning useful abstractions for hierarchical planning [Knoblock, 1989], and by acquiring knowledge from domain experts via graphically oriented static and dynamic knowledge acquisition interfaces [Joseph, 1989]. Our work is focused on the acquisition of the domain theory through external feedback from targeted actions—execution monitoring of plans as they unfold and targeted experiments to resolve apparent indeterminacies in the environment.

Of the possible imperfections in a domain theory described in the previous section, we focus our work on the refinement of incomplete theories. The specification of a domain can be incomplete in several different ways:

- Attributes of objects in the world could be unknown—factual properties could be missing (size, color, category, functional properties, etc.) or even knowledge about to which objects the operators may be applied to achieve the desired effects. Totally new attributes could be learned, or the range of already known ones could be further specified. Additionally, attributes of objects can be combined to form new attributes. For example, density and volume under constant gravity define the attribute "weight." Inference rules can also define new attributes expressing more complex relations.

- Entire operators could be missing—the planner may not know all the capabilities of the performance component.

- Operators could be partially specified—the planner may know only some of their preconditions or some of their consequences.

- Interactions among operators could be unknown, causing planning failures or planning inefficiencies.

Our goal is to develop learning methods and experimentation strategies to acquire missing domain knowledge in general. This paper focuses on one central approach, the operator refinement method, to acquire missing pre- and post-conditions of operators in the domain theory. In a forthcoming paper [Carbonell, *et al.*, forthcoming], we describe other techniques for learning by experimentation in the context of problem solving that address other types of incompleteness in the domain theory.

We first present a detailed implemented example of the operator refinement method in action. Then, we describe the method itself more formally.

OPERATORS

```
(GRIND-CONCAVE                          (CLEAN
   (params (<obj>))                        (params (<obj>))
   (preconds                               (preconds
      (is-solid <obj>))                       (is-solid <obj>))
   (effects (                              (effects (
      (add (is-parabolic <obj>)))))          (add (is-clean <obj>)))))

(POLISH                                 (ALUMINIZE
   (params (<obj>))                        (params (<obj>))
   (preconds                               (preconds
      (and (is-clean <obj>)                   (and (is-clean <obj>)
           (is-glass <obj>)))                      (is-solid <obj>)))
   (effects (                              (effects (
      (add (is-polished <obj>)))))            (add (is-reflective <obj>)))))
```

INFERENCE RULES

```
(IS-TELESCOPE-MIRROR                    (IS-MIRROR
   (params (<obj>))                        (params (<obj>))
   (preconds                               (preconds
      (and (is-mirror <obj>)                  (and (is-reflective <obj>)
           (is-parabolic <obj>)))                  (is-polished <obj>)))
   (effects (                              (effects (
      (add (is-telescope-mirror <obj>)))))    (add (is-mirror <obj>)))))
```

Figure 7–1: Incomplete domain theory, as given initially to the system

7.2.1 The Operator Refinement Method: A Detailed Example

Consider an example domain of expertise: crafting a primary telescope mirror from raw materials (such as pyrex glass, pure aluminum, distilled water, etc.) and pertinent tools (such as grinding equipment, aluminum vaporizers,[3] etc.). A telescope mirror will be considered here as a reflective and polished surface that has a parabolic shape. The operators in the domain include: GRIND-CONCAVE, POLISH, ALUMINIZE, and CLEAN and are presented in detail in Figure 7–1 with the inference rules. As we will see through the example, this is an incomplete specification of the domain.

Let us suppose that the goal of producing a telescope mirror arises, and we have glass blanks and wood pieces to work with, none of them with clean or polished

---

[3] Aluminum is placed on the primary reflecting surface of a glass mirror blank by placing the blank in a vacuum chamber and passing a strong current through a thin pure aluminum strip, which then vaporizes and is deposited evenly, several molecules thick, on the glass surface to produce optical-quality mirrors. For simplicity in our discussion, these details of the aluminizing process are suppressed, as are internal details of the grinding and polishing processes. Hence, though the domain we have chosen is very much a real one, we discuss it at suitable level of abstraction and simplification.

surfaces. PRODIGY starts back-chaining by matching the goal state against the right-hand side of operators and inference rules, concluding that in order to make a telescope mirror it should first make a mirror, and then make its shape parabolic. Then seeing how to make a mirror, it concludes that it should make it reflective and then polish it (by matching IS-MIRROR against the right-hand side of the second inference rule). Let us assume for now that PRODIGY correctly selected the glass blank (it was listed first) as the starting object. Now it must apply the operator ALU-MINIZE to the glass, which requires that it be a solid and that it be clean. The first precondition is satisfied (glass is a solid), and the second one requires applying the CLEAN operator, which succeeds because any solid thing may be cleaned. These conditions enable the ALUMINIZE operator to apply successfully, and go on to the next goal in the conjunctive subgoal set: IS-POLISHED. Thus far (as shown in Figure 7–2), there have been no surprises and no learning, just locally successful performance.

However, whereas PRODIGY believed that the POLISH operator preconditions were satisfied (it believes in temporal persistence of states, such as IS-CLEAN, unless it learns otherwise), the environment states the contrary: The glass was not clean. The first learning step occurs in the attribution of this state change (the glass becoming dirty again) to one of the actions that occurred since the state IS-CLEAN was brought about. Since there was only one intervening operator invocation (ALU-MINIZE), it infers that a previously unknown consequence of this operator is ~IS-CLEAN (meaning retracting IS-CLEAN from the current state). If there had been many intermediate operators, specific experiments to perform some but not other steps would have been required to isolate the culprit operator. The operator ALUMI-NIZE is corrected, and PRODIGY tries now to achieve its goal of making a telescope mirror with the new domain knowledge.

Since the glass is dirty, the CLEAN operator is applied once more. It again attempts to POLISH, but the operator does not result in the expected state: IS-POLISHED. This means that either it is missing some knowledge (some other precondition for POLISH is required), or its existing knowledge is incorrect (IS-POLISHED is not a consequence of POLISH). Always preferring to believe its knowledge correct unless forced otherwise, it prefers to examine the former alternative. But, how can it determine what precondition could be missing?

It is time to formulate an experiment: Are there other objects on which it could attempt the POLISH operation? The only possibilities are unaluminized, dirty glass blanks and dirty wood blanks. Only glass can be polished (see the preconditions of POLISH), and all the glass blanks are identical to each other, but different from the current object in that they are both dirty and unaluminized, so it chooses a glass blank. After cleaning it, the POLISH operator succeeds, and PRODIGY must establish a reason for the operator succeeding this time, but failing earlier: The only difference is the glass not being aluminized. Thus a new precondition for POLISH is

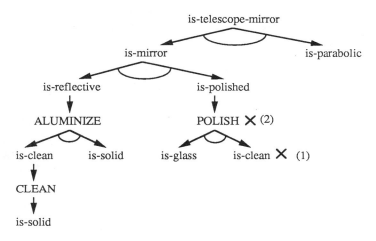

Figure 7-2: Initial planning attempts. PRODIGY learns that ~(IS-CLEAN <obj>) is a new postcondition of ALUMINIZE (from failure 1) and ~(IS-REFLECTIVE <obj>) is a new precondition of POLISH (from failure 2).

learned as a result of a simple directed experiment: ~IS-REFLECTIVE(<OBJ>), meaning that once coated with aluminum, the substrate substance (e.g. the glass) cannot be polished.

Now back to the problem at hand. In order to POLISH the glass it must un-aluminize it, but there is no known operator that removes aluminum (see Figure 7–2).[4] So the IS-POLISHED subgoal fails, and failure propagates to the IS-MIRROR subgoal, with the cause of failure being that the IS-REFLECTIVE prevented POLISH from applying. Here there is a goal interaction[5] that can be solved by reordering the interacting components:

> If the cause of failure of one conjunctive subgoal is a consequence of an operator in an earlier subgoal in the same conjunctive set, try reordering the subgoals.

That heuristic succeeds by POLISHing before ALUMINIZing. Having obtained success in one ordering and failure in another, the system tries to prove to itself that this ordering is always required, and succeeds by constructing the proof: ALUMINIZE

---

[4] If its domain knowledge were greater, it would know that grinding removes aluminum and well as changing shape and removing surface polish. In fact, this knowledge is acquired later in the example, as an unfortunate side effect of attempting to make a flat mirror into a parabolic one by grinding it.

[5] Sussman would call it a "clobber-brother-subgoal" interaction in HACKER [Sussman, 1973].

will always produce IS-REFLECTIVE which blocks POLISH, and since there are no other known ways to achieve IS-POLISHED, failure is guaranteed. The present version of PRODIGY is capable of producing such proofs in failure-driven EBL mode [Minton and Carbonell, 1987]. Thus, a goal-ordering control rule is acquired for this domain: Always choose POLISH before ALUMINIZE, if both are in the same conjunctive goal set and both apply to the same object.

PRODIGY tries again to produce a telescope mirror. The system succeeds in producing a mirror but now needs to make it parabolic. The only operator to make IS-PARABOLIC true is GRIND-CONCAVE. Its only precondition is that the object be solid, and so it applies. At this point the system checks whether it finally has achieved the top-level goal IS-TELESCOPE-MIRROR, and discovers (much to its dismay, were it capable of emotions), that all its work polishing and aluminizing has disappeared (see Figure 7–3). The only operator that applied since the mirror was polished and aluminized was GRIND-CONCAVE, and so it learns two new consequences for GRIND-CONCAVE: ~IS-POLISHED and ~IS-REFLECTIVE. No explicit experiment was needed as only one operator (GRIND-CONCAVE) could have caused those changes.

At this point PRODIGY spawns off the subgoal to make the parabolic glass back into a mirror, using all it learned earlier (POLISH before ALUMINIZE, etc.) to produce the plan more efficiently. Finally, the top level goal of IS-TELESCOPE-MIRROR is achieved (see Figure 7–4).

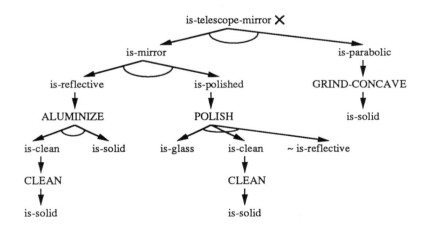

Figure 7–3:   Second planning attempt. New postconditions of GRIND-CONCAVE are learned: ~(IS-REFLECTIVE <obj>) and ~(IS-POLISHED <obj>)

Figure 7–4:   Final search tree after learning

The learning system, however, is seldom quiescent, and though global success was achieved, some states (IS-MIRROR, IS-REFLECTIVE, IS-POLISHED, IS-CLEAN) had to be achieved multiple times. Retrospective examination of the less-than-optimal solution suggests that another goal reordering heuristic applies:

> If a result of a subgoal was undone when pursuing a later subgoal in the same conjunctive set, try reordering these two subgoals.

So, PRODIGY goes off and tries the experiment of achieving IS-PARABOLIC before achieving IS-MIRROR, resulting in a more efficient plan. (In general we are measuring relative efficiency by requiring fewer total steps and no repeated subgoals. In the instance case we have a stronger condition: The leaf-node actions of the more efficient plan constitute a proper subset of the leaf-node actions of the previous less efficient plan.) A proof process is again invoked to determine whether to make it a reordering rule, concluding that it is always better to achieve IS-PARABOLIC first.

Figure 7–5 summarizes the new knowledge acquired (in italics) as a result of the problem solving episodes, experiments, and proofs. Such is the process of fleshing out incomplete domain and control knowledge through experience and focused interaction with the task environment. We present now a formal description of the method used through this example.

7.2.2 The Operator Refinement Method

In the current implementation, PRODIGY continually monitors the outside world for external compliance when operator preconditions are matched in the inter-

OPERATORS

```
(GRIND-CONCAVE                          (CLEAN
   (params (<obj>))                         (params (<obj>))
   (preconds                               (preconds
       (is-solid <obj>))                        (is-solid <obj>))
   (effects (                              (effects (
       (add (is-parabolic <obj>))               (add (is-clean <obj>)))))
       (del (is-planar <obj>))
       (del (is-reflective <obj>))
       (del (is-polished <obj>)))))
```

```
(POLISH                                  (ALUMINIZE
   (params (<obj>))                         (params (<obj>))
   (preconds                               (preconds
       (and (is-clean <obj>)                    (and (is-clean <obj>)
            (is-glass <obj>))                        (is-solid <obj>)))
       (~ (is-reflective <obj>))))     (effects (
   (effects (                                   (add (is-reflective <obj>))
       (add (is-polished <obj>)))))             (del (is-clean <obj>)))))
```

INFERENCE RULES

```
(IS-TELESCOPE-MIRROR                     (IS-MIRROR
   (params (<obj>))                         (params (<obj>))
   (preconds                               (preconds
       (and (is-mirror <obj>)                   (and (is-reflective <obj>)
            (is-parabolic <obj>)))                   (is-polished <obj>)))
   (effects (                              (effects (
       (add (is-telescope-mirror <obj>)))))     (add (is-mirror <obj>)))))
```

LEARNED CONTROL RULES

Select IS-POLISHED(<obj>) before IS-REFLECTIVE(<obj>) if both are present in the same conjunctive subgoal set.

Select IS-PARABOLIC(<obj>) before IS-MIRROR(<obj>) if both are present in the same conjunctive subgoal set.

Figure 7–5:   Complete domain theory after experimentation. Items in italics denote new knowledge acquired through the operator refinement method.

nal state, and when new effects (adds and deletes) are asserted upon operator application. In doing this, for each precondition or effect P we obtain a value of the predicate **Consistent(World, State, P)** as follows:

Consistent(World, State, P)
if P is satisfied in both the internal state and the external world
    or P is not satisfied in either the internal state or external world
then True
else False

The predicate **Consistent** is false whenever **P** is satisfied in either **world** or **state** but not in the other, signifying a discrepancy between internal belief and external reality.

PRODIGY applies an operator **O** only after establishing that all its preconditions are satisfied in the internal state. If these are verified in the external world, planning proceeds normally, but if not, it attempts to extend the domain theory as follows:

For every operator O selected

for every precondition P of operator O
  if Consistent(World, State, P)
    then continue planning

if NOT(Consistent(World, State, P))
  then one of the operators applied
  after P was established has a
    previously unknown postcondition.

Case 1
  1. *Select candidate operators.* The candidate set consists of all operators applied since the consistency of P was last checked.
  2. *Identify responsible operator.* Formulate experiments by selecting an operator in a binary search over the ordered candidate set, applying it and then checking P in the World. If as result of an experiment with operator O_E, P is unexpectedly changed in the World, then O_E is E incompletely specified.
  3. *Add P as a new postcondition of operator O_E.*

This case corresponds to the first discrepancy discussed in our example: The planner's internal state contained the belief that the glass was clean, while in reality it was not. PRODIGY learned that ALUMINIZE should delete the literal IS-CLEAN from the internal state.

Whenever an operator **O** is applied, PRODIGY verifies that its postconditions have been realized in the external world. If not, the domain theory is refined as follows:

for every postcondition P of operator O
  if Consistent(World, State, P)
  then continue planning

if NOT(Consistent(World, State, P))
  then

    if ∃ Q precondition of O such that NOT(Consistent(World, State, Q))
      then one of the operators applied after Q was established
      should have had a postcondition affecting Q.

Case 2
1. *Select candidate operators.* The candidate set consists of all operators applied since the consistency of Q was last checked.
2. *Identify responsible operators.* Formulate experiments by selecting an operator. Each experiment will consist of applying one of the operators and checking Q in the World. If as a result of an experiment with operator O_E Q is unexpectedly changed in the World, O_E is incompletely specified.
3. *Add Q as a new postcondition of operator O_E.*

> **if $\forall$ preconditions Q of O Consistent(World, State, Q)**
> **then a precondition of operator O might be missing.**

Case 3
1. *Select candidate preconditions.* The candidate set $\Delta(S_{old}, S_{current})$ is formed by calculating all the differences between the most similar earlier state in the previous problem-solving history in which O was applied successfully S_{old} and the current state $S_{current}$ (an unsuccessful application of O).
2. *Identify missing precondition.* Formulate experiments using a binary search over $\Delta(S_{old}, S_{current})$ by generating new state $S_{experiment}$ which contains half of the differences between S_{old} and $S_{current}$ and determining whether O produces the desired effect. If so, continue the binary search over that half of $\Delta(S_{old}, S_{current})$, and if not, over the other half until only one condition R is left in the Δ set.
3. *Add R as a new precondition of operator O.*

Case 2 corresponds to the last situation described in our example. After applying GRIND-CONCAVE the planner assumed that the glass was still a mirror (i.e., that it was still REFLECTIVE and POLISHED). Since the external world did not confirm this expectation, the planner acquired the previously unknown consequences of the grinding operator.

Case 3 also occurred in our example. When the system applied the operator POLISH, its effects were not realized in the external world. The method hypothesizes that a precondition must be missing from the operator. Through experimentation, the new precondition is found, and the hypothesis is confirmed.

Although in the example all the learned preconditions are negated predicates (absence tests) and the new consequences are deletions from the current state, the same basic process applies to acquiring nonnegated preconditions and consequences that add assertions to the state.

In addition the system used the following heuristics for cases of goal interaction and plan optimization:

- If the cause of failure of one conjunctive subgoal is a consequence of an operator in an earlier subgoal in the same conjunctive set, try reordering the subgoals.
- If a result of a subgoal was undone when pursuing a later subgoal in the same conjunctive set, try reordering these two subgoals.

The method for acquiring the missing pre- and postconditions of operators are summarized in Table 7–1 below. In essence, plan execution failures trigger the experimentation and replanning process. Thus, each method is indexed by the failure condition to which it applies, encoded as differences between expected and observed outcomes. The first two cases are the focus of the current chapter. A forthcoming paper [Carbonell, *et al.*, forthcoming] expands the method to address the last case on the table.

Table 7–1

EXPECTED OUTCOME	OBSERVED BEHAVIOR	RECOVERY STRATEGY	LEARNING METHOD (EXPERIMENT GENERATOR)
all the known preconditions satisfied earlier	at least one precondition is violated at present	plan to achieve the missing precondition	binary search on operator sequence from establishment of precondition to present, adding negated precondition as postcondition of the culprit operator
all the known preconditions satisfied earlier	all the known preconditions satisfied but operator fails to apply; postconditions remain undone	attempt to plan without this operator, or failing that, suspend plan till the experiment is complete	compare present failure to the last time operator applied successfully, generating in a binary search intermediate world descriptions to identify the necessary part of the state, adding it to the operator preconditions
operator applies and all the postconditions are satisfied	at least one postcondition fails to be satisfied	if the unmet postcondition is incidental ignore it, but if it is a goal state try different operator(s)	compare to last time all postconditions were met, perform binary search on world state to determine necessary part to achieve all postconditions - then replace operator with two new ones: one with the new precondition and all the postconditions, the other with the new precondition negated and without the postcondition in question

Operator refinement is always applied in an active planning context: There is a goal, a state, and a (partially) formulated plan. We are not modeling idle curiosity. Thus, we characterize our work as purposeful and task-driven experimentation. Experiments are always directed at overcoming a current impasse in the planning processes.

7.3 RELATED WORK

Experimentation techniques have been used in recent work on various areas of machine learning, including learning from examples [Gross, 1985] and discovery programs [Langley, et al., 1987; Nordhaussen and Langley, 1989]. Kulkarni and Simon [Kulkarni, 1988; Kulkarni and Simon, 1989] developed a system called KEKADA that simulates the reasoning process followed by scientists when they encounter surprising phenomena. In essence, they developed a set of heuristics to propose experiments to confirm, magnify, and elaborate the extent of a previously unexpected observation.

In similar spirit to the work reported here, Rajamoney focused on on the problem of refining incorrect theories of qualitative physics in the ADEPT system [Rajamoney, 1986]. When a contradiction arises in the process of explaining an observation, ADEPT proposes hypotheses, and experimentation is used to confirm or reject a single hypothesis at a time. Several kinds of experiments are proposed to test these hypotheses. In COAST [Rajamoney, 1988], experimentation-based hypothesis refutation is also used to revise an incorrect theory. Experiments are designed using the predictions made by the current hypothesized theory, and their results are used to reject possible theories. Rajamoney proposes four dimensions to evaluate the design of experiments: efficacy, efficiency, tolerance in the presence of unavailable data, and feasibility.

In contrast with these systems, our work is focused on learning by experimentation to improve the domain theory of a planning system, and more specifically to overcome impasses when external reality differs from planning expectations. The LIVE system, by Shen and Simon [Shen, 1989; Shen and Simon, 1989] shares some of our objectives. LIVE acquires new operators and refines old ones by interacting with the environment in order to formulate indirectly observable features of objects in the domain and uses these features in creating new preconditions to split overgeneral operators. This method differs from our work in several ways. First, in order to gather information about the world, LIVE checks every instantiated predicate that is known to the system. In our system, the only predicates that are attended to in the external world are those that the planner checks or changes in the internal state. We consider this a more practical approach to larger domains. Second, the definition of new features causes a real overload for the system, since it must find out the value of every new feature for every object in order to apply its operators. Nevertheless, this capability for defining new features gives the system the ability to acquire a more powerful language to express the domain knowledge. Finally, LIVE keeps no history of its past behavior, retaining only the current set of operators, objects and features.

There is a significant amount of work on recovery from planning failures, both in the context of case-based reasoning and of reactive systems ([Hammmond, 1984; Schoppers, 1987; Georgeff and Lansky, 1987; Kaelbling, 1986], and others). However our work is more focused on the techniques for learning from these failures rather than the process of plan recovery itself.

There are a number of systems that use different techniques to learn in the context of planning and interacting with an external environment. Robo-SOAR [Laird, et al., 1989] is a system implemented in SOAR that learns control knowledge from outside guidance. The Theo-Agent [Blythe and Mitchell, 1989] is an autonomous robot that starts out building plans to solve new problems and learns rules that allow it to have a reactive behavior.

7.4 DISCUSSION AND FURTHER WORK

The operators in the domains that we have used to test our methods are expressed using only conjunction and negation. Further work should expand these techniques to learn more complex expressions of the preconditions of operators. The method was also described assuming that only one condition is acquired in each learning episode. To increase efficiency, we are currently extending it to consider cases where the experimentation phase can find several unknown preconditions or postconditions.

More comprehensive learning could occur by attempting to generalize the newly acquired preconditions and consequences to other sibling operators in the operator hierarchy (see Figure 7–6). For instance, the newly learned consequences of destroying a polished or aluminized surface apply not just to GRIND-CONCAVE, but to any GRIND operation (such as GRIND-CONVEX, GRIND-PLANAR). However, these consequences do not apply to other RESHAPE operations such as BEND, COMPRESS, etc. The process to determine the appropriate level of generalization again requires experimentation (or asking focused questions to a human expert). For instance, observing the consequences of GRIND-PLANAR on a previously aluminized mirror, provides evidence that all GRINDs behave alike with respect to destroying surface attributes, and observing the consequences of bending a polished reflective glass tube without adverse effects on surface attributes prevents generalization above GRIND.

In addition to proposing experiments to guide generalization, we are starting to investigate trade-offs between experimentation and resource consumption (minimizing the latter, while maximizing the information gained from the former), and trade-offs between experimentation and other goals such as safety of the robot or person

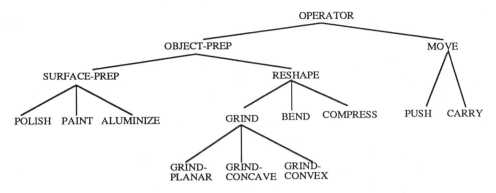

Figure 7–6:   Fragment of operator "isa" hierarchy

conducting the experiment. The entire planning context can be used to formulate and guide the experiment, in order to focus on the most direct and economical way of inferring the missing knowledge. Thus, experiment formulation, once invoked with the appropriate constraints, becomes itself a metaproblem amenable to all the methods in the general purpose planner. The EBL method (or perhaps a similarity-based method—SBL) may then be invoked to retain not just the result of the instance experiment, but its provably correct generalization (or empirically appropriate one if SBL is used).

The experimentation methods discussed here focused only on operator refinement (both preconditions and consequences), but not on acquiring new operators, new features of the state or domain, or new meta-level control structures. In a forthcoming paper [Carbonell, *et al.*, forthcoming], we present other techniques for learning by experimentation in the context of problem solving. That paper describes how PRODIGY can acquire knowledge about the state, such as values of attributes not known when needed to expand the current plan. Another method allows the system to learn multiple more specific versions of overgeneral operators that failed to predict outcomes consistently.

The methods described here and in [Carbonell, *et al.*, forthcoming] apply when PRODIGY is given a correct but incomplete domain theory, and learning is always incremental: The initial knowledge is monotonically augmented. This metaprinciple of *cognitive inertia* dictates that monotonic changes (adding new information) be preferred over nonmonotonic ones (changing previous information), so long as no overt inconsistencies are discovered. Further work should address the problem of modifying an incorrect domain theory.

In order to avoid the complexities of full interleaving of planning and execution, we constructed an expository domain where environmental feedback can be provided by a domain-knowledgeable user (that answers only yes-or-no questions about the state of the external environment), and one where the search space is of manageable size (e.g., there are no difficult decision points with multiple applicable operators). Moreover, we assume environmental feedback is correct and deterministic. Clearly, not every domain permits such a limited manipulation and interchange of information as the one used to describe the *operator refinement method*. In other work on experimentation we connected PRODIGY to a full 3D Newtonian kinematics robotic simulator [Carbonell and Hood, 1986; Carbonell, *et al.*, 1989] for more realistic environmental feedback [Carbonell, *et al.*, forthcoming]. The MAX system (a PRODIGY progeny) exhibits a richer communication channel [Knokka, 1990]. Finally, we assume that the environment is only affected by the actions of our system. There are no environmental changes unless PRODIGY produces them, although of course PRODIGY is not always aware of all the changes that each of its actions may produce.

Our ultimate aim is to develop a set of general techniques for an AI system to acquire knowledge of its task domain systematically under its own initiative, starting from a partial domain theory and little if any *a priori* control knowledge. The impact of this work should be felt in robotic and other autonomous planning domains, as well as in expert systems that must deal with a potentially changing environment of which they cannot possibly have complete and accurate knowledge beforehand. The *operator refinement method* is but the first step in this long-term endeavor.

ACKNOWLEDGMENTS

This research was sponsored in part by the Defense Advanced Research Projects Agency (DOD), ARPA order No. 4976, monitored by the Air Force Avionics Laboratory under contract F33615-84-K-1520, in part by the Office of Naval Research under contract N00014-84-K-0345, and in part by a gift from the Hughes Corporation. The views and conclusions contained in this document are those of the authors and should not be interpreted as representing the official policies, either expressed or implied, of DARPA, AFOSR, ONR, or the U.S. government. The authors would like to acknowledge other past and present members of the PRODIGY project at CMU: Daniel Borrajo, Oren Etzioni, Robert Joseph, Craig Knoblock, Dan Kuokka, Steve Minton, Henrik Nordin, Alicia Perez, Santiago Rementeria, Hiroshi Tsuji, and Manuela Veloso, and the help of Dan Kahn, Michael Miller, and Ellen Riloff in implementing the PRODIGY system. Dan Kuokka and Raul Valdes-Perez provided some very helpful criticisms of an earlier draft of this chapter.

APPENDIX I   THE PRODIGY ARCHITECTURE

PRODIGY is a general problem solver combined with several learning modules. The PRODIGY architecture, in fact, was designed both as a unified testbed for different learning methods and as a general architecture to solve interesting problems in complex task domains. Let us now focus on the architecture itself, as diagrammed in Figure 7–7.

The operator-based problem solver produces a complete search tree, encapsulating all decisions—right ones and wrong ones—as well as the final solution. This information is used by each learning component in different ways. In addition to the central problem solver,[6] PRODIGY has the following learning components:

- A user-interface that can participate in an apprentice-like dialogue, enabling the user to evaluate and guide the system's problem solving and learning. The interface is graphic based and tied directly to the problem solver, so that it can accept advice as it is solving a problem (i.e., coaching) or replay and analyze earlier solution attempts, while refining the factual or control knowledge.

- An explanation-based learning facility [Minton, 1988] for acquiring control rules from a problem-solving trace, as indicated in Figure 7–7. Explanations are constructed from an axiomatized theory describing both the domain and relevant aspects of the problem solver's architecture. Then the resulting descriptions are expressed in control rule form, and control rules whose utility in search reduction outweighs their application overhead are retained.

- A method for learning control rules by analyzing PRODIGY's domain descriptions prior to problem solving. This investigation has culminated in the STATIC program [Etzioni, 1990], which produces control rules without utilizing any training examples. STATIC matches EBL's performance on some domains but exhibits a learning rate one to two orders of magnitude faster. However, not all problem spaces permit purely static learning, requiring EBL to learn control rules dynamically.

- A derivational analogy engine [Carbonell and Veloso, 1988; Veloso and Carbonell, 1989] that is able to replay entire solutions to similar past problems, calling the problem solver recursively to reduce any new subgoals brought about by known differences between the old and new problems. As indicated in

---

[6] The problem solver is an advanced operator-based planner that includes a simple reason-maintenance system and allows operators to have conditional effects. The problem solver's search (means-ends analysis) is guided by explicit domain-independent and domain-specific control rules. All of PRODIGY's learning modules share the same general problem solver and the same knowledge representation language, PDL.

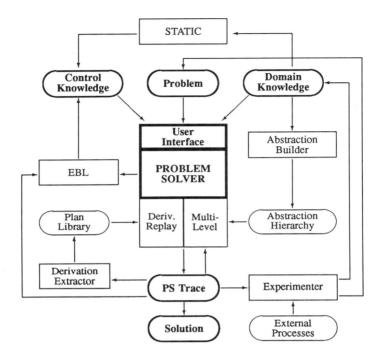

Figure 7–7: The PRODIGY architecture: multiple learning modules unified by a common representation language and a shared general problem solver.

Figure 7–7, both analogy and EBL are independent mechanisms to acquire domain-specific control knowledge. They coexist in PRODIGY and should be more tightly coupled than in the present architecture.

- A multilevel abstraction planning capability [Knoblock, 1989]. First, the axiomatized domain knowledge is divided into multiple abstraction layers based on an in-depth analysis of the domain. Then, during problem solving, PRODIGY proceeds to build abstract solutions and refine them by adding back details from the domain, solving new subgoals as they arise. This method is orthogonal to analogy and EBL, in that both can apply at each level of abstraction.

- A learning-by-experimentation module for refining domain knowledge that is incompletely or incorrectly specified (as described in the body of this chapter). Experimentation is triggered when plan execution monitoring detects a divergence between internal expectations and external expectations. As indicated in

Figure 7–7, the main focus of experimentation is to refine the factual domain knowledge, rather than the control knowledge.

The problem solver and EBL component of PRODIGY have been fully implemented and tested on several task domains including an augmented version of the STRIPS domain, a machine shop scheduling domain, and a robotics domain. The abstraction learning method and the static control rule learner are virtually complete and proven effective. The other learning components, while successfully prototyped, are at various stages of development and implementation. A complete nonlinear planner has been developed [Veloso, 1989] as a more general, alternative problem-solving engine. A more complete description of PRODIGY's architecture can be found in [Minton, *et al.*, 1989b].

References

Blythe, J. and Mitchell, T.M. 1989. On Becoming Reactive. *Proc. of the Sixth International Workshop on Machine Learning*, Ithaca, New York. Morgan Kaufmann, San Mateo, CA.

Carbonell, J.G. 1983. Learning by Analogy: Formulating and Generalizing Plans from Past Experience. In R.S. Michalski, J.G. Carbonell and T.M. Mitchell (editors), *Machine Learning, An Artificial Intelligence Approach*. Morgan Kaufmann, San Mateo, CA.

Carbonell, J.G. and Hood, G. 1986. The World Modelers Project: Learning in a Reactive Environment. In R.S. Michalski, J.G. Carbonell and T.M. Mitchell (editors), *Machine Learning: A Guide to Current Research*, pp. 29–34. Kluwer Academic Press.

Carbonell, J.G. and Veloso, M.M. 1988. Integrating Derivational Analogy into a General Problem-Solving Architecture. *Proc. of the First Workshop on Case-Based Reasoning*, Tampa, FL. Morgan Kaufmann, San Mateo, CA.

Carbonell, J., Gross, K., Hood, G., Shell, P., and Tallis, H. 1989. *The World Modeling System User Guide*. Technical Report, Department of Computer Science, Carnegie Mellon University, Pittsburgh, PA. Internal document.

Carbonell, J.G., Knoblock, C.A., and Minton, S. 1990. PRODIGY: An Integrated Architecture for Planning and Learning. In Kurt VanLehn (editor), *Architectures for Intelligence*. Erlbaum, Hillsdale, NJ.

Carbonell, J.G., Gil, Y., and Rementeria, S. Forthcoming. *Experimentation in PRODIGY: Acquiring Domain and State Knowledge*. Technical Report, School of Computer Science, Carnegie Mellon University, Pittsburgh, PA.

Carbonell, J.G. 1986. Derivational Analogy: A Theory of Reconstructive Problem Solving and Expertise Acquisition. In R.S. Michalski, J.G. Carbonell and T.M. Mitchell (editors), *Machine Learning, An Artificial Intelligence Approach, Volume II*. Morgan Kaufmann, San Mateo, CA.

Cheng, P.W. and Carbonell, J.G. 1986. Inducing Iterative Rules from Experience: The FERMI Experiment. In *Proc. of the Fifth National Conference on Artificial Intelligence*, Philadelphia, PA.

DeJong, G.F. and Mooney, R. 1986. Explanation-Based Learning: An Alternative View. *Machine Learning* 1(2):145–176.

Etzioni, O. 1990. *A Structural Theory of Search Control*. PhD Thesis, School of Computer Science, Carnegie Mellon University, Pittsburgh, PA. In preparation.

Fikes, R.E. and Nilsson, N.J. 1971. STRIPS: A New Approach to the Application of Theorem Proving to Problem Solving. *Artificial Intelligence* 2:189–208.

Georgeff, M.P. and Lansky, A.L. 1987. Reactive Reasoning and Planning. *Proc. of the Sixth National Conference on Artificial Intelligence*, Seattle, WA.

Gross, K.P. 1988. Incremental Multiple Concept Learning Using Experiments. *Proc. of the Fifth International Conference on Machine Learning*, Ann Arbor, MI.

Hammond, K. 1989. *Case-based Planning: Viewing Planning as a Memory Task*. Academic Press.

Joseph, R.L. 1989. Graphical Knowledge Acquisition. *Proceedings of the 4th Workshop on Knowledge Acquisition for Knowledge-Based Systems*, Banff, Canada.

Kaelbling, L. 1986. *An Architecture for Intelligent Reactive Systems*. Technical Report Technical Note 400, Artificial Intelligence Center, SRI International, Menlo Park, CA.

Knoblock, C.A. 1989. Learning Hierarchies of Abstraction Spaces. *Proc. of the Sixth International Workshop on Machine Learning*, Ithaca, NY, June 1989. Morgan Kaufmann, San Mateo, CA.

Kulkarni, D.S. 1988. *The Process of Scientific Research: The Strategy of Experimentation*. PhD Thesis, School of Computer Science, Carnegie Mellon University, Pittsburgh, PA.

Kulkarni, D. and Simon, H.A. 1989. The Role of Experimentation in Scientific Theory Revision. *Proc. of the Sixth International Workshop on Machine Learning*, Ithaca, New York. Morgan Kaufmann, San Mateo, CA.

Kuokka, D.R. 1990. *The Deliberate Integration of Planning, Execution and Learning*. PhD Thesis, School of Computer Science, Carnegie Mellon University, Pittsburgh, PA, Forthcoming.

Laird. J.E., Rosenbloom, P.S., and Newell, A. 1986. Chunking in SOAR: The Anatomy of a General Learning Mechanism. *Machine Learning* 1(1):11–46.

Laird, J.E., Yager, E.S., and Tuck, C.M. 1989. Learning in Tele-autonomous Systems using SOAR. *Proc. of the NASA Conference on Space Telerobotics*. Pasadena, CA.

Langley, P., Simon, H.A., Bradshaw, G.L., and Zytkow, J.M. 1987. *Scientific Discovery: Computational Explorations of the Creative Processes*. MIT Press.

Michalski, R.S., Carbonell, J.G., and Mitchell, T.M. (Eds). 1983. *Machine Learning, An Artificial Intelligence Approach*. Morgan Kaufmann, San Mateo, CA.

Michalski, R.S., Carbonell, J.G., and Mitchell, T.M. (Eds). 1986. *Machine Learning, An Artificial Intelligence Approach, Volume II*. Morgan Kaufmann, San Mateo, CA.

Minton, S. and Carbonell, J.G. 1987. Strategies for Learning Search Control Rules: An Explanation-Based Approach. *Proc. of the Tenth International Joint Conference on Artificial Intelligence*, Milan, Italy. Morgan Kaufmann, San Mateo, CA.

Minton, S., Carbonell, J.G., Knoblock, C.A., Kuokka, D.R., Etzioni, O., and Gil, Y. 1989. Explanation-Based Learning: A Problem-Solving Perspective. *Artificial Intelligence* 40(1–3):63–118.

Minton, S., Knoblock, C.A., Kuokka, D.R., Gil, Y., Joseph, R.L., Carbonell, J.G. 1989. *PRODIGY 2.0: The Manual and Tutorial*. Technical Report CMU-CS-89-146, School of Computer Science, Carnegie Mellon University, Pittsburgh, PA.

Minton, S., Carbonell, J.G., Etzioni, O, Knoblock, C.A., Kuokka, D.R. 1987. Acquiring Effective Search Control Rules: Explanation-Based Learning in the PRODIGY System. *Proc. of the Fourth International Workshop on Machine Learning*, Irvine, CA. Morgan Kaufmann, San Mateo, CA.

Minton, S. 1988. *Learning Search Control Knowledge: An Explanation-based Approach*. Kluwer Academic Publishers, Boston, Massachusetts. Limited availability as Carnegie Mellon CS Tech. Report CMU-CS-88-133.

Mitchell, T.M., Keller, R.M. and Kedar-Cabelli, S.T. 1986. Explanation-Based Generalization: A Unifying View. *Machine Learning* 1(1).

Mitchell, T.M., Utgoff, P.E. and Banerji, R.B. 1983. Learning by Experimentation: Acquiring and Refining Problem-Solving Heuristics. In R.S. Michalski, J.G. Carbonell and T.M. Mitchell (editors), *Machine Learning, An Artificial Intelligence Approach.* Morgan Kaufmann, San Mateo, CA.

Nordhaussen, B. and Langley, P. 1989. *An Integrated Approach to Empirical Discovery.* Technical Report 89–20, Department of Information and Computer Science, University of California, Irvine, CA.

Rajamoney, S. 1986. *Automated Design of Experiments for Refining Theories.* M.S. thesis, Department of Computer Science, University of Illinois, Urbana, IL.

Rajamoney, S.A. 1988. *Explanation-Based Theory Revision: An Approach to the Problems of Incomplete and Incorrect Theories.* PhD Thesis, University of Illinois at Urbana-Champaign.

Schoppers, M.J. 1987. Universal Plans for Reactive Robots in Unpredictable Environments. *Proc. of the Tenth International Joint Conference on Artificial Intelligence*, Milan, Italy. Morgan Kaufmann, San Mateo, CA.

Shen, W.M. 1989. *Learning from the Environment Based on Percepts and Actions.* PhD Thesis, School of Computer Science, Carnegie Mellon University, Pittsburgh, PA.

Shen, W.M. and Simon, H.A. 1989. Rule Creation and Rule Learning through Environmental Exploration. *Proc. of the Eleventh International Joint Conference on Artificial Intelligence*, Detroit, Michigan. Morgan Kaufmann, San Mateo, CA.

Sussman, G. J. 1973. *A Computational Model of Skill Acquisition.* PhD Thesis, Massachusetts Institute of Technology.

Veloso, M.M. 1989. *Nonlinear Problem Solving Using Intelligent Casual Commitment.* Technical Report, School of Computer Science, Carnegie Mellon University, Pittsburgh, PA.

Veloso, M.M. and Carbonell, J.G. 1989. Learning Analogies by Analogy—The Closed Loop of Memory Organization and Problem Solving. *Proc. of the Second Workshop on Case-Based Reasoning*, Pensacola, FL, May 1989. Morgan Kaufmann, San Mateo, CA.

8

LEARNING FAULT
DIAGNOSIS HEURISTICS
FROM DEVICE DESCRIPTIONS

Michael J. Pazzani
(University of California, Irvine)

Abstract

This chapter describes a technique for the construction of the knowledge base of a diagnostic expert system. Diagnosis heuristics (i.e., efficient rules that encode empirical associations between atypical device behavior and device failures) are learned from information implicit in device models. This approach is desirable since less effort is required to obtain information about device functionality and connectivity to define device models than to encode and debug diagnosis heuristics provided by a domain expert. This approach to learning integrates failure-driven learning and explanation-based learning.

8.1 INTRODUCTION

This chapter describes an approach to learning efficient heuristics for diagnosing faults in complex systems. This technique is applicable to the learning heuristics for the identification of failures of components of large systems whose status is monitored for unusual or atypical features, such as a power plant or a satellite. When one or more atypical features are detected, a diagnosis process seeks to find an explanation for the atypical features. This explanation typically involves isolating the cause of the atypical features to the failure of a component. Occasionally, the explanation may be that system is in a normal but unusual mode.[1] The focus of our investigation is the attitude control system of the DSCS-III satellite.[2] The system is implemented in a combination of LISP and PROLOG.

Two different approaches have been used for fault diagnosis. In one approach [Davis, *et al.*, 1982B; Genesereth, *et al.*, 1981; Scarl, *et al.*, 1985], the observed functionality of devices are compared to their predicted functionality, which is specified by a quantitative or qualitative model of the device [de Kleer and Brown, 1984; Kuipers, 1984; Forbus, 1984]. For a large system whose status is changing rapidly, comparing observed to predicted functionality can be costly. The alternative approach [Shortliffe, 1976; Nelson, 1982; Wagner, 1983] encodes empirical associations between unusual behavior and faulty components as heuristic rules. This approach requires extensive debugging of the knowledge base to identify the precise conditions that indicate a particular fault is present. In previous work, [Pazzani and Brindle, 1985, 1986] we have described the Attitude Control Expert System (ACES) in which these two approaches are integrated. Heuristics examine the atypical features and hypothesize potential faults. Device models confirm or deny hypothesized faults. Thus, heuristics focus diagnosis by determining which device in a large system might be at fault. Device models determine if that device is indeed responsible for the atypical features.

In this chapter, we address the problem of revising the fault diagnosis heuristics when they hypothesize a fault that is later denied. This occurs when all of the possible exceptions to a heuristic are not explicitly stated. When a fault is proposed, and later denied by device models, the reasons for this hypothesis failure are noted; and the heuristic that suggested the fault is revised so that the hypothesis will not be proposed in future similar cases. This is a kind of failure-driven learning [Schank, 1982] that enables a diagnostic expert system to start with heuristics that indicate some of the signs (or symptoms) of a failure. As the expert system solves problems, the heuristics are revised to determine what part of the device model should be consulted to distinguish one fault from another fault with similar features. This approach is desirable for several reasons:

- Device models are a natural way of expressing the functionality of a component. However, they are not the most natural or efficient representation for diagnosis [Sembugamoorthy and Chandrasekaran, 1985].
- Determining some of the signs of a fault (i.e., the initial diagnostic heuristics) is a relatively easy task. Typically, the initial diagnosis heuristics are definitional.

---

[1] It is often the case that the monitor is designed to have a tolerable number of false alarms, rather than miss an actual failure.

[2] The attitude control system is responsible for detecting and correcting deviations from the desired orientation of the satellite.

For example, ACES starts with a heuristic that states that if a tachometer is reading 0, then it is faulty. Later this heuristic is revised to include conditions to distinguish a fault in a tachometer from a fault in the component measured by the tachometer.

The following example illustrates failure-driven learning of diagnosis heuristics. I once noticed that the left taillight of my car was not working. I knew of two reasons that a taillight could be out, which might be expressed as the following two heuristics in an expert system:

```
IF a taillight is not working
THEN the fuse of the taillight's circuit is blown.

IF a taillight is not working,
THEN the bulb of the taillight is burned out.
```

I was able to rule out a blown fuse. If the fuse were blown, then all of the lights on the same fuse would be out. Consulting my owner's manual, I discovered that the right-front parking light would also be out if the fuse were blown. The first fault diagnosis heuristic could be modified to prevent considering this hypothesis in the future:

```
IF a taillight is not working
AND the opposite front parking light is not working
THEN the fuse of the taillight's circuit is blown.
```

One way to view this type of learning is as an extension of dependency-directed backtracking [Stallman and Sussman, 1977]. In dependency-directed backtracking, when a hypothesis failure occurs, the search tree of the current problem is pruned by removing those states that would lead to failure for the same reason. In failure-driven learning, the reason for hypothesis failure is recorded, so that the search tree of future similar problems does not include states that would lead to failure for the same reason.

In the remainder of this chapter, we first discuss some related work in machine learning on improving performance with experience. Next, we describe our approach to learning efficient diagnosis heuristics. Finally, we present an example of the approach applied to the attitude control system of DSCS-III.

8.2 PREVIOUS WORK

8.2.1 R1-Soar

R1-Soar [Rosenbloom, *et al.*, 1985] is an attempt to duplicate the performance of R1 [McDermott, 1982], an expert system that configures computers, by learning configuration strategies. R1-Soar utilizes a learning mechanism called *chunking* as implemented in Soar [Laird, *et al.*, 1984]. R1-Soar starts with an initial *base* representation, which indicates the goal to be achieved and operators that can be used to achieve the goal state. In Soar, all basic operations are represented as subgoals. For example, subgoals will be spawned to select among applicable operators, to test if a goal has been achieved, and to find the result of applying an operator to a state. With the base representation and subgoaling strategy, R1-Soar can search for the solution to any configuration problem, but this search may be expensive. In Soar, efficiency is achieved by rules that guide the search. These rules are automatically acquired by creating chunks of knowledge implicit in the base representation. Chunking is a technique for recording the solution of a subgoal so that the chunk can substitute for the subgoal processing the next time the same subgoal is encountered. For example, chunking a goal to select among operators will result in a chunk that selects the proper operator in that state. Chunking is accomplished by creating a new rule. The test of the rule is found by noting which facts were accessed to solve the subgoal. The action of the rule is computed by noting which facts were added to memory during the processing of the subgoal that are needed by the parent goal.

R1-Soar presents an interesting approach to learning, which we share. Expert systems can be viewed as knowledge-intensive programs, as opposed to domain-independent, general purpose, problem-solving programs. Much work is required to build and debug the knowledge base of an expert system. In contrast, less effort is required to define the general knowledge needed by a problem solver, but the general problem solver is bound to be more inefficient since it must search for a solution. A primary difference between R1-Soar and our work is the mechanism that creates a knowledge-intensive expert system from a general problem solver. R1-Soar uses a general technique that records the solution to every subgoal. One question unanswered by R1-Soar is when learning is beneficial. Clearly, it is not valuable to remember that on March 4, 1984 at 10:35 the momentum was within normal bounds. Even though it may take 50 primitive operations to recalculate this fact, it is not worth learning since it will not be used again. Our more specific approach only learns one thing: how to avoid making the same mistake. An additional problem with Soar is that it can overgeneralize. For example, R1-Soar learned that a module could not be put in any backplane, where it should have learned that the module could not be put in a particular backplane. Overgeneralization is a serious problem that must be addressed before Soar can be used in a practical application.

8.2.2 Failure-driven Learning

Schank [1982] has proposed failure-driven learning as the mechanism by which a person's memory of events and generalized events evolves with experience. A person's memory provides expectations for understanding natural language understanding and inferring other's plans and goals. When a new experience fails to conform to these expectations, it is stored in memory along with the explanation for the failure to prevent the generation to the erroneous expectation in the future. In

Schank's theory, the reason for the expectation failure can be a *motivational explanation* (i.e., an actor is pursuing a different goal than inferred) or an *error explanation* (i.e., an actor was not able to accomplish his goal which was inferred correctly). The correction to memory so that the failure does not occur again is to remember the event causing the failure indexed by the explanation for the failure. In future similar situations, this event will be the source of expectations rather than the generalized event whose expectations were incorrect. In failure-driven learning as applied to fault diagnosis, the failures are of fault hypotheses rather than expectations. The reason for failure is identified as some aspect of the device's function that disagrees with the fault hypothesis. The correction is to modify the heuristic rule that proposed the incorrect hypothesis to check that aspect of the device before proposing the fault.

8.2.3 Explanation-based Learning

Failure-driven learning dictates two important facets of learning: *when* to learn (when a hypothesis failure occurs) and *what* to learn (features that distinguish a fault in one component from faults in other components). What is not specified is *how* to learn. For example, a learning system could learn to distinguish a faulty tachometer from failures with similar features by correlation over a number of examples (e.g., [Michie, 1983; Mitchell, 1982; Vere, 1975]). Device models (or a teacher) could classify a large number of examples as positive or negative examples of broken tachometers. For example, the heuristic that suggests broken tachometers could be revised to include a description of those combinations of features that are present in a number of examples when a tachometer is faulty, but not present when the tachometer is working properly.

In contrast, ACES learns how to avoid a hypothesis failure after just one example. The conditions that need to be tested to avoid a hypothesis failure are exactly those features of the one example that were needed by the device models to deny the hypothesis. The device models serve a dual role here. First, they identify when to learn by denying a hypothesis. More importantly, they provide an explanation for the hypothesis failure. The device models indicate which features would have been needed to be present (or absent) to confirm the hypothesis. This deductive approach to learning is called *explanation-based learning* [DeJong, 1983; Minton, 1984; Mitchell, *et al.*, 1986]. Explanation-based learning improves the performance of ACES by creating fault diagnosis heuristics that explicate information implicit in the device models.

8.3 FAILURE-DRIVEN LEARNING OF FAULT DIAGNOSIS HEURISTICS

In this section, we describe our approach to learning fault diagnosis heuristics by finding symptoms of faults implicit in device models. First, let us clarify what we mean by a device model. Following Chandrasekaran [Sembugamoorthy and Chandrasekaran, 1985], we represent the following aspects of a device:

- *Structure:* Specifies the connectivity of a device.
- *Functionality:* Specifies the output of a device as a function of its inputs (and possibly state information).

It is not important to the expert system or the learning module that the functionality be expressed quantitatively or qualitatively. The important part is that, given the observed inputs of a device, the device model can make a prediction about the output. The predicted value of the output may be compared to the observed value or may be treated as an input to another device.

8.3.1 Reasons for Hypothesis Failure

We have identified three different reasons for failing to confirm a hypothesis. For each reason we have implemented a correction strategy.

- *Hypothesized Fault—Inconsistent Prediction:* The hypothesized failure is inconsistent with observed behavior of the system. The strategy for correction is to check for other features that the proposed fault might cause. The hypothesis failure in the example of the taillight discussed earlier is of this type.

- *Hypothesized Unusual Mode—Enablement Violated:* The atypical features can be explained by the system being in a normal but unusual mode. However, the enabling conditions for that mode are not met. For example, once the EGR (Exhaust Gas Recirculation) warning light on my car went on indicating that the emission system needs servicing. In an expert system this might be expressed:

```
IF the EGR light is on
THEN the emission control system needs service
```

When I read the owner's manual for my car, I found that the light goes on every 25,000 miles. Since the car had around 18,000 miles on it, the emission control system didn't need service (although the light did).

The strategy for correcting the heuristic that proposed the faulty hypothesis is simply to consider one of the enabling conditions of the unusual state. In general, there may be several conditions that define such an unusual state. Only those conditions that would be true if the system were in an atypical mode but are not true in the current example are used to revise the fault diagnosis heuristic. The above rule would be changed by this strategy:

```
IF the EGR light is on
AND the odometer is near a multiple of 25,000
THEN the emission control system needs service
```

- *Hypothesized Fault—Unusual Input:* The device hypothesized to be faulty is in fact functioning properly. This typically occurs when the input to a device is very unusual. In this case, the output of the device may also be unusual, and the device might be assumed to be faulty unless the input is considered. For example, when I was a young child living in New Jersey, my television stopped working; only static appeared on all of the stations. I tried to fix it by adjusting the fine-tuning knob and finally asked my mother for help. My mother assumed that I had broken the tuner by twisting it so much. Apparently, she has a heuristic that might be expressed as:

```
IF there is static on all stations
THEN the tuner is broken
```

Several hours later, she discovered that there was a power failure in New York, and none of the television stations were broadcasting. The problem with this heuristic is that it doesn't consider that the input to the television might be at fault. Revising the above rule to account for the input relationship would result in the following:

```
IF there is static on all stations
AND the stations are broadcasting
THEN the the tuner is broken
```

Whenever a hypothesis is denied by consulting a device model, the reason for the denial must be found to avoid the failure in future similar cases. We have identified these three sources of hypothesis failure and use a different correction strategy for each failure.

8.3.2 Revising Fault Diagnosis Heuristics

When there is a hypothesis failure, the explanation for the failure is found and the heuristic rule that proposed the hypothesis is revised. A heuristic rule that proposes a fault can apply to one particular component (e.g., the light bulb of the left taillight) or a class of components (e.g., light bulbs). Similarly, the correction strategy can apply to a particular component or a class of components. The manner in which the knowledge base of heuristic rules is revised depends on the generality of the heuristic rule and correction. These interact in the following manner:

- *Heuristic rule not more general than the correction:* The correction is added to the heuristic rule, and this new, more specialized rule replaces the old rule.
- *Heuristic rule more general than the correction:* The correction is added to the heuristic rule and applied only in the specialized case. The old rule is retained for use in other cases.

Consider the case of the taillight discussed earlier. This example assumed that the explanation for ruling out the fuse was expressible as, "If the fuse for a taillight is blown, then the front parking light on the opposite side will be out." Since the rule and the revision both applied to any taillight (i.e., same level of generality), the rule is replaced by the revised version. On the other hand, if the explanation were expressed as, "If the fuse for a left taillight is blown, then the right-front parking light will be out," then the new rule could not replace the previous rule:

```
IF a left taillight is not working
AND the right front parking light is not working
THEN the fuse of the taillight's circuit is blown.
```

In a similar manner, if the original fault diagnosis heuristic were expressed more generally, about car lights in general instead of about taillights, then it would need to be specialized about taillights but remain to diagnose problems with other lights. The knowledge base would then need to contain the following two rules:

```
IF a taillight is not working
AND the opposite front parking light is not working
THEN the fuse of the taillight's circuit is blown.

IF a light is not working
THEN the fuse of the light's circuit is blown.
```

There are two other issues to be considered in revising heuristic rules. First, since some testing is being added to hypothesis generation, it would be wasteful to repeat the same test during confirmation. To avoid this potential problem, the revision to a rule caches the results of a test. Second, the amount of search necessary to prove a conjunction of subgoals in PROLOG (the language we use to implement our rules) is dependent on the order in which the subgoals are attempted. We use a strategy to order the tests in a revised rule similar to one proposed by Naish [1985]. This strategy minimizes the size of the search space by detecting the ultimate failure of a rule as soon as possible. This assumes that decreasing the search space is the best means of increasing performance. This is true in our application since testing for the presence or absence of any feature is equally expensive. Cantone [Cantone, *et al.*, 1983] gives an approach for ordering tests based in part on the cost of the test.

8.3.3 A Definition of Fault Diagnosis with Heuristics and Device Models

The goal of diagnosis is to find a hypothesis **H**, which accounts for the abnormal functionality of a device. The process of diagnosis can be viewed as applying the following inference rule to conclude **H**:

$$\frac{\text{F and F} \rightarrow \text{H}}{\text{H}}, \text{ if consistent(H,M,O)}$$

where **F** is a set of features, **F** → **H** is a fault diagnosis heuristic, **H** is a fault hypothesis, **M** is a set of implications that represents a device model, **O** is the set of observed data (**F** is a subset of **O**), and **consistent(H,M,O)** is true if **H** is consistent with the device model and the observed data. In the discussion of the blown fuse in Section 8.1, **F** is the feature indicating that the taillight is not working, **H** is the hypothesis that the fuse is blown, **F** → **H** is the diagnosis heuristic which indicates a blown fuse if a taillight is not working, **M** is the device model of the circuit (two lights protected by a fuse), and **O** is the set of observed features (the taillight is not working, and the parking light is working). Note that the above inference rule is similar to *modus ponens* except that the conclusion **H** must be consistent with the model and the observed data. This is necessary because the implication **F** → **H** may not be correct.

In our approach to learning and fault diagnosis, **consistent(H,M,O)** corresponds to confirming a hypothesis with device models. It is computed by first finding M_H, a model of a new device which is identical to **M** except that a faulty component has a different functionality. In the discussion of the blown fuse in Section 8.1, M_H, corresponds to a device similar to two lights in parallel protected by a fuse, but the fuse is replaced by a broken wire. This new model, M_H, has a number of predictions, P_i. M_H can be viewed as a number of implications:

H and **M** → M_H
M_H → P_1
M_H → P_2
...
M_H → P_n

In the blown fuse example in Section 8.1, P_i might be the feature indicating that the opposite parking light is not working.

A hypothesis **H** is not consistent (i.e., **consistent(H,M,O)** is false) if there is an implication M_H → P_i and P_i is false. Here, the inconsistency arises because from M_H → P_i and M_H, it is possible to deduce P_i. However, P_i is known to be false.

To summarize, we view diagnosis as consisting of two processes: generating a fault hypothesis **H** from diagnosis heuristics of the form **F** → **H**, and then confirming or denying **H** by evaluating **consistent(H,M,O)**.

8.3.4 A Definition of Learning Fault Diagnosis Heuristics

When a diagnosis heuristic (**F** → **H**) proposes a fault hypothesis **H** which is denied because **consistent(H,M,O)** is false, the diagnosis heuristic can be revised to not propose the fault in future similar conditions. By similar, we mean those conditions that would result in the same inconsistency. Recall that an inconsistency is detected when P_i and **not**(P_i) can be derived. The following is an example of an inconsistent theory:

F
F → H
M
H and M → M$_H$
M$_H$ → P$_i$
not(P$_i$)

We blame **F → H** for the inconsistency, because we are assuming that the observed data (**not(P$_i$)** and **F**) and the implication from the device model **M$_H$ → P$_i$** are correct. To avoid this inconsistency the diagnosis heuristic is revised to:

F and P$_i$ → H

The new theory, given below, no longer allows **H** and, therefore, **P$_i$** to be derived:

F
F and P$_i$ → H
M
H and M → M$_H$
M$_H$ → P$_i$
not(P$_i$)

In some cases, checking the consistency of a hypothesis with the device models is more properly viewed as the following implication:

B and M$_H$ → P$_i$

The situation when **B** is true and **P$_i$** is false and corresponds to the case that the revised heuristic is used in addition to the old heuristic. The form of the revised heuristic in this case is:

F and P$_i$ and B → H

The point of failure-driven learning of diagnosis heuristics is that it is simpler to rule out a hypothesis by testing for **P$_i$** than proving **consistent(H,M,O)**.

8.4 FAILURE-DRIVEN LEARNING OF DIAGNOSIS HEURISTICS

In this section, we describe an example of how the performance of the expert system to diagnose faults in the attitude control system is increased through failure-driven learning. To follow this example, it is necessary to know a little about attitude control.

8.4.1 Attitude Control

The attitude control system consists of a number of sensors which calculate the satellite's orientation on the three axes (called *yaw*, *pitch*, and *roll*) by detecting the

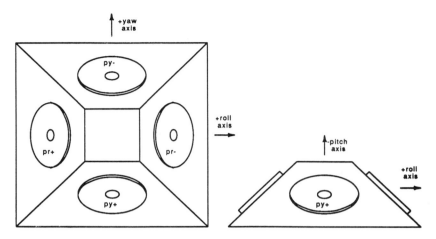

Figure 8–1:   The reaction wheels of the DSCS-III satellite. All four reaction wheels contribute to momentum on the pitch axis. Opposing wheel pairs contribute to momentum on the roll and yaw axes.

location of the earth and the sun and a set of reaction wheels which can change the satellite orientation if it deviates from the desired orientation. There are four reaction wheels (PY+, PY–, PR+, and PR–), arranged on the four sides of a pyramid (see Figure 8–1). Pitch momentum is stored as the sum of all four wheel speeds; roll momentum is stored as the difference between the PR+ and PR– speeds; and yaw momentum is stored as the difference between the PY+ and PY– speeds.

A diagram of the attitude control system appears in Figure 8–2. The signals YATT, RATT, and PATT represent the attitude on the yaw, roll, and pitch axes respectively. The wheel drive signal-processing component issues drive signals to the motor of the reaction wheels to change the wheel speeds. The wheel drive signals are WDPY+, WDPY–, WDPR+ and WDPR– for the PY+, PY–, PR+ and PR– wheels, respectively. The wheel speeds are measured by tachometers yielding the signals WSPY+, WSPY–, WSPR+ and WSPR– for the PY+, PY–, PR+ and PR– wheels, respectively. The tachometer signal-processing module converts the four wheel speeds to the three values representing the equivalent wheel speeds on the yaw, roll, and pitch axes. These equivalent wheel speeds are also combined with the attitude information from the sensors to yield the estimated attitudes (YATT, RATT, and PATT).

The attitude control system contains the logic necessary to maintain the desired attitude. For example, to compensate for a disturbance on the roll axis, the difference between the speed of PR+ and PR– wheels must change.

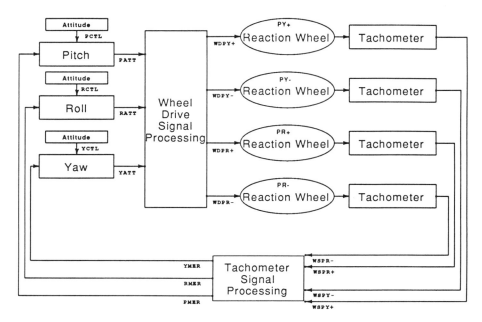

Figure 8–2: Block diagram of the attitude control system of the DSCS-III satellite. Sensor and tachometer data are combined to produce an estimate of the attitude on the roll (RATT), pitch (PATT) and yaw (YATT) axes. Wheel drive signals are produced to change the wheel speeds to correct for any attitude disturbances.

8.4.2 ACES: The Attitude Control Expert System

One reason that our particular satellite was chosen for this research is that The Aerospace Corporation possesses a simulator for the attitude control system, which generates telemetry tapes reflecting faulty behaviors to aid engineers in faults diagnosis. In addition, these tapes serve as input to our expert system. ACES consists of two major modules:

- *Monitor.* This module converts the raw telemetry data to a set of features that describe the atypical aspects of the telemetry. In ACES, the features detected include:
  - *(value-violation signal start-time end-time value)*: Between *start-time* and *end-time* the average *value* of *signal* has taken on an illegal *value*.
  - *(jump signal start-time end-time amount start-value end-value slope)*: The *signal* has changed from *start-value* to *end-value* between *start-time* and

end-time. Amount is the difference between *start-value* and *end-value* and *slope* is *amount* divided by the difference between *start-time* and *end-time*.

- *Diagnostician.* This module finds an explanation for the atypical features.

In this chapter, we focus on the learning in the diagnostician. The diagnostician illustrated in Figure 8–3 is composed of several cooperating modules:

- *Fault Identification.* The atypical features are used as symptoms of faults by heuristic rules to postulate a hypothesis that could account for the behavior of the satellite. Typically, the hypothesis isolates the atypical behavior to a failure of a single component.
- *Fault Confirmation.* This step compares the actual device functionality to the functionality as specified by a device model. This process can either confirm or deny that a hypothesized fault is present. If a hypothesis is denied, an attempt is made to identify another fault.
- *Fault Implication Analysis.* After a fault has been confirmed, the effect of the fault on the values of other telemetry signals is assessed. A model of the attitude control system predicts the values of telemetry signals that might be af-

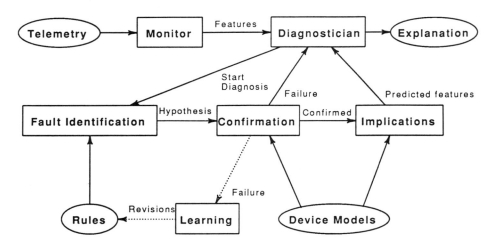

Figure 8–3:   Block diagram of the Attitude Control Expert System. The monitor detects unusual features in the telemetry data stream. The diagnostician attempts to find an explanation for the usual features (e.g., a reaction wheel is ignoring its drive signal). Diagnosis is accomplished by heuristic rules that suggest faults and device models that confirm or deny faults. When a heuristic rule suggests a fault that is denied by device models, the learning procedure is initiated to revise the heuristic.

fected by the fault. The predicted telemetry values are analyzed by the monitor to see if they are atypical. Descriptions of atypical, predicted values are then compared against the set of atypical features to explain any features which are a result of a confirmed fault.

8.4.3 Refining Fault Diagnosis Heuristics

For this example, the initial fault diagnosis heuristics are quite simple. These rules implement two very crude heuristics: "If the speed of a reaction wheel is 0, then the tachometer is broken"; and "If the speed of a reaction wheel is 0, then the wheel drive is broken." Figure 8–4 presents the definition of two fault diagnosis rules. These PROLOG rules have a LISP-like syntax since our PROLOG is implemented in LISP. The first element of a list is the predicate name. Variables are preceded by ":–" The part of the rule preceded by ":–" is a fault hypothesis, and the part of the rule after ":–" are those conditions that are necessary to be proved to propose the hypothesis.

Since ACES is implemented in PROLOG, it tries the heuristic rules in the order they are defined. However, for the purposes of learning, we find it more convenient to have the ordering of the rules undefined.[3] This prevents one heuristic from relying on the fact that another fault proposed by an earlier heuristic has been ruled out.

```
1: (problem (problem wheel-tach ?from
                      (broken-wheel-tach ?wheel ?from)))  :-
;there is a tachometer stuck at 0
(feature (value-violation ?sig ?from ?until 0))
(measurement ?sig ?wheel speed ?tach)
(isa ?wheel reaction-wheel)
;if the speed of a wheel is 0

2: (problem (problem wheel drive ?from
                      (broken-wheel drive ?wheel ?from ?sig)))  :-
;there is a wheel drive motor not responding to the drive signal
(feature (value-violation ?sig ?from ?until 0))
(measurement ?sig ?wheel speed ?tach)
(isa ?wheel reaction-wheel)
;if the speed of a wheel is 0
```

Figure 8–4:   Initial fault diagnosis heuristics. Comment lines are preceded by ";.". The first rule suggests a faulty tachometer when there is a value-violation of a reaction wheel speed signal. The second rule suggests that the wheel drive is ignoring its input signal.

---

[3] This is implemented by randomly changing the order of the rules before each run.

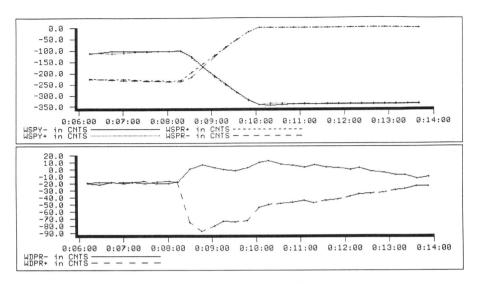

Figure 8–5:   Telemetry data after a broken wheel drive. The upper graph indicates the speed of the reaction wheels. The lower graph indicates the wheel drive signals of the pitch-roll wheels.

An example will help to illustrate some of the strategies for revising fault diagnosis heuristics. Figure 8–5 contains the relevant telemetry data. For this telemetry tape, the monitor notices several atypical features:

1. WSPR–, WSPR+, WSPY+ and WSPY– have changed an unusual amount.
2. WSPR+ and WSPR– are 0.

The first hypothesis proposed by the first rule in Figure 8–4 is that the tachometer of the PR– wheel is stuck at 0. The confirmation module denies this hypothesis for the following reason: If the tachometer were stuck at 0, the attitude of the satellite would change drastically.[4] Since the attitude did not change, the heuristic must be revised to avoid generation of this hypothesis in future similar cases. The hypothesis failure is caused by not checking the implications of a faulty tachometer (Hypothe-

---

[4]The attitude control system would believe that the wheel was not storing any momentum when in fact it is. To compensate for the erroneous report of loss of momentum, the attitude control system would adjust the momentum of the other wheels, changing the attitude of the satellite.

```
(problem (problem wheel-tach ?from
                  (broken-wheel-tach ?wheel ?from))) :-
(FEATURE (VALUE-VIOLATION YATT ?FROM-32 ?END-33 ?VALUE-34))
;MAKE SURE THE YAW ATTITUDE HAS BEEN DISTURBED
(feature(value-violation ?sig ?from ?until 0))
(AFTER ?FROM-32 ?FROM)
;MAKE SURE THE ATTITUDE DISTURBANCE IS AFTER THE VALUE VIOLATION
(measurement ?sig ?wheel speed ?tach)
(isa ?wheel reaction-wheel)
(CACHE-PROVED ATTITUDE-DISTURBANCE)
```

Figure 8–6:   Revised faulty tachometer heuristic changes in CAPITALS. Variables in the revision (e.g., ?FROM-32) are created by renaming variables from the device models to avoid name conflicts. If this rule succeeds, it is not necessary to test the attitude-disturbance model since this rule caches the result of that model.

sized Fault–Inconsistent Prediction). Checking any of the attitude signals would suffice to distinguish a faulty tachometer from the actual fault. In Figure 8–6, the revision tests YATT.

After the heuristic has been revised, diagnosis continues. The next hypothesis proposed by the second rule in Figure 8–4 is that the wheel drive of the PR– is broken. The device model of a wheel drive includes the following information: The wheel speed is proportional to the integral of the wheel drive signal. If the wheel drive signal is positive, the wheel speed should increase.

During the time that WSPR– increased from –100 to 0, WDPR– was positive (see Figure 8–4). Therefore, the PR– wheel was not ignoring its drive signal and the hypothesis is denied. The hypothesis failure is caused by the fact that WSPR– wheel is indeed doing something very unusual by changing so rapidly and stopping. However, it is doing this because it is responding to WDPR–. The heuristic that proposed this fault is revised to consider the functionality of the device (Hypothesized Fault–Unusual Input).

In Figure 8–7, the revised heuristic checks that change of the wheel speed as it approaches 0 is not due to the drive signal. Since our heuristic rules and our device models are implemented in the same language, it is possible to move code from the device model to a heuristic rule by renaming variables. In other systems, this may not be possible. However, this strategy would still apply if the rule could be revised to indicate what part of the device model to check for (e.g., test that the observed wheel speed could not be produced given the wheel drive between $time_1$ and $time_2$). In ACES, it is possible to revise the rule to specify *how* the test should be performed instead of *what* test should be performed.

```
(problem (problem wheel drive ?from
                    (broken-wheel drive ?wheel ?from ?sig))) :-
(FEATURE(JUMP ?SIG ?FROM-37 ?UNTIL-38 ?JUMP-39 ?START-40
              ?END-41 ?SLOPE-42))
;THERE IS A CHANGE IN THE WHEEL SPEED>
(feature(value-violation ?sig ?from ?until 0))
(AFTER ?FROM ?FROM-37)
;THE WHEEL SPEED REACHES 0 AFTER IT CHANGES>
(measurement ?sig ?wheel speed ?tach)
(isa ?wheel reaction-wheel)
(DRIVES ?DRIVE-43 ?WHEEL)
(MEASUREMENT ?DRIVE-SIGNAL-44 ?DRIVE-43 AMPLITUDE DIRECT)
;FIND THE WHEEL DRIVE SIGNAL OF THE ?WHEEL
(IS ?DRIVE-SIGNAL-SIGN-45
      (TELEMETRY-SIGNAL-SIGN ?DRIVE-SIGNAL-44 ?FROM-37 ?UNTIL-38))
;FIND THE SIGN OF THE THE DRIVE SIGNAL DURING THE JUMP
(IS ?SLOPE-SIGN-46 (REPORT-SIGN ?SLOPE-42))
;FIND THE SIGN OF JUMP
(NOT (AGREE ?SLOPE-SIGN-46 ?DRIVE-SIGNAL-SIGN-45))
;MAKE SURE THE DIRECTION OF THE JUMP DISAGREES WITH THE DRIVE-
      SIGNAL.
(CACHE-DISPROVED WHEEL-DRIVE-STATUS)
```

Figure 8–7:   Revised wheel drive heuristic—changes in CAPITALS

After the heuristic has been revised, another hypothesis is found to account for the atypical features: The faulty wheel drive heuristic proposes that the PR+ drive is ignoring its input since WSPR+ is 0, and when it increased to 0, WDPR+ was negative indicating that the speed should decrease (see Figure 8–5). The confirmation of this hypothesis is trivial since the heuristic already proved that the drive was not functioning according to its device description. After the fault is confirmed, the effects on the rest of the attitude control system are assessed. Since roll momentum is stored as the difference between the speed of the PR+ and PR– reaction wheels, when WSPR+ goes to 0, WSPR– should change by the same amount. The satellite was in a very unusual state prior to the failure: WSPR+ and WSPR– were equal. When the PR+ drive broke, WSPR– went to 0 to compensate for the change in WSPR+. In addition, since the pitch momentum is stored as the sum of all four wheels, to maintain pitch momentum WSPY+ and WSPY– decreased by the amount that WSPR+ and WSPR– increased. While WSPY+ and WSPY– decreased, the difference between them remained constant to maintain the yaw momentum. The broken PR+ wheel drive accounts for the atypical features and the diagnosis process terminates.

CASE	Fault	Naive-ACES	Naive-ACES after learning	Expert-ACES
1	tachometer	21	1	1
2	wheel drive	4	1	2
3	wheel unload	1	1	1
4	wheel drive	2	1	1

Figure 8–8:   Number of fault hypotheses

8.4.4 Results

There are two standards for evaluating the effects of learning in ACES. First, there is the performance of ACES using the rules in Figure 8–4. We call this version *naive-ACES*. Additionally, there is the performance of ACES using rules hand-coded from information provided by an expert. We call this version of the system *expert-ACES*. The performance of the naive-ACES after learning is compared to naive-ACES and expert-ACES in Figure 8–8 and Figure 8–9. There are four test cases used for comparison:

1. A tachometer stuck at 0.
2. A wheel drive ignoring its input when the opposite wheel is at the same speed. Data from this example is in Figure 8–5.
3. A wheel unload (i.e., the speed of the reaction wheels is changed by the firing of a thruster). This is not actually a failure, but it changes the wheels speeds and momentum so that the monitor detects atypical features.
4. A wheel drive ignoring its input in the usual case where the opposite wheel is at a different speed.

The data in Figure 8–8 demonstrate that the failure-driven learning technique presented in this chapter improves the simple fault diagnosis heuristics to the extent that the performance of ACES using the learned heuristics is comparable to the system using the rules provided by an expert. In one case, the performance of the learned rules is even better than the expert-provided rules. This particular case is the previous example in which a wheel drive broke when the satellite was in an unusual state. The heuristic provided by the expert did not anticipate the rare condition that two opposing wheel speeds were equal.

CASE	Fault	Naive-ACES	Naive-ACES after learning	Expert-ACES
1	tachometer	2268	211	584
2	wheel drive	1238	616	910
3	wheel unload	870	861	947
4	wheel drive	745	409	643

Figure 8–9:   Number of inferences to generate and confirm fault

The data in Figure 8–9 reveal that the number of logical inferences required by the expert system decreases after learning. This demonstrates that after learning, the expert system is doing less work to identify a failure rather than moving the same amount of work from hypothesis confirmation to hypothesis generation. Comparing the number of inferences required by naive-ACES after learning to those of expert-ACES is not actually fair since it appears that the expert's rules at times test some information retested by the confirmation process. Recall that retesting is avoided by a revised rule since the revision contains information to cache the results of consulting a device model. It has been our experience that this cache reduces the number of inferences by approximately 10%. An additional 10% of the inferences are saved through intelligent ordering of clauses of revised rules compared to our initial simple approach of appending the revision to the end of a rule.

8.5 CONCLUSION

We have presented an approach to refining fault diagnosis heuristics by determining what aspect of a device model must be consulted to distinguish one fault from another fault with similar features. This approach relies on explaining why a heuristic does not apply in a certain case and correcting the heuristic to avoid proposing an erroneous fault hypothesis. Applying this technique to a simple version of the ACES expert system for the diagnosis of faults in the attitude control system yields performance comparable to and in some cases better than the performance of ACES with expert fault diagnosis heuristics.

ACKNOWLEDGMENTS

Comments by Anne Brindle, Jack Hodges, Steve Margolis, Rod McGuire, and Carl Kesselman helped clarify this article. This research was supported by the U.S. Air Force Space Division under contract F04701-85-C-0086 and by the Aerospace Sponsored Research Program.

References

Cantone, R., Pipitone, F., Lander, W., and Marrone, M. 1983. Model-based probabilistic reasoning for electronics troubleshooting. In *Proceedings of the Eighth International Joint Conference on Artificial Intelligence*, Vancouver.

Davis, R., *et al*. 1982. Diagnosis based on description of structure and function. In *Proceedings of the National Conference on Artificial Intelligence*, Pittsburgh, PA.

de Kleer, J. and Brown, J. 1984. A qualitative physics based on confluences. *Artificial Intelligence*, Vol. 24(1).

DeJong, G. 1983. Acquiring schemata through understanding and generalizing plans. In *Proceedings of the Eighth International Joint Conference on Artificial Intelligence*, Karlsruhe, West Germany.

Forbus, K. 1984. Qualitative process theory. *Artificial Intelligence*, Vol. 24(1).

Genesereth, M., Bennett, J.S., and Hollander, C.R. 1981. DART: Expert systems for automated computer fault diagnosis. In *Proceedings of the Annual Conference*. Baltimore, MD: Association for Computing Machinery.

Kuipers, B. 1984. Commonsense reasoning about causality: Deriving behavior from structure. *Artificial Intelligence*, Vol. 24(1).

Laird, J., Rosenbloom, P., and Newell, A. 1984. Towards chunking as a general learning mechanism. In *Proceedings of the National Conference on Artificial Intelligence*, Austin, TX.

McDermott, J. 1982. R1: A rule-based configurer of computer systems. *Artificial Intelligence*, Vol. 19(3).

Michie, D. 1983. Inductive rule generation in the context of the fifth generation. In *Proceedings of the International Machine Learning Workshop*, Monticello, IL.

Minton, S. 1984. Constraint-based generalization: Learning game-playing plans from single examples. In *Proceedings of the National Conference on Artificial Intelligence*, Austin, TX.

Mitchell, T. 1982. Generalization as search. *Artificial Intelligence*, Vol. 18(2).

Mitchell, T., Kedar-Cabelli, S., and Keller, R. 1986. Explanation-based learning: A unifying view. *Machine Learning*, Vol. 1(1).

Naish, L. 1985. Prolog control rules. In *Proceedings of the Ninth International Joint Conference on Artificial Intelligence*, Los Angeles, CA.

Nelson, W.R. 1982. REACTOR: An expert system for diagnosis and treatment of nuclear reactor accidents. In *Proceedings of the National Conference on Artificial Intelligence*, Pittsburgh, PA.

Pazzani, M. and Brindle, A. 1985. An expert system for satellite control. In *Proceedings of ITC/USA/85, the International Telemetering Conference*, Las Vegas, NV.

————, 1986. Automated diagnosis of attitude control anomalies. In *Proceedings of the Annual AAS Guidance and Control Conference*, Keystone, CO. American Astronautical Society.

Rosenbloom, P., Laird, J., McDermott, J., Newell, A., and Orciuch, E. 1985. R1-SOAR: An experiment in knowledge-intensive programming in a problem-solving architecture. *IEEE Transactions on Pattern Analysis and Machine Intelligence*, Vol. 7(5).

Scarl, E.A., Jamieson, J., and Delaune, C. 1985. A fault detection and isolation method applied to liquid oxygen loading for the space shuttle. In *Proceedings of the Ninth International Joint Conference on Artificial Intelligence*. Los Angeles, CA.

Schank, R. 1982. *Dynamic Memory: A Theory of Reminding and Learning in Computers and People*. Cambridge University Press.

Sembugamoorthy, V. and Chandrasekaran, B. 1985. *Functional Representation of Devices and Compilation of Diagnostic Problem-Solving Systems* (Tech. Rep). Ohio State University.

Shortliffe, E.H. 1976. *Computer-based Medical Consultation: MYCIN*. New York, NY: American Elsevier.

Stallman, R.M. and Sussman, G.J. 1977. Forward reasoning and dependency-directed backtracking in a system for computer-aided circuit analysis. *Artificial Intelligence*, Vol. 9(2), 135–196.

Vere, S. 1975. Induction of concepts in the predicate calculus. In *Proceedings of the Fourth International Joint Conference on Artificial Intelligence*, Tbilisi, USSR.

Wagner, R.E. 1983. Expert system for spacecraft command and control. In *Computers in Aerospace IV Conference*, Hartford, CT. American Institute of Aeronautics and Astronautics.

9

CONCEPTUAL CLUSTERING AND CATEGORIZATION:

Bridging the Gap between Induction and Causal Models

Stephen José Hanson
(Siemens Research Center and Princeton University)

Abstract

Categorization processes are central to many human capabilities; e.g., language, reasoning, problem solving. The concept of categorization is also at the base of many kinds of phenomenon which AI researchers have attempted to model; e.g., induction, analogy, and the use of causal models. Most approaches to induction can be characterized on a single dimension such as model driven, "top-down" to data driven, "bottom-up." At the one end a large amount of preconstructed information (knowledge rich) is used while on the other end the featural similarity is analyzed of a given set of objects or events in the absence of other knowledge structures. These two kinds of approaches, represented recently by explanation-based learning (EBL) and similarity-based learning (SBL), conflict in terms of the proper approach to categorization and construction of causal theories.

One view central to the present approach is that featural information is instrumental in formation of knowledge structures. Knowledge structures can be more general than objects and can possess more complex information than features (e.g., abstract concepts, actions, relations). Such knowledge structures are hypothesized to be both created and further manipulated by the SBL mechanism that learned them in the first place. The present approach is related to the discovery of category structure and the use of feature intercorrelations and their interaction with generalization, inheritance, retrieval, and memory organization.

9.1 INTRODUCTION

Research in induction using conceptual clustering [Michalski, 1980; Hanson and Bauer, 1989] has focused on data-driven, similarity-based, "knowledge-poor" problems. A criticism of this sort of induction approach has been that the clustering of objects or events without a context, goal, or some information concerning the *function* of the derived clusters is not likely to be useful for real-world problems. Furthermore, such clustering is not likely to provide information about knowledge structures that might be more abstractly represented in clusters of objects and their relationships. It is just not clear how conceptual clustering would be able to deal with more complex phenomena like analogy, explanation, reasoning, motivated planning or problem solving (but see [Stepp and Michalski, 1986]).

On the other hand, induction approaches that tend to focus on complex human behavior like problem-solving or natural language domains [Mitchell, Keller, and Kedar-Cabelli, 1986; Dejong and Mooney 1986; Schank, Collins, and Hunter, 1987], require a large amount of previously organized knowledge and featural information. This kind of information about the task can include what features are important in a given context, how features are related in a given context, and what other features one might expect to find in new instances. Given such elaborate information prior to seeing some data, it is perhaps not too surprising that learning can occur "…with one example…" (compare [Mitchell, *et al.*, 1986]). It is also not surprising that significant inferences can be made with such elaborate information. But the question, of course, still remains: How do such featural relations, object, type relations, and context bindings get learned in the first place?

It would seem there is a gray area in between the knowledge-poor conceptual clustering kind of induction and the knowledge-rich type of induction associated with explanation-based learning (EBL) approaches. Of course, having lots of knowledge about the world is useful for all kinds of intelligent behavior. However, the *learning* problem is not solved by instantiating a system with a complex, large knowledge base, which cannot easily be added to, deleted from, or reorganized in any significant way. This seems to be at least one of the potential contributions of conceptual clustering approaches: the promise of the construction of complex knowledge structures from featural information, object clusters, and category structure.

Unfortunately, most conceptual clustering to date tends to produce what might be termed "syntactic" clusters: ones that make sense for some general general criteria independent of the particular context in which the learning system is found. Such conceptual clustering is not motivated because such groupings produce particular relations between objects, or between classes of objects, or between features. That is, the *structure* of the category has not been the motivation for the clustering process. Nor does past work in conceptual clustering tend to focus on the goals or functions of the category, which would help in *a priori* feature selection or feature weighting (compare [Schank, Collins, and Hunter, 1987]).

The role that is envisioned here for conceptual clustering, therefore, is somewhat unusual and difficult. It involves learning category structure from little previous information outside some featural analysis and using a domain-general ("syntactic"), similarity-based method to refine and construct new knowledge structures.

9.2 LEARNING BY OBSERVATION (INDUCTION)

Learning by observation might, therefore, be interpreted in these two, polarized ways, one involving a more reflective, top-down process and the other a more automatic, bottom-up process. For example, suppose a system is exposed to or allowed to observe a number of instances. Such instances may be related to a rule, concept, or category. With an SBL approach a system may use common features that allow instances to cluster together satisfying some external constraint. In contrast, an EBL approach has more flexibility in the way in which it may work. For example, the system may attempt to retrieve some memory event or episode that reminds it of the present one and invoke an action similar to the one it had used in the past. It may also attempt to incorporate the new event into existing memory structures based on the reminded one. More generally, EBL approaches might provide the system with a model, or causal structure, that might help the system explain the present instance in the context on this model. This would allow the EBL system to store the new instance with some appropriate links or indices that locate the new instance in relation to other instances determined by the causal model that it had invoked. Presumably this makes the instance easier to retrieve and the memory more efficiently organized.

Suppose you are given instances of the two categories of people shown in Figure 9–1. These are hypothetical people who can be described with feature values on attributes such as where they live, their profession, their marital status, and the car they drive. For example, John in category B, lives in NYC, is a lawyer is married and drives a Porsche. George in category A, lives in San Francisco, is a lawyer, is divorced, and drives a Porsche. Mary, also in John's category lives in SF, is a lawyer, is married, and drives a VW. An SBL approach might note that there is a number of common features in category A but ones that also appear in category B. In fact, without some feature weightings, an SBL approach might find many other categorizations equivalent, since each of these "people" can be seen to represent the vertices of cube in their first three attribute values (111, 110, 101, 011 represents the first group, for example—assume the car driven is an incidental feature). A cut through one of the diagonals of cube creates the two categories of people.

A system employing an EBL approach might wonder why Mary is driving a VW, given she is a lawyer. And in general, an EBL system would make many associations about the *relation* of the features to one another. Using background informa-

Category A

George	Joan	Sally	Henry
SF	NYC	SF	SF
Lawyer	Accountant	Accountant	Accountant
Divorced	Divorced	Married	Divorced
Porsche	Honda	VW	Honda

Category B

John	Mary	Bill	Fred
NYC	SF	NYC	NYC
Lawyer	Lawyer	Accountant	Lawyer
Married	Married	Married	Divorced
Porsche	VW	Porsche	Honda

Figure 9–1: Two out of three polymorphy example adapted from [Dennis, Hampton, and Lea, 1973] using arbitrary features of people

tion, a system would be able to note that particular feature relations may be more predictive of a category then another, partly due to the observed correlations within these three features and partly due to the potential correlations with other features not mentioned. In some sense, each of these features invoke many other features concerning economic status, social relationships, and general personality features about each person.

If the goals of the categorizer are known (for instance suppose the categorizer is interested in hiring one of these people for a job or is instead looking for a roommate) certain features may be seen as more important (many that aren't listed) and given more weight in the categorization. Nonetheless, the system at some point will have to use the features to construct a similarity relation on which the goals of the context—outside of feature selection or weighting—will have no affect.

The kinds of categories represented by the people in Figure 9–1 are what Wittgenstein [1953] referred to as *exhibiting family resemblance*. He claimed there was a simple property that was at the basis of all "natural" categories called *polymorphic* or *polythetic* features, [Dennis, Hampton, and Lea, 1973; Smith and Medin, 1981; Sneath and Sokal, 1973], that of neither necessary nor sufficient features. Polymorphy represents a weakening of the conjunction operator by allowing at least *m* out of *n* features rather then *n* out of *n* features (compare [Michalski and Stepp, 1985]). Thus, a polymorphy operator can be seen to be somewhere in between a conjunction and disjunction operator. Exemplars of such categories tend to have a family resemblance in the sense referred to by Wittgenstein as category *criteria*—criteria which must be satisfied for category membership.

We will argue that family resemblance (e.g., polymorphy) of such categories provides the basis for the coherence and rationale of a set of exemplars. Polymorphy can be described in a number of different complementary ways. For example, polymorphy can arise from decision processes involving distributed monitors or evidence detectors in a noisy or complex environment. It is also possible to show how recent connectionist models also use polymorphy operators [Rumelhart and McClelland, 1986] in that their combination rule (e.g., thresholded-weighted sum of a unit) is a polymorphy operator (also referred to as *majority logic*).

Finally, the concept description underlying a category can be seen as either allowing polymorphy operators or not. For example, a Hamming distance measure (or any common feature measure or conjunction rule) will tend to minimize polymorphy in the concept description, since feature descriptions will tend to reference features that appear in all exemplars but not in others ("disjoint coverage"). Feature intercorrelation measures, on the other hand, tend to introduce polymorphy in the concept space since feature descriptions can reference subsets of features that can be non-overlapping.[1] Moreover, feature relations seem to be a more natural kind of information in as much as they are typically embedded (not learned) in an EBL approach.

The argument that feature intercorrelations can be used as a basis for similarity and explanation requires some context for the notion of conceptual clustering in at least two other disciplines. One area concerns the relation between conceptual clustering and statistical clustering and the claim that they pertain to different domains or data structures. The second area concerns the relation of human categorization to conceptual clustering approaches. In what follows, an attempt will be made to show how these two areas (statistical clustering and human categorization) intersect with and constrain conceptual clustering research.

9.3 CONCEPTUAL CLUSTERING VERSUS STATISTICAL CLUSTERING

Michalski [1980] (also see [Michalski and Stepp, 1983]) has defined conceptual clustering as "…grouping objects into conceptually simple classes based on attribute values." This has been contrasted with statistical clustering by the claim that statistical clustering involves a predefined measure of similarity and does not take

---

[1]This is of course true of any sort of disjunction as well; however, note that what is being advocated is a strengthening of a disjunction operator, which is more constrained about what sorts of disjunctive features are allowed to enter the concept description: In fact, it tends to allow features that are *correlated* with other features while any disjunction can introduce features that may seem incidental. Further, note that conceptual clustering approaches have used disjunction, but both EBL and SBL approaches have tended to focus on common feature or conjunctive rules.

into consideration "...any background knowledge about the semantic relations among object attributes or global concepts that could be used for characterizing object configurations..." [Stepp and Michalski, 1986].

A simple example of this distinction can be illustrated by having prior knowledge that a particular geometric shape (like a circle) is sought in the clustering solution. This "background knowledge" should bias the clustering procedure to find circles in the object space even if the discovery of circles does not optimize within and between cluster distances of the data set.

On the other hand, statistical researchers in standard clustering [Everitt, 1971] and numerical taxonomy [Sneath and Sokal, 1973] texts, also discuss the desire to produce conceptually simple classes based on attribute values. Furthermore, these researchers have always stressed the importance of taking as much information of the data set into account as possible. For example, Everitt points out that "...the ultimate criterion for evaluating the meaning of such terms as 'cluster' or 'similarity' is the value judgment of the data analyst." Indeed where features are known to be more important than others, similarity measures and appropriate weightings should be used to reflect this knowledge.

Part of the confusion concerning the relation between statistical and conceptual clustering comes from assuming that there is a small number of approaches in statistical clustering that produce basically the same result. Actually, there are hundreds of different ways to do a cluster analysis, and given the same data, it would be relatively easy to find conflict in performance among many of the various methods [Wishart, 1969]. For example, consider the circles shown in Figure 9–2. These were clustered by their coordinate positions with a standard centroid method using Euclidian distance (see Section 9.4). As predicted by Michalski and his colleagues, the method failed to find the circles as indicated by the solid lines in Figure 9–2(a). However with a small modification in the group membership rule, using a method called nearest neighbor (see Section 9.4), now the circles were not only clustered together (see solid lines in Figure 9–2(b)) but in the absence of background knowledge. This represents a much more powerful result—the discovery of the circle concept!

Actually, we now have a different problem. Instead of selecting the appropriate background information for the given task we now must select a similarity measure that best reflects the background information whether it is available or not. The conceptual clustering problem is still with us—it is just not as easy to distinguish it from the goals of statistical clustering, and perhaps it shouldn't be. Conceptual clustering could be seen as a specific variation of statistical clustering, where the process of the clustering and focus on the type of categories formed is more important then the discovery of new structures and the exploration of data (see [Shepard, 1980] for other types of clustering and proximity models and related issues).

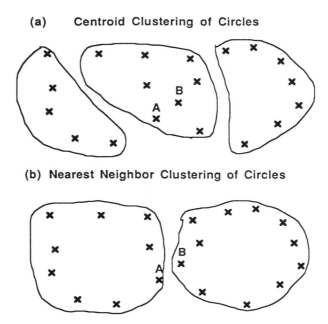

(a)   Centroid Clustering of Circles

(b) Nearest Neighbor Clustering of Circles

Figure 9–2:   A clustering example showing the sensitivity of the solution to the group
membership rule

9.4 WHAT IS NORMATIVE?

But this leaves the question of what should count as *normative* in a conceptual
clustering model. If, as suggested above, normative criteria must be reflected in the
clustering process or the similarity measure chosen, then it should be chosen on
some grounds other then simplicity, robustness, or generality, since these are typical
reasons for choosing a statistical measure or model. Normative criteria might be chosen on the basis of what sorts of measures are retained from the data and how general
such measures are. For example, various group membership rules in statistical clustering can be ordered on a sort of "abstractness" measure.

One of the simplest group membership rules is based on the nearest neighbor.
In determining the closeness of a point to a particular group relative to some other
group an exemplar in the feature space is compared using some metric (e.g., Euclidian distance) to an exemplar in the group which happens to be closest (see Figure
9–3(a)). This type of nearest neighbor measure tends to overgeneralize and create

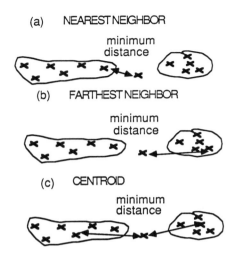

Figure 9–3:   Clustering examples illustrating three different but commonly used methods for determining group membership: (a) nearest neighbor, (b) farthest neighbor, (c) centroid

links where there shouldn't be links. It also uses minimal information about the aggregate or category information collected about each cluster.

Another group membership rule, called *farthest neighbor*, uses more information about the cluster groups than nearest neighbor in determining closeness of exemplars (see Figure 9–3(b)). In this case, the exemplar farthest away in the cluster determines closeness of the exemplar of interest. And in the example shown in Figure 9–3(b), it reverses the choice of group membership. This type of rule tends to undergeneralize and avoids creating clusters when it should. It, like nearest neighbor, could be said to be minimally abstract in that no further information is abstracted about the data set as the clusters are forming. Nor is there abstracted information that gets used further in determining group membership.

A third group membership rule, called *centroid*, illustrates one the simplest kind of abstractions from clusters that can be used to effect group membership. In this case, an average value is computed from each group and used to determine the closeness of the exemplars of interest. Using the centroid criterion now makes the choice of group membership indifferent between the two groups (see Figure 9–3(c)). This type of rule can produce misrepresentations of the cluster if it is not symmetric about the center point and thus can bias the clustering in ways that may not best represent each cluster. Other types of abstractions can be taken from the cluster and used in the group membership decision. These may be more representative, like the variance of the cluster or ones that use various statistical measures that may optimize some other measure. A general measure of abstractness has been proposed by Lance and Williams [1969] called the *flexible beta measure*, which for different values of beta can simulate nearest, farthest, centroid, variance measures, and anything in between.

Conceptual clustering can be seen as abstracting concept descriptions in a way that is similar to the centroid and variance measures described above. It is possible to construct any sort of abstraction from a set of concept descriptions, that involve nominal (substitutive variables) or metric variables that "stand in" for the clustering structure at any point in time. Michalski's [1980] approach involves just such a strategy. He developed a description language (APC), which constrains possible concept descriptions ("LEF" conditions) that might be determined from a set of examples. Thus, for Michalski, LEF conditions are normative conditions on the kinds of clusters that are allowed to emerge during conceptual clustering. These kind of conditions involve limitations on the sentence length of the concept description, the number of allowable disjunctions in the sentence length, and so on—conditions on the simplicity of the concept descriptions and therefore the clusters recovered.

9.5 CONSTRAINTS ON CATEGORIES

Another set of hypotheses about what might be normative for conceptual clustering arises from work in human categorization. Here, a set of constraints on the kinds of concept descriptions that are allowable in the description space is needed. Such constraints can delimit the type of within-category structure (e.g., aggregate, generalization behavior, default attributes), the type of descriptors, and the between-category preference (number of categories, level of description).

Although the details about human categorization are complex, several simple ideas seem to be relevant. First, people tend to form relative "contrasts" between categories; that is, people tend to minimize variance within clusters while maximizing variance among clusters [Rosch and Lloyd, 1978; Tversky, 1977; Smith and Medin, 1981]. Second, people also tend to have best or prototypical members of a category as opposed to equivalence classes [Homa, 1978; Posner and Keele, 1968]. Third, people tend to impose a category structure on a set of objects with a set of rich semantic properties. In general, it seems clear that people tend to elaborate the exemplars they are shown relative to other exemplars; they place the exemplars in the context of some set of category relations.

These trends can be summarized by the four following properties, which represent some minimal set of constraints on human categorization.

1. Categories arise as contrasts between one another; in other words, categorization is relative to the existing context of other putative categories.

2. Categories have a distribution of members, some more representative, some less. Furthermore, there tends to be one best member, or a set of best members, or an abstracted member (prototype) that may be used to represent the entire category.

3. Categories tend to possess members that have features that are neither necessary nor sufficient (polymorphy). Polymorphy seems to arise in real-world contexts, that is, when there is either natural variation in members or when the category is supported by a rational or causal account of the underlying relations between objects in the category.

4. Categories can be represented by the intercorrelation between feature sets; such intercorrelations can be used as a measure of the coherence of the concept underlying a category. The "similarity" of categories is in terms of the uncertainty reduction between feature sets identified within each category.

9.6 INTERCORRELATION HYPOTHESIS AND BASIC LEVELS

Some 10 years ago, Rosch [Rosch, *et al.*, 1976] posited a preferred level for object reference, knowledge representation, and perception in a taxonomy of concepts which she called the *basic level*. Imagine for example, a taxonomy of animals:

superordinate: mammals

basic: birds: dogs: cats

subordinate: robin, sparrow: golden retriever, dachshund: persian, lion

There is ample converging evidence for what is called in psychology the *basic-level effect*. It is known, for example, that a level somewhere between the superordinate and subordinate level (e.g., birds, dogs, cats) is learned first by children, is recognized faster by adults, and evokes many more features during description than the other levels. Apparently, there is a type of categorization that is basic to taxonomic information and helps organize other knowledge about the world. For Eleanor Rosch,

> Basic categories are those which carry the most information, possess the highest cue validity and are thus, the most differentiated from one another... . Basic-level categories possess the greatest bundle of features... . Basic objects are the most inclusive categories which delineate the correlational structure of the environment. [Rosch, *et al.*, 1976]

Rosch, in fact, explicitly stated a predictive function for the basic level. It was to be that level in a hierarchy that maximized something like the conditional probability of a category given a feature. This measure was dubbed "cue validity" and could be denoted by $\sum p(c \mid f_i)$ (although Rosch was careful to avoid the probability interpretation). Thus, within a hierarchy of possible cluster groups the cluster groups with the largest number of predictive features would be those that should provide basic-level effects. For conceptual clustering, then, basic levels can provide information about the group membership, the similarity between objects, and the number of categories that may be present in a set of objects.

9.7 SIMILARITY MATTERS!

Recently, however, it has been pointed out that the conditional probability interpretation of the cue validity measure cannot be correct (although Rosch was also apparently aware of this problem). Murphy [1983] argued that if one examines what cue validity will select from a hierarchy it will always be the superordinate or most general level. This follows since the

$$p(mammal \mid hair) > p(dog \mid hair) > p(golden \; retriever \mid hair).$$

It is much more likely that a thing with hair is a mammal and less likely it is a golden retriever since possession of hair isn't particularly predictive of a golden retriever.

It is possible that simple variations on cue validity might correct the lack of identification of the basic level. Suppose we reverse the relation and consider the probability of a feature given a category, "category validity." This sort of measure is sensitive to the predictiveness of a category for a feature. Unfortunately, the reverse selection occurs, and the subordinate or most specific level becomes preferred. Consider the cases

$$p(flies \mid mammal) < p(flies \mid bird) < p(flies \mid robin).$$

It is much more likely to find a flying robin then a flying mammal; that is, being a robin is particularly predictive for flying.

Jones [1985] suggested a measure involving both category validity and cue validity that did select the basic level or at the very least tended to be nonmonotonic over taxonomic levels. This was done by multiplying cue validity by category validity, a measure Jones called *collocation*. Although this strategy does produce a symmetric measure about the basic level and does seem to be similar to certain statistical measures of association, it is not psychologically motivated.

Recently, this measure (or more accurately a variation of it) was derived by Gluck and Corter [1986] with some simple psychological assumptions about feature frequency estimation and uncertainty reduction about categories given features. Their measure maximizes the difference between the feature uncertainty when the feature predicts the category and when it does not—a sort of "category utility."

$$p(c) * (\Sigma p(f_i \mid c)^2 - \Sigma p(f_i)^2) \tag{1}$$

However, the category utility measure can be shown to be a variation of the collocation measure with some rearrangement of the terms, noting that first, for a given data set the second term of the equation is a constant, we can thus deal with the first term. Now noting that,

$$p(c) = \frac{p(f_i)*p(c \mid f_i)}{p(f_i \mid c)} \qquad (2)$$

Substituting $p(c)$ in equation (1) above reduces category utility to a weighted version of collocation:

$$\sum p(f_i)*p(c \mid f_i)*p(f_i \mid c) \qquad (3)$$

This particular relationship was first shown by Fisher [1987] who also uses the category utility measure in a conceptual clustering model (COBWEB).

The importance of these types of similarity measures relates to their ability to account for the basic-level effect and to produce sensible, graded family membership effects as a function of feature predictability within and between categories. Presumably, these category relations help determine the coherence of categories and their explanatory power in the domain.

9.8 BUT ARE FEATURES INDEPENDENT?

All the previous measures assume independence of the features and independently combine feature predictiveness for all features and all categories. However, if features are not independent such measures will tend to overestimate the predictiveness of features. More importantly, such measures misrepresent feature-to-feature relations or fail to represent them at all. Recent research concerning the categorization abilities of people implicate feature intercorrelations at some level in determining the comprehensibility and similarity relations in categories [Murphy and Medin, 1985; Medin, Wattenmaker, and Hampson, 1986; Estes, 1986; Lewicki, 1985].

Stated simply, the present hypothesis is that basic levels and the similarity between objects is a function of the intercorrelations of features within the object set. This particular hypothesis can be found in much of Rosch's writing; in fact, she refers many times to the "correlational structure of the environment" and to "bundles of correlated features" at the basic level. What is proposed here specifically relates to a family of measures that directly incorporates some measure of correlation or relation between attributes in an object set.

The representation of categories proposed in the present model is to be a set of indices or pointers of features to other features. Formally, this can be represented by feature to feature uncertainty reduction:

$$\sum p(f_i \mid f_j) \text{ for all } i \neq j \qquad (4)$$

Feature intercorrelation measures (FI) have been entertained in possible accounts of theories that laypeople tend to hold about categories and further seem to play an in-

Metric Comparisons

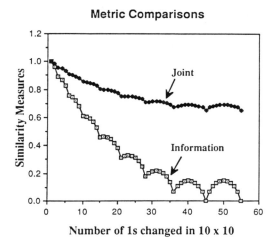

Number of 1s changed in 10 x 10

Figure 9–4:   Comparison of a Common Features (CF) metric and a Feature Intercorrelation (FI) metric, using an *n by n* binary matrix in which the bits in the matrix are incrementally turned off until they are half on and half off

creasing role in accounting for recent categorization effects [Murphy and Medin, 1985; Estes, 1986]. Such intercorrelation measures could include the effects of common feature measures (CF) like cue validity or Hamming distance measures (which, by the way, tend to be used in some SBL programs as well as EBL programs; compare [Lebowitz, 1986]), since the presence of a large number of common features will also produce a large number of intercorrelated features.

One difference between CF and FI measures concerns the way each type of measure might grade family membership. For example, as common features diminish, the CF measure falls very quickly, while a FI measure grades much more slowly due to its sensitivity to the *structure* in the data. This is easily demonstrated by transforming an *n by n* binary matrix starting with all bits on, to half of the bits on and off, by changing contiguous bits cumulatively per row (first one bit in row 1, then two bits in row 2, etc., until the diagonal is completely off). A Hamming distance measure or CF information measure grades quite quickly, while a simple FI (see Section 9.13) measure grades more slowly (see Figure 9–4).

It is also possible to compare the feature intercorrelation measure with the category utility or collocation measure. Gluck and Corter [1986] provide a test of their model using archival data from an object-verification task by Murphy and Smith [1982]. In this type of experiment, subjects are asked to identify a picture as one of three possible levels from a previously learned hierarchy of types. Subjects are typi-

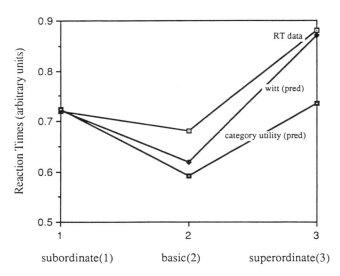

Figure 9–5: Comparison of category utility, within and between category intercorrelation measure with the Murphy and Smith [1982] reaction time verification data

cally fastest at verification for the intermediate level in the previously learned hierarchy. In order to apply these models, Gluck and Corter made featural analyses of the Murphy and Smith stimuli, and these feature values for each stimulus were used for the predictions in Figure 9–5. Shown are the reaction time verification data, the predictions for the category utility measure and the predictions for a simple intercorrelation measure that contrasts within-group intercorrelations and between-group intercorrelations (see below). The purpose of this demonstration is not to rule out particular models but to show the general shape of the predictions of each of the metrics as a function of the category levels. Apparently, the intercorrelation measure can model a similar basic level effect as the category utility measure and may also provide a better description of the reaction time data due to its asymmetry about the basic level (see Figure 9–5).

9.9 CONNECTIONIST MODELS AND INTERCORRELATION OF FEATURES

For perspective it is worth placing the present approach in the context of connectionist models [Rumelhart and McClelland, 1986]. In such models a unit is defined that represents the weighted sum of input features from other units. These combinations of input features may be recombined later in the network producing even more feature reduction. The first level of combination could, in fact, produce complete power set combinations on the input features. In fact, it is well known now that a single layer of units intermediate to input and output units can produce arbitrary half-space cuts in the feature space [Hanson and Burr, 1987] producing arbitrary nonconvex regions. Much of the power of these networks has come, in fact, from being able to represent and manipulate higher order correlations in the feature set. Thus, the present motivation for feature intercorrelations could be just as appropriate for a connectionist model.

Conceptual clustering models are what connectionists would refer to as non-supervised techniques, while many connectionist algorithms require teacher signals independent of the feature space. When such supervision is relaxed, decisions must be made concerning the size, type, number of intercorrelations, and various other constraints concerning the desired category structure.

Heuristics for unsupervised learning connectionist models, tend to be similar to the simple category heuristics listed earlier. Thus, Grossberg's models [1976] stress the notion of competitive interactions amongst categories as they are formed. Rumelhart and Zipser's [1986] competitive learning model explicitly uses architectural constraints (reciprocal inhibition) to induce competition among hypotheses about the feature space as they are forming. Other models might provide more general clustering abilities as a function of the statistics available in the feature space. The relation between these various connectionist models and the previously outlined categorization literature is less clear and will require specific analysis of the prototype or aggregate behavior of the network and the preferred level of abstraction and the generalization behavior relative to human behavior (see in particular [Anderson, *et al.*, 1987; McClelland and Rumelhart, 1987]). The similarity measure within the network is particularly complicated since it is a function of the basic unit computation, learning rule and architecture.

9.10 WHAT'S WRONG WITH STATISTICS?

What we have been discussing so far may seem much too statistical to really apply to human learning or the semantics of complex human behavior. It is worth trying to defend general statistical approaches or at least to provide a possible context for their use in what are typically thought of as symbolic arenas.

Criticisms of "syntactic" or statistical approaches to semantics usually presuppose a type of model in which default statistical assumptions are made (Bernoulli trials, representative sample statistics, arithmetic averages, etc.). When, in fact, Kahneman and Tversky [Kahneman, Slovic, and Tversky, 1982] have amply demonstrated that people tend to violate simple normative statistical assumptions. People, in fact, seem to make judgments about the world that are riddled with statistical problems such as being biased toward dependence, using small samples, and weight-

ing recent events more than distant events. Nonetheless, we argue that such judgments, although likely to cause trouble in the statistician's world, are apparently adequate for detecting causal relationships some reasonable amount of the time.

Statistical accounts of people's abilities need not employ normative statistical
arguments (law of large numbers, independence, etc.). Nor need they be independent
of the context in which they are formed. Statistical arguments are typically quite sophisticated, relatively context dependent, and can involve assumptions that make the
results optimal under narrowly defined conditions. Therefore, it is critical to understand the difference between default statistical reasoning employed in general models and modeling that employs statistical arguments in the context of assumptions
relevant to a set of phenomena and various external criteria [Cheeseman, 1986].

9.11 COMPREHENSIBILITY MATTERS!

It is important to realize that the similarity measure constrains the conceptual
simplicity and comprehensibility of the category. One of the criticisms leveled
against the statistical clustering techniques is that they are likely to produce categories that will be difficult to interpret, since they do not use any background information. However, it is possible to construct similarity measures that might be more
likely to produce clusters that are more comprehensible. Similarity metrics that
could produce basic-level effects would be associated with categories that have a
higher density of predictable features, thus producing more expectations about the
exemplars in the category and making categories more comprehensible.

People tend to be very good at making judgments about what is comprehensible and what is not. Consider the trains shown in Figure 9–6. These have been used
by Medin, Wattenmaker, and Michalski [1987] in a set of experiments with conceptual clustering and judgments of human subjects. One of Michalski's conceptual
clustering programs (AQ11) has produced concept descriptions that are common to
all members within each set of trains and disjoint between each set of trains. The top
set is described in the conjunction as trains with one small car with a closed top,
while the bottom set is described by the program with the disjunction as trains with
either two cars or trains with a car with a jagged top.

In some of Medin's experiments [Medin, et al., 1987], people were given these
trains to sort, and they found that people did not produce the sets shown but rather
found other categorizations that typically involved only one attribute, thus trains
with a car with a triangle were all grouped together, or trains with cars that had two
wheels, or trains that were all red and so on.

In order to get a fair comparison of the AQ11 description with people's sorts it
is worth considering a variation on this experiment. It is possible that people did not
use more than one feature because they had no reason to do so. We replicated this
experiment with two changes: First, subjects had to repeat the category sort five

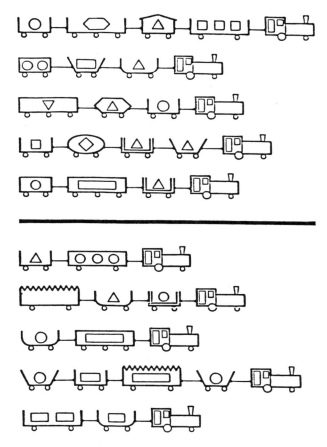

Figure 9–6: Michalski and Stepp [1983] trains example. Shown across the line is a disjoint cover solution. (Reproduced from [Michalski, 1983] with permission of the publisher.)

more times in a row producing unique sorts each time, thus forcing them to use more information about the trains. Second, subjects were asked to state what rule was being used as pairs of trains (randomly chosen) from each group in Figure 9–6 were laid before them. There were two groups of subjects, 10 subjects with at least a college education, and six more subjects from mathematics and computer science research departments at Bellcore.

In part one of the experiment none of the 16 subjects produced categorizations similar to Figure 9–6. Typically, the number of features subjects used increased from one feature to two or three in a conjunction but never in a disjunction. By the fifth sort, concept descriptions supplied by more than half (9/15) of the subjects began using qualifications like "at least one..." or "not more than..."—types of descriptions that are consistent with a polymorphous category. In none of the sorts did subjects attempt to produce a disjoint conjunctive description, and were tolerant of exceptions to their categorization schemes in terms of unattended features or even attended features.

Since no subjects produced the AQ11 result, in part 2 of the experiment the same subjects from experiment 1 were now asked to attempt to induce the rule that AQ11 had produced as a description of the concepts underlying the two groups of trains. Only one subject (a computer scientist) was able to come close to the description that AQ11 had produced. Generally subjects found the concept descriptions produced by AQ11 to be incomprehensible and tended to produce descriptions involving hedges similar to ones they had used before to describe their own sorts.

The lesson to be learned from these train sorts is that not all similarity metrics will produce comprehensible categories and that constraints on categories must result in sets of exemplars that can be described in simple, general terms that reduce uncertainty about the next exemplar to be encountered.

9.12 AN ALGORITHM USING FEATURE INTERCORRELATIONS: WITT

What follows is an implementation of a conceptual clustering algorithm using feature intercorrelations, and contrasts between categories as objects are added to existing categories. Concept descriptions (prototypes, see Section 9.13) are extracted and used as clustering continues to stand in for the exemplars so far clustered in a group.

9.13 WITT STRUCTURE

The present conceptual clustering algorithm (WITT)[2] attempts to automatically cluster a set of objects that have been defined previously in a feature space. WITT's primary goal is to discover concepts in the object set by forming hypotheses and testing the resulting putative concepts for cohesiveness. Failure of one hypothesis leads WITT to test other hypotheses that involve creating new concepts or merging old ones. Various hypotheses are attempted in sequence (an escalation over hypothe-

---

[2] Named for the philosopher Ludwig Wittgenstein who argued persuasively for "family resemblance" and polymorphy as the basis for categorization and language. His classic example of this problem is the nature of the category "game." WITT is implemented in zeta-LISP on a Symbolics 3600, the version described here is an early version of WITT using various feature intercorrelation methods; these had improved in later versions (see [Hanson and Bauer, 1989]).

sis states) in order to achieve better overall cohesiveness within all categories and simultaneously increase the distinctiveness between categories. At present, acceptable levels of cohesiveness are indicated to WITT through two parameters that index the relative "coherence" (normalized to 0,1) within and between categories.

WITT's control structure is modeled after a person attempting to sort or categorize an arbitrary number of objects into a set of disjoint, coherent categories. An example of the kinds of tasks that WITT would attempt to model might be an expert in a field of research attempting to file away some recent documents relevant to a particular subarea of research while at the same time trying to maximize the probability of retrieving the document again in an appropriate context. Another example of a task WITT models is a problem solver attempting to decide whether the problem it is presently dealing with is similar to another problem that it has already solved in the past and subsequently deciding that it should attempt to apply the same sort of problem-solving technique (these might be domain-specific solutions or so-called "weak" methods; compare [Laird, Rosenblum, and Newell 1985]).

WITT has three major components: a search procedure, several selection operators, and an information metric to detect significant interrelationships among features. The search procedure is similar to *K-Means clustering*, in that seeds (protoseeds) are selected in the feature space and further clustering is done relative to these initial seeds. Selection operators then act on objects, protoseeds, and categories in the feature space.

There are only three such operators: object selection, protoseed creation, and protoseed merging. Each has its specific procedures, although each operator employs an information metric in some specific way. WITT cycles within each state until it hits an impasse; that is, until it finds that it cannot apply the present operator. Then the next operator is invoked.

Given a set of objects defined on a (binary or multivalued) feature space, WITT first attempts to form local estimates of dense regions by looking for very similar objects based on an information-loss metric (compare [Orloci, 1969; Lance and Williams, 1967; Wallace and Boulton, 1968]). This defines a preclustering process that gathers identical or relatively identical objects together until a threshold is reached relative to the initial pair of objects joined. Each of these regions is then assigned as a "protoseed." This region may consist of no less then two protoseeds consisting of no less then two objects each.

The protoseed measure is a standard information-loss type measure in which the information content in terms of features of the objects when they are separate is compared with the content when they are joined. If information loss is relatively small they are subsequently assigned to a new protoseed. This is done across objects and is consequently expensive. We have tried incremental variations of this, which seem to work well, that involve picking seeds randomly and then looking in the neighborhood of the seed as new objects appear. This procedure can be done with and without memory but seems more robust with a small (8 to 10) object memory buffer. The protoseed measure is used first for the sake of efficiency and speed. The protoseed measure also avoids having to calculate intercorrelations of a small number of objects that are likely to be misleading. The metric that is used by other operators is a joint information measure among the features within a set of objects, between sets of objects (say, o_x and o_y) and between objects and protoseeds. Such measures are usually defined in terms of independence within the feature space as a function of an information content measure (H):

$$J(f_x, f_y) = H(f_x) + H(f_y) - I(f_x; f_y) \tag{5}$$

J refers to joint or shared information in the features while I refers to intersection or mutual information in the features. We invert I and call it a feature predictability measure (W). It indicates the predictability of one feature given another. This measure is used in WITT to establish relationships between pairs of features within sets of objects.

At each cycle WITT tests whether it is possible to add members to each protoseed without affecting the "identity" of each putative concept. The identity of each protoseed is determined by coherence of feature values that support, and at the same time, distinguish it from all other existing concepts. A ratio of the coherence within a category to the coherence outside the category is formed at each pass to test this trade-off between the cohesion and distinctiveness of the category. The effect on the category cohesion for the protoseed from adding the object is calculated by the feature predictability (W) of the combined object and protoseed (WC = within-category cohesion).

$$WC = W(C_1; o_x) \tag{6}$$

Next the effect of adding the object to the category relative to other existing categories is determined. This consists of two parts: First, the combination of the protoseed pairwise with other protoseeds normalized against the worst case which has $W(C_1; o_x) = W(C_2)$, that is, the protoseeds being indistinguishable. So the cohesion outside the tested category is defined to be:

$$OC = (W(C_1; o_x) + W(C_j) - 2 * W(C_1; C_j; o_x))^{-1} \tag{7}$$

This measure is averaged over all existing protoseeds. Finally the two measures are combined to predict the relative change in feature predictability for the tested category:

$$\textit{Relative Change in Category Cohesion} = \frac{WC}{OC} \tag{8}$$

This measure is a more complex version of the measure used for the basic level predictions in Figure 9–5. This ratio measures the coherence among features in each category relative to the coherence among features to other categories currently available. If this object selection fails, WITT tries a new hypothesis and attempts to create new dense regions, which are assigned to new protoseeds. If the identities of all present protoseeds are maintained or improved, then the protoseed is instantiated, and the object selection operator is tried.

If, on the other hand, the new protoseed fails, it is assumed that the protoseeds are too close together to yield improvement (although we should note there are other possibilities). At this point, the protoseed merging operator is invoked and identities of the protoseeds are again checked. If successful, WITT returns to object selection; otherwise WITT gives up, since further search violates input values of the requested relative tension between categories. WITT then announces that the protoseeds are well formed and indicates whether some objects are left unclustered. WITT then describes each concept in turn and the overall structure of the cluster solution.

At the end of the process several properties of the category are likely to be achieved:

1. At least one best member is identified for each category;

2. the cohesion of the category and its relative distinctiveness are reported;

3. a relative contrast between all categories is chosen to maximize identity within a category and minimize overgeneralization between categories;

4. feature relations are indicated by the correlation structure within each category;

5. and labels for the hierarchical relations of the objects are indicated at each branch of the tree including common features, distinctive features, and necessary and sufficient features (if any).

9.14 SOME RESULTS: WITT STUDIES

9.14.1 Detection of Polymorphy

In order to demonstrate some of the category properties we have been discussing, we first examine a difficult kind of artificial stimuli that has been used in a categorization experiment with human subjects [Dennis, Hampton, and Lea, 1973]. Recall these are the stimuli that were described earlier of people that have different cars, professions, location, and marital status. In this case the car owned is an incidental feature and the other three features form a perfect example of 2 out of 3 polymorphy for the categories. As stated earlier, a property of polymorphous categories is that the feature set that defines the inclusion rule is based on neither necessary, sufficient nor necessary and sufficient feature sets. Thus, there is no feature common to all members of the category nor is there one that is not in one category without being present in the other.

Subjects (in some of our experiments) will provide similarity ratings between pairs of exemplars that seem to indicate they are sensitive to the overlapping feature sets. Subjects can also successfully categorize these exemplars into the two indicated sets in Figure 9–1, although they will generally not be able to state the rule they are using to do the sorting.

WITT was given these same stimuli in a binary matrix (including the incidental feature, car driven) and different clustering parameters were used in seven separate runs. Five of these seven runs resulted in unique clusterings that cover most of the significant range of the clustering parameters, which are shown in Table 9–1. Shown in each column are the parameter values for the cohesion (Tc), distinctiveness (Td) the ratio of distinctiveness and cohesion (Tc/Td; $T_{c/d}$), the resultant distinctiveness ("Dis") and cohesiveness ("Coh") of the clusters.

If one looks for both the largest cohesiveness and concurrently the smallest distinctiveness of the solution, it is clear that the intermediate ratio of cohesiveness and distinctiveness (9; starred cluster value) produces the best outcome.

This particular solution has an extremely good distinctiveness in terms of transmission between categories (almost 0) and the largest cohesion distributed equally across the two clusters. In many ways this is an ideal cluster solution. Further note that the feature-to-feature intercorrelations for all eight stimuli considered together is 0. That is, the solution to this problem must involve agglomerative or local views of the data in order to find the optimal intercorrelation set. Other standard multivariate techniques would have a difficult time with such an intercorrelation matrix.

Finally in Figure 9–7 is the complete dendrogram of the eight stimuli showing the cluster history as a function of transmission between features. Notice that the two centers first isolated provide the strongest possible contrast in the space, although there are other possible choices. Thereafter, members are added that reduce the overall cohesion but not beneath a tolerable threshold (we actually allowed WITT to chose a relatively high value of cohesion if it could). WITT stopped because it ran out of objects to cluster. No one of the exemplars was considered by WITT to be more prototypical of the discovered categories than any other.

Table 9–1:   Polymorphy runs

Tc	Td	Tc/Td	Dis	Coh	#Clusters
.5	.2	2.5	.1,.1,.03	.16,.16,.5	3
.8	.2	4	.1,.1,.03	.17,.17,.35	3
.9	.1	9	.0001	.23,.23	2*
.7	.05	40	.0001	.16,.10	2
.8	.005	140	none	.10	1

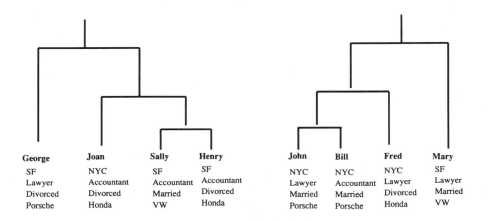

George	Joan	Sally	Henry	John	Bill	Fred	Mary
SF	NYC	SF	SF	NYC	NYC	NYC	SF
Lawyer	Accountant	Accountant	Accountant	Lawyer	Accountant	Lawyer	Lawyer
Divorced	Divorced	Married	Divorced	Married	Married	Divorced	Married
Porsche	Honda	VW	Honda	Porsche	Porsche	Honda	VW

Figure 9–7:   A dendrogram for the two out of three polymorphy example shown in
Figure 9–1

9.15 WHERE DO SCRIPTS COME FROM?

The following demonstration is intended to show how semantic net construction might be accomplished by using machine-readable resources and conceptual clustering. In this type of approach, semantic relations are inferred from the featural relations discovered during cluster formation. Following from the psychological evidence discussed earlier, we argue that semantic categories are those that are supported by a set of feature intercorrelations within each cluster. These may also correspond to basic levels that may underlie the data set and simulate the kind of learning children might do. The comprehensibility and underlying rationale of each category depends on the constellation of feature values that supports one category and distinguishes it from another.

In this approach we also assume that semantic primitives, semantic links in a type hierarchy (e.g., ISA and "kindof" links) and slot-filler structures such as scripts or frames have analogues in conceptual clustering. If conceptual clustering semantic primitives are to be found in the category structure, they are most likely to be represented by objects or metalevels that provide the greatest support for the other members of a category. Links can be represented by those common, distinctive and polymorphous features that induce category membership. Scripts and other slot-filler structures are represented in conceptual clustering by the feature interrelations; such covariation is analogous to "expectations" that cause a conceptual structure to be used to predict, using attribute "criteria," that an object is of a certain type rather than another.

Various approaches to conceptual modeling have appeared in AI. Schank and his colleagues have argued for a conceptual-dependency approach. This involves using some primitive concepts in a domain and representing more complex concepts with these primitives. So "liar," for example, might be represented as someone who transfers false knowledge from one person (himself) to another (M-TRANS). In this approach, each concept might possess expectations about information it is receiving; so for example, in the canonical approach, if the "earthquake concept" has been activated then certain expectations about the size, the location, the extent of the destruction, and the likelihood of further tremors may also be activated. In such a way scripts or frames can take advantage of possible (preenumerated) attribute correlations by "expecting" other features once a correlate has been observed.

The main disadvantage to semantic network construction is that these approaches tend to be *ad hoc*. Many of the so-called fundamental problems in machine learning, for example the "bottleneck" problem and the "brittleness" problem, arise from the unprincipled construction of knowledge bases, which makes the addition of new knowledge complicated and the generalization to new domains intractable.

In order to illustrate the current approach and contrast it with other approaches, we consider a specific example of using of an archival distribution of semantic features for the nations of the world. We stress that we are not looking for one particular organization or the "right" set of categories, but rather any organization of object types that is comprehensible and provides specific, sensible hypotheses about the group membership based on feature sets. Thus, it should be noted that random organizations of nations are generally not sensible and that higher order descriptions such as "superpowers," "third world" and "poor but technologically advanced" are unlikely to arise by chance organizations alone.

The following example uses a machine-readable version of the *1985 World Almanac* in which three tuples of the form:

<country attribute value>

were extracted[3] from the running text in each section describing a particular country. In each description there turned out to be 17 usable, multivalued features (453 binary features) for each country. These are shown in Table 9–2, with their descriptions; they consisted of attributes like "defense budget," "religions" and "infant mortality." Thirty-seven countries were arbitrarily chosen with the constraint that they cover a

---

[3] R.A. Amsler is responsible for the automatic extraction of the S-expressions from the machine-readable text. This was accomplished by parsing both the phototypesetting symbols and the resultant noun phrases. This example is used by permission and and originally appeared in Hanson and Bauer [1989].

Table 9–2: Features for nations of the world

AREA	area of the country (hi,mid,lo)
LOCATION	location of the nation in the world (N-africa,indochina...)
INDUSTRIES	primary industries in the country (iron, cars, electronics...)
DEFENSE	amount spent of GNP on defense (hi,mid,lo)
CURRENCY	name of the currency of the country (dollar, riel, kyat...)
LITERACY	number in population literate (hi,mid,low)
CHIEF-CROPS	primary crops farmed by population (grains, wine, potatoes...)
MINERALS	primary minerals in the country (oil, iron, coal...)
IMPORTS	countries from which this country imports (usa, france ...)
EXPORTS	countries to which this country exports (usa, w-germany...)
TYPE	the type of government in place in the country in 1985 (republic, communist...)
LANGUAGE	the primary languages spoken by population (english, french...)
RELIGIONS	the primary religions practiced by the population (hindu, christian...)
TELEVISION-SETS	the number of tvs in the country (hi,mid,low)
NATIONAL-BUDGET	the size of the national budget as reported in 1985 (hi,mid,low)
PER-CAPITA-INCOME	the average income for a member of the population (hi,mid,low)
INFANT-MORTALITY	the rate of infant death from birth, disease etc. ... (hi,mid,low)

large range of continents and provide a large range of variation in featural values. Although more nations could have been included, we felt it was not necessary since we were interested in constructing metalevel categories, which should not be necessarily based on complete coverage (i.e., you may know the concept "third world" countries but not be able to name them all). And in any case, the *World Almanac* does not really provide comprehensive coverage over the entire world.

The variables taken from the almanac were further cleaned up and quantitative variables such as "percent literacy of population" were transformed to ordinal values. This was done automatically by examining the frequency histogram of the variable and looking for nodes in the data that would suggest a break for multivalued variables like "hi," "mid," or "low." Approximately one-half the variables were quantitative and transformed accordingly. Nonetheless, WITT, only uses the nominal or semantic value of the variable without note of possible order information, although the value is reported along with feature correlations.

WITT was given the 37 nations of the world with their corresponding attribute values. Several runs were attempted, some with conservative categorization (low $T_{c/d}$) and some with more liberal (high $T_{c/d}$) criteria. Most of the runs settled in relatively stable local minima, similar to what was found in Figure 9–8.[4] This figure shows the complete dendrogram for the 37 nations of the world. Examination of the dendrogram reveals that WITT did discover reasonable and comprehensible groupings. For example, at the top of the dendrogram note the first cluster of two countries including the U.S.A. and Canada. This set seems to be broken off from a European cluster including Italy, Spain, United Kingdom, and France, which in turn are distinct from a larger cluster starting near the bottom of the dendrogram with Cambodia, Vietnam, and Bangladesh. Toward the center of the dendrogram we have some interesting clusters such as Ireland and Israel, and a separate cluster involving China, Iran, and Iraq.

Roughly the structure of the dendrogram can be broken into seven or eight groups. At the highest level we see a split between countries that may be described as "third world" and countries that are technologically advanced and have a relatively high quality of life. Finer distinctions can be made as we move down the dendrogram and notice a cluster having to do with European countries and another cluster down the tree in Southeast Asia or Africa. However, geography seems to have less to do with the finer groupings than do some abstract qualities having to do with economy, quality of life, and industries.

Each cluster group can be examined in terms of the feature correlations representing the groups that WITT found. Figure 9–9 shows two cluster groups at the lowest level of the tree. These include for contrast, the U.S.A. cluster and the Southeast Asia cluster. In this figure correlations are shown that were among the top five to 10 in characterizing the cluster. For example, in the U.S.A. group we see correlates that might be related to a "high quality of life" seem to predominate. This seems indicated by the large number of television sets (related to leisure time, recreation, etc.) and the large national budgets each of these countries has. Also location in the world and industries seem to be a good predictor of this group, although, one that might be expected to change when other locations outside of North America were found to contain similar values. Finally, a third predictor set was the predominate literacy of the population and the democratic type of government. Each of these sets was above .6 in correlation and indicates what is considered "important" to these clusters. In the next group, in which Cambodia is the prototype, we see lots of features that might indicate a "low quality of life." Economic factors also seem to be an important attribute of the cluster. For example, the pair low national budget and low per capita income seem to be included in a number of correlations with other variables like literacy, defense, and number of televisions—a seeming mix of economic, govern-

---

[4] In fact, from experience we have found there are typically only a few numbers of clusters that WITT can find, and they are generally in a small neighborhood of possible groupings. This must partly reflect WITT's conservative control structure and partly the given distribution of attribute values in a given data set.

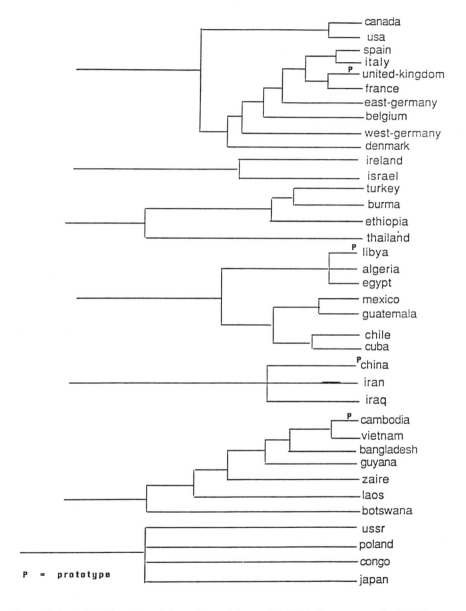

Figure 9–8:   WITT sorting of the nations of the world. "P" indicates countries WITT selected as closest to prototype.

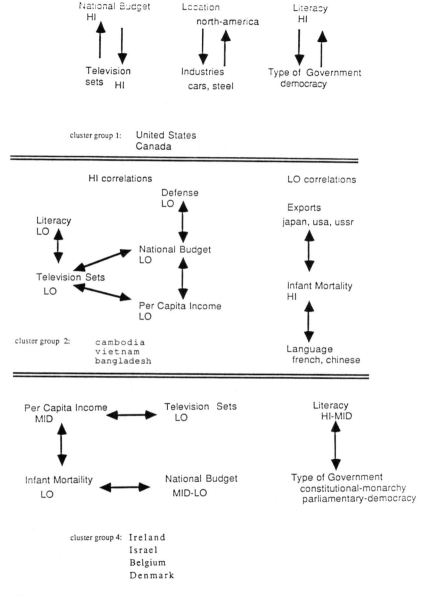

Figure 9-9:   A more structural view of three selected groups of the nations of the world clustering. Shown are the feature intercorrelations on which the group was based.

mental, educational, and technological variables. A third set of variable correlations seem significant involving infant mortality with location, exports, and language. Such covariates would seem to implicate not only quality-of-life issues but hospital care, local health conditions, and education.

Human judgments of the nations of the world provide a similar picture of the categories. Both the number of categories and the gross overall group structure is similar to WITT's clustering. Figure 9–10 shows the results of clustering the sortings of 10 subjects who were given either just the nation labels (e.g., "France"), the feature values for that nation, or both. Subjects were first analyzed individually showing few differences (partly due to the small number of subjects per group) and thus collapsed to obtain a co-occurrence matrix (i.e., the number of subjects that agreed that nation i belonged with nation j). This was submitted to a hierarchical clustering algorithm for complete linkage clustering. The average number of categories used by subjects was about 11, while the tree shown in Figure 9–10 suggests a cut at about seven to nine clusters. Overall, the main partitions seem very similar to WITT's groups including Europe, the U.S.A. and Canada, and many of the same third-world countries. Some clusters that WITT missed involved more complicated political features (USSR, Poland, East Germany) and possibly simpler geographically motivated clusters (Zaire, Botswana, Congo).

9.16 SUMMARY: FEATURE INTERCORRELATIONS, CATEGORIZATION, AND SEMANTICS

In this chapter, several interrelated arguments have been made:

1. Correlations of features are important for the support and elaboration of categories. They can be used to discover the structure of semantic domains (also see [Deerwester, *et al.*, 1987]) and are probably used to reduce uncertainty about events in the domain. It would thus be possible to construct a similarity-based method that would use results of its clustering to do category-to-feature and feature-to-category predictability in order to construct expectations and generate hypotheses about the domain.

2. Although computational and mathematical models with various similarity metrics, are potentially many, they can be constrained by their category properties, including the prototype information they employ, their relation to the basic level, and how they grade family resemblance within the category.

3. Explanation-based learning models and semantic models more generally tend to employ the sort of information captured by feature correlations. Analogy and problem solving tends to have this flavor; for example, it is possible to interpret relations and other sorts of domain information as other kinds of fea-

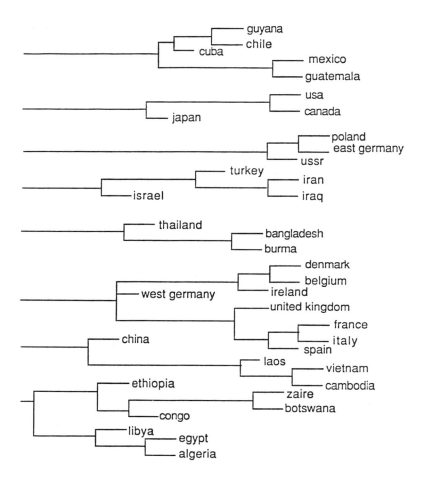

Figure 9–10:   The resultant dendrogram from 10 human subjects sorting the nations of the world by features, using labels and combination of features and labels

tures and use them with property features in correlation-based learning systems (e.g., constraint satisfaction paradigms; compare [Holyoke and Thagard, 1987]).

4. Finally, it remains to be seen how the inductive gap will be filled between bottom-up, data-oriented approaches and top-down, theory-guided methods. One

step in the right direction must involve the sort of "causal" knowledge that is commonly embedded in top-down methods, which may be possible to discover in bottom-up methods that entertain complex similarity hypotheses about domain features and their relations.

ACKNOWLEDGMENTS

Malcolm Bauer implemented various versions of WITT and has helped in the design and theory regarding later versions of WITT. I am also grateful to R.B. Allen, G.W. Furnas, C. Hanson, G.A. Miller, and D. Walker for reading and commenting on earlier versions of this chapter.

References

Anderson, J.A., Silverstein, J.W., Ritz, S.A., and Jones, R.S. 1977. Distinctive features, categorical perception, and probability learning: Some applications of a neural model, *Psychological Review* 84, pp. 413–451.

Hanson, S.J. and Burr, D.J. 1987. Knowledge representation in connectionist networks, Bellcore Technical Report.

Deerwester, S., Dumais, S., Furnas, G., Landauer, T., and Harshman, R. 1987. Indexing by latent semantic analysis, Bellcore Technical Report.

Dennis, I., Hampton, J.A., and Lea, S.E.G. 1973. New problem in concept formation, *Nature* 243, pp. 101–102.

Cheeseman, P. 1986. In defense of probability. *Proceedings of the AAAI*.

DeJong, G. and Mooney, 1986. Explanation based learning: an alternative view, *Machine Learning* 1,2, pp. 145–176.

Estes W.K. 1986. Memory storage and retrieval processes in category learning, *Journal of Experimental Psychology: General* 22, pp. 155–174.

Everitt, B. 1977. *Cluster Analysis*, Heinemann Educational Books, London.

Fisher, D. 1987. Conceptual Clustering, Learning from Examples, and Inference. Machine Learning Conference, Irvine, pp. 38–48.

Gluck, M.A. and Corter, J.A. 1985. Information and category utility, *Seventh Annual Cognitive Science Conference*, Irvine, August.

Grossberg, S. 1976. Adaptive pattern classification and universal recoding I: Parallel development and coding of neural feature detectors, *Biological Cybernetics* 23, pp. 121–134.

Holyoke, K. and Thagard, P. 1987. Analogical Mapping by Constraint Satisfaction, unpublished manuscript.

Homa, D. 1978. Abstraction of ill-defined form, *Journal of Experimental Psychology: Human Learning and Memory* 4, pp. 407–416.

Jones G.V. 1983. Identifying basic categories, *Psychological Bulletin* 94, pp. 423–428.

Kahneman, D., Slovic, P., and Tversky, A. 1982. *Judgement Under Uncertainty: Heuristics and Biases*, Cambridge University Press, NY.

Laird, J.E., Rosenbloom, P.S., and Newell, A. 1985. Towards chunking as a general learning mechanism, *Technical Report cmu-cs–85-110,* Department of Computer Science, CMU, January.

Lance, G.N. and Williams, W.T. 1967. Note on a new information-statistic classificatory program, *Computer Journal* 195.

Lebowitz, M. 1986. Concept learning in a rich input domain: Generalization-based memory. In *Machine Learning: An Artificial Intelligence Approach, Volume II,* R.S. Michalski, J.G. Carbonell, and T.M. Mitchell (Eds.), Morgan Kaufmann, San Mateo, CA.

McClelland, J.J. and Rumelhart, D. 1985. Distributed memory and the representation of general and specific information, *Journal of Experimental Psychology: General,* 114, pp. 159–188.

Medin, D.L., Wattenmaker W.D., and Hampson S.E. In press. Family resemblance, conceptual cohesiveness and category construction, *Cognitive Psychology.*

Medin, D.L., Wattenmaker, W.D., and Michalski, R.S. 1987. Constraints and preferences in inductive learning: An experimental study of human and machine performance, *Cognitive Science* 11, pp. 299–339.

Michalski, R.S. 1980. Knowledge acquisition through conceptual clustering: A theoretical framework and an algorithm for partitioning data into conjunctive concepts, *International Journal of Policy Analysis and Information Systems* 4, pp. 219–244.

Michalski, R.S. and Stepp, R.E. 1983. Learning from observation: Conceptual clustering. In R.S. Michalski, J.G. Carbonell, and T.M. Mitchell (Eds.), *Machine*

Learning: An Artificial Intelligence Approach, Morgan Kaufmann, San Mateo, CA., pp. 331–363.

R.S. Michalski, J.G. Carbonell, and T.M. Mitchell (Eds.), 1983. *Machine Learning: An Artificial Intelligence Approach*, Morgan Kaufmann, San Mateo, CA

Mitchell T., Keller, R., and Kedar-Cabelli, S. 1986. Explanation-based generalization: A unifying view, *Machine Learning* 1, pp. 47–80.

Murphy, G.L. 1982. Cue validity and levels of categorization, *Psychological Bulletin* 91, pp. 174–177.

Murphy, G.L. and Medin, D.L. 1985. The role of theories in conceptual coherence, *Psychological Review* 92, pp. 289–316.

Murphy, G.L. and Smith, E.E. 1982. Basic level superiority in picture categorization, *Jounal of Verbal Learning and Verbal Behavior* 21, pp. 1–20.

Orloci, L. 1969. Information analysis of structure in biological collections, *Nature* 223, pp. 483–484.

Posner, M.I. and Keele, S.W. 1968. On the genesis of abstract ideas, *Journal of Experimental Psychology* 77, pp. 353–363.

Rosch, E. and Lloyd, B.B. (Eds.). 1978. *Cognition and Categorization*, Erlbaum, Hillsdale, NJ.

Rosch, E., Mervis, C., Gray, W., Johnson, D,. and Boyes-Braem. 1976. Basic objects in natural categories. *Cognitive Psychology* 7, pp. 382–439.

Rumelhart, D. and McClelland, J.J. 1986. *Parallel Distributed Processing: Explorations in the Microstructure of Cognition*, MIT Press, Cambridge, MA.

Rumelhart, D.E. and Zipser, D. 1985. Competitive learning, *Cognitive Science,* 9, pp. 75–112.

Schank, R.C., Collins, G.C., and Hunter, L. 1987. Transcending inductive category formation in learning. *Behavioral and Brain Sciences*.

Shepard, R.N. 1980. Multidimensional scaling, tree-fitting and clustering, *Science* 210, pp. 390–398.

Smith, E.E. and Medin, D.L. 1981. *Categories and Concepts*, Harvard Univ. Press, Cambridge, MA.

Sneath, E. and Sokal, E. 1973. *Numerical Taxonomy*, San Francisco: W.H. Freeman.

Stepp, R. and Michalski, R. 1986. Conceptual clustering: Inventing goal-oriented classifications of structured objects. In *Machine Learning: An Artificial Intelli-*

gence Approach, Volume II, R.S. Michalski, J.G. Carbonell, and T.M. Mitchell (Eds.), Morgan Kaufmann, San Mateo, CA.

Wallace, C.S. and Boulton, D.M. 1968. An information measure for classification, *Computer Journal* 11, pp. 185–194.

Wishart, D. 1969. Numerical classification method for deriving natural classes, *Nature* 221, pp. 97–98.

Wittgenstein, L. 1953. *Philosophical Investigations*, Basil Blackwell, Oxford.

Tversky, A. 1977. Features of similarity, *Psychological Review* 84, pp. 327–352.

PART
THREE

ANALYTICAL LEARNING METHODS

10

LEAP:

A LEARNING APPRENTICE
FOR VLSI DESIGN

Tom M. Mitchell
(Carnegie Mellon University)

Sridbar Mabadevan
Louis I. Steinberg
(Rutgers University)

Abstract

It is by now well recognized that a major impediment to developing knowl-edge-based systems is the knowledge-acquisition bottleneck: The task of building up a complete enough and correct enough knowledge base to provide high-level perfor-mance. This chapter proposes a new class of knowledge-based systems designed to address this knowledge-acquisition bottleneck by incorporating a learning compo-nent to acquire new knowledge through experience. In particular, we define *learning apprentice systems* as the class of *interactive*, knowledge-based consultants that di-rectly assimilate new knowledge by observing and analyzing the problem-solving steps contributed by their users through their *normal* use of the system. This chapter describes a specific learning apprentice system, called LEAP, which is currently being developed in the domain of VLSI design. We also discuss design issues for learning apprentice systems more generally, as well as restrictions on the generality of our current approach.

10.1 LEARNING APPRENTICE SYSTEMS

It is by now well recognized that a major impediment to developing knowl-edge-based systems is the knowledge-acquisition bottleneck: The task of building up a complete enough and correct enough knowledge base to provide high-level performance. In an effort to reduce the cost and increase the level of performance of current knowledge-based systems, a number of researchers have developed semi-automated tools for aiding in the knowledge-acquisition process. These tools include interactive aids to help pinpoint and correct weaknesses in existing sets of rules (e.g., [Davis, 1981; Politikas, 1982]), as well as aids for the acquisition of new rules (e.g., [Kahn, et al., 1984]). Others have studied automated learning of rules from databases of stored cases, but with few exceptions (e.g., [Buchanan and Mitchell, 1978; Michalski and Chilauskym, 1980]), work on machine learning has not yet led to useful knowledge-acquisition tools.

This chapter proposes a new class of knowledge-based consultant systems designed to overcome the knowledge-acquisition bottleneck, by incorporating recently developed machine learning methods to automate the acquisition of new rules. In particular, we define *learning apprentice systems* as the class of *interactive* knowledge-based consultants that directly assimilate new knowledge by observing and analyzing the problem-solving steps contributed by their users through their *normal* use of the system. This chapter discusses issues related to the development of such learning apprentice systems, focusing on the design of a particular learning apprentice system (called LEAP) for VLSI circuit design.

One key aspect of learning apprentice systems as we define them is that they are designed to continually acquire new knowledge without an explicit "training mode." For example, the LEAP system provides advice on how to refine the design of a VLSI circuit, while allowing the user to override this advice and to manually refine the circuit when he so desires. In those cases where the user manually refines the circuit, LEAP records this problem-solving step as a training example of some rule that it should have had. LEAP then generalizes from this example to form a new rule summarizing this refinement tactic.

In task domains for which learning apprentice systems are feasible, we expect that they will offer strong advantages over current architectures for knowledge-based systems. Many copies of a learning apprentice system distributed to a broad community of users could acquire a base of problem-solving experience very large compared to the experience from which a human expert learns. For example, by distributing copies of LEAP to a thousand circuit designers, the system (collection) would quickly be exposed to a larger number of example circuit designs than a human designer could hope to see during a lifetime. Such a large experience base would offer the potential for acquiring a very strong knowledge base, provided effective learning methods can be developed.

The following section describes the design of the LEAP learning apprentice system for VLSI design, focusing on its mechanism for capturing training examples, and on its methods for generalizing from these examples to form new rules. The final section discusses some of the major choices made in the initial design of LEAP, limitations on the applicability of our initial approach, and several basic issues that we see as central to developing learning apprentice systems in a variety of task domains.

10.2 LEAP: A LEARNING APPRENTICE FOR VLSI DESIGN

LEAP is currently being constructed as an augmentation to a knowledge-based VLSI design assistant called VEXED [Mitchell, *et al.*, 1985]. VEXED provides interactive aid to the user in implementing a circuit given its functional specifications, by suggesting and carrying out possible refinements to the design. A large part of its knowledge about circuit design is composed of a set of *implementation rules*, each of which suggests some legal method for refining a given function. For example, one implementation rule states that *IF the required function is to convert a parallel signal to a serial signal, THEN one possible implementation is to use a shift register*. It is these rules that LEAP is designed to learn. This section describes the VEXED system, the type of training examples that it can capture from its users, and two generalization methods that allow LEAP to form general rules from these examples.

10.2.1 The VEXED Design Consultant

VEXED is a prototype knowledge-based design consultant that provides a convenient editor and user interface that helps the user design digital circuits beginning with functional specifications and leading to implementation. VEXED maintains an agenda of design subtasks (e.g., "implement the module that must multiply two numbers"), which initially contains the top-level task of implementing the entire circuit. VEXED repeatedly selects a subtask from the agenda, examines its implementation rules to determine whether it can suggest possible implementations for the corresponding circuit module, then presents any such suggestions to the user. The user may select one of the suggested implementation rules—in which case that rule is executed to refine the module. Alternatively, the user may disregard VEXED's suggestions and instead use the editor to refine the circuit module manually. It is in this latter case that LEAP will add to its knowledge of circuit design, by generalizing from the implementation step contributed by the user to formulate a new rule that summarizes a previously uncatalogued implementation method.

As an example of this kind of learning scenario, suppose that at some point during the design VEXED and the user are considering the task of implementing a particular circuit module. In the example, this circuit module must compute the Boolean product of sums of four particular input signals that appear in the context of the larger circuit. Assume further that these input signals are regular streams of Boolean values arriving every 100 nanoseconds, remaining stable for approximately 70 nanoseconds, and encoded in positive logic.[1] Assume furthermore, that the stream of input values for Input1 is known to be an alternating stream of logical ones and zeros. The exact definitions of the function to be implemented and of the signals for which it must work are given in the top half of Figure 10–1.[2]

Given this information about the module to be implemented, the system searches its set of implementation rules for advice regarding possible refinements of this circuit. In this case, the system may have a rule that suggests implementing the circuit module using an AND gate and two OR gates. Suppose, however, that the user disregards the advice of the system in this case, choosing instead to implement the module using the circuit shown in Figure 10–1. This implementation contributed by the user provides the system with precisely the kind of training example that LEAP needs for learning a new implementation rule. In general, then, each training example consists of

1. a description of the function to be implemented,

2. a description of the known characteristics of the input signals, and

3. a circuit entered by the user to implement the given function for the given input signals.[3]

Given such a training example, there are two kinds of changes that one might expect the system to make to its knowledge base. First, LEAP has the opportunity to acquire a new implementation rule that can be used in subsequent cases to suggest the user's NOR-gate circuit where it is a *possible* implementation. Second, the system also has an opportunity to learn a fragment of control knowledge for selecting between the NOR-gate implementation and the previously known AND-OR-gate implementation, depending on which is *preferred* according to some cost criterion. In VEXED, we have cleanly separated out these two kinds of knowledge. Implementation rules characterize only the *possible* correct implementations, while a separate body of control knowledge will be used to select the *preferred* implementation from among several possible alternatives. In our work to date and in this chapter, we consider only learning of new implementation rules that characterize the general conditions under which the user's circuit can be correctly used.

---

[1] That is, a logical one is encoded as five volts, and a logical zero as zero volts.

[2] Signals or "datastreams" in VEXED are described as an array of data elements, each defined in terms of its value, start-time, duration, data type, and encoding.

[3] Although in this example the user's circuit has been refined down to the gate level, in general it need only be one step more refined than the submodule it is implementing.

Function to be Implemented:
Inputs: Input1, Input2. Input3. Input4
Outputs: Output
Function: (Equals (Value Output(i))
    (And (Or (Value Input1(i)) (Value Input2(i)))
        (Or (Value Input3(i)) (Value Input4(i)))))

Where Input Signals Satisfy:
(Datatype Input1(i)) = Boolean
(Value Input1(i)) = i Mod 2
(Encoding Input1(i)) = Positive-Logic
(Start-Time Input1(i)) = $i \cdot 100 + t_0$
(Duration Input1(i)) = 75 nsec.
(Datatype Input2(i)) = Boolean
(Value Input2(i)) = unknown
(Encoding Input2(i)) = Positive-Logic
(Start-Time Input2(i)) = $i \cdot 100 + t_0$
(Duration Input2(i)) = 65 nsec.
(Datatype Input3(i)) = Boolean
(Value Input3(i)) = unknown
(Encoding Input3(i)) = Positive-Logic
(Start-Time Input3(i)) = $i \cdot 100 + t_0$
(Duration Input3(i)) = 58 nsec.
(Datatype Input4(i)) = Boolean
(Value Input4(i)) = unknown
(Encoding Input4(i)) = Positive-Logic
(Start-Time Input4(i)) = $i \cdot 100 + t_0$
(Duration Input4(i)) = 75 nsec.

User's Solution:

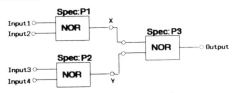

Figure 10–1: A training example for LEAP

Given this training example, the most straightforward method of acquiring a new implementation rule is to create a rule that suggests the given circuit can be used to implement the given module function in precisely this context (e.g., whenever the input signals are precisely the same as in the training example). Such a rule would clearly be so specific that it would add little of general use to the system's knowledge of implementation methods. A better approach would be to generalize the pre-

IF the Function to be Implemented is of the form:
Inputs: Input1, Input2, Input3, Input4
Outputs: Output
Function: (Equals (Value Output(i))
  (And (Or (Value Input1(i)) (Value Input2(i)))
       (Or (Value Input3(i)) (Value Input4(i))))))

Where Input Signals Satisfy:
((Datatype Input1(i) = Boolean)
((Encoding Input1(i)) = Positive-Logic)
((Datatype Input2(i) = Boolean)
((Encoding Input2(i)) = Positive-Logic)
((Datatype Input3(i) = Boolean)
((Encoding Input3(i)) = Positive-Logic)
((Datatype Input4(i) = Boolean)
((Encoding Input4(i)) = Positive-Logic)
(Length (Intersection (Interval Input1(i))
       (Interval Input2(i))
       (Interval Input3(i))
       (Interval Input4(i)))) > 3 nsec.

THEN one possible implementation is:

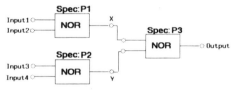

Figure 10–2:   Inferred rule with generalized left-hand side

conditions (left-hand side) of the implementation rule, so that it characterizes the general class of input signals for which the given circuit correctly implements the specified function. Such a generalized rule is shown in Figure 10–2 and the method for producing such generalizations in LEAP is described in the following subsection. A further step in generalizing the implementation rule would be to generalize the user's circuit as well as the function it implements. (e.g., the essential idea behind the NOR-gate implementation can be used to implement a class of functions related to the one encountered in this training example). Such a generalization of the implementation rule is shown in Figure 10–3, and the method used by LEAP for generalizing the rule in this fashion is described in Section 10.2.3.

    LEAP computes a justifiably general rule precondition by using its theory of digital circuits to analyze the single training example. In particular, LEAP first explains (verifies) for itself that the circuit does in fact work for the example input signals, then generalizes from this example by retaining only those features of the

IF the Function to be Implemented is of the form:
  Inputs: < inputs >
  Outputs: < out >
  Function: (Equals (Value <out>(i))
                    (And <bool-fn2> <bool-fn1>))

THEN one possible implementation is:

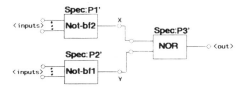

With Specifications of the three modules as follows:

P_1': (Equals (Value X(i)) (Not <bool-fn2>))

P_2': (Equals (Value Y(i)) (Not <bool-fn1>))

P_3': (Equals (Value <out>(i)) (Not (Or X(i) Y(i))))

Figure 10–3:   Inferred rule with generalized right-hand side

signals that were mentioned in this explanation. It is this set of signal features that is required for the explanation to hold in general, and which therefore characterizes the class of input signals for which the circuit will correctly implement the desired function. This explain-then-generalize method for producing justifiable generalizations from single examples is based on our previous work on goal-directed generalization [Mitchell, 1983], and is also similar to the generalization methods employed in [De-Jong, 1982; Salzberg and Atkinson, 1984; Minton, 1984].

To illustrate this generalization method, consider again the training example introduced in Figure 10–1. LEAP begins by verifying that the example circuit will operate correctly for the example input signals. In order to do this, it examines its definitions of the primitive components that make up the example circuit. Figure 10–4 shows the description of the primitive NOR gate used in the present example circuit. The *Operating Conditions* in this description summarize characteristics of the input signals that are required for the component to have a well-defined output. For example, the constraint

(Length (Intersection (Interval Input1(i)) (Interval Input2(i)))) > 3 nsec.

```
Inputs:  Input1, Input2
Outputs: Output

Operating Conditions:
  (Equals (Datatype Input1(i)) Boolean)
  (Equals (Encoding Input1(i)) Positive-Logic)
  (Equals (Datatype Input2(i)) Boolean)
  (Equals (Encoding Input2(i)) Positive-Logic)
  (Length (Intersection (Interval Input1(i))
                        (Interval Input2(i)))) > 3 nsec.

Mapping:
  (Equals (Value Output(i))
          (Not (Or (Value Input1(i)) (Value Input2(i)))))
  (Equals (Encoding Output(i)) Positive-Logic)
  (Equals (Start-Time Output(i))
          (+ 10 (Latest (Start-Time Input1(i))
                        (Start-Time Input2(i)))))
  (Equals (Duration Output(i))
          (Length (Intersection (Interval Input1(i))
          (Interval Input2(i)))))
```

The *Operating Conditions* describe minimum
requirements on input signals to assure the component
will produce a well-defined output. The *Mapping*
describes how features of the output signal depend on
the inputs.

Figure 10–4:   Known behavior of a NOR gate

indicates that for the NOR gate to operate correctly, its inputs must overlap in time
by at least 3 nanoseconds.[4]

These operating conditions of the individual circuit components are constraints
that must be verified for the example circuit and the given input signals. Some of
these operating conditions can be tested directly against the descriptions of the
global circuit inputs (e.g., the operating conditions for the leftmost NOR gates in the
example circuit can be tested against the known characteristics of the circuit inputs).
The operating conditions associated with components internal to the example circuit
must be restated in terms of the equivalent constraints on the global circuit inputs.
These constraints are therefore *propagated* to (reexpressed in terms of) the global
inputs of the circuit network, then tested to see that they are satisfied by the example
input signals. For instance, the constraint

   (Length (Intersection (Interval X(i)) (Interval Y(i)))) > 3 nsec.

---

[4]The *Interval* of a data element is defined here as the time interval beginning at the *Start-time*
of the data element, and continuing for the *Duration* of that element.

which follows from the operating conditions of the rightmost NOR gate, is re-expressed in terms of the four global circuit inputs to produce the equivalent constraint

(Length (Intersection (Interval Input1(i))(Interval Input2(i))
(Interval Input3(i)) (Interval Input4(i)))) > 3 nsec.[5]

By propagating the constraints arising from the operating conditions of the circuit components, as well as the original constraint on the circuit output (e.g., that it produces the Boolean sum of products of the input, LEAP can then verify that the user-introduced circuit will correctly implement the desired function for the given inputs. More importantly, the constraints that are propagated to the inputs of the circuit network characterize precisely the class of inputs for which the circuit will operate correctly, and therefore constitute the desired general preconditions for the newly acquired implementation rule.

In summary, the procedure for computing the generalized preconditions for the new rule is

1. to propagate each constraint derived from the operating conditions of each primitive circuit component, along with constraints on the global circuit output, back to the global inputs to the circuit network, then

2. to record the resulting constraints on the global inputs, with appropriate substitution of variable names, as the generalized preconditions for the new implementation rule.

Figure 10–2 illustrates the resulting generalization for the training example from Figure 10–1. Notice that in comparing this generalized rule with the original training example, values of several features of the circuit inputs have been generalized. Only the constraints on data type and on signal encodings remain intact, while the detailed values for the signal start-times and durations have been replaced by the general constraint on overlapping time intervals.

10.2.3 Generalizing Rule Right-Hand Side

The previous section describes how LEAP is able to generalize the left-hand side (LHS) of the rule by determining the class of input signals for which the given circuit will work. This section describes how LEAP can also generalize the right-hand side (RHS) of the rule; that is, generalize the circuit schematic along with the functional specifications to be implemented.

---

[5] This constraint propagation step is performed in the VEXED system by a set of routines called CRITTER [Kelly, 1984] which is able to propagate and check signal constraints in loop-free digital circuits by examining the function definition of the primitive circuit elements.

The key to generalizing the RHS is to first verify that the circuit correctly implements the desired function. This verification can then be examined to determine the general class of circuits and functional specifications to which the same verification steps will apply. This method, which we call *verification-based learning*, is described more generally in [Smith, *et al.*, 1988]. That paper discusses the general applicability of this method to learning problem decomposition rules, or planning schema. Here we discuss the application of this method to generalizing circuit implementation rules and illustrate the method using the training example and rule discussed above.

10.2.3.1 Step 1: Forming the Composed Specification from Rule RHS

The first step in the process of inferring a general circuit design rule from a training example is verification—ensuring that the function computed by the user's circuit meets the original circuit specification.

We can derive a description of the circuit's function from its structure by composing the functions of the submodules constituting the circuit, according to the configuration in which they are interconnected. For the user's NOR-gate circuit, this *composed specification* is given as

```
(EQUALS (VALUE Output(i))
        (NOT (OR (NOT (OR (VALUE Input1 (i))
                          (VALUE Input2(i))))
                 (NOT (OR (VALUE Input3(i))
                          (VALUE Input4(i))))
)))
```

Note that, in general, the composed specification will be a *syntactically re-expressed* version of the original specification. For example, the above composed specification is not syntactically identical to the functional specifications in the training example, even though it does represent the same Boolean function. This frequently occurs in VLSI circuits in which, for example, functional specifications in terms of AND and OR Boolean expressions are often implemented in terms of NAND and NOR gates.

10.2.3.2 Step 2: Verifying the Circuit Function

To verify the correctness of the user-suggested NOR-gate circuit, LEAP must show the equivalence between the *composed specification* for this circuit and the *original specification* of the circuit being implemented. Thus, it seeks to verify that

```
(IMPLIES <composed-spec> <original-spec>
```

or in this case

```
(IMPLIES
     (NOT (OR (NOT (OR (VALUE Input1(i))
                        (VALUE Input2(i)))))
              (NOT (OR (VALUE Input3(i))
                        (VALUE Input4(i)))))))
     (AND (OR (VALUE Input1(i))
              (VALUE Input2(i)))
          (OR (VALUE Input3(i))
              (VALUE Input4(i))))))
```

LEAP verifies that the composed specification meets the original specification by determining a sequence of algebraic transformations which, when applied to the composed specification, will yield the original specification. Each transform has a *precondition*, which describes the class of situations to which it can be applied, and a *postcondition*, which specifies the result of the transformation. The two transforms that will be used for the current example in the circuit domain are given below.

de Morgan's Law

Precondition:
```
(NOT (OR <bool-fn1> <bool-fn2>))
```

Postcondition:
```
(AND (NOT <bool-fn1>) (NOT <bool-fn2>))
```

Remove-Double-Negation:

Precondition:
```
(NOT (NOT <bool-fn>))
```

Postcondition:
```
<bool-fn>
```

Here "<bool-fn>" represents an arbitrary Boolean function. Shown below is the veririration as a sequence of transformations.

Verification

```
(NOT (OR (NOT (OR (VALUE Input1(i))
                   (VALUE Input2(i))))
          (NOT (OR (VALUE Input3(i))
                   (VALUE Input4(i)))))))
         ↓
    de Morgan
         ↓
(AND (NOT (NOT (OR (VALUE Input1(i))
                    (VALUE Input2(i)))))
     (NOT (NOT (OR (VALUE Input3(i))
                    (VALUE Input4(i)))))))
```

↓
Remove-Double-Negation
↓
```
(AND (OR (VALUE Input1(i))
         (VALUE Input2(i)))
     (NOT (NOT (OR (VALUE Input3(i))
                   (VALUE Input4(i)))))))
```
↓
Remove-Double-Negation
↓
```
(AND (OR (VALUE Input1(i))
         (VALUE Input2(i)))
     (OR (VALUE Input3(i))
         (VALUE Input4(i))))
```

10.2.3.3 Step 3: Determining the Generalized Composed Specification

Given the verification tree shown above, the next step is to determine the general class of expressions for which this sequence of verification steps will correctly apply. This is essentially a problem of viewing the transformation sequence as an operator and of determining the necessary preconditions for the operator sequence. LEAP accomplishes this by back-propagating the precondition of each transform in the sequence, to determine the necessary conditions on the starting expression. This process is described in greater detail in [Mahadevan, 1985]. The sequence shown below illustrates this back-propagation and indicates the resulting generalization of the composed specification.

Computing the Generalized Composed Specification
```
(AND (OR (VALUE Input1(i))
         (VALUE Input2(i)))
(OR (VALUE Input3(i))
         (VALUE Input4(i))))
```
↓
Remove-Double-Neg
↓
```
(AND (OR (VALUE Inputi(i))
         (VALUE Input2(i)))
     (NOT (NOT <bool-in1>)))
```
↓
Remove-Double-Neg
↓
```
(AND (NOT (NOT <bool-fn2>))
     (NOT (NOT <bool-fn1>)))
```
↓

de Morgan
↓

```
(NOT (OR (NOT <bool-fn2>)
         (NOT <bool-fn1>)))
```

Notice that the final expression in the above sequence describes the generalized composed specification for which the verification will correctly apply. From it, we see that the important feature of the two submodule specifications P_1 and P_2 (the two leftmost NOR gates in Figure 10–1) is that they both compute the *negation of some Boolean function*, while the specifications of the third component cannot be generalized.

Generalized Specifications of Submodules

```
P₁': (EQUALS (VALUE X(i)) (NOT <bool-fn2>))
P₂': (EQUALS (VALUE Y(i)) (NOT <bool-fn1>))
P₃': (EQUALS (VALUE <out>(i))
             (NOT (OR X(i) Y(i))))
```

10.2.3.4 Step 4: Determining the Generalized Original Specification

Having determined the generalized specifications of the circuit submodules, the RHS of the new rule can now be formed. However, LEAP must also produce a corresponding generalization of the original functional specification in the rule LHS. This generalized original specification can be computed in a relatively straightforward manner, either by reapplying the sequence of verification transforms or by using the variable bindings generated when computing the generalized composed specification. Following either of these two approaches, the result is that the new, original specification becomes

```
(EQUALS (VALUE Output(i))
        (AND <bool-fn2> <bool-fn1>))
```

Comparing the generalized original specification above with the original specification of the circuit implementation in Figure 10–1, it is seen that a generalization of the original specification has been achieved from a conjunction of disjunctions to a *conjunction of any Boolean functions*.

10.2.3.5 Step 5: Forming the New Implementation Rule

We have shown in the last few paragraphs how the original specification of a circuit module as well as the functional specifications of each of the submodules P_i in its implementation could be generalized. The final step is to form the new implementation rule, which is based on these generalized specifications. The preconditions for this new rule are formulated to require (1) that the function to be implemented match the generalized original specification, and (2) that the input signals satisfy the constraints that are determined as shown in the previous subsection. The right-hand side of the new rule is formulated so that it produces the submodules with their corresponding submodule specifications P_i'. For the present example, the new implementation rule formed in this fashion is shown in Figure 10–3.[6]

10.3 DISCUSSION

The previous section describes in some detail how LEAP captures training examples from its users, and how it forms general rules from these examples. This section discusses more broadly the architectural issues involved in designing knowledge-based systems that can incorporate such learning methods. In particular, we discuss the major design features of LEAP that appear important to the design of learning apprentice systems more generally. Three design features that have a major impact on the capabilities of LEAP are:

1. the interactive nature of the problem solving system,

2. the use of analytic methods for generalizing from examples, and

3. the separation of knowledge about when an implementation technique can be used from knowledge about when it *should* be used.

10.3.2 Interactive Nature of the Apprentice Consultant

A fundamental feature of LEAP is that it embeds a learning component within an *interactive* problem-solving consultant. This allows it to collect training examples that are closely suited to refining its rule base. In particular, training examples collected by a learning apprentice have two attractive properties:

1. Training examples focus only on knowledge that is missing from the system. The need for the user to intervene in problem solving occurs only when the system is missing knowledge relevant to the task at hand, and the resulting training examples therefore focus specifically on this missing knowledge.

2. The training examples correspond to single problem-solving steps. This is in contrast to the type of training examples used by other rule learning systems such as Meta-DENDRAL [Buchanan and Mitchell, 1978] and INDUCE-PLANT [Michalski and Chilausky, 1980], in which training examples are complete problem solutions. By working with training examples that are single steps, LEAP circumvents many difficult issues of credit assignment that arise in cases where the training example corresponds to a chain of several rules.

---

[6] Notice that in this rule, there are no final constraints that must be satisfied by the input signal. This is because the leftmost circuit modules in the figure are defined so abstractly that they pose no constraints on the signal formats of their inputs.

While to first order, LEAP acquires training examples that correspond to single-rule inferences, this is only approximately true. We expect that LEAP will encounter training examples in which its existing rules will correspond to finer grained decisions than the user thinks of as a single step. For instance, the system may have a sequence of rules to implement a serial–parallel converter by first selecting a shift register, then a general class of shift registers (e.g., dynamic), and only then a specific circuit, while the user may think of the whole series of decisions as a single step, implementing the converter with a specific circuit.

In such cases, LEAP could just go ahead and learn the larger grained rule that will follow from the user's training example, but doing so could cause a number of problems. One problem is that it will result in a ruleset with rules of greatly varying grain. Such inconsistency in grain is likely to lead to redundancy and lack of generality in the rules. A second potential problem associated with large-grain training examples is that our analytical methods of generalization may be too expensive to use on steps of large grain. Since the methods depend on constructing a verification of the step, there is reason to fear the cost may grow very quickly as the size of the step gets large compared to the size of the transformations used in the verification process.

Thus, the question of how to handle grain-size mismatch may be an important issue for future research. One possible direction would be to develop methods for examining a training example that corresponds to a large step, then determining which existing rules correspond to parts of this inference step, leaving only the task of acquiring the missing finer grain rules.

10.3.2 Use of Analytical Methods for Generalization

A second significant feature of the design of LEAP is that it uses analytical methods to form general rules from specific training examples, rather than more traditional empirical, data-intensive methods. LEAP's explain-then-generalize method, based on having an initial domain theory for constructing the explanation of the example, allows LEAP to produce justifiable generalizations from single training examples. This capability is particularly important for LEAP since it is not at all clear how LEAP could tell that two different training examples involving different circuit specifications and different resulting circuits, were in fact two examples of the same rule.

One significant advantage of the analytical methods involves learning in the presence of error-prone training data. An issue that seems central to research on learning apprentice systems, and one that LEAP must confront immediately, is that the users who (unwittingly) supply its training examples are likely to make mistakes. In particular, since we hope to first introduce LEAP to a user community of university students who are themselves learning about VLSI design, the issue of dealing with error-prone examples is a major one. Our initial plan for dealing with this problem is straightforward. LEAP will form general rules *only* from the training example circuits that it can verify in terms of its knowledge of circuits. Since its generalization method requires that it explain an example circuit before it can generalize it, LEAP will be a very conservative learner. Since it will be unable to verify incorrect circuit examples that it encounters, there is little danger of its learning from incorrect examples.[7] This method of dealing with errorful data is attractive, but may be insufficient if we need to include empirical learning methods along with analytical methods for generalization.

While analytical generalization methods offer a number of advantages, they require that the system begin with a domain theory to explain/validate the training examples. This requirement, then, constrains the kind of domain for which our approach can be used. In the domain of digital circuit design, the required domain theory corresponds to a theory for verifying the correctness of circuits. In certain other domains, such a theory may be difficult to come by. For example, in domains such as medical diagnosis the underlying theory to explain/verify an inference relating symptoms to diseases is often unknown even to the domain experts. In such domains, the system would lack a domain theory to guide the analytical generalization methods, and would have to rely instead on empirical generalization methods that generalize by searching for similarities among a large number of training examples. In fact, our current methods for utilizing domain theories to guide generalization are limited to cases where there is a strong enough theory to "prove" the training example is correct. One important research problem is thus to develop methods for utilizing more approximate, incomplete domain theories to guide generalization, and for combining analytical and empirical generalization methods in such cases. One new research project that is interesting in this light is an attempt to construct a learning apprentice for well-log interpretation [Smith, *et al.*, 1985]. In this domain, the underlying theory necessary to learn new rules involves geology and response of well-logging tools. Since these theories are inherently approximate and incomplete, that research project must face the issue of generating and utilizing approximate explanations of training examples to infer general rules.

10.3.3 Partitioning of Control and Basic Domain Knowledge

A third significant feature in the design of LEAP is the partitioning of its knowledge base into (1) implementation rules that characterize *correct* (though not necessarily preferred) circuit implementations, and (2) control knowledge for selecting the *preferred* implementation from multiple legal options. This partitioning is

---

[7] Even this is not quite true. Since the domain theory is only approximate (as will probably be true for learning apprentice systems in general), there may be incorrect circuits that it succeeds in verifying (say, because it overlooks parasitic capacitances).

important because it helps deal with the common problem that when one adds a new rule to a knowledge base one must often adjust existing rules as well.

The first of these two parts of the knowledge base has the convenient property that its rules are logically independent; that is, when one adds a new implementation rule characterizing a new implementation method, it does not alter in any way the correctness of the existing implementation rules. Thus, when a new implementation rule is added, the only portion of the knowledge base that might require an update is the control knowledge for selecting among alternative implementations. This logical independence of implementation rules is also important when combining sets of rules that may have been learned from various users by different copies of the learning apprentice. While the problem of combining multiple rulesets learned from different sources is in principle simply a matter of forming the union of the rulesets, in fact the resulting set of correct rules may be overly redundant and disorganized. Thus, we anticipate that we may have to develop methods for merging and reorganizing sets of correct rules to make them more manageable.

To date, we have only considered learning the first type of knowledge. In some sense, learning these rules is easier than learning the control knowledge, because the complexity of explaining a training example is much less for implementation rules than for control rules. To explain/verify an example of an implementation rule, the system need only verify the correctness of the circuit fragment mentioned in the training example. However, to learn a control rule that characterizes when some implementation is *preferred*, it is necessary to compare this implementation with all the alternative possibilities. Thus, the complexity of constructing the explanations is quite different in these two cases. In the longer term, we see learning of control knowledge as an important task for LEAP, and a task for which it can easily capture useful training examples.

10.4 CONCLUSION

We have presented the notion of a learning apprentice system as a framework for automatically acquiring new knowledge in the context of an interactive knowledge-based consultant. The initial design of a learning apprentice for VLSI design has been described. In particular, we have detailed the methods that LEAP employs for learning new implementation rules, and for generalizing both the left- and right-hand side of these rules. Whereas, previous attempts at automatic knowledge acquisition have met with little success, the proposed learning apprentice system differs in two important respects: It utilizes more powerful analytical learning methods, and it is restricted to interactive knowledge-based systems that can easily capture useful training examples.

ACKNOWLEDGMENTS

We thank several people who provided useful criticisms of earlier drafts of this chapter: Rich Keller, Yves Kodratoff, John McDermott, Jack Mostow, Reid Smith, and Timothy Weinrich. We also thank the members of the Rutgers AL/VLSI project for many useful discussions regarding the design of LEAP, and for creating the VEXED system on top of which LEAP is being constructed. Schlumberger-Doll Research has made the STROBE system available as a representation framework in which VEXED and LEAP are being implemented. This chapter was reprinted from *Proceedings of the International Conference on Artificial Intelligence*, 1985, with permission of IJCAI, Inc. This material is based on work supported by the Defense Advanced Research Project Agency under Research Contract N00014-81-K-0394, and by the National Science Foundation under grant DCS83-51523. The views and conclusions in this document are those of the authors and should not be interpreted as necessarily representing the official policies, either expressed or implied, of the Defense Advanced Research Projects Agency, the National Science Foundation, or the U.S. Government.

References

Davis, R. 1981. "Application of meta level knowledge to the construction and use of large knowledge bases." In *Knowledge-based Systems in Artificial Intelligence*, Davis, R. and Lenat, D., eds., McGraw-Hill, NY.

Politakis, P. 1982. *Using Empirical Analysis to Reline Expert System Knowledge Bases*, PhD Dissertation, Rutgers University, August 1982.

Kahn, G., Nowlan, S., and McDermott, J. 1984. "A Foundation for Knowledge Acquisition." In *Proceedings of the IEEE Workshop of Principles of Knowledge-based Systems*. IEEE, December 1984, pp. 89–96.

Buchanan, B.G. and Mitchell, T.M. 1978. "Model-directed learning of production rules," in *Pattern-directed Inference Systems*, Waterman, D, A. and Hayes-Roth, F., eds., Academic Press, NY.

Michalski, R.S. and Chilausky R.L. 1980. "Knowledge Acquisition by Encoding Expert Rules Versus Computer Induction from Examples: A Case Study using Soybean Pathology." *Intl. Jrnl. for Man-Machine Studies* 12:63.

Mitchell, T.M., Steinberg, L.I., and Shulman, J.S. 1984. "A Knowledge-based Approach to Design." In *Proceedings of the IEEE Workshop of Principles of Knowledge-based Systems*. IEEE, December 1984, pp. 27–34. Revised version appeared *IEEE Transactions on Pattern Analysis and Machine Intelligence*, September 1985.

Mitchell, T. 1983. "Learning and Problem-Solving." In *IJCAI-83*, August 1983, pp. 1139–1151.

DeJong, G. 1982. "Automatic Schema Acquisition in a Natural Language Environment." In *Second National Conference on Artificial Intelligence*. Pittsburgh, PA, August 1982, pp. 410–413.

Salzberg, S. and Atkinson, D.J. 1984. "Learning by Building Causal Explanations." In *ECAI-84*. September 1984, pp. 497–500.

Minton, S. 1984. "Constraint-based Generalization." In *AAAI-84*. Austin, Texas, August 1984, pp. 251–254,

Kelly, Van E. 1984. "The CRITTER System—Automated Critiquing of Digital Circuit Designs." In *Proceedings of the elat Design Automation Conference*. IEEE, June 1984, pp. 419–425. Also Rutgers AI/VLSI Project Working Paper No. 13

Mahadevan, S. 1985. "Verification-based Learning: A Generalization Strategy for Inferring Problem Decomposition Methods." In *Proceedings of the Ninth International Joint Conference on Artificial Intelligence*, August 1985.

Smith, R.G., Winston, H.A., Mitchell, T.M., and Buchanan, B.G. 1985. "Representation, Use and Generation of Explicit Justifications for Knowledge Base Refinement." In *Proceedings of the Ninth International Joint Conference on Artificial Intelligence*, August 1985.

COMMENTARY

Pavel B. Brazdil
(University of Porto, Portugal)

1 MAIN FEATURES OF LEAP

One reason I think the learning apprentice system is an interesting project is that it tries to apply the techniques of machine learning to a rather complex domain. The domain of VLSI design is indeed sufficiently complex for us to be able to ask questions like: What methodology should we adopt so as to obtain a knowledge base that is sufficiently complete and correct? This is one of the questions that concerns Tom Mitchell and other participants of the project working on LEAP.

The learning apprentice system provides the user with advice about how he should refine the design. The user has a choice of accepting or ignoring the advice. If the user decides to ignore the advice, the problem-solving step is recorded and used as a new training example from which the system tries to learn. That is, the system acquires new knowledge while it is interacting with the user. As the authors point out, the system does not have to go through a specific training phase, nor through a testing phase. In my view this approach has certain advantages and certain drawbacks.

As the system keeps acquiring new knowledge it does not shut itself off and say, "I have passed your tests so I will not accept new knowledge now." However, what the system seems to be lacking is the ability to reason about what it knows. It is unable to consider a problem and tell us, "I am not too good at designing multipliers, although I know quite a lot about adders!" Information of this kind helps us to determine whether the advice should really be taken seriously. However, very few systems are able to provide us with this kind of information anyway.

2 ORGANIZATION OF THE KNOWLEDGE BASE

It is to be expected that if LEAP were to interact with a number of users as it is intended to, the system would acquire a large body of knowledge in the long run.

The objective of subjecting the system to a wide range of experience is to construct a knowledge base that is in some sense complete. However, what may be won on the completeness front may be lost on other fronts instead.

If the system were allowed to learn from different users, the resulting knowledge base would most likely contain a lot of redundant knowledge. The knowledge base would probably be also rather badly structured. As the authors suggest, new techniques have to be worked out for reorganizing knowledge coming from different knowledge sources. Although no suggestions are made in Chapter 10 as to how these issues ought to be tackled, one contribution of this work is that it leads to these interesting questions.

3 KNOWLEDGE-ACQUISITION BOTTLENECK

We think that there is also a danger that the system could acquire various "training examples" that are really of no use. This could easily happen if the system were used by novices, who may propose steps that are actually wrong.

The authors have noticed this problem, and they propose the following solution: Any step that differs from LEAP's is stored and analyzed in detail later. As we can see later in the chapter, new generalized rule is created only if the system is capable of justifying to itself (or explaining) that the step is correct.

Here we think is LEAP's weak point. If LEAP cannot find a justification for what the user does, the system is unable to learn from it. Yet the user is provided with no means of convincing the system that her step is correct. Without de Morgan's Law, for example, LEAP would be unable to obtain the generalized specification shown in Chapter 10. The user's step would have no effect on LEAP's state of knowledge.

We see that LEAP is a somewhat more conservative learner than one would expect after reading the introduction: If no explanation is found for the user's step, the system is unable to learn. It would seem that one ought to provide some means for updating the knowledge used in explanations. However, this is a difficult problem. We do not want to go to the other extreme and let the novices provide an easy way of proving that what they do is simply right!

4 CAN SPECIFICATIONS BE MODIFIED?

It seems that a tacit assumption has been followed in the sense that the specifications do not really need to be changed as the circuit is being designed. People that have been involved with design know that changing the specification during the design can create lots of difficulties later. This is why most people go to a great length to avoid this. Yet, in our experience many "bugs" were not resolved by changing the design, but instead by changing the specification.

Errors in specifications arise due to similar reasons as errors in programs do. It is simply difficult to think of everything up front. Specification can turn out to be incomplete or even incorrect.

From a certain standpoint the specification shown in Chapter 10 could also be regarded as incomplete. The function to be implemented does not contain any restriction on admissible time delay. It is clear that this could be simply amended by the addition of the appropriate conditions to the specification. But the problem is that if this is done during the design, some part of the design may get invalidated.

So what we think we need in the future is some means for updating the existing specification, together with means for revising the corresponding parts of the design.

Now follow excerpts of the discussion that took place between the author, R. Holte, M. Lebowitz, R. Michalski, T. Mitchell, and various people in the audience during the presentation.

5 HOW FAR SHOULD WE GENERALIZE?

Holte:

Because generalization plays an important role in LEAP, I would like to ask one concrete question: Do you always generalize as far as you can? Are the very general operators useful?

Mitchell:

You have made a few good points, but let me answer your last point first. Operators that are general are not automatically better than the operators that are more specific. Operators that are general have perhaps wider applicability than the operators that are more specific, but they give you weaker advice.

Suppose, for example, that you are trying to implement "AND of two Boolean functions." You can imagine one implementation in which you use "NOR of two circuits,"[8] In another implementation you can use "NOR of two NOR circuits." The first implementation is more abstract than the second one. It does not give you a strong recommendation as to how you should design the circuit.

So you have made a good point: Just because it is possible to formulate a rule in a very general form, it is not necessarily most useful for the system to have the rule in this form.

---

[8] NOR represents a circuit which is sometimes called a "Negative OR." Using de Morgan's Law we can show that X AND Y is equivalent to ~X ~OR ~Y.

6 LEARNING CONTROL KNOWLEDGE

Audience:

If you have several versions of the same rule (from the most specific to the most general one), will you not have an indexing problem? That is, how do you decide which rule should be chosen?

Mitchell:

At the moment LEAP will chose all the versions, and let the user make the choice. I suppose if the system had hundreds of versions, the system ought to be more helpful and recommend a particular rule.

Holte:

I have collected a few questions from the audience on this point. Someone has suggested that the system could see what the user does and try to learn from it: If the user has ignored some rules, then the suggestion was that the system could use these cases as negative training examples. The negative examples can then be eliminated by specializing some of the existing rules.

Mitchell:

As I have mentioned the current version of LEAP provides the user with all the alternatives. But several people at Rutgers are currently studying this problem. Jack Mostow, for example, is concerned with the issue of incorporating advice from the user into the system's knowledge base.

Suppose you wanted to tell the system that the slowest parts of the circuit ought to be designed first. If you are trying to optimize the design for speed, this is a reasonable strategy to adopt. However, it is not easy to make systems take the advice in this form. Jack Mostow has been concerned with the problem of how such advice could be transformed into more concrete operational statements. Maybe a statement of the kind, "When implementing a multiplier, work on the half adder first" is more specific and more operational version of the general advice "Work on the slowest parts of the circuit first."

7 REVISION OF CONTROL KNOWLEDGE

Holte:

If you decide to add control knowledge to the implementation rules, then you have to face another problem. Every time a new rule is added, you need to reexamine all the existing implementation rules!

Mitchell:

Very important observation! We have decided to deal with the problem of learning possible implementation rules, which is similar to the problem of learning the legal moves of a game. This problem is somewhat easier than the problem of learning which of these legal moves are in fact good moves. Legal moves can really grow monotonically, whereas the control knowledge cannot.

However, we have a good deal of experience in learning control knowledge for guiding search. The LEX system, for example, learned heuristics for guiding search in the domain of symbolic integration. Clearly, keeping explanations around helps you to identify the items that are relevant when you are trying to revise the control knowledge.

For example, suppose that the system has learned that Shift-Register-2 is better than Shift-Register-1, if you are interested in speed. Presumably the explanation for forming this rule will refer to the implementation of the two registers, and how the implementation affects speed. Therefore the explanation provides you with a dependency network, which is useful when you need to revise your control knowledge after you have modified your knowledge base.

Audience:

Suppose the user has chosen a particular implementation rule. Have you thought of asking him to justify his choice? That is, explaining not only why his method works, but also how it compares to the other alternatives?

Mitchell:

This information could be important if we decided that the system should be concerned with learning control knowledge.

8 PROBLEMS OF COMMUNICATION

Lebowitz:

People frequently choose one method of implementing a circuit in preference to another one, because it is cheaper to do it this way. Considerations of this kind introduce a whole new set of concepts. None of the explanations you have shown mentioned cost. Could you extend your system to be able to accept advice from the user that mentions cost?

Mitchell:

You can imagine setting up a restricted language enabling the system and the user to communicate.

Lebowitz:

I do not only mean to say that the language might be deficient. Sometimes it is necessary to provide the system with a whole set of new concepts!

Mitchell:

In order to be able to accept advice the system has to understand meaning. Explaining the meaning is, however, a difficult problem.... Maybe some interesting results will come out of the work at Schlumberger, as their system works with incomplete theories.[9] So if the system cannot fully explain a particular training example, it could try to stretch the explanation in a plausible way. For example, the system could try to find out why the user thought there was a "late fault" in some region, and how this is related to the "red pattern."

9 DEALING WITH MULTIPLE EXPLANATIONS

Holte:

It seems that explanations enable you to focus on the relevant attributes. But what do you do when there are potentially multiple explanations?

Mitchell:

If they are inconsistent, you are in trouble. If they are not inconsistent, and if you think your theory is right, you can select one and use it to generate a generalization. By the way, LEAP works in this manner. In general you may want to consider various explanations, generate a generalization from each one, and then form a disjunction. You may also try to see whether one generalization subsumes another.

To be realistic, you have to consider that most domains do not have a perfect theory. If you notice that you have more than one explanation, then maybe you can select one to refine one of your imperfect theories. Work in this area might really be interesting.

10 DEALING WITH IMPERFECT THEORIES

Brazdil:

So far not many people in this field have been concerned with imperfect theories. I think there is a big gap between the techniques that have been worked out so far, and the techniques I think are needed for dealing with imperfect theories.

---

[9]Tom Mitchell is referring here to the work described, for example, in [Smith, *et al.*, 1985] in his chapter.

Mitchell:

I think you are absolutely right, and I think a lot more effort of this community should go into extending the techniques. One direction we could follow is this one: We could try to merge what we know about inductive inference, which normally deals with imperfect data, and explanation-based learning.

You can work on extending explanation-based learning to be able to deal with imperfect theories, by giving the system, say, more data. Alternatively, you can work on extending the methods of inductive inference. For example, if you look at Michalski's work on inductive inference, you could consider giving the system more knowledge about the domain, or about the goals you are trying to achieve.

11 TRADE-OFFS BETWEEN SIMPLICITY AND COMPLETENESS

Holte:

It seems that a simple incomplete theory is sometimes preferable to a complex complete theory that is correct. Consider, for example, a theory that contains a fact that birds can fly. This theory is useful in most cases, as most birds can fly. Would you not agree?

Mitchell:

I do not think it is so much a question of choice. One does not need to sacrifice completeness and correctness for simplicity. It is more realistic to think that the system should be organized in such a way so that it could take as much knowledge as possible in, and use the appropriate part at the appropriate time.

Holte:

The idea was that the theory would say that birds could fly. We know, of course, that some birds do not fly.

Mitchell:

I guess I could imagine a theory that has assertions like "Birds fly" as well as "Penguins do not fly."

Holte:

But penguins are birds!

Mitchell:

I do not mean that you are not going to get into the usual problems. We must be careful about how we go about dealing with inconsistent theories or default reasoning.

12 THEORY OF GEOLOGY IS INCOMPLETE

Holte:

The theory of geology you have described earlier is incomplete or incorrect?[10]

Mitchell:

It is both incomplete and incorrect. It is incorrect in the sense that it contains statements like, "Faults produce distortion regions." Well, sometimes they do not. In addition to this assertion the theory contains this statement:

> The subclass of faults called "normal faults" produce above them a subclass of "distortion regions" called "down-dip thickening" with probability of 0.8.

This assertion is a little bit less abstract, and a little bit less incorrect. But it exists in parallel with the first assertion mentioned, which cannot be easily empirically verified.

Someone has made a comment to the effect that this theory is incomplete in a very specific sense. It cannot be obtained from a complete theory by taking away one assertion. It is not a problem of a missing rule. Our theory is imperfect, because it is an abstract theory of geology, which is going to make a prediction about almost anything, any kind of "fault."

13 DEEP AND SHALLOW THEORIES

Brazdil:

The imperfect theory of geology could be regarded as a shallow theory that is concerned with the operational aspects of the domain. A deep theory, on the other hand, is said to describe the inherent causal relationship in the domain. It seems that so far this community has been concerned mainly with the problem of how we can learn shallow theories.

Mitchell:

In a sense Newtonian physics or quantum physics are complete theories of geology. The problem is these theories do not help you much when you try to answer questions in geology.

---

[10]In his presentation Tom Mitchell discussed the problem of acquiring knowledge about geology.

A similar situation arises in chess. Knowing the rules of chess gives you enough knowledge to be able to answer, for example, this question, "Does the opening move 'pawn to king forward' ensure you a win?" It is also not easy to provide an explanation for why the game was lost after 23 moves!

There are a few projects going on in this area. Tadepalli, for example, has been concerned with the issue of learning in intractable domains.[11] He has been trying to determine how one might compile out a part of given theory in order to obtain a theory which is more tractable. The explanations you will get with the new theory are more reasonable, but they might not be complete. The theory is less correct, however. So this might be an interesting attempt to learn from what you call a deep theory, which is complete but intractable.

I think it is important to understand in what ways the theories may not be useful to you. First, they can be intractable. Second, they can be incomplete. Third, they may be complete but too abstract; complete in the sense of making predictions about anything, and abstract in the sense that they do not give you a precise enough prediction. As you see theories may be unusable for different reasons. What we need to understand now is how to make unusable theories useful. This is a good area for further research.

14 RESPONSE TIME AND OFF-LINE PROCESSING

Holte:

Do you think it is important to continue studying the systems that do not interact with the user? As far as the response time is concerned, is it significantly affected by LEAP's work on generalization?

Mitchell:

To answer your first question, I think it is important to study both interactive and noninteractive systems. To answer your second question I would say that in LEAP the response time is not really affected by its attempt to process examples, since this is done off-line. As new examples are encountered, they are stored in a file, and so the user does not have to wait while she is designing her circuit. The system tries to generalize the examples during a night run.

---

[11] Tadepalli's paper has appeared in *Machine Learning: A Guide to Current Research* (eds. T. Mitchell and J. Carbonell), Kluwer, 1986.

15 BACKTRACKING

Holte:

You mentioned that the user is able to backtrack and effectively undo a part of the design. What happens to the corresponding training examples? Are they eliminated after the user has changed his mind?

Mitchell:

Actually, at the moment all training examples are retained, even if the designer has changed his mind later. However, the system must be able to explain to itself that the example correctly implements a given specification for the example to have any effect.

16 WHAT IS AN EXPLANATION?

Audience:

I would like to ask, "What exactly is an explanation?"

Mitchell:

Explanation can be considered synonymous with the word "proof." For example, if you represent your knowledge in the form of, say, PROLOG clauses, the proof you will get may be regarded as the system's explanation for why something is true. So, for example, you might prove that some Boolean function is equivalent to another. The proof you will get explains why this is so.

The part of LEAP that generates the explanations concerning timings is quite interesting. It is based on a circuit-verification system. This system uses various timing constraints that one might impose on the circuit, together with the description of the individual components used in the circuit to answer questions like this one:

Tell me what are the sufficient conditions on this wire over here so as to satisfy the global timing constraint!

The system gets the answer essentially by constraint propagation.

17 RELATION OF EBL TO ANALOGY

Audience:

There is a strong connection between explanation-based learning (EBL) and analogy. I guess one could consider that explanation-based learning is anticipating the work that will be done by analogy.

Mitchell:

You can look at things this way. After you have solved a few design problems, you can base your next solution on what you have done before. You can either use analogy or generalized rules.

If you use analogy, you have to deal with two issues: First, you have to determine which of the earlier solutions is applicable to the current situation. This is called the retrieval problem. Then the second issue is how you actually use what you have found. For example, how do you use the knowledge about how to design a multiplier in the design of an adder, for example.

In explanation-based learning some results get preprocessed and stored for later use. For example, one can try to determine the general class of circuit specifications for which a particular design technique works.

In practice very few problems are perfectly analogous, in the sense that they require the same sequence of steps in the solution. If you are dealing with an imperfect analogy, you may have to build an abstraction of the original sequence of steps before applying it. On a certain level of abstraction the two problems become perfectly analogous.

18 GENERALIZATION AND PROPAGATION OF CONSTRAINTS

Audience:

After you have generalized the right-hand side, you propagate the constraints. Is that right?

Mitchell:

I am glad that you have asked this question, because I forgot to point out that LEAP does it like this, although I have mentioned these issues in the opposite order here. LEAP generalizes the circuit first, and then propagates the constraints across the generalized circuit.

19 RELATIONSHIP OF EXAMPLES AND WEAK THEORIES

Audience:

When dealing with a strong theory it is not difficult to identify false training instances. Weak theories seem to complicate matters, however. How do you recognize a false training instance when you are dealing with a weak theory?

Mitchell:

The advantage of having strong theories is that you can eliminate some examples you think are wrong, and you can justify that by assuming that the user has made a mistake. You cannot do this when you have a weak theory. You no longer have a simple way of accepting or rejecting examples. What is important is the degree to which the examples conform to the theory; or in other words, the degree to which the theory can corroborate the examples.

20 EXTENDING EBL TO DEAL WITH UNCERTAIN REASONING

Michalski:

It has been mentioned here that many theories we use are not perfect: They may be incomplete, inconsistent, intractable or uncertain. If you have, say, uncertain theories, you have to have mechanisms for manipulating uncertainty. Do you think it is worthwhile research to try to extend explanation-based learning to handle uncertainty?

Mitchell:

It is certainly a worthwhile research topic, and some work has already been done on "probabilistic induction." One of the questions addressed in this work is, for example, this one: "Which probabilities can be attributed to individual assertions, provided we have attributed certain probabilities to interpretations (explanations)?" I think a lot of interesting work can be done here.

ACKNOWLEDGMENTS

This text is an edited version of the discussion that took place at IMAL after the talk delivered by Tom Mitchell. The discussion was initiated by the two commentators, Pavel Brazdil and Robert Holte, the second of whom collected a number of questions from the audience.

I think that I would have been unable to give such a vivid account of all the arguments without the written transcriptions prepared by Michel Manago. Having read through the text, I have taken the liberty of altering it at various places. Apart from filling in the words not captured during the recording I have made various other alterations as well. The purpose of all these alterations was merely to improve the presentation of the text without changing its spirit.

11

ACQUIRING GENERAL ITERATIVE CONCEPTS BY REFORMULATING EXPLANATIONS OF OBSERVED EXAMPLES

Jude W. Shavlik
(University of Wisconsin, Madison)

Gerald F. DeJong
(University of Illinois)

Abstract

In *explanation-based learning*, a specific problem's solution is generalized into a form that can be later used to solve conceptually similar problems. Most research in explanation-based learning involves relaxing constraints on the variables in the explanation of a specific example, rather than generalizing the *structure* of the explanation itself. However, this precludes the acquisition of concepts where an iterative process is implicitly represented in the explanation by a fixed number of applications. Such explanations must be reformulated during generalization. The fully implemented BAGGER system analyzes explanation structures and detects extensible, repeated, interdependent applications of rules. When any are found, the explanation is extended so that an arbitrary number of repeated applications of the original rule are supported. The final structure is then generalized and a new rule, which embodies a crucial shift in representation, is produced. An important property of the extended rules is that their preconditions are expressed in terms of the initial state—

they do not depend on the results of intermediate applications of the original rule. BAGGER's generalization algorithm is presented and empirical results that demonstrate the value of generalizing to N are reported. To illustrate the approach, the acquisition of a plan for building towers of arbitrary height is discussed in detail.

11.1 INTRODUCTION

Often a person will, in the course of solving a problem, repeatedly employ an action or collection of actions. It is an important, but difficult, problem, to correctly generalize this sequence, once observed. Sometimes the number of repetitions should be the subject of generalization. Other times it is quite inappropriate to alter the number of repetitions. This article addresses the important issue in explanation-based learning (EBL) of *generalizing to N* [Shavlik and DeJong, 1985; 1987b; 1987c]. This can involve generalizing such things as the number of entities involved in a concept or the number of times some action is performed. Generalizing number has been largely ignored in previous explanation-based learning research. Instead, other research has focused on changing constants into variables and determining the general constraints on those variables.

In explanation-based learning [DeJong and Mooney, 1986; Mitchell, Keller, and Kedar-Cabelli, 1986], a specific problem solution is generalized into a form that can be later used to solve conceptually similar problems. The generalization process is driven by the *explanation* of why the solution worked. Knowledge about the domain allows the explanation to be developed and then generalized.

Consider the LEAP system [Mitchell, Mahadevan, and Steinberg, 1985]. The system is shown an example of using NOR gates to compute the Boolean AND of two ORs. It discovers that the technique generalizes to computing the Boolean AND of any two inverted Boolean functions. However, LEAP cannot generalize this technique to allow constructing the AND of an arbitrary number of inverted Boolean functions using a multi-input NOR gate. This is the case even if LEAP's initial background knowledge were to include the general version of de Morgan's Law and the concept of multi-input NOR gates. Generalizing the number of functions requires alteration of the original example's explanation.

Ellman's [1985] system also illustrates the need for generalizing number. From an example of a 4-bit circular shift register, his system constructs a generalized design for an arbitrary 4-bit permutation register. A design for an N-bit circular shift register cannot be produced. As Ellman points out, such generalization, though desirable, cannot be done using the technique of changing constants to variables.

Many important concepts, in order to be properly learned, require generalization of number. For example, physical laws such as momentum and energy conservation apply to arbitrary numbers of objects; constructing towers of blocks requires an arbitrary number of repeated stacking actions; and setting a table involves a range of possible numbers of guests. In addition, there is recent psychological evidence [Ahn, *et al.*, 1987] that people can generalize number on the basis of one example.

Repetition of an action is not a sufficient condition for generalization to N to be appropriate. Generalizing to N is necessary in one but inappropriate in the other. Compare two simple examples:

- Observing a previously unknown method of moving an obstructed block, and
- seeing, for the first time, a toy wagon being built.

Suppose a learning system observes an expert achieving the desired states. In each case, consider what general concept should be acquired.

In the first example, the expert wishes to move, using a robot manipulator, a block with four other blocks stacked in a tower on top of it. The manipulator can pick up only one block at a time. The expert's solution is to move all four of the blocks in turn to some other location. After the underlying block has been cleared, it is moved. In the second example, the expert wishes to construct a movable rectangular platform, one that is stable while supporting any load whose center of mass is over the platform. Given the platform and a bin containing two axles and four wheels, the expert's solution is to first attach each of the axles to the platform. Next all four of the wheels are grabbed in turn and mounted on an axle protrusion.

This comparison illustrates an important problem in explanation-based learning. Generalizing the block unstacking example should produce a plan for unstacking *any* number of obstructing blocks, not just four as observed. The wagon-building example, however, should not generalize the number 4. It makes no difference whether the system is given a bin of five, six, or 100 wheels, because only four wheels are needed to fulfill the functional requirements of a stable wagon.

Standard explanation-based learning algorithms [DeJong and Mooney, 1986; Fikes, Hart, and Nilsson, 1972; Hirsh, 1987; Kedar-Cabelli and McCarty, 1987; Mitchell, Keller, and Kedar-Cabelli, 1986; Mooney and Bennett, 1986; O'Rorke, 1987a] and similar algorithms for chunking [Laird, Rosenbloom, and Newell, 1986] cannot treat these cases differently. These algorithms, possibly after pruning the explanation to eliminate irrelevant parts, replace constants with constrained variables. They cannot significantly augment the explanation during generalization. Thus, the *building-a-wagon* type of concept will be correctly acquired but the *unstacking-to-move* concept will be undergeneralized. The acquired schema will have generalized the identity of the blocks so that the target block need not be occluded by the same four blocks as in the example. Any four obstructing blocks can be unstacked. However, there must be exactly four blocks.[1] Unstacking five or more blocks is beyond the scope of the acquired concept.

Note that EBL systems do not work correctly on the *building-a-wagon* kind of problem either—they just get lucky. They do nothing to augment explanation structures during generalization. It just happens that to acquire a schema to build a wagon, *not* generalizing the explanation structure is the appropriate thing to do.

One can, of course, simply define the scope of EBL-type systems to exclude the *unstacking-to-move* concept and those like it. This is a mistake. First, the problem of augmenting the explanation during generalization, once seen, is ubiquitous. It is manifested in one form or another in most real-world domains. Second, if one simply defines the problem away, the resulting system could never guarantee that any of its concepts were as general as they should be. Even when such a system correctly constructed a concept like the *building-a-wagon* schema, it could not know that it had generalized properly. The system itself could not tell which concepts fall within its scope and which do not.

Observations of repeated application of a rule or operator may indicate that generalizing the number of rules in the explanation may be appropriate. However, alone this is insufficient. To be conducive to number generalization there must be a certain recursive structural pattern. That is, each application must achieve preconditions for the next. For example, consider stacking blocks. The same sort of repositioning of blocks occurs repeatedly, each building on the last. In this article, the vocabulary of predicate calculus is adopted to investigate this notion of structural recursion. The desired form of structural recursion is manifested as repeated application of an inference rule in such a manner that a portion of each consequent is used to satisfy some of the antecedents of the next application.

The next section introduces an implemented system designed to generalize the structure of explanations. Subsequent sections describe the algorithm used and illustrate it with a detailed example. Finally, before the conclusion, there are an empirical validation of the merits of generalizing the structure of explanations (including a comparison to the results of a standard EBL algorithm), a discussion of related work, and descriptions of several open research problems.

_____

[1] The SOAR system [Laird, *et al.*, 1986] would seem to acquire a number of concepts that together are slightly more general. As well as a new operator for moving four blocks, the system would acquire new operators for moving three blocks, two blocks, and one block, but not five or more. Anderson's [1986] knowledge-compilation process would acquire a similar set of rules.

11.2 THE BAGGER SYSTEM

The BAGGER system (Building Augmented Generalizations by Generating Extended Recurrences) analyzes predicate calculus proofs and attempts to construct concepts that involve generalizing to N. Most of the examples under study use the situation calculus [McCarthy, 1963] to reason about actions, in the style of Green [1969]. (Green's formulation is also discussed in [Nilsson, 1980].)

11.2.1 Situation Calculus

In situation calculus, predicates and functions whose values may change over time are given an extra argument that indicates the situation in which they are being evaluated. For example, rather than using the predicate $On(x,y)$, indicating that x is on y, the predicate $On(x,y,s)$ is used, indicated that in situation s, x is on y. In this formulation, operators are represented as functions that map from one situation to another situation.

Problem solving with BAGGER's situational calculus rules can be viewed as transforming and expanding situations until one is found in which the goal is known to be achieved. The BAGGER system has two types of inference rules: *intersituational* rules, which specify attributes that a new situation will have after application of a particular operator; and *intrasituational* rules, which can embellish BAGGER's knowledge of a situation by specifying additional conclusions that can be drawn within that situation.

Each intersituational inference rule specifies knowledge about one particular operator. However, operators are not represented by exactly one inference rule. A major inference rule specifies most of the relevant problem-solving information about an operator. But it is augmented by many lesser inference rules, which capture the operator's frame axioms and other facts about a new situation. This paradigm contrasts with the standard STRIPS [Fikes and Nilsson, 1971] formalism.[2] The inference rules of a STRIPS-like system are in a one-to-one correspondence with the system's operators. Each inference rule fully specifies an operator's add- and delete-lists. These lists provide all of the changes needed to transform the current situation into the new situation. Any state not mentioned in an add- or delete-list is assumed to persist across the operator's application. Thus, the new situation is completely determined by the inference rule. In the BAGGER system this is not the case. Many separate inference rules are used to fully characterize the effect of an operator.

---

[2] Fahlman [1974] and Fikes [1975] augmented the standard STRIPS model by allowing a distinction between primary and secondary relationships. Primary relationships are asserted directly by operators while secondary relationships are deduced from the primary ones as needed. While this serves the same purpose as BAGGER's intrasituational rules, multiple intersituational rules for an operator are not allowed [Waldinger, 1977].

The advantage of the STRIPS approach is that the system can always be assured that it has represented all that there is to know about a new situation. However, this can also be a disadvantage. A STRIPS-like system must always muddle through all there is to know about a situation, no matter how irrelevant many facts may be to the current problem. Conversely, the advantages of BAGGER's approach are that the inference rules are far less complex and therefore more manageable, the system's attention focusing is easier because it does not bog down in situations made overly complex by many irrelevant facts, and a programmer can more easily write and update knowledge about operators. Furthermore, STRIPS-style operators do not allow disjunctive nor conditional effects in their add- or delete-lists.

A potential disadvantage of BAGGER's approach is that to completely represent the effects of applying an operator in a particular situation, the system must retrieve all of the relevant inference rules. However, this is not a task that arises in BAGGER's problem solving. Indeed, there has been no attempt to guarantee the completeness of the system's inferential abilities. This means that there may be characteristics of a situation which BAGGER can represent but cannot itself infer.

11.2.2 Some Sample Problems

One problem solution analyzed by BAGGER is shown in Figure 11–1. The goal is to place a properly supported block so that its center is above the dotted line and within the horizontal confines of the line. BAGGER is provided low-level domain knowledge about blocks, including how to transfer a single block from one location to another and how to calculate its new horizontal and vertical position. Briefly, to move a block, the block must have nothing on it, and there must be free space at which to place it. The system produces a situation calculus proof validating the actions shown in Figure 11–1, in which three blocks must be moved to build the tower.

If a standard explanation-based generalization algorithm is applied to the resulting proof, a plan for moving *three* blocks will result. They need not be these same three blocks; any three distinct ones will do. Nor is it necessary that the first block moved be placed on a table; any flat, clear surface is acceptable. Finally, the height of the tower need not be the same as that in the specific example. Given appropriately sized blocks, towers of any height can be constructed. Many characteristics of the problem are generalized. However, the fact that exactly three blocks are moved would remain.

If one considers the universe of all possible towers, as shown in Figure 11–2, only a small fraction of them would be captured by the acquired rule. Separate rules would need to be learned for towers containing two blocks, five blocks, etc. What is desired is the acquisition of a rule that describes how towers containing any number of blocks can be constructed.

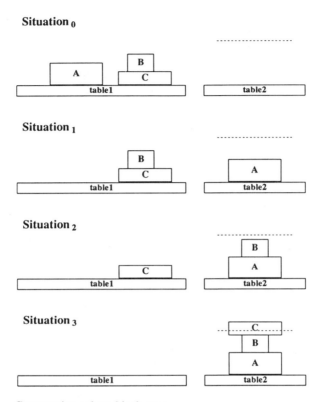

Figure 11–1:   Constructing a three-block tower

By analyzing the proof of the construction of the three-block tower, BAGGER acquires a general plan for building towers by stacking *arbitrary* numbers of blocks, as illustrated in Figure 11–3. This new plan incorporates an indefinite number of applications of the previously known plan for moving a single block.

In another example, the system observes three blocks being removed from a stack in order to satisfy the goal of having a specific block clear. Extending the explanation of these actions produces a plan for unstacking any number of blocks in order to clear a block within the stack. Figure 11–4 illustrates this general plan. The plan includes the system's realization that the last unstacked block is currently clear and thus makes a suitable destination to place the next block to be moved. This knowledge is incorporated into the plan and no problem solving need be performed to find destinations once the first free location is found.

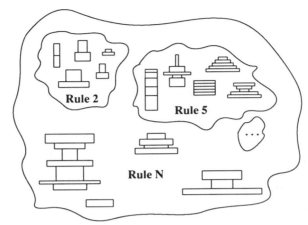

Figure 11–2:   Universes of constructible towers

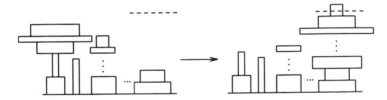

Figure 11–3:   The effects of a general plan for constructing towers

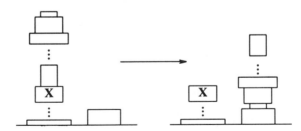

Figure 11–4:   The effects of a general plan for unstacking towers

Unlike many other block-manipulation examples, these examples do *not* assume that blocks can support only one other block. This means that moving a block does not necessarily clear its supporting block. Another concept learned by BAGGER, by observing two blocks being moved from on top another, is a general plan

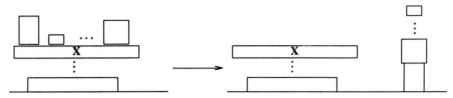

Figure 11–5:   The effects of a general plan for clearing objects

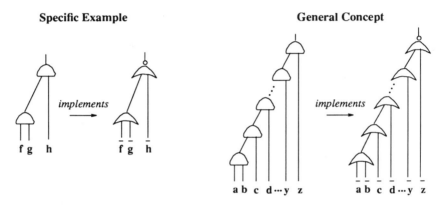

Figure 11–6:   A circuit implementation example

for clearing an object directly supporting any number of clear blocks. This plan is illustrated in Figure 11–5.

The domain of digital circuit design also contains many examples where a fixed number of rule applications should be generalized into an arbitrary number. By observing the repeated application of de Morgan's Law to implement two cascaded AND gates using OR and NOT gates, BAGGER produces a general version of de Morgan's Law which can be used to implement N cascaded AND gates with N OR and one NOT gate. This example, which does not use situation calculus, is shown in Figure 11–6.

The next section presents the BAGGER generalization algorithm. Following that, there is a detailed presentation of the tower-building example, including the full proof tree and the acquired rule. The inference rules used in this example are described in the appendix. Complete details on the other examples, including the complete set of initial inference rules, the situation calculus proofs, and the acquired inference rules, can be found in [Shavlik, 1988].

11.3 GENERALIZATION IN BAGGER

Generalizing number, like more traditional generalization in EBL, results in the acquisition of a new inference rule. The difference is that the sort of rule that results from generalizing number describes the world after an indefinite number of world changes or other inferences have been made. Each such rule subsumes a potentially infinite class of standard situation calculus rules. Thus, with such rules the storage efficiency can be dramatically improved, the expressive power of the system is increased, and, as shown in Section 11.5, the system's performance efficiency can also be higher than without these rules. This section describes how BAGGER generalizes number.

11.3.1 Sequential Rules

Like its standard inference rules, number-generalized rules in the BAGGER system are usually represented in situational calculus. In the previous section, two types of BAGGER inference rules are discussed: intrasituational rules and intersituational rules. To define number-generalized rules, the intersituational rules are further divided into two categories: simple intersituational rules and sequential intersituational rules (or simply *sequential rules*). Sequential rules apply a variable number of operators. Thus, within each application of a sequential rule, many intermediate situations may be generated. The actual number of intermediate situations depends on the complexity of the problem to be solved. The rule for building towers is an example of a sequential rule. This rule is able to construct towers of any number of blocks in order to achieve a specified goal height. The rule itself decides how many blocks are to be used and selects which blocks to use from among those present in the current situation.

Sequential rules, like their simple intersituational counterparts, have an antecedent and a consequent. Also, like the simple versions, if the antecedent is satisfied, the consequent specifies properties of the resulting situation. Unlike the simple rules, the resulting situation can be separated from the initial situation by many operator applications and intermediate situations. For example, building a tower requires many block-moving operations. It is an important feature of sequential rules that no planning need be done in applying the intermediate operators. That is, if the antecedent of a sequential rule is satisfied, its entire sequence of operators can be applied without the need for individually testing or planning for the preconditions. The preconditions of each operator are guaranteed to be true by the construction of the sequential rule itself. Thus, the consequent of a sequential rule can immediately assert properties that must be true in the final situation. A sequential rule behaves much as a STRIPS-like macro-operator. It is termed a *sequential rule* and not a *macro-operator* because it is, in fact, a situational calculus rule and not an operator. It has a situation variable, does not specify add and delete lists, etc.

Sequential rules can be much more efficient than simply chaining together simple constituents. This improved efficiency is derived from three sources: (1) collecting together antecedents so that redundant and subsumed operator preconditions are eliminated, (2) heuristically ordering the antecedents, and, especially, (3) eliminating antecedents that test operator preconditions which, due to the structure of the rule, are known to be satisfied.

11.3.2 Representing Sequential Knowledge

A representational shift is crucial to this chapter's solution to the generalization to N problem. While objects in the world are represented within simple inference rules directly as predicate calculus variables, this is not possible for BAGGER's sequential rules. A standard operator interacts with a known number of objects. Usually, this number is small. The rule representing the operator that moves blocks, for example, might take as arguments the block to be moved and the new location where it is to be placed. A simple intersituational rule for this operator might specify that in the resulting situation, the block represented by the first argument is at the location specified by the second. This rule represents exactly one application of the move operator. There are always two arguments. They can be conveniently represented by predicate calculus variables. That is, each of the world objects with which a simple operator interacts can be uniquely named with a predicate calculus variable. Sequential rules cannot uniquely name each of the important world objects. A rule for building towers must be capable of including an arbitrary number of blocks. The uninstantiated rule cannot know whether it is to be applied next to build a tower of five blocks, seven blocks, or 24 blocks. Since the individual blocks can no longer be named by unique variables within the rule, a shift to a scheme that can represent aggregations of world objects is necessary. Such a representational shift, similar to Weld's [1986], makes explicit attributes that are only implicitly present in the example. Thus, it shares many characteristics of constructive induction [Michalski, 1983; Rendell, 1985].

A new object called an RIS (for Rule Instantiation Sequence) is introduced to represent arbitrarily large aggregations of world objects. A sequential rule works directly with one of these generalized structures so that it need not individually name every world object with which it interacts. A sequential rule's RIS is constructed in the course of satisfying its antecedent. Once this is done, the RIS embodies all of the constraints required for the successive application of the sequence of operators that make up the plan.

11.3.3 The BAGGER Algorithm

Figure 11–7 schematically presents how BAGGER generalizes the structure of explanations. On the left is the explanation of a solution to a specific problem. In it,

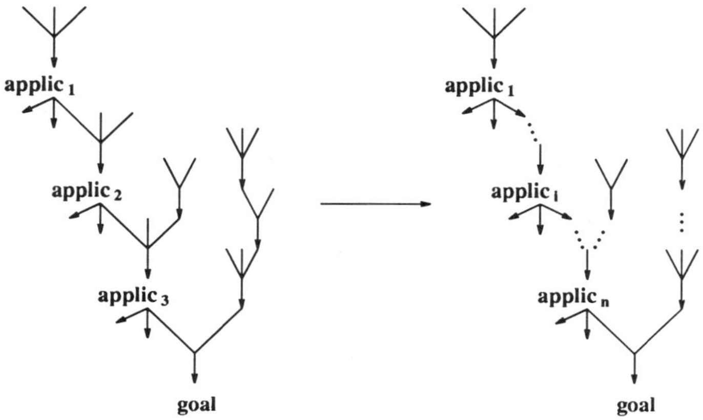

Figure 11–7:   Generalizing the structure of an explanation

some inference rule is repeatedly applied a fixed number of times. In the generalized explanation, the number of applications of the rule is unconstrained. In addition, the properties that must hold in order to satisfy each application's preconditions, and to meet the antecedents in the goal, are expressed in terms of the initial situation. This means that portions of the explanation not directly involved in the chain of rule applications must also be expressed in terms of the initial state. When the initial situation has the necessary properties, the results of the new rule can be immediately determined, without reasoning about any of the intermediate situations.

The generalization algorithm appears in Figure 11–8. This algorithm is expressed in a pseudocode, while the actual implementation is written in LISP. The remainder of this section elaborates the pseudocode. In the algorithm back arrows (←) indicate value assignment. The construct

for each *element* **in** *set* **do** *statement*

means that *element* is successively bound to each member of *set*, following which *statement* is evaluated. The functions *AddDisjunct* and *AddConjunct* alter their first argument. If either of *AddConjunct*'s arguments is *fail*, its answer is *fail*. *AddRule* places the new rule in the database of acquired rules.

The algorithm begins its analysis of a specific solution at the goal node. It then traces backward, looking for repeated rule applications. To be a candidate, some consequent of one instantiation of a rule must support the satisfaction of an antecedent of another instantiation. These repeated applications need not directly connect— there can be intervening inference rules. Once a candidate is found, all the interconnected instantiations of the underlying general rule are collected.

procedure BuildNewBAGGERrule (goalNode)

focusNodes ← CollectFocusRuleApplications(goalNode)
antecedentsInitial ← BuildInitialAntecedents(Earliest(focusNodes))
antecedentsIntermediate ← φ
for each focusNode **in focusNodes do**
    answer ← ViewAsArbitraryApplic(focusNode, focusNodes)
    if answer ≠ *fail* **then** AddDisjunct(antecedentsIntermediate, answer)
antecedentsFinal ← ViewAsArbitraryApplic(goalNode, focusNodes)
consequents ← CollectGoalTerms(goalNode)
if antecedentsIntermediate ≠ φ ∧ antecedentsFinal ≠ *fail*
    then AddRule(antecedentsInitial, antecedentsIntermediate, antecedentsFinal,
        consequents)

procedure ViewAsArbitraryApplic (node, focusNodes)

result ← φ
for each antecedent **in** Antecedents(node) **do**
    if Axiom?(antecedent) **then** *true*
    else if SupportedByEarlierNode?(antecedent, focusNodes) **then**
        AddConjunct(result, CollectNecessaryEqualities(antecedent,
            Supporter(antecedent)))
    else if SituationIndependent?(antecedent) **then** AddConjunct(result, antecedent)
    else if SupportedByPartiallyUnwindableRule?(antecedent) **then**
        AddConjunct(result, CollectResultsOfPartiallyUnwinding(antecedent))
        AddConjunct(result, ViewAsArbitraryApplic(PartiallyUnwind(antecedent),
            focusNodes))
    else if SupportedByUnwindableRule?(antecedent) **then**
        AddConjunct(result, CollectResultsOfUnwinding(antecedent))
    else if SupportedByRuleConsequent?(antecedent) **then**
        AddConjunct(result, CollectNecessaryEqualities(antecedent,
            Supporter(antecedent)))
        AddConjunct(result, ViewAsArbitraryApplic(SupportingRule(antecedent),
            focusNodes))
    else return *fail*
return result

Figure 11–8:   The BAGGER generalization algorithm

The general rule repeatedly applied is called a *focus rule*. After a focus rule is
found, BAGGER ascertains how an *arbitrary* number of instantiations of this rule
and any intervening rules can be concatenated together. This indefinite-length col-

lection of rules is conceptually merged into the explanation, replacing the specific-length collection, and a new rule is produced from the augmented explanation.

A specific solution contains several instantiations of the general rule chosen as the focus rule. Each of these applications of the rule addresses the need of satisfying the rule's antecedents, possibly in different ways. For example, when clearing an object, the blocks moved can be placed in several qualitatively different types of locations. The moved block can be placed on a table (assuming the domain model specifies that tables always have room), it can be placed on a block moved in a previous step, or it can be placed on a block that was originally clear.

BAGGER analyzes all applications of the general focus rule that appear in the specific example. When several instantiations of the focus rule provide sufficient information for different generalizations, BAGGER collects the preconditions for satisfying the antecedents of each in a disjunction of conjunctions (one conjunct for each acceptable instantiation). Common terms are factored out of the disjunction. If none of the instantiations of the focus rule provide sufficient information for generalizing the structure of the explanation, no new rule is learned by BAGGER.

Three classes of terms must be collected to construct the antecedents of a new rule. First, the antecedents of the initial rule application in the arbitrary length sequence of rule applications must be satisfied. To do this, the antecedents of the focus rule are used. Second, the preconditions imposed by chaining together an arbitrary number of rule applications must be collected. These are derived by analyzing each interconnected instantiation of the focus rule in the sample proof. Those applications that provide enough information to be viewed as the arbitrary ith application produce this second class of preconditions. Third, the preconditions from the rest of the explanation must be collected. This determines the constraints on the final applications of the focus rule.

In order to package a sequence of rule applications into a single sequential rule, the preconditions that must be satisfied at each of the N rule applications must be collected and combined. The preconditions for applying the resulting extended rule must be specifiable in terms of the initial state, and *not* in terms of intermediate states. This ensures, given that the necessary conditions are satisfied in the initial state, a plan represented in a sequential rule will run to completion without further problem solving, regardless of the number of intervening states necessary. For example, there is no possibility that a plan will lead to moving $N - 2$ blocks and then get stuck. If the preconditions for the ith rule application were expressed in terms of the result of the $(i - 1)$th application, each of the N rule applications would have to be considered in turn to see if the preconditions of the next are satisfied. This is not acceptable. In the approach taken, extra work during generalization and a possible loss of generality are traded off for a rule whose preconditions are easier to check.

When a focus rule is concatenated an arbitrary number of times, variables need to be chosen for each rule application. The RIS, a sequence of p-dimensional *vectors*, is used to represent this information. The general form of the RIS is:

$$<v_{1,1} ,..., v_{1,p}>, <v_{2,1} ,..., v_{2,p}> ,..., <v_{n,1} ,..., v_{n,p}> \qquad (1)$$

In the tower-building example of Figure 11–1, initially $p = 3$: the current situation, the object to be moved, and the object on which the moved object will be placed.

Depending on the rule used, the choice of elements for this sequence may be constrained. For example, certain elements may have to possess various properties, specific relations may have to hold among various elements, some elements may be constrained to be equal to or unequal to other elements, and some elements may be functions of other elements. Often choosing the values of the components of one vector determines the values of components of subsequent vectors. For instance, when building a tower, choosing the block to be moved in step i also determines the location to place the block to be moved in step $i + 1$.

To determine the preconditions in terms of the initial state, each of the focus rule instantiations appearing in the specific proof is viewed as an arbitrary (or ith) application of the underlying rule. The antecedents of this rule are analyzed as to what must be true of the initial state in order that it is guaranteed the ith collection of antecedents are satisfied when needed. This involves analyzing the proof tree, considering how each antecedent is proved. An augmented version of a standard explanation-based generalization algorithm [Mooney and Bennett, 1986] is used to determine which variables in this portion of the proof tree are constrained in terms of other variables.

Once this is done, the variables are expressed as components of the p-dimensional vectors described above, and the system ascertains what must be true of this sequence of vectors so that each antecedent is satisfied when necessary. All antecedents of the chosen instantiation of the focus rule must be of one of the following types for generalizing to N to be possible:

1. The antecedent may be an *axiom*. Since an axiom always holds, it need not appear as a precondition in the final rule.

2. The antecedent may be supported by a consequent of an earlier application of the focus rule. Terms of this type place intervector constraints on the sequence of p-dimensional vectors. These constraints are computed by unifying the general versions of the two terms.

3. The antecedent may be *situation-independent*. Terms of this type are unaffected by actions.

4. The antecedent may be supported by an *unwindable* or partially *unwindable* rule. When this happens, the antecedent is unwound to an arbitrary earlier state

and all of the preconditions necessary to ensure that the antecedent holds when needed are collected. A *partially unwindable* rule goes back an indefinite number of situations, from which the algorithm continues recursively. If no other inference rules are in the support of the unwindable rule, then it is unwound all the way to the initial state. The process of unwinding is further elaborated later. It, too, may place intervector constraints on the sequence of p-dimensional vectors.

5. The antecedent is supported by other terms that are satisfied in one of the above ways. When traversing backward across a supported antecedent, the system collects any intervector constraints produced by unifying the general version of the antecedent with the general version of the consequent that supports it.

Notice that antecedents are considered satisfied when they can be expressed in terms of the initial state, and *not* when a leaf of the proof tree is reached. Conceivably, to satisfy these antecedents in the initial state could require a large number of inference rules. If that is the case, it may be better to trace backwards through these rules until more *operational* terms are encountered. This *operationality/generality* trade-off [DeJong and Mooney, 1986; Keller, 1987; Mitchell, Keller, and Kedar-Cabelli, 1986; Segre, 1987; Shavlik, DeJong, and Ross, 1987] is a major issue in explanation-based learning but will not be discussed further here. Usually the cost of increased operationality is more limited applicability. An empirical analysis of the effect of this trade-off in the BAGGER system appears in [Shavlik, 1988].

A second point to notice is that not all proof subtrees will terminate in one of the above ways. If this is the case, this application of the focus rule cannot be viewed as an arbitrary ith application.[3]

The possibility that a specific solution does not provide enough information to generalize to N is an important point in explanation-based approaches to generalizing number. A concept involving an arbitrary number of substructures may involve an arbitrary number of substantially different problems. Any specific solution will only have addressed a finite number of these subproblems. Due to fortuitous circumstances in the example some of the potential problems may not have arisen. To generalize to N, a system must recognize all the problems that exist in the *general* concept and, by analyzing the specific solution, surmount them. Inference rules of a

---

[3] An alternative approach to this would be to have the system search through its collection of unwindable rules and incorporate a relevant one into the proof structure. To study the limits of this chapter's approach to generalizing to N, it is required that *all* necessary information be present in the explanation; no problem-solving search is performed during generalization. Another approach would be to assume the problem solver could overcome this problem at rule application time. This second technique, however, would eliminate the property that a learned plan will always run to completion whenever its preconditions are satisfied in the initial state.

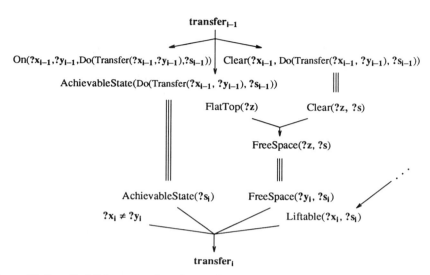

Figure 11–9:   Satisfying antecedents by previous consequents

certain form (described later) elegantly support this task in the BAGGER system. They allow the system to reason backwards through an arbitrary number of actions.

Figure 11–9 illustrates how consequents of an earlier application of a focus rule can satisfy some antecedents of a later instantiation. This figure contains a portion of the proof for the tower-building example. (The full proof tree is presented and discussed later.) Portions of two consecutive transfers are shown. All variables are universally quantified. Arrows run from the antecedents of a rule to its consequents. Triple parallel lines represent terms that are equated in the specific explanation. The generalization algorithm enforces the unification of these paired terms, leading to the collection of equality constraints.

There are four antecedents of a transfer. To define a transfer, the block moved (x), the object on which it is placed (y), and the current state (s) must be specified, and the constraints among these variables must be satisfied. One antecedent, the one requiring that a block not be placed on top of itself, is type 3—it is *situation-independent*. The next two antecedents are type 2. Two of the consequents of the $(i-1)$th transfer are used to satisfy these antecedents of the ith transfer. During *transfer*$_{i-1}$, in state s_{i-1} object x_{i-1} is moved on to object y_{i-1}. The consequents of this transfer are that a new state is produced, the object moved is clear in the new state, and x_{i-1} is on y_{i-1} in the resulting state.

The state that results from $transfer_{i-1}$ satisfies the second antecedent of $transfer_i$. Unifying these terms defines s_i in terms of the previous variables in the RIS.

Another antecedent requires that, in state s_i, there be space on object y_i to put block x_i. This antecedent is type 5, and, hence, the algorithm traverses backwards through the rule that supports it. An inference rule specifies that a clear object with a flat top has free space. The clearness of x_{i-1} after $transfer_{i-1}$ is used. Unifying this collection of terms leads, in addition to the redundant definition of s_i, to the equating of y_i with z and x_{i-1}. This means that the previously moved block always provides a clear spot to place the current block, which leads to the construction of a tower.

The fourth antecedent, that x_i be liftable, is also type 5. A rule (not shown) states that an object is liftable if it is a clear block. Block x_i is determined to be clear because it is clear in the initial state and nothing has been placed on it. Tracing backwards from the liftable term leads to several situation-independent terms and the term $Supports(?x_i, \phi, ?s_i)$. Although this term contains a situation variable, it is satisfied by an *unwindable rule*, and is type 4.

Equation (2) presents the form required for a rule to be unwindable. The consequent must match one of the antecedents of the rule. Hence, the rule can be applied recursively. This feature is used to *unwind* the term from the *i*th state to an earlier state, often the initial state. Occasionally there can be several unwindable rules in a support path. For example, a block might support another block during some number of transfers, be cleared, remain clear during another sequence of transfers, and finally be added to a tower.

$$P(x_{i,1},...,x_{i,\mu},y_{i-1,1},...,y_{i-1,v},s_{i-1}) \tag{2}$$
$$\text{and}$$
$$Q(x_{i,1},...,x_{i,\mu},y_{i-1,1},...,y_{i-1,v},y_{i,1},...,y_{i,v},...,z_{i,1},...,z_{i,\omega})$$
$$\text{and}$$
$$s_i = Do(x_{i,1},...,x_{i,\mu},y_{i-1,1},...,y_{i-1,v},...,z_{i,1},...,z_{i,\omega},s_{i-1})$$
$$\rightarrow$$
$$P(x_{i,1},...,x_{i,\mu},y_{i,1},...,y_{i,v},s_i)$$

The variables in the rule are divided into three groups. First, there are the x variables. These appear unchanged in both the consequent's term P and the antecedent's term P. Second, there are the y variables, which differ in the two P's, and the z variables that only appear in the antecedents. Finally, there is the state variable (s). There can be additional requirements of the x, y, and z variables (via predicate Q), however, these requirements cannot depend on a state variable.

Applying equation (2) recursively produces equation (3).

$$P(x_{i,1},...,x_{i,\mu},y_{j,1},...,y_{j,v},s_1) \text{ and } 0 < j < i \tag{3}$$
$$\text{and}$$

$\forall\, k \in j+1\,,..., i$

$\qquad Q\,(x_{i,1}\,,...,\, x_{i,\mu},\, y_{k-j,1}\,,...,\, y_{k-j,v},\, y_{k,1}\,,...,\, y_{k,v}\,,...,\, z_{k,1}\,,...,\, z_{k,\omega})$

$\qquad$ and

$\qquad s_k = Do\,(x_{i,1}\,,...,\, x_{i,\mu},\, y_{k-j,1}\,,...,\, y_{k-j,v}\,,,...,\, z_{k-j,1}\,,...,\, z_{k-j,\omega},\, s_{k-1}\,)$

$\rightarrow$

$P\,(x_{i,1}\,,...,\, x_{i,\mu},\, y_{i,1}\,,...,\, y_{i,v},\, s_i)$

This rule determines the requirements on the earlier state so that the desired term can be guaranteed in state i. Except for the definition of the next state, none of the antecedents depends on the intermediate states. Notice that a collection of y and z variables must be specified. Any of these variables not already contained in the RIS are added to it. Hence, the RIS is also used to store the results of intermediate computations. Since the predicate Q does not depend on the situation, it can be evaluated in the initial state.

The requirements on the predicate Q are actually somewhat less restrictive. Rather than requiring this predicate to be situation-independent, all that is necessary is that any term containing a situation argument be supported (possibly indirectly) by an application of a focus rule. The important characteristic is that the satisfaction of the predicate Q can be specified in terms of the initial situation only. Separately unwinding a predicate Q while in the midst of unwinding a predicate P is not possible with the current algorithm, and how this can be accomplished is an open research issue.

Frame axioms often satisfy the form of equation (2). Figure 11–10 shows one way to satisfy the need to have a clear object at the ith step. Assume the left-hand side of Figure 11–10 is a portion of some proof. This explanation says block x_i is clear in state s_i because it is clear in state s_{i-1} and the block moved in *transfer*$_{i-1}$ is not placed on x_i. Unwinding this rule leads to the result that block x_i will be clear in state s_i if it is clear in state s_1 and x_i is never used as the new support block in any of the intervening transfers.

To classify an instantiation of a rule as being unwindable, the rule must be applied at least *twice* successively. This heuristic prevents generalizations that are likely to be spurious. Just like when looking for multiple applications of the focus rule, multiple applications are required for unwindable rules. The intent of this is to increase the likelihood that a generalization is being made that will be prove useful in the future. For example, imagine some rule represents withdrawing some money from a bank and also imagine this rule is of the form of equation (2). Assume that in state 5, John withdraws $500 to buy a television, while in states 1 to 4, the amount of money he has in the bank is unaffected. While it is correct to generalize this plan to include any number of trips to the bank in order to get sufficient money for a purchase, it does not seem proper to do so. Rather, the generalization should be to a

A Portion of the Explanation   **Unwound Subgraph**

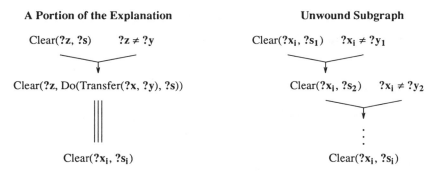

Figure 11–10:   Unwinding a rule

single trip to the bank at *any* time. Frame axioms are exceptions to this constraint—they only need to be applied once to be considered unwindable. Since frame axioms only specify what remains unchanged, there is no risk in assuming an arbitrary number of successive applications.

Once the repeated rule portion of the extended rule is determined, the rest of the explanation is incorporated into the final result. This is accomplished in the same manner as the way antecedents are satisfied in the repeated rule portion. The only difference is that the focus rule is now viewed as the *Nth* rule application. As before, antecedents must be of one of the five specified types. If all the terms in the goal cannot be satisfied in the arbitrary *Nth* state, no rule is learned.

The consequents of the final rule are constructed by collecting those generalized final consequents of the explanation that directly support the goal.

Even though all the antecedents of a sequential BAGGER rule are evaluated in the initial state, substantial time can be spent finding satisfactory bindings for the variables in the rule. Simplifying the antecedents of a rule acquired using EBL can increase the efficiency of the rule [Minton, *et al.*, 1987; Prieditis and Mostow; 1987]. After a rule is constructed by the BAGGER generalization algorithm, duplicate antecedents are removed and the remainder are rearranged by the system in an attempt to speedup the process of satisfying the rule. This involves several processes. Heuristics are used to estimate whether is better to construct sequences from the first vector forward or from the last vector backward. Terms not effected by the intermediate antecedent are moved so that they are tested as soon as possible. Terms involving arithmetic are placed so that all their arguments are bound when they are evaluated. Finally, within each grouping, antecedents are arranged so that terms involving the same variable are near each other.

The next section discusses the sequential-rule produced by this algorithm when applied to the problem of building a tower.

11.4 DETAILS OF THE STACKING EXAMPLE

This section presents the details of one of BAGGER's sequential rules. The proof that explains the tower-building actions of Figure 11–1 appears in Figure 11–11. This graph is produced by the BAGGER system, however nodes have been rearranged by hand for the sake of readability. Since the situation arguments are quite lengthy, they are abbreviated, and a key appears in the figure. Arrows run from the antecedent of a rule to its consequent. When a rule has multiple antecedents or consequents, an ampersand (&) is used. Descriptions of all the rules used in this structure are contained in the appendix. The primed ampersands are the instantiations of the focus rule, while the lowest ampersand is the goal node.

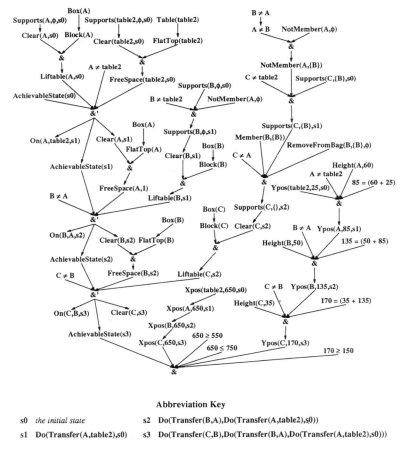

Abbreviation Key

s0 *the initial state*	s2 Do(Transfer(B,A),Do(Transfer(A,table2),s0))
s1 Do(Transfer(A,table2),s0)	s3 Do(Transfer(C,B),Do(Transfer(B,A),Do(Transfer(A,table2),s0)))

Figure 11–11:   Situation calculus plan for stacking three blocks

The goal provided to the backward-chaining theorem prover that produced this graph is:

$\exists$ AchievableState(?state) $\land$
   Xpos(?object, ?px, ?state) $\land$?px $\geq$ 550 $\land$?px $\leq$ 750 $\land$
   Ypos(?object, ?py, ?state) $\land$?py $\geq$ 150.

This says that the goal is to prove the existence of an achievable state, such that in that state the horizontal position of some object is between 550 and 750 and the vertical position of that same objects is at least 150.

The sequential rule produced by analyzing this explanation structure appears in Table 11–1. The remainder of this section describes how each term in this table is produced. Line numbers have been included for purposes of reference. For readability, the new rule is broken down into components, as shown in equation (4).

$$Antecedents_{initial} \land Antecedent_{intermediate} \land Antecedents_{rest} \rightarrow Consequents \qquad (4)$$

Table 11–1:   The components of the learned rule

Antecedents$_{initial}$
(1)   Sequence(?seq) $\land$ InitialVector(?v_1, ?seq) $\land$ State(s0) $\land$?$v_{1,1}$ = s0 $\land$
(2)   FreeSpace(?$v_{1,3}$, s0) $\land$ Liftable(?$v_{1,2}$, s0) $\land$ Height(?$v_{1,2}$, ?$v_{1,4}$) $\land$
(3)   Xpos(?$v_{1,3}$, ?px, s0) $\land$ Ypos(?$v_{1,3}$, ?new, s0) $\land$?$v_{1,2} \neq$?$v_{1,3}$ $\land$
(4)   ?$v_{1,5}$ = (?$v_{1,4}$ + ?new) $\land$?px $\geq$?xmin $\land$?px $\leq$?xmax $\land$

Antecedent$_{intermediate}$
(5)   [Member(?v_i, ?seq) $\land$?$v_i \neq$?v_1 $\land$ Member(?v_{i-1}, ?seq) $\land$
      Predecessor(?v_{i-1},?v_i, ?seq)

         $\rightarrow$

(6)   ?$v_{i,3}$ = ?$v_{i-1,2}$ $\land$?$v_{i,1}$ = Do(Transfer(?$v_{i-1,2}$, ?$v_{i-1,3}$), ?$v_{i-1,1}$) $\land$ FlatTop(?$v_{i,3}$) $\land$
(7)   Block(?$v_{i,2}$) $\land$ Height(?$v_{i,2}$, ?$v_{i,4}$) $\land$?$v_{i,2} \neq$?$v_{i,3}$ $\land$?$v_{i,5}$ = (?$v_{i,4}$ + ?$v_{i-1,5}$) $\land$
(8)   [[[Member(?v_j,?seq) $\land$ Earlier(?v_j,?v_i,?seq) $\rightarrow$?$v_{i,2} \neq$?$v_{j,3}$] $\land$ Supports(?$v_{i,2}$,ϕ,s0)]
(9) $\lor$ [[Member(?v_j,?seq) $\land$ Earlier(?v_j,?v_{i-1},?seq) $\rightarrow$
         NotMember(?$v_{i,2}$, {?$v_{i-1,2}$})] $\land$
(10)   [Member(?v_j, ?seq) $\land$ Earlier(?v_j, ?v_{i-1}, ?seq) $\rightarrow$?$v_{i,2} \neq$?$v_{j,3}$] $\land$
(11)   Supports(?$v_{i,2}$, {?$v_{i-1,2}$}, s0) $\land$?$v_{i,2} \neq$?$v_{i-1,3}$]]] $\land$

Antecedents$_{final}$
(12)   FinalVector(?v_n,?seq) $\land$?py = ?$v_{n,5}$ $\land$?state = Do(Transfer(?$v_{n,2}$, ?$v_{n,3}$), ?$v_{n,1}$) $\land$
(13)   ?object = ?$v_{n,2}$ $\land$?py $\geq$?ymin

Consequents
(14)   State(?state) $\land$ Xpos(?object, ?px, ?state) $\land$?px $\leq$?xmax $\land$?px $\geq$?xmin $\land$
(15)   Ypos(?object, ?py, ?state) $\land$?py $\geq$?ymin

This rule extends sequences 1 $\rightarrow$ N.

While BAGGER's reordering of a new rule's antecedents means the presented rule is somewhat harder to read, Table 11–1 accurately reflects the rule acquired and used by the system.

11.4.1 Producing the Initial Antecedents

The initial antecedents in the first line of the rule establish a sequence of vectors, the initial state, and the first vector contained in the sequence. Subscripts are used to indicate components of vectors, as a shorthand for functions that perform this task. For example, $?v_{1,3}$ is shorthand for $ThirdComponent(?v_1)$. Lines 2 and 3 contain the antecedents of the first application in the chain of applications. These are the same terms that appear in the focus rule (the first rule in Table 11–A2), except that the components of v_1 are used. The system has knowledge of which arguments are situation variables and the initial state constant is placed in these positions. The other terms in this grouping are produced by the unwinding process ($Height,$~$Xpos,$~$Ypos$, and the addition term) or are moved ($\geq$ and $\leq$) from the final antecedents to the initial antecedents because their variables are not influenced by the intermediate antecedents. The terms produced by unwinding are described further in what follows.

11.4.2 Analyzing the Applications of the Focus Rule

Lines 5 through 11 contain the preconditions derived by analyzing the three instantiations of the focus rule. In this implication, v_i, an arbitrary vector in the sequence (other than the first), is used, as these constraints must be satisfied for each of the applications that follow the first. Vector v_{i-1} is the vector immediately preceding v_i. It is needed because some of the antecedents of the ith application are satisfied by the $(i-1)$th application. Although some preconditions in the new rule involve v_i and v_{i-1}, these preconditions all refer to conditions in the initial state. They do *not* refer to results in intermediate states.

The final two of the three instantiations of the focus rule produce sufficient information to determine how the antecedents of the rule can be satisfied in the ith application. In the first application (upper left of Figure 11–11), neither the support for *Liftable* nor the support for *FreeSpace* provide enough information to determine the constraints on the initial state so that these terms can be satisfied in an arbitrary step. In both cases, the proof only had to address clearness in the current state. No information is provided within the proof as to how clearness can be guaranteed to hold in some later state.

The two other instantiations of the focus rule provide sufficient information for generalization. Two different ways of satisfying the antecedents are discovered, and, hence, a disjunction is learned. The common terms in these two disjuncts appear in lines 6 and 7, while the remaining terms for the first disjunction are in line 8 and for the second in lines 9–11.

The third term in line 7 is the vector form of the inequality that is one of the antecedents of the focus rule. This, being situation-independent, is a type 3 antecedent. In vector form, it becomes $v_{i,2} \neq v_{i,3}$. It constrains possible collections of vectors to those that have different second and third members. This constraint stems from the requirement that a block cannot be stacked on itself.

Both of the successful applications of the focus rule have their *AchievableState* term satisfied by a consequent of a previous application. These terms are type 2 and require collection of the equalities produced by unifying the general versions of the matching consequents and antecedents. (See Figure 11–9 for the details of these matchings.) The equality that results from these unifications is the second term of line 6. Thus, the next state is always completely determined by the previous one. No searching needs to be done in order to choose the next state. (Actually, no terms are ever evaluated in these intermediate states. The only reason they are recorded is so that the final state can be determined, for use in setting the situation variable in the consequents.)

Both successful applications have their *FreeSpace* term satisfied in the same manner. Traversing backwards across one rule leads to a situation independent term (*FlatTop*—line 6) and the consequent of an earlier application (*Clear*). Unifying the two clear terms (again, see Figure 11–9) produces the first two equalities in line 6. This first equality means that the block to be moved in the ith step can always be placed on top of the block to be moved in the $(i - 1)$th step. No problem solving need be done to determine the location at which to continue building the tower.

The *Block* term in line 7 is produced during the process of analyzing the way the *Liftable* term is satisfied. The remaining portion of the analysis of *Liftable* produces the terms in the disjunctions. As in the initial antecedents, the *Height* and addition terms in line 7 are produced during the analysis of the terms in the goal, which is described later.

In the second application of the focus rule, which produces the first disjunct, a clear block to move is acquired by finding a block that is clear because it supports nothing in the initial state, and nothing is placed on it later. The frame axiom supporting this is an unwindable rule. Unwinding it to the initial state produces line 8. The *Supports* term must hold in the initial state and the block to be moved in step i can never be used as the place to locate a block to be moved in an earlier step. The general version of the term *NotMember(A,ϕ)* does not appear in the learned rule because it is an axiom that nothing is a member of the empty set. (An earlier unification, from the rule involving *Clear*, requires that the second variable in the general version of *NotMember* term be ϕ.)

Notice that this unwinding restricts the applicability of the acquired rule. The first disjunct requires that if an initially clear block is to be added to the tower, nothing can ever be placed on it, even temporarily. A more general plan would be learned, however, if in the specific example a block is temporarily covered. In that case, in the proof there would be several groupings of unwindable rules; for a while the block would remain clear, something would then be placed on it, and it would remain covered for several steps. Finally it would be cleared and remain that way until moved. Although this clearing and unclearing can occur repeatedly, the current BAGGER algorithm is unable to generalize number within unwindable subproofs.

The second disjunct (lines 9–11) results from the different way a liftable block is found in the third application of the focus rule. Here a liftable block is found by using a block that initially supported one other block, which is moved in the previous step, and where nothing else is moved to the lower block during an earlier rule application. Unwinding the subgraph for this application leads to the requirements that initially one block is on the block to be moved in step i, that block be moved in step $(i-1)$, and nothing else is scheduled to be moved to the lower block during an earlier rule applications. Again, some terms do not appear in the learned rule (*Member* and *RemoveFromBag*) because, given the necessary unifications, they are axioms. This time *NotMember* is not an axiom, and hence, appears. If the specific example were more complicated, the acquired rule would reflect the fact that the block on top can be removed in some *earlier* step, rather than necessarily in the *previous* step.

11.4.3 Analyzing the Rest of the Explanation

Once all of the instantiations of the focus rule are analyzed, the goal node is visited. This produces lines 12 and 13, plus some of the earlier terms. The *AchievableState* term of the goal is satisfied by the final application of the focus rule, leading to the third term in line 12.

The final X-position is calculated using an unwindable rule. Tracing backwards from the *Xpos* in the goal to the consequent of the unwindable rule produces the first term in line 13, as well as the third term in line 12. When this rule is unwound it produces the first term of line 3 and the second term of line 6. Also, matching the *Xpos* term in the antecedents with the one in the consequents, so that equation (2) applies, again produces the first term in line 6. Since there are no "Q"-terms (equation (2)), no other preconditions are added to the intermediate antecedent.

The inequalities involving the tower's horizontal position are state-independent; their general forms are moved to the initial antecedents because their arguments are not effected by satisfying the intermediate antecedent. These terms in the initial antecedents involving $?px$ insure that the tower is started underneath the goal.

Unwindable rules also determine the final Y-position. Here "Q"-terms are present. The connection of two instantiations of the underlying general rule appears in Figure 11–12. This general rule is unwound to the initial state, which creates the second term of line 3 and the second term of line 6. The last three terms of line 7 are also produced, as the "Q"-terms must hold for each application of the unwound rule. This process adds two components to the vectors in the RIS. The first ($?v_{i,4}$) comes

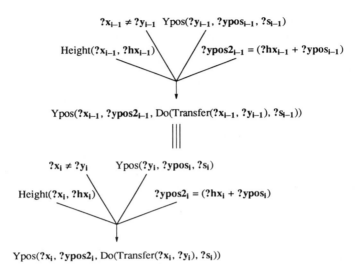

Figure 11–12: Calculating the vertical position of the *i*th stacked block

from the ?*hx* variable, which records the height of the block being added to the tower. The other (?$v_{i,5}$) comes from the variable ?*yPos2*. It records the vertical position of the block added, and hence, represents the height of the tower. The ?*ypos* variable does not lead to the creation of another RIS entry because it matches the ?*yPos2* variable of the previous application. All that is needed is a ?*ypos* variable for the first application. Similarly, matching the *Ypos* term in the antecedents with the one in the consequents produces the first term in line 6.

The last conjunct in the goal produces the second term on line 13. This precondition insures that the final tower is tall enough. Finally, the general version of the goal description is used to construct the consequents of the new rule (lines 14 and 15).

11.5 EMPIRICAL ANALYSIS

An empirical analysis of the performance of the BAGGER system is presented in this section. This system is compared to an implementation of a standard explanation-based generalization algorithm and to a problem-solving system that performs no learning. Two different training strategies are analyzed.

The major issue these experiments investigate is whether generalizing explanation structures is worthwhile. Generalizing explanation structures leads to acquiring more general rules, but because the resulting rules are more complicated, applying them entails more work. The experiments are designed to investigate is whether it is better to the learn the more general rule or whether it would be better to learn individually the subsumed rules as they are needed. The results demonstrate the efficacy of generalizing to N.

11.5.1 Experimental Methodology

Experiments are run using blocks-world inference rules. An initial situation is created by generating 10 blocks, each with a randomly chosen width and height. One at a time, they are dropped from an arbitrary horizontal position over a table; if they fall in an unstable location, they are picked up and rereleased over a new location. Once the 10 blocks are placed, a randomly chosen goal height is selected, centered above a second table. The goal height is determined by adding from one to four average block heights. In addition, the goal specifies a maximum height on towers. The difference between the minimum and maximum acceptable tower heights is equal to the maximum possible height of a block. This reason for this upper bound is explained later. A sample problem situation can be seen in Figure 11–13. The goal is to place a block so that its top is centered within the confines of the dotted lines.

Once a scene is constructed, three different problem solvers attempt to satisfy the goal. The first is called NO-LEARN, as it acquires no new rules during problem solving. The second, called STD-EBL, is an implementation of a standard explanation-based generalization algorithm, called EGGS [Mooney and Bennett, 1986]. (Explanation structures are pruned at terms that are either situation-independent or describe the initial state.) BAGGER is the third system. All three of these systems use a backward-chaining problem solver to satisfy the preconditions of rules. When the two learning systems attack a new problem, they first try to apply the rules they have acquired, possibly also using existing intrasituational rules. No intersituational rules are used in combination with acquired rules in order to limit searching, which would quickly become intractable. Hence, to be successful, an acquired rule must directly lead to a solution without using other intersituational rules.

BAGGER's problem solver, in order to construct the RIS, is a slightly extended version of the standard backward-chaining problem solver—basically a version of PROLOG [Clocksin and Mellish, 1984]—used by the other two systems. First, the

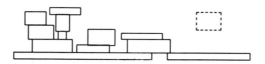

Figure 11–13:   A sample problem

constraints on $?v_1$ are checked against the initial state. This leads to the binding of other components of the first vector in the sequence. Next, the problem solver checks if the last vector in the sequence (at this point, $?v_1$) satisfies the preconditions for $?v_n$. If so, a satisfactory sequence has been found and back-chaining terminates successfully. Otherwise, the last vector in the sequence is viewed as $?v_{i-1}$, and the problem solver attempts to satisfy the intermediate antecedent. This may lead to vector $?v_i$ being incorporated into the sequence. If a new vector is added, the final constraints on the sequence are checked again. If they are not satisfied, the new head of the sequence is viewed as $?v_{i-1}$, and the process repeats. This cycle continues until either the current sequence satisfies the rule's antecedents or the initial state cannot support the insertion of another vector into the sequence. When the current sequence cannot be further extended, chronological backtracking is performed, moving back to the last point where there are choices as to how to lengthen the sequence.

The problem solver is used is rather naive. A more sophisticated one could take advantage of sophisticated matching algorithms (such as RETE [Forgy, 1982]), complicated conflict resolution strategies, metalevel control strategies, etc. However, using these enhancements would require that more parameters be set for the experiments and that the experiments also evaluate the enhancements. Fortunately, the same problem-solving strategy is used by all three systems, so that improved problem solving would help each of them. However, the amount each would be helped by improvements may differ. Investigating the overall impact of problem-solving enhancements is an area for future research. It is possible that the gains from learning reduce the need to have a complicated problem solver.

Two different strategies for training the learning systems are employed. In one, called *autonomous mode*, the learning systems resort to solving a problem from "first principles" when none of their acquired rules can solve it. This means that the original intersituational rules can be used, but learned rules are not used. When the proof of the solution to a problem is constructed in this manner, the systems apply their generalization algorithm and store any general rule that is produced. In the other strategy, called *training mode*, some number of solved problems (the *training set*) is initially presented to the systems, and the rules acquired from generalizing these solutions are applied to additional problems (the *test set*). Under this second strategy, if none of a system's acquired rules solves the problem at hand, the system is considered to have failed. No problem solving from first principles is ever performed by the learning systems in this mode.

Unfortunately, constructing towers containing more than two blocks from first principles exceeds the limits of the computers used in the experiments (Xerox Dandelions). For this reason, the performance of the NO-LEARN system is estimated by fitting an exponential curve to the data obtained from constructing towers of size one and two. This curve is used by all three systems to estimate the time needed to construct towers from first principles when required, and a specialized procedure is used to generate a solution.

Data collection in these experiments is accomplished as follows. Initially, the two learning systems possess no acquired rules. They are then exposed to a number of sample situations, building up their rule collections according to the learning strategy applied. (At each point, all three systems address the same randomly generated problem.) Statistics are collected as the systems solve problems and learn. This continues for a fixed number of problems, constituting an experimental run. However, a single run can be greatly effected by the ordering of the sample problems. To provide better estimates of performance, multiple experimental runs are performed. At the start of each run, the rules acquired in the previous run are discarded. When completed, the results of all the runs are averaged together. Unless otherwise noted, the data presented in this section is the result of superimposing 25 experimental runs and averaging. In all of the curves, solid circles represent data from BAGGER, open circles from STD-EBL, and x's from NO-LEARN.

Each learning system stores its acquired rules in a linear list. During problem solving, these rules are tried in order. When a rule is successful, it is moved to the front of the list. This way, less useful rules will migrate toward the back of the list. Analysis of other indexing strategies is presented in [Shavlik, 1988], where a more comprehensive experimental analysis of EBL is presented.

This indexing strategy is the reason that, in the goal, tower heights are limited. The STD-EBL system would sooner or later encounter a goal requiring four blocks, and a rule for this would migrate to the front of its rule list. From that time on, regardless of the goal height, a four-block tower would be constructed. With a limit on tower heights, the rules for more efficiently building towers of lower heights have an opportunity to be tried. This issue would be exacerbated if the goal were not limited to four-block towers due to simulation time restrictions.

11.5.2 Experimental Results

In this section the performance of the three systems in the two basic modes of operation—*autonomous* and *training*—is presented. The autonomous mode is considered first. In this mode, whenever a system's current collection of acquired rules fails to solve a problem, a solution from first principles is constructed and generalized. Figure 11–14 shows the probability that the learning systems will need to resort to first principles as a function of the number of sample problems experienced. As more problems are experienced, this probability decreases. (On the first problem the probability is always 1.) BAGGER is less likely to need to resort to first principles than is STD-EBL because, as a result of generalizing structure, BAGGER produces a more general rule by analyzing the solution to the first problem. (The increase of BAGGER in the 42 to 50 range is due to statistical fluctuations.)

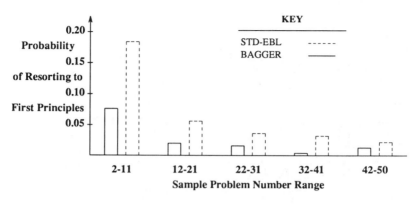

Figure 11–14:   Probability of resorting to first principles in autonomous mode

On average, BAGGER learns 1.72 sequential rules in each experimental run, while STD-EBL learns 4.28 rules. It takes BAGGER about 50 seconds and STD-EBL about 45 seconds to generalize a specific problem's solution. Averaging over problems 26 to 50 in each run (to estimate the asymptotic behavior), produces a mean solution time of 3720 seconds for BAGGER, 8100 seconds for STD-EBL, and 79,300 seconds[4] for NO-LEARN. For BAGGER, this is a speedup of 2.2 over STD-EBL and 21.3 over NO-LEARN, where speedup is defined as follows:

$$Speedup\ of\ A\ over\ B = \frac{mean\ solution\ time\ for\ B}{mean\ solution\ time\ for\ A}$$

Figure 11–15 presents the performance during a *single* experimental run of the two learning systems in the autonomous mode. The average time to solve a problem is plotted, on a logarithmic scale, against the number of sample problems experienced. The time taken to produce a solution from first principles dominates the time taken to apply the acquired rules, accounting for the peaks in the curves.

Because the cost of solving a big problem from first principles greatly dominates the cost of applying acquired rules, the autonomous mode may not be an acceptable strategy. Although learning this way means many problems will be solved quicker than without learning, the time occasionally taken to construct a solution when a system's acquired rules fail can dominate the performance. The peaks in Figure 11–15 illustrate this. A long period may be required before a learning system

---

[4] One day contains 86,400 seconds.

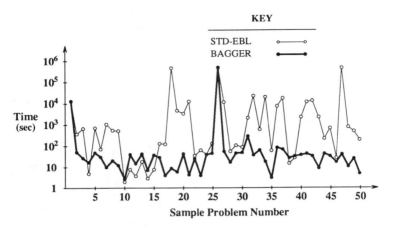

Figure 11–15:   Performance comparison in the autonomous mode

acquires enough rules to cover all future problem-solving episodes without resorting to first principles.

The second learning mode provides an alternative. If an expert is available to provide solutions to sample problems and an occasional failure to solve a problem is acceptable, this mode is attractive. Here, a number of sample solutions are provided and the learning systems generalize these solutions, discarding new rules that are variants[5] of others already acquired. After training, the systems use their acquired rules to solve new problems. No problem solving from first principles is performed when a solution cannot be found using a system's acquired rules. Occasional failures to solve a problem are assumed to be more acceptable than long times spent solving from first principles. This methodology means that BAGGER and STD-EBL are compared independent of the issue of how much time each spends reasoning from first principles. Only the amount of search among their acquired rules is considered.

The performance results in the training mode are shown in Figure 11–16. After 10 training problems, the systems solve 20 additional problems. In these 20 test problems, the two learning systems never resort to using first principles. BAGGER

---

[5] The algorithm for detecting variants determines if two rules exactly match, given some renaming of variables. This means, for instance, that $a \vee b$ and $b \vee a$ are *not* variants. Hence, semantically equivalent rules are not always considered variants. A more sophisticated variant algorithm would reduce the number of saved rules. However if the variant algorithm considered associativity and commutativity, it would be much less efficient [Benanav, Kapur, and Narendran, 1985].

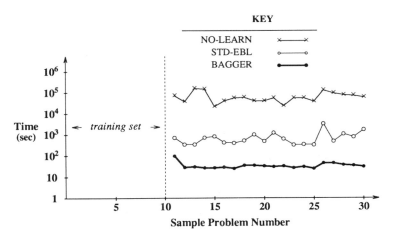

Figure 11–16:   Performance comparison of the trained problem solvers

takes, on average, 36.6 seconds on the test problems (versus 3720 seconds in the autonomous mode), STD-EBL requires an average of 828 seconds (versus 8100 seconds), and NO-LEARN averages 68,400 seconds (versus 79,6300 seconds).

Since NO-LEARN operates the same in the two modes, these statistics indicate the random draw of problems produced an easier set in the second experiment. The substantial savings for the two learning systems (99% for BAGGER and 90% for STD-EBL) are due to the fact that in this mode these systems spend no time generating solutions from first principles. In this experiment, BAGGER has a speedup of 23 over STD-EBL (versus 2.2 in the other experiment) and 1870 over NO-LEARN (versus 21.3).

One of the prices of using the training mode is that occasionally the learning systems will not be able to solve a problem. Figure 11–17 plots the number of failures as a function of the size of the training set. In each experimental run used to construct this figure, 20 test problems are solved after the training examples are presented. With 10 training solutions, both of the systems solve over 98.5% of the test problems.

The final figure, Figure 11–18, summarizes the performance of the three systems in the two training modes. Note that a logarithmic scale is used.

11.5.3 Summary

The empirical results presented in this section demonstrate the value of generalizing to N. In the two training strategies investigated, BAGGER performs substan-

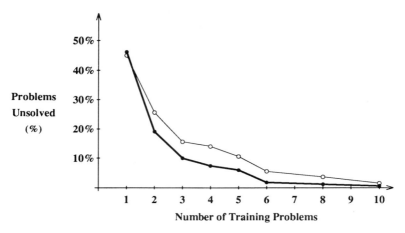

Figure 11–17:   Failure comparison of the trained problem solvers

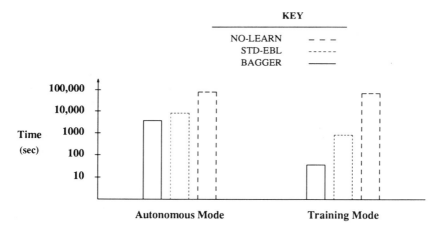

Figure 11–18:   Performance of the three systems in the two modes

tially better than a system that performs no learning. BAGGER also outperforms a standard explanation-based learning system.

Other researchers have also reported on the performance improvement of standard EBL systems over problem solvers that do not learn [Fikes, Hart, and Nilsson, 1972; Minton, 1985; Mooney, 1988; O'Rorke, 1987b; Prieditis and Mostow, 1987;

Steier, 1987]. One major issue is that as more new concepts are learned, problem-solving performance can *decrease*. This occurs because substantial time can be spent trying to apply rules that appear promising, but ultimately fail [Minton, 1985; Mooney, 1988]. Also, a new, broadly applicable rule, which can require substantial time to instantiate, may block access to a more restricted, yet often sufficient, rule whose preconditions are easier to apply [Shavlik, DeJong, and Ross, 1987]. While the non-learning system outperforms the learning systems on some problems, in the experiments reported in this section the overall effect is that learning is beneficial.

It may seem that investigating only tower-building problems unfairly favors explanation-based learning. An alternative would be to investigate a more diverse collection of problem types. However, the negative effects of learning are manifested most strongly when the acquired concepts are closely related. If the effects of some rule support the satisfaction of a goal, substantial time can be spent trying to satisfy the preconditions of the rule. If this cannot be done, much time is wasted. To the STD-EBL system, a rule for stacking two blocks is quite different from one that moves four blocks. Frequently a rule that appears relevant fails. For example, often STD-EBL tries to satisfy a rule that specifies moving four blocks to meet the goal of having a block at a given height, only to fail after much effort because all combinations of four blocks exceed the limitations on the tower height. When the effects of a rule are clearly unrelated to the current goal, much less time is wasted, especially if a sophisticated data structure is used to organize rules according to the goals they support.

The BAGGER algorithm leads to the acquisition of fewer rules, because one of its rules may subsume many related rules learned using standard EBL. In this section's experiments, this decreases the likelihood that time will be wasted on rules that appear to be applicable. The probability that, in the training mode, a retrieved rule successfully solves a problem is 0.595 for STD-EBL and 0.998 for BAGGER. Additionally, fewer training examples are needed for BAGGER to acquire a sufficient set of new rules. These advantages over standard EBL magnify if the range of possible tower heights is increased [Shavlik, 1988].

The two training modes demonstrate the importance of external guidance to learning systems. In the autonomous mode, the systems must solve all problems on their own. The high cost of doing this when no learned rule applies dissipates much of the gain from learning. Substantial gain can be achieved by initially providing solutions to a collection of sample problems and having the learners acquire their rules by generalizing these solutions. The usefulness of this depends on how representative the training samples are of future problems and how acceptable are occasional failures. Again, since BAGGER requires fewer training examples and produces more general rules, it addresses these issues better than does standard EBL.

11.6 RELATED WORK

The need to generalize number in EBL was first pointed out in [Shavlik and DeJong, 1985], where the knowledge that momentum is conserved for any N objects is learned from an example involving the collision of a fixed number of balls. Besides BAGGER, several other explanation-based approaches to generalizing number have been recently proposed.

Prieditis [1986] has developed a system that learns macro-operators representing sequences of repeated STRIPS-like operators. While BAGGER is very much in the spirit of Prieditis's work, STRIPS-like operators impose unwarranted restrictions. For instance, BAGGER's use of predicate calculus allows generalization of repeated structure and repeated actions in a uniform manner. In addition, the BAGGER approach accommodates the use of additional inference rules to reason about what is true in a state. Everything does not have to appear explicitly in the focus rule. For example, in the stacking problem, other rules are used to determine the height of a tower and that an object is clear when the only object it supports is transferred. Also, instantiations of the focus rule do not have to directly connect—intervening inference rules can be involved when determining that the results of one instantiation partially support the preconditions of another. Prieditis's approach only analyzes the constraints imposed by the connections of the precondition, add, and delete lists of the operators of interest. There is nothing that corresponds to BAGGER's unwinding operation nor are disjunctive rules learned.

In the FERMI system [Cheng and Carbonell, 1986], cyclic patterns are recognized, using empirical methods and the detected repeated pattern is generalized using explanation-based learning techniques. A major strength of the FERMI system is the incorporation of conditionals within the learned macro-operator. However, unlike the techniques implemented in BAGGER, the rules acquired by FERMI are not fully based on an explanation-based analysis of an example, and so are not guaranteed to always work. For example, FERMI learns a strategy for solving a set of linear algebraic equations. None of the preconditions of the strategy check that the equations are linearly independent. The learned strategy will appear applicable to the problem of determining x and y from the equations $3x + y = 5$ and $6x + 2 = 10$. After a significant amount of work, the strategy will terminate unsuccessfully.

Cohen [1987] has recently developed and formalized another approach to the problem of generalizing number. His system generalizes number by constructing a finite-state control mechanism that deterministically directs the construction of proofs similar to the one used to justify the specific example. One significant property of his method is that it can generate proof procedures involving tree traversals and nested loops. A major difference between Cohen's method and other explanation-based algorithms is that in his approach no "internal nodes" of the explanation are eliminated during generalization. In other explanation-based algorithms, only the leaves of the operationalized explanation appear in the acquired rule. The generalization process guarantees that all of the inference rules within the explanation apply in the general case, and the final result can be viewed as a compilation of the effect of combining these rules as generally as possible. Hence, to apply the new rule, only the general versions of these leave nodes need be satisfied. In Cohen's approach, every inference rule used in the original explanation is explicitly incorporated into the final result. Each rule may again be applied when satisfying the acquired rule. Hence, there is nothing in this approach corresponding to unwinding a rule from an arbitrary state back to the initial state, and the efficiency gains obtained by doing this are not achieved. Finally, because the final automaton is deterministic, it incorporates disjunctions only in a limited way. For example, if at some point two choices are equally general, the ordering in the final rule will be the same as that seen in the specific example.

A fourth system, PHYSICS 101 [Shavlik and DeJong, 1985, 1987a; Shavlik, 1988], differs from the above approaches in that the need for generalizing number is motivated by an analytic justification of an example's solution and general domain knowledge. This system learns such concepts as the general law of conservation of momentum (which is applicable to an arbitrary collection of objects) by observing and analyzing the solution to a specific three-body collision. In the momentum problem, information about number, localized in a single physics formula, leads to a global restructuring of a specific solution's explanation. However, PHYSICS 101 is designed to reason about the use of mathematical formulae. Its generalization algorithm takes great advantage of the properties of algebraic cancellation (e.g., $x - x = 0$). To be a broad solution of the generalization to N problem, nonmathematically based domains must also be handled.

Another aspect of generalizing the structure of explanations involves generalizing the *organization* of the nodes in the explanation, rather than generalizing the *number* of nodes. An approach of this form is presented in [Mooney, 1988], where the temporal order of actions is generalized in plan-based explanations. The approach is limited to domains expressed in the STRIPS-formalism [Fikes and Nilsson, 1971].

The problem of generalizing to N has also been addressed within the paradigms of similarity-based learning [Andreae, 1984; Dietterich and Michalski, 1983; Dufay and Latombe, 1984; Michalski, 1983; Sammut and Banerji, 1986; Whitehall, 1987; Wolff, 1982) and automatic programming [Biermann, 1978; Kodratoff, 1979; Summers, 1977; Siklossy and Sykes, 1975]. A general specification of number generalization has been advanced by Michalski [1983]. He proposes a set of generalization rules including a *closing interval rule* and several *counting arguments rules* that can generate number-generalized structures. The difference between such similarity-based approaches and BAGGER's explanation-based approach is that the newly formed similarity-based concepts typically require verification from corroborating examples, whereas the explanation-based concepts are immediately supported by the domain theory.

11.7 SOME OPEN RESEARCH ISSUES

The BAGGER system has taken important steps towards the solution to the "generalization to N" problem. However, the research is still incomplete. From the vantage point of current results, several avenues of future research are apparent.

One issue in generalizing the structure of explanations is deciding when there is enough information in the specific explanation to usefully generalize its structure. Due to the finiteness of a specific problem, fortuitous circumstances in the specific situation may have allowed shortcuts in the solution. Complications inherent in the general case may not have been faced. Hence the specific example provides no guidance as to how they should be addressed. In BAGGER, the requirement that, for an application of a focus rule to be generalized, it must be viewable as the arbitrary ith application addresses the problem of recognizing fortuitous circumstances. If there is not enough information to view it as the ith application, it is likely that some important issue is not addressed in this focus rule application. However, more powerful techniques for recognizing fortuitous circumstances need to be developed.

Related to this, BAGGER's method for choosing a focus rule needs improvement. Currently the first detected instance of interconnected applications of a rule is used as the focus rule. However, there could be several occurrences that satisfy these requirements. Techniques for comparing alternative focus rules are needed. Inductive inference approaches to detecting repeated structures [Andreae, 1984; Dietterich and Michalski, 1983; Dufay and Latombe, 1984; Weld, 1986; Whitehall, 1987; Wolff, 1982] may be applicable to the generation of candidate focus rules, from which the explanation-based capabilities of BAGGER can build.

A second research topic is performing multiple generalizations to N in a single problem. Especially interesting is *interleaved generalization to N*. Here, in the final result, each application in an arbitrary length sequence would be supported by another sequence of arbitrary length. In other words, a portion of the intermediate antecedent of a BAGGER rule would be the antecedents of another BAGGER rule. Learning an interleaved sequential rule from one example may be too ambitious. A more reasonable approach may be to first learn a simple sequential rule, and then use it in the explanation of a later problem. Managing the interactions between the two RIS's is a major issue. See Cohen [1987] for a promising approach to the problem of interleaved generalization to N.

A third area of future research is to investigate how BAGGER and other such systems might acquire accessory intersituational rules, such as frame axioms, to complement their composite rules. Currently, each of BAGGER's new sequential inference rules specifies how to achieve a goal involving some arbitrary aggregation of objects by applying some number of operators. These rules are useful in directly achieving goals that match the consequent, but do not effectively improve BAGGER's backward-chaining problem-solving ability. This is because currently BAGGER does not construct new frame axioms for the rules it learns. (This problem is not specific to generalizing to N—standard EBL algorithms must also face it when dealing with situation calculus.)

There are several methods of acquiring accessory rules. They can be constructed directly by combining the accessory rules of operators that make up the sequential rule. This may be intractable, since the number of accessory rules for initial operators may be large, and they may increase combinatorially in sequential rules. Another, potentially more attractive, approach is to treat the domain theory, augmented by sequential rules, as intractable. Since the accessory rules for learned rules are derivable from existing knowledge of initial operators, the approach in [Chien, 1987] might be used to acquire the unstated but derivable accessory rules when they are needed.

Investigating the generalization of operator application orderings within learned rules is a fourth opportunity for future research. Currently, in the rules learned by the BAGGER algorithm, the order interdependence among rule applications is specified in terms of sequences of vectors. However, this is unnecessarily constraining. When valid, these constraints should be specified in terms of *sets* or *bags*[6] of vectors. This could be accomplished by reasoning about the semantics of the system's predicate calculus functions and predicates. Properties such as symmetry, transitivity, and reflexivity may help determine constraints on order independence.

If a set satisfies a learned rule's antecedents, then *any* sequence derived from that set suffices. Conversely, if the vectors in a set fail to satisfy a rule's antecedents, there is no need to test each permutation of the elements. Unfortunately, testing all permutations occurs if the antecedents are unnecessarily expressed in terms of sequences. For example, assume the task at hand is to find enough heavy rocks in a storehouse to serve as ballast for a ship. A sequential rule may first add the weights in some order, find out that the sum weight of all the rocks in the room is insufficient, and then try another ordering for adding the weights. A rule specified in terms of sets would terminate after adding the weights once.

---

[6] A bag (or multiset) is an *unordered* collection of elements in which an element can appear more than once.

A fifth area of future research involves investigating the most efficient ordering of conjunctive goals. Consider an acquired sequential rule that builds towers of a desired height, subject to the constraint that no block can be placed on a narrower block. The goal of building such towers is conjunctive: The correct height must be achieved and the width of the stacked blocks must be monotonically nonincreasing. The optimal ordering is to select the blocks subject only to the height requirement, and then sort them by size to determine their position in the tower. The reason this works is that a nonincreasing ordering of widths on any set of blocks is guaranteed so that no additional block-selection constraints are imposed by this conjunct. The system should ultimately detect and exploit this kind of decomposability to improve the efficiency of the new rules.

Satisfying global constraints poses a sixth research problem. The sequential rules investigated in this chapter are all *incremental* in that successive operator applications converge toward the goal. This is not necessarily the case for all sequential rules. Consider a sequential rule for unstacking complex block structures subject to the global constraint that the partially dismantled structure always be stable. Removing one block can drastically alter the significance of another block with respect to the structure's stability. For some structures, only the subterfuge of adding a temporary support block or a counterbalance will allow unstacking to proceed. A block may be safe to remove at one point but be essential to the overall structural stability at the next, even though the block actually removed was physically distant from it. Such *nonincremental* effects are difficult to capture in sequential rules without permitting intermediate problem solving within the rule execution.

The RIS, besides recording the focus rule's variable bindings, is used to store intermediate calculations, such as the height of the tower currently planned. Satisfying global constraints may require that the information in an RIS vector increase as the sequence lengthens. For example, assume that each block to be added to a tower can only support some block-dependent weight. The RIS may have to record the projected weight on each block while BAGGER plans the construction of a tower. Hence, as the sequence lengthens, each successive vector in the RIS will have to record information for one additional block. Figuratively speaking, the RIS will be getting longer and wider. The current BAGGER algorithm does not support this.

Often a repeated process has a closed-form solution. For example, summing the first N integers produces

$$\frac{N(N+1)}{2}.$$

There is no need to compute the intermediate partial summations. A recurrence relation is a recursive method for computing a sequence of numbers. Recognizing and solving recurrence relations during generalization is a seventh area for additional research.

Many recurrences can be solved to produce efficient ways to determine the nth result in a sequence. It is this property that motivates the requirement that BAGGER's preconditions be expressed solely in terms of the initial state. However, the rule instantiation sequence still holds intermediate results. While often this information is needed (if, for instance, the resulting sequence of actions is to be executed in the external world), BAGGER would be more efficient if it could produce, whenever possible, number-generalized rules that did not require the construction of an RIS. If BAGGER observes the summation of, say, four numbers it will not produce the efficient result mentioned above. Instead it will produce a rule that stores the intermediate summations in the RIS. One extension that could be attempted is to create a library of templates for soluble recurrences, matching them against explanations. A more direct approach would be more appealing. Weld's [1986] technique of *aggregation* may be a fruitful approach. Aggregation is an abstraction technique for creating a continuous description from a series of discrete events.

The issue of termination is an eighth research area. One important aspect of generalizing number is that the acquired rules may produce data structures whose size can grow without bound (for example, the rule instantiation sequence in BAGGER) or the algorithms that satisfy these rules may fall into infinite loops [Cohen, 1987]. Although the *halting problem* is "undecidable" in general, in restricted circumstances termination can be proved [Manna, 1974]. Techniques for proving termination need to be incorporated into systems that generalize number. A practical, but less appealing, solution is to place resource bounds on the algorithms that apply number-generalized rules [Cohen, 1987], potentially excluding successful applications.

Finally, it is important to investigate the generalization to N problem in the context of imperfect and intractable domain models [Mitchell, Keller, and Kedar-Cabelli, 1986; Rajamoney and DeJong, 1987]. In any real-world domain, a computer system's model can only approximate reality. Furthermore, the complexity of problem solving prohibits any semblance of completeness. Thus far BAGGER's sequential rules have relied on a correct domain model, and it has not addressed issues of intractability, other than the use of an outside expert to provide sample solutions when the construction of solutions from first principles is intractable.

11.8 CONCLUSION

Most research in explanation-based learning involves relaxing constraints on the variables in an explanation, rather than generalizing the number of inference rules used. This chapter presents an approach to the task of generalizing the structure of explanations. The approach relies on a shift in representation, which accommodates indefinite numbers of rule applications. Compared to the results of standard explanation-based algorithms, more general rules are acquired, and since less rules need to be learned, better problem-solving performance gains are achieved.

A situation calculus example from the blocks world is analyzed to illustrate the approach. This leads to a plan in which the number of blocks to be placed in a tower is generalized to N. In this example, the system observes three blocks being stacked on one another, in order to satisfy the goal of having a block located at a specified height. Initially, the system has rules specifying how to transfer a single block from one location to another, and how the horizontal and vertical position of a block can be determined after it is moved. By analyzing the explanation of how moving three blocks satisfies the desired goal, BAGGER learns a new rule that represents how an unconstrained number of block transfers can be performed in order to satisfy future related goals.

The fully implemented BAGGER system analyzes explanation structures (in this case, predicate calculus proofs) and detects repeated, interdependent applications of rules. Once a rule on which to focus attention is found, the system determines how an *arbitrary* number of instantiations of this rule can be concatenated together. This indefinite-length collection of rules is conceptually merged into the explanation, replacing the specific-length collection of rules, and an extension of a standard explanation-based algorithm produces a new rule from the augmented explanation.

Rules produced by BAGGER have the important property that their preconditions are expressed in terms of the initial state—they do not depend on the situations produced by intermediate applications of the focus rule. This means that the results of multiple applications of the rule are determined by reasoning only about the current situation. There is no need to apply the rule successively, each time checking if the preconditions for the next application are satisfied.

The specific example guides the extension of the focus rule into a structure representing an arbitrary number of repeated applications. Information not contained in the focus rule, but appearing in the example, is often incorporated into the extended rule. In particular, *unwindable* rules provide the guidance as to how preconditions of the i_{th} application can be specified in terms of the current state.

A concept involving an arbitrary number of substructures may involve any number of substantially different problems. However, a specific solution will have necessarily only addressed a finite number of them. To generalize to N, a system must recognize all the problems that exist in the general concept and, by analyzing the specific solution, surmount them. If the specific solution does not provide enough information to circumvent all problems, generalization to N cannot occur because BAGGER is designed not to perform any problem-solving search during generalization. When a specific solution surmounts, in an extensible fashion, a subproblem in different ways during different instantiations of the focus rule, disjunctions appear in the acquired rule.

An empirical analysis of the benefit of generalizing the structure of explanations has been performed. These experiments indicate a performance improvement of at least an order of magnitude over standard explanation-based algorithms and several orders of magnitude over a problem solver that does not learn.

Generalizing to N is an important property currently lacking in most explanation-based systems. This research contributes to the theory and practice of explanation-based learning by developing and testing methods for extending the structure of explanations during generalization. It brings this field of machine learning closer to its goal of being able to acquire the full concept inherent in the solution to a specific problem.

ACKNOWLEDGMENTS

The authors wish to thanks the other members of the explanation-based learning group at Illinois. Interactions with Raymond Mooney, Shankar Rajamoney, Scott Bennett, Steve Chien, and Melinda Gervasio have stimulated many interesting ideas. This research was partially supported by the Office of Naval Research under grant N00014-86-K-0309, by the National Science Foundation under grant NSF IST 85-11542, and by a University of Illinois Cognitive Science/Artificial Intelligence Fellowship to the first author. All of the work was done in the Coordinated Science Laboratory of the University of Illinois.

Since this paper was written, the BAGGER2 algorithm has been created [Shavlik, in press a]. BAGGER2 essentially is the result of making the original BAGGER recursive; the major result of this is that recursive, rather than only iterative, concepts can now be learned. A longer description of both BAGGER and BAGGER2, including a more extensive empirical study, appears in [Shavlik, in press b].

Table 11-A1:   Intra-situation rules used in the stacking example

Rule	Description
Clear(?x,?s) ∧ → FreeSpace(?x,?s) FlatTop(?x)	If an object is clear and has a flat top, space is available.
Clear(?x,?s) → Liftable(?x,?s) Block(?x)	A block is liftable if it is clear.
Box(?x) → FlatTop(?x)	Boxes have flat tops.
Table(?x) → FlatTop(?x)	Tables have flat tops.
Box(?x) → Block(?x)	Boxes are a type of block.
Supports(?x,φ,?s) → Clear(?x,?s)	An object is clear if it is supporting nothing.
?x ≠ ?y → ?y ≠ ?x	Inequality is reflexive.
?x ≠ ?y ∧ NotΜεμβερ(?ξ,?βαγ) → NotMember(?x,{?y | ?bag})	If two objects are distinct, and the first is not in a collection of objects, then the first is not a member of the collection that results from adding the second object to the original collection.
NotMember(?x,φ)	Nothing is a member of the empty set.
Member(?x,{?x})	Everything is a member of the singleton set containing it.
RemoveFromBag(?x,{?x | ?bag},?bag)	Remove this object from a collection of objects, producing a new collection of objects.

APPENDIX: THE INITIAL INFERENCE RULES

The inference rules used in the tower-building (stacking) example are presented in this appendix. Not all the rules in the system are presented. However, a complete collection of the rules can be found in [Shavlik, 1988]. The first table contains those rules that describe *intra*-situation inferences, while *inter*-situation inferences appear in the second table. The first rule in the second table is the definition of the transfer action. This rule is the *focus rule* of the stacking example. (The construct {?a | ?b} matches a list with head ?a and tail ?b. For example, if matched with {x,y,z}, ?a is bound to x and ?b to {y,z}.)

Table 11A–1: Intra-situation rules used in the stacking example

AchievableState(?s) ∧ Liftable(?x,?s) ∧ FreeSpace(?y,?s) ∧ ?x ≠ ?y → AchievableState(Do(Transfer(?x,?y),?s)) ∧ Clear(?x,Do(Transfer(?x,?y),?s)) ∧ On(?x,?y,Do(Transfer(?x,?y),?s))	If the top of an object is clear in some achievable state and there is free space on another object, then the first object can be moved from its present location to the new location. However, an object cannot be moved onto itself. Moving creates a new state in which the moved object is still clear but (possibly) at a new location.
Xpos(?y,?xpos,?s) → Xpos(?x,?xpos,Do(Transfer(?x,?y),?s))	After a transfer, the object moved is centered (in the X-direction) on the object on which it is placed.
?x ≠ ?y ∧ Height(?x,?hx) ∧ Ypos(?y,?ypos,?s) ∧ ?ypos2 = (?hx + ?ypos) → Ypos(?x,?ypos2,Do(Transfer(?x,?y),?s))	After a transfer, the Y-position of the object moved is determined by adding its height to the Y-position o the object on which it is placed.
?u ≠ ?y ∧ Supports(?u,?items,?s) ∧ NotMember(?x,?items) → Supports(?u,?items,Do(Transfer(?x,?y),?s))	If an object neither supports the moved object before the transfer, nor is the new supporter, then the collection of objects it supports remains unchanged.
?u ≠ ?y ∧ Supports(?u,?items,?s) ∧ Member(?x,?items) ∧ RemoveFromBag(?x,?items,?new) → Supports(?u,?new,Do(Transfer(?x,?y),?s))	If an object is not the new support of the moved object, but supported it before the transfer, then the moved object must be removed from the collection of objects being supported.

References

Ahn, W., Mooney, R.J., Brewer, W.F., and DeJong, G.F. 1987. "Schema Acquisition from One Example: Psychological Evidence for Explanation-based Learning," *Proceedings of the Ninth Annual Conference of the Cognitive Science Society*, pp. 50–57, Seattle, WA, July 1987.

Anderson, J.R. 1986. "Knowledge Compilation: The General Learning Mechanism" in R.S. Michalski, J.G. Carbonell, and T.M. Mitchell (Eds.), *Machine Learning: An Artificial Intelligence Approach, Volume II*, pp. 289–310, Morgan Kaufmann, San Mateo, CA.

Andreae, P.M. 1984. "Justified Generalization: Acquiring Procedures from Example," PhD Thesis, Department of Electrical Engineering and Computer Science, MIT, Cambridge, MA, January 1984. (Also appears as Technical Report 834, MIT AI Laboratory).Benanav, D., Kapur, D., and Narendran, P. 1985. "Complexity of Matching Problems," *Proceedings of the First International Conference on Rewriting Techniques and Applications*, Dijon, France, May 1985.

Cheng, P., and Carbonell, J.G. 1986. "The FERMI System: Inducing Iterative Macro-operators from Experience," *Proceedings of the National Conference on Artificial Intelligence*, pp. 490–495, Philadelphia, PA, August 1986.

Chien, S.A. 1987. "Simplifications in Temporal Persistence: An Approach to the Intractable Domain Theory Problem in Explanation-based Learning," MS Thesis, Department of Computer Science, University of Illinois, Urbana, IL, September 1987. (Also appears as Technical Report UILU-ENG-87-2255, AI Research Group, Coordinated Science Laboratory.)

Cohen, W.W. 1987. "A Technique for Generalizing Number in Explanation-based Learning," Technical Report ML-TR-19, Department of Computer Science, Rutgers University, New Brunswick, NJ, September 1987.

Clocksin, W.F. and Mellish, C.S. 1984. *Programming in PROLOG,* Springer-Verlag, Berlin.

DeJong, G.F. and Mooney, R.J. 1986. "Explanation-based Learning: An Alternative View," *Machine Learning*, Vol. 1, No. 2, pp. 145–176, April 1986.

Dietterich, T. and Michalski, R.S. 1983. "Discovering Patterns in Sequences of Objects," *Proceedings of the 1983 International Machine Learning Workshop*, Urbana, IL, pp. 41–57, June 1983.

Dufay, B. and Latombe, J. 1984. "An Approach to Automatic Robot Programming Based on Inductive Learning," in *Robotics Research: The First International Symposium*, MIT Press, pp. 97–115, Cambridge, MA.

Ellman, T. 1985. "Generalizing Logic Circuit Designs by Analyzing Proofs of Correctness," *Proceedings of the Ninth International Joint Conference on Artificial Intelligence*, pp. 643–646, Los Angeles, CA, August 1985.

Fahlman, S. 1974. "A Planning System for Robot Construction Tasks," *Artificial Intelligence*, Vol. 5, No. 1, pp. 1–49, 1974.

Fikes, R. 1975. "Deductive Retrieval Mechanisms for State Description Models," *Proceedings of the Fourth International Joint Conference on Artificial Intelligence*, pp. 99–106, Tbilisi, Georgia, USSR, August 1975.

Fikes, R.E., and Nilsson, N.J. 1971. "STRIPS: A New Approach to the Application of Theorem Proving to Problem Solving," *Artificial Intelligence*, Vol. 2, No. 3/4, pp. 189–208.

Fikes, R.E., Hart, P.E., and Nilsson, N.J. 1972. "Learning and Executing Generalized Robot Plans," *Artificial Intelligence*, Vol. 3, No. 4, pp. 251–288.

Forgy, C.L. 1982. "Rete: A Fast Algorithm for the Many Pattern/Many Object Pattern Match Problem," *Artificial Intelligence*, Vol. 19, pp. 17–37.

Green, C.C. 1969. "Application of Theorem Proving to Problem Solving," *Proceedings of the First International Joint Conference on Artificial Intelligence*, pp. 219–239, Washington, D.C., August 1969.

Hirsh, H. 1987. "Explanation-based Generalization in a Logic-Programming Environment," *Proceedings of the Tenth International Joint Conference on Artificial Intelligence*, pp. 221–227, Milan, Italy, August 1987.

Kedar-Cabelli, S.T., and McCarty, L.T. 1987. "Explanation-based Generalization as Resolution Theorem Proving," *Proceedings of the 1987 International Machine Learning Workshop*, pp. 383–389, Irvine, CA, June 1987.

Keller, R.M. 1987. "Defining Operationality for Explanation-based Learning," *Proceedings of the National Conference on Artificial Intelligence*, pp. 482–487, Seattle, WA, July 1987.

———, 1988. "Operationality and Generality in Explanation-based Learning: Separate Dimensions or Opposite Endpoints?," *Proceedings of the AAAI Explanation-based Learning Symposium*, pp. 153–157, Stanford, CA, March 1988.

Kodratoff, Y. 1979. "A Class of Functions Synthesized from a Finite Number of Examples and a LISP Program Scheme," *International Journal of Computer and Information Sciences*, Vol. 8, No. 6, pp. 489–521.

Laird, J., Rosenbloom, P., and Newell, A. 1986. "Chunking in Soar: The Anatomy of a General Learning Mechanism," *Machine Learning*, Vol. 1, No. 1, pp. 11–46.

Manna, Z. 1974. *Mathematical Theory of Computation*, McGraw-Hill, New York, NY.

McCarthy, J. 1968. "Situations, Actions, and Causal Laws," memorandum, Stanford University, Stanford, CA, 1963. (Reprinted in *Semantic Information Processing*, M. Minsky (Ed.), MIT Press, pp. 410–417, Cambridge, MA.

Michalski, R.S. 1983. "A Theory and Methodology of Inductive Learning" in *Machine Learning: An Artificial Intelligence Approach*, R.S. Michalski, J.G. Carbonell, and T.M. Mitchell (Eds.), pp. 83–134, Morgan Kaufmann, San Mateo, CA.

Minton, S.N. 1985. "Selectively Generalizing Plans for Problem-Solving," *Proceedings of the Ninth International Joint Conference on Artificial Intelligence*, pp. 596–599, Los Angeles, CA, August 1985.

Minton, S.N., Carbonell, J.G., Etzioni, O., Knoblock, C. A., and Kuokka, D.R. 1987. "Acquiring Effective Search Control Rules: Explanation-based Learning in the PRODIGY System," *Proceedings of the Fourth International Workshop on Machine Learning*, pp. 122–133, Irvine, CA, June 1987.

Mitchell, T.M., Mahadevan, S., and Steinberg, L.I. 1985. "LEAP: A Learning Apprentice for VLSI Design," *Proceedings of the Ninth International Joint Conference on Artificial Intelligence*, pp. 573–580, Los Angeles, CA, August 1985.

Mitchell, T.M., Keller, R., and Kedar-Cabelli, S. 1986. "Explanation-based Generalization: A Unifying View," *Machine Learning*, Vol. 1, No. 1, pp. 47–80, January 1986.

Mooney, R.J. 1988. "A General Explanation-based Learning Mechanism and its Application to Narrative Understanding," PhD Thesis, Department of Computer Science, University of Illinois, Urbana, IL, 1988. (Also appears as Technical Report UILU-ENG-87–2269, AI Research Group, Coordinated Science Laboratory.)

Mooney, R.J. and Bennett, S.W., 1986. "A Domain Independent Explanation-based Generalizer," *Proceedings of the National Conference on Artificial Intelligence*, pp. 551–555, Philadelphia, PA, August 1986.

Nilsson, N.J. 1980. *Principles of Artificial Intelligence*, Morgan Kaufmann, San Mateo, CA.

O'Rorke, P.V. 1987a. "Explanation-based Learning via Constraint Posting and Propagation," PhD Thesis, Department of Computer Science, University of Illinois, Urbana, IL. (Also appears as Technical Report UILU-ENG-87-2239, AI Research Group, Coordinated Science Laboratory.)

———, 1987b. "LT Revisited: Experimental Results of Applying Explanation-based Learning to the Logic of Principia Mathematica," *Proceedings of the 1987 International Machine Learning Workshop*, pp. 148–159, Irvine, CA, June 1987.

Prieditis, A.E. 1986. "Discovery of Algorithms from Weak Methods," *Proceedings of the International Meeting on Advances in Learning*, pp. 37–52, Les Arcs, Switzerland. (An updated version appears in *Machine Learning: An Artificial*

Intelligence Approach, Volume III, R.S. Michalski and Y. Kodratoff (Eds.), Morgan Kaufmann, San Mateo, CA.

Prieditis, A.E. and Mostow, J. 1987. "PROLEARN: Towards a PROLOG Interpreter that Learns," *Proceedings of the National Conference on Artificial Intelligence*, pp. 494–498, Seattle, WA, July 1987.

Rajamoney, S., and DeJong, G.F. 1987. "The Classification Detection and Handling of Imperfect Theory Problems," *Proceedings of the Tenth International Joint Conference on Artificial Intelligence*, pp. 205–207, Milan, Italy, August 1987.

Rendell, L. 1985. "Substantial Constructive Induction using Layered Information Compression: Tractable Feature Formation in Search," *Proceedings of the Ninth International Joint Conference on Artificial Intelligence*, pp. 650–658, Los Angeles, CA, August 1985.

Sammut, C.B. and Banerji, R.B. 1986. "Learning Concepts by Asking Questions," in R.S. Michalski, J.G. Carbonell, and T.M. Mitchell (Eds.), *Machine learning: An Artificial Intelligence Approach, Volume II*, pp. 167–191, Morgan Kaufmann, San Mateo, CA.

Segre, A.M. 1987. "On the Operationality/Generality Trade-off in Explanation-based Learning," *Proceedings of the Tenth International Joint Conference on Artificial Intelligence*, pp. 242–248, Milan, Italy, August 1987.

Shavlik, J.W. 1988. "Generalizing the Structure of Explanations in Explanation-based Learning," PhD Thesis, Department of Computer Science, University of Illinois, Urbana, Ill. (Also appears as Technical Report UILU-ENG-87-2276 AI Research Group, Coordinated Science Laboratory.)

———, in press a. "Acquiring Recursive and Iterative Concepts with Explanation-based Learning," *Machine Learning* 5:1, pp. 39–70.

———, in press b. "Extending Explanation-based Learning by Generalizing the Structure of Explanations," copublished by Pitman, London and Morgan Kaufmann, San Mateo, CA.

Shavlik, J.W. and DeJong, G.F. 1985. "Building a Computer Model of Learning Classical Mechanics," *Proceedings of the Seventh Annual Conference of the Cognitive Science Society*, pp. 351–355, Irvine, CA, August 1985.

———, 1987a. "Analyzing Variable Cancellations to Generalize Symbolic Mathematical Calculations," *Proceedings of the Third IEEE Conference on Artificial Intelligence Applications*, Orlando, FL, February 1987.

————— , 1987b. "BAGGER: An EBL System that Extends and Generalizes Explanations," *Proceedings of the National Conference on Artificial Intelligence*, pp. 516–520, Seattle, WA, July 1987.

————— , 1987c. "An Explanation-based Approach to Generalizing Number," *Proceedings of the Tenth International Joint Conference on Artificial Intelligence*, pp. 236–238, Milan, Italy, August 1987.

Shavlik, J.W., DeJong, G.F., and Ross, B.H. 1987. "Acquiring Special Case Schemata in Explanation-based Learning," *Proceedings of the Ninth Annual Conference of the Cognitive Science Society*, pp. 851–860, Seattle, WA, July 1987.

Siklossy, L. and Sykes, D.A. 1975. "Automatic Program Synthesis from Example Problems," *Proceedings of the Fourth International Joint Conference on Artificial Intelligence*, pp. 268–273, Tbilisi, Georgia, USSR.

Steier, D. 1987. "CYPRESS-Soar: A Case Study in Search and Learning in Algorithm Design," *Proceedings of the Tenth International Joint Conference on Artificial Intelligence*, pp. 327–330, Milan, Italy, August 1987.

Summers, P.D. 1977. "A Methodology for LISP Program Construction from Examples," *Journal of the Association for Computing Machinery*, Vol. 24, pp. 161–175.

Waldinger, R. 1977. "Achieving Several Goals Simultaneously," in *Machine Intelligence 8*, E. Elcock and D. Michie (Eds.), Ellis Horwood Limited, London,.

Weld, D.S. 1986. "The Use of Aggregation in Casual Simulation," *Artificial Intelligence*, Vol. 30, No. 1, pp. 1–34, October 1986.

Whitehall, B.L. 1987. "Substructure Discovery in Executed Action Sequences," M.S. Thesis, Department of Computer Science, University of Illinois, Urbana, IL, September 1987. (Also appears as Technical Report UILU-ENG-87-2256, AI Research Group, Coordinated Science Laboratory).

Wolff, J.G. 1982. "Language Acquisition, Data Compression and Generalization," *Language and Communication*, Vol. 2, No. 1, pp. 57–89.

12

DISCOVERING ALGORITHMS
FROM WEAK METHODS[1]

Armand E. Prieditis

(Rutgers University)

Abstract

This chapter describes a system that discovers iterative STRIPS-style macro-operators from single example plans. This work suggests that a weak method (e.g., a backward-chaining planner) can become stronger by acquiring such algorithmic knowledge. The system differs from other machine learning systems because it generalizes over the example plan rather than over the objects manipulated by the plan's operators. It limits the search space of possible algorithm inferences to only those algorithms described in general terms by macro-operator templates.

12.1 INTRODUCTION AND MOTIVATION

What knowledge is necessary to discover algorithms of arbitrary complexity from single example plans? The research on automatic programming from example traces has shown that inferring complex algorithms may require many examples, much debugging, and an enormous search space [Bauer, 1975; Phillips, 1977; Siklossy, 1975; Biermann, 1972; Petry, 1976]. In contrast, machine learning research has shown that simple algorithms (sequential macro-operators) can be inferred justifiably from single example plans without further debubbing [Fikes, *et al.*, 1972; Minton, 1984; Mitchell, 1986; Mooney, 1986].

---

[1]This work was originally published in the *Proceedings of the International Meeting on Advances in Learning*. Les Arcs, July. 1986. Since then, others [Shavlik, 1987; Cheng, 1986] have pursued similar work—the references are included here for the interested reader.

This work shows that algorithmic macro-operator templates can limit the search space of algorithm discovery as well as provide a justifiable basis for inferring more complex algorithms from single example plans without further debugging. The system described here discovers iterative STRIPS-style macro-operators [Fikes, et al., 1972] from plans generated by a backward-chaining planner with goal protection. Iterative macro-operators are generalizations over the example plan rather than over the objects manipulated by the plan's operators.

The rest of this chapter is organized as follows: Section 12.2 shows two iterative macro-operators that the system discovers from example plans. Section 12.3 describes how the system discovers iterative macro-operators. Section 12.4 discusses some open problems. Finally, Section 12.5 summarizes the contributions of this work.

12.2 DISCOVERING ITERATIVE MACRO-OPERATORS: EXAMPLES

This section shows how the system discovers two particular iterative blocks-world macro-operators: for unstacking any number of given blocks and for stacking any number of given blocks. Each blocks-world operator consists of three predicate sets: the precondition set, which describes what must be true in the world before application; and the deletion and addition sets, which describe how the world changes after application:[2]

putdown(x)
P & D: {HOLDING(x)}
A: {ONTABLE(x),CLEAR(x),HANDEMPTY}

pickup(x)
P & D: {ONTABLE(x),CLEAR(x),HANDEMPTY}
A: {HOLDING(x)}

unstack(x,y)
P & D: {HANDEMPTY,CLEAR(x),ON(x,y)}
A: {HOLDING(x),CLEAR(y)}

stack(x,y)
P & D: {HOLDING(x),CLEAR(y)}
A: {HANDEMPTY,CLEAR(x),ON(x,v)}

---

[2] After [Nilsson, 1980].

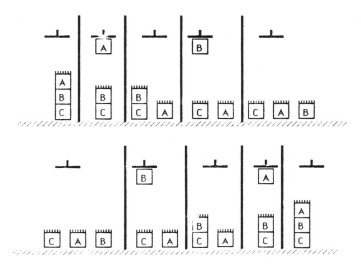

Figure 12–1:   Top: Destroying a tower; Bottom: Building a tower (Bristles symbolize "CLEAR")

Given the sequence of operators produced by the planner, shown from left to right in the upper-half of Figure 12–1, the user identifies an instance of repeated behavior in curly braces: {**unstack(A,B)**, **putdown(A)**} followed by {**unstack(B,C)**, **putdown(B)**}.[3] (Here, **unstack-putdown** repeats twice in a certain way.) The system then learns the iterative macro-operator **rep-unstack-putdown**, which represents **unstack-putdown** applied an *arbitrary* number of times:

rep-unstack-putdown(1)

P: **p**(1)

D: **d**(1)

A: **a**(1)

where

$p([(x,y)]) = \{HANDEMPTY, CLEAR(x), ON(x,y)\}$

$p([(y,z),(x,y)|t]) = \{ON(x,z)\} \cup p([(x,y)|t])$

---

[3] The goal of this research was to understand how algorithms could be inferred rather than identified; user-provided identification simplified matters considerably. Other recent work [Riddle, 1986] discusses how such plans can be parsed automatically in certain domains.

$$\mathbf{d}([x,y)]) = \{ON(x,y)\}$$
$$\mathbf{d}([y,z),(x,y)|t]) = \{ON(x,z)\} \cup \mathbf{d}([x,y)|t])$$
$$\mathbf{a}([(x,y)]) = \{ONTABLE(x),ONTABLE(y)\}$$
$$\mathbf{a}([(y,z),(x,y)|t]) = \{CLEAR(z),ONTABLE(y)\} \cup \mathbf{a}([(x,y)|t])$$

The macro-operator's argument list, l, consists of pairs of blocks that are arguments for each **unstack-putdown** application. Arguments to the recursive functions **p**, **d**, and **a**, return the precondition, deletion, and addition sets of **rep-unstack-putdown** and specify l's structure. The list [(y,z),(x,y)|t] specifies that the first element must be (y,z), the second (x,y), and the rest t.[4] Since each function calls itself again with [(x,y)|t], t maintains the same structure.

The general effects of **rep-unstack-putdown**, shown from left to right in the top-half of Figure 12–2, can be interpreted as "for each element (x,y) of the reverse of [(y,z),(x,y)|t], unstack x from y and put x on the table." For example, if **rep-unstack-putdown** were applied to the list [(B,C),(A,B)], **unstack-putdown** would first be applied to (A,B) and then to (B,C) producing the original plan. The recursive functions ensure that the pattern (y,z) followed by (x,y) matches every consecutive pair of elements in the argument list of **rep-unstack-putdown**. As an example of the generalization over the original plan, if **rep-unstack-putdown** were applied to the list [(D,E),(C,D),(B,C),(A,B)], A would be unstacked and put down from B, B from C, C from D and finally D from E.

The bottom block z is shown as "floating" above the table since **rep-unstack-putdown** does not require it to be explicitly on top of another block or on the table. Recall that in the example plan, the bottom block was actually on the table. Other systems capable of learning only sequential macro-operators [Fikes, *et al.*, 1972; Minton, 1984; Mitchell, 1986; Mooney, 1986] also generalize similarly over the example plan's objects.

As a second example, given the sequence shown in the lower-half of Figure 12–1, and with the appropriate user identification of {**pickup(B),stack(B,C)**} followed by {**pickup(A),stack(A,B)**}, the system learns **rep-pickup-stack(l)**:

rep-pickup-stack(l)

P: **p(l)**
D: **d(l)**
A: **a(l)**

where

---

[4] Since the planning and discovery systems are implemented in PROLOG, this chapter assumes some familiarity with PROLOG.

$p([(x,y)]) = \{ONTABLE(x),CLEAR(x),HANDEMPTY,CLEAR(y)\}$
$p([(z,x),(x,y)|t]) = \{ONTABLE(z),CLEAR(z) \cup p([(x,y)|t])$

$d([(x,y)]) = \{ONTABLE(x),CLEAR(y)\}$
$d([(z,x),(x,y)|t]) = \{ONTABLE(z),CLEAR(x)\} \cup d([x,y)|t])$

$a([(x,y)]) = \{ON(x,y)\}$
$a([(z,x),(x,y)|t]) = \{ON(x,z)\} \cup a([(x,y)|t])$

The effects of **rep-pickup-stack**, shown in the bottom half of Figure 12–2, can be interpretd as "for each element (x,y) of the reverse [(z,x),(x,y)|t], pickup x from the table and stack it on y." If **rep-pickup-stack** were applied to [(A),(B,C)], **B** would be picked up and stacked on C and then **A** would be picked up and stacked on **B**, producing the original plan. As an example of generalization over the original plan, if **rep-pickup-stack** were applied to [(A,B), (B,C), (C,D), (D,E)], D would be picked up and stacked on E, C on D, B on C and finally A on B.

Each macro-operator compactly captures the algorithmic behavior in the example plan and embodies an infinite number of macro-operators—one for each iteration.

12.3 DISCOVERING ITERATIVE MACRO-OPERATORS: THE METHOD

Given an example trace of some iterative behavior, the system infers the two macro-operators equivalent to the two user-identified subsequences, notes their interaction, and then instantiates an iterative macro-operator template according that interaction. The rest of this section shows how the system learns **rep-unstack-putdown**.

First, the system applies a standard version of explanation-based generalization (Mitchell, 1986; Fikes, *et al.*, 1972) to infer the two macro-operators equivalent to the two user-identified sequences, {**unstack**(A,B), **putdown**(A)} followed by {**unstack**(B,C), **putdown**(B)}. Explanation-based generalization finds the weakest precondition and greatest postcondition of each user-identified sequence; these conditions define uninstantiated and instantiated versions of the macro-operators **unstack-putdown**$_1$ and **unstack-putdown**$_2$:

unstack-putdown$_1$(A,B)
P: {HANDEMPTY,CLEAR(A),ON(A,B)}
D: {ON(A,B)}
A: {CLEAR(B),ONTABLE(A)}

unstack-putdown$_1$(x,y)
P: {HANDEMPTY,CLEAR(x),ON(x,y)}
D: {ON(x,y)}
A: {CLEAR(y),ONTABLE(x)}

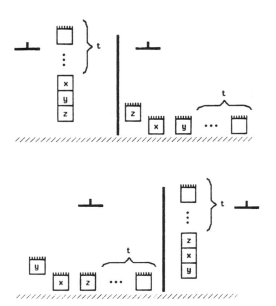

Figure 12–2: Top: Effects of **rep-unstack-putdown([y,z].(x,y)|t|)**
Bottom: Effects of **rep-pickup-stack([z,x],(x,y)|t|)**

unstack-putdown₂(B,C)
P: {HANDEMPTY,CLEAR(B),ON(B,C)}
D: {ON(B,C)}
A: {CLEAR(C),ONTABLE(B)}

unstack-putdown₂(w,z)
P: {HANDEMPTY,CLEAR(w),ON(w,z)}
D: {ON(w,z)}
A: {CLEAR(z),ONTABLE(w)}

Instantiated **unstack-putdown₁**, when applied, produces the first user-identified sequence; instantiated **unstack-putdown₂**, the second.

Next, the system determines how the two instantiated macro-operators interact and forces the same interaction onto the uninstantiated macro-operators. Since **unstack-putdown₁(A,B)** adds CLEAR(B) and **unstack-putdown₂(B,C)** requires CLEAR(B), they *interact* at CLEAR(B). To ensure the same interaction pattern between **unstack-putdown₁(x,y)** and **unstack-putdown₂(w,z)**, the variable y *must be* unified with w since **unstack-putdown₁(x,y)** adds CLEAR(y) and **unstack-putdown₂(w,z)** requires CLEAR(w).

Finally, the system instantiates the iterative macro-operator template, shown below, as the iterative macro-operator shown immediately below the template. The template describes the precondition, addition and deletion sets for applying *op* (any STRIPS-style operator) iteratively to the elements of a list. The functions

$$P(op_i(args_i)), D(op_i(args_i)), A(op_i(args_i))$$

return the precondition, deletion, and addition sets of op_i with $args_i$ ($i \in \{1,2\}$). (From the previous unification, $op_1(args_1)$ is **unstack-putdown$_1$**(x,y) and $op_2(args_2)$ is **instack-putdown$_2$**(y,z)). They specify one particular type of iterated behavior by constraining the interaction between the precondition, addition and deletion sets:

1. The addition set of each operator intersects only with the very next operator's precondition set (the recursive line of **p**) or the very next operator's deletion set (the recursive line of **d**).

2. The deletion set of each operator intersects only with the very next operator's addition set (the recursive line of **a**).

$\mathbf{p}([args_1]) = P(op_1(args_1))$
$\mathbf{p}([args_2args_1/t]) = \{[P(op_2(args_2)) - P(op_1(args_1))] - A(op_1(args_1))\} \cup \mathbf{p}([args_1/t])$

$\mathbf{d}([args_1]) = D(op_1(args_1))$
$\mathbf{d}([args_2,args_1/t]) = \{D(op_2(args_2)) - A(op_1(args_1))\} \cup \mathbf{d}([args_1/t])$

$\mathbf{a}([args_1]) = A(op_1(args_1))$
$\mathbf{a}([args_2,args_1/t]) = [A(op_2(args_2)) - D(op_1(args_1))] \cup \mathbf{a}([args_1/t])$

rep-unstack-putdown(l)

P: **p**(1l
D: **d**(l)
A: **a**(l)

where

$\mathbf{p}([(x,y)]) = \{HANDEMPTY,CLEAR(x),ON(x,y)\}$
$\mathbf{p}([(y,z),(x,y)|t]) = \{ON(y,z)\} \cup \mathbf{p}([(x,y)|t])$

$\mathbf{d}([(x,y)]) = \{ON(x,y)\}$
$\mathbf{d}([(y,z),(x,y)|t]) = \{ON(y,z)\} \cup \mathbf{d}([(x,y)|t])$

$\mathbf{a}([(x,y)]) = \{ONTABLE(x),CLEAR(y)\}$
$\mathbf{a}([(y,z),(x,y)|t]) = \{CLEAR(z),ONTABLE(y) \cup \mathbf{a}([(x,y)|t])$

The iterative macro-operator template justifies generalizing from a single instance of repeated behavior to the general case of an arbitrary number of repeated behaviors.

12.4 OPEN PROBLEMS

This work raises an important question: Can a system discover algorithms of arbitrary complexity from single example plans? Before this question can be answered, many open problems have to be attacked. One problem that remains is choosing the right language to describe a desired algorithmic behavior. Although this work describes interaction using a simple PROLOG-based syntax, more complex interactions may require more complex description languages. Furthermore, the description language may have to be different from the identification language, because compact descriptions of algorithmic behavior may not necessarily be efficient identifiers of the behavior. Another problem, not considered here, is choosing among a large number of candidate algorithmic macro-operator templates.

12.5 SUMMARY

This chapter has described a system that discovers one particular type of algorithmic macro-operator—an iterative macro-operator—from a single example plan. The system differs from other machine learning systems because it generalizes over the example plan rather than over the objects manipulated by the plan's operators. It limits the search space of possible algorithm inferences to only those algorithms described in general terms by macro-operator templates.

How problem-solving systems change from weak (search-based) to strong (algorithmic) is still unclear, but this work suggests one way that a weak problem-solving system (backward-chaining planner) can become stronger by acquiring algorithmic knowledge.

ACKNOWLEDGMENTS

Thanks go to Tom Mitchell, Chris Tong, Jack Mostow, Christina Chang, Lou Steinberg, Pat Langley, Yves Kodratoff, and Ryszard Michalski for comments on earlier versions of this chapter. Thanks also go to Jaizhen Cai for many thoughtful discussions on set theory.

References

Bauer, M.A. 1975. *Basis for the Acquisition of Procedures From Protocols*, pp. 226–231. Proceedings IJCAI-4, Tbilisi, Georgia, USSR.

Biermann, A. 1972. On the Inference of Turing Machines from Sample Computations. *Artificial Intelligence*, 3(1), 181–198.

Cheng, P. and Carbonell, J. 1986. *The FERMI System: Inducing Iterative Macro-Operators from Experience*, pp. 490–495. Proceedings AAAI-86, Philadelphia, Pennsylvania, August, 1986.

Fikes, R., Hart, P., and Nilsson, N.J. 1972. Learning and Executing Generalized Robot Plans. *Artificial Intelligence*, 3(4), 251–288. Also in *Readings in Artificial Intelligence*, Webber, B.L. and Nilsson, N.J., (Eds.). San Mateo: Morgan Kaufmann.

Minton, S. 1984. *Constraint Based Generalization: Learning Game-Playing Plans From Single Examples*, pp. 251–254. Proceedings AAAI-84, Austin, TX, August, 1984.

Mitchell, T., Keller, R. and Kedar-Cabelli, S. 1986. Explanation-based Generalization: A Unifying View. *Machine Learning*, 1(1), 47–80.

Mooney, R. and Bennett, S. 1986. *A Domain Independent Explanation-based Generalizer*, Proceedings AAAI-86, Philadelphia, Pennsylvania, August, 1986.

Nilsson, N.J. 1980. *Principles of Artificial Intelligence*. San Mateo: Morgan Kaufmann.

Petry. F. and Biermann, A. 1976. *Reconstruction of Algorithms from Memory Snapshots of their Execution*, pp. 530–534. Proceedings 1976 Annual ACM Conference, NY.

Phillips, J. 1977. *Program Inference from Traces using Multiple Knowledge Sources*. Proceedings IJCAI-5, Cambridge, MA, August, 1977.

Riddle, P. 1986. *An Overview of Problem Reduction: A Shift of Problem Representation*. Proceedings of the Workshop on Knowledge Compilation, Otter Crest. Oregon.

Shavlik. J. and Dejong, G. 1987. *BAGGER: An EBL System that Extends and Generalizes Explanations*. Proceedings AAAI-87, Seattle, Washington.

Siklossy, L. and Sykes, D.A. 1975. *Automatic Program Synthesis From Example Problems*, pp. 268–273. Proceedings IJCAI-4, Tbilisi, Georgia, USSR.

13

OGUST:

A SYSTEM THAT LEARNS USING DOMAIN PROPERTIES EXPRESSED AS THEOREMS

Christel Vrain
(LRI, Université de Paris-Sud)

Abstract

In this chapter, we present a system, called OGUST, which learns concepts from sets of examples. Presently, most such systems use only properties of the domain expressed as taxonomies or use only a few simple theorems. First, we show that for learning "good" generalizations, we must use all kinds of theorems and not only those expressed by taxonomies. Then we explain how in OGUST, we control the use of theorems to apply only those that may improve the generalization, how we avoid the problem of loops, and how the use of theorems enables to increase the explicability of the system.

13.1 INTRODUCTION

13.1.1 Explanation-based Learning and Inductive Learning

From the point of view of the strategies they use, machine learning systems tend to fall under two different headings. One can be called *deductive learning* in that its main engine is deduction or theorem proving. It has been recently illustrated by EBG [Mitchell, 1986] and EBL [Dejong, 1986]. Its goal is the following:

- given a training example of a concept, a definition of this concept, and a complete background knowledge,
- obtain a new, more efficient, more operational definition of the concept.

This method proceeds in two steps. First, it proves that the training example is actually an instance of the concept it illustrates. Second, it applies goal regression techniques to the proof tree, in order to obtain an explanation of the proof, which leads to a new definition of the concept. This new definition is more operational than the old one since it is expressed in terms of the descriptors of the example—instead of being expressed in terms of the (old) descriptors of the concept. EBL strategy therefore relies on deduction, and its more visible feature is the need for an exhaustive knowledge of the object whose description it is improving.

The other systems can be called *inductive learning* because their main engine is an inductive mechanism. They can use very little background knowledge. In that case, they belong to *empirical learning*, and they always need a big number of examples to provide some justification to their inductive steps. One must be aware that these systems can also use as much background knowledge as can be provided. In that case, they can be classified as belonging to *constructive learning* [Kodratoff and Michalski—Chapter 1, this volume] in which the inductive hypotheses are validated by the background knowledge, at least partially. Our approach belongs to this last kind of learning since it shows how large amounts of knowledge have to be used in order to find better similarities between different examples. Because we are able to justify the inductive hypotheses, we can find some kind of explanations that are different from the ones EBL finds. They follow from the proof that the examples are instances of the generalization one has obtained. This last point will not be emphasized in this chapter, which is devoted to the description of the peculiarities a theorem prover must show in order to be usable in the context of learning similarities between examples.

We have developed a system, called OGUST (from the French: Outil de Généralisation Utilisant Systématiquement les Théorèmes), which learns a recognition function for a concept from a set of examples. The examples are expressed in a subset of first-order logic, which contains only predicates; i.e., Boolean functions of any arity and constants.

Let us now give a very simple, but not totally trivial, example of the difficulties that one can meet when using domain properties expressed as theorems.

13.1.2 On the Use of the Theorems

In this section, we will show how all kinds of theorems must be used. For this, consider the two following examples:

$E_1 = $ (mammalian A) & (bred-by-man A)
$E_2 = $ (domestic B) & (viviparous B)

where (mammalian x) is a predicate which is true if x is a mammalian; (bred-by-man x) is true if x is bred by a man; (domestic x) is true if x is a domestic animal; and (viviparous x) is true if x is viviparous.

Suppose also that you know the three following theorems:

R_1: $\forall$x   [(mammalian x) & (bred-by-man x) $\Rightarrow$ (domestic x)]
R_2: $\forall$x   [(domestic x) & (viviparous x) $\Rightarrow$ (mammalian x)]
R_3: $\forall$x   [(domestic x) $\Rightarrow$ (inoffensive x)]

where (inoffensive x) is true if x is in general, inoffensive.

The example is simple enough, and the reader will find easily that a generalization of E_1 and E_2 is:

(mammalian x) & (domestic x)

Nevertheless, you should be also aware that the above theorems were not applied without being driven by the goal of obtaining some generalization of the examples. This chapter is about an algorithmization of the intuitive behavior the reader has to have. In Section 13.3.3, we shall illustrate our algorithm by applying it to this example.

13.1.3 Structural Matching

The method used to detect similarities between examples, in this chapter, has been called *structural matching*. Its aim is to minimize the loss of information on the examples. The basic idea is to transform the representation of the examples, using axioms of first-order logic, domain properties, ... , until there is no need to use the dropping condition rule to generalize them. Actually, we have to use the dropping conjunction rules but their use is rejected at the last step of the generalization.

For instance, consider the two following examples:

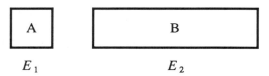

$$E_1 \qquad\qquad\qquad E_2$$

They can be represented by the formulae:

$RE_1 = (square\ A)$
$RE_2 = (rectangle\ B)$

RE_1 and RE_2 are not similar because in RE_1 there is the predicate 'square', and in RE_2, there is the predicate 'rectangle'. Suppose now that we know the theorem:

$\forall\ x\ [(square\ x) \Rightarrow (rectangle\ x)]$

which expresses the proposition that a square is a kind of rectangle.

The goal of structural matching is to improve the matching between the two examples. Applying the theorem into RE_2 will introduce the predicate 'rectangle' and is therefore expected to improve the matching.

Applying this theorem, we obtain a new equivalent expression of RE_1:

$RE_1' = (square\ A)\ \&\ (rectangle\ A)$

Of course, we are unable to find an expression equivalent to RE_2 that would contain the predicate 'square'. The process of structural matching stops and we apply the dropping condition rule to RE_1' to obtain:

$RE_1'' = (rectangle\ A)$

RE_1'' and RE_2 are now similar: If we consider the formula $F = (rectangle\ x)$ and the substitutions σ_1, defined by $\sigma_1(x) = A$ and σ_2, defined by $\sigma_2(x) = B$, $\sigma_1(F) = RE_1''$ and $\sigma_2(F) = RE_2$. We say that RE_1'' and RE_2 *match structurally*. We now know that the objects in E_1 and in E_2 are rectangles and that a generalization G of these two examples is:

$G = (rectangle\ x)$

Definition 0

Let $E_1, E_2, \dots , E_n$ be n examples. We say that $E_1, E_2, \dots ,E_n$ *match structurally* if there exists a formula F and n substitutions σ_i such that for each i, $\sigma_i(F) = E_i$.

In our previous example, RE_1 and RE_2 did not match structurally. However, RE_1'' and RE_2 match structurally.

When examples match structurally, it is easy to find a generalization of them: The formula F is already a kind of generalization. We can find a better generalization by analyzing the substitutions σ_i. For instance, if we consider the two following examples:

$E_1 = (book\ A)\ \&\ (red\ A)\ \&\ (on\ A\ TABLE)\ \&\ (pen\ B)\ \&\ (on\ B\ TABLE)$
$E_2 = (book\ C)\ \&\ (red\ C)\ \&\ (on\ C\ TABLE)\ \&\ (pen\ D)\ \&\ (on\ D\ C)$

These two examples match structurally, for if we consider the formula G defined by:

$G = (book\ x)\ \&\ (red\ x)\ \&\ (on\ x\ u)\ \&\ (pen\ y)\ \&\ (on\ y\ v)$

and the substitutions σ_1 defined by $\sigma_1(x) = A$, $\sigma_1(y) = B$, $\sigma_1(u) = TABLE$, $\sigma_1(v) = TABLE$ and σ_2 defined by $\sigma_2(x) = C$, $\sigma_2(y) = D$, $\sigma_2(u) = TABLE$, $\sigma_2(v) = C$, we have $\sigma_1(G) = E_1$ and $\sigma_2(G) = E_2$. We notice that in σ_1 and in σ_2, the variable u is instantiated by the same constant $TABLE$. By generalizing this fact, we find a better generalization G' of E_1 and E_2:

$G' = G\ \&\ (=\ u\ TABLE)$

We could further refine our generalization by analyzing the instantiations of the variables in each substitution. For instance, we can compare the instantiations of the variables having the relation '='. The generalization of G would be improved into:

$G'' = G\ \&\ (=\ u\ TABLE)\ \&\ (\neq x\ y)\ \&\ (\neq x\ u)\ \&\ (\neq y\ v)\ \&\ (\neq y\ u),$

where the link '$(\neq x\ y)$' generalizes the fact that in each example, the variables x and y have different values, and so on.

There is no end to the process of generalization refinement [Michalski, 1984], but this chapter is rather devoted to the study of the task of putting the examples into structural matching.

13.2 OGUST

A first-generalization algorithm, AGAPE, based on the principle of structural matching, was implemented in our group by T. Bollinger [Bollinger, 1986]. To put the examples into structural matching, idempotency was used, as well as some specific properties of the universe (those that express relations of generality between objects). Our system OGUST uses the same algorithm as AGAPE, but it has improved this system to deal with all kinds of theorems.

13.2.1 Representation of the Examples and of the Domain Properties

We work in first-order logic. The examples are represented as conjunctions of atoms, which are either predicates of arity zero, or terms ($p\ C_1 \ldots C_n$) where p is a predicate of arity n and $C_1, \ldots, C_n$ are constants. For instance, the following example:

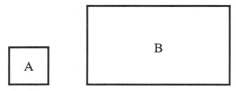

may be represented by the conjunction of atoms:

(square A) & (small A) & (rectangle B) & (large B)

In the representation of the examples, we do not allow the presence of non-Boolean functions, but only of constants. Sometimes, because of this restriction, some characteristics of the objects in the examples cannot be described. For instance, suppose that we want to represent the following example:

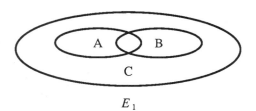

E_1

we can express that A is included in C by the atom *(included A C)*, we can also express that B is included in C but we cannot express that $A \cup B$ is also included in C, because $A \cup B$ is not a constant. We should allow functions in the representation of the examples and our last example could be represented by:

(included A C) & *(included B C)* & *(included (union A B) C)*

The theorems are universally quantified. Their left-hand side is a conjunction of atoms, which like the examples, are either predicates of arity zero, or terms (p x_1 ... x_n), where p is a predicate and x_1, ... , x_n are variables or constants. Their right hand side consists of a single atom of the same form. The taxonomies are used as sets of theorems. For instance, the following taxonomy:

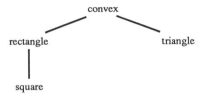

represents the set of theorems:

$\forall x$ *[(square x)* $\Rightarrow$ *(rectangle x)]*
$\forall x$ *[(rectangle x)* $\Rightarrow$ *(convex x)]*
$\forall x$ *[(triangle x)* $\Rightarrow$ *(convex x)]*

Their representation as taxonomies is kept only to increase the efficiency of the system. In this chapter, we shall therefore suppose that all the domain properties are expressed as theorems. To simplify our presentation, we shall moreover suppose that there are no predicates of arity 0. We can easily extend our algorithm to the case where this assumption is removed.

In the next sections, we give an example of the generalization algorithm, and then we describe the main steps of this algorithm.

13.2.2 Example

Suppose that we have the two following examples:

E_1 = *(square A)* & *(blue A)* & *(ellipsoid B)*
E_2 = *(rectangle C)* & *(blue C)* & *(circle D)*

In each example, there are two constants. Suppose that we choose to match the constants A and C because the objects represented by these constants are blue, and because we know that a square is a kind of rectangle. We replace all the occurrences of the constant A in E_1, and all the occurrences of the constant C in E_2 by the pseudo-variable x. This is not a true variable, since its value is kept in the formula in brackets. This gives the substitution that should be applied to find the original example again. But, it will perhaps become a generalization variable during the second step of the process. Therefore, we shall call it a TGV (Tentative Generalization Variable).

E_1 = *(square x) & (blue x) & (ellipsoid B) [(= x A)]*
E_2 = *(rectangle x) & (blue x) & (circle D) [(= x C)]*

In this chapter, we are not interested in the information concerning links between the TGVs and the constants kept in the brackets, it has already been treated by J.G. Ganascia [1985]. So, we only take into account the occurrences of x, which appear in the conjunction of atoms.

In E_1, we consider the two occurrences of the variable x defined: as an argument of the predicate 'square', and as an argument of the predicate 'blue'. In E_2, we consider the two occurrences of the variable x defined: as an argument of the predicate 'rectangle' and as an argument of the predicate 'blue'. In E_1, the occurrence of x in the atom *(square x)* discriminates E_1 in E_2, because we do not find it in E_2. In the following, we shall name such an occurrence a *discriminating occurrence*. In E_2, the occurrence of x in the atom *(rectangle x)* is also discriminating. If we know no theorems, we cannot make these discriminating occurrences disappear and therefore we shall be obliged to use the dropping conditions rule to generalize the examples. But, if we know that a square is a rectangle, we can transform E_1 into E_1':

E_1' = *(square x) & (rectangle x) & (blue x) & (ellipsoid B) [(= x A)]*

Of course, we are unable to find an expression equivalent to E_2 that would contain the predicate 'square'. We shall see in Section 13.3.2 more precisely how theorems are used.

We now choose the last constants C and D and replace them with the TGV y.

E_1' = (square x) & (rectangle x) & (blue x) & (ellipsoid y) [(= x A) (= y B)
   ($\neq$ x y)]
E_2 = (rectangle x) & (blue x) & (circle y) [(= x C) (= y D) ($\neq$ x y)]

We have added, for each example, the link *($\neq$ x y)* in brackets, because the values of x and y are different. In E_1', there is only an occurrence of y in the atom *(ellipsoid y)*. It is a discriminating one, because we do not find such an occurrence in E_2. In E_2, there is only an occurrence of y in the atom *(circle y)*. It is also a discriminating one. If we know the theorem: $\forall x [(circle\ x) \Rightarrow (ellipsoid\ x)]$, we can transform E_2 into E_2':

E_2' = *(rectangle x) & (blue x) & (circle y) & (ellipsoid y) [(= x C) (= y D)
   ($\neq$ x y)]*

There are no more constants to be chosen. The two examples E_1' and E_2' do not match structurally, and we have to apply the dropping conjunction rule. We obtain:

E_1'' = *(rectangle x) & (blue x) & (ellipsoid y) [(= x A) (= y B) ($\neq$ x y)]*
E_2'' = *(rectangle x) & (blue x) & (ellipsoid y) [(= x C) (= y D) ($\neq$ x y)]*

We have transformed E_1 into E_1'' and E_2 into E_2'' so that E_1'' and E_2'' match structurally. Moreover, we know that in E_1 and in E_2, the instantiations of x and y are different. A generalization of E_1 and E_2 is therefore:

G = *(rectangle x) & (blue x) & (ellipsoid y) & (≠ x y)*

which means that in E_1 and in E_2, there are two different objects: a blue rectangle and an ellipsoid.

13.2.3 The Algorithm

Suppose we have n examples $E_1, E_2, \ldots, E_n$ that we want to generalize. Our generalization method consists of two steps:

First step: We put the examples into structural matching.

Second step: When the examples match structurally, we can then generalize them. There exists a formula F and n substitutions σ_i so that for each i, $\sigma_i(F) = E_i$. A generalization of the examples is made from the common formula F and the common links between the variables.

In fact, we shall see in Section 13.3.2 that we cannot really always put the examples into structural matching. Most of the time, after the first step, the examples consist of a formula F common to all the examples and of a conjunction of discriminating atoms. The generalization of the examples is then composed of the common formula F and of the common links between the variables. It means that at this last step of generalization, we may use the dropping conjunction rules on the remaining discriminating atoms.

In this chapter, we are interested in the first step: how to improve the structural matching of the examples. The algorithm used is quite simple: We repeat the following operations until there are no more constants to choose:

1. At each step, according to some heuristics, we choose a constant in each example.

2. We replace all the occurrences of these constants by a unique Tentative Generalization Variable (TGV).

3. We compare the occurrences of this TGV in the examples, and we try to make all the discriminating occurrences disappear. The notion of discriminating occurrence will be defined in Section 13.3.1.

4. If constants remain, we perform the same operations 1, 2, and 3 with new constants; otherwise we stop.

This algorithm is still a little simplified. In fact, during the algorithm, we may use axioms of first order logic like:

$\forall$ x [(A x) $\Leftrightarrow$ (A x) & (A y) & (= x y)], A being a given predicate.

Such axioms introduce new variables, these variables are not TGVs and are treated as constants. These axioms are used in very specific cases, precisely defined and controlled, but we shall not speak about that in this chapter.

From now on, we suppose that we have n examples to generalize, and that we are at step 3 of the algorithm of structural matching; that is to say that we have chosen a constant in each example, replaced it by a TGV, named x, and we are interested in trying to make the discriminating occurrences of x disappear. Our definitions will be illustrated by these examples:

E_1 = *(book A) & (pen x) & (on A x) & (near B x) [(= x D)]*
E_2 = *(book x) & (on x TABLE) & (near C x) [(= x E)]*

which mean that, at the beginning, the examples were:

E_1 = *(book A) & (pen D) & (on A D) & (near B D)*
E_2 = *(book E) & (on E TABLE) & (near C E)*

We have chosen to match the constants D and E and replaced them by the TGV x. Moreover, to simplify the examples, we shall not write the links between the variables.

13.3 THE ELIMINATION OF DISCRIMINATING OCCURENCES

13.3.1 Definitions

Consider now an example E_1 and an occurrence of x in that example. That occurrence is completely determined by the atom (P cv_1 ... x ... cv_n) of E_1 in which it occurs and by its position in that atom. It is important also to give the position of the occurrence in the atom, because the same atom can have several occurrences of x. In our notation, cv_i represents either a constant or a TGV for, at a previous step, it is possible that we chose a constant that occurred in that atom and renamed it with a TGV.

Definition 1
Let E_1 and E_2 be two examples, and o_1, o_2 be occurrences of x in E_1, E_2. The occurrences o_1 and o_2 are given by the atoms in which they appear; i.e., atom$_1$ = (P$_1$ cv$_{11}$ ... x ... cv$_{n1,1}$) and atom$_2$ = (P$_2$ cv$_{12}$ ... x ... cv$_{n2,2}$) respectively, and by their positions p_1 and p_2 in these atoms. We say that the occurrence o_2 *matches the occurrence* o_1 if atom$_1$ and atom$_2$ are formed with the same predicate; i.e., $P_2 = P_1$ and if the occurrences have the same position; i.e., $p_1 = p_2$.

This definition is symmetrical: If o_2 matches o_1 then o_1 matches o_2 too. We say that o_1 and o_2 match structurally.

Consider the two following examples:

$E_1 = (book\ A)\ \&\ (pen\ x)\ \&\ (on\ A\ x)\ \&\ (near\ B\ x)$
$E_2 = (book\ x)\ \&\ (on\ x\ TABLE)\ \&\ (near\ C\ x)$

Let o_1 be the occurrence of x in the atom *(near B x)* of E_1, and o_2 the occurrence of x in the atom *(near C x)* of E_2. The occurrences o_1 and o_2 match structurally. The occurrence of x in E_1 defined by *(pen x)* and the occurrence of x in E_2 defined by *(book x)* do not match structurally, because the atoms, in which they occur, do not have the same predicate. The occurrence of x in E_1 defined by the atom *(on A x)* and the occurrence of x in E_2 defined by the atom *(on x TABLE)*, do not match structurally, because x does not occur at the same position in these atoms.

Definition 2

Suppose that we have a set E of n examples $E_1, \ldots, E_n$. Consider an example E_i belonging to E and an occurrence o_i of x in E_i. We say that o_i is a *discriminating occurrence* of x in E_i if there exists an example E_j, $j \neq i$, belonging to E such that no occurrences of x in E_j match o_i. In such a case, E_j is called a *critical example* of o_i.

Suppose that we have three examples:

$E_1 = (book\ A)\ \&\ (pen\ x)\ \&\ (on\ x\ A)$
$E_2 = (book\ x)\ \&\ (on\ x\ TABLE)$
$E_3 = (book\ x)\ \&\ (paper\ B)\ \&\ (on\ B\ x)$

The occurrence o_1 of x in E_1, defined by *(pen x)*, is a discriminating occurrence, because there are no occurrences of x either in E_2 or in E_3 whose predicate is 'pen', and hence which match this occurrence. Its critical examples are E_2 and E_3. The occurrence o_2 of x in E_1 defined by *(on x A)* is a discriminating occurrence, because the only occurrence of x in E_3, whose predicate is 'on', is defined by *(on B x)*, and x is not at the same place as in E_1. The example E_3 is the only critical example of o_2.

This example shows us that we can see two kinds of critical examples for a given discriminating occurrence: predicate-critical examples and position-critical examples.

Definition 3

Suppose that we have a set E of n examples $E_1, \ldots, E_n$. Consider an example E_i belonging to E and a discriminating occurrence o_i of x in E_i. The occurrence o_i is determined by the atom $(Q\ cv_1 \ldots x \ldots cv_n)$ in which it appears, and its position in that atom. Consider E_j, a critical example of o_i. We say that E_j is a *predicate-critical example* of o_i, if no occurrences of x in E_j occur in an atom whose predicate is Q.

In our previous example, E_2 and E_3 are predicate-critical examples of o_1.

Definition 4

In the circumstances given in definition 3, we say that E_j is a *position-critical example* of o_i, if there exist in E_j occurrences of x whose atoms are formed with the predicate Q but which do not have the same position as o_i.

In our previous example, E_3 is a position-critical example of o_2.

We distinguish the position-critical examples of a discriminating occurrence o_i from the predicative ones, for we may think that, since in the position-critical examples we already have occurrences of x whose predicate is the same as for o_i, it will perhaps be sufficient to use theorems, like the commutativity, to solve these critical examples. If this is not possible, we shall treat them as predicate-critical examples.

13.3.2 Using the Theorems

We suppose that in the example E_i, there is a discriminating occurrence o_i of the TGV x. The occurrence o_i is defined by the atom (P $cv_{i,1}$ ... x ... $cv_{i,n}$) in which it appears and by its position p_i in this atom.

As heuristics, we treat first the position-critical examples of o_i, since there exist occurrences of x in a position-critical example, whose atoms are formed with the same predicate P as o_i and which therefore seem rather similar to o_i. So, as a first step, we deal with the position-critical examples.

Position-Critical Examples

Consider E_x, a position-critical example of o_i.

This example, E_x, contains atoms (P $cv_{j,1}$ ... x ... $cv_{j,n}$), but x is never in the position p_i in these atoms.

The goal is to try to apply theorems, like commutativity, to the atoms (P $cv_{j,1}$ ... x ... $cv_{j,n}$) to deduce a new atom in which the variable x would be at the same position as the variable x in the occurrence o_i.

Since we try to treat the position-critical examples of a *fixed* discriminating occurrence o_i, *the position p_i of the TGV x in this occurrence is fixed.* At this step, we try to introduce in the position-critical examples, an occurrence of x at this position p_i. Therefore, we do not have the problem of modifying the position of the TGV x in a position-critical example of o_i and of modifying differently the position of the variable x in another position-critical example of o_i.

We try to apply theorems like commutativity, which inverts the position of the variables. The most general form of such theorems is:

$$\forall x_1, \ldots, x_n \, [(P \, x_1 \ldots x_n) \Rightarrow (P \, x_{\sigma(1)} \ldots x_{\sigma(n)})], \text{ where } \sigma \text{ is a permutation.}$$

If we cannot apply such theorems, we treat E_x as a predicate critical example of o_i, since it means that the presence of occurrences of x in E_x, whose predicate is the same as for o_i is not helpful.

For instance, if we have the two following examples:

$E_1 = (near \; x \; B) \; \& \; (left \; x \; B)$
$E_2 = (near \; C \; x) \; \& \; (left \; C \; x) \; \& \; (right \; D \; x)$

All the occurrences of x in E_1 and in E_2 are discriminating ones. But if we know the theorem:

$R_1 : \forall \; x \; \forall \; y \; [(near \; x \; y) \Leftrightarrow (near \; y \; x)]$

we can improve the matching of E_1 and E_2.

The example E_2 is a position-critical example for the occurrence of x, defined in E_1 by the atom *(near x B)*. But, in E_2, we can apply R_1 to deduce from the atom *(near C x)* the atom *(near x C)*. We have now:

$E_1 = (near \; x \; B) \; \& \; (left \; x \; B)$
$E_2 = (near \; x \; C) \; \& \; (left \; C \; x) \; \& \; (right \; D \; x)$

The two occurrences of x in the atoms *(near x B)* and *(near x C)* match structurally. Let us notice that the occurrence of x, defined in E_2 by the atom *(near C x)* was a discriminating occurrence. It was transformed into a matching occurrence at the same time as the occurrence of x in the atom *(near x B)*.

The example E_2 is a position-critical example of the occurrence of x, defined in E_1 by the atom *(left x B)*. But the predicate 'left' is not commutative. At this step, we cannot make appear an occurrence of x in E_2, which matches this occurrence of x. Likewise, E_1 is a position critical example of the occurrence of x, defined in E_2 by the atom *(left C x)* and we cannot treat it at this step.

General Method

In this chapter, we call the set of leftover critical examples of o_i, *leftover set*. This set consists of the predicate-critical examples of o_i, and of the remaining position ones which have not yet been treated.

First Step   First of all, we try to see if, in each critical example, we can introduce an occurrence of the TGV x which matches o_i. We try then to deduce, in each example of the leftover set, an atom (P $cv_{j,1}$ ... x ... $cv_{j,n}$) where the TGV x appears at position p_i. If we can, we say that *the discriminating occurrence o_i can be put into structural matching*.

Second Step   We can justify this step by the following idea: To find, in each example an occurrence of the TGV x matching the occurrence o_i, defined by the atom (P $cv_{i,1}$ ... $cv_{i,n}$), means that all the objects represented by the TGV x in the examples satisfy the property P. If we cannot match this occurrence of x, it means, of course, that some objects represented by the TGV x do not satisfy this property but, from this property P satisfied by x only in some examples, we may perhaps find a new property satisfied by x in all the examples.

So, we try to see if there exist on the one hand, theorems which can be applied to E_i with the atom (P cv_1 ... x ... cv_n), in which the occurrence o_i appear, to generate an atom (Q $cv_{i,1}$ ... x ... $cv_{i,p}$) and, on the other hand, theorems which can be applied to all the examples E_j to generate atoms (Q $cv_{j,1}$ ... x ... $cv_{j,p}$), where the occurrence of x is at the same position as in (Q $cv_{i,1}$ ... x ... $cv_{i,p}$).

The new atom (Q $cv_{i,1}$ ... x ... $cv_{i,p}$), generated in E_i must not be already present in E_i, since it would bring redundant information.

Suppose that we have the two following examples:

E_1 = *(rectangle x)* & *(near A x)*
E_2 = *(rhombus x)* & *(on x B)*

All the occurrences of *x* in each example are discriminating occurrences. For the occurrence of *x* defined in E_1 by the atom *(near A x)*, we can apply the theorems:

$\forall\ u\ \forall\ v\ [(on\ u\ v) \Rightarrow (near\ u\ v)]$
$\forall\ u\ \forall\ v\ [(near\ u\ v) \Leftrightarrow (near\ v\ u)]$

to deduce from the atom *(on x B)* the atom *(near B x)* in E_2. This new occurrence of x matches the occurrence of *x*, defined in E_1 by the atom *(near A x)*.

For the occurrence of *x* defined in E_1 by the atom *(rectangle x)*, we can apply the theorems:

$\forall\ u\ [(rectangle\ u) \Rightarrow (parallelogram\ u)]$
$\forall\ u\ [(rhombus\ u) \Rightarrow (parallelogram\ u)]$

to transform the atom *(rectangle x)* into *(parallelogram x)* in E_1 and the atom *(rhombus x)* into *(parallelogram x)* in E_2.

Therefore, we transform E_1 and E_2 into

E_1' = *(parallelogram x)* & *(near A x)*
E_2' = *(parallelogram x)* & *(near B x)*

There are no longer any discriminating occurrences.

Remarks

- We must take care when applying the theorems, because at previous steps, we may have introduced other TGVs and put them into structural matching. We must avoid to modify these structural matchings, and so we have some constraints on the application of theorems. We shall not go into further details about this point in this chapter, for more details, see [Vrain, 1987].
- This last example shows us that often when we treat a discriminating occurrence in an example, the effected transformations modify some discriminating occurrences in other examples and may treat these discriminating occurrences or prevent them from being treated.

For instance, in our previous example, when we treat the occurrence of x defined by the atom *(near A x)* in E_1, we dealt at the same time with the discriminating occurrence of x, defined in E_2 by the atom *(on x B)*: We have transformed the atom *(on x B)* in order to match them.

But if we were in an universe where all the rectangles were put on the same table, called TAB, that is to say if the following theorem were valid,

$R: \forall u [(rectangle\ u) \Rightarrow (on\ u\ TAB)]$,

we could have introduced in E_1 an occurrence of x which would have matched the occurrence of x in E_2 defined by the atom *(on x B)*, since we had

$E_1 = (rectangle\ x) \& (near\ A\ x)$,

and we could apply the previous theorem to get

$E_1 = (rectangle\ x) \& (near\ A\ x) \& (on\ x\ TAB)$.

But, we have transformed E_1 and E_2 in:

$E_1{}' = (parallelogram\ x) \& (near\ A\ x)$
$E_2{}' = (parallelogram\ x) \& (near\ B\ x)$.

We have lost the information that in E_1, the TGV x was a rectangle and we can no more apply the theorem R to $E_1{}'$. We have also lost the fact that in E_2 there was an occurrence of x in the atom *(on x B)*.

This example illustrates how the application of a theorem, which is not an equivalence, produces information lost. If we had an occurrence defined by the atom $(P\ cv_{i,1} \ldots x \ldots cv_{i,n})$ and if we apply the universally quantified theorem:

$(P\ u_1 \ldots u_n) \Rightarrow (Q\ v_1 \ldots v_q)$

we lose the information that there was an occurrence of x in an atom whose predicate is P, and we may need this occurrence to match other occurrences.

To avoid this,

• when we use a theorem which is not an equivalence,

MG $\Rightarrow$ MD,

we use idempotency, and we always apply it as,

MG $\Rightarrow$ MG & MD

• when, to treat a discriminating occurrence, defined by the atom $(P\ cv_{i,1} \ldots x \ldots cv_{i,n})$ and which cannot be put into structural matching (second step of the general method), we deduce a new atom $(Q \ldots x \ldots)$, then we replace $(P\ cv_{i,1} \ldots x \ldots cv_{i,n})$ by $(P\ cv_{i,1} \ldots x \ldots cv_{i,n}) \& (Q \ldots x \ldots)$, and we mark the atom $(P\ cv_{i,1} \ldots x \ldots cv_{i,n})$ by a star to recall that this discriminating occurrence has already been treated.

In our previous example,

E_1 = *(rectangle x) & (near A x)*
E_2 = *(rhombus x) & (on x B),*

to treat the discriminating occurrences of the TGV x defined by the atoms *(near A x)* and *(rectangle x)*, the examples E_1 and E_2 are transformed into:

E_1 = **(rectangle x) & (near A x) & (parallelogram x)*
E_2 = *(rhombus x) & (on x B) & (parallelogram x) & (near B x),*

and we have to treat the remaining discriminating occurrences defined in E_2 by the atoms *(rhombus x)* and *(on x B)*.

13.3.3 Example

Let us consider now the examples in Section 13.1.2. We have given a generalization of them, but let us see how we can get it.

The examples are:

E_1 = *(mammalian A) & (bred-by-man A)*
E_2 = *(domestic B) & (viviparous B),*

and we know the three following theorems:

R_1: $\forall x$ *[(mammalian x) & (bred-by-man x)* $\Rightarrow$ *(domestic x)]*
R_2: $\forall x$ *[(domestic x) & (viviparous x)* $\Rightarrow$ *(mammalian x)]*
R_3: $\forall x$ *[(domestic x)* $\Rightarrow$ *(inoffensive x)]*

First of all, we have to choose a constant in each example and replace it with a TGV. There is only one constant in the examples, so we choose it and replace it with the TGV x.

E_1 = **(mammalian x)** & **(bred-by-man x)** *[(= x A)]*
E_2 = **(domestic x)** & **(viviparous x)** *[(= x B)]*

We write the discriminating occurrences in bold, and we mark the discriminating occurrences, which have been already treated, by a star.

All the occurrences of x are discriminating ones. We consider the first occurrence of E_1, defined by the atom *(mammalian x)*. Since all the discriminating occurrences will be treated, the order in which we treat them has no importance, and we only follow the order in which the examples and the atoms are given. We see that we can deduce the atom *(mammalian x)* from E_2, using the theorem R_2. We get:

E_1 = *(mammalian x)* & **(bred-by-man x)** *[(= x A)]*
E_2 = **(domestic x)** & **(viviparous x)** & *(mammalian x) [(= x B)]*

There are still three discriminating occurrences defined by the atoms *(bred-by-man x)*, *(domestic x)*, and *(viviparous x)*.

We consider the discriminating occurrence of E_1 defined by the atom *(bred-by-man x)*.

- No theorem can be applied to E_2 to make appear *(bred-by-man x)*.
- We can apply the theorem R_1 to E_1 using the atom *(bred-by-man x)*. It generates the atom *(domestic x)* and there is an occurrence of x in E_2 which matches this occurrence. Therefore, we apply R_1 and we mark the atom *(bred-by-man x)* with a star to remember it has already been treated.

E_1 = *(mammalian x)* & ***(bred-by-man x)*** & *(domestic x) [(= x A)]*
E_2 = *(domestic x)* & **(viviparous x)** & *(mammalian x) [(= x B)]*

There remains only one discriminating occurrence, which has not yet been treated—the occurrence defined in E_2 by the atom *(viviparous x)*.

- No theorems can be applied to E_1 to make appear the atom *(viviparous x)*.
- The only theorem, which can be applied to E_2 with the atom *(viviparous x)* is the theorem R_1. But it would introduce the atom *(mammalian x)* which is already present in E_2: It would bring no new information.

No theorems can be applied, therefore we mark the atom *(viviparous x)* by a star to remember that the occurrence of x in this atom has already been dealt with. We get:

E_1 = *(mammalian x)* & ***(bred-by-man x)*** & *(domestic x) [(= x A)]*
E_2 = *(domestic x)* & ***(viviparous x)*** & *(mammalian x) [(= x B)]*

All the discriminating occurrences have been dealt with. We drop the remaining discriminating occurrences, which can never be put into structural matching. We get:

E_1 = *(mammalian x)* & *(domestic x) [(= x A)]*
E_2 = *(domestic x)* & *(mammalian x) [(= x B)]*

The two examples match structurally. A generalization of them consists of the common formula and the common links between the variables. There are no common links. A generalization G is therefore:

G = *(domestic x)* & *(mammalian x)*

13.3.4 Discussion

In our general method, at the second step, (see Section 13.3.2), it is not obvious how we should search for an atom $(Q \ cv_{i,1} \ ... \ x \ ... \ cv_{i,p})$, which satisfies the given conditions.

13.3.4.1 The Number of Different Atoms Is Finite

Our langage of description is composed only of predicates and of constants, and given a knowledge base, the number of theorems is finite, so the number of atoms that we can deduce from an example is finite. Nevertheless, we could generate the same atom an infinite number of times. In the next section, we show that the strategy we use prevents loops.

13.3.4.2 The Number of Applications of Theorems Is Finite

Given an example E_i and a discriminating occurrence of the TGV x, defined by the atom (P $cv_{i,1}$ ... x ... $cv_{i,n}$), the strategy used to get the atoms (Q ... x ...) that we can deduce from E_i using the atom (P $cv_{i,1}$ ... x ... $cv_{i,n}$) can be expressed as follows:

Let TH be the set of theorems of our knowledge base and n its number of elements.

Let TH_1 be the set of theorems in which the predicate P is used to express at least a precondition, and let n_1 be the number of elements of TH_1.

We try to apply each theorem of TH_1 to the atom (P $cv_{i,1}$ ... x ... $cv_{i,n}$) and to other atoms of E_i. That means that we match the precondition whose predicate is P to the atom (P $cv_{i,1}$ ... x ... $cv_{i,n}$) and in this environment, we try to prove in E_1 the other preconditions of the theorems. If possible, by applying the theorem, we get a new occurrence of x in a new atom (Q ... x ...) of E_i. We call this new occurrence of x defined by the atom (Q ... x ...), o_2. If the theorem has several atoms in its preconditions each with the predicate P, we try all the matches of these atoms with the atom (P $cv_{i,1}$ ... x ... $cv_{i,n}$) and therefore, we may deduce several new occurrences of x. We call this operation a *first-step-forward chaining operation* on (P $cv_{i,1}$ ... x $cv_{i,n}$) using TH_1.

Then, two cases may happen:

- The new occurrence o_2 can be put into structural matching, that is to say in each example, either there is an occurrence of x which matches o_2, or we can deduce an occurrence of x which matches it. We add this new atom (Q ... x ...) to E_i and if necessary we add new atoms to match o_2, in the other examples also.

- The new occurrence o_2 cannot be put into structural matching. Let TH_2 be the set of theorems in which at least one precondition is expressed with the predicate Q and for which no preconditions are expressed with the predicate P. Let n_2 be its number of elements. We have:

$$TH_1 \cap TH_2 = \varnothing$$
$$n_1 + n_2 < n$$

We make the first step forward chaining on $(Q \dots x \dots)$ using the theorems TH_2, and we go on with the new occurrences generated.

Our process must stop since at each step we consider only new theorems that have not been considered at a previous step, and the number of theorems is finite.

We can sum up the process by the following tree:

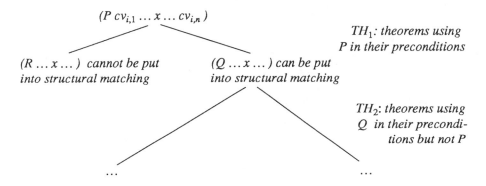

13.3.4.3 Tools for Reducing the Search Space

Moreover, to decrease the search and to increase the efficiency, we have developed several tools. We just mention them and for further details, see [Vrain, 1987].

Predicative Generalization of a Set of Examples   The predicative generalization of examples $E_1, \dots, E_n$ is a set of predicates which satisfies the following condition:

if a predicate Q does not belong to the predicative generalization of $E_1, \dots, E_n$, it cannot be put into structural matching in the examples.

In the example of the Section 13.3.3, we had:

$E_1 = (mammalian\ A)\ \&\ (bred\text{-}by\text{-}man\ A)$
$E_2 = (domestic\ B)\ \&\ (viviparous\ B),$

and we knew the three following theorems:

$R_1:$ $\forall\ x\ [(mammalian\ x)\ \&\ (bred\text{-}by\text{-}man\ x) \Rightarrow (domestic\ x)]$
$R_2:$ $\forall\ x\ [(domestic\ x)\ \&\ (viviparous\ x)\ \Rightarrow (mammalian\ x)]$
$R_3:$ $\forall\ x\ [(domestic\ x)\ \Rightarrow (inoffensive\ x)]$

The predicative generalization of E_1 and E_2 is:

$PG(E_1, E_2) = \{mammalian, domestic, inoffensive\}$

We shall not explain in this chapter how the predicative generalization of a set of examples is constructed.

This set is very useful to treat an occurrence o_i defined by an atom (P cv_1 ... cv_n): If the predicate P does not belong to the predicative generalization of the examples, we know without any search that the occurrence cannot be put into structural matching. It is therefore a discriminating occurrence and we have to treat it using the method described in Section 13.3.2. Moreover, we know that we have to do at least a first step of forward chaining.

Classes of Predicates   We define disjoint classes of predicates so that for two predicates P_1 and P_2 belonging to two different classes C_1 and C_2, there exist no theorems expressed with the two predicates P_1 and P_2. Therefore, the classes of predicates do not depend on the examples but on the knowledge base.

Let us suppose that we have the following knowledge base:

$$\forall x \qquad [\ (square \ x) \qquad \Rightarrow (rectangle \ x)]$$
$$\forall x \qquad [\ (rectangle \ x) \qquad \Rightarrow (convex \ x)]$$
$$\forall x \qquad [\ (triangle \ x) \qquad \Rightarrow (convex \ x)]$$
$$\forall x \qquad [\ (blue \ x) \qquad \Rightarrow (colored \ x)]$$
$$\forall x \qquad [\ (red \ x) \qquad \Rightarrow (colored \ x)]$$
$$\forall x \ \forall y \qquad [\ (on \ x \ y) \qquad \Rightarrow (near \ x \ y)]$$
$$\forall x \ \forall y \qquad [\ (near \ x \ y) \qquad \Rightarrow (near \ y \ x)]$$

We have 3 classes of predicates:

$C_1 = \{square, rectangle, triangle, convex\}$,
$C_2 = \{blue, red, colored\}$
$C_3 = \{on, near\}$.

Let us suppose that we want to treat a discriminating occurrence o_i defined in E_i by the atom (P cv_1 ... cv_n) and that the predicate P belongs to the class C.

- If in another example E_j, j ≠ i, there are no atoms whose predicate belongs to the class C, we know that it will not be possible to put this occurrence into structural matching, and moreover we know that none of the occurrences that we could deduce from this occurrence could be put into structural matching. Therefore, it is useless to apply our method.

- In the other cases, to treat o_i, we reduce the search space to the atoms whose predicate belongs to the class C.

13.4 CONCLUSION

One of the main points claimed for OGUST is to take into account all the available theorems that can be expressed in our description language, without applying all the applicable theorems to the examples. A theorem is used only if it improves the similarity of the examples; i.e., similarity measured by the structural matching between the examples (Section 13.1.3). Another important characteristic of the system is its explicability: As outputs of the system, we do not only get a recognition function of the concept, but we also have for each example—the proof that the example is really an instance of the obtained recognition function.

We have shown in this chapter how to use all the domain knowledge, represented either by taxonomies or by theorems, without preferring one representation to the other. We have only developed a part of the system: how to use theorems to erase discriminating occurrences. Another difficult point was the choice of the constants to match. Heuristics have been developed to choose the constants automatically—they take the theorems into account and evaluate the possible common properties of the objects.

Moreover, when the system generalizes examples, it keeps the trace of the way the constants have been generalized and of the theorems used on each example. It can then justify its generalization.

The system OGUST has been implemented in Lelisp, v.15.2, on a Sun workstation. Currently, our system is not incremental: If we learn a new example after we have obtained a generalization, we are not able to improve our generalization to take into account the new example, and we have to start a generalization of the whole set of examples including the new one again. Moreover, if we have a great number of examples, there is a problem of combinatorial explosion, and incremental learning may be a solution to these problems.

The explanations can help us to do incremental learning with new examples, "relatively similar" to some of our previous examples. If we know that a new example, called E_j, is similar to the old example E_i, we can use analogical reasonings, based on the justification that the example E_i is really an instance of the obtained generalization, to test if E_j is an instance of the generalization and if necessary to improve the generalization.

We illustrate the use of analogical reasonings by a very simple example:
Suppose that we have two examples:

$E_1 = (rectangle A)$ & $(red A)$,
$E_2 = (parallelogram B)$ & $(red B)$

A generalization of these two examples is:

$G = (parallelogram x)$ & $(red x)$

Let us suppose now that we learn the new example:

$E_3 = (rhombus C)$ & $(red C)$

We have to test if this example is covered by the generalization. In order to do this, let us find analogies between E_1 and E_3. The two examples have the common feature 'red' but in E_1, the object is a rectangle and in E_3, it is a rhombus.

The example E_1 is an instance of the generalization G, because we can apply the following theorem to E_1:

$\forall x \, [\, (rectangle \; x) \Rightarrow (parallelogram \; x) \,]$

We cannot apply this theorem to E_3, since it is based on the discriminant feature 'rectangle', but we can search for a "similar" theorem, based on the corresponding feature of E_3—'rhombus'. If we know the theorem

$\forall x \, [\, (rhombus \; x) \Rightarrow (parallelogram \; x) \,]$,

we can immediately deduce that E_3 is an instance of G.

A new version of OGUST, called OGUST+, based on these ideas, is currently under development [Vrain, 1988; 1989].

As a conclusion, we shall speak about a very important extension of our system to treat the problem of *negative examples*. It provides us with new heuristics to those given in Section 13.3.4.3.

Our system OGUST is able, given a set of examples, to learn a complete description of the corresponding concept, expressed as conjunctions of atoms. Currently, it is not able to deal with negative examples and to learn a complete and consistent description, as systems like Michalski's INDUCE [Michalski, 1984] do. It is certainly not possible to learn complete and consistent generalizations expressed as conjunctions of atoms, and we need to introduce disjunctions. But we have developed new heuristics, not yet implemented, to choose the constants—not on the basis of their similarities but on the basis of the negative examples—and therefore to guide the generalization towards a consistent generalization. Work must still be done on this topic to see how we can reject the remaining negative examples, still covered by the generalization. We only illustrate this by a very simple example:

Let us suppose that we have the following examples:

$E_1 = (rectangle \; A) \; \& \; (red \; A) \; \& \; (circle \; B) \; \& \; (on \; B \; A)$
$E_2 = (ellipse \; C) \; \& \; (red \; C) \; \& \; (triangle \; D) \; \& \; (on \; D \; C)$

Let us suppose that we know the following negative example:

$NE_1 = (square \; E) \; \& \; (red \; E) \; \& \; (triangle \; F) \; \& \; (on \; F \; E)$

To generalize E_1 and E_2, we would choose, according to the similarities of the constants, to match the constants A and C on the one hand, and the constants B and D on the other hand.

According to the negative example NE_1, we should choose to match the constants B and C, since in the generalization we shall then get the predicate 'ellipse', which is not satisfied by NE_1. For further details about these heuristics, see [Vrain, 1987].

In this chapter we have described a tool for using background knowledge expressed as theorems in order to improve the quality of the similarities found among positive examples of a concept. Besides the simple fact that background knowledge must be used when available, we are currently using our tool to improve the state of two very difficult problems:

1. To ensure that incremental learning from sets of examples need not behave erratically,
2. To use negative examples in order to decrease the complexity of the generalization from positive examples.

References

Bollinger, T. 1986. "Généralisation en apprentissage à partir d'examples" *Thèse de troisième cycle soutenue le 30 Janvier 1986*, Université Paris Sud.

DeJong, G. and Mooney, R. 1986. "Explanation based learning: An alternative view," *Machine Learning Journal*, Vol. 1, Number 2, pp. 145–176, Kluwer Academic Publisher.

Ganascia, J.G. 1985. "Comment oublier a l'aide de contres examples," *Proceedings du 5ème congrès Reconnaissances des Formes et Intelligence Artificielle*, AFCET, Tome 2, pp. 1085–1098, Grenoble.

Kodratoff, Y. 1983. "Generalizing and particularizing as the techniques of learning," *Computers and Artificial Intelligence 2*, pp. 417–441.

——— , 1985. "A theory and a methodology for symbolic learning," *COGNITIVA 85*. June 4–7, pp. 639–651.

Kodratoff, Y. and Ganascia, J.G. 1986. "Improving the generalization step in learning," *Machine Learning: An Artificial Intelligence Approach, Volume II*, Michalski, R.S., Carbonell, J.G., Mitchell, T. M. (Eds). Morgan Kaufmann Publishers, pp. 215–244.

Michalski, R.S. 1984. "A theory and methodology of inductive learning," *Machine Learning, an Artificial Intelligence Approach*. Michalski R.S., Carbonell J.G., Mitchell T.M. (Ed.s). Springer Verlag, pp. 83–129.

Mitchell, T.M. 1983. "Learning and problem solving," *Proceedings IJCAI-83*, Karlsruhe, pp. 1139–1151.

Mitchell, T.M., Utgoff P.E., and Banerji, R. 1983. "Learning by experimentation, acquiring and refining problem-solving heuristics," *Machine Learning: An Artificial Intelligence Approach*, Michalski, R.S., Carbonell, J.G., Mitchell, T.M. (Eds), Morgan Kaufmann Publishers, pp. 163–190.

Mitchell, T, Keller, R.M., and Kedar-Cabelli, S.T. 1986. "Explanation based learning, a unifying view," *Machine Learning Journal*, Vol.1, Number 1, pp 47–80, Kluwer Academic Publishers.

Vere, S.A. 1980. "Multilevel counterfactuals for generalizations of relational concepts and productions," *Artificial Intelligence* 14, pp. 139–164.

Vrain, C. 1987. "Un Outil de Généralisation Utilisant Systématiquement les Théorèmes: le système OGUST," *Thèse de troisième cycle*, 25 février 1987, Université de Paris-Sud.

Vrain, C. and Kodratoff, Y. 1989. "The use of analogy in incremental SBL," in *Knowledge Representation and Organization in Machine Learning*, K. Morik (Ed.), Springer-Verlag, Berlin, pp. 231–246.

Vrain, C., Lu, C.-R. 1988. "An analogical method to do incremental learning of concepts," *Proceedings of the European Working Session on Learning*, D. Sleman (Ed.), Pitman, London, pp. 227–235, 1988.

14

CONDITIONAL OPERATIONALITY AND EXPLANATION-BASED GENERALIZATION

Haym Hirsh
(Rutgers University)

Abstract

Explanation-based generalization (EBG) finds the weakest preconditions of a proof to form a generalization covering all cases for which the proof succeeds. The generalization must be *operational*; that is, it must satisfy some criterion on the merit of the generalization for the problem solver. When the generalizations created by EBG are conditionally operational for fine-grained definitions of operationality, the conditions on the operationality of a generalization should be determined and included with the generalization. This chapter describes an implementation of EBG called ROE (Reasoning about Operationality for EBG) that proves that the predicates used in a generalization are operational for the particular situation on which it is based, and generalizes the proof of operationality to determine the weakest conditions on when the generalization should be used. These conditions are included in the results of ROE to restrict their use to situations in which they are operational. Reasoning about and generalizing operationality is accomplished by using ROE itself on a domain theory that concludes whether predicates are operational for whatever notion of operationality the user encodes.

14.1 INTRODUCTION

Explanation-based generalization (EBG) [Mitchell, Keller, and Kedar-Cabelli, 1986; DeJong and Mooney, 1986] proves that a *goal concept* holds for an example of the concept called the *training instance*, using a *domain theory* of rules and facts about the goal concept. EBG forms a generalization of the instance, defining the class of instances that are examples with the same proof as the training instance. It does so by finding the weakest preconditions on the proof, restricting such conditions to expressions that satisfy an *operationality criterion* on the merit of the generalization for the problem solver.

The operationality criterion judges how well a generalization satisfies the purpose for learning. It should guarantee that the results of EBG meet the needs of the problem solver. In general, predicates may be operational for only some argument values. For example (from [DeJong and Mooney, 1986]), the predicate Provable is operational if its argument is 2 + 2 = 4 but not if its argument is Fermat's Last Theorem (for a definition of operationality based on computational ease). In such cases the conditions of operationality on the predicates used in a generalization must be determined and included with the generalization, since EBG must only form operational definitions.

This chapter presents an implementation of explanation-based generalization called ROE (Reasoning about Operationality for EBG) that, in addition to generalizing proofs that some property holds for a given training instance, determines the general conditions of operationality for its results. A user of ROE specifies a set of rules and facts about operationality that are used to prove predicates operational. For example, instance-language predicates could be specified operational (e.g., to form rules that conclude the goal concept directly from instances with no additional processing). However, more sophisticated theories of operationality enable predicates to be conditionally operational. Therefore ROE generalizes its proofs of operationality, using ROE itself on the user's theory of operationality, and includes the conditions so formed in its results. Rather than committing to a generalization as unconditionally good or bad, such reasoning about and generalizing of the operationality of generalizations can restrict a generalization to the cases for which it is operational.

14.2 EBG

As an example of EBG consider the Safe-To-Stack problem presented by Mitchell, Keller, and Kedar-Cabelli [1986], which will be used throughout this chapter. The domain theory has rules about the safety of stacking one object on another (goal concept Safe-To-Stack):[1]

---

[1] This chapter uses the logical formalism utilized by Mitchell, Keller, and Kedar-Cabelli [1986] and developed further elsewhere [Hirsh, 1987]. Throughout this chapter variables begin with lowercase letters and are assumed to be universally quantified. All relations, including $<$, are written in prefix form, and n-ary functions are written as $n+1$-nary relations, with the result as the additional $n+1$st argument. The Unprovable in the fifth rule is a built-in predicate that succeeds if there is no proof for its argument (i.e., it represents negation-as-failure). It makes the rule explicitly a default rule [Hirsh, 1987].

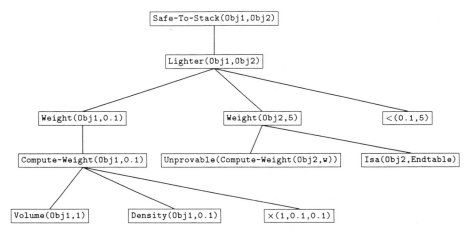

Figure 14–1: Proof for `Safe-To-Stack(Obj1,Obj2)`

```
Not(Fragile(y))  →  Safe-To-Stack(x,y)
Lighter(x,y)  →  Safe-To-Stack(x,y)
Weight(p1,w1) ∧ Weight(p2,w2) ∧ <(w1,w2)  →  Lighter(p1,p2)
Compute-Weight(p,w)  →  Weight(p,w)
Unprovable(Compute-Weight(p,w)) ∧  Isa(p,Endtable)  →  Weight(p,5)
Volume(p,v) ∧ Density(p,d) ∧ ×(v,d,w)  →  Compute-Weight(p,w).
```

The training-instance facts describe two objects, `Obj1` and `Obj2`, that satisfy `Safe-To-Stack(Obj1,Obj2)`:

```
On(Obj1,Obj2)
Isa(Obj1,Box)
Isa(Obj2,Endtable)
Color(Obj1,Red)
Color(Obj2,Blue)
Volume(Obj1,1)
Density(Obj1,0.1).
```

Finally, the operationality criterion states what predicates may appear in rules:

```
Operational(Volume(p,v))
Operational(Density(p,d))
Operational(On(x,y))
Operational(Color(p,c))
Operational(Isa(x,o))
Operational(×(x,y,z))
Operational(<(x,y)).
```

EBG forms both a proof that the training instance is a correct example of `Safe-To-Stack` (Figure 14–1), and a generalized proof that will apply to other examples of

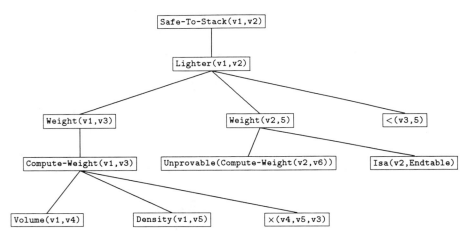

Figure 14–2:   Generalized proof for `Safe-To-Stack(Obj1,Obj2)`

`Safe-To-Stack` (Figure 14–2). From this generalized proof EBG forms a rule specifying a larger set of cases that are `Safe-To-Stack`:

```
Volume(v1,v4) ∧ Density(v1,v5) ∧ ×(v4,v5,v3)
    ∧ Isa(v2,Endtable)∧ <(v3,5)
    ∧ Unprovable(Compute-Weight(v2,v6))
  → Safe-To-Stack(v1,v2).
```

If EBG also had `Operational(Weight(x,w))`, it would instead form the rule

```
Weight(v1,v3) ∧ Weight(v2,v4) ∧ <(v3,v4) → Safe-To-Stack(v1,v2).
```

Operationality selects the vocabulary in which the final rule will be expressed. Details on specific implementations of EBG can be found elsewhere (e.g., [Hirsh, 1987; Kedar-Cabelli, 1987; and Mooney and Bennett, 1986]).

14.3 REASONING ABOUT OPERATIONALITY

Although operationality is a general property on the merit of a learning result for the problem solver, the only definition used by Mitchell, Keller, and Kedar-Cabelli [1986] is: "The concept definition must be expressed in terms of the predicates used to describe examples ... or other selected, easily evaluated, predicates from the domain theory." This notion of operationality assumes a particular problem solver and purpose for learning in which forming rules that summarize a chain of processing from training-instance facts to goal concept is desired. DeJong and Mooney [1986] point out that such simple selection of operational predicates is insufficient, and provide examples in which operationality is a function of the proof structure. But they, too, assume a particular purpose for learning for their problem solver, reflected in their particular operationality criterion.

A previous paper [Hirsh, 1987] described an EBG system enabling more robust operationality criteria. It proposed making the criterion for deciding operationality *explicit* for use by EBG. The paper describes a mechanism for explicit reasoning about operationality, using theorem proving on a set of facts and rules about the predicate Operational. This allows the user to specify explicitly whatever operationality criterion is consistent with the problem solver and the purpose for learning. The EBG system uses this theory to prove predicates Operational, which can then be used to prune proofs that, although successful, do not yield operational generalizations. For example, the user's theory of operationality might simply check if a predicate is known to be true (i.e., rules aren't used to prove it), or if a rule has already been learned for concluding it (e.g., [DeJong and Mooney, 1986]). More sophisticated definitions of operationality might even perform experimentation or lookahead search to determine whether a predicate will be both usable and useful, in a manner similar to MetaLEX [Keller, 1987]. The key idea is to allow the user to axiomatize whatever notion of operationality is desired.

14.4 GENERALIZING OPERATIONALITY

One difficulty that the earlier paper [Hirsh, 1987] overlooked is that Operational need not hold for predicates regardless of argument value. Arbitrary reasoning about operationality may make a predicate operational only for a subset of its possible argument values. Thus ROE determines the conditions on when a generalization is truly operational, by proving that each of its predicates is Operational for the particular training instance and finding the weakest preconditions on the proof. This process of determining the weakest preconditions on a proof is precisely what EBG does, and thus ROE uses itself on these proofs of the goal concept Operational to determine the conditions of operationality for its base-level results. Whenever a predicate is operational (and hence will appear in the learned rule) ROE places its conditions of operationality immediately before the predicate in the final rule to restrict its use to when it is operational.

For example, as mentioned earlier the predicate Provable is easy to determine if its argument is 2+2=4, but difficult if its argument is Fermat's Last Theorem. A user might specify a theory of operationality for which

```
Arithmetic(p)  →  Operational(Provable(p)).
```

If a proof that ROE generalizes uses Provable(2+2=4), the resulting rule would include Provable as a condition of the generalization. However, Arithmetic— the weakest preconditions on the proof of Operational(Provable(2+2=4))— would also appear, preceding the Provable to guarantee that the learning result will only attempt `Provable` when the user's theory of operationality says it is operational.

14.5 ROE

The basic algorithm of ROE follows that of other implementations of EBG (e.g., [Hirsh, 1987; Kedar-Cabelli and McCarty, 1987]). The system attempts to prove that the instance is an example of the goal concept (such as `Safe-To-Stack(Obj1,Obj2)` above) by backward chaining on the goal through rules until training-instance facts are reached. However, each time a rule is used, it is simultaneously applied backward to the variablized goal concept (such as `Safe-To-Stack(v1,v2)`), creating in parallel with the instantiated proof the generalized proof from which the final rule is extracted. ROE differs from past implementations in that it proves predicates `Operational`. Whenever this occurs, ROE applies itself to the operationality proof, gathers the conditions of operationality, and includes them in the final learned rule before the condition imposed by the base-level proof.

If in the `Safe-To-Stack` example `Weight` were known to be operational when its first argument has small dimensions (e.g., so that it could be placed on a scale, guaranteeing that there will always be some easy way to determine `Weight`) rather than universally operational, `Weight` is used in the rule ROE creates because it is operational for `Obj1`, a box. But the unconditional use of `Weight` would not be correct, since a rule using `Weight` is only operational for objects with small dimensions. Therefore ROE includes in its final rule restrictions on the size of the first argument of `Safe-To-Stack` for which the rule is actually operational.

Thus if ROE had the rule

```
Small-Dimensions(x)  →  Operational(Weight(x,w)),
```

with the additional training instance fact `Small Dimensions(Obj1)` and operationality fact `Operational(Small Dimensions(x))`, it would learn the rule

```
Small-Dimensions(v1) ∧ Weight(v1,v3) ∧ Isa(v2,Endtable)
    ∧ Unprovable(Compute-Weight(v2,v4)) ∧ <(v3,5)
    → Safe-To-Stack(v1,v2)
```

by not only proving that `Safe-To-Stack` holds for the training instance, but also that each predicate used in the result, including `Weight`, is operational for the training instance. The generalized proof of operationality, as computed by ROE itself on the user's domain theory for operationality, determines that `Small-Dimensions` is a necessary condition on the operationality of `Weight`, and thus on the operationality of the final rule. ROE fails if there is no proof terminating in operational predicates, even if nonoperational proofs do exist. Furthermore, ROE checks operationality during proof creation to prune proofs of subgoals that would yield nonoperational results.

Small-Dimensions is only used in the learned rule if it is *also* operational. The predicates used in checking operationality, such as Small-Dimensions, must themselves be operational. Although it appears that ROE must be recursively applied on each subsequent level of operationality, the process does bottom out. ROE is only applied recursively when *rules* are used for operationality. If we simply know that Volume is operational, there is no need to apply ROE, since there is no reasoning taking place. Of course, if the user provides a definition of operationality that utilizes rules with the very predicates whose operationality is being tested, cyclic behavior can result. But in general no cyclic behavior need occur.

Note that there is no need to check that the additional conditions imposed by operationality are consistent with the other conditions of the generalization. All conditions appearing in the final result must have been true for the instance, regardless of whether they appear for the goal concept or for conditions of operationality. The only way contradictory conditions will appear in a learned rule is if there are contradictory facts supplied for the training instance.

14.6 GENERALITY OF RESULTS

The user's theory of operationality can cause ROE to form rules specialized beyond what is required by the domain theory alone. If a predicate is operational for specific argument values or when certain arguments are equal, the final rule must be made consistent with operationality. An operationality fact can force a constant to appear as the value of a predicate's argument (where a variable would have appeared) if the predicate is only operational for that value. For example (from [Mostow, 1983]), in a theory of card games Has-Card(Me,card) is operational (players can see their own cards), whereas the more general Has-Card (player,card) is not (players do not know what cards their opponents have). Operationality facts can similarly force two arguments to be equal, if necessary for operationality. For example, Like(x,x) might be operational, whereas the more general Like(y,x) is not (a person can determine whether he likes himself more easily than he can determine whether someone else likes him). Anything more general would be nonoperational at times. If the restriction imposed by operationality is not true for the training instance, ROE will instead continue its search for alternative proofs that will yield a generalization operational for the training instance.

ROE forms the operationality conditions from the proof of why the generalization was operational *for the instance*. The resulting full conditions of the generalization will cover those instances not only with the same base-level proof, but also with the same operationality proof. This need not cover all cases for which the rule is operational. The results of ROE are conservative—it will guarantee that the result is only applied to operational situations, restricting the rule to the extent that it may not consider using it on some other operational situation that requires a different proof of operationality. Thus not only do the additional conditions exclude nonoperational situations, they also may exclude operational situations that require a different proof.

ROE forms rules using the first successful operational predicates found. However, the selection of higher level nodes in an explanation as operational need not lead to the most general possible definitions as in standard EBG. For example, if the small dimensions of `Obj1` were inferred by the rule

```
Isa(x,Box) → Small-Dimensions(x),
```

with `Isa` operational instead of `Small-Dimensions`, ROE would form the rule

```
Isa(v1,Box) ∧ Weight(v1,v3) ∧ Isa(v2,Endtable)
  ∧ Unprovable(Compute-Weight(v2,v4)) ∧ <(v3,5)
  → Safe-To-Stack(v1,v2).
```

Despite the use of the more general predicate `Weight` that can be inferred from any rule that concludes `Weight`, this rule may or may not apply in as many situations as the rule from Section 14.2 that uses the volume-times-density `Weight` rule, since incorporating the conditions of operationality restricts the learned rule to boxes. This issue is considered further by Braverman and Russell [1988].

14.7 REMOVING CONDITIONAL OPERATIONALITY

An alternative approach to the problem of conditional operationality due to reasoning about operationality asks whether conditional operationality can be removed so that standard EBG techniques will apply, yielding correct results. Domain theories with conditionally operational predicates can always be rewritten using predicates that are universally operational or nonoperational. Operationality depends on the vocabulary in which a domain theory is expressed, and a new vocabulary can always be defined from the original one so that operationality is a universal property. For example, given the following new domain and operationality theories for `Safe-To-Stack`:

```
Not(Fragile(y)) → Safe-To-Stack(x,y)
Lighter(x,y) → Safe-To-Stack(x,y)
Weight(p1,w1) ∧ Weight(p2,w2) ∧ <(w1,w2)
  → Lighter(p1,p2)
Small-Dimensions(p) ∧ Op-Weight(p,w) → Weight(p,w)
Weight0(p,w) → Weight(p,w)
Weight0(p,w) → Op-Weight(p,w)
Compute-Weight(p,w) → Weight0(p,w)
Isa(p,Endtable) ∧ Unprovable(Compute-Weight(p,w))
  → Weight0(p,5)
Volume(p,v) ∧ Density(p,d) ∧ ×(v,d,w)
  → Compute-Weight(p,w)
```

```
Operational(Op-Weight(p,w))
Operational(Small-Dimensions(p))
Operational(Isa(x,o))
Operational(Unprovable(p))
Operational(<(x,y))
```

standard EBG will generate correct, universally operational results, with a domain theory equivalent to the original one, with no need for reasoning about operationality. For `Obj1` and `Obj2` EBG generates the rule

```
Small-Dimensions(v1) ∧ Op-Weight(v1,v3) ∧ Isa(v2,Endtable)
   ∧ Unprovable(Compute-Weight(v2,v4)) ∧ <(v3,5)
   → Safe-To-Stack(v1,v2).
```

Since `Op-Weight` is equivalent to `Weight` in the original theory, the resulting rules is equivalent to that given in Section 14.5.

The task of automating the reformulation process is an interesting problem in its own right, providing an alternative solution to conditional operationality due to reasoning about operationality. However, one shortcoming of the approach is that since operationality is now part of the domain theory, whenever operationality changes the entire theory must be reformulated again to reflect the new conditional operationality.

14.8 LIMITATIONS

This chapter has described how conditional operationality requires determining the conditions of operationality on the results of EBG. It further describes how this is done by one particular EBG system, ROE, for one class of conditional operationality, when it is defined using explicit theories of operationality. However, not all forms of operationality can use the approach taken here. The addition of new conditions may change the operationality analysis of the other conditions generated earlier. ROE assumes that the operationality of the new conditions can be tested independent of the other conditions imposed by the base-level proof of the goal concept.

For example, if the operationality criterion tests pattern-matching expenses, the addition of further conditions to a rule changes the overall pattern-matching costs, and thus changes the overall operationality of the rule. The new conditions cannot then be tested for operationality independent of the other conditions. A theory of operationality for entire rules could be tried and applied to the new, longer rule, but this process must be repeated again and again until the resulting rule is unconditionally operational. The difficulty is that there is no guarantee that the iterations will end. In the pattern-matching case costs can continue to increase as more conditions are added, taking the rule farther and farther from operationality.

14.9 RELATED WORK

ROE provides the capabilities for explicit reasoning about operationality, and thus has many similarities to MetaLEX [Keller, 1987]. MetaLEX reasons about and compares the operationality of competing definitions of a concept. Keller views learning systems as exploring a space of possible concept definitions. MetaLEX explicitly investigates the merit—operationality—of concept definitions with respect to the goals of learning. ROE can be viewed as a concrete instance of the ideas proposed by Keller. Keller argues for general reasoning about operationality; ROE provides a language and mechanism for doing so.

Similarly, Mostow's [1987, 1983] BAR system explicitly reasons about operationality. BAR explores a space of advice operationalizations using domain knowledge and a theory of operationality. Operationalizing the advice `Get void in suit s` for the card game "Hearts" is done by transforming the advice to something that matches the pattern `@IsAchievable` (i.e., that `IsAchievable` would succeed when evaluated on the operationalized advice). Domain-level rules and definitions are applied in searching the space of possible operationalizations.

The relevance of BAR to ROE is that it suggests how to get BAR-like behavior out of EBG, clarifying the distinction between operationalization as done by Mostow versus that done by EBG. A ROE version of BAR would use Mostow's domain knowledge for Hearts as a domain theory to analyze retrospectively a completed game in which some advice was warranted. ROE's theory of operationality would be based on BAR's operationality theory, and would state things like `Operational (Has(Me,card))` but not the more general `Operational(Has(player, card))`. The final rule learned by ROE would only use `Has` if its first argument is restricted to the agent using the rule. Other occurrences of `Has` (those not testing the agent's own cards) would require further processing to reach operational form since they cannot be proven operational for the training instance.

Finally, Braverman and Russell [1988] independently recognized the need to consider conditional operationality in their work on IMEX. Their technique allows conditional operationality if the conditions are themselves already part of the overall generalization. However, they do not impose further restrictions on the results of EBG to make a conditionally operational result operational, as is done by ROE.

14.10 CONCLUSION

This chapter has argued that since the generalizations created by explanation-based generalization may be conditionally operationality for finer grained definitions of operationality, the conditions on the operationality of a generalization should be determined and included with the generalization. ROE proves that the predicates used in a generalization are operational for the training instance on which it is based, and generalizes the proof of operationality to determine the weakest conditions on when the generalization should be used. These conditions are included in the results of ROE to restrict their use to situations in which they are operational. Reasoning about and generalizing operationality is accomplished by using ROE itself on a domain theory that concludes whether predicates are operational for whatever notion of operationality the user encodes.

ACKNOWLEDGMENTS

Discussions with and comments from Michael Braverman, Rich Keller, Jack Mostow, Armand Prieditis, Paul Rosenbloom, Stuart Russell, Devika Subramanian, and Monte Zweben were invaluable. An earlier draft of this chapter appeared elsewhere [Hirsh, 1988].

APPENDIX I   PROLOG IMPLEMENTATION OF ROE

ROE is based on the PROLOG implementation of MRS-EBG [Hirsh, 1987] given by Kedar-Cabelli and McCarty [1987], which uses a metainterpreter that simultaneously creates instantiated and generalized explanations.

The predicate `ebg(P,R)` is the top-level call to ROE. It creates a generalized version `G` of the goal `P`, and uses `ebg1` to do the major work, with the final rule bound to `R` at the end. The predicate `ebgs(P,Rs)` finds all results possible with ROE along each possible proof path.

```
ebg(P,R):-variablize(P,G),!,ebg1(P,G,Op),mkrule(G,Op,R).
ebgs(P,Rs):-variablize(P,G),!,bagof(R,ebgs1(P,G,R),Rs).
ebgs1(P,G,R):-ebg1(P,G,Op),mkrule(G,Op,R).
```

The core of ROE is `ebg1(P,G,C)`: `C` is the list of general conditions on `G` based on the proof of `P`. It applies rules in a depth-first, backward-chaining manner to both the instantiated (`P`) and generalized (`G`) form of goal predicates. The first clause applies ROE on each of a list of subgoals and combines the results. The second uses `ebgop` when a subgoal is operational. Otherwise backward-chaining occurs.

```
ebg1((PA,PB),(GA,GB),C):-!,ebg1(PA,GA,C1),ebg1(PB,GB,C2),
                 append(C1,C2,C).
ebg1(P,G,C):-operational(P),ebgop(P,G,C).
ebg1(P,G,C):-clause(G,GB),unprovable(GB==true),
             copy((G:-GB),(P:-PB)),ebg1(PB,GB,C).
```

When a subgoal is operational, `ebgop` determines its conditions of operationality. If the operationality is concluded without a rule (the first clause) ROE need not be recursively applied. When operationality is concluded by a rule, ROE is used recursively.

```
ebgop(P,G,[G]):-clause(operational(G),true),
                copy(operational(G),operational(P)),P.
ebgop(P,G,C):-clause(operational(G),GB),unprovable(GB==true),
              copy((operational(G):-GB),(operational(P):-PB)),
              ebg1(PB,GB,C1),P,append(C1,[G],C).
```

The predicate `variablize` generalizes predicates using `varargs` to variablize arguments. The clause for `copy`, which creates a copy of an expression with new variable names, is based on code by Shapiro and corrects a minor error in the Kedar-Cabelli and McCarty code (which occurs when `Old` and `New` are not unifiable, leaving temporary assertions in memory). Next, `mkrule` forms a rule given its head and a list of the predicates that will form its body. It uses `parenify` to convert the list of predicates into a parenthesized list of subgoals. Finally, `\+` is `Unprovable` in PROLOG-20.

```
variablize(P,G):-P=..[H|A],varargs(A,V),G=..[H|V],!.
varargs([],[]):-!.
varargs([X|Y],[A|B]):-varargs(Y,B).

copy(Old,New):-assert('$marker'(Old)),
               retract('$marker'(Temp)),
               !,New=Temp.

mkrule(H,[C],(H:-C)):-!.
mkrule(H,L,(H:-B)):-parenify(L,B).
parenify([X],X):-!.
parenify([X|T],(X,Y)):-parenify(T,Y).

unprovable(P):- \+ P.
```

References

Braverman, M.S. and Russell, S.J. 1988. Boundaries of operationality. In *Proceedings of the Fifth International Conference on Machine Learning*. Ann Arbor, MI. Morgan Kaufmann Publishers.

DeJong, G.F. and Mooney, R.J. 1986. Explanation-based learning: An alternative view. *Machine Learning*, 1:2, 145–176.

Hirsh, H. 1987. Explanation-based generalization in a logic-programming environment. In *Proceedings of the Tenth International Joint Conference on Artificial Intelligence* (pp. 221–227), Milan, Italy. Morgan Kaufmann Publishers.

————— , 1988. Reasoning about operationality for explanation-based learning. In *Proceedings of the Fifth International Conference on Machine Learning* (pp. 214—220), Ann Arbor, MI. Morgan Kaufmann Publishers.

Kedar-Cabelli, S.T. and McCarty, L.T. 1987. Explanation-based generalization as resolution theorem proving. In *Proceedings of the Fourth International Workshop on Machine Learning* (pp. 383–389), Irvine, CA. Morgan Kaufmann Publishers.

Keller, R.M. 1987. Concept learning in context. In *Proceedings of the Fourth International Workshop on Machine Learning* (pp. 376–382), Irvine, CA. Morgan Kaufmann Publishers.

Mitchell, T.M., Keller, R.M., and Kedar-Cabelli, S.T. 1986. Explanation-based generalization: A unifying view. *Machine Learning*, 1:1, 47–80.

Mostow, D.J. 1983. Operationalizing advice: A problem-solving model. In *Proceedings of the International Machine Learning Workshop* (pp. 110–116), Urbana-Champaign, IL.

————— , 1987. Searching for operational concept descriptions in BAR, MetaLEX, and EBG. In *Proceedings of the Fourth International Workshop on Machine Learning* (pp. 376–382), Irvine, CA. Morgan Kaufmann Publishers.

PART
FOUR

INTEGRATED
LEARNING SYSTEMS

15

THE UTILITY OF SIMILARITY-BASED LEARNING IN A WORLD NEEDING EXPLANATION

Michael Lebowitz
(Morgan Stanley and Company)

Abstract

A large portion of the research in machine learning has involved a paradigm of comparing many examples and analyzing them in terms of similarities and differences. The assumption is made, usually tacitly, that the resulting generalizations will have applicability to new examples. While such research has been very successful, it is by no means obvious why similarity-based generalizations should be useful, since they may simply reflect coincidences. Proponents of explanation-based learning—a knowledge-intensive method of examining single examples to derive generalizations based on underlying causal models—could contend that their methods are more fundamentally grounded, and that there is no need to look for similarities across examples. In this chapter, we present the issues, and then show why similarity-based methods are important. We include a description of the similarity-based system UNIMEM and present four reasons why robust machine learning must involve the integration of similarity-based and explanation-based methods. We argue that: (1) it may not always be practical or even possible to determine a causal explanation; (2) similarity usually implies causality; (3) similarity-based generalizations can be refined over time; (4) similarity-based and explanation-based methods complement each other in important ways.

15.1 INTRODUCTION

Until recently, machine learning has emphasized a single paradigm—the generalization of concepts through the comparison of examples in terms of similarities and differences. The assumption has been made, though often tacitly, that the generalization of similarities will lead to concepts that can be applied in other contexts. Despite its ubiquity, this paradigm has one real problem: There is no obvious reason why the underlying assumption should hold. In other fields people have called into doubt the utility of noticing similarities in the world and assuming them to be important. Naturalist Stephen Jay Gould, in discussing the nature of scientific discovery comments that:

> The human mind delights in finding pattern—so much so that we often mistake coincidence or forced analogy for profound meaning. No other habit of thought lies so deeply within the soul of a small creature trying to make sense of a complex world not constructed for it.
>
> "Into this Universe, and why not knowing // Nor whence, like water willy-nilly flowing" as the Rubaiyat says. No other habit of thought stands so doggedly in the way of any forthright attempt to understand some of the world's most essential aspects—the tortuous paths of history, the unpredictability of complex systems, and the lack of causal connection among events superficially similar.
>
> Numerical coincidence is a common path to intellectual perdition in our quest for meaning. [Gould, 1984]

Further doubt has been cast upon the use of similarity-based learning by a new methodology that has been developed in recent years: the extensive application of knowledge to single examples to determine the underlying mechanism behind an example, and the use of this causal explanation to derive generalized concepts. By learning from single examples, this knowledge-based approach calls into question the need for similarity-based approaches.

Despite Gould's warning and the recent successes of explanation-based methods, learning methods that concentrate on seeking out similarities have had remarkable success across a variety of tasks. Furthermore, as Gould implies above, people (and other creatures) do seem to be optimized for such learning. Given this evidence, it worth trying to explain why such methods work. In this chapter we will illustrate why similarity-based learning not only works, but is a crucial part of learning. For researchers using similarity-based methods, our main message is that people should be looking at the underlying rationale for such techniques; for those using explanation-based methods, we hope to illustrate the need to include similarity-based elements for robust learning.

15.2 EXPLANATION AND SIMILARITY: TWO APPROACHES TO LEARNING

Considerable research has been done involving *similarity-based learning* (SBL).[1] [Winston, 1972; 1980; Michalski, 1980; 1983; Michalski and Stepp, 1983; Lebowitz, 1983; 1986; Dietterich and Michalski, 1986] are just a few examples. Other examples can be found in [Michalski, *et al.*, 1983; 1986]. While there are many variations to such learning research, the basic idea is that a program takes a number of examples, compares them in terms of similarities and differences, and creates a generalized description by abstracting out similarities. A program given descriptions of Columbia University and Yale University and told that they were Ivy League universities and that the University of Massachusetts was not would define "Ivy League university" in terms of the properties that the first two examples had and that the third did not—e.g., as being private, expensive, and old. Similarity-based learning has been studied for cases where the input is specially prepared by a teacher; for unprepared input; where there are only positive examples; where there are both positive and negative examples; for a few examples; for many examples; for determining only a single concept at a time; and for determining multiple concepts. In a practical sense, SBL programs have learned by comparing examples more or less syntactically, using little "high-level" knowledge of their domains (other than in deciding how to represent each example initially).

In the settings where SBL has been used with teachers, it clearly makes sense that the concepts derived will be useful. We assume the teacher is trying to make a point. The cases we are concerned with, however, involve *learning by observation* where there is no teacher. Conceptual clustering [Michalski and Stepp, 1983] and our own concept formation work [Lebowitz, 1983; 1986] fall into this classification. Here we must consider more carefully why the methods developed produce useful concepts.

Explanation-based learning (EBL), in contrast, views learning as a knowledge-intensive activity, much like other tasks in artificial intelligence (AI). [DeJong, 1986; DeJong and Mooney, 1986; Ellman, 1985; Mitchell, 1983a; Mitchell, *et al.*, 1986; Mostow, 1983; Minton, 1984; Silver, 1986] are a few examples of explanation-based learning research. An EBL program takes a single example, builds up an explanation of how the various components relate to each other by using traditional AI understanding or planning methods, and then generalizes the properties of various components of the example as long as the explanation remains valid. What is left is then viewed as a generalized description of the example that can be applied in understanding further examples. This kind of learning is tremendously useful, as it allows

---

[1]Most of this work actually involved analysis in terms of both similarities and differences. We use the abbreviation SBL for simplicity.

generalized concepts to be determined on the basis of a single example. On the other hand, the building and analysis of explanations does require extremely detailed knowledge of the domain (which may minimize the need to learn). In addition, virtually all current EBL work is in the "perfect learner" paradigm that assumes that all input is consistent and fits the correct final generalization.

It is important to make clear here exactly the sense in which EBL is concept learning. It might be contended that all that is being done is the application of pre-existing information to a problem—unlike SBL, which is clearly a form of inductive learning. The key is in the generalization phase, where the EBL learner loosens constraints on its representation and determines whether the explanation that it has built up still holds. This generalized concept can then serve as a form of compiled knowledge that simplifies the processing of later input. This can be a way to learn structures such as frames [Minsky, 1975] and scripts [Schank and Abelson, 1977]. The view of using EBL to produce knowledge structures that make later processing more efficient has been called *operationalization* [Mostow, 1983]. Even though it might in some sense be possible to understand later examples just using low-level rules, realistically it is crucial to have a set of knowledge structures at various levels of complexity.

It does not make sense to consider learning in isolation from other elements of intelligent processing. While certain aspects of learning, e.g., curiosity, may not be in service of an immediate goal, at some point there must be a task involved to make use of what is learned. In general, the idea is for an organism or program to be able to carry out a task better (either be able to do more examples or do examples more efficiently) than it did before learning. It is particularly important to keep in mind the eventual presence of a task when considering concept learning, which has often been studied without regard to the future utility of the concepts created.

For most tasks that people or intelligent programs carry out, the most obvious way to be able to improve performance is to develop a *causal model* that explains how elements of the domain work. Such a model will allow the learner to *predict* what is likely to happen in later situations, which will clearly be useful. The model will allow the learner to *understand* further input. Although we will consider later whether it is possible in all domains, the construction of a causal model is clearly a worthy goal in learning. [Schank, 1975] and [Schank, 1986] present reasons for constructing explanatory causal models even in domains with incomplete information. Explanation-based learning methods strike directly at the problem of creating causal models. Similarity-based methods do not, but yet seem to lead to useful generalizations. This leads us to the central question of this chapter.

Having decided that the construction of a causal model for a domain is important, or perhaps even crucial, as part of learning, we are left with the key question, "Is there any role for similarity-based learning in a comprehensive learning model, and if so, why?" Even if we assume that there must be something to SBL, since, after all, so many people have worked on it with impressive results, we must ask why it works—why it helps a learner perform better. That generalizations from explanation-based learning are valid and useful makes sense intuitively, since they are derived from causal analyses. Similarity-based generalizations could just be the result of the coincidences that arise in a complex world.

Note that similarity-based learning is not merely an artifact of researchers in machine learning. As pointed out in the Gould quote above, people delight in noticing similarities in disparate situations. Indeed, in many ways human processing seems to be optimized for such learning. An anecdotal example immediately comes to mind: On one airline flying between New York and Boston, passengers are given a sequence number for boarding. On one round trip, I received the same sequence number going in each direction. Even though the first number was not in front of me when I received the second, I noticed the similarity immediately, despite the apparent irrelevance of the coincidence to my performance on later shuttle trips. Virtually everyone has experienced, and noticed, similar coincidences. When people have a powerful cognitive mechanism, there always seems to be a good reason. We will see shortly why the recognition of similarities is important, though—to reiterate, the utility is not obvious and should not simply be assumed by SBL researchers.

15.3 A SIMILARITY-BASED LEARNING PROGRAM: UNIMEM

We can most easily look at the utility of SBL in the context of a specific learning program. UNIMEM [Lebowitz, 1982; 1986a; 1986b] takes examples represented as sets of features (essentially property/facet/value triples) and automatically builds up a generalization hierarchy using similarity-based methods. It is not told in advance which examples to compare or what concepts to form, but instead learns by observation. One domain on which we have tested UNIMEM involves data about universities that was collected from students in an AI class at Columbia.[2]

Figure 15–1 shows the information used by UNIMEM for two universities, Columbia and Carnegie Mellon. Each university is represented by a set of triples that describe features of the university, a property name, facet, and value. So, Columbia is in New York state while Carnegie Mellon is in Pennsylvania. Both are urban and private, and Columbia has a 7:3 male/female ratio compared to Carnegie Mellon's 6:4. Some features, like quality of life, involve arbitrary numeric scales.

The goal of UNIMEM is to take similar instances and abstract them to form a hierarchy of generalizations that we hope are useful concepts and will be used to

---

[2]Other domains UNIMEM has been tested on include information about states of the United States, congressional voting records, software evaluations, biological data, football plays, universities, and terrorist events.

Property	Facet	Value for COLUMBIA	Value for CMU
STATE	VALUE	NEW-YORK	PENNSYLVANIA
LOCATION	VALUE	URBAN	URBAN
CONTROL	VALUE	PRIVATE	PRIVATE
MALE:FEMALE	VALUE	RATIO:7:3	RATIO:6:4
NO-OF-STUDENTS	VALUE	THOUS:5-	THOUS:5-
STUDENT:FACULTY	VALUE	RATIO:9:1	RATIO:10:1
SAT	VERBAL	625	600
SAT	MATH	650	650
EXPENSES	VALUE	THOUS$:10+	THOUS$:10+
%-FINANCIAL-AID	VALUE	60	70
NO-APPLICANTS	VALUE	THOUS:4-7	THOUS:4-7
%-ADMITTANCE	VALUE	30	40
%-ENROLLED	VALUE	50	50
ACADEMICS	SCALE:1-5	5	4
SOCIAL	SCALE:1-5	3	3
QUALITY-OF-LIFE	SCALE:1-5	3	3
ACAD-EMPHASIS	VALUE	LIB-ARTS	ENGINEERING

Figure 15–1: Information about two universities

organize the instances. The manner in which generalizations are combined to form a concept hierarchy is illustrated in Figure 15–2, using universities as examples. The concept hierarchy can be either the final output of the program or used for other understanding techniques. We can see in Figure 15–2 how the basic concept of a university is broken down into a number of more specialized versions and that the instances are stored with the generalizations. Both subgeneralizations and instances are recorded using some form of efficient indexing.[3] The generalizations themselve are sets of features abstracted from similar instances.

An important part of the UNIMEM methodology is that the more specialized versions of a given concept need not be mutually exclusive. In Figure 15–2, for example, the concepts of "universities in the northeast United States" and "universities with machine learning projects" are obviously not exclusive as one university could fit both descriptions. As a result of this, an instance can be stored in several places in memory. This is an important point, as most clustering techniques, conceptual or otherwise, force an example to appear in only one category. Forcing disjoint categories

---

[3] We have experimented both with discrimination networks [Feigenbaum, 1963; Charniak, *et al.*, 1980] and hash tables for indexing.

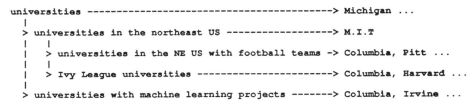

```
universities -----------------------------------------> Michigan ...
 |
 > universities in the northeast US ------------------> M.I.T
 |    |
 |    > universities in the NE US with football teams -> Columbia, Pitt ...
 |    |
 |    > Ivy League universities -----------------------> Columbia, Harvard ...
 |
 > universities with machine learning projects -------> Columbia, Irvine ...
```

Figure 15–2:   Hypothetical university generalization hierarchy

does not seem to be the best way to maximize the inferential power of the concepts created. For example, universities that have machine learning projects might share many other features, but those without such projects may not. Practically, the generalizations created by UNIMEM are overlapping, but do not seem to be extensively so.

Figure 15–2 shows a typical piece of UNIMEM's memory after about 150 universities have been processed, including Columbia and Carnegie Mellon. It shows one "top-level" generalization and several more specific versions of it. GND2, the top-level generalization in Figure 15–2, is a set of features that describe a class of universities. They include: average math SAT of 625, 60% of students getting financial aid, academic level 4 out 5, and so on. The generalization could be summarized as "high-quality private universities." At this point in the run, no instances were stored directly under GND2 as those from which it was created had all been used to create subgeneralizations. The UNIMEM representation includes only specific feature values, although the matching process does not require perfect correspondence. Generalized features involving ranges, such as "social level greater than 2" cannot be represented, though they would be a straightforward extension of UNIMEM.

As part of its representation, UNIMEM includes numeric ratings that indicate its confidence in each feature of each generalization. These numbers start at 0 and are adjusted upward and downward depending on whether future instances agree or disagree with the generalization. The values in parentheses in the right-hand column of Figure 15–2 are the confidence levels.[4] The features with "xxx" in the confidence field reached a sufficiently low confidence level and were removed from the generalization. Thus the last two features of GND2 are no longer really part of the generalization. By removing these features, UNIMEM came up with a generalization applicable to a wider range of instances, and yet that still provides useful information.

The numbers in square brackets indicate how often that feature appears in other generalizations. This information is used for *predictability* analysis, a method for de-

---

[4] Naturally, all the decimal places should not be taken too seriously. They are the product of the numeric evaluation procedure used and the version of LISP.

```
GND2
SAT                 MATH            625.0           [1]     (4.87)
%-FINANCIAL-AID     VALUE           60              [2]     (3.54)
ACADEMICS           SCALE:1-5       4               [3]     (15.0)
SOCIAL              SCALE:1-5       3               [3]     (15.0)
NO-APPLICANTS       ALUE            THOUS:4-         [4]     (9.0)
LOCATION            VALUE           URBAN           [6]     (15.0)
CONTROL             VALUE           PRIVATE         [6]     (15.0)
%-ENROLLED          VALUE           20                      (xxx)
SAT                 VERBAL          625.0                   (xxx)
[]

    GND18
    %-ADMITTANCE        VALUE           60              [1]     (-1.98)
    ACAD-EMPHASIS       VALUE           LIBERAL-ARTS    [1]     (-.3)
    MALE:FEMALE         VALUE           RATIO:1:1       [1]     (-.76)
    SAT                 MATH            592.5           [1]     (.09)
    EXPENSES            VALUE           THOUS$:10+      [2]     (4.5)
    QUALITY-OF-LIFE     SCALE:1-5       3.5             [2]     (3.0)
    [BARNARD BOSTON-UNIVERSITY]

    GND21
    SAT                 MATH            620.0           [1]     (1.2)
    EXPENSES            VALUE           THOUS$:7-10     [1]     (-2.7)
    %-ADMITTANCE        VALUE           35.0            [1]     (.9)
    SAT                 VERBAL          612.5           [1]     (3.37)
    QUALITY-OF-LIFE     SCALE:1-5       3.5             [2]     (3.0)
    [CARNEGIE-MELLON COLORADO-COLLEGE COLUMBIA UNIVERSITY-OF-CHICAGO]
```

Figure 15–3:   A university domain example

termining which features are likely to indicate a generalization's relevance. While we will not discuss predictability in depth here—it is discussed more fully in [Lebowitz, 1983]—the basic idea is that only the presence of some features of a concept in an instance indicate the relevance of the concept. These features can be identified quite easily using a generalization hierarchy as the features that do not appear in many generalizations (in a given context). Predictability analysis can also be important in determining causal explanations for generalizations as we will indicate below. A complicating factor in applying predictability is that combinations of features may be predictive while the individual ones are not. We are currently looking at ways to determine which combinations of features to consider.

Shown under GND2 in Figure 15–2 are two more specific version of it, GND18, which describes expensive, liberal arts schools, and GND21, which describes highly selective universities. These classes are not exclusive, and a university could plausibly fall under both. We can see that each of these generalizations has actual instances (universities) stored with it. When future instances are found to be described by these generalizations, they will be compared to the examples stored there. Also notice that UNIMEM is still very much in the process of evaluating these generalizations, as many of the confidence levels are quite low. Should most of its features be removed given enough examples, UNIMEM may conclude that GND18 does not describe a general enough class of instances to be worth keeping.

An interesting observation about GND18 and GND21 is that the names of the universities stored under GND18 both start with "B" and all those under GND21 with "C." This is, one assumes, purely a coincidence. Had we coded up "first letter of name" as a feature, UNIMEM would have added it to the generalizations. However, UNIMEM's confidence evaluation methods would eventually have removed the anomalies from the generalizations. Alternatively, this is the kind of coincidence that we would expect to be removed from a generalization by explanation-based methods.

The generalizations in Figure 15–2 are not that unlike those that might be formed by statistical clustering techniques, e.g., [Anderberg,1973]. The key differences are that UNIMEM's generalizations are done incrementally (without waiting for all the instances to be available) and that the use of conceptual modeling techniques leads to generalizations that make more intuitive sense and are more likely to correspond to actual regularities in the world than those produced by most statistical clustering techniques. The advantages of conceptual clustering are outlined by Michalski and Stepp [1983] and Fisher and Langley [1985].

The use of a hierarchy of generalizations as a method of memory organization allows efficient storage of information. Information in a generalization does not have to be repeated for each instance that it describes, since it can be inherited. The use of concept hierarchies with inheritance to intelligently and efficiently organize information about concepts is a standard one in AI. Semantic networks [Quillan, 1968], frame systems [Minsky, 1975], MOPs [Schank, 1982] (which inspired many aspects of our work, but, practically, involved smaller numbers of more complexly represented examples; see also [Kolodner, 1984]), among many other formalisms include inheritance. What is important here is the dynamic formation of the concept hierarchy, and its use to guide the development of further concepts.

The basic UNIMEM concept-formation process makes direct use of the memory organization that has been defined. Before beginning to describe the UNIMEM incorporation algorithm we should note that the algorithm includes a number of adjustable parameters, noted by a superscript P in the text. We fully parameterized the program since we do not wish to take any given number too seriously. So, when we mention a "small" value, "small" is simply a parameter that a user can set. We do, of course, have to set all the parameters.

At the top level, the structure of UNIMEM's update algorithm is:

- Take new input instance (as list of features).
- Search the generalization hierarchy for the most specific GEN-NODE(s) describing the instance by calling SEARCH(<u>root node, input features</u>).
- Add the new instance to the node or nodes found by SEARCH, generalizing if possible by calling UPDATE(<u>most-specific-node, input features</u>).

As UNIMEM processes each new instance, it first finds the most specific generalizations that describe it. UNIMEM's memory can be thought of as a large discrimination net [Feigenbaum, 1963; Charniak, *et al.*, 1980], so it starts with the most general node and does a type of controlled depth-first search to find the most specific generalization (or generalizations) that legitimately describe the new instance. When the search begins, none of the features have yet been accounted for. As UNIMEM searches down the generalization tree, features are excluded from the unexplained list as they are accounted for by generalizations. During the search, UNIMEM also updates feature confidence levels.

The major steps of the function SEARCH applied to <u>gen-node</u> and <u>unexplained features</u> are:

- Increase confidence in any features of <u>gen-node</u> also in <u>unexplained features</u>. Decrease the confidence of those that contradict it. Delete any features with confidence levels that go low enough[P].
- If the features in <u>unexplained features</u> are not "close enough"[P] to those in <u>gen-node</u> to assume that it describes the instance then return the empty list.
- Otherwise, for each potentially relevant sub-gen-node, <u>sx</u>, of <u>gen-node</u> (determined using the sub-gen-node index) call SEARCH(<u>sx</u>,[<u>unexplained features</u> − gen-node features]).
- If SEARCH returns a list of nodes that describe the new instance for any <u>sx</u>, then return the union of those lists.
- Otherwise, return the singleton list of <u>gen-node</u>.

During the search process, feature values can do more than match or mismatch—they can exist in various degrees of closeness. Although we developed categorization algorithms for numeric input that allowed a "match or no match" regimen to work [Lebowitz, 1985], UNIMEM currently makes use of distance *metrics* of the sort used in statistical clustering techniques, but for individual features, not whole instances. Instead of values simply matching or not, we allow the quality of matches to vary between 0 (perfect mismatch) and 1 (perfect match).[5] This produces an effect much like the use of a category utility function as described in [Gluck and Corter,

---

[5] The system is set up so that the user can easily define different metrics for various features, if desired.

1985] and applied to conceptual clustering in [Fisher, 1986], except still allowing multiple classification.

In order to utilize distance metrics, when UNIMEM matches a new instance to a generalization, it asks whether the combined distances of the features in the generalization from those in the new instance is small enough[P] to assume that the generalization "describes" the instance.[6] This allows the generalization to be used even if there are some small differences from the instance. Contradicting features simply override the values in the generalization. This contrasts with many learning techniques that assume that all the features of any generalization are necessarily true for each instance of it. Allowing contradiction does potentially leave UNIMEM open to problems of the sort described by Brachman [1985], e.g., describing an instance as "an Ivy League-type school except it's not in the East, not private, not expensive...." However, as long as we keep the allowed-difference parameter small, this does not seem to happen.

Once the best location for a new instance is found, before it is indexed under that generalization, the instance is compared against instances already stored there to determine whether further generalizations should be made. UNIMEM looks for other instances that have some features in common with the new one. If there are "enough" features in common[P], a new concept is generalized, based on the standard SBL assumption that it represents a meaningful underlying relation about the world, and the contributing instances indexed there. If no similar existing instances are found, the new instance is simply stored under the existing generalization.

The main steps in the UPDATE of an <u>new-instance</u> to a <u>gen-node</u> are:

- Define <u>new features</u> as the features of <u>new-instance</u> that are not part of <u>gen-node</u> (or its parent nodes). This information is retained from SEARCH.
- Look at the set of instances currently stored under <u>gen-node</u>. If none of these instances share enough else in common[P] with <u>new-instance</u> to warrant a new generalization then store <u>new-instance</u> under <u>gen-node</u>.
- Otherwise, for each instance with enough in common with <u>new-instance</u>, create a new gen-node with any members of <u>new features</u> with values similar to the instance and:
  - Store the new gen-node in the <u>gen-node</u>'s sub-gen-node list.
  - Store both instances under the new gen-node.
  - Remove the old instance from the original gen-node.

------

[6] We also add in a penalty for any feature of the generalization simply missing from the instance. This is possible since instance descriptions can be incomplete in UNIMEM.

In deciding which features to include in a generalization, UNIMEM will select any with values that are close^P (including exact matches, of course). In the case where features have close, but not identical values, UNIMEM includes the feature in the generalization, giving it an "average" value appropriate for that feature (typically the arithmetic or geometric mean for continuous data and one of the two values for ordinal or nominal data).

15.4 THE KEY QUESTION

Having seen the kinds of processing performed by UNIMEM for the university domain, we will consider what it would mean in general to "understand" or learn from the examples in Figure 15–1. While the exact nature of understanding would depend on the ultimate task that we had in mind, presumably what a person or system learning from these examples would be after is a causal model that relates the various features to each other.

In understanding Figure 15–1, we might wish to know how the fact that both universities are private relates to the fact that they are both expensive or why Carnegie Mellon offers financial aid to more people. A causal model that answers questions of this sort would be extremely useful for almost any task involving universities. Typical of the causation that we would look for is, for example, that private universities get less government support and hence have to raise more money through tuition. (At least that is how private universities explain it!) Similarly, a model might indicate that Carnegie Mellon's emphasis on engineering leads to the acceptance of more students who need financial aid. Notice, however, that it will certainly not be possible to build a complete causal model solely from the information in Figure 15–1, but will require additional domain knowledge.

An EBL program would create a low-level causal model of a university using whatever methods were available and then would use the model to develop a generalized concept. For example, it might decide that the Columbia explanation could be generalized by removing the requirement of being in New York state and by allowing the numeric values to vary within ranges, if none of these changes would affect the underlying explanation. It might be, however, that the liberal arts emphasis is crucial for some aspect of the explanation. In any case, by relaxing constraints in the representation, an EBL program would develop—using a single, causally motivated example—a generalized concept that may apply to a wide range of situations.

Let us now compare the desired causal explanation with the kind of generalization made by UNIMEM. Figure 15–2 showed several generalizations that UNIMEM had made from the university representations in Figure 15–1 (among others). They simply consisted of sets of features values that the instances shared (or had similar values for). Presumably these generalizations would be used in processing information about other universities. If we identified an instance where a generalization was thought to be relevant, we would assume that any of the generalization's features that were not known would apply to the instance. The assumption is made by all similarity-based learning programs, including UNIMEM, that they have created usable concepts from which default values may be inherited. Even when learning is described in terms of classification, the task only makes sense if there is ultimately default inference involved.

We can now state our problem quite clearly in terms of the UNIMEM generalizations: *What reason do we have to believe that a new example that fits part of a similarity-based generalization will have the rest of the features?* With explanation-based methods we at least have the underlying causal model as justification for making this sort of inference. But what is the inferential support for similarity-based generalizations?

15.5 ELEMENTS OF A SOLUTION

There are four main elements to our explanation of why SBL produces generalized concepts that can be profitably applied to other problems, and why it should be so used:

- While the goal of learning is indeed a causal model, it is often not possible to determine underlying causality, and even where it is possible it may not be practical.
- Similarity usually implies causality and is much easier to determine.
- There are ways to *refine* generalizations to mitigate the effects of coincidence.
- Explanation-based and similarity-based methods complement each other in crucial ways.

15.5.1 Causality Cannot Always Be Determined

In order to achieve their impressive results, the EBL methods that have been developed to date assume that a complete model of a domain is available and thus a full causal explanation can be constructed, although discussion about incomplete models has begun to appear; e.g., [Mitchell, *et al.*, 1986; DeJong and Mooney, 1986]. In addition, it is assumed that it is always computationally feasible to determine the explanation of any given example. While these assumptions may be acceptable for some learning tasks, they do not appear reasonable for situations where we are dealing with incomplete, complex, possibly inconsistent data—characteristics of most real-world problems. It is also unreasonable to expect to have a complete domain model available for a new domain that we are just beginning to explore. Even in our university example, it is hard imagine all the information being available to build a complete model.

Most EBL work has not addressed these issues. Some of the domains used, like integration problems [Mitchell, 1983a], logic circuits [Mitchell, 1983b; Ellman,

1985] or chess games [Minton, 1984] do indeed have complete domain models, and the examples used are small enough for the explanation construction to be tractable. Even in a domain such as the news stories of [DeJong, 1986; DeJong and Mooney, 1986], the assumption is made, perhaps with less assurance, that it is always possible to build up a complete explanation.

In domains where a detailed explanation cannot reasonably be constructed, a learner can only rely on similarity-based methods. By looking for similarities, the learner can at least bring some regularity to its knowledge base. The noticing of co-occurrence is possible even the absence of a complete domain model. Further, much research, including our own, has shown that SBL can be done efficiently in a variety of different problem situations. In the university example of Section 15.3, UNIMEM was able to come up with a variety of similarity-based generalizations with minimal domain information. Further, as we noted above, people seem to be optimized for SBL.

15.5.2 Similarity Usually Implies Causality

The regularity that is detected using SBL is not worthwhile if it cannot be used to help cope with further examples. Such help is not likely if there is no connection between the similarities and the underlying causal explanation. Fortunately, such a connection will usually exist.

Put as simply as is possible, similarities among examples usually occur because of some underlying causal mechanism. Clearly if there is a consistent mechanism, it will produce consistent results that can be observed as similarities. While the infinite variety of the world will also produce many coincidental similarities, it is nonetheless true that among the observed similarities are the mechanisms that we desire.

So, in the air travel sequence number example used above, while it is almost certain that the duplicate seat numbers I received were coincidental, if there was a mechanism involving seat numbers, say the numbers were distributed in alphabetical order, it would manifest itself in this sort of coincidence. Similarly, when discussing the university domain, we indicated possible causal mechanisms that would lead to the kind of schools that were described.

Two recent "real-world" examples illustrate how causal understanding frequently relates to similarity-based processing. The first involves scientific research, an attempt to understand a complex meteorological phenomenon, and the second an investigation into a mysterious crime. In Section 15.5.4 we will show how explanation and similarity can be integrated in UNIMEM.

In recent years weather researchers have been trying to explain a set of possibly related facts. Specifically: (1) the average temperature in 1981 was very high; (2)

the El Chichon volcano erupted spectacularly in early 1982; (3) El Niño (a warm Pacific current) lasted an exceptionally long time starting in mid-1982; (4) there have been severe droughts in Africa since 1982.

One might expect researchers to immediately attempt to construct a causal model that explains all these phenomena. However, weather systems are extremely complex, and by no means fully understood. Author Gordon Williams, writing in *The Atlantic Monthly*, discusses the attempt to gain understanding as follows: "How could so much human misery in Africa be caused by an errant current in the Pacific? *Records going back more than a century show that the worst African droughts often come in El Niño years.*" (Emphasis added.) Furthermore, Williams quotes climate analyst Eugene Rasmusson as saying, "It's disturbing because we don't understand the process" [Williams, 1986].

We can see clearly in this example that although the ultimate learning goal is a causal model, the construction of such a model is not immediately possible. So, researchers began by looking for correlations (although some sort of simple explanatory model may have been used to select features to look at). They expect correlations to lead eventually to deeper understanding.

The second example involves investigators trying to determine how certain extra-strength Tylenol capsules became laced with poison. *The New York Times* of February 16, 1986 reported:

> Investigators tracing the routes of two bottles of Extra-Strength Tylenol containing cyanide-laced capsules have found that both were handled at the same distribution center in Pennsylvania two weeks apart last summer. Federal officials and the product's manufacturer said that the chance that the tainting occurred at the distribution facility was remote, but the finding prompted investigators to examine the possibility as part of their inquiry. [McFadden, 1986]

This is another case where a causal explanation is desired, and yet there is not enough information available to construct one. So, the investigators began by looking for commonalities among the various poisoned capsules. Again a crude model may have helped select relevant features. When they found the distribution facility in common, that became an immediate possible contributor to the explanation. Although no final explanation was discovered, it is clear that the explanation process began with the noticing of similarities.

There is one further connection between noticing similarities and generating explanations that is worth making. This involves the idea of *predictability*, which was mentioned earlier. It turns out that the kinds of similarities that are noticed provide clues not only to what features should be involved in an explanation but what the direction of causality might be (e.g., what causes what). As we have described elsewhere [Lebowitz, 1983; 1986c], features that appear in just a few generalizations, which we call *predictive*, are the only ones that indicate a generalization's relevance to a given situation, and, further, are those likely to be the *causes* in an underlying explanation. This becomes clear when we realize that a feature present in many different situations cannot cause the other features in any single generalization, or it would cause the same features to appear in *all* the other generalizations that it is in.

In the weather example above, if we knew of many generalizations involving droughts, but only one with a volcano, then the volcano might cause the drought, but the drought could not cause the volcano. Of course, it may be that neither direction of causality is right, there being a common cause of both, but at least predictability provides a starting point.

The power of predictability is that it can be determined quite simply, basically as a by-product of the normal SBL process. The various indexing schemes used in a generalization-based memory allow the simple counting of features in context. While there are many problems to be explored, particularly that of predictive combinations of features, the ability to know the likely initial causes when determining a mechanism is an important advantage of SBL. Further, even when no explanation can be found, the use of predictability often allows us to make predictions from a generalization at the correct moments, even without any deep understanding of the generalization

15.5.3 Refining Generalizations

The third part of our explanation as to the utility of similarity-based learning is that generalizations, once made, are not immutable—they can be *refined* in the light of later information. This means that the aspects of a generalizations that are due to coincidence can be removed. As indicated in our description of UNIMEM's learning algorithm, we have developed various techniques for doing this that work essentially by noticing during processing when various elements of a generalization are contradicted by new examples. If we remove the features that are frequently contradicted, we have a concept that is more widely applicable and still contains meaningful information.

As an example of this, we will look again at our university generalizations (Figure 15–2 from Section 15.3). Suppose that there were a wide range of universities with most of the features of GND2, but with different levels of SAT verbal score. This contradiction of the SAT score in the original generalization would have prevented it from being applicable. However, our refinement methods allowed UNIMEM to remove this feature, leaving a more widely applicable generalization. In this way similarity-based methods can overcome some of the coincidences that might seem to require explanation-based methods. Notice, however, that UNIMEM makes this refinement without having any real idea of why it is doing so, other than the pragmatic rationale that it allows the generalization to fit more examples, but does not reduce it so much that it carries no information.

15.5.4 Integrated Learning

The final element of our analysis of the importance of similarity-based methods lies in the need for an integrated approach employing both similarity-based and explanation-based approaches. This point is really a corollary of the relation between similarity and causality described in Section 15.5.2.

The basic idea is to use EBL primarily upon the generalizations that are found using SBL rather than trying to explain every aspect of every instance. This drastically cuts down the search necessary for constructing an explanation, particularly in domains where we have very little specific knowledge and have to rely on general rules for the explanations. Basically, we use SBL as a bottom-up control on the top-down processing of EBL.

The "real-world" weather and crime investigation examples in Section 15.5.2 illustrate clearly how human problem solvers make use of this form of integrated learning—trying to explain the coincidences that are noted, rather than explaining every element of a situation from scratch. We will describe briefly how we have implemented a simple form of such integrated learning for UNIMEM. More details can be found in [Lebowitz, 1986c]. This implementation was done in a domain of congressional voting records.

We used for this simple example of integrated learning a "backward-chaining" explanation mechanism that applies simple rules to the generalizations that are made by UNIMEM. To apply explanation-based methods, we must supply rules that capture our initial understanding of the domain. The obvious way to do this for UNIMEM is with implications that capture hypothesized low-level causal connections among features. We have rules that indicate that the presence of one set of features causes the presence of another set of features, i.e., $F_c \rightarrow F_r$. Such rules can be used in understanding the causality underlying a set of features in one of two ways: (1) from the presence of one feature (F_c) we "explain" the presence of another (F_r); (2) from the known absence of one feature (F_r) "explain" the absence of another feature (F_c) whose presence would have forced the presence of the first.

The second usage of our rules is particularly important in "closed-world" domains, like the congressional votes in our example. Absences are easy to detect; a "yes" vote by a given congressman indicates conclusively that a "no" vote did not occur. For example, one of our rules is that "a congressman from a state with a major defense industry will vote against the MX-cut." Using this rule, we can "explain" a "no" MX-cut vote from a defense industry in the congressman's state. We can also "explain" the lack of a defense industry from a "yes" MX-cut vote, although the complete underlying causality is, of course, more complicated. We cannot, though, explain a "yes" MX-cut vote from the absence of a defense industry (the rules are one-directional).

```
(STATE TYPE RURAL) (STATE INDUSTRY LOWTECH) =>
  (STATE VOTERS PRO-WILDLIFE)
(STATE TYPE RURAL) => (STATE SIZE (< SIZ4:6))
(STATE INDUSTRY DEFENSE) => (MX-CUT VOTE A)
(DISTRICT TYPE BOOMDIST) => (DISTRICT POP-DIR UP)
(NOT (DISTRICT PHILOSOPHY FREE-ENT)) => (HOSP-COST-CONT VOTE F)
(DISTRICT PHILOSOPHY FREE-ENT) (DISTRICT PHILOSOPHY HIGH-TECH) =>
  (DISTRICT TYPE BOOMDIST)
```

Figure 15–4: Rules about the congressional district voting record domain

Figure 15–4 illustrates a few of the rules used in the experiments described here. It is important to recognize that in this experiment we were primarily trying to indicate how causal explanation rules could be applied to SBL learning. While we tried to make the rules plausible, their details are not critical to this presentation. Although the rules were not specifically created to explain just this one generalization, they were created with an eye on a small number of examples. Each rule indicates that if the features on the left of the "=>" describe a congressional district then they can be used to plausibly explain the features on the right. The first rule, for example, indicates that we believe that a rural state with low-tech industry will be pro-wildlife.

The rules in Figure 15–4 indicate a believed direction of causality for relations among features. They reflect an informal level of explanation that people often use. The rules may hide a number of steps in the true underlying causal mechanism. This is quite important when we are using the rules in a contrapositive sense, since a full explanation then involves what would have happened in other cases. Note that we do *not* view the rules as being guaranteed correct. Rather, they are considered to be heuristic and tentative, representing our best, current information about the domain. This would be the best we could do for many domains.

With initial rules in hand, UNIMEM can engage in a simplified form of EBL. We have ignored so far the problem of deciding when during SBL a generalization should be explained, and simply show how we would process a typical generalization. Figure 15–5 shows one generalization made by UNIMEM. It describes congressional districts that gained population since the last census, that are located in medium-sized states with low tax rates, high farm value, and low minority population, and where the congressman voted "yes" on the windfall profits and draft votes and "no" on the hospital cost-containment and MX-cut votes.

As mentioned earlier, an EBL analysis of GND1 would begin by developing a plausible causal explanation of the various features. Finding such an explanation would be nontrivial, as many different rules would apply at each stage of the analy-

```
GND1
WIND-TAX-LIM      VOTE       F         [1]      (16)
DRAFT             VOTE       F         [1]      (9)
HOSP-COST-CONT    VOTE       A         [2]      (12)
MX-CUT            VOTE       A         [2]      (16)
STATE             TAXES      TAX2:5    [2]      (18)
DISTRICT          POP-DIR    UP        [3]      (26)
STATE             FARM-VAL   FAR5:6    [4]      (20)
STATE             SIZE       SIZ3:6    [4]      (10)
STATE             MIN-PCT    MIN1:2    [6]      (44)
```

Figure 15–5:   Another typical generalization—GND1

sis. Indeed, in some cases, the rules may be mutually contradictory, due to their heuristic nature.

The UNIMEM analysis tries to build an explanation of why the features it believes are predictive explain the other features, in terms of the production rules. It then proceeds through an iterative procedure that tries to explain apparently predictive features that were not involved in the explanation. All this is done using simple backward-chaining methods that in parallel try to connect one set of features to another. Figure 15–6 shows the output from this analysis displayed in graphical form, with the arrows indicating features believed to cause others. The features marked with "c" are the assumed causes (initially determined using predictability); the results are marked with "r." The links marked with *'s involve the application of the contrapositive forms of the original rules. That is, the absence of the right side of the rule (usually the presence of a contradictory feature, often an opposite vote) is being used to explain the negation of the left side.

Figure 15–6 makes clear that we have found the kinds of relationships we are looking for. We see that since GND1 describes low tax states, the states are probably rural, small and high income. The windfall and hospital cost-containment votes would only be cast by congressmen from districts that are high-tech-conscious and pro-free-enterprise. Such districts would normally be "boom" areas. This, in turn, implies that the districts are likely to have high farm values and rising populations (due to the "high-tech" boom). The low minority level is simply a default (46 of the 50 states fall in this class). If it seems a little strange that the explanation has several votes at the beginning of the causal chains (as if they directly caused properties of the states), notice that in each case the relevant rules are being used in contrapositive form, meaning that there are really underlying factors inhibiting the opposite vote.

The current version of UNIMEM does not follow up on the causal explanation that it has built. If we were to continue the EBL process, we would use the explanation built for the specific generalization and see if we could abstract it and determine

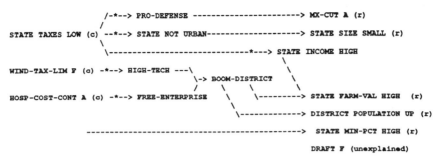

Figure 15–6:   An "explanatory" analysis of GND1

the essential features of the explanation. So, for example, we might infer that the windfall tax-limit vote is not necessary to conclude that a district is interested in high tech, but instead any positive vote on limiting taxes is satisfactory. We would, of course, need further presupplied domain knowledge to allow us to analyze in this way (although our existing rules can be used to some degree; for example, the rules that require only a range of values, e.g., less that than the third category out of 6, would allow us to relax a specific category to a range).

There are several ways we could use our explanatory analysis directly within UNIMEM, or indeed as part of any integrated learning system. The most obvious is to drop from a generalization any features that were not involved in our analyses (e.g., the draft vote in the example above). This adds a new way to detect coincidence in generalizations. This is the way that we would hope to remove the "B" and "C" college name generalizations that we ran into earlier. In addition, features that we thought were predictive, but did not explain anything else and were explainable themselves (MX-cut vote was an example of this), could be marked as nonpredictive, even though they appear to be predictive from their frequency in different generalizations. This has a significant effect on the application of generalizations to new instances, as only predictive features can indicate a generalization's potential relevance. In this case, a "no" MX-cut vote would no longer be used to indicate the applicability of GND1. We can also imagine splitting up generalizations based on the explanations, and other uses involving the details of the analysis.

There are several important points to be gleaned from the example in this section. Predictability provided significant control on the explanation process. We did not have to use brute force and try all the possible explanatory rule sequences. If we had a more detailed knowledge of the domain with very specific explanatory rules, this would not be so important; but in a new domain, where rules are very general and perhaps contradictory, it is crucial. We can also see how the SBL and EBL processes naturally complement each other. SBL gives us generalizations to explain and help control the explanation. The explanation, in addition to the main EBL purpose of detailed understanding, can be used to make further SBL processing more efficient.

15.6 CONCLUSION

We have shown in this paper a number of ways that similarity-based learning and explanation-based learning can each contribute to the ultimate learning goal of building a coherent causal explanation of a situation. Indeed, we feel both methods are necessary. While we would not contend that first generalizing and then explaining is always the way to go—in fact, we have begun a project involving learning from a series of terrorist bombings where we first do a simple explanation for each event, then generalize, then attempt a more detailed explanation—we do think that such an approach is correct for domains where our knowledge is quite limited.

From the analysis we have provided in this paper, it should not be surprising that people seem to be optimized for noticing similarities, as such processing leads to the understanding that helps deal with the world. Generalizations made by noticing similarities can be used when explanations are not available (since there usually is an underlying causal mechanism) and can help derive explanations. Our computer programs should equally be equipped with both methods. Similarity-based learning is definitely not the path to perdition.

ACKNOWLEDGMENTS

This research was supported in part by the Defense Advanced Research Projects Agency under contract N00039-84-C-0165 and in part by the United States Army Research Institute under contract MDA903-85-0103. Comments by Kathy McKeown, Yves Kodratoff, and Jerry DeJong on an earlier draft of this paper were quite useful. This paper is a substantially expanded version of one that appeared in the Proceedings of AAAI-86, while the author was a member of the Department of Computer Science at Columbia University.

References

Anderberg, M.R. 1973. *Cluster Analysis for Applications*. Academic Press, New York.

Brachman, R.J. 1985. I lied about the trees. *AI Magazine* 6:80–93.

Charniak E., Riesbeck, C.K., and McDermott, D.V. 1980. *Artificial Intelligence Programming*. Lawrence Erlbaum Associates, Hillsdale, New Jersey.

DeJong, G.F. 1986. An approach to learning from observation. *Machine Learning: An Artificial Intelligence Approach, Volume II*. Morgan Kaufmann, San Mateo, CA, pp. 571–590.

DeJong, G.F. and Mooney, R. 1986. Explanation-based learning: An alternative view. *Machine Learning* 1(2):145–176.

Dietterich, T.G. and Michalski, R.S. 1986. Learning to predict sequences. *Machine Learning: An Artificial Intelligence Approach, Volume II*. Morgan Kaufmann, San Mateo, CA, pp. 63–106.

Ellman, T. 1985. Generalizing logic circuit designs by analyzing proofs of correctness. In *Proceedings of the Ninth International Joint Conference on Artificial Intelligence*, pp. 643–646. Morgan Kaufmann, San Mateo, CA.

Feigenbaum, E.A. 1963. The simulation of verbal learning behavior. *Computers and Thought*. McGraw-Hill, New York, pp. 297–309.

Fisher, D. 1986. The acquisition of basic level concepts via incremental conceptual clustering. Technical Report, Irvine Computational Intelligence Project.

Fisher, D. and Langley, P. 1985. Approaches to conceptual clustering. In *Proceedings of the Ninth International Joint Conference on Artificial Intelligence*, pp. 691–697. Morgan Kaufmann, San Mateo, CA.

Gluck, M. and Corter, J. 1985. Information, uncertainty, and the utility of categories. In *Proceedings of the Seventh Annual Conference of the Cognitive Science Society*, pp. 283–287. Irvine, CA.

Gould, S.J. 1984. The rule of five. *Natural History* 93(10):14–23, October.

Kolodner, J.L. 1984. *Retrieval and Organizational Strategies in Conceptual Memory: A Computer Model*. Lawrence Erlbaum Associates, Hillsdale, New Jersey.

Lebowitz, M. 1982. Correcting erroneous generalizations. *Cognition and Brain Theory* 5(4):367–381.

———— , 1983. Generalization from natural language text. *Cognitive Science* 7(1):1–40.

———— , 1985. Classifying numeric information for generalization. *Cognitive Science* 9(3):285–308.

———— , 1986a. Concept learning in a rich input domain: Generalization-based Memory. *Machine Learning: An Artificial Intelligence Approach, Volume II*. Morgan Kaufmann, San Mateo, CA, pp. 193–214.

————, 1986b. UNIMEM, a general learning system: An overview. In *Proceedings of ECAI-86*. Brighton, England.

————, 1986c. Integrated learning: Controlling explanation. *Cognitive Science* 10(2):219–240.

McFadden, R. 1986. Two bottles of poisoned Tylenol were shipped by the same distributor. *New York Times* 135(February 16):1.

Michalski, R.S. 1980. Pattern recognition as rule-guided inductive inference. *IEEE Transactions on Pattern Analysis and Machine Intelligence* 2(4):349–361.

————, 1983. A theory and methodology of inductive learning. *Artificial Intelligence* 20:111–161.

Michalski, R.S. and Stepp, R.E. 1983. Automated construction of classifications: Conceptual clustering versus numerical taxonomy. *IEEE Transactions on Pattern Analysis and Machine Intelligence* 5(4):396–409.

Michalski, R.S., Carbonell, J.G. and Mitchell, T.M. (Eds.). 1983. *Machine Learning, An Artificial Intelligence Approach*. Morgan Kaufmann, San Mateo, CA.

————, 1986. *Machine Learning, An Artificial Intelligence Approach, Volume II*. Morgan Kaufmann, San Mateo, CA.

Minsky, M. 1975. A framework for representing knowledge. *The Psychology of Computer Vision*. McGraw-Hill, New York.

Minton, S. 1984. Constraint-based generalization. In *Proceedings of the Fourth National Conference on Artificial Intelligence*, pp. 251–254. Morgan Kaufmann, San Mateo, CA.

Mitchell, T.M. 1983a. Learning and problem solving. In *Proceedings of the Eighth International Joint Conference on Artificial Intelligence*, pp. 1139–1151. Morgan Kaufmann, San Mateo, CA.

————, 1983b. An intelligent aid for circuit redesign. In *Proceedings of the Third National Conference on Artificial Intelligence*, pp. 274–278. Morgan Kaufmann, San Mateo, CA.

Mitchell, T.M., Keller, R.M. and Kedar-Cabelli, S.T. 1986. Explanation-based generalization: A unifying view. *Machine Learning* 1(1):47–80.

Mostow, J. 1983. Operationalizing advice: A problem-solving model. In *Proceedings of the 1983 International Machine Learning Workshop*, pages 110–116. Urbana-Champaign, Illinois.

Quillian, M.R. 1968. Semantic memory. *Semantic Information Processing*. MIT Press, Cambridge, MA.

Schank, R.C. 1975. The structure of episodes in memory. *Representation and Understanding: Studies in Cognitive Science*. Academic Press, New York, pp. 237–272.

———— , 1982. *Dynamic Memory: A Theory of Reminding and Learning in Computers and People*. Cambridge University Press, New York.

———— , 1986. *Explanation Patterns*. Lawrence Erlbaum Associates, Hillsdale, New Jersey.

Schank, R.C. and Abelson, R.P. 1977. *Scripts, Plans, Goals and Understanding*. Lawrence Erlbaum Associates, Hillsdale, New Jersey.

Silver B. 1986. Precondition analysis: Learning control information. *Machine Learning: An Artificial Intelligence Approach, Volume II*. Morgan Kaufmann, San Mateo, CA, pp. 647–670.

Williams, G. 1986. The weather watchers. *Atlantic* 257:69 –73.

Winston, P.H. 1972. Learning structural descriptions from examples. *The Psychology of Computer Vision*. McGraw-Hill, New York, pp. 157–209.

———— , 1980. Learning and reasoning by analogy. *Communications of the ACM* 23:689–702.

COMMENTARY:

SOME ISSUES IN CONCEPT LEARNING

Larry Rendell
(University of Illinois)

1 INTRODUCTION

This commentary is a distillation of the discussion that followed Lebowitz's presentation of his paper "The Utility of Similarity-based Learning in a World Needing Explanation" at IMAL/86 at Les Arcs, France. The discussion, led by myself with help from Bob Stepp and the audience, was followed by Lebowitz's responses to our comments and questions. The quality of the recording has led to a slightly different emphasis in this written version, although I have tried to incorporate many points of the original discussion.

The next section is a reiteration and development of Lebowitz's argument for similarity-based learning (SBL). Section 3 discusses the general problem of concept learning and some of its components. Section 4 is an attempt to clarify the issue of similarity. Section 5 examines the question of where the knowledge resides in SBL systems. The final section returns to Lebowitz's concern of using similarity to discover cause.

2 THE IMPORTANCE OF SIMILARITY

Lebowitz presents some convincing arguments that similarity is indispensable. I would like to reiterate and elaborate these arguments. The following incorporates some material appearing since the time Lebowitz originally wrote his paper.

The Relationship of Similarity to Causality, Uncertainty, etc. One of Lebowitz's points is that in human endeavors the investigation of similarity often precedes the discovery of causality. For example, a theory of climate may begin by noticing the coincidence of events such as volcanic eruption, altered oceanic currents, and severe droughts. Even before any theory is formed, the coincidence of such events may often be used to find significant correlations among variables (e.g., using statistical techniques). Hence SBL might be used for prediction immediately. Meanwhile, the patterns of similarity might be also used for the eventual formation of a more complete and useful theory, which is evidenced by some of Lebowitz's programs.

Another of Lebowitz's points is that because techniques for SBL can easily incorporate probability and statistics, these methods can be error-resilient and can improve generalizations over a period of time. Thus SBL is well suited for real world application.

Finally, as Lebowitz states, "similarity-based and explanation-based methods can complement each other in important ways." SBL and EBL mesh well because they both use abstract attributes to describe objects, and each method has something the other does not. For example, EBL incorporates domain theories to guide the discovery of a concept, although most methods do not learn in the presence of noise (see [Mitchell, *et al.*, 1986; DeJong and Mooney, 1986]). On the other hand, SBL can manage noisy data but not domain knowledge (see [Rendell, 1986] for a detailed study of SBL methods).

Kinds of Similarity and Kinds of Objects There have been increasing attempts to merge system designs. Whereas Lebowitz's current programs are designed to follow SBL with EBL, other systems reverse the order [Dietterich, recent talks]. Future methods may mesh SBL and EBL in more complex and powerful ways, performing better than either of these paradigms as currently understood.

The arguments for the utility of similarity have perhaps been further substantiated since Lebowitz's paper was written. For example, Dietterich has discussed the idea of using SBL to generalize explanations (an extension of [Flann and Dietterich, 1986]). In other words, similarities may exist among objects other than the input data. While early SBL methods [Duda and Hart, 1973; Samuel, 1959] coalesced data objects according to their similarity in *instance space*, recent methods have coalesced "higher order" objects based on their similarity in more abstract spaces. Meta-DENDRAL can be viewed as grouping similar explanations in a space of hypothetical bond cleavages [Buchanan and Feigenbaum, 1978]. Rendell, *et al.*, [1987] coalesce other kinds of abstract objects: In their system, similar inductive biases and similar problem domains are grouped in "bias space" and "problem space."

In addition to the different kinds of objects, there may be different measures of similarities between them. As Steve Hanson reminded us during the discussion, many metrics exist even for instance space SBL (see [Duda and Hart, 1973]). To examine some of the basic ideas behind similarity-based learning, let us try to clarify the fundamental problem.

3 THE PROBLEM OF CONCEPT LEARNING

To begin, we are given a set of instances which are often described in terms of a k-tuple of attributes x, whose k elements $x_1, x_2, \ldots x_k$ may vary within a predefined range (this is Lebowitz's case). The problem is to partition not only the instances but the whole universe U describable by any $\mathbf{x}$, including instances not yet observed. The size of U depends on k and the range of each x_i; the number of sets or *classes* in U depends on the problem.

Even if the number n of classes is large, the problem may be broken down into n problems each of which is to find some subset of U and its description. The description of the desired class is is the target *concept*. Shown in Figure 1(a), this is a common AI view of concept formation (e.g., see [Dietterich, *et al.*, 1982; Mitchell, *et al.*, 1986]), although it is actually more complex in several ways.

Class Descriptions for Uncertain Situations   While the "all-or-none" logic view of Figure 1(a) is sufficient for some problems, other AI problems are less well behaved. Available attributes may be insufficient to describe the data and various types of uncertainties may degrade their observation; consequently class membership becomes graded, as in Figure 1(b) (see [Rendell, 1986]). For example, the various attributes of universities in Figure 15–1 may be inadequate to unequivocally distinguish the ones that produce the best research; hence, the concept changes from a Boolean function to the more general multivalued form. In either (a) or (b) the function maps an object $\mathbf{x}$ into its *class membership* value u($\mathbf{x}$).

Dynamic Descriptions for Complex Problems   While a concept is a function defined over the attributes of data objects, there is also the question of what the attributes $x_1, x_2, \ldots x_k$ should be. In simpler problems, the attributes are fixed by the user, although even Samuel's early work [Samuel, 1959] allowed their selection from a

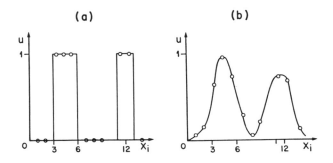

(a)   **(b)**

Figure 1:   Concepts or class membership functions

larger set. Different k-tuples $(x_1, x_2, \ldots x_k)$ can result in very different kinds of functions, some much better behaved than others. For example, some concepts about universities may depend on their location (see Figure 15–1). If location is expressed as urban or rural, the effect this attribute on the class membership function is controlled, but consider the effect if location is expressed in terms of latitude and longitude.

One way to broaden our view of the concept-learning problem is to say that we need to find not only the class membership function (Figure 1(a) or (b)), but also a well-behaved set of attributes $\{x_1, x_2, \ldots x_k\}$ to begin with. In other words, in addition to searching for the target concept in a space representing possible classes, we can also search for a desirable concept *description,* chosen from a space of possible descriptions all of the same concept. While all the descriptions represent the same class, they vary in their suitability for representation and learning. Some aspects of these ideas are generalized by Keller [1987] and by Rendell [1987]. In the case of SBL, a suitable description is one that identifies similarity directly with the attributes.

4 DEFINITIONS AND CONSEQUENCES OF SIMILARITY

The Primary but Disguised Definition   What is similarity? The most direct and sensible way to define it in the context of concept learning is as follows: Two objects **x** and **y** are *similar* if the differences in their class membership values are small; in other words the dissimilarity

$$d = |\, u(x) - u(y)|$$

is very close to zero (consider Figure 1). Similarity is the opposite of dissimilarity; i.e., similarity = 1 – d. This is the most basic definition of similarity; any other definition is (or should be) derivative.

Common but Secondary Definitions   An immediate result of our primary definition is that since the individual objects of a class must be similar by definition, all concept learning is "similarity-based." But this is not what is meant by SBL. What is normally understood is that the class membership u is strongly related to the attributes. This means that even if we do not know u, we can replace it with some smooth function of the attributes. In other words, the dissimilarity $d = |\, u(x) - u(y)|$ becomes

$$d = \|\, x - y\|$$

where "‖ ‖" denotes some metric such as Euclidean or Hamming distance. For example, in Lebowitz's university problem (see Figure 15–1), we would expect that two instances might gradually become more dissimilar as the difference in their student-to-faculty ratio increases.

(Given our primary definition of similarity we can derive common distance measures. For example, if the attributes are binary, the result might be the Hamming distance. *If* we believe that the class membership u is a well-behaved function of the attributes, then we might assert that the relationship is of the form

$u(x) = c_1 x_1 + c_2 x_2 + ... + c_k x_k$ (where the c_i are constants).

Using this expression for the two instances **x** and **y** in the primary definition

$d = | u(x) - u(y) |,$

we obtain

$$d = c_1 (x_1 - y_1) + c_2 (x_2 - y_2) + ... + c_k (x_k - y_k) \leq d'$$
$$= c_1 | x_1 - y_1 | + c_2 | x_2 - y_2 | + ... + c_k | x_k - y_k |,$$

a weighted Hamming distance. If the c_i are assumed to have the same magnitude, then we can make $c = 1$ without loss of generality, giving $d' = \sum | x_i - y_i |$, which is the (unweighted) Hamming distance. If the attributes are continuous, then the Euclidean distance follows similarly. The result is the usual understanding of similarity-based learning.)

The Extreme Constraint Required by SBL   SBL requires explicit or implicit assumptions about instance space distance, which in turn means that class membership had better be a well-behaved function of the attributes. Only when the attributes of **x** bear a smooth relationship to the class membership function $u(x)$ (Figure 1) are these assumptions valid. They are extremely strong assumptions that amount to a strong inductive bias (see [Rendell, 1986]). This bias works for typical SBL applications because the user chooses the attributes accordingly. For Lebowitz's university problem an appropriate attribute is "location" expressed as urban versus rural but not expressed in terms of latitude and longitude (see Figure 15–1).

The next section continues this discussion in terms of the difficulties of problems and the amount of knowledge in their formulations.

5 WHERE IS THE KNOWLEDGE?

We have seen that the concept formation problem has at least two components:

1. Find appropriate attributes which give a well-behaved class membership function u.
2. Given the attribute vector **x**, find this (Boolean or graded) function u.

SBL has been primarily concerned with (2), yet (1) may be at least as important.

The Problem of Knowing the Attributes   Whether (1) or (2) is the more difficult of the two subproblems depends on the domain, the data, and the knowledge supplied to the program. Consider two extreme examples of relative difficulty:

i. Attribute selection: a small set of attributes is given, some of which are salient (relevant for class discrimination). For example the program selects the best 16 from 40 predefined attributes for checkers [Samuel, 1959] or a salient subset of 17 given attributes for concepts about universities (Figure 15-1). In such cases expressing the appropriate attributes is relatively easy and techniques for finding them are well known. Standard statistical techniques (e.g., see [Anderberg, 1973; Draper and Smith, 1981]) can be adapted to AI use (some are discussed in [Rendell, 1986]). The inductive aspect of explanation-based learning is to select features (see [Mitchell, *et al.*, 1986]).

ii. Attribute construction from primitives: a set of low-level attributes is given, whose relationship to the class membership function is highly irregular, necessitating their transformation into better behaved attributes. For example, the program might be given only the rules of checkers and low-level attributes that are simply the board contents (though no existing program can learn much at this level). Then the problem of knowing suitable attributes becomes the hard problem of "constructive induction" or "new terms." In such domains, finding appropriate attributes (subproblem 1) seems much more difficult than finding the class membership function once the appropriate high-level attributes are known (subproblem 2).

We might identify the ability to handle difficulty with the "amount of knowledge" a system is given or can induce. In typical SBL applications most of the knowledge is contained in the attributes themselves. (This can be shown quantitatively; see [Rendell, 1986].)

Knowing the attributes is an important problem for learning from examples (supervised learning) and also for learning from observation (unsupervised learning or clustering). Even in the more difficult problem of learning from observation, the user normally specifies the attributes; hence the user supplies much of the knowledge. One goal of recent work is to transform knowledge into new terms in effective and efficient ways [Rendell, 1988].

Learning from Examples versus Learning from Observation   Concept learning is the discovery of the class membership function u (Figure 1). In learning from examples the data are usually given as positive and negative training instances; then the class membership value u is 1 or 0, as shown in Figure 2(a). However, the data may be noisy or uncertain; e.g., a checkers position may be strong but not a guaranteed win. In such a case u might have the range [0,1] (Figure 2(b)). Moreover, the uncertain class membership value u may itself be uncertain; for example some familiar

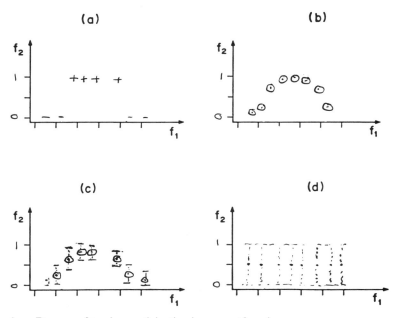

Figure 2:   Degrees of teacher participation in concept learning

board position may be known to win $80\% \pm 5\%$ of the time, whereas another, unfamiliar position may be guessed to win with a probability of $60\% \pm 30\%$. Such a situation is shown in Figure 2(c). In the most extreme case, the u value is completely unknown (in Figure 2(d) it is 0.5 ± 0.5). At which point does the teacher's role disappear; i.e., when does learning from examples change to learning from observation? and how does the magnitude of knowledge about class membership compare with that of the appropriate attributes to begin with?

We can begin to answer such questions using a simple analysis of the quantities involved. In checkers, for example, expressing a board position in primitive, low-level terms as the contents of each board square gives about 10^{18} possibilities. The number of ways of dividing these into hypothesized wins and losses is $2^{[10^{18}]}$! In contrast, using typical abstract attributes such as piece advantage and center control [Samuel, 1959] compresses all these positions into about 10^6 high level objects (a compression factor of a trillion). The number of ways of dividing these into hypothesized wins and losses now becomes $2^{[10^6]}$. Because of this drastic reduction (relative to the work remaining), and because the abstract attributes are much better behaved than the primitive ones, we can say that most of the knowledge is in the abstract attributes.

Even so, the number of ways of hypothesizing wins and losses is still immense: $2^{[10^6]}$. In contrast, in a typical learning problem, a relatively small number of data are given, perhaps 10,000 at most. This "simplifies" the problem so that the number of possible hypotheses is reduced from $2^{1,000,000}$ to "only" $2^{990,000}$. Now consider this as a problem of learning from observation and suppose that the 10,000 data remain unclassified. If we happen to know that the number of final classes is still two, then the number of hypotheses remains at $2^{[10^6]}$. This is much closer to $2^{990,000}$ than $2^{[10^8]}$ is to $2^{[10^6]}$. (For more detailed and accurate analyses of such problems see [Anderberg, 1973; Rendell, 1986].) Compared with the amount of knowledge in the abstract attributes, the amount of knowledge in the examples is relatively small. So, in the context of the whole problem, which includes knowing the attributes (Section 4), is learning from observation much different from learning from examples?

This suggests that the research into constructive induction is rather important if we eventually are to develop fully intelligent learning systems [Rendell, 1988]. But there are many other problems, some of which we shall consider in the following section as we return to Lebowitz's ideas about the uses of similarity.

6 AFTER THE SBL

The function of similarity-based learning is to discover the concept in the form of a Boolean class membership function (Figure 1(a)) or a graded function (Figure 1(b)). (This is for the two-class case; for the n-class case, n functions are needed.) If the graded form represents probability (as it often does) then this information may be written in the form $u(x) = Pr(C \mid x)$ where C means "class membership" and x represents the example.

Knowing the concept means knowing $u(x) = Pr(C \mid x)$ for all x. From u, class membership is immediately available. But many other kinds of information may also be computed, such as (when attribute x_i is binary) the category validity $Pr(C \mid x_i)$ and the cue validity $Pr(x_i \mid C)$ (see [Smith and Medin, 1981]).

One interesting use of the concept is to discover feature correlations, in the strict statistical sense [Draper and Smith, 1981] or using measures such as $Pr(x_i \mid x_j)$ (see [Watanabe, 1969]). This raises one of the most important issues that Lebowitz has made: that similarity-based learning determines attribute correlations and that they are related to causality.

Suppose that two attributes A and B are found to be correlated, and suppose that the underlying situation is that A implies B. (For example A might be "fever" and B "flu.") Although we do not know the direction of the implication, we can hypothesize that fever implies flu or flu implies fever (or still other relationships). In general, we can hypothesize theories based on SBL.

7 SUMMARY

To summarize these aspects of Lebowitz's chapter and the emphases of this commentary: We have seen that for many reasons similarity is indispensable. It meshes well with other approaches such as explanation-based learning. Moreover, a clear understanding of similarity can help to guide research. Many interesting and important avenues remain, some of which have been developed or suggested in these two chapters.

References

Anderberg, M.R. 1973. *Cluster Analysis for Applications*, Academic Press.

Buchanan, B.G. and Feigenbaum, E.A. 1978. DENDRAL and Meta-DENDRAL: Their applications dimension, *Artificial Intelligence* 11:5–24.

DeJong, G. and Mooney, R. 1986. Explanation-based learning: An alternative view, *Machine Learning Journal* 1, 2.

Dietterich, T.G., London, B., Clarkson, K., and Dromey, G. 1982. Learning and inductive inference, STAN-CS-82-913, Stanford University, also Chapter XIV of *The Handbook of Artificial Intelligence*, Cohen, P.R. and Feigenbaum, E.A. (Eds.), Addison-Wesley.

Dr.aper, N.R. and Smith, H. 1981. *Applied Regression Analysis* (Second Edition), Wiley.

Duda, R.O. and Hart, P.E. 1973. *Pattern Classification and Scene Analysis*, Wiley.

Flann, N.S. and Dietterich, T.G. 1986. Selecting appropriate representations for learning from examples, *Proc. Fifth National Conference on Artificial Intelligence*, pp. 460–466.

Keller, R.M. 1987. Defining operationality for explanation-based learning, *Proc. Sixth National Conference on Artificial Intelligence*, Seattle, Washington, July 1987.

Mitchell, T.M., Keller, R.M., and Kedar-Cabelli, S.T. 1986. Explanation-based generalization—a unifying view, *Machine Learning* 1, 1 (January 1986).

Rendell, L.A. 1986. A general framework for induction and a study of selective induction, *Machine Learning* 1, 2:177–226.

Rendell, L.A. 1987. Similarity-based Learning and Its Extensions, *Computational Intelligence* 3, 4 (special issue on learning), November 1987, pp. 241–266.

Rendell, L.A. 1988. Learning Hard Concepts, European Working Session on Learning, Glasgow, Scotland, October 1988, pp. 177–200.

Rendell, L.A., Seshu, R.M., and Tcheng, D.K. 1987. Layered concept learning and dynamically variable bias management, *Proc. Tenth International Joint Conference on Artificial Intelligence*, Milan, Italy, August 1987.

Samuel, A.L. 1963. Some studies in machine learning using the game of checkers, *IBM Journal of Research and Development*, 1959, reprinted in in Feigenbaum, E.A. and Feldman, J. (Ed.), *Computers and Thought*, McGraw-Hill, pp. 71–105.

Smith, E.E. and Medin, D.L. 1981. *Categories and Concepts*, Harvard University Press.

Watanabe, S. 1969. *Knowing and Guessing: A Formal and Quantitative Study*, Wiley.

16

LEARNING EXPERT KNOWLEDGE BY IMPROVING THE EXPLANATIONS PROVIDED BY THE SYSTEM

Yves Kodratoff
(CNRS , Université de Paris-Sud and
George Mason University)

Abstract

This chapter presents a framework for integrating all possible sources of explications: those stemming from explanation-based learning (EBL) and those describing the relationships of a recognition function with the positive or negative examples of the concept it is supposed to cover. For those directly obtained from a human expert, refer to Chapter 19. The deep analogy between these different explanatory sources is explained and carefully exemplified. The chapter starts with a description of what expert knowledge, a knowledge fit to symbolic approaches, is, as opposed to casual knowledge, fit to numeric approaches. Our main point is that expert knowledge is almost as much devoted to efficiency as to explication. We then explain how much the improvement and progressive refinement of a generalization depends on the quality of the explanations one can get—"why the generalization is good or bad." Finally, we propose some general methodology to improve the explanations themselves.

16.1 INTRODUCTION

The word "learning" is currently used in such a wide variety of meanings that the research area attracts people that have different or even opposite interests. Most people claiming to belong to artificial intelligence (AI) tend to be oriented towards a symbolic approach, which can be characterized by its care for providing explanations in the user's language. This demands intensive and explicit use of background knowledge and symbolic reasoning. It can possibly lead to some lack of efficiency and accuracy.

On the other hand, most other techniques, like data analysis, connectionism, operations research, and all statistical methods emphasize the needs for efficiency and accuracy. They fulfill these needs by using a knowledge representation, the semantics of which is the closest possible to the semantics of numbers. Therefore, these approaches make implicit use of background knowledge, and they usually are unable to provide explanations in the user's language.

Actually, there seems to be not only a double, but a triple misunderstanding of the expression "machine learning" (ML) that arises on the one hand, between specialists in artificial intelligence (called *AI-learnists* in the rest of this chapter) and, on the other hand, between more psychology-oriented people (called *psy-learnists* in the rest of this chapter), and non-AI-oriented learnists (called *NOT-AI-learnists* in this chapter). We shall attempt to qualify AI-learnists by two features. The first feature concerns the topic they are working on.

First Criterion **There exists a body of explicit knowledge in the field in which learning takes place, expressed in the expert's language.** Having expertise in this field means mastering the field's language (i.e., the symbolic representation of the domain knowledge) and being able to explain to another expert the reasons for one's choices. There may be some disagreement among experts, but the disagreement is over the reasons rather than the choices themselves. In everyday life, this is enough to define expert knowledge, as opposed to casual knowledge. Typically, mathematics is expert knowledge, and bicycle riding is casual knowledge.

We need to add here a second feature concerning the way these approaches are working on their topic. Within AI-learning itself many discussions take place, like the recent one between explanation-based learning (EBL) and empirical learning. These discussions tend to hide that both approaches are issued from the AI approach, and both are characterized by the following.

Second Criterion **Their results are expressed in the language of the expert him/herself.** The other approaches to ML, illustrated by statistics, and also, more recently, by the connectionist approach [Hinton—Chapter 20, this volume], whose aim is rather *efficiency and accuracy*, and where explanations hardly can be expressed in the vocabulary of the expert. More generally, all sciences aim to develop their own language with which they can describe the behavior of their observables. AI indeed develops its own vocabulary as well, but it must include the expert's language. Statistics do provide explanations of their results, but, typically, these reasons are expressed in terms of "quadratic squares," or other statistical concepts. They are expressed in the vocabulary of the expert in statistics, not in the vocabulary of the expert of the field on which statistics are done. In opposition, all the AI-inspired, EMYCIN-like expert systems provide explanations in the vocabulary of the expert in the field under study even though they are well known for providing bad explanations of their behavior because of the way they combine positive and negative beliefs.

Definitions We shall say that one is doing *expert knowledge acquisition* when the two following requirements are fulfilled.

- First, the acquisition concerns a field that possesses a body of theory such that the expert in this theory can provide explanations.
- Second, the acquisition provides explanations of its behavior and uses the vocabulary of the human experts.

When one of these conditions is not fulfilled, then we define the acquisition of knowledge as *casual knowledge acquisition* (or *non-conceptual* knowledge acquisition).

Let us give three examples of NOT-AI-learning, ordered by their distance from AI-learning.

- Riding a bicycle is an example of everyday life casual knowledge, its learning therefore belongs to casual knowledge acquisition.
- A diagnosis system that would rely on thousands of clinical cases, store all of them, and provide a diagnosis by a template-matching mechanism does not provide explanations, therefore it belongs to NOT-AI-learning. It is similar to rote-learning, which clearly is of little concern to AI specialists.
- A diagnosis system that uses pure numerical techniques in order to perform its clusterings, and generate its recognition functions, cannot give explanations in the vocabulary of the expert.

There are here some (fortunate!) shadows on the limits between AI- and NOT-AI-learning, since the clustering algorithm may or may not include, as parameters, some semantics of the field. Michalski's *conceptual clustering* [Michalski and Stepp, 1983] is very typical of a numerical technique that falls into AI-learning because it can provide some explanations of its clusters in the expert's vocabulary. NOT-AI-learnists are interested in casual knowledge acquisition, because they do not mind explanations but efficiency.

Psy-learnists mind explanations but they are interested in the way humans actually store their knowledge, which seems to be very far from the way existing knowledge-based systems store it.

One necessary condition to the generation of explanations is that the system is able to *prove* that its actions obey some constraints; the quality of this proof is another matter that will be discussed later. Section 16.3 will illustrate how proving things may be a first step towards explanations. These explanations look different when coming from EBL or from empirical learning. Actually, there has been recently a considerable emphasis on the difference between the two. EBL works by using classical theorem-proving and goal-regression techniques, while empirical learning usually looks for recognition functions obtained by a generalization from a set of positive and negative examples. This chapter will show that their essential difference does not lie in using one (as generally EBL does) or several (as generally empirical learning does) examples, but in the way each uses background knowledge. It just happens that empirical learning may hide, and often has hidden, its background knowledge into the representation of the examples. When empirical learning does not use explicit background knowledge at all, our definitions place it in NOT-AI-learning. Conversely, as soon as one is willing to pay the price for an explicit representation of the background knowledge, then empirical learning is also able to provide explanations to its user. In order to avoid confusions, we shall call *learning from examples by empirical induction* the empirical learning that does not use explicitly background knowledge, and *learning from examples by constructive induction* the one with explicit background knowledge (see the first chapter of this book for precise definitions). We therefore also want to illustrate that, contrary to the "EBL versus empirical learning" way of looking at machine learning, constructive learning from examples must also provide explanations and needs some theorem proving.

EBL is born from techniques that are efficient on a very well-defined domain. For instance, the recently defined EBG (G for *generalization*), [Mitchell, *et al.*, 1986] requires both

1. a complete theory (including a definition of the concept under learning), and

2. an instance of the concept. It would be useful to be able to define generalization in a domain where the concept to be reached is still unknown, or the theory still to be completed. This has been done by Michalski [Michalski, 1983, 1984], in his formalization of generalization. Our aim is to push forward this theory, and attempt to encompass both EBL and constructive learning from examples into it, by showing that the last also should provide explanations of its generalizations. In less formalized domains, one should at least be able to take into account human experts' explanations. This last topic is discussed in Chapter 19 of this book.

In this chapter, we hope to reach two different goals. The first is to show how a formal theorem prover can help in providing explanations that improve the concept under learning, the learning being deductive (as it should be) or, a bit more unexpectedly, inductive as well. We shall differentiate the use of theorem proving done during inductive learning from the one done during deductive learning. The second goal is to show how these formalities are actually simple, and in many cases, easy to use, once one disposes of a theorem prover. The most widely available being the language PROLOG, we used its formalism in the rest of the chapter.

16.2 NOTATIONS

In this chapter, we shall use a PROLOG-like notation of the clauses. A Horn clause has the form A:- B, C, D, ... which means, A is TRUE IF (B is TRUE, and C is TRUE, and D is TRUE, ...). A is called the *conclusion* of the clause, and B, C, D, ... are called the *conditions* of the clause. A clause without condition, i.e., a pure positive clause, is often called a *fact*, or a datum. A clause without a conclusion, i.e., a pure negative clause, is called a *question*. It is clear that nothing special is brought by this representation as such. Its interest comes from the fact that an inference mechanism is included in it. For instance, consider the clauses

```
(C₁)   MORTAL(x)          :-   HUMAN(x)
(C₂)   HUMAN(SOCRATES)     :-
```

In general, one should be able to resolve C_2 and C_1, which means that one should remark that C_2 fulfills the condition of C_1, x being instantiated by SOCRATES. Using PROLOG representation implicitly says that this kind of reasoning, usually called *forward chaining*, will not be used. On the contrary, one will only use *backward chaining*; i.e., a question (represented by a pure negative clause) will have to match some conclusions and will generate new questions etc. ... up to the moment where all questions have been answered. In other words, PROLOG uses a refutation strategy; therefore a question will be stated in the form of a pure negation, as already defined. The original question and all subquestions have been answered when all of them have been put in contradiction with some parts of the data basis. One then says that one has derived the empty clause from the data basis and the question; i.e., that the question is inconsistent with the data basis. For example, the only way to deduce something about Socrates's mortality, is asking the question "Is Socrates mortal?" by adding a pure negative clause in the form

```
(C₃)   :-   MORTAL(SOCRATES)
```

The refutation will then proceed by resolving C_3 against C_1, with the substitution [x ← SOCRATES], therefore generating the new question

```
(C₄)   :-   HUMAN(SOCRATES)
```

which resolves with C_2 to the empty clause. The refutation procedure thus concludes that it was led to a contradiction by negating MORTAL (SOCRATES), it has therefore proven that asserting it leads to no contradiction.

All that explains why PROLOG programmers say that the proof "succeeds" when the interpreter finds a contradiction, and that the proof "fails" when it does not.

16.3 IMPROVING A GENERALIZATION

In the following, we shall suppose that we reached a given state of knowledge acquisition, and that we are trying to improve it by checking the current state of the learned recognition function against new positive or negative examples. When they do not fit together, the problem is then to be able to improve this recognition function. Said in an intuitive way, one expects from a recognition function to "recognize" new examples and to "reject" new negative examples. Let us now give one possible definition for recognition and rejection. We choose here a quite intuitive way of defining these words. More details have been given in [Kodratoff and Ganascia, 1986; Kodratoff, 1988]. This definition has also been extensively used by J. Nicolas [1986]. The reader is asked to accept these definitions as temporary hypotheses: other definitions would lead to other proofs, but the essential step that we want to illustrate here; for instance, how a proof can be the basis for an explanation, does not depend on these definitions. Let E, NE, and f(x) be an example, a negative example, and a recognition function, respectively.

16.3.1 Recognition of an Example

16.3.1.1 Definitions

Definition 1   One says that a function f(x) *recognizes (1)* an example E when there is an instance of "x," say [x ← A] such that f(A) = E. This definition fits well our intuitive feeling of "recognition" but, in view of our goal of generating explanations, it is quite inefficient. We shall generalize it somewhat in order to obtain explanation of "why f(x) recognizes E."

Definition 2   Suppose that definition 1 holds; i.e., there is a [x ← A] such that f(A) = E. Then A is the very instance that exemplifies that both E and ∃x [f(x)] are TRUE. Therefore, one says that a function f(x) *recognizes (2)* an example E when there is no contradiction to assert both E and ∃x [f(x)] together.

Definition 3   Definition 2 is not very computation efficient, this is why we shall choose to perform the proof by refutation. We shall make the choice to assert E and to refute ∃x [f(x)]; while the converse, asserting ∃x [f(x)] and refuting E could have been also quite possible. Reasons for this choice are discussed at length in Chapter 6 of [Kodratoff, 1988], we shall skip them here. We shall therefore try to prove that asserting both E and ¬∃x [f(x)] together leads to a contradiction. Since ¬∃x [f(x)] is logically equivalent to ∀x [¬f(x)]. This gives our third definition. One says that a function f(x) *recognizes (3)* an example E when there is a contradiction to assert both E and ∀x [¬f(x)] together.

This third definition is very computation efficient since E and $\forall x\,[\neg f(x)]$ can be put in clause form, following classical rules [Kowalski, 1979]. Then, if these clauses are Horn clauses, they can be directly given to a PROLOG interpreter,

$$\forall x\,[\neg f(x)]$$

being seen as a question. The proof that E and $\forall x\,[\neg f(x)]$ contradict each other is completed when PROLOG succeeds in finding the empty clause out of their clausal form.

Example 1

Let us suppose that we have so far obtained the following recognition function $f_1(x, y) = \text{SPHERE}(x)\ \&\ \text{RED}(y)$ which means: "there are two objects, one is a sphere, the other one is red." Suppose that a further example is given as

$$E_1 = \text{SPHERE}(A)\ \&\ \text{RED}(A)$$

where "A" is the name of an object that happens to be a red sphere, then E_1 is clearly an instance of $f_1(x, y)$ since the substitution $\sigma_1 = [x \leftarrow A, y \leftarrow A]$ is such that

$$\sigma_1 {}^\circ f_1(x, y) = E_1.$$

Once in clausal form, E reads

```
C₁:    SPHERE(A)              :-
C₂:    RED(A)                 :-
```

and $\forall x\,[\neg f_1(x)]$ becomes

```
C₃:                          :-  SPHERE(x), RED(y)
```

Proving that $[\forall x\,[\neg f_1(x)]\ \&\ E_1]$ is contradictory amounts to proving that

$$\{C_1, C_2, C_3\}$$

is contradictory. In order to prove this last statement, one uses resolution [Kowalski, 1979] as follows. $\text{SPHERE}(x)$ in C_3 resolves with C_1, with the substitution $[x \leftarrow A]$, leading to the new set of clauses

```
C₂:    RED(A)                 :-
C'₃:                         :-  RED(y)
```

$\text{RED}(y)$ in C'_3 resolves with C_2, with the substitution $[y \leftarrow A]$, thus leading to the empty clause. This proves that $\{C_1, C_2, C_3\}$ is contradictory. Therefore, $f_1(x, y)$ recognizes E_1 according to definition 3.

The above example illustrates why we can use the definition of "recognition" we just gave, but it still does not explains its use, since the direct proof by substitution is possible. It may happen that the substitution is very hard or impossible (as Example 2 shows) to find because, in order to make sure that E is an instance of $f(x)$, one must use semantic properties of the microworld one is learning in. In that case, the proof that $[\forall x \ [\neg f_1(x)] \ \& \ E_1]$ leads to a contradiction may become quite lengthy. An analysis of this proof will show why it succeeds, and explain why f(x) is recognition function for E.

Example 2

Suppose now that the recognition function is $f_2(x) = \text{ELLIPSOID}(x) \ \&$ RED(x), which means that we have memorized that "there is a red ellipsoid" in all the scenes we are learning from. Suppose that we are given a further example

$$E_2 = \text{SPHERE}(B) \ \& \ \text{RED}(B)$$

where "B" is the name of a red sphere. Since ELLIPSOID and SPHERE do not match, the proof by substitution is useless. Suppose now that the semantics of the microworld where learning is taking place are such the following theorem is known

$$\text{Th}_1: \forall x \ [\text{SPHERE}(x) \Rightarrow \text{ELLIPSOID}(x)].$$

We shall add Th_1 in our knowledge base and attempt to prove that

$$[\forall x \ [\neg f_2(x) \ \& \ \text{Th}_1] \ \& \ E_1]$$

leads to a contradiction. This reads

```
C_4:   SPHERE(B)          :-
C_5:   RED(B)             :-
C_6:   ELLIPSOID(x)       :-   SPHERE(x)
C_7:                      :-   ELLIPSOID(x), RED(x)
```

C_7 resolves with C_6, leading to the new clause

```
C_8:                      :-   SPHERE(x), RED(x)
```

and C_8 resolves with C_4 and C_5 to lead to the empty clause with the substitution [x ← B]. Therefore, E_2 is recognized by $f_2(x)$.

As suggested by this example, it must be understood that the proof that

$$[E \ \& \ \forall x \ [\neg f(x)]]$$

leads to the empty clause has to make use of all the available knowledge. Actually, definition 3 tells it implicitly. For the sake of clarity, let us accept some redundancy and introduce explicitly the use of background knowledge in definition 3.

Definition 4 Let BK be the available background knowledge. One says that a function f(x) *recognizes (4)* an example E when there is a contradiction to assert both E and $\forall x \ [\neg f(x) \ \& \ BK]$ together. When they are in clausal form, this amounts to say that $[E \ \& \ \forall x \ [\neg f(x) \ \& \ BK]]$ leads to the empty clause.

16.3.2 Rejection of a Negative Example

16.3.2.1 Definitions

As in Section 16.3.1, and for the same reasons, we shall give four definitions of rejection.

Definition 1′   One says that a function f(x) *rejects (1)* an example E when there are no instances of "x," say [x ← A] such that f(A) = E.

Definition 2′   One says that a function f(x) *rejects (2)* an example E when there is a contradiction to assert both E and ∃x [f(x)] together.

Definition 3′   One says that a function f(x) *rejects (3)* an example E when there is no contradiction to assert both E and ∀x [¬f(x)] together. The proof that E and ∀x [¬f(x)] do not contradict each other is completed when PROLOG is unable to find the empty clause out of their clausal form.

Definition 4′   Let us call BK the background knowledge. One says that a function f(x) *rejects (4)* an example E when there is a no contradiction to assert both E and ∀x [¬f(x) & BK] together. When they are in clausal form, this is equivalent to saying that [E & ∀x [¬f(x) & BK]] fails to lead to the empty clause.

Example 3

Suppose that the recognition function is $f_3(x) = $ SPHERE(x) & RED(x) and that $NE_3 = $ SPHERE(C) & RED(D) is a negative example to f_3. Clearly, NE_3 is not an instance of f_3 since x cannot be substituted by both C and D. Using the above formalism, one checks that the system of clauses

```
C₉:   SPHERE(C)              :-
C₁₀:  RED(D)                 :-
C₁₁:                         :-  SPHERE(x), RED(x)
```

does not lead to the empty clause. Resolving C_{11} with C_9, one obtains

```
C₁₀:  RED(D)                 :-
C₁₂:                         :-  RED(C)
```

because "x" has been instantiated by "C" during the resolution. C_{10} and C_{12} cannot be reduced since "C" and "D" are different constants. This proves that NE_3 is a negative example for $f_3(x)$.

All the above illustrates our definitions and the proof procedure but is not very significant as an explanation generator just because there is indeed little to explain. This happens because the amount of background knowledge we are using in these examples is almost zero. However, in Example 2, the proof that

E_2 and $\forall x\ [\neg f_2(x)\ \&\ Th_1]$

contradict each other uses clause

```
C₆:  ELLIPSOID(x)          :-  SPHERE(x).
```

Therefore, we can say that $f_2(x)$ *recognizes* E_2 because a sphere is a kind of ellipsoid. This constitutes a simple but not trivial explanation, which happens to be the trace of a formal proof. The next section will show that EBL works in a quite similar way. This will show that both deductive and inductive learning use theorem proving to generate explanations. In the case of inductive learning, the inductive process will generate some recognition function from a set of examples and, once it has been generated by induction, a proving process exactly the same as the one shown in Sections 16.3.1 and 16.3.2 will "explain" why this function recognizes the positive examples and rejects the negative ones it has been learned from.

16.3.3 Improvement of a Formula by an Explanation of its Success to Recognize a New Example

In cases less toy-like than the examples above, it often happens that the recognition function is too much "hairy"; i.e., it contains irrelevant information that does not harm the recognition of the given example, but could be harmful in other situations. One must then prune it from its irrelevant information. This pruning, an essential part of explanation-based learning, will be exemplified below when we shall analyze level 3_3 of the "safe-to-stack" example.

In order to illustrate the necessity for pruning, imagine a recognition function for "man" that contains a predicate "beard" taking the value TRUE when the man has a beard. It may be that only bearded men have been seen so far by the system, which recognizes "man" only if its description gives the value TRUE to "beard."

- Given a complete theory of "man," in this case, a detailed description of what are secondary sexual features, and about some social shaving habits,
- Given a complete description of a bearded man, the system should be able to prove that the predicate "beard" is not necessary to assert that this bearded man is actually a man, because it is a secondary feature often erased by social habits.

As this example shows, since irrelevant information is dropped, another consequence is that some generalization is performed on the given formula. This is the topic of *goal regression* [Waldinger, 1977; Nilsson, 1980], and of explanation-based generalization (EBG) [Mitchell, *et al.*, 1986].

EBG is very clearly described in [Mitchell, *et al.*, 1986]. We shall insist here on the importance of proof traces in performing it. For that purpose, we shall use a PROLOG version of the "safe-to-stack" example, taken from [Mitchell, *et al.*, 1986].

Such a PROLOG version has been implemented by Kedar-Cabelli [1987]. We have implemented [Touchais, 1987; Siqueira and Puget, 1988; Kodratoff, 1988] a conversational version in which the operationality criterion can be changed at any step by a request of the user. Let us summarize EBG as follows. Given

- a complete theory,
- a training example,
- an operationality criterion given as a list of "operational" predicates. Do the following:
  - prove that the training example fits the theory,
  - gather the corresponding proof tree,
  - prune the proof tree according to the operationality criterion by cutting off any branch containing a predicate that does not belong to the list of operational predicates,
  - generalize the pruned tree while keeping the information sufficient to prove that the training example fits the theory,
  - gather the leaves of the generalized pruned tree: They form a new, operational, description of the general concept described in the training instance.

We shall exemplify this procedure by using the Mitchell, *et al.*, [1986] "safe-to-stack" example. It amounts to learn a more efficient rule to perform stacking. Given

- an example of a particular box "BOX_1 stacked on a particular table "ENDTABLE$_1$."
- a "complete" theory of stacking
- an operationality criterion: Are all predicates met in the theory and the training instance operational?

Find

- an operational rule for stacking objects.

Learning proceeds from three kinds of information. The first kind of information is the "complete" knowledge of the specific box, "BOX_1," and the specific table "$ENDTABLE_1$."

```
C₁ ON(BOX₁, ENDTABLE₁)        :-
C₂ COLOR(BOX₁, RED)           :-
C₃ COLOR(ENDTABLE₁, BLUE)     :-
C₄ VOLUME(BOX₁, 10)           :-
C₅ DENSITY(BOX₁, 1)           :-
C₆ FRAGILE(ENDTABLE₁)         :-
C₇ OWNER(ENDTABLE₁, CLYDE)    :-
C₈ OWNER(BOX₁, BONNIE)        :-
```

The second kind of information is the "complete" background knowledge about stacking things, also called the theory of the domain.

```
C9   SAFE-TO-STACK(x, y)       :- NOT FRAGILE(y)
C10  SAFE-TO-STACK(x, y)       :- LIGHTER(x, y)
C11  WEIGHT(x, w)              :- VOLUME(x, v),DENSITY(x, d), w is v*d, !
C12  WEIGHT(ENDTABLE1, 50)     :-
C13  LIGHTER(x, y)             :- WEIGHT(x, w1),WEIGHT(y, w2), LESS(w1, w2)
C14  LESS(x, y)                :- x < y
```

The reader may be surprised to find C_{12} placed in the background knowledge. This is due to PROLOG's clumsiness in expressing default values. In new versions of PROLOG that include data typing, it would be possible to declare that "END-TABLE$_1$" is of type "ENDTABLE" in the above first kind of information and to declare in the second one that the default value of the weight of the type ENDTABLE is 50. Since our aim is not the illustration of typed PROLOGs (that would require a paper by itself), let us go on with a standard PROLOG language and notice that there is no real contradiction to put C_{12} in the background knowledge.

The third kind of information is expressing that one can safely stack "BOX$_1$" on "ENDTABLE$_1$." Since we want to prove that by PROLOG; i.e., by a refutation procedure, this knowledge will be given as question to the PROLOG interpreter. It reads

```
C15      :-  SAFE-TO-STACK(BOX1, ENDTABLE1)
```

Clauses C_9 and C_{10} are supposed to represent a complete knowledge about stacking. Therefore, we already know how to prove or disprove whether an object "x" is stacked on an other "y." What we want to learn from this example is a more efficient (here, this means "more operational") way to stack "x" on "y" than the one given by C_9 and C_{10}.

Most clauses are straightforward rewritings of those in [Mitchell, *et al.*, 1986], but three differences must be pointed out. The first difference is that we use integers; therefore we multiply by 10 the values given in [Mitchell, *et al.*, 1986]. The second difference is that the "ISA" links are dropped. This would have to be expressed as types in a typed PROLOG—as already pointed out, typing PROLOG is not our present topic. The third difference is that the default value is given in clause C_{12} as a "normal" value. The fact that it is a default value is expressed by the "!" at the end of clause C_{11}. If C_{11} succeeds, this "!" tells to "jump over" clause C_{12}. Therefore C_{12} is used only when C_{11} fails as it should be for a default value.

The proof proceeds as the following trace shows. This trace is provided by most PROLOG interpreters. The comment "Call" means that the predicate has been used as a question to the system. The comment "Exit" means that the predicate (with the instances in the "Exit") has been proven TRUE. The comment "Fail" means that the predicate has been proven FALSE. The comment "Back to" means that back-

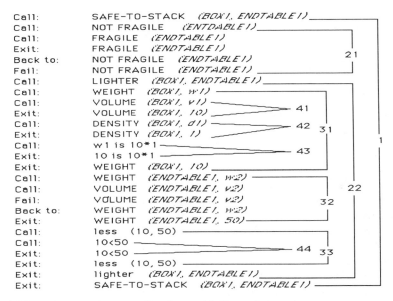

Figure 16-1:   An execution trace directly provided by an interpreter

tracking is taking place. The numbers to the left are those provided by an actual C-PROLOG compiler, we have put on the right the level of embedding they actually represent. For instance, call "NOT FRAGILE(ENDTABLE$_1$)" is indexed by "2" and call LIGHTER(BOX$_1$, ENDTABLE$_1$) is indexed by "4" in the computer output. Actually, they are at the same level of embedding and are labeled respectively 2$_1$ and 2$_2$ on the right.

Let us now analyze the above proof trace and show that it actually gives a set of explanations why it is safe to stack BOX$_1$ on ENDTABLE$_1$; which, in the rest of this section will be abbreviated by "expl.stack." A level always begins with a question, labelled as a "Call." When it succeeds, it ends with an "Exit." The exit contains the reason why the call succeeded. This is why we say that each level provides an "expl.stack," that becomes more and more refined as one goes down the levels.

Level 1 is the most outside. In a sense it says

it is safe to stack BOX$_1$ on ENDTABLE$_1$ because I have proven it just now.

It is the most superficial level of explanations. Children use it quite often!

Level 2 contains sublevel 2$_1$ and sublevel 2$_2$. Sublevel 2$_1$ is a failure sublevel: it tells that "NOT FRAGILE" has nothing to do with "expl.stack." We disregard it here, but one must be aware that, when explanations for failures are looked for, then failure sublevels only can provide that information.

Sublevel 2$_2$ provides the "expl.stack":

It is safe to stack BOX_1 on $ENDTABLE_1$ because BOX_1 is lighter than END-TABLE$_1$.

Level 3 contains three sublevels 3_1, 3_2, and 3_3. The explanations obtained from each one must be conjuncted to obtain the explanation. They provide the "expl.stack":

It is safe to stack BOX_1 on $ENDTABLE_1$ because the weight of BOX_1 is 10, the weight of $ENDTABLE_1$ is 50, and 10 is less than 50.

One can be tempted to generalize at once by saying that the weight of BOX_1 is w_1, the weight of $ENDTABLE_1$ is w_2, and w_1 is less than w_2. This is not allowed by EBG, which says that one can generalize further only if the numerical values come from example data. If some numerical value is issued from theory data, then this value should be kept as such. In this case, the default value—the weight of END-TABLE$_1$ = 50—is part of the theory data, not of the example data. Another way to look at this is to say that one must keep them where there is no deeper explanation to the numerical values. In this case, there is no deeper explanation to the fact that the weight of $ENDTABLE_1$ = 50, since sublevel 3_2 contains no inner sublevel. Therefore, this value will be kept in the final result.

Sublevel 3_1 says that the weight of BOX_1 is 10 because its volume is 10, its density is 1, and because $10*1 = 10$. In this case, the numerical values are issued from the example and can be generalized. The value of the volume is called v_1, the value of the density is called d_1, which gives the partial "expl.stack" :

The weight of BOX_1 is $w_1 = v_1 * d_1$.

Sublevel 3_3 contains an explanation given by 4_4. This explanation is disregarded because it uses a function, like $<$, of low level. Deciding what is at "low level" is a strategic decision that must always be made beforehand. In EBG this decision is made by the choice of an *operationality criterion* given by the user, as defined above. In this particular example and choice of operationality criterion, the function $<$ is not an operator that appears in the background knowledge; therefore it does not belong to the list of operational descriptors; therefore we have to prune out level 4_4, which contains it.

Applying this generalization into the explanation of level 3 (which is the last "expl.stack" found) leads to the final "expl.stack":

It is safe to stack BOX_1 on $ENDTABLE_1$" because the weight of BOX_1 is $w_1 = v_1 * d_1$, the weight of $ENDTABLE_1$" is 50, and w_1 is less than 50.

The process we describe here, is nothing but a paraphrasing of EBG, with two differences from the original paper [Mitchell, *et al.*, 1986]. First, our presentation has a stronger theorem-proving orientation, similar to the one of [Kedar-Cabelli, 1987]. Second, instead of forcing the variables down to elementary facts, we force the constants up to some level where they can be generalized. In an implementation, EBG is the correct way to realize the transmission of the relations among variables. We felt nevertheless it is easier to understand why this process is an explanation of something when presented the other way round.

DeJong and Mooney [1986] have been presenting a set of criticisms to EBG. We shall not comment here on their criticism except on the one concerning the case where two or more explanations are possible. This point will be more detailed in Section 16.4, since it arises also in the context of explaining the failures. At any rate, as useful as it is, goal regression alone hardly provides the possibility for a progressive improvement of the quality of the explanations. This will be possible only when the theory itself will be improved: Explanations for failures are necessary to improve the theory.

16.3.4 Improvement of a Recognition Function by an Explanation of its Failure to Recognize a New Example

Let us suppose that $f(x)$ cannot recognize a new example E. As definition 4 says, this means failure to prove that E and $\forall x \ [\neg f(x) \ \& \ BK]$; i.e., one cannot deduce the empty clause from the clause form of $[E \ \& \ \forall x \ [\neg f(x) \ \& \ BK]]$. The problem is now to explain why. This process is usually difficult to implement, as the following example shows.

Example 4

Let $f_4(x) = SPHERE(x) \ \& \ RED(x)$ and suppose that a new example is E_4: $SPHERE(E) \ \& \ RED(F)$. One fails to prove that E_4 and $\forall x \ [\neg f(x)]$ contradict each other, as the following set of equivalent clauses shows.

```
C13:   SPHERE(E)          :-
C14:   RED(F)             :-
C15:                      :-  SPHERE(x), RED(x)
```

Remember that in Example 3, NE_3 was considered as a negative example to f_3, therefore failing to prove that it was leading to the empty clause was just fitting definition 4'. Now, since we are considering E_4 as an example, we should have been able to prove it. We must find an explanation for the failure. This is more or less equivalent to finding a new function, $f_4'(x)$, that is "the closest possible" to f_4 but allows the proof to succeed.

The failure can originate from two very different sources. Either there is a problem with the predicates themselves (one cannot find a predicate in the conclusion of the clauses (further called *conclusion-predicate*) to match another one in the conditions of the clauses (further called *condition-predicate*), or there is a problem with the substitutions. Example 4 illustrates the second case. Both condition-predicates SPHERE and RED can match their conclusion counterparts in C_{13} and C_{14}, but "x" must be instantiated either by "E" or by "F."

Example 4'

Imagine that, instead of $f_4(x)$, one would start with

$f_4'(x) = \text{SPHERE}(x) \ \& \ \text{RED}(y) \ \& \ \text{RELIGIOUS}(z)$.

Then E_4 would not be recognized by $f_4'(x)$ since the set of clauses

```
C₁₃:    SPHERE(E)        :-
C₁₄:    RED(F)           :-
C₁₅':                    :-    SPHERE(x), RED(y), RELIGIOUS(z)
```

fails to lead to the empty clause. In this case, the variables "x" and "y" could be correctly instantiated by E and F, but no conclusion-predicate could match "RELIGIOUS." Thus E_4 is not recognized by $f_4'(x)$ because E_4 does not contain any information about RELIGIOUS.

When the reason for the failure of the proof is a substitution problem, then one has to introduce variables at the right places to ensure the success of the proof with the new generalization. When the reason for the failure of the proof is a predicate problem, it can be easily found in some cases where one only misses, in the middle of many others that match. When the reason for the failure of the proof mixes substitution and predicate problems, then finding the reason for the failure becomes more or less intractable. This is why we have developed an algorithm described elsewhere [Kodratoff, 1983; Kodratoff, *et al.*, 1985; Kodratoff and Ganascia, 1986; Vrain— Chapter 13, this volume], the role of which is to trace down the possible failures in a given set of examples. The central mechanism for this has been called *structural matching*: It preserves as much as possible the structure of the examples before attempting any generalization.

16.3.5 A Simple Example of Structural Matching (SM)

Consider the two examples in Figure 16–2. Using his intuition, the reader may notice that he can find two different generalizations from these examples. He sees that either

- there are two different objects touching each other, and a small polygon;
- there are two different objects touching each other, one of them is a square.

Both generalizations are true and there is no reason why one of them should be chosen rather than the other. We shall now see that one of the interesting features of SM is that it keeps all the available information, and therefore constructs a formula containing both the above two "concepts."

The examples can be described by the following formulas

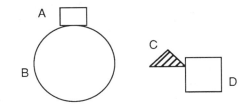

Figure 16-2:   Two scenes to be generalized

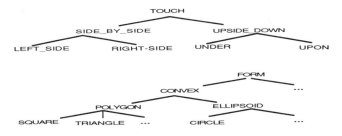

Figure 16-3:   A simple hierarchy of geometrical shapes

E_1 = SQUARE(A) & CIRCLE(B) & ON(A, B) & SMALL(A) & BIG(B)
E_2 = TRIANGLE(C) & SQUARE(D) & TOUCH(C, D) & SMALL(C) &
        BIG(D)

Let us suppose that the hierarchy shown in Figure 16–3 is provided to the system together with the theorems

$\forall x \, \forall y \, [ON(x, y) \Rightarrow TOUCH(x, y)]$
$\forall x \, \forall y \, [TOUCH(x, y) < \Rightarrow [TOUCH(y, x)]$

This taxonomy and the theorems represent our background knowledge of the semantics of the microworld in which learning is taking place. The SM of E_1 and E_2 proceeds by transforming them into equivalent formulas E_1' and E_2', such that E_1' is equivalent to E_1, and E_2' is equivalent to E_2 in this microworld (i.e., taking into account its semantics). When the process is completed, E_1' and E_2' are made of two parts. One is a variablized version of E_1 and E_2. It is called the body of the SM-ized formulas. When SM succeeds, the bodies of E_1' and E_2' are identical. The other part, called the bindings (of the variables), gives all the conditions at which the bodies might become the examples again. In our example,

Body of $E_1' =$ POLYGON(u, y) & SQUARE(x) & CONVEX(v_1, v_2, z) &
ON(y, z) & TOUCH(y, z) & SMALL(y) & BIG(z)

Bindings of $E_1' =$ ((x = y) & (y $\neq$ z) & (x $\neq$ z) & (v_1 = ELLIPSOID) &
(v_2 = CIRCLE) & (u = SQUARE) & (x = A) & (z = B))

Body of $E_2' =$ POLYGON(u, y) & SQUARE(x) & CONVEX(v_1, v_2, z) &
TOUCH(y, z) & SMALL(y) & BIG(z)

Bindings of $E_2' =$ ((x $\neq$ y) & (y $\neq$ z) & (x = z) & (v_1 = POLYGON) &
(v_2 = SQUARE) & (u = TRIANGLE) & (x = D) & (y = C))

The algorithm that constructs E_1' and E_2' is explained in [Kodratoff, 1983; Kodratoff and Ganascia, 1986; Kodratoff, et al., 1985]. The reader can check that E_1' and E_2' are equivalent to E_1 and E_2. E_1' and E_2' contain exactly the information extracted from the hierarchy and the theorems which is necessary to put the examples into SM. For instance, in E_1', the expression "(POLYGON(u, y)" means that there is a polygon in E_1, and since we have the binding (u = SQUARE), it says that this polygon is a square, which is redundant in view of the fact that SQUARE(x) & (x = y) says that x is a square and is the same as y. This redundancy is not artificial when one considers the polygon in E_2, which is a TRIANGLE.

Once this SM step has been performed, the generalization step becomes trivial: We keep in the generalization all the bindings common to the SM-ized formulas and drop all those not in common. The generalization E_1 and E_2 is therefore

Eg: POLYGON(u, y) & SQUARE(x) & CONVEX(v_1, v_2, z) &
TOUCH(y, z) & SMALL(y) & BIG(z) with bindings (y $\neq$ z).

In "English," this formula means that there are two different objects (named y and z), y and z touch each other, y is a small polygon, z is a big convex, and there is a square (named x), which may be identical to y or z.

The last implementation of SM [Vrain—Chapter 13, this volume] is not tuned to incremental learning. Nevertheless, changes evoked by Vrain would make it work incrementally, as long as the structural matching is preserved. An explanation of each change due to a new example would then be possible. In other words, it would not be too difficult to include OGUST into an apprentice system as long as the "good" structural matching has been found with the first set of examples. In that case, the explanations provided by OGUST would be of increasing quality as the number of new examples increases. On the contrary, if a new example differs widely from the present generalization, then a completely new generalization process would have to take place, thus providing no explanations.

16.3.6 Improvement of a Recognition Function by an Explanation of Its Failure to Reject a New Negative Example

Let us suppose that f(x) recognizes a new negative example NE (as it should not). This means that the proof that [NE & $\forall$x [$\neg$f(x)]] leads to the empty clause instead of failing as it should if the negative example were rejected. Explaining a success, if not easy, is usually less complicated than explaining a failure. This is why we think that a method can be devised for incremental learning in this case. The simplest way to forbid a proof to succeed is to collect the substitutions that lead to a success and forbid them. Since a substitution can be represented by an equality, the new function will be obtained from the old one, by adding the condition that its variables do not take the values as in the substitution.

Example 5

Suppose that the recognition function is $f_5(x, y) = \text{SPHERE}(x)\ \&\ \text{RED}(y)$ and that NE_5: $\text{SPHERE}(G)\ \&\ \text{RED}(G)$ is a negative example to f_5. Writing it as clauses, one sees at once that one cannot deduce $\neg f_5$ from NE_5 since

```
C₁₆:   SPHERE(G)              :-
C₁₇:   RED(G)                 :-
C₁₈:                          :-  SPHERE(x),  RED(y)
```

leads to the empty clause with the substitution $[x \leftarrow G, y \leftarrow G]$. Therefore, as defined in Section 16.3.2, NE_5 is recognized by f_5. As one can see the success of the proof is easy to explain: Any substitution that leads to the result is a kind of explanation. The simplest way to change f_5 in order to obtain a new function f_5', that forbids the success of the proof, is to forbid to x and y to take the value G. From f_5 and the new negative example NE_5, one obtains the new recognition function

$$f_5'(x, y) = \text{SPHERE}(x)\ \&\ \text{RED}(y)\ \&\ \neg[[x = G]\ \&\ [y = G]].$$

Let us now see how this can help solve the problems of incremental learning and explanations.

16.3.7 Relative Role of Positive and Negative Examples

Positive examples will generalize to a recognition function containing all the properties common to them. On the other hand, the negative examples express the fact that none of the positive ones may possess such or such property. Therefore, the positive examples must verify the theorem obtained by negating the one that best expresses the properties of the negative examples.

In other words, let us call $\{E_i\}$ the set of positive examples, and $\{\text{NE}_i\}$ the set of the negative ones. Let NP_j (Negative Property) be a property common to all NE_is. Then, none of the E_is should show NP_j. Let us call $f(x)$ a tentative recognition function of the positive examples, one has to prove that $\forall x\ [f(x) \Rightarrow \neg\text{NP}_j]$. This can be done for each j, each proof being necessary to the control of the validity of $f(x)$.

Let us now suppose that we have been able to find $f_N(x)$, the "best" recognition function of all the negative examples. None of the examples should be recognized by this function, then none should be compatible with $\exists x\ [f_N(x)]$, therefore all of them should be compatible with $\neg\exists x\ [f_N(x)] = \forall x\ [\neg f_N(x)]$.

This proves that examples allow us to find recognition functions and that the negative examples allow us to find theorems, like

$$\forall x \ [f(x) \Rightarrow \neg NP_j] \text{ and } \forall x \ [f(x) \Rightarrow \neg f_N(x)],$$

that must be verified by all correct instances of the recognition function. Let then $f(x)$ be a tentative recognition function of the positive examples, one has to prove

$$\forall x \ [f(x) \Rightarrow \neg f_N(x)]$$

as a condition necessary for $f(x)$ to be a valid recognition function. From this proof one can of course retrieve explanations for why $f(x)$ is a good recognition function.

Note that this formula is valid only for an $f(x)$ that is supposed to be the "best" one; i.e., *the* one that characterizes the domain of the examples. Starting from an $f(x)$, which is not the best one, failure to prove one of the above theorems will help us improve $f(x)$.

In conclusion, negative examples can be used to improve the recognition function. The "best" one must verify $fj \ [\forall x \ [f(x) \Rightarrow \neg NP_j]]$ and $\forall x \ [f(x) \Rightarrow \neg f_N(x)]$.

Example 6

For the remainder of this section, let $f_6(x, y) = SPHERE(x) \ \& \ BLACK(y)$. Suppose that the negative example is

$$NE_6 = [BLACK(A) \ \& \ SPHERE(A)].$$

The best theorem is NE_6 itself, the theorem that must be verified by the examples is $\forall x \forall y \ [f_6(x, y) \Rightarrow \neg NE_6]$; i.e., one must attempt to prove

$$\forall x \forall y \ [[BLACK(x) \ \& \ SPHERE(y)] \Rightarrow \neg [BLACK(A) \ \& \ SPHERE(A)]]$$

and one will, of course, fail.

Let us now see how this progressive refinement of $f(x)$ through failures to prove some $\forall x \ [f(x) \Rightarrow \neg NP_j]$ may be handled. We must attempt to construct a new generalization $f'(x)$ which implies $\neg f_N(x)$. Our method for doing so uses an attempt to prove a particular theorem, henceforth called Th. The reason Th is chosen cannot be understood beforehand; the reader is asked to wait a little before seeing the interesting consequences of its proof.

Th: $\exists x \ [f(x) \Rightarrow f_N(x)]$.

Example 7 (Start)

In this example, we shall attempt to prove that

$$\exists x \exists y \ [[BLACK(x) \ \& \ SPHERE(y)] \Rightarrow [BLACK(A) \ \& \ SPHERE(A)]]$$

When attempting to prove Th, there are three possible cases.

First Case Th is not provable.

The reason may be that $\forall x \, [f(x) \Rightarrow \neg f_N(x)]$ has been proven. In that case, the new property of the negative examples actually does not cover any example, and nothing has to be changed. It may also be so we are unable to prove both Th and

$$\forall x \, [f(x) \Rightarrow \neg f_N(x)].$$

This is the failure case, where nothing can be learned. It shows that we ignore an essential property of the domain, but does not tell where to find it.

Second Case Th is provable and its normal form is the empty clause. We prove it by refutation, attempting to prove that one can deduce the empty clause from ¬Th. Since Th is provable, one will succeed and each success delivers a substitution s, which is an instance of the substitutions to be made to x in order to verify Th. By carrying out all the possible proofs, in the case where there is a finite number of them; or, in infinite cases, by inventing a function that covers all the cases (this part is not emphasized here but is of course very difficult), one defines the set of all the x_i such that $f(x_i) \Rightarrow f_N(x_i)$.

Let us call P_i this set

$$P_i = \{ x_i \, / \, f(x_i) \Rightarrow f_N(x_i) \}.$$

We now claim that

$$\forall x \, [[f(x) \,\&\, \{x/ \neg[x \in P_i]\}] \Rightarrow \neg f_N(x)].$$

This theorem is valid since it simply says that when $f(x)$ is true, and that x belongs to the set for which the implication $f(x) \Rightarrow f_N(x)$ is FALSE, then $f_N(x)$ is FALSE. Though very simple, this theorem gives us the $f'(x)$ we have been looking for:

$$f'(x) = [f(x) \,\&\, \{x/ \neg[x \in P_i]\}].$$

Example 7 (continued 1)

In order to prove

$$\exists \, x \, y \, [[BLACK(x) \,\&\, SPHERE(y)] \Rightarrow [BLACK(A) \,\&\, SPHERE(A)]]$$

we shall try to derive the empty clause from its negation ¬Th. As usually [Kowalski, 1979], the theorem is transformed into clauses as follows:

$$\neg\exists x\exists y \, [[BLACK(x) \,\&\, SPHERE(y)] \Rightarrow [BLACK(A) \,\&\, SPHERE(A)]] =$$
$$\neg\exists x\exists y \, [\,\neg[BLACK(x) \,\&\, SPHERE(y)] \vee [BLACK(A) \,\&\, SPHERE(A)]] =$$
$$\forall x\forall y \, [[BLACK(x) \,\&\, SPHERE(y)] \,\&\, \neg[BLACK(A) \,\&\, SPHERE(A)]]$$

which is equivalent to the set of clauses:

```
BLACK(x)    :-
SPHERE(y)   :-
            :- BLACK(A),  SPHERE(A)
```

This set generates once only the empty clause with the substitution

$$\sigma = [x \leftarrow A, y \leftarrow A] \ .$$

It follows that the set $\{x = A, y = A\} = P_i$ is the set for which Th is valid. As proven above, conjuncting $\neg[(x = A) \& (y = A)]$ to [BLACK(x) & SPHERE(y)] will yield the looked for generalization

[BLACK(x) & SPHERE(y)] & [(x≠A) <186 (y≠A)].

This is the generalization that keeps as much as possible what has been deduced from the examples and excludes the negative example.

One should be aware that this is the best particularization that can be made from the negative examples. If one attempted to derive a more general law, one could overgeneralize and lose some vital information.

Example 7 (continued 2)
Suppose the following further negative example is added

NE_7 = BLACK(A) & SPHERE(D)

then our method shows that the generalization from f_6 and NE_6 and NE_7 must be

[BLACK(x) & SPHERE(y) & (x ≠ A)].

Third Case   Th is provable but does not reduce to the empty clause. One must then analyze the failure. Since we suppose that we use resolution to deduce the empty clause from $\neg$Th, it follows that the failure will be caused by a subset of irreducible clauses that do not reduce to the empty clause. Let us call LO(x) (Left-Over) this subset. We shall not give here many details about LO(x), nor comment on the fact that it is not unique in general. Section 16.4 is devoted to an analysis of this kind of problems.

Let us suppose in this section that it is unique. Consider the expression

f(x) & ¬LO(x)

and attempt to prove

Th′: $\exists x$ [f(x) & ¬LO(x)] ⇒ f_N(x)]

Its negation is $\forall x$ [[f(x) & ¬LO(x) & ¬f_N(x)] and, since LO(x) is precisely the left-over of the resolution of $\forall x$ [f(x) & ¬f_N(x)], the empty clause will always follow from it. Let us now call P_i the set of values that verify Th′.

Drawing a conclusion from the above reasoning requires us to take a somewhat closer look at LO. Due to the conjunctive form of the theorem

$\forall x$ [f(x) & ¬LO(x) & ¬f_N(x)],

one can always assume that each clause contains atoms that originate from and only from $f(x)$ or from and only from $f_N(x)$. It follows that $LO(x)$ has the form

$LO'(x)$ & $\neg LO''(x)$ where $f(x) = f'(x)$ & $LO'(x)$ and $f_N(x) = f_N'(X)$ & $LO''(x)$.

During the proof of Th', LO' (respectively $\neg LO''$) resolves some predicates of $\neg f_N$ (respectively f). It follows that from the proofs of $\exists x\ [[f(x)$ & $\neg LO(x)\ ] \Rightarrow f_N(x)]$ one can deduce that

$\forall x\ [[f'(x)$ & $\{x/\neg[x \in P_i]\}] \Rightarrow \neg f_N'(x)]$

by the same reasoning as above.

Let us now use the two following trivialities

from $A \Rightarrow C$, deduce that A & $B \Rightarrow C$
from $A \Rightarrow C$, deduce that A & $D \Rightarrow C \vee D$

in order to find that

$\forall x\ [[f(x)$ & $\{x/\neg[x \in P_i]\}$ & $\neg LO''(x)] \Rightarrow \neg f_N(x)\ ]$

which is the "interesting" form we wanted to construct.

The final definition we can now give for the best formula that can be learned from formula $f(x)$ and negative examples generalizing to $f_N(x)$ is

$[\ f(x)$ & $\neg LO''(x)$ & $\{x/\neg[x \in P_i]\}]$.

This is the correct recognition function.

We now describe two simple examples showing that our definitions contain the well-known intuitive learning behavior when the positive and negative examples mismatch by a predicate. There are two cases.

First Case The generalization from examples contains more predicates than the negative example.

Example 7 (continued 3)
        Recall that $f_6(x, y)$ is: $BLACK(x)$ & $SPHERE(y)$, and suppose that the negative example is now $BLACK(A)$. The attempt to prove

$\exists x\ y\ [[BLACK(x)$ & $SPHERE(y)] \Rightarrow BLACK(A)]$

fails with $SPHERE(y)$ as $LO = LO'$. Conjuncting $\neg LO$ to $f_6(x, y)$, one attempts now to prove

$\exists x \exists y\ [[BLACK(x)$ & $SPHERE(y)$ & $\neg SPHERE(y)] \Rightarrow BLACK(A)]$,

i.e., that $\neg \exists x \exists y\ [\ BLACK(x) \Rightarrow BLACK(A)\ ]$ contains a contradiction. The substitution $[x \leftarrow A]$ describes the domain where this contradiction holds, and it follows that

$\forall x \forall y\ [[BLACK(x)$ & $SPHERE(y)$ & $\neg SPHERE(y)$ & $(x \neq A)] \Rightarrow$
        $\neg BLACK(A)]$.

This shows that the final generalization is

[BLACK(x) & SPHERE(y) & SPHERE(y) & (x ≠ A)] = [BLACK(x) &
SPHERE(y) & (x ≠ A)]

Second case   The generalization from examples contains fewer predicates than the negative example.

Example 8
Let the generalization from examples be $f_7(x) = $ BLACK(x), and the negative example be SPHERE(A) & BLACK(A). The left-over is ¬SPHERE(A) = ¬LO″, conjuncting its negation to BLACK(x) allows us to find the empty clause with

[x ← A].

It follows that the best recognition function is

BLACK(x) & ¬SPHERE(A) & (x ≠ A).

16.4 IMPROVING THE EXPLANATIONS

16.4.1 Improving the Quality of the Generalization

Instead of applying the above techniques to the recognition function and a negative example, one can also attempt to compare it to a generalization of the negative examples. Since their generalization will be used in order to expel some information from the recognition function of the examples, it may be that the modified recognition function no longer recognizes all the examples after its modification. This will happen when one uses an overgeneralization of the negative examples. It is therefore extremely important to avoid this overgeneralization. Structural matching, the role of which is to avoid such kind of overgeneralization, is important when generalizing examples, but it is even more important when generalizing negative examples.

Example 9
Consider again $f_6 = $ BLACK(x) & SPHERE(y).Consider now the case where one wants to find the correct generalization associated to f_6 and

$NE_8 = $ BLACK(A) & SPHERE(A)
$NE_9 = $ BLACK(B) & SPHERE(B).

The recognition function deduced from NE_8 and NE_9 is

$f_N(x) = $ BLACK(x) & SPHERE(x)

In this case, Th is

∃x∃y [[BLACK(x) & SPHERE(y)] ⇒ [BLACK(x) & SPHERE(x)]]

which is TRUE for the unique substitution [y ← x], therefore P_i is characterized by $x = y$ and $\neg[x \in P_i]$ if $x \neq y$. It follows that the correct generalization is, in this case,

[BLACK(x) & SPHERE(y) & (x ≠ y)].

Notice that overgeneralizing NE_1 and NE_3 to BLACK(x) & SPHERE(y) for instance would lead to total disappearance of the recognition function—a case clearly difficult to overcome by further modifications!

16.4.2 Improving of the Quality of the Proof

As seen in preceding sections, an explanation procedure can always be attached to a proof of recognition or rejection. There are often several possible proofs. Each of them will provide new different explanations. Explanations relative to successes will enrich the recognition functions. Explanations relative to failures will allow modifying the data basis. For instance, in the example of Section 16.3.3, the default values of an ENDTABLE can be modified in case the system fails to recognize that a given BOX_1 can be stacked on a given $ENDTABLE_1$. In a real situation, where we will have to handle numerous explanations, one will be able to modify the data theory by learning.

16.4.2.1 The System Generates Several Explanations from One Example

Suppose that, as in Section 16.3.3, it finds that BOX_1 can be stacked on END-$TABLE_1$ because the weight of BOX_1 is less than 50. Suppose also that, by using another reasoning path, it finds also the other explanation: because $ENDTABLE_1$ is "very stiff" (one should have defined this predicate in the data of the theory). The system will have first to prove that there is no mutual implication between "BOX_1 is less than 50" and "$ENDTABLE_1$ is very stiff." Then it will have to improve its explanation by providing a disjunction of these two cases. As another example, suppose that one obtains the two explanations

Ex_1: the weight of BOX_1 is less than 50
Ex_2: the weight of $ENDTABLE_1$ is more than twice the weight of BOX_1

depending on the reasoning path that is used during the proof. In this case, one would have to check that the weight of BOX_1 is less than 25; i.e., that the two explanations are not contradicting each other. None of them imply the other, they would have both to be kept.

16.4.2.2 The System Generates Several Explanations from Several Examples

We shall present here the ideas underlying a system currently under construction [Duval and Kodratoff, 1990] in our French group. This system performs EBL on a set of several training examples and combines the explanations. Let us illustrate our approach on the "suicide" example of DeJong and Mooney [1986]. Suppose that a first example describes the suicide of Peter with a gun. For a given operationality criterion and given schemes for "killing," let us suppose that EBL generalizes this instance to "a man self-killing with a shot-gun." Suppose that we get now the story of Mary's suicide with a gun and that we generalize it to "a woman self-killing with a shot-gun." Using a standard learning procedure (here, by using the "climbing the generalization tree" rule), we can combine the two above generalizations into the unique one "a human self-killing with a shot-gun." The same kind of mechanisms, now including structural matching or even some analogy-based reasoning [Vrain and Kodratoff, 1987; 1988] can be used when getting new examples of suicide with, say, a dagger or with butane gas (shot-gun would then have to be generalized to "harmful object"). A more difficult case will be met when the system will see a suicide committed by jumping from the Eiffel tower, which is not normally a harmful object. The learning would then proceed by recognizing the analogies between "pushing someone from a cliff" and "jumping from the Eiffel tower." The whole "killing" scheme would then have to be refined by including the situations where an actor place an other one in a potentially harmful situation etc. ...

This example shows that we need a system able to refine the theory it starts with; i.e., that includes new rules into the theory, in order to avoid proof failures. The next section describes some of the ideas underlying such a system.

16.4.3 Refinement of Incomplete Theories

A stringent requirement of EBL is that it demands a complete theory of the domain of learning. One can easily imagine that this case seldom holds in reality. This is why a great deal of work has been done on the topic of error recovery by explanations, which is quite similar to explanation improvement. The interested reader should consult the chapters in this volume by Carbonell and Gil, DeJong and Mooney, Hirsh, and also [Hill, 1987; Rajamoney and DeJong, 1987; Mostow and Bhatnagar, 1987].

For the management of incomplete theories, the central idea is to complete the failure proofs by an abduction[1] mechanism guided by analogical reasoning about explanations and enables to discover new rules that refine the domain theory. We shall illustrate this by the following example drawn from DeJong and Mooney [1986]. In this example, our aim is learning a definition of the concept of suicide $Kill(x,x)$. The domain theory TH_0 contains the following rules

---

[1] Technically, an abduction is the process that, given a B, finds some A's such that $A \Rightarrow B$. In practice, this amounts to finding the conditions that would allow a failed proof to succeed.

```
KILL(a,b)        :-  HATE(a,b), POSSESS(a,c),
                     WEAPON(c)
HATE(w,w)        :-  DEPRESSED(w)
POSSESS(u,v)     :-  BUY(u,v)
WEAPON(z)        :-  SHOT-GUN(z)
```

where a, b, c, w, u, v, z are variables.

The training instance TR1 is a suicide, described by the following facts.

```
TR1
DEPRESSED(JOHN)    :-
BUY(JOHN,OBJ1)     :-
SHOT-GUN(OBJ1)     :-
                   :-  KILL(JOHN, JOHN)
```

DeJong and Mooney have shown that applying EBL to the training instance leads to building the generalized proof of the fact that John has been committing suicide, that we shall from now on call S (Source) in which x and c are variables (see Figure 16–4).

This produces the rule

```
KILL(x,x)  :-              DEPRESSED(x), BUY(x,c), SHOT-GUN(c)
```

which is "added" to TH_0 in order to define the concept C of suicide. Nothing is actually added since this new rule is a consequence of TH_0. It happens that this rule seems to be more operational to define suicide that applying KILL(a, b) with a = b.

Suppose now that the system is provided with an example TR2 of concept C, which is not recognized by the theory. In other words, some oracle will have been telling the system that TR2 does belong to the suicide case, but the PROLOG solver failed to prove it. Nevertheless, it may happen (this is the case we are actually considering here) that partial proofs might be obtained. They will provide partial proof trees that may match parts of S. Let us call Ti (Target incomplete) incomplete proof trees that can be viewed as partial explanations as explained with more details in [Duval and Kodratoff, 1990]. Our aim will then be to complete each of these Ti into Tc (Target complete) in such a way that S and Tc are as "close" as possible.

Figure 16-4:   Generalized proof that John has been committing suicide

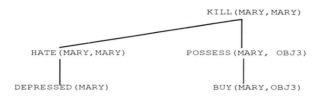

Figure 16–5:   Ti: Partial explanation of Mary's suicide

As an illustration of such a Ti, consider an other suicide instance TR2 described by the following facts.

```
DEPRESSED(MARY)                  :-
BUY(MARY,OBJ1)                   :-
SLEEPING-PILLS(OBJ1)             :-
PRICE(SLEEPING-PILLS, 6)  :-
BUY(MARY, OBJ2)                  :-
BOOK(OBJ2)                       :-
PRICE(BOOK, 5)                   :-
...
```

where OBJ1 and OBJ2 are constants.

We will be unable to prove KILL(MARY, MARY) because she has no shotgun. Nevertheless we obtain one, and only one in this case, partial proof (see Figure 16–5).

Ti obviously matches a subtree of S.

In order to achieve the completion of Ti into Tc, and to achieve it so that Tc is "close" to S, we propose to use two different abductions. In general, the mechanism underlying this abduction process is analogy. We shall not speak of analogy here—see [Duval and Kodratoff, 1990] for more details.

First Abduction   We attempt to complete Ti by viewing it as an instance of S (this is one of the possible definitions of "closeness"). Therefore, Ti will be completed by taking the missing pieces from S, appropriately instantiated.

In our example, such a forced matching leads to Tc1 (see Figure 16–6).

This first abduction can be seen as interpreting the fact that Mary possesses an object that is in fact a shot-gun, but our knowledge about shot-guns is not sufficient to identify this object. The cause of the preceding failure is attributed to our supposed "ignorance" that OBJ3 (i.e., sleeping pills) are actually shot-guns. Notice that this first mechanism is the only one considered in other works about abduction such as [Cox, 1986], and note how easily it can lead to absurd results, as here.

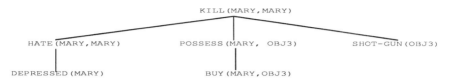

Figure 16–6:   Tc1: Proof tree completed. S matches Tc1 with the substitutions
[x ← MARY, c ← OBJ3].

Second Abduction In this case, we try to add a new rule that will allow us to complete the proof. One can easily understand why this mechanism has not been taken into account so far; in principle one can add so many ridiculous rules that this approach seems to be hopeless.

For instance, in our example adding to TH_0 the rule

```
KILL(x,x)   :-   PRICE(SLEEPING-PILLS, 6)
```

will indeed allow us to prove Mary's suicide. But it means that everyone will commit suicide when the price of sleeping pills reaches the value 6, which is totally irrelevant to the preceding suicide case, notwithstanding its strange meaning.

In order to avoid adding such ridiculous rules as above, we define a new notion of distance between S and Tc. Given two possible completed proof trees, Tc and Tc′, consider an attempt to match S and Tc, and S and Tc′. In this second abduction, we do not consider the case where they match (this would be the first kind of abduction). We shall therefore collect the mismatches between S and Tc on the one hand, and between S and Tc′ on the other hand. We shall say that that Tc is closer to S than Tc if the number of mismatches between Tc and S is less than the number of mismatches between Tc′ and S. When they are equal, we shall say that Tc is closer to S than Tc′ when the conceptual distance (supposedly defined) between the mismatches is less for Tc than for Tc′.

In our example, it is clear that the number of mismatches between S and the proof tree obtained by using

```
KILL(x,x)   :-   PRICE(SLEEPING-PILLS, 6)
```

to prove Mary's suicide is very high.

On the other hand, completing Ti by SLEEPING-PILL(OBJ3), obtaining thus the proof tree Tc2, shown in Figure 16–7, leads to one mismatch only, namely

[SHOT-GUN(OBJ3) ← SLEEPING-PILLS(OBJ3)].

Notice that we speak here of mismatch since SHOT-GUN(OBJ3) is not a variable. Applying EBG to this proof leads to add the new rule

```
KILL(x,x)   :-   DEPRESSED(x), BUY(x,c), SLEEPING-PILLS(c)
```

to TH_0.

Figure 16–7: Sleeping pills are viewed as the cause of Mary's death

Figure 16–8: Books are viewed as the cause of Mary's death

One can complete it as well by BOOK(OBJ4), obtaining the proof tree Tc3 shown in Figure 16–8.

Applying EBG to this proof leads to add the new rule

```
KILL(x,x)   :-   DEPRESSED(x),  BUY(x,c),  BOOK(c)
```

to TH_0.

From our semantic knowledge, it is clear that Tc2 is the good answer, but this result is not so easy to obtain. It needs to have some ways to prove that sleeping pills are more likely to kill someone than books.[2] Proving this would ask a large amount of extra-knowledge not contained in TH_0. Anyhow, we simply suppose here that one has been able to set up some way of evaluating the semantic distance between SHOT-GUN and SLEEPING-PILLS, and between SHOT-GUN and BOOK, and that the first is less than the second. Then, we would choose Tc3 as other possible abduction.

We will leave here open the two following points. One is the way to measure the semantic distance between concepts, which can be taken care of completely independently of this chapter. The second one is to choose between the results of the above two kinds of abductions. A a simple hint, let us point out that the new rule

---

[2] Consider however that a French writer recently published a book entitled *A Cheap Guide to Happy Suicide*. He is regularly sued by families of suicides arguing that his book is the cause of the suicide's death, and the families always win their cases.

should be checked against other knowledge of different granularity, for instance finding if shot-guns and sleeping pills generalize to a rich concept or not.

As conclusion to this section, let us acknowledge first that the difficult problems of completing the theory from experiences and explanation are visibly very hard to tackle with. Nevertheless, we can see that proposing sound abduction is quite feasible, and that choosing the best among them is a matter of good structuration of the background knowledge.

16.5 CONCLUSIONS

This chapter advocates an integrated approach to machine learning in which inductive and deductive learning enhance each other. The key concept to link them is *explanations*, and the source of explanations is a theorem prover. We have shown how much EBL relies on the trace of proof, and how much the construction of a recognition function relies as well on theorem proving. EBL uses a proof that some goal may be achieved, like the goal of stacking BOX_1 on $ENDTABLE_1$ as shown in Section 16.3.3. We have shown that learning from examples needs to prove or disprove that an instance belongs to a concept, in exactly the same way as EBL does.

In other words, this chapter can be considered a detailed illustration of how constructive learning is going to be achieved. One may have to learn rules to solve a problem, to achieve a goal, to recognize a concept but, in all cases, constructive learning will proceed as follows.

1. Choose a representation language for the examples of concept or behavior.

2. Find a generalization that will describe some of the properties they share.

3. Prove, or disprove, that other examples are instances of the generalization obtained at step 2.

4. Analyze the proof, or proof failures, in order to obtain an explanation for why the new example is recognized or rejected.

5. Use these explanations to improve the representation language of the examples (i.e., use new explanations to perform again, and better, step 1 above) and their generalization (i.e., use new explanations to perform again, and better, step 2 above).

In the description of this closed-loop process, the first four steps have already received much attention in the current literature. Step 5 has to be somehow implemented in all the systems described in the *Integrated Learning* part of this book. We have shown here that the whole integration hinges on explanations. Our main argument is that being able to refine explanations will, in turn, allow us to refine the generalizations. We did not argue here about the representation changes, but we are convinced that explanations of failures are the best way to drive the search in the best direction whenever representation changes are needed.

References

Duval, B. and Kodratoff, Y. 1990. "A Tool for the Management of Incomplete Theories: Reasoning about Explanations," in *Machine Learning, Meta-Reasoning and Logics*, P. Brazdil and K. Konolige (eds), Kluwer Academic Press, Amsterdam, pp. 135–158.

Hill, W. L. 1987. "Machine Learning for Software Reuse," *Proc. IJCAI-87*, pp. 338–344, John McDermott (ed), Morgan Kaufmann, San Mateo, CA.

Kedar-Cabelli, S.T. and McCarthy, L.T. 1987. "Explanation-Based Generalization as Resolution Theorem Proving," *Proc. 4th International Workshop on Machine Learning*, pp. 383–389, Irvine, June 1987, Langley, P. (ed), Morgan Kaufmann, San Mateo, CA.

Kodratoff, Y. 1983. "Generalizing and Particularizing as the Techniques of Learning," *Computers and Artificial Intelligence* 2, pp. 417–441.

Kodratoff, Y., Ganascia, J.-G., Clavieras, B., Bollinger, T., and Tecuci, G. 1984. "Careful generalization for concept learning," in *Advances in Artificial Intelligence*, T. O'Shea (ed), pp. 229–238, North-Holland Amsterdam, 1985.

Kodratoff, Y. and Ganascia, J.-G. 1986. "Improving the Generalization Step in Learning," in *Machine Learning: An Artificial Intelligence Approach, Volume II*, Michalski, R.S., Carbonell, J.G., and Mitchell, T.M. (eds), Morgan-Kaufmann, San Mateo, CA, pp. 215–244.

Kodratoff, Y. and Tecuci, G. 1987a. "DISCIPLE-1: Interactive Apprentice System in Weak Theory Field," McDermott, J. (ed), *IJCAI 1987*, Morgan Kaufmann, San Mateo, CA, pp. 271–273.

————— , 1987b. Techniques of design and DISCIPLE learning apprentice. *International Journal of Expert Systems*, 1, pp. 39–66.

Kodratoff, Y. 1988. *Introduction to Machine Learning*, Pitman, London. Available in the U.S. from Morgan Kaufmann, San Mateo, CA.

Kowalski, R. 1979. *Logic for Problem Solving*, North Holland.

Michalski, R.S. 1983. "A theory and a methodology of inductive learning." *Artificial Intelligence*, 20, pp. 111–161.

————— , 1984. "Inductive learning as rule-guided transformation of symbolic descriptions: A theory and implementation," in *Automatic Program Construction Techniques*, Biermann, A.W., Guiho, G., Kodratoff, Y. (eds), Macmillan Publishing Company, pp. 517–552.

Michalski, R.S. and Stepp, R.E. 1983. "Learning from Observation: Conceptual Clustering," in *Machine Learning: An Artificial Intelligence Approach*, Michalski, R.S., Carbonell, J.G., Mitchell, T.M. (eds), Morgan Kaufmann, San Mateo, CA, pp. 163–190.

Mitchell, T.M. 1983. "Learning and Problem Solving" *Proc. IJCAI-83*, pp. 1139–1151, Karlsruhe.

Mitchell, T.M., Mahadevan, S., and Steinberg, L.I. 1985. "Leap: A Learning Apprentice for VLSI Design," *Proc. IJCAI-85*, Los Angeles, pp. 573–580.

Mitchell, T.M., Keller, R.M., and Kedar-Cabelli, S.T. 1986. "Explanation-Based Generalization: A Unifying View," *Machine Learning* 1, pp. 47–80.

Mostow, J. and Bhatnagar, N. 1987. "Failsafe—A Floor Planner that Uses EBG to Learn from its Failures," *Proc. IJCAI-87*, McDermott, J. (ed), pp. 249–255, Morgan Kaufmann, San Mateo, CA.

Nicolas, J. 1986. "Learning as Search: A Logical Approach," *CIIAM'86*, Marseille, Hermes, Paris, pp. 441–459.

Nilsson, N. J. 1980. *Principles of Artificial Intelligence*, Morgan Kaufmann, San Mateo, CA.

Rajamoney, S. and DeJong, G. 1987. "The Classification, Detection and Handling of Imperfect Theory Problems," *Proc. IJCAI-87*, McDermott, J. (ed), Morgan Kaufmann, San Mateo, CA, pp. 205–207.

Siqueira, J.L. and Puget, J.F. 1988. "Explanation-Based Generalization of Failures," *Proc. ECAI*, Munich, Kodratoff, Y. (ed), Pitman, London.

Touchais, R. 1987. "Généralisation à partir de l'explication," Rapport de stage DEA, Orsay Univ.

Vrain, C. and Kodratoff, Y. 1989. "The Use of Analogy in Incremental SBL," in *Knowledge Representation and Organization in Machine Learning*, Lecture Notes in Computer Science, No. 347, Morik, K. (ed), Springer-Verlag, Berlin, pp. 231–246.

Waldinger, R. 1977. "Achieving Several Goals Simultaneously," in *Machine Intelligence* 8, Elcock, E.W. and Michie, D. (eds), Ellis Horwood.

COMMENTARY

Robert E. Stepp
(University of Illinois)

1 OVERVIEW OF THE PAPER

Kodratoff describes an approach to machine learning that performs in a manner he calls an "explicatory apprentice"; i.e., a system designed for building and improving explanations of events. The paper focuses on theorem-proving techniques that bring together the two polar notions in machines learning: similarity-based learning (SBL) and explanation-based learning (EBL). It is pointed out that these approaches are actually closely related—both aim at producing good explanations of events, and both can be practiced using theorem-proving techniques (although doing so naturally introduces powerful preferences and biases, a topic not considered).

Kodratoff notes that SBL and EBL operate in problem-dependent microworlds. In traditional SBL approaches, the microworld is the background knowledge provided to the learning system. In traditional EBL approaches, the microworld is the domain theory by which the system understands the concept being explained.

First, an explanation can be viewed as a *generalized proof*. In EBL, explanation as logical proof provides the constraints that must be maintained for the explanation to hold. It is this proof mechanism that requires EBL applications to include complete domain knowledge. In SBL systems, explanation is the mechanism of performance. By the explanation, SBL systems can ultimately identify the categories to which events should be assigned, and thereby explain them.

Second, an explanation can be viewed as a learning/generalizing tool. In EBL, explanation maintenance is the tool by which the boundary between generalization and overgeneralization is defined. EBL works because generalization is never taken to the point that the explanation ceases to hold. In SBL, generalization (and inverse generalization, i.e., specialization) is a mechanism for explanation repair. New events that do not receive the desired decision (those that are misidentified) call for explanation repair.

In the language of covering algorithms [Michalski, 1984], this situation is described as finding one or more events that are either uncovered or covered by the wrong category description. Kodratoff presents a theorem-proving approach involving cases where an explanation proof fails when it should succeed or succeeds when it should fail. In both cases, repair is required.

From a theorem-proving standpoint, the mechanisms of SBL and EBL are related. For EBL systems, the main inference rule is *modus ponens*:

if A *and* A $\Rightarrow$ B *then deduce* B.

For SBL systems, Kodratoff says the main inference rule is *classical generalization*:

if A *and* A $\rhd$ B *then deduce* B

where the symbol $\rhd$ means "is more general than." In each case, the mechanisms are to be used to generate proofs (and generalized proofs) called *explanations*, which are in the language of the problem domain. Guidance on how to do this is embodied in the preferences and biases of the algorithms, and in "explanation kits" provided by domain knowledge. In EBL, the explanation kit is the knowledge needed to do goal regression. In SBL, the explanation kit is a forest of concept generalization trees to climb (e.g., squares, rectangles, triangles are generalize to the concept *polygon*).

2 THE SBL VIEW

In this section of the commentary, the link between Kodratoff's approach and Michalski's approach is explored. Michalski has presented the formula (see Chapter 3, this volume):

Hypotheses + Background-Knowledge $\rhd$ Facts

By this statement he means that the hypotheses and the background knowledge taken together account for or *explain* the facts. If one makes the background knowledge implicit rather than explicit (by operating in the *context* of the background knowledge), and if one calls the hypotheses the *recognition rules*, then one can arrive at this commentator's interpretation of the view taken by Kodratoff, illustrated in the following diagram in which the box encloses the context within which the background knowledge is available to be applied.

```
┌─────────────────────────────────────┐
│ Recognition rules ▷ Examples         │
│ Background Knowledge                  │
└─────────────────────────────────────┘
```

Thus, Kodratoff's SBL approach can be described by Michalski's formula; the goal is the generation of recognition rules. An EBL approach is described by the same formula; the goal is to add to the background knowledge an improved/generalized explanation proof.

Kodratoff's approach is to develop a system to manage explanations. Learning is by explanation repair. To do this, one must have at least four basic knowledge management tools:

- a generalization operator
- a specialization operator
- a consistency maintenance mechanism
- preference criteria

3 AN ILLUSTRATION AND BRIEF REVIEW OF EXPLANATION REPAIR

According to Kodratoff, a learning system needs to perform at least three tasks:

- learn to recognize positive examples,
- learn to reject negative examples, and
- manage consistency

Here are a few thoughts about each, drawn from the paper.

3.1 Learning to Recognize Positive Examples

Suppose there is a rule (a recognizer) of the form

R_1: $\exists$ x y (sphere x) (red y)
"There exists a part x that is a sphere and a part y that is red"

and there are examples such as

E_1: (sphere A) (red B)   {covered}
E_2: (sphere A) (red A)   {covered}
E_3: (rectangle A) (red B)   {not covered}

Examples E_1 and E_2 are properly explained (covered) by R_1. Example E_3 causes R_1 to fail. The system needs to generalize on failure to repair its recognizer and explain all the examples, based on the fact that the system cannot explain how E_3 is an instance of R_1.

From the microworld (background knowledge) the following useful inferences are retrieved.

$\forall$ x (sphere x) $\Rightarrow$ (ellipsoid sphere x)
$\forall$ x (ellipsoid sphere x) $\Rightarrow$ (convex ellipsoid sphere x)
$\forall$ x (rectangle x) $\Rightarrow$ (polygon rectangle x)
$\forall$ x (polygon rectangle x) $\Rightarrow$ (convex polygon rectangle x)

By applying these inference rules to the examples, discarding unlike forms, and changing constants into variables within the like forms, a process Kodratoff calls *structural mapping* produces the form

$$R_2: \exists\ v_1\ v_2\ x\ y\ (convex\ v_1\ v_2\ x)\ (red\ y)$$

R_2 is the repaired version of R_1 and recognizes all examples *when operated in the context of the background knowledge*. This rule is interpreted as "there is a convex part and a red part." *Structural mapping* is the process for making the minimum (most specific) generalization using the transformations of climbing a specificity hierarchy and variablizing forms. Climbing the specificity hierarchy uses deductive inference over implications that define the hierarchy. It is thus one type of knowledge-based generalization transformation. Vrain [Chapter 13, this volume] describes another knowledge-based generalization mechanism.

Structural mapping makes inductive leaps (when discarding unlike forms and doing variablizing) and is an SBL mechanism. Not explained in Kodratoff's paper is how structural mapping can limit its generalization to avoid describing negative events (and how to do this efficiently). Kodratoff provides references to papers that do investigate this [Ganascia, 1985; Vrain, 1985]. Since the resulting rules are already maximally specific under this paradigm, the introduction of negative events could lead to a disjunctive statement or (if disjunction is not allowed) to only a partial explanation of a subset of the examples.

3.2 Learning to Reject Negative Examples

Suppose we have arrived at rule R_2, and we encounter negative example E_4:

$$E_4: (sphere\ A)\ (red\ A)\ (rectangle\ B)$$

E_4 is recognized by R_2, and this is incorrect. Here specialization is driven by explanation failure. A proof of R_2 given the examples shows that E_4 supports R_2 under two bindings of variables, namely (x/A, y/A) and (x/B y/A). To repair the rule, both bindings must be defeated. This is done using specialized binding and idempotency to get

$$R_3: \exists\ v_1\ v_2\ v_3\ v_4\ x\ y\ z\ (convex\ v_1\ v_2\ x)\ (convex\ v_3\ v_4\ z)\ (red\ y)$$
$$([x{\neq}A]\ v\ [y{\neq}A])\ ([x{\neq}B][y{\neq}A])$$

This appears to be a rather awkward notation. The approach is similar to Winston's [1975] introduction of *must not* conditions in his blocks-world learning algorithm. Learning a generalized constraint on bindings requires considering several negative examples. Kodratoff proposes that constraints on bindings, such as in R_3 above, be generalized by requiring conjunctive forms that are maximally specific. This eliminates the full enumeration of all binding constraint combination without additionally restricting the concept.

3.3 Managing Consistency

Given a rule R that explains positive examples, a rule R_c is consistent with R if R can be shown to be more specific than (not R_c). Let R involve a set of variables denoted as *vars* and let R_c involve a set of variables denoted as *cvars*. Consistency could be demonstrated in one of the three ways:

$\forall$ vars R $\Rightarrow$ $\exists$ cvars (not R_c)
$\forall$ vars R $\Rightarrow$ $\forall$ cvars (not R_c)
$\forall$ vars R $\Rightarrow$ (not R_c)

In the illustration above, there is only one negative event, so R_c equals E_4. To see if R_2 is consistent with R_c the proof must be in the last of the three forms above because R_c contains no variables.

Consider our example:

$\forall$ v_1 v_2 x y (convex v_1 v_2 x) (red y) $\Rightarrow$ (not (sphere A)) v (not (red A)) v (not (rectangle B))

This cannot be proved; R_2 is not consistent with E_4. Therefore it may be possible to prove the negation of the consistency constraint, namely that "R generalizes to R_c," in one of two possible forms:

$\exists$ vars R $\Rightarrow$ $\exists$ cvars R_c
$\exists$ vars R $\Rightarrow$ R_c

In general let A and B be implications of the forms:

A: $\exists$ vars (R vars) $\Rightarrow$ (R_c vars)
B: $\forall$ vars (R vars) $\Rightarrow$ (not (R_c vars))

There are four cases to consider:

1. A is not proved, and B is proved,
2. A is proved, and B is not proved,
3. A is provable, but not proved and B is not proved, and
4. A is not provable, and B is not proved.

Kodratoff explains that the last situation is a fundamental inconsistency that cannot be repaired. The first case indicates that R is consistent with R_c and thus no repair is needed. In the second case each binding under which the proof holds is a problem of inconsistency between R and R_c. Let the bindings that result from this set of problems be called P. The recognition rule is repaired under this scheme by a specialization that conjoins the form (not (intersects P *binding*)) where *binding* is the set of variable bindings and P is the set of disallowed bindings. The repair for case 3 involves harvesting leftover clauses in two groups LO and LO_c such that one can prove

$\exists$ vars R & LO $\Rightarrow$ R$_c$ & LO$_c$

Then R can be redefined as R anded with (NOT LO$_c$), which fits the second case above.

4 SBL AS EBL EXPLANATION REPAIR

Normally one wants rules generated by an SBL algorithm to be consistent and complete. Given n positive events E$_i$ and m negative events F$_i$, we can take R$_c$ in Kodratoff's approach to be

$$R_c: G_1 \lor G_2 \lor \ldots \lor G_n$$

where the G$_i$ are generalizations of the negative events, and n depends on the degree of generalization performed by structural mapping: n = m and G$_i$ = F$_i$ for no generalization of negative examples; n = 1 when negative examples are described by one generalized conjunctive formula.

Showing consistency requires proving that R is a specialization of (NOT R$_c$) as is outlined above. Showing completeness requires proving that each positive event is a specialization of R. Using repair mechanisms, one finds a provable theorem that is the conjunction of all the constraints. On finding such a theorem, one has the maximally specific consistent and complete explanation of the class of positive events. Standard EBL generalization can now be used to generalize this result.

Deep bias for generating consistent rules is normally built into SBL learning algorithms. Here it is a constraint on a proof. When this constraint is applied via formal logic, explanation-based generalization (EBL) can generalize against this constraint while giving the effect of SBL learning. It is the placement of the bias that has shifted, and such hard biases as consistency appear to be applicable as a kind of *operationality*.

That this transmutation of algorithms is possible should not be a surprise. But just because it is possible to twist one into performing like the other (to some degree at least) does not mean that doing so will be rewarding. The EBL approach is an incremental approach that fits the notion of *repair* fairly well. However, as mentioned above, it is also convenient to have a technique for generalizing over positive examples while working *against* known negative examples (rather than having to repair again later). This trade-off is one more reason why repair techniques perform the minimum generalization; using more generalization would open them up to the need for more repair.

5 STRENGTHS

There are two fundamental strengths to the method of learning by explanation repair: (1) it is stimulated to learn by failure, and (2) it is based in crisp, formal logic.

The former strength places this approach among general models of human learning that might also turn out to be good AI models. The latter strength helps bring deep biases towards the surface where they will be more obvious in their impact on results and more open to inference over the biases themselves.

The method for explanation repair has another important feature: It can generate multiple candidate repairs and associated explanations. More and more, in inference systems of all kinds, it is important to be able to consider several interpretations under a range of contexts and heuristics. Perhaps this is a small trend towards a more parallel computation model in which several views of the same situation are considered at more or less the same time.

6 POTENTIAL WEAKNESSES AND POSSIBLE EXTENSIONS

It is not clear that consistency and completeness ought to be absolute targets of machine learning. Likewise, explanation repair might not need to be the paramount goal of a system. Many concepts are fuzzy, with probabilistic behavior, and yet humans do not seem perturbed by this. Explanations that are known to fail on anomalous cases might not warrant repair.

When many learning systems are confronted by real-sized problems, they break under combinatorial demands unless they can make wide use of heuristics. The question of how to use heuristic knowledge, or to do plausible rather than complete deductive inference, is important. The method of explanation repair is a straight deductive mechanism on its outside. On the inside lie the critical processes such as the pruning of candidate binding lists for generating repairs. These processes could make widespread use of heuristics, but acquiring, revising, and applying the heuristics is as yet an unsolved problem. The point is this: If the power of the algorithm lies in the performance of interior parts for which good heuristics are critical, then how important or critical is the outside formality, no matter how elegant? Perhaps a formal approach can lead Kodratoff's "AI-learnists" towards elegant techniques for acquiring, applying, and managing heuristic metaknowledge at just the places where today's approaches show it to be critical. That would certainly be a worthy challenge.

References

Ganascia, J.-G. 1985. "Comment oublier a l'aide de contre-exemples," *Actes du congres AFCET RFIA*, Grenoble, November 1985.

Michalski, R.S. 1984. "Inductive Learning as Rule-guided Transformation of Symbolic Descriptions: A Theory and Implementation," *Automatic Program Con-*

struction Techniques, Biermann, A.W., Guiho G., Kodratoff, Y. (eds), Macmillan Publishing, pp. 517–552.

Mitchell, T.M. 1983. "Learning and Problem Solving," *Proc. IJCAI-83*, Karsruhe, pp. 1139–1151.

Vrain, C. 1985. "Contre-examples: Explications deduites do l'etude des predicats," *Actes du congres AFCET RFIA*, Grenoble, November 1985, pp. 145–159.

Winston, P.H. 1975. "Learning Structural Descriptions from Examples," *The Psychology of Computer Vision*, Winston, P.H. (ed), Ch. 5, McGraw Hill.

17

GUIDING INDUCTION WITH DOMAIN THEORIES[1]

Francesco Bergadano
Attilio Giordana
(Universitá di Torino, Italy)

Abstract

In this chapter we present a concept-acquisition methodology that uses data (concept examples and counterexamples), domain knowledge, and tentative concept descriptions in an integrated way. Domain knowledge can be incomplete and/or incorrect with respect to the given data; moreover, the tentative concept descriptions can be expressed in a form that is not operational. The methodology is aimed at producing discriminant and operational concept descriptions, by integrating inductive and deductive learning. In fact, the domain theory is used in a deductive process, that tries to operationalize the tentative concept descriptions, but the obtained results are tested on the whole learning set rather than on a single example. Moreover, deduction is interleaved with the application of data-driven inductive steps. In this way, a search in a constrained space of possible descriptions can help overcome some limitations of the domain theory (e.g., inconsistency). The method has been tested in the framework of the inductive learning system "ML-SMART," previously developed by the authors, and a simple example is also given.

17.1 INTRODUCTION

The automated acquisition of concept descriptions is a classical topic of machine learning, to which a large amount of research effort has been devoted (see [Mi-

---

[1]This chapter is a longer version of a paper printed in *Proceedings of the Fifth International Conference on Machine Learning*, 1988, Morgan Kaufmann Publishers, San Mateo, CA

chalski, Carbonell, and Mitchell, 1983 and 1986] for a deep introduction in the field).

In the recent literature, a differentiation between two major approaches to concept learning emerges: empirical learning (or similarity-based learning, according to some authors), and analytic learning (or explanation-based learning, according to the definition given in [Mitchell, 1986; DeJong, 1986]). The empirical learning approach uses mostly induction and produces concept descriptions by generalizing a training set of concept instances. One of the best-known examples of this approach is the system INDUCE by Michalski [Michalski, 1980; 1983]. On the other hand, analytic learning is a deductive method, which produces a generalized and operational concept description starting from a domain theory, a good nonoperational concept description, and just one concept instance. The meaning of operationality is slightly different according to different authors [Mitchell, 1986; DeJong, 1986; Keller, 1987] and a comparison of the different definitions can be found in [Mostow, 1987].

However, this approach, in its early formulation, may be difficult to apply to many real-world problems, because of the strong requirement that the domain theory be perfect. Nevertheless, it has received a lot of attention because of its attractive, knowledge-intensive nature, and it is actively investigated in order to develop extensions to the case of incomplete and inconsistent domain theories. On the other hand, inductive learning also has a number of limitations. First, the correctness of its results cannot be proven, since induction is not truth preserving [Michalski, 1983]. This means that even if we find a common characteristic of a large number of examples, we are not sure that the same phenomenon will occur in future cases. As a consequence, we have no objective criteria for preferring one hypothesis over the other, when both are consistent with the data. Second, we do not know how confident we can be in the obtained results. For this reason, different approaches to induction have been studied, which allow us to compute a limitation of the probability of error for the acquired classification rules [Valiant, 1984]. Finally, induction is usually slow [Simon, 1983] and this problem is related to the need of evaluating a very large number of possible hypotheses. Some concept-acquisition problems have been shown to be NP-hard, when only examples and counterexamples are available [Valiant, 1985; Haussler, 1986].

The interest in investigating empirical learning seems diminished. Some authors (see for instance, [Van de Velde, 1986]) consider it data driven and blind. However, some papers that recently appeared in the literature, for instance [Schlimmer, 1986; Dieterich, 1986; Ginsberg, 1985], seem to disconfirm these critics, because they propose knowledge-based methodologies to guide the induction process. Successful examples of this new approach can also be found in [Bergadano, et al., 1988; 1989], where the inductive system, ML-SMART, organized as a problem solver, is presented. Nevertheless, none of the above-mentioned systems is really knowledge intensive.

Finally, other authors agree that analytic learning and empirical learning are not intended as competing approaches, but, rather, as complementary ones to be integrated in the same learning paradigm. Proposals in this sense came from [Lebovitz, 1986 and 1987; Pazzani, 1985; Danyluk, 1987; Kodratoff, 1987]. This integration does not lead to provably correct results, especially if the domain theory is not perfect, but the acquired knowledge can be considered more reliable, since it is also partially justified by domain-specific criteria. Moreover, by using the domain theory during the inductive process, the computational complexity of the problem might be improved, since the number of possible hypotheses is smaller (not all of them are meaningful in the given domain).

This chapter makes proper the belief that a good integration between empirical and analytic learning could be the right approach to concept acquisition in many real problems, and extends the learning paradigm adopted in ML-SMART, in order to integrate both inductive and deductive techniques in the same framework. In particular, the system described here (a modified version of ML-SMART) searches for discriminant concept descriptions [Michalski, 1983] starting from a set of examples and counterexamples. The learning process is formalized as a top-down search in a space of logical formulas, performed using specialization. This search process is guided by strategies exploiting multiple sources of information, including statistical information, general learning heuristics, and domain theory. Then, in such a framework, both pure similarity-based inductive learning, and pure explanation-based learning are possible as special cases, but, more generally, they can be used in cooperation, obtaining in this way a true integration between the two approaches.

Another contribution of this chapter concerns the explanation-based methodology. In fact, in this framework the explanation is generated for many examples at a time. This allows criteria to be defined, founded on a statistical basis, in order to choose one explanation among a set of alternatives and then guide the operationalization process. Moreover, working with examples and counterexamples it is possible to deal with inconsistencies and incompletenesses of the domain theory, in order to correct the concept descriptions obtained through analytic learning techniques.

As a last point, this chapter sets a link between the fields of machine learning and deductive databases. Techniques of both fields can be exploited in the proposed framework. Such relationships are analyzed in the conclusion.

17.2 A FRAMEWORK FOR INDUCING CONCEPT DESCRIPTIONS

In this section, the induction of discriminant concept descriptions, from a set of examples, will be formalized as a search problem in a space of logical formulas. To this aim, a logical framework (similar to the one used by deductive databases) in which both induction and deduction are possible, will be introduced. The same framework was already adopted in [Bergadano, *et al.*, 1988] where a system able to find both discriminant and characterizing concept descriptions is presented.

Let $H_0 = \{h_i | 1 \leq i \leq N\}$ be a set of concepts to be discriminated and let $F_0 = \{f | class(f) \in H_0\}$ be a set of instances of the concepts in H_0, where *class(f)* is a classification given by a teacher. Moreover, let L be a logical language for describing the concepts. In many learning systems, such as INDUCE or ML-SMART, the concept-description language is a first-order logical language, using quantifiers and functors. Here, we will adopt a simpler language, for the sake of conciseness; nevertheless, the methodology described in the following can be extended to the concept-description language used in ML-SMART.

Thus, the language L is defined in a way similar to PROLOG; its terms can be constants or variables and its connectives are $\wedge$, $\rightarrow$. The assertions admissible in L will be of this type:

$$P_1 \wedge P_2 \wedge \ldots \wedge P_k \rightarrow Q \tag{1}$$

according to the usual syntax of the Horn clause logic languages. Finally, the set **P** of the predicates of L consists of two disjoint subsets $\mathbf{P^o}$ and $\mathbf{P^n}$ ($\mathbf{P} = \mathbf{P^o} \cup \mathbf{P^n}$). For each predicate $P_i \in \mathbf{P^o}$ a semantic function

$$v_{P_i} : X^k \rightarrow \{0,1\}$$

is defined, where k is the arity of P_i and X is the set of elementary objects present in the instances to be classified. This means that a deterministic procedure for computing the truth value of the predicate is actually given. The semantic function

$$v_{P_i}$$

could also be defined extensionally. On the contrary, the predicates in $\mathbf{P^n}$ can be used only on the right hand side of assertions of type (1); i.e., their truth value can only be deduced from predicates in the set $\mathbf{P^o}$. In other words, the predicates $\mathbf{P^o}$ are operational, according to the definition of Mitchell [Mitchell, 1986] whereas the ones in $\mathbf{P^n}$ are not operational. This corresponds to an *operationality theory* [Hirsh, 1987; Braverman, 1988] containing only rules of the type "operational(P)," where P is any predicate, plus the combination rule

operational(p) $\wedge$ operational(q) $\rightarrow$ operational(p$\wedge$q)

[Braverman, 1988].

It should be noted that the examples are described as complex objects consisting of elementary components related to each other. This representation and the use of existentially quantified variables in the clauses of L are appropriate for pattern recognition applications [Michalski, 1980; Bergadano, *et al.*, 1988], and are important for the computational complexity of the learning problem [Valiant, 1985]. As an example, we will use the concept instances given in Figure 17–1.

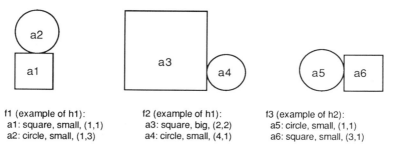

f1 (example of h1):
a1: square, small, (1,1)
a2: circle, small, (1,3)

f2 (example of h1):
a3: square, big, (2,2)
a4: circle, small, (4,1)

f3 (example of h2):
a5: circle, small, (1,1)
a6: square, small, (3,1)

Figure 17–1:   Instances of two concepts

In particular, we have two concepts, namely h_1 and h_2, two instances for concept h_1 (f_1 and f_2) and one instance for concept h_2 (f_3). In this example, every instance has two components, and every component is described with its shape, size and co-ordinates of the center, as given in Figure 17–1. As an example of an operational predicate we give $P = above(x,y)$ by defining its semantic function as

$$v_P (x,y): y - coordinate(x) > y - \text{coordinate(y)}$$

(here we assume that components cannot overlap). Instead of writing a procedure for computing the truth value of the predicate we could have given its extensional definition. For example, $above(x,y)$ is satisfied by $x = a_2$, $y = a_1$ in the instance f_1 and is not satisfied elsewhere. For nonoperational predicates neither the procedure nor the extensional specification of the predicate are given, but only rules such as (1), allowing us to deduce their truth value from the operational predicates and from other rules.

A concept description, discriminant for a concept h_i, is a conjunction of operational predicates which is verified only by a nonnull set $F \subset F_0$ of instances of the concept h_i. In the following we will use the notation:

$$P_1 \wedge P_2 \wedge ... \wedge P_n \rightarrow h_i \tag{2}$$

to indicate a discriminant description of the concept h_i. Moreover, if a conjunctive formula $\psi = Q, \wedge ... \wedge Q_r$ is verified for a nonnull subset F of F_0 such that

$$class(f_j) \in H \subseteq H_0, \forall f_j \in F,$$

we will write:

$$Q_1 \wedge Q_2 \wedge ... \wedge Q_r \rightarrow H \tag{3}$$

By considering h_i and H as predicates belonging to $\mathbf{P^n}$, expressions (2) and (3) are well-formed formulas of language L. Disjunction is of course possible by giving more than one rule such as (2) for the same concept. This is equivalent to disjunctive, normal form expressions. Here are some examples of concept descriptions (corresponding to the learning problem given in Figure 17–1):

$small(x) \rightarrow h_1, h_2, above(x,y) \rightarrow h_1, right\text{-}of(x,y) \wedge square(x)$
$\rightarrow h_2, right\text{-}of(x,y) \rightarrow h_1, h_2.$

The problem of inducing discriminant descriptions for the concepts in H_0 can then be seen as the problem of finding a set of formulas Φ, of type (2), such that the union of the sets of examples that they cover is F_0. The above given formulas do not have this property, for the examples of Figure 17–1, since f_2 is not covered.

17.2.1 A Relational Calculus for Evaluating the Extension of Formulas

In order to discover formulas $\varphi = P_1 \wedge \ldots \wedge P_k$ of type (1), it is necessary to evaluate the extension of a formula $\varphi \in L$ over the finite universe of the concept instances F_0. The simplest way to obtain the extension of φ consists in matching φ on all the examples in F_0; nevertheless, a more efficient method based on a relational calculus can be used.

For every formula $\varphi (x_1, \ldots, x_k)$ a $(k + 2)$-ary relation $\varphi^* = (F, H, X_1, \ldots, X_k)$ can be constructed, where each tuple t_j in φ^* corresponds to a different binding of the variables $x_1, \ldots, x_k$, which satisfy φ. The field F contains the identifier f_j of the example in which the binding has been obtained (notice that more than one tuple for each example can exist); the binding is then a function from the variables in φ to the elementary objects contained in the example f_j. The field H contains the classification $class(f_j)$ given by the teacher, and $X_1, \ldots, X_k$ contain the constant values bound to the variables $x_1, \ldots, x_k$, respectively. Relation φ^* contains the complete information about the extension of φ on F_0. For example, the formula

$right\text{-}of(x,y) \wedge square(x)$

will correspond to the relation containing the only tuple $F = f_3$, $H = h_2$, $x = a_6$, $y = a_5$. The formula $small(x)$ corresponds to the following relation:

F	H	x
f_1	h_1	a_1
f_1	h_1	a_2
f_2	h_1	a_4
f_3	h_2	a_5
f_3	h_2	a_6

As it is obvious from the last example, the relation can contain more than one tuple for every instance.

Particularly useful information, which can be extracted from φ^*, is the so-called *sample distribution histogram*, consisting of a vector **m** of $N = |H_0|$ integers

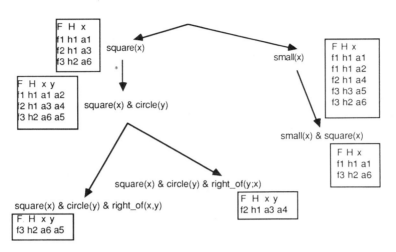

Figure 17–2:   Specialization tree

such that each m_i corresponds to the number of different instances of h_i in F_0 verifying the condition φ. From **m** (φ), it is immediate to induce assertions of type (2) or (3), corresponding to φ. In an analogous way, a vector **m'** (φ) is also defined, whose i-th component m'_i is the number of tuples in φ^* corresponding to instances of h_i. For example, m($right$-$of(x,y) \wedge square(x)$) = m'($right$-$of(x,y) \wedge square(x)$) = (0,1) and m($small(x)$) = (2,1) but m'($small(x)$) = (3,2).

A relation φ^* can be computed incrementally starting from preexisting relations ψ^*_i corresponding to subformulas ψ_i of φ; as a particular case φ^* can be computed starting from the relations $\mathbf{P}^*_i$ of the predicates in $\mathbf{P}^o$ which are always known by definition. For example, the relation corresponding to $above(x,y)$ is known or can be computed from the given definition of the predicate. It consists of the single tuple $F = f_1$, $H = h_1$, $x = a_2$, $y = a_1$. Now, suppose "square" is also an operational predicate and therefore the corresponding relation is given by definition. Then, the relation corresponding to the formula $square(x) \wedge above(x,y)$ can be computed by intersecting the two relations or by applying a database selection operation [Maier, 1983], according to the semantic function associated to the predicate "above." Nonoperational predicates represent virtual relations and deductive steps are needed to obtain the actual data.

These operations can be formalized in the framework of relational databases. This technology offers tools for handling the relational calculus in a suitable way. An efficient but problem oriented solution has also been implemented in the system ML-SMART.

17.2.2 The Specialization Tree

Let us consider a tree of formulas, having a form of type (3) (or in the best case of type (2)) and a nonempty extension over the set F_0:

- The root of the tree is the most general formula *true* $\rightarrow H_0$.
- The sons nd_j of a generic node $nd_i : \varphi \rightarrow H$ are obtained by making more specific φ, in every possible way, with one of the predicates in $\mathbf{P^o}$.

Such a kind of tree will be called the *specialization tree* of L, ST(L), and the following relations hold for all pairs of nodes nd_1, nd_2 such that nd_1 is an ancestor of nd_2:

$$H_2 \subseteq H_1, \qquad \mathbf{m_1} \geq \mathbf{m_2} \tag{4}$$

Figure 17–2 shows part of the specialization tree corresponding to the concepts of Figure 17–1, with the above given predicates. Formulas are generated from most general to most specific, and this makes it more efficient to compare the relations (every specialization corresponds to a selection operation).

The induction of formulas of type (2) can be seen as a search process that visits the tree ST(L) starting from the root. Nevertheless, the size of ST(L) is excessively large and then heuristics must be used in order to limit the visit to the nodes that are possible "good" discriminant descriptions or that are possible ancestors of "good" discriminant descriptions. The concept of a "good" description has been formalized in [Bergadano, *et al.*, 1988; 1989]; briefly, a concept description is "good" if it is verified by a statistically significant set of samples belonging to F_0.

Here, we will distinguish three kinds of heuristics in order to drive the search on ST(L):

1. **Statistical Heuristics:** From the statistical definition of a "good" description, it is possible to derive an estimate of the probability of moving toward a discriminant concept description by applying a given specialization on a node of ST(L). In this way it is possible to follow a purely data-driven, best-first search strategy.

2. **Domain Independent Heuristics:** We could define some theory of learning, or, more simply, a set of criteria suggesting how to drive the search process in order to minimize the effort or to find more reliable and less complex concept descriptions. For instance, some of the criteria used in [Bergadano, *et al.*, 1988] aim to contain the size of the relations associated with the formulas, by suggesting to apply first the specializations producing formulas having a small number of alternative bindings for any given example; other criteria aim to produce expressions that are easy for a human expert to read, etc.

3. **Domain Specific Heuristics**: All the *a priori* knowledge available for a particular domain can, in principle, be exploited in order to formulate such heuristics.

Examples of an intensive use of heuristics of types 1 and 2 can be found in [Bergadano, *et al.*, 1988; 1989] where they have been formalized in terms of meta-rules, which are used to control the induction process. Nevertheless, knowledge of type 3 is still poorly exploited in this kind of system. Basically, it has been used only to determine a precedence order in the use of the predicates or to define a taxonomy among the predicates, as it is done in INDUCE [Michalski, 1980]. However, the domain knowledge is much more powerful if used to suggest possible (also partial) concept descriptions that allow the system to expand the specialization tree $ST(L)$ quickly toward a promising description, or, alternatively, if it is used to prune those branches in $ST(L)$ corresponding to formulas not in agreement with the domain theory. Such use of the domain theory can be made only using deduction (from the theory) as it is made in EBL.

A very limited use of deductive rules has been already made in INDUCE in order to introduce capabilities of constructive learning [Michalski, 1983]. Nevertheless, this is still insufficient for our purposes, and we will introduce a method for using deduction in a general way, in the framework described in this section.

17.3 USING DEDUCTION TO DRIVE INDUCTION

Let us suppose we are given a domain theory, expressed in the language L and containing both operational and nonoperational predicates. Moreover, suppose that some nonoperational, tentative inductive assertions are suggested by a human expert. We will show how such assertions can be exploited to drive the induction through a deductive process. In the introduced framework, operationalizing an assertion A, consisting of the conjunction of some predicates $P_i \in \mathbf{P}$ (as a particular case, only one predicate can be present), means to deduce the relation A^*. The deductive process uses the operational predicates in $\mathbf{P}^0$ and the available domain theory. Such a capability is typically provided by deductive database systems, for which algorithms have been developed, capable of handling recursion (even if this is not always true for full first-order logic), as described in [Ullman, 1985; Lozinskii, 1985; Vieille, 1986]. In the following, a simple deductive algorithm, derived from the LOGLISP logic programming environment [Robinson, 1982] will· be introduced. Although there are some limitations, this approach has been sufficient to test the proposed methods on some applications.

17.3.1 The Deductive Algorithm

This algorithm uses a best-first strategy and expands an OR tree of goals. Every goal is, in general, a conjunction of operational and nonoperational predicates (subgoals); we will then write

$$g_i = P^o_1 \wedge \ldots \wedge P^o_r / P^n_1 \wedge \ldots \wedge P^n_t \tag{5}$$

with $P^o_i \in \mathbf{P^o}$ and $P^n_i \in \mathbf{P^n}$; this is done in order to separate the operational part of the goal from the predicates that are still to be operationalized. For every goal g the system creates the relation g^* corresponding to the conjunction of the operational predicates. This can be easily done since procedural calls correspond to these predicates. The root of the tree is the assertion A and the frontier of the tree is kept in a list OPEN, for further expansion. The algorithm proceeds as follows:

1. Select a node g_i from OPEN, according to some heuristic criterion.

2. Select the leftmost, nonoperational predicate P^n_j in g_i.

3. Unify P^n_j with the head of some assertion in the domain theory, and create a new goal g_k containing the same predicates that were listed in g_i, but where P^n_j has been replaced by the body of the assertion, after unification. If more than one assertion whose head can be unified is found, alternative (OR) nodes are generated.

4. If the new node g_k contains some new operational predicates, a new relation g_k^* is created, otherwise g_k inherits the relation from g_i. Notice that, in this way, the deduction step corresponds to one or more steps along a branch of ST(L).

The heuristic criterion, used in step 1, to select the node to be expanded, trades off statistical criteria (e.g., completeness and consistency) against the ratio between the number of operational and nonoperational predicates in the goal. The process stops, when an assigned *halt criterion* is satisfied or when no goal g_i, such that the relation g_i^* satisfies the minimal requirements posed by the statistical heuristics, exists in OPEN. The halt criterion, depending on the decision of strategies at higher level, can be assigned as:

1. At least one complete proof has been found.

2. All the proofs whose statistical relevance is higher than a given threshold th have been completed (or failed).

3. All the acceptable proofs (according to the statistical heuristics) have been completed (or failed).

The problem of infinite recursion loops is simply handled, as it is done in [Robinson, 1982], by posing a limit on the maximum number of deductions allowed along a given branch. An example will be given in Section 17.4.

17.3.2 Pure EBL

The described algorithm can be used to execute a pure EBL strategy, although the whole learning set is used rather than a single example. In this way, we obtain the advantage that the proofs can be chosen by using a better operationality criterion (in the line of [Keller, 1987]), which also takes into account the number of samples verifying the proof. Some degree of generalization in the proof is automatic, since proofs are done on many examples, and the predicates in the nodes contain variables. If a solution node is the only son of its father node, further generalization can be obtained by using the father node as a solution. Finally, more general proofs can be obtained by making operational (moving from $\mathbf{P^n}$ to $\mathbf{P^o}$) a predicate $P(x_1, \dots, x_n)$, which is defined in a taxonomy as a direct generalization of operational predicates. This can be done by constructing the relation P^*, which is the union of the projections on $x_1, \dots, x_k$ of the relations corresponding to all the final goals obtainable starting from the assertion P.

17.3.3 Using Deduction with Imperfect Theories

Dealing with imperfect theories requires induction. In fact, in order to fix the bugs in a theory, it is necessary to make assumptions on the basis of other knowledge (external to the theory) collected from experimental evidence (data) or other theories.

An informal classification of the imperfect theory problems is proposed by Rajamoney and DeJong [Rajamoney, 1987] in which *multiple explanations*, *broken explanations*, *contradiction*, and *resources exceeded* (intractable theories) are mentioned. We will analyze here how the proposed framework is useful in order to help cope with the first three types of problems, by exploiting the empirical information contained in the training set. Our goal is only to obtain a good operational concept description, whereas the harder problem of correcting the theory is not faced here.

Multiple Explanations   The cause of this problem is considered to be the lack of sufficient details in the theory, which allows some ambiguities. However, reasoning with multiple examples offers a statistical basis in order to choose among the explanations (see Section 17.3.1).

It is unlikely, in fact, that a missed detail in the theory concerns the most frequent events (the best known to the expert of the domain). Moreover, this statistical information can also be the start point for improving the theory according to the scientific discovery approach.

Broken Explanations   In our framework an explanation can be broken essentially for two reasons: (a) because there is no way to operationalize some assertion (missed information), or, (b) because the theory has some internal contradiction that makes it impossible (or possible only in exceptional cases) to be applied; for instance, to require that a bird be very heavy and capable of flying will be unsuccessful, almost always. The case (a) can be solved by exploiting the induction capability. In fact, when an explanation is interrupted at a subgoal g because of this reason, usually, it exists a partial operationalization g^o of g, which can be completed, using the other specialization techniques, in order to obtain a concept description.

The second reason, (b), (not considered by [Rajamoney, 1987]) is detected because the operationalization process leads to an empty relation and is a particular case of inconsistency in the theory, which must be handled by retracting some assertions from the partially operationalized goal.

Contradictions They are due to the fact that an obtained concept description is true both for some examples of a concept h_i and also for some examples of another concept $h_j \neq h_i$. The reason for that can be due (see [Rajamoney, 1987]) to missing information and/or wrong assertions in the theory. The first case can be solved again by using induction to further specialize the concept description in order to exclude the counterexamples that are covered. The second case, however, must be handled again by retracting some assertion.

In the implementation that has been done, inductive and deductive steps can be interleaved and combined in a flexible way, under the control of a high-level, global strategy. The search starts from the tentative inductive assertions, as they are given by the expert. Then, the domain theory is used in a deductive process that tries to operationalize the given assertions. If the operationalization of the goals fails for some of the reasons mentioned above, the system tries to recover it by using one of the following strategies on some interrupted or inconsistent proof selected according to a global strategy (see [Bergadano, *et al.*, 1988; 1989]):

1. The proof is interrupted, or is complete (i.e., the operationalization is concluded) but inconsistent, and is associated with a relation g^* covering many examples (and also some counterexample) of the concept h_i that we are trying to operationalize. In this case it is assumed that the problem is due primarily to lack of knowledge in the domain theory, and then the specialization is continued by means of the inductive search strategies of ML-SMART. If the proof is an interrupted one, then the predicate P^n (in g^n), which failed to be operationalized, is removed.

2. The proof is associated with a relation g^* containing too few examples of the concept h_i (possibly none). It means that some contradictory predicate is present in the operationalized part of the goal g. Then the branch of $ST(L)$ ending in g is revisited by looking for those specialization steps going from a node nd_j to a node nd_k such that $m^*_i(nd_j) >> m^*_i(nd_k)$ i.e., where the assertion of a predi-

cate P^o caused a significant reduction of the tuples corresponding to instances of the concept h_i. These specializations are considered as possible contradictions and, for every one of these cases a new, partially operationalized concept description is created, in which the suspect predicate has been dropped. All these new concept descriptions are then proposed for specialization by induction.

Some specialization steps, driven by inductive heuristics, can then be performed. After this, for the goals that still have a nonempty and nonoperationalized assertion, also the possibility of continuing again with deduction is considered, and a new attempt is made by restarting the deductive process. If the deductive strategy fails (it does not produce any helpful operationalization of the concept description), the search is continued using only the inductive learning strategy.

17.4 AN EXAMPLE

The example presented in this section is a modification of the "CUP" classification problem proposed by [Winston, *et al.*, 1983] and used by [Mitchell, 1986]. In this case, though, since we are integrating induction and deduction, we are given both a domain theory and a set of examples and counterexamples of the concept "CUP." The domain theory is the same as in [Mitchell, 1986] except that one more clause is present:

$CUP(x) \leftarrow Liftable(x) \wedge Stable(x) \wedge Open\text{-}vessel(x)$
$Liftable(x) \leftarrow is(x,Light) \wedge part\text{-}of(x,y) \wedge isa(y,Handle)$
$Stable(x) \leftarrow part\text{-}of(x,y) \wedge isa(y,Bottom) \wedge is(y,Flat)$
$Stable(x) \leftarrow part\text{-}of(x,y) \wedge isa(y,Support) \wedge$
$\qquad\qquad \wedge part\text{-}of(x,w) \; isa(w,Body) \wedge above(w,y)$
$Open\text{-}vessel(x) \leftarrow part\text{-}of(x,y) \wedge isa(y,Concavity) \wedge is(y,Upward\text{-}pointing)$

The examples and counterexamples of the concept "CUP" are given in Figure 17–3, where the examples are events a,b,c,d and the counterexamples are events e,f,g,h.

First, it should be noted that the domain theory, although it intuitively describes the examples of cups, is neither complete nor correct. In fact, the predicate CUP(x) is only true for examples a and b, since c and d do not have a handle. Moreover, CUP(x) is true for counterexample g, and therefore the description is not consistent. Finally, the domain theory handles correctly the other counterexamples, because CUP(x) is false for e, that is not Light, for f, that does not have a handle and for h, whose body, h3, is not an Open-vessel.

The learning process is based on the expansion of the specialization tree, as it was described in Section 17.3. The tree for this example is shown in Figure 17–4.

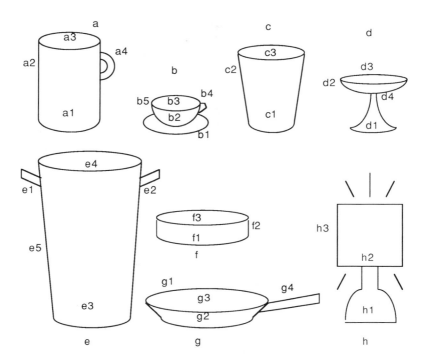

a: light; a1: bottom, small, flat; a2: body; a3: concavity, upward; a4: handle

b: light; b1: support; b2: bottom, small; b5: body; b3: concavity, upward; b4: handle; b5,b1: above

c: light; c1: bottom, small,flat; c2: body; c3: concavity, upward

d:light; d1: bottom, small; d4: bottom,small; d2: body; d3: concavity, upward: d2,d1: above

e: heavy; e1: handle; e2: handle; e3: bottom, small, flat; e4: concavity, upward; e1 :body

f: light; f1: bottom, flat; f2: body; f3: concavity, upward

g: light; g1: body; g2: bottom, flat; g3: concavity, upward; g4: handle

h: light; h&: support; h2: bottom, small; h: body; h3,h1: above

Figure 17–3:   Examples and counterexamples of the concept "CUP"

The search starts from a node containing only the nonoperational predicate CUP(x), shown in the root of the tree. Nonoperational predicates (starting with capital letters and listed below the horizontal bar in every node of Figure 17–4) are handled through a deductive step, which replaces them with their precondition in the domain theory. If more than one rule exists for a given predicate, alternate search branches are followed in the tree.

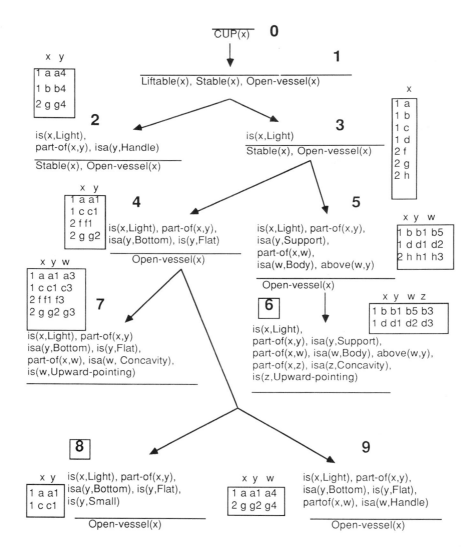

Figure 17–4: Specialization tree

The root is then expanded by substituting CUP(x) with its definition in the domain theory: Liftable(x) ∧ Stable(x) ∧ Open-vessel(x). At this point, the predicate Liftable(x) is handled in the same way, and node 2 is generated. This node already contains operational predicates, and therefore a relation in the database is generated and shown in Figure 17–4, next to the node. The predicates above the horizontal line in node 2 are satisfied by examples a and b and by counterexample g; the bindings for the variable y are also kept in the relation (see Section 17.2). The description given in node 2 is already incomplete, and operationalizing the rest of the predicates below the line will not produce any improvement. The reason is that some examples of cup do not have a handle; this requirement is then retracted, and node 3 is generated. (See strategy 2 at the end of Section 17.3.3.)

The predicate Stable(x) is then operationalized in two possible ways, as defined in the domain theory, and nodes 4 and 5 are generated and expanded. Operationalization of Open-vessel leads to nodes 7 and 6, respectively. Node 6 is a terminal node, since it corresponds to a consistent description of CUP; but node 7 is not, since it covers counterexamples f and g. At this point, normal search in the space of possible specializations is continued, in order to obtain a consistent description. Nevertheless, this is done by expanding node 4, rather than node 7, since 7 is more complicated but no better than 4 with respect to consistency. Among many other possibilities, node 8 could be generated, which corresponds to a consistent solution. Descriptions 6 and 8, taken together, are a complete a consistent solution of the discrimination problem:

$$is(x,Light) \wedge part\text{-}of(x,y) \wedge isa(y,Support) \wedge part\text{-}of(x,w) \wedge$$
$$\wedge\ isa(w,Body) \wedge above(w,y) \wedge part\text{-}of(x,z) \wedge$$
$$\wedge\ isa(z,Concavity) \wedge is(z,Upward\text{-}pointing) \rightarrow CUP(x)$$
$$is(x,Light) \wedge part\text{-}of(x,y) \wedge isa(y,Bottom) \wedge is(y,Flat) \wedge is(y,Small) \rightarrow CUP(x)$$

On the one hand, if the domain theory was not available, the search space in the specialization tree would have been much larger, since every possible predicate would have to be tested. On the other hand, the domain theory alone was not able to produce correct discriminant rules and classify the instances of the given concept. The proposed methodology allows for an integration of domain knowledge and data, in a natural and relatively efficient way.

17.5 CONCLUSIONS

We have presented a learning methodology which is an extension of the one used in [Bergadano, et al., 1988; 1989] which can exploit an incomplete and inconsistent domain theory in order to drive the induction through a deductive process. The method is basically an EBL approach but has the important novelty that the "explanation" is obtained on many examples at the same time rather than on a single one. This allows the system to evaluate both the consistency and the completeness of the assertions generated during the proof. It is then possible, on one hand, to choose the explanations according to an extended operationality criterion (in the sense of

[Keller, 1987]), and, on the other, to exploit results, even if partial, which are deducible from imperfect theories. The method has been developed in a framework related to deductive databases, and a simple deduction algorithm has been described, although it can be limited in the way it handles recursion in large knowledge bases; nevertheless, deductive database technology can be very helpful for improving this solution. From a more general point of view, this paper shows how the research in machine learning and databases can be cross-fertilized, to develop powerful systems for learning with full memory.

The method has been tested on some cases such as the one described in Section 17.4 and has been successfully applied to a problem of fault diagnosis in electro-mechanical industrial systems.

References

Bergadano, F., Giordana, A. and Saitta, L. 1988. Concept Acquisition in Noisy Environments. *IEEE Transaction on Pattern Analisys and Machine Intelligence* Vol. PAMI-10, number 4, pp. 555–578.

Bergadano, F., Gemello, R., Giordana, A., and Saitta, L. 1989. ML-SMART: A Problem Solver for Learning from Examples. *Fundamenta Informaticae*, Vol. XII, pp. 29–50.

Braverman, M.S. and Russel, S.J. 1988. Boundaries of Operationality. In *Proceedings Int. Conference on Machine Learning* (pp. 221–234). Ann Arbor, MI.

Danyluk, A.P. 1987. The Use of Explanations for Similarity-based Learning. In *Proceedings Int. Joint Conference on Artificial Intelligence IJCAI-87* (pp. 274–276). Milano, Italy.

DeJong, G. and Mooney, R. 1986. Explanation-based Learning: An Alternative View. *Machine Learning*, 1, 145–176.

Dietterich, T.G. and Michalski, R.S. 1986. Learning to Predict Sequences. In Michalski, R.S., Carbonell, J.G. and Mitchell, T.M. (Eds.), *Machine Learning: An Artificial Intelligence Approach, Volume II* (pp. 41–81). San Mateo, CA: Morgan Kaufmann Publishers.

Ginsberg, A., Weiss, S.M., and Politakis, P. 1985. SEEK2: A Generalized Approach to Automatic Knowledge Base Refinement. In *Proceedings Int. Joint Conference on Artificial Intelligence IJCAI-85* (pp. 367–374). Los Angeles, CA.

Hirsh, H. 1987. Explanation-based generalization in a logic programming environment. In *Proceedings Int. Joint Conference on Artificial Intelligence IJCAI-87* (pp. 271–273). Milano, Italy.

Keller, R. 1987. Defining Operationality for Explanation Based Learning. In *Proceedings of Conference of American Association for Artificial Intelligence AAAI-87* (pp. 482–487). Seattle, WA.

Kodratoff, Y.K. and Tecuci, G. 1987. DISCIPLE-1: Interactive apprentice system in weak theory fields In *Proceedings Int. Joint Conference on Artificial Intelligence IJCAI-87* (pp. 271–273). Milano, Italy.

Lebowitz, M. 1987. Experiments with the Incremental Concept Formation: UNIMEM. *Machine Learning*, 2, 103–138.

———, 1986. Integrated Learning: Controlling Explanations. *Cognitive Science*, 10.

Lozinskii, E.L. 1985. Evaluating Queries in Deductive Databases by Generating. In *Proceedings Int. Joint Conference on Artificial Intelligence* (pp. 173–177). Los Angeles, CA.

Maier, D. 1983. *The Theory of Relational Data Base*, Computer Science Press, Potomac, MD

Michalski, R.S. 1983. A Theory and Methodology of Inductive Learning. *Artificial Intelligence*, 20, 111–161.

———, 1980. Pattern Recognition as Rule-guided Inductive Inference. *IEEE Transaction on Pattern Analysis and Machine Intelligence*, 2, 349–361.

Michalski, R.S., Carbonell, J.G. and Mitchell, T.M. (Eds). 1983. *Machine Learning: An Artificial Intelligence Approach*. San Mateo, CA: Morgan Kaufmann Publishers.

———, 1986. *Machine Learning: An Artificial Intelligence Approach, Volume II*. San Mateo, CA: Morgan Kaufmann Publishers.

Mitchell, T.M., Keller, R.M. and Kedar-Cabelli, S.J. 1986. Explanation-based Generalization: A unifying view. *Machine Learning*, 1, 47–80.

Mostow, J. 1987. Searching for Operational Concept Descriptions in BAR, MetaLEX and EBG. In *Proceedings of the Fourth International Workshop on Machine Learning* (pp. 376–382). Irvine, CA.

Pazzani, M. 1985. *Explanation and Generalization Based Memory*. Technical Report UCLA-AI-85-13. University of California at Los Angeles, Los Angeles, CA. *International Journal of Intelligent Systems*.

Rajamoney, S. and DeJong, G. 1987. The Classification, Detection and Handling of Imperfect Theory Problems. In *Proceedings Int. Joint Conference on Artificial Intelligence IJCAI-87* (pp. 205–207). Milano, Italy.

Robinson, J.A. and Siebert, E.E. 1982. LOGLISP: An Alternative to PROLOG. In Hayes, J.E. and Michie, D. (Eds.) *Machine Intelligence*, 10 (pp. 399–419).

Schlimmer, J.C. and Granger, R.H. 1986. Incremental Learning from Noisy Data. *Machine Learning*, 1, 317–354.

Ullman, J.D. 1985. Implementation of Logical Query Languages for Databases. *ACM Transaction on Database Systems*, 10, 289–321.

Van de Velde, W. 1986. Explainable Knowledge Production. In *Proceedings of The European Conference on Artificial Intelligence ECAI-86* (pp. 8–21). Brighton, UK.

Vieille, L. 1986. Recursive Axioms in Deductive Databases: the Query Subquery Approach. In *Proceedings of First Int. Conference on Expert Database Systems*. Charleston, SC.

Winston, P.H., Binford, T.O., Katz, B. and Lowry, M. 1983. Learning Physical Descriptions from Functional Definitions, Examples and Precedents. In *Proceedings of Int. Joint Conference on Artificial Intelligence IJCAI-83* (pp. 433–439). Karlsruhe, Germany.

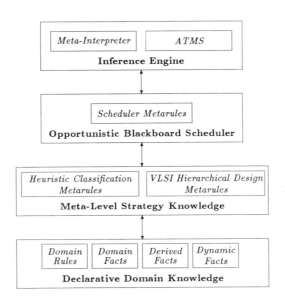

Figure 18–1:   MINERVA system architecture

Domain knowledge consists of MYCIN-like rules and simple frame knowledge for an application domain (e.g., medicine, geology). An example of rule knowledge in Horn clause format is

```
conclude(migraine-headache, yes, .5) :- finding(photophobia,
yes)
```

meaning "to conclude the patient has a migraine headache with a certainty .5, determine if the patient has photophobia." An example of frame knowledge is

```
subsumed-by(viral-meningitis, meningitis)
```

meaning "hypothesis viral meningitis is subsumed by the hypothesis meningitis." *Problem-state knowledge* is generated during execution of the expert system. Examples of problem-state knowledge are `rule-applied(rule163)`, which says that rule 163 has been applied during this consultation, and

```
differential(migraine-headache, tension-headache)
```

which says that the expert system's active hypotheses are migraine headache and tension headache.

Strategy knowledge is contained in the shell, and it approximates a cognitive model of problem solving. For heuristic classifcation problems, this model is often referred to as hypothesis-directed reasoning [Elstein, 1978]. The different problem-solving strategies that can be employed during problem solving are explicitly represented, which facilitates use of the model to follow the line of reasoning of a human problem solver. The strategy knowledge determines what domain knowledge is relevant at any given time, and what additional information is needed to solve the problem. The problem-state and domain knowledge, including rules, are represented as tuples, and strategy metarules are quantified over these tuples.

The strategy knowledge needs to access the domain and problem-state knowledge. To achieve this, the domain and problem-state knowledge is represented as tuples. Even rules are translated into tuples. For example, if rule 160 is

```
conclude(hemorrhage yes .5) :- finding (diplopia, yes) ∧
finding(aphasia, yes)
```

it would be translated into the following four tuples:

```
evidence.for(diplopia hemorrhage rule160 .5),
evidence.for(aphasia hemorrhage rule160 .5),
antecedent(diplopia rule160),
antecedent(aphasia, rule160).
```

Strategy metarules are quantified over the tuples. Figure 18–4 (page 501) presents four strategy metarules in Horn clause form; the tuples in the body of the clause quantify over the domain and problem-state knowledge. The rightmost metarule in Figure 18–4 encodes the strategy to find out about a symptom by finding out about a symptom that subsumes it. The metarule applies when the goal is to find out symptom P1, and there is a symptom P2 that is subsumed by P1, and P2 takes Boolean values, and it is currently unknown, and P2 should be asked about instead of being derived from first principles. This is one of eight strategies in HERACLES that is also used in MINERVA for finding out the value of a symptom; this particular strategy of asking a more general question has the advantage of cognitive economy: a "no" answer provides the answer to a potentially large number of questions, including the subsumed question.

18.2.1 The Evolution from HERACLES to MINERVA

MINERVA is a reworking of HERACLES, similar to the way that HERACLES is a reworking of EMYCIN. The ultimate objective in both these efforts has been a more declarative and modular representation of knowledge. This facilitates construction of a learning program to examine and reason about the knowledge structures of the metalevel strategy in the expert system, to interpret better a user's strategy in terms of the metalevel strategy knowledge in the expert system, and to allow the same shell to encode strategy knowledge for the generic problem tasks of analysis (e.g., heuristic classification) and synthesis (e.g., VLSI circuit design).

There are four principal differences between MINERVA and HERACLES at the strategy level. In determining which task to perform next, HERACLES uses a fixed order goal tree; by contrast MINERVA employs an opportunistic blackboard scheduler. This facilitates interpreting a user's strategy in terms of the expert system's strategies, and better integrates top-down and bottom-up strategic reasoning. Second, in controlling metalevel reasoning, HERACLES uses dynamic control flags and variables, such as task end conditions. In MINERVA a pure, functional programming style and a deliberation-action loop have been used; this eliminates all flags and variables at the strategy level. So, in MINERVA the system state is completely determined by the state of the domain-level static and dynamic knowledge. Third, in Heracles, strategy metarule premises sometimes change the state of the system, invoke subgoals, and use procedural attachment to LISP code; and HERACLES strategy metarule actions can invoke several goals. In conrast, MINERVA metarules do not follow any of these practices, which allows a pure deliberation-action cycle for strategic reasoning. The MINERVA style of metarules reduces side effects, thus making it easier for the learning program to reason about the strategy knowledge. Fourth, in MINERVA, more of the expert system's reasoning, such as the rule interpreter code, has been encoded in strategy metarules.

Other changes are as follows: The MINERVA system has been completely implemented in PROLOG; by contrast, HERACLES uses a combination of PROLOG-like clauses with with procedural attachment to LISP for each of the PROLOG clause predicates in metarules. The more uniform representation in MINERVA moves us toward our long-term goal of allowing a learning program to reason about all knowledge structures in the expert system shell. MINERVA incorporates an ATMS to maintain consistency of the knowledge base, uses a logic metainterpreter, and supports both certainty factors and Pearl's method to represent rule uncertainty and for propagation of information in a hierarchy of diagnostic hypotheses [Pearl, 1986a; 1986b]. As can be seen, all of the changes mentioned have resulted in a more declarative and functional knowledge representation.

18.3 ODYSSEUS'S METHOD FOR EXTENDING AN INCOMPLETE DOMAIN THEORY

We have developed two methods for extending an incomplete domain theory; an apprenticeship learning approach and a case-based reasoning approach. This section will only describe the former approach. Table 18–1 shows the major refinement steps and the method of achieving them for apprenticeship and case-based learning. The techniques will be elaborated below.

Table 18–1:   Comparison of case-based and apprenticeship learning method for extending an incomplete domain theory

Learning method	Case-based learning (similarity-based)	Apprenticeship learning (explanation-based)
Scope	Heuristic rules.	Heuristic rules. 4 types of frame knowledge.
Detect knowledge-base deficiency	Select and run a case. Deficiency exists if case is misdiagnosed.	Observe expert solving a case. Deficiency exists if action of expert cannot be explained.
Suggest knowledge-base deficiency	Generalize or specialize rules. Induce new rules.	Find tuples that allow explanation to be completed under single fault assumption.
Validate knowledge-base repair	Use underlying domain theory to validate repairs.	Use underlying domain theory to validate repairs.

The solution approach of the ODYSSEUS apprenticeship program for extending an incomplete domain theory in a learning-by-watching scenario is illustrated in Figure 18–2. As Figure 18–2 shows, the learning process involves three distinct steps: detect domain theory deficiency, suggest domain theory repair, and validate domain theory repair. This section defines the concept of an explanation and then describes the three learning steps.

The main observable problem-solving activity in a diagnostic session is finding out values of features of the artifact to be diagnosed—we refer to this activity as asking *findout questions*. An *explanation* in ODYSSEUS is a proof that demonstrates how an expert's findout question is a logical consequence of the current problem state, the domain and strategy knowledge, and one of the current high-level strategy goals. An explanation is created by backchaining the metalevel strategy metarules; Figure 18–4 provides examples of these metarules represented in Horn clause form. The backchaining starts with the findout metarule and continues until a metarule is reached whose head represents a high-level problem-solving goal. To backchain a metarule requires unification of the body of the Horn clause with domain and problem-state knowledge. Examples of high-level goals are: to test a hypothesis, to differentiate between several plausible hypotheses, to ask a clarifying question, and to ask a general question.

Apprenticeship learning is a form of learning by watching, in which learning occurs as a by-product of building explanations of human problem-solving actions. An apprenticeship is the most powerful method that human experts use to refine and debug their expertise in knowledge-intensive domains such as medicine. The major accomplishment of our method of apprenticeship learning is a demonstration of how an explicit representation of the strategy knowledge for a general problem class,

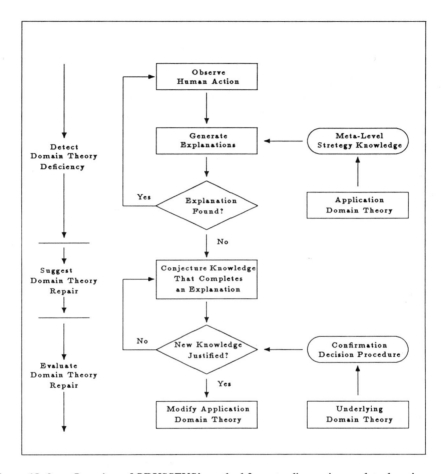

Figure 18–2: Overview of ODYSSEUS's method for extending an incomplete domain theory in a learning-by-watching apprentice situation. This chapter describes techniques that permit automation of each of the three stages of learning shown on the left edge of the figure. An explanation is a proof that shows how the expert's action achieves a problem-solving goal.

such as diagnosis, can provide a basis for learning the knowledge that is specific to a particular domain, such as medicine.

18.3.1 Detection of Knowledge Base Deficiency

The first stage of learning involves the detection of a knowledge base deficiency. An expert's problem solving is observed and explanations are constructed for

Patient's Complaint and Volunteered Information:
1. Alice Ecila, a 41 year old black female.
2. Chief complaint is a headache.

Physician's Data Requests:
3. Headache duration?
   focus=tension headache.   7 days.
4. Headache episodic?
   focus=tension headache.   No.
5. Headache severity?
   focus=tension headache.   4 on 0-4 scale.
6. Visual problems?
   focus=subarachnoid hemorrhage.   Yes.
7. Double vision?
   focus=subarachnoid hemorrhage, tumor.   Yes.
8. Temperature?
   focus=infectious process.   98.7 Fahrenheit.
   . . . . . .

Physician's Final Diagnosis:
25. Migraine Headache.

Figure 18–3:   An example of what the ODYSSEUS apprentice learner sees. The data requests in this problem-solving protocol were made by John Sotos, MD. The physician also provides information on the focus of the data requests. The answers to the data requests were obtained from an actual patient file from the Stanford University Hospital, extracted by Edward Herskovits, MD.

each of the observed problem-solving actions. An example will be used to illustrate our description of the three stages of learning, based on the NEOMYCIN knowledge base for diagnosing neurology problems. The input to ODYSSEUS is the problem-solving behavior of a physician, John Sotos, as shown in Figure 18–3. In our terminology, Dr. Sotos asks findout questions and concludes with a final diagnosis. For each of his actions, ODYSSEUS generates one or more explanations of his behavior.

When ODYSSEUS observes the expert asking a findout question, such as asking if the patient has visual problems, it finds all explanations for this action. When none can be found, an explanation failure occurs. This failure suggests that there is a difference between the knowledge of the expert and the expert system, and it provides a learning opportunity. The knowledge difference may lie in any of the three types of knowledge that we have described: strategy knowledge, domain knowledge, or problem-state knowledge. Currently, ODYSSEUS assumes that the cause of the explanation failure is that the domain knowledge is deficient. In the current example, no explanation can be found for findout question number 7 in Figure 18–3 (asking about visual problems), and an explanation failure occurs.

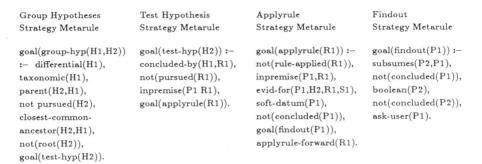

Group Hypotheses Strategy Metarule	Test Hypothesis Strategy Metarule	Applyrule Strategy Metarule	Findout Strategy Metarule
goal(group-hyp(H1,H2)) :— differential(H1), taxonomic(H1), parent(H2,H1), not pursued(H2), closest-common- ancestor(H2,H1), not(root(H2)), goal(test-hyp(H2)).	goal(test-hyp(H2)) :— concluded-by(H1,R1), not(pursued(R1)), inpremise(P1 R1), goal(applyrule(R1)).	goal(applyrule(R1)) :— not(rule-applied(R1)), inpremise(P1,R1), evid-for(P1,H2,R1,S1), soft-datum(P1), not(concluded(P1)), goal(findout(P1)), applyrule-forward(R1).	goal(findout(P1)) :— subsumes(P2,P1), not(concluded(P1)), boolean(P2), not(concluded(P2)), ask-user(P1).

Figure 18–4:   Learning by completing failed explanations. The illustrated strategy-level Horn clause metarules can chain together to form an explanation of how the findout action of ask-user(P1) relates to the high-level goal of group-hypoth(H1,H2). In this particular case, all the tuples in the chain cannot be instantiated with domain knowledge. ODYSSEUS attempts to complete this and other failed explanation chains by adding domain knowledge to the knowledge base so that all the tuples unify.

18.3.2 Suggesting a Knowledge Base Repair

The second step of apprenticeship learning is to conjecture a knowledge base repair. A confirmation theory (which will be described in the discussion of the third stage of learning) can judge whether an arbitrary tuple of domain knowledge is erroneous, independent of the other knowledge in the knowledge base.

The search for the missing knowledge begins with the single fault assumption. It should be noted that the missing knowledge is conceptually a single fault, but because of the way the knowledge is encoded, we can learn more than one tuple when we learn rule knowledge. For ease of presentation, this feature is not shown in the following examples. Conceptually, the missing knowledge could be eventually identified by adding a random domain knowledge tuple to the knowledge base and seeing whether an explanation of the expert's findout request can be constructed. How can a promising piece of such knowledge be effectively found? Our approach is to apply backward chaining to the findout question metarule, trying to construct a proof that explains why it was asked. When the proof fails, it is because a tuple of domain or problem-state knowledge needed for the proof is not in the knowledge base. If the proof fails because of problem-state knowledge, we look for a different proof of the findout question. If the proof fails because of a missing piece of domain knowledge, we temporarily add this tuple to the domain knowledge base. If the proof then goes through, the temporary piece of knowledge is our conjecture of how to refine the knowledge base.

Figure 18–4 illustrates one member of the set of failed explanations that ODYSSEUS examines in connection with the unexplained action

```
ask-user(visual problems)
```

that is contained in the tail of the rightmost metarule. These strategy metarules create a chain between the high-level goal in the head of the leftmost metarule,

```
group-hypotheses(Hypothesis1, Hypothesis2)
```

and the low-level observable action in the tail of the rightmost metarule

```
ask-user(visual problems).
```

Note that this chain is but one path is a large explanation graph that connects the observable action of asking about visual problems to all high-level goals. Each path in the graph is a potential explanation, and each node in a path is a strategy metarule. The failed explanation that ODYSSEUS is examining consists of the four metarules shown in Figure 18–4: Group Hypothesis, Test Hypothesis, Applyrule, and Findout. For a metarule to be used in a proof, its variables must be instantiated with domain or problem-state tuples that are present in the knowledge base. In this example, the `evidence.for` tuple is responsible for the highlighted chain not forming a proof. It forms an acceptable proof if the tuple

```
evidence.for(photophobia acute.meningitis $rule $cf)
```

is added to the knowledge base. During the step that generates repairs, neither the form of the left-hand side of the rule (e.g., number of conjuncts) or the strength is known. In the step to evaluate repairs, the exact form of the rule is produced in the process of evaluation of the worth of the tuple.

18.3.3 Validation of Knowledge Base Repair

The task of the third step of apprenticeship learning is to evaluate the proposed repair. To do this, we use the *confirmation decision procedure* (CDP) method. CDPs are constructed for each type of tuple in the domain theory and can determine if the tuple is an acceptable tuple. Of the 19 different types of tuples in the NEOMYCIN knowledge base, we have implemented CDPs for three of them:

```
evidence.for, clarifying.question, and ask.general.question
```

tuples. In addition to their use for validating knowledge base repairs, CDPs are also used to modify or delete incorrect parts of the initial domain theory; they are described in greater detail in Section 18.4.

`Evidence.for` tuples were generated in the visual problems example. In order to confirm the first candidate tuple, ODYSSEUS uses an empirical induction system that generates and evaluates rules that have photophobia in their premise and acute meningitis in their conclusion. A rule is found that passes the rule "goodness" measures, and it is automatically added to the object-level knowledge base. All the tuples that are associated with the rule are also added to the knowledge base. This completes our example.

The CDP method also validates frame-like knowledge. An example of how this is accomplished will be described for clarify question tuples, such as

```
clarify.questions(headache-duration headache).
```

This tuple means that if the physician discovers that the patient has a headache, she should always ask how long the headache has lasted. The confirmation theory must determine whether headache duration is a good clarifying question for the "headache" symptom. To achieve this, ODYSSEUS first checks to see if the question to be clarified is related to many hypotheses (the ODYSSEUS explanation generator allows it to determine this), and then tests whether the clarifying question can potentially eliminate a high percentage of these hypotheses. If these two criteria are met, then the clarify questions tuple is accepted.

18.4 ODYSSEUS'S METHOD FOR IMPROVING AN INCORRECT DOMAIN THEORY

The main focus of this chapter is on extending an incomplete domain theory via apprenticeship learning. However, it is clearly helpful if we are extending a domain theory that is correct and consistent. This section describes the methods that we have developed to improve the correctness of the domain theory. These methods are applied to the domain theory prior to the use of apprenticeship learning.

The key to addressing the problem of incorrect knowledge is the use of the *confirmation decision procedure* (CDP) method, which connects tuples in the domain theory to underlying theories of the domain that are capable of judging their correctness. In this approach, a CDP is created for each type of domain theory tuple in the knowledge base. Given an arbitrary instantiated tuple, the CDP calculates whether the tuple is true or false. In some cases the CDP can suggest how the tuple can be modified so as to make it true.

Of the 19 different types of domain theory tuples in the NEOMYCIN domain theory, we have created CDPs for three types of tuples. These tuples comprise approximately 70% of all tuples in the domain theory. For example, a CDP has been implemented for `evidence.for` tuples. These tuples are derived from the heuristic domain rules provided by a user that relate evidence to hypotheses. Validating `evidence.for` tuples therefore consists of validating the heuristic associational rules in the knowledge base.

The CDP `evidence.for` consists of an induction system, a set of rule biases, and a representative case library for the application domain. It accepts or rejects heuristic rules, whether they are rules in the initial knowledge base or rules conjectured during apprenticeship learning. In addition to accepting or rejecting rules, the CDP for `evidence.for` can modify a given rule to make it correct; it does this by adding conjuncts or modifying the rule strength. A rule can be modified to be "correct" by using probability and decision theory and representative sets of cases to determine its correct weight or strength (in contrast to trusting the weight provided by the user). If a rule lacks sufficient strength, the CDP will try to add conjuncts to the rule to increase its specificity.

When given an `evidence.for` tuple, its corresponding heuristic associational rule, which is indicated by the third argument of the `evidence.for` relation, is tested in five ways by the `evidence.for` CDP. A test for *simplicity* ensures that the number of antecedent conditions of the rules are less than the specified number. The test for *strength* accepts rules whose certainty factors (CF) are greater than a threshold value. The third bias is to test the *generality* of the rules. It succeeds only if the rules cover a certain percentage of the cases in a representative case library. The test for *colinearity* ensures that the proposed rules are not similar to any existing rules in performing classification of the induction set of cases. Finally the bias for *uniqueness* will check that the rules fire on a training case and that there exist no rules in the current domain rule set that also succeed for that case. Good rules are those recommendations that pass the verification process. This rule may then be added into the system.

It is often difficult to create CDPs for some types of tuples in the domain theory. For example, consider the tuple type `askfirst(PARM)`. This tuple says that a particular feature of the system being diagnosed should be obtained from a user instead of derived from first principles. It is difficult to imagine how to do this for an arbitrary feature, although eventually a way must be found if knowledge acquisition is to be completely automated.

Note that most knowledge bases are much more heterogeneous than LEAP, a learning apprentice for acquiring a domain theory that consists of VLSI circuit implementation rules. In this system, the domain theory only contains implementation rules (in our parlance, only contains one type of domain tuple). LEAP can verify the implementation rules using Kirkhoff's laws as its underlying domain theory. The challenge of using this idea for knowledge-base systems is that most domain theories contain many different types of domain knowledge, not just one type as in LEAP.

The CDPs were originally constructed to validate repairs during apprenticeship learning. However, they nicely allow the initial knowledge base to be validated prior to apprenticeship learning. As will be reported in Section 18.6, about half of the existing knowledge base is modified during the processing stage that focuses on ensuring that the domain theory contains correct knowledge.

18.5 ODYSSEUS'S METHOD FOR IMPROVING AN INCONSISTENT DOMAIN THEORY

A processing stage prior to apprenticeship learning also removes a form of inconsistent knowledge from the domain theory, which is responsible for deterioration of the performance of the system due to sociopathic interactions between elements of the domain theory. A domain theory is *sociopathic* if and only if (1) all the rules in the knowledge base individually meet some "goodness" criteria; and (2) a subset of the knowledge base gives better performance than the original knowledge base. The five biases described in Section 18.4 provide an example of goodness criteria for heuristic rules in the domain theory.

The significance of the phenomena of sociopathicity is as follows. First, most extant expert systems have sociopathic knowledge bases. Second, traditional methods to correct missing and wrong rules, e.g., the general TEIRESIAS approach [Davis, 1982], cannot handle the problem. Third, sociopathicity imposes a limit on the quality of knowledge base performance. And last, it implies that some kind of global refinement for the acquired knowledge is essential for machine learning systems.

The phenomena of sociopathicity is addressed at length in another paper, [Wilkins and Ma, 1989], wherein we show that the best method for dealing with this form of inconsistency is to find a subset of the original domain theory that is not sociopathic (which must exist by our definition of sociopathicity). A summary of our results are as follows: The process of finding an optimal subset of a sociopathic knowledge base is modeled as a bipartite graph minimization problem and shown to be NP-hard. A heuristic method, the *sociopathic reduction algorithm*, has been developed to find a suboptimal solution for sociopathic domain theories. The heuristic method has been experimentally shown to give good results.

18.6 RELATED RESEARCH

18.6.1 ODYSSEUS and Explanation-based Learning

The ODYSSEUS apprenticeship learning method involves the construction of explanations, but it is different from explanation-based learning as formulated in EBG [Mitchell, *et al.*, 1986] and EBL [DeJong, 1986]; it is also different from explanation-based learning in LEAP [Mitchell, *et al.*, 1989], even though LEAP also focuses on the problem of improving a knowledge-based expert system. In EBG, EBL, and LEAP, the domain theory is capable of explaining a training instance, and learning occurs by generalizing an explanation of the training instance. In contrast, in our apprenticeship research, a learning opportunity occurs when the domain theory, which is the domain knowledge base, is incapable of producing an explanation of a training instance. The domain theory is incomplete or erroneous, and all learning occurs by making an improvement to this domain theory.

18.6.2 Case-based versus Apprenticeship Learning

In empirical induction from cases, a training instance consists of an unordered set of feature-value pairs for an entire diagnostic session and the correct diagnosis. In contrast, a training instance in apprenticeship learning is a single feature-value pair given within the context of a problem-solving session. This training instance is therefore more fine-grained, can exploit the information implicit in the order in which the diagnostician collects information, and allows obtaining many training instances from a single diagnostic session. Our apprenticeship learning program attempts to construct an explanation of each training instance; an explanation failure occurs if none is found. The apprenticeship program then conjectures and tests modifications to the knowledge base that allow an explanation to be constructed. If an acceptable modification is found, the knowledge base is altered accordingly. This is a form of learning by completing failed explanations.

The case-based learning approach currently modifies or adds heuristic rules to the knowledge base. It runs all the cases in the library and locates those that are misdiagnosed. Given a misdiagnosed case, the local credit assignment problem is solved as follows: The premises of the rules that concluded the wrong final diagnosis are weakened by specialization, and the premises of the rules that concluded the correct diagnosis are strengthened. If this does not solve the problem, new rules will be induced from the patient case library that apply to the misdiagnosed case and that conclude the correct final diagnosis. The verification procedure used to test all knowledge-base modifications is identical to that described for apprenticeship learning.

18.7 EXPERIMENTAL RESULTS

Our knowledge-acquisition experiments centered on improving the knowledge base of the NEOMYCIN expert system for diagnosing neurology problems. The initial NEOMYCIN knowledge base was constructed manually over a 7-year period; the first test of this system on a representative suite of test cases was performed in conjunction with the ODYSSEUS system. The NEOMYCIN vocabulary includes 60 diseases; our physician, Dr. John Sotos, determined that the existing data request vocabulary of 350 manifestations only allowed diagnosis of 10 of these diseases. Another physician, Dr. Edward Herskovits, constructed a case library of 115 cases for these 10 diseases from actual patient cases from the Stanford Medical Hospital, to be used for testing ODYSSEUS. The validation set consisted of 112 of these cases.

Let us begin our performance analysis by considering the baseline system performance prior to any ODYSSEUS knowledge base refinement. The expected diagnostic performance that would be obtained by randomly guessing diagnoses is 10%, and the performance expected by always choosing the most common disease is 18%. Version 2.3 of HERACLES with the NEOMYCIN knowledge base initially diagnosed 31% of the cases correctly, which is 3.44 standard deviations better than always selecting the disease that is *a priori* the most likely. On a student t-test, this is significant at a $t = .001$ level of significance. Thus we can conclude that NEOMYCIN's initial diagnostic performance is significantly better than guessing. Version 3.1 of MINERVA, with the manually constructed NEOMYCIN knowledge base gave almost identical performance results; it initially diagnosed 32 of the 112 cases correctly (28.5% accuracy).

Table 18–2 shows the various diseases and their sample sizes in the evaluation set. The result of each test suite are described along three dimensions. TP (true-positive) refers to the number of cases that the expert system correctly diagnosed as present, FN (false-negative) to the number of times a disease was not diagnosed as present but was indeed present, and FP (false-positive) to the number of times a disease was incorrectly diagnosed as present.

Table 18–2: Summary of MINERVA experiments. The KB1 column is the performance using the manually constructed domain theory. KB2 shows performance after use of methods that correct an incorrect domain theory.

Disease	Number of cases	KB1			KB2		
		TP	FN	FP	TP	FN	FP
Bacterial meningitis	16	14	2	49	14	2	21
Brain abscess	7	0	7	1	0	7	1
Cluster headache	10	1	9	0	7	3	4
Fungal meningitis	8	0	8	0	4	4	0
Migraine	10	4	6	6	1	9	0
Myco-TB meningitis	4	0	4	2	4	0	0
Primary brain tumor	16	0	16	0	0	16	0
Subarach hemorrhage	21	1	20	0	15	6	0
Tension headache	9	7	2	5	7	2	6
Viral meningitis	11	5	6	11	10	1	12
None	0	0	0	6	0	0	6
Totals	112	32	80	80	62	50	50

18.7.1 Improving an Incorrect and Inconsistent Domain Theory

The first stage of improvement involves locating and modifying *incorrect* domain knowledge tuples. Our method modified 48% of the heuristic rules in the knowledge base. The improvement obtained using the refined knowledge base is shown in column KB2 of Table 18–2; MINERVA diagnosed 62 cases correctly (55.3% accuracy), showing an improvement of about 27%. The second stage of improvement involves correcting inconsistent domain knowledge. No experimental results are reported here, although our methods have been previously shown to lead to significant improvement [Wilkins and Ma, 1989].

18.7.2 Extending Incomplete Domain Theory via Case-based Reasoning

The third stage of improvement involves extending a correct but incomplete domain knowledge base. Two experiments were conducted. The first used case-based learning. All the cases were run, and two misdiagnosed cases in areas where the knowledge base was weak were selected. The case-based learning approach was applied to these two cases. This refinement, shown in column KB3 of Table 18–3, enabled the system to diagnose 68 cases correctly (60.7% accuracy), showing an aggregate improvement of 32%.

18.7.3 Extending Incomplete Knowledge Base via Apprenticeship Learning

The second experiment used apprenticeship learning. For use as a training set, problem-solving protocols were collected by Dr. Sotos's solving two cases, consisting of approximately 30 questions each. ODYSSEUS discovered 10 pieces of knowledge by watching these two cases being solved; eight of these were domain rule knowledge. These eight pieces of information were added to the NEOMYCIN knowledge base of 152 rules, along with two pieces of frame knowledge that classified two symptoms as "general questions"; these are questions that should be asked of every patient. This refinement, shown in column KB4 of Table 18–3, enabled the system to diagnose 73 cases correctly (65.2% accuracy), an aggregate improvement of about 37%. Compared to NEOMYCIN's original performance, the performance of NEOMYCIN after improvement by ODYSSEUS is 2.86 standard deviations better. On a student t-test, this is significant for $t = .006$. One would expect the improved NEOMYCIN to perform better than the original NEOMYCIN in better than 99 out of 100 sample sets.

Table 18–3: Summary of MINERVA experiments. KB3 and KB4 show the performance after using case-based learning and apprenticeship learning, respectively, to extend the incomplete domain theory.

Disease	Number of cases	KB3			KB4		
		TP	FN	FP	TP	FN	FP
Bacterial meningitis	21	12	4	4	14	2	13
Brain abscess	7	5	2	15	1	6	0
Cluster headache	10	7	3	4	8	2	0
Fungal meningitis	8	3	5	0	3	5	0
Migraine	10	4	6	0	6	4	0
Myco-TB meningitis	4	4	0	0	4	0	1
Primary brain tumor	16	0	16	0	3	13	0
Subarach hemorrhage	21	16	5	2	16	5	3
Tension headache	9	7	2	6	8	1	3
Viral meningitis	11	10	1	6	10	1	12
None	0	0	0	7	0	0	7
Totals	112	68	44	44	73	39	39

It is important to note that the improvement occurred despite the physician's only diagnosing one of the two cases correctly. The physician correctly diagnosed a cluster headache case and misdiagnosed a bacterial meningitis case. As is evident from examining Tables 18–2 and 18–3, the improvement was over a wide range of cases. And the accuracy of diagnosing bacterial meningitis cases actually decreased. These counterintuitive results confirm our hypothesis that the power of our learning method derives from following the line of reasoning of a physician on individual findout question and is not sensitive to the final diagnosis as is the case in learning by empirical induction from examples.

All of this new knowledge learned by apprenticeship learning was judged by Dr. Sotos as plausible medical knowledge, except for a domain rule linking aphasia to brain abscess. Importantly, the new knowledge was judged by our physicians to be of much higher quality than when straight empirical induction was used to expand the knowledge base, without the use of explanation-based learning.

More experimental work remains. Our previous experiments with ODYSSEUS suggest that the apprenticeship learning approach is better than a case-based approach for producing a user-independent knowledge base to support multiple problem-solving goals such as learning, teaching, problem-solving, and explanation generation.

18.8 CONCLUSIONS

In this chapter, we presented three distinct methods used by ODYSSEUS to improve a domain theory.

Our method of extending an incomplete domain theory is a form of failure-driven explanation-based learning, which we refer to as apprenticeship learning. Apprenticeship is the most effective means for human problem solvers to learn domain-specific problem-solving knowledge in knowledge-intensive domains. This observation provides motivation to give apprenticeship learning abilities to knowledge- based expert systems. The paradigmatic example of an apprenticeship period is medical training, in which we have performed our investigations.

With respect to the incomplete theory problem, the research described illustrates how an explicit representation of the strategy knowledge for a general problem class, such as diagnosis, provides a basis for learning the domain-level knowledge that is specific to a particular domain, such as medicine, in an apprenticeship setting. Our approach uses a given body of strategy knowledge that is assumed to be complete and correct with the goal of learning domain-specific knowledge. This contrasts with learning programs such as LEX and LP where the domain-specific knowledge (e.g., integration formulas) is completely given at the start, and the goal is to learn strategy knowledge (e.g., preconditions of operators) [Mitchell, et al., 1983]. Two sources of power of the ODYSSEUS approach are the method of completing failed explanations, called the *metarule chain completion method*, and the use of underlying domain theories to evaluate domain-knowledge changes via the *confirmation decision procedure method*. Our approach complements the traditional method of empirical induction from examples for refining a knowledge base for an expert system for heuristic classification problems. With respect to learning certain types of heuristic rule knowledge, empirical induction from examples plays a significant role in our work. In these cases, an apprenticeship approach can be viewed as a new method of biasing selection of which knowledge is learned by empirical induction.

An apprenticeship learning approach, such as described in this chapter, is perhaps the best possible bias for automatic creation of large "user-independent" knowledge bases for expert systems. We desire to create knowledge bases that will support the multifaceted dimensions of expertise exhibited by some human experts, dimensions such as diagnosis, design, teaching, learning, explanation, and critiquing the behavior of another expert.

The long-term objectives of this research are the creation of learning methods that can harness an explicit representation of generic shell knowledge and that can lead to the creation of a user-independent knowledge base that rests on deep underlying domain models. Within this framework, this chapter described specialized methods that address three major types of knowledge base pathologies: incorrect, inconsistent, and incomplete domain knowledge. We believe that the use of *specialized methods* for different domain knowledge pathologies minimizes the interactions between pathologies, thereby making the problem much more tractable.

ACKNOWLEDGMENTS

Many people have greatly contributed to the evolution of the ideas presented in this chapter. We would especially like to thank Bruce Buchanan, Bill Clancey, Tom Dietterich, Haym Hirsh, John Holland, John Laird, Pat Langley, Bob Lindsay, John McDermott, Ryszard Michalski, Roy Rada, Tom Mitchell, Paul Rosenbloom, Ted Shortliffe, Paul Scott, Devika Subramanian, Marianne Winslett, the members of the Grail learning group, and the Guidon tutoring group. This work would not have been possible without the help of physicians Eddy Herskovits, Kurt Kapsner, and John Sotos.

We would also like to express our deep gratitude to Lawrence Chachere, Ziad Najem, Young-Tack Park, and Kok-Wah Tan, and other members of the Knowledge-based Systems group at the University of Illinois for their major role in the design and implementation of the MINERVA shell and for many fruitful discussions. This research was principally supported by NSF grant MCS-83-12148, and ONR grants N00014-79C-0302 and N00014-88K0124.

References

Boose, J.H. 1984. Personal construct theory and the transfer of human expertise. In *Proceedings of the 1983 National Conference on Artificial Intelligence*, pp. 27–33, Washington, D.C.

Buchanan, B.G. and Shortliffe, E.H. 1984. *Rule-Based Expert Systems: The MYCIN Experiments of the Stanford Heuristic Programming Project*. Reading, MA: Addison-Wesley.

Clancey, W.J. 1984. NEOMYCIN: Reconfiguring a rule-based system with application to teaching. In Clancey, W.J. and Shortliffe, E.H., editors, *Readings in Medical Artificial Intelligence*, Chapter 15, pp. 361–381. Reading, MA: Addison-Wesley.

Clancey, W.J. 1985. Heuristic classification. *Artificial Intelligence*, 27:289–350.

Clancey, W.J. 1986. From GUIDON to NEOMYCIN to HERACLES in twenty short lessons. *AI Magazine*, 7:40–60.

Davis, R. 1982. Application of meta level knowledge in the construction, maintenance and use of large knowledge bases. In Davis, R. and Lenat, D.B., editors, *Knowledge-Based Systems in Artificial Intelligence*, pp. 229–490. NY: McGraw-Hill.

DeJong, G. 1986. An approach to learning from observation. In Michalski, R.S., Carbonell, J.G., and Mitchell, T.M., editors, *Machine Learning: An Artificial Intelligence Approach, Volume II*, pp. 571–590. San Mateo, CA: Morgan Kaufmann.

Elstein, A.A., Shulman, L.S., and Sprafka, S.A. 1978. *Medical Problem Solving: An Analysis of Clinical Reasoning*. Cambridge: Harvard University Press.

Fu, L.M. and Buchanan, B.G. 1985. Learning intermediate concepts in constructing a hierarchical knowledge base. In *Proceedings of the 1985 IJCAI*, pp. 659–666, Los Angeles, CA.

Ginsberg, A., Weiss, S., and Politakis, P. 1985. SEEK2: A generalized approach to automatic knowledge base refinement. In *Proceedings of the 1985 IJCAI*, pp. 367–374, Los Angeles, CA.

Kahn, G., Nowlan, S., and McDermott, J. 1985. MORE: An intelligent knowledge acquisition tool. In *Proceedings of the 1985 IJCAI*, pp. 573–580, Los Angeles, CA.

Michalski, R.S. 1983. A theory and methodology of inductive inference. In Michalski, R.S., Carbonell, J.G., and Mitchell, T.M., editors, *Machine Learning: An Artificial Intelligence Approach*, pp. 83–134. San Mateo, CA: Morgan Kaufmann.

Mitchell, T., Utgoff, P.E., and Banerji, R.S. 1983. Learning by experimentation: Acquiring and refining problem-solving heuristics. In Michalski, T.M., Carbonell, J.G., and Mitchell, T.M., editors, *Machine Learning: An Artificial Intelligence Approach*, pp. 163–190. San Mateo, CA: Morgan Kaufmann.

Mitchell, T.M., Keller, R.M., and Kedar-Cabelli, S.T. 1986. Explanation-based generalization: A unifying view. *Machine Learning*, 1(1):47–80.

Mitchell, T.M., Mahadevan, S., and Steinberg, L.I. 1989. LEAP: A learning apprentice for VLSI design. In Kodratoff, Y. and Michalksi, R.M., editors, *Machine Learning: An Artificial Intelligence Approach, Volume III*, pp. 271–289. San Mateo, CA: Morgan Kaufmann.

Park, Y.T., Tan, K.W., and Wilkins, D.C. 1989. ProHCD: A knowledge based system shell with declarative representation and flexible control: For heuristic classification and VLSI design tasks. Working Paper KBS-89-01, Department of Computer Science, University of Illinois, Urbana-Champaign, Illinois.

Pearl, J. 1986a. Fusion, propagation, and structuring in belief networks. *Artificial Intelligence*, 29(3):241–288.

Pearl, J. 1986b. On evidential reasoning in a hierarchy of hypotheses. *Artificial Intelligence*, 28(1):9–15.

Quinlan, J.R. 1983. Learning efficient classification procedures and their application to chess end games. In Michalski, R.S., Carbonell, J.G., and Mitchell, T.M., editors, *Machine Learning: An Artificial Intelligence Approach*, pp. 463–482. San Mateo, CA: Morgan Kaufmann.

Tecuci, G. and Kodratoff, Y. 1990. Apprenticeship learning in imperfect domain theories. In Kodratoff, Y. and Michalski, R.S., (eds), *Machine Learning: An Artificial Intelligence Approach, Volume III*, pp. 514–551. San Mateo: CA, Morgan Kaufmann.

Wilkins, D.C. 1987. *Apprenticeship Learning Techniques For Knowledge Based Systems*. PhD Thesis, University of Michigan. Also, Report No. STAN-CS-88-1242, Dept. of Computer Science, Stanford University, 1988.

Wilkins, D.C. and Ma, Y. 1989. Sociopathic knowledge bases. Technical Report UIUCDCS-R-89-1538, Department of Computer Science, University of Illinois. Submitted to *Artificial Intelligence*.

19

APPRENTICESHIP LEARNING IN IMPERFECT DOMAIN THEORIES

Gheorghe Tecuci
(Research Institute for Computers and Informatics, Bucharest))

Yves Kodratoff
(CNRS, Université de Paris-Sud, and
George Mason University)

Abstract

This chapter presents DISCIPLE, a multistrategy, integrated learning system illustrating a theory and a methodology for learning expert knowledge in the context of an imperfect domain theory. DISCIPLE integrates a learning system and an empty expert system, both using the same knowledge base. It is initially provided with an imperfect (nonhomogeneous) domain theory and learns problem-solving rules from the problem-solving steps received from its expert user, during interactive problem-solving sessions. In this way, DISCIPLE evolves from a helpful assistant in problem solving to a genuine expert. The problem-solving method of DISCIPLE combines problem reduction, problem solving by constraints, and problem solving by analogy. The learning method of DISCIPLE depends on its knowledge about the problem-solving step (the example) from which it learns. In the context of a complete theory about the example, DISCIPLE uses explanation-based learning to improve its performance. In the context of a weak theory about the example, it synergistically combines explanation-based learning, learning by analogy, empirical learning, and learning by questioning the user, developing its competence. In the context of an incomplete theory about the example, DISCIPLE learns by combining the above-mentioned methods, improving both its competence and performance.

19.1 INTRODUCTION

The present success of AI is mostly due to the knowledge-based systems that proved to be useful almost anywhere. As the name suggests, the power of a knowledge-based system comes from its knowledge. However, building a knowledge base for such a system is a very complex, time-consuming, and error-prone process. Moreover, the resulting system lacks or has only poor abilities to update its knowledge or to acquire new knowledge.

One promising solution to this "knowledge-acquisition bottleneck" is represented by the Learning Apprentice Systems (LAS). An LAS is an interactive knowledge-based consultant that is provided with an initial domain theory and is able to assimilate new problem-solving knowledge by observing and analyzing the problem-solving steps contributed by its users, through their normal use of the system [Mitchell, Mahadevan, and Steinberg, 1985].

Representative examples of this approach are the systems LEAP [Mitchell, Mahadevan, and Steinberg, 1985] and GENESIS [DeJong and Mooney, 1986]. LEAP's domain of expertise is the VLSI design and GENESIS's is story understanding. A common feature of LEAP and GENESIS is that they are based on a strong (complete) domain theory that allows them to learn a general rule or schemata from a single example by reducing learning to deductive reasoning.

Nevertheless, such beautifully tailored domains are seldom available. *A typical real-world domain theory is nonhomogeneous* in that it provides complete descriptions of some parts of the domain, and only incomplete or even poor (weak) descriptions of other parts of the domain. A learning episode, however, uses only one part of the domain theory; and this part may have the features of a complete, incomplete or weak theory even if, globally, the theory is nonhomogeneous. Therefore, a learning system should be able to learn a general rule or concept not only when disposing of a complete theory about an example, but also when disposing of an incomplete or even weak theory about it. An illustration of such a learning system is DISCIPLE. *DISCIPLE is a multistrategy, integrated learning system.* It has the same general purpose as a learning apprentice system, but it is based on a multistrategy approach to learning, instead of on deductive reasoning.

DISCIPLE is a tool for building practical expert systems. It integrates an empty expert system and a learning system, both using the same knowledge base. To build an expert system with DISCIPLE, one has to first introduce elementary knowledge about an application domain into DISCIPLE's knowledge base—knowledge constituting a nonhomogeneous theory of the domain. Next, DISCIPLE may be used to solve problems interactively, according to the following scenario:

The user gives DISCIPLE the problem to solve, and the expert subsystem starts solving this problem by showing the user each problem-solving step (which we shall call *partial solution*). The user may agree with or reject it. In the latter case, or when DISCIPLE is unable to propose any partial solution, the user is compelled to give his own solution. Once this solution is given, a learning process will take place. DISCI-PLE will try to learn a general rule so that, when faced with problems similar to the current one (which it has been unable to solve), it will become able to propose a solution similar to the solution, given by the user, to the current problem. In this way, DISCIPLE progressively evolves from a useful assistant in problem solving to a genuine expert.

19.2 DISCIPLE AS AN EXPERT SYSTEM

In DISCIPLE we have adopted a *problem-reduction* approach to problem solving. That is, a problem is solved by successively reducing it to simpler subproblems. This process continues until the initial problem is reduced to a set of elementary problems; that is, problems with known solutions. Moreover, the problem to solve may be initially imprecisely formulated, becoming better and better formulated as the problem-solving process advances. To this purpose, DISCIPLE formulates, propagates, and evaluates constraints [Tecuci, 1988; Tecuci, *et al.*, 1987].

Problem reduction is a general method, suitable for solving a large variety of problems. In the following, however, we shall consider only problems of designing action plans for achieving partially specified goals. These problems are similar to those solved by PLANX10 [Sridharan and Bresina, 1982], NONLIN [Tate, 1977], and others. An example of such a problem is:

- given the incomplete specifications of a loudspeaker;
- design the actions needed to manufacture the loudspeaker.

DISCIPLE may start with the following top-level operation, which can be seen as the current goal:

MANUFACTURE OBJECT loudspeaker

It will try to solve this problem by successive decompositions and specializations, as illustrated in Figure 19–1 and in Figure 19–2. DISCIPLE will combine such decompositions and specializations, building a problem-solving tree like the one in Figure 19–3. This process continues until all the leaves of the tree are elementary actions, that is, actions that can be executed by the entity manufacturing the loudspeaker.

Figure 19–3 shows a standard AND tree, the solution to the problem from the top of this tree consisting of the leaves of the tree. That is, to manufacture the loudspeaker, one has to perform the following sequence of operations:

FIX OBJECTS contacts ON chassis

In order to solve the problem
MANUFACTURE OBJECT loudspeaker
solve the subproblem
1. MAKE OBJECT chassis-assembly
    In order to solve this subproblem solve the sub-subproblems
    1.1 FIX OBJECT contacts ON chassis

    1.2 MAKE OBJECT mechanical-chassis-assembly

    1.3 FINISHING-OPERATIONS ON entrefer

    In order to solve this subproblem solve the sub-subproblems
    1.3.1 CLEAN OBJECT entrefer

    1.3.2 VERIFY OBJECT entrefer
2. MAKE OBJECT membrane-assembly
3. ASSEMBLE OBJECT chassis-assembly WITH membrane-assembly

    In order to solve this subproblem solve the sub-subproblems
    3.1 ATTACH OBJECT membrane-assembly ON chassis-assembly

    3.2 ATTACH OBJECT ring ON chassis-membrane-assembly

    In order to solve this subproblem solve the sub-subproblems
    3.2.1 APPLY OBJECT mowicoll ON ring

    3.2.2 PRESS OBJECT ring ON chassis-membrane-assembly
4. FINISHING-OPERATIONS ON loudspeaker

Figure 19–1:   Problem-solving operations: Decompositions of problems into simpler sub-problems

In order to solve the problem
CLEAN OBJECT entrefer
solve the specialization
CLEAN OBJECT entrefer WITH air-jet-device

In order to solve this problem solve the specialization
CLEAN OBJECT entrefer WITH air sucker

In order to solve the problem
APPLY OBJECT mowicoll ON ring
solve the specialization
APPLY OBJECT mowicoll-C107 ON ring

Figure 19–2:   Problem-solving operations: specializations of problems

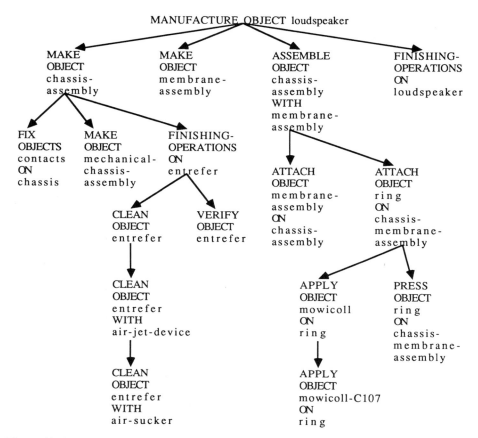

Figure 19–3:   A problem-solving tree. It was built by using the decompositions and the specializations from Figures 19–1 and 19–2.

MAKE OBJECT mechanical-chassis-assembly

CLEAN OBJECT entrefer WITH air-sucker

VERIFY OBJECT entrefer

MAKE OBJECT membrane-assembly

ATTACH OBJECT membrane-assembly ON chassis-assembly

APPLY OBJECT mowicoll-C107 ON ring

PRESS OBJECT ring ON chassis-membrane-assembly

FINISHING-OPERATIONS ON loudspeaker

Let us notice that the decompositions and the specializations model, in fact, the main operations used in design, where one usually starts with a very general specification of an object, successively imposes different constraints on the specification, and reduces object design to subparts design.

19.3 THE LEARNING PROBLEM

The decompositions and the specializations from Figure 19–3 were the result of the application of general reduction rules or were directly indicated by the user. From each solution received from the user, DISCIPLE is trying to learn a general problem-solving rule. Therefore, the learning problem of DISCIPLE may be formulated as shown in Figure 19–4.

For instance,

Given:
The theory of loudspeaker manufacturing;
The problem of attaching two parts of the loudspeaker (the 'ring' and the 'chassis-membrane-assembly') *and the decomposition of this problem into two simpler subproblems* expressing the gluing of the two parts with 'mowicoll' (see Figure 19–5).

Determine:
A general decomposition rule indicating the conditions under which one may reduce an 'attachment' problem to a process of gluing (see Figure 19–6).

As one may notice, the structure of **General Rule 1** in Figure 19–6 is identical with the structure of **Example 1** in Figure 19–5. Therefore, rule learning is reduced to learning the features that the objects 'x', 'y', and 'z' should have so that the attachment of 'x' and 'y' may be reduced to a process of gluing them with 'z'. Otherwise stated, one should learn the concepts represented by these objects.

The method of learning this rule depends on the system's theory (knowledge) about **Example 1**. We distinguish between three types of theories: *complete, weak,* and *incomplete*.

A *complete theory* about Example 1 consists of the complete descriptions of the objects and actions from this problem-solving episode. In such a case, DISCIPLE uses an explanation-based learning method, being able to learn at once a general rule from Example 1 alone.

A *weak theory* about Example 1 consists only of incomplete descriptions of the objects. It differs qualitatively from a complete theory in that it does not contain action descriptions. In this case, DISCIPLE uses an interactive learning method that synergistically combines explanation-based learning, learning by analogy, empirical learning, and learning by questioning the user.

Given:

Domain Theory

The domain theory contains:

- o a specification of the types of objects in the world and their properties and relations;

- o a set of inference rules for inferring properties and relations from other properties and relations;

- o a set of action models describing the actions that may be performed in the domain. An action model specifies the preconditions of the action (i.e., the states of the world in which the action may be executed), the effects of the action (i.e., the states that result after the execution of the action), as well as the objects that may play certain roles in the action (the agent executing the action, the object on which the action is performed, the instrument used, etc.).

Problem-Solving Episode

It consists of

- o P, a problem to solve, and

- o S, a (partial) solution to P.

Determine:

A General Problem-Solving Rule.

According to this rule, problems similar to P will receive solutions similar to S.

Figure 19–4:   The learning problem of DISCIPLE

Example 1:

Solve the problem

ATTACH OBJECT ring ON chassis-membrane-assembly

by solving the subproblems

APPLY OBJECT mowicoll ON ring

PRESS OBJECT ring ON chassis-membrane-assembly

Figure 19–5:   A decomposition indicated by the user

The intermediate case, between a complete theory and a weak theory, is the *incomplete theory*. It contains incomplete descriptions of the objects and the actions from Example 1. In the case of an incomplete theory about Example 1, DISCIPLE learns a general rule by combining the method corresponding to the weak theory with the one corresponding to the complete theory.

IF

> (x TYPE solid) & (y TYPE solid) & (x PARTIALLY-FITS y) &
> (z ISA adhesive) & (z TYPE fluid) & (z GLUES x) & (z GLUES y)

THEN
General Rule 1:
solve the problem
> ATTACH OBJECT x ON y

by solving the subproblems
> APPLY OBJECT z ON x
> PRESS OBJECT x ON y

Figure 19–6: The general decomposition rule learned from Example 1: If 'x' and 'y' are two solid objects that partially fit each other, and there is a fluid adhesive 'z' that glues both 'x' and 'y', then one may attach 'x' on 'y' by first applying 'z' on 'x' and then by pressing 'x' on 'y'

A side effect of rule learning in the context of a weak or incomplete theory is that of developing the domain theory. In the following sections we shall present these three learning methods of DISCIPLE.

19.4 LEARNING IN A COMPLETE THEORY DOMAIN

19.4.1 A Sample of a Complete Theory

In the case of DISCIPLE, a complete theory of a domain consists of complete descriptions of all the objects and actions of the domain. In particular, a complete theory about the problem-solving episode in Figure 19–5, contains the complete descriptions of the objects 'ring', 'chassis-membrane-assembly', and 'mowicoll', as well as the complete descriptions (models) of the actions 'ATTACH', 'APPLY', and 'PRESS'.

The objects are described by specifying all the relevant factual properties and relations. Some of these may be explicitly specified, as indicated in Figure 19–7.

Other properties and relations may be implicitly specified by using inference rules for deducing them from other properties and relations, as indicated in Figure 19–8.

The action models describe the actions that may be performed in the domain. A complete action model specifies all the necessary preconditions of the action (i.e., all the states of the world in which the action may be executed), all its effects (i.e., the states that result after the execution of the action), as well as all the objects that may play certain roles in the action (the agent executing the action, the object on which the action is performed, the instrument used, etc.).

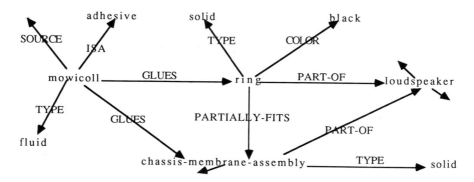

Figure 19–7:   A hierarchical semantic network containing explicit representations of object properties and relations

$$\forall x \; \forall y \; [(x \; \text{GLUED-ON} \; y) \Rightarrow (x \; \text{ATTACHED-ON} \; y)]$$
$$\forall x \; \forall y \; \forall z \; [(z \; \text{ISA adhesive}) \& (z \; \text{GLUES} \; x) \& (z \; \text{GLUES} \; y) \&$$
$$(z \; \text{BETWEEN} \; x \; y) \Rightarrow (x \; \text{GLUED-ON} \; y)]$$
$$\forall x \; \forall y \; [(x \; \text{GLUES} \; y) \Rightarrow (x \; \text{ADHERENT-ON} \; y)]$$

Figure 19–8:   Inference rules for deducing new properties and relations of objects

Action	Preconditions	Effects
ATTACH OBJECT x ON y	(x TYPE solid) & (y TYPE solid)	(x ATTACHED-ON y)
APPLY OBJECT z ON x	(z TYPE fluid) & (z ADHERENT-ON x) & (x TYPE solid)	(z APPLIED-ON x)
PRESS OBJECT x ON y	(z APPLIED-ON x) & (x PARTIALLY-FITS y) & (y TYPE solid)	(z BETWEEN x y)

Figure 19–9:   Action models

Figure 19–9 presents the models of the actions from the problem-solving episode in Figure 19–5. For instance, the action 'APPLY' may be performed if and only if 'x' is a solid object and 'z' is a fluid object that is adherent on 'x'. As an effect of performing this action, 'z' will be applied on 'x'. Notice that the necessary features of the objects are specified in the action's preconditions.

19.4.2 General Presentation of the Learning Method

In the case of a complete theory about Example 1, the learning method of DIS-CIPLE follows the explanation-based learning paradigm developed by [DeJong and Mooney, 1986; Fikes, Hart, and Nilsson, 1972; Mitchell, Keller, and Kedar-Cabelli, 1986] and others:

1. Prove that the solution indicated by the user is indeed a solution of the problem to solve. This proof isolates the relevant features of the objects in Example 1; that is, those features that will be present in the condition of General Rule 1.

2. Generalize the proof tree as much as possible so that the proof still holds. This is done as in [Mooney and Bennet, 1986] by replacing each instance of action model or inference rule with its general pattern and by unifying these patterns. By generalizing the proof tree, one generalizes the problem, its solution, and the relevant features.

3. Formulate the learned rule from the generalized proof by extracting the generalized problem, its generalized solution, and the generalized relevant features, which constitute the applicability condition of the rule.

In the following sections we shall briefly illustrate this method with the aid of **Example 1** (Figure 19–5).

19.4.3 Proving the Example

To prove **Example 1** means to show that the sequence of the actions

APPLY OBJECT mowicoll ON ring

PRESS OBJECT ring ON chassis-membrane-assembly achieves
the goal of the action

ATTACH OBJECT ring ON chassis-membrane-assembly that is,
achieves the goal

(ring ATTACHED-ON chassis-membrane-assembly).

The proof is indicated in Figure 19–10. It was obtained by using the object descriptions in Figure 19–7, the inference rules in Figure 19–8, and the action models in Figure 19–9.

The leaves of the tree in Figure 19–10 are those features of 'ring', 'chassis-membrane-assembly', and 'mowicoll' that allowed one to reduce the problem of attaching the 'ring' on the 'chassis-membrane-assembly' to the process of gluing them with 'mowicoll'. Thus, by proving the example, one isolates the relevant features of it (see Figure 19–11). The 'color' of the 'ring' or the 'source' of the 'mowicoll' were not useful in proving the validity of the example. Therefore, these features are not important for this example.

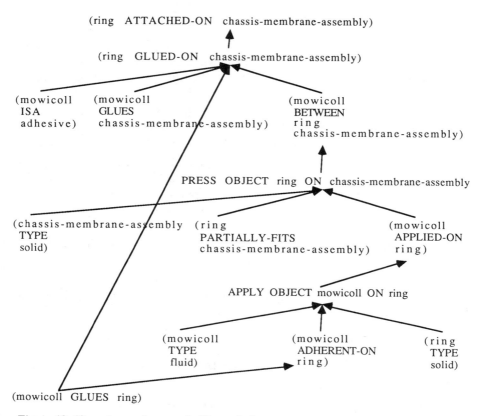

Figure 19–10:   A complete proof of Example 1

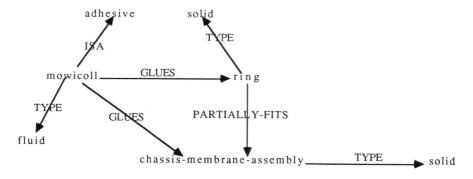

Figure 19–11:   The relevant features of Example 1

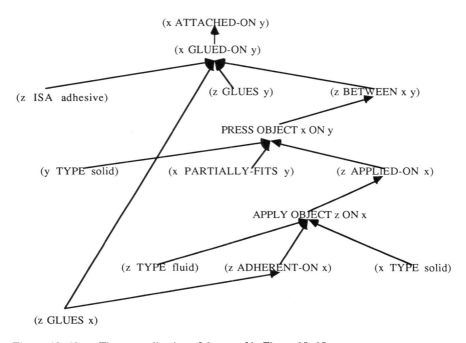

Figure 19–12: The generalization of the proof in Figure 19–10

19.4.4 Generalization of the Proof

The next step consists in the generalization of the proof, as much as possible, so that the proof still holds. Since the proof in Figure 19–10 was obtained by using instances of inference rules and action models, one may generalize the proof by generalizing these instances. One way to do this is to first replace each instantiated inference rule or action model with its general pattern, and then to unify these patterns [Mooney and Bennet, 1986] (see Figure 19–12). The leaves of this generalized tree represent a justified generalization of the relevant features in Figure 19–11:

(x TYPE solid) & (y TYPE solid) & (x PARTIALLY-FITS y) &
(z ISA adhesive) & (z TYPE fluid) & (z GLUES x) & (z GLUES y)

They also represent a general precondition for which the sequence of the actions 'APPLY OBJECT z ON x', 'PRESS OBJECT x ON y' achieves the goal of the action 'ATTACH OBJECT x ON y'. That is, one has learned the general decomposition rule in Figure 19–6.

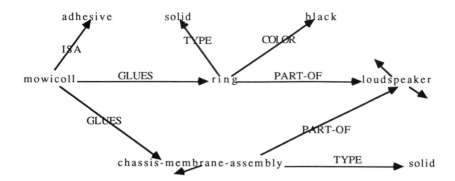

Figure 19–13:   Fragment of a weak theory

19.5 LEARNING IN A WEAK THEORY DOMAIN

19.5.1 A Sample of a Weak Theory

A weak theory about the problem-solving episode in Figure 19–5 (Example 1) consists of the incomplete descriptions of the objects from this episode. It does not contain any action model. A sample of such a theory is represented in Figure 19–13.

Considering such a theory is justified because it is very difficult for an expert to describe the actions in terms of their preconditions and effects. On the other hand, it is much easier for him to describe the objects and to give examples of decompositions and specializations.

Therefore, instead of forcing the expert to completely formalize his knowledge, we decided to accept the theory that was easily provided by him and to learn the rest of the necessary knowledge.

19.5.2 General Presentation of the Learning Method

In the context of a weak theory, DISCIPLE will try to balance the lack of knowledge by using an integrated learning method whose power comes from the synergism of different learning paradigms: explanation-based learning, learning by analogy, empirical learning, and learning by questioning the user. Rule learning takes place in several stages, which are illustrated in Figure 19–14.

More formally, the learning method is the following one:

Explanation-based Mode

1. Find an explanation of the user's solution (Example 1) and call it Explanation 1.

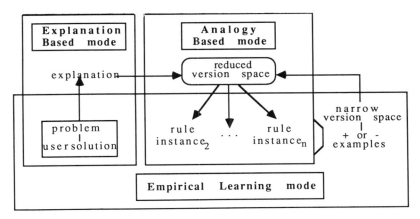

Figure 19–14: The learning method in the context of a weak theory. First DISCIPLE looks for a shallow explanation of the user's solution. Then it uses this explanation to formulate a reduced version space for the rule to be learned. Each rule in this space covers only instances analogous to the user's example. DISCIPLE carefuly generates analogous instances to be characterized as positive examples or as negative examples by the user. These are used to further narrow the version space until it contains only the rule illustrated by the user's solution.

Analogy-based Mode

2. Overgeneralize Example 1 by simply turning all the objects into variables, and call it General Rule 1.

3. Take Explanation 1 as a Lower Bound for the applicability condition of General Rule 1.

4. Overgeneralize Explanation 1 to the most general expression that may still be accepted by the user as an explanation of General Rule 1.

5. Take the overgeneralized explanation as an Upper Bound for the applicability condition of General Rule 1. The Upper Bound, the Lower Bound, and the General Rule 1 define a reduced version space for the rule to be learned.

6. Look in the knowledge base for tuples of objects that satisfy the Upper Bound but do not satisfy the Lower Bound.

   If there are such objects then call Explanation-i the properties of these objects that were used to prove that they satisfy the Upper Bound and go to step 7.

   If there are no such objects then show the Upper Bound, the Lower Bound, and the General Rule 1 to the user as an uncertain rule and stop.

7. Use the objects found in step 6 to generate an instance of General Rule 1. Call it Instance-i. This instance is analogous to Example 1.

8. Propose Instance-i to the user and ask him to characterize it as a valid or as an invalid reduction. If Instance-i is rejected by the user then go to step 9. Otherwise go to step 14.

Explanation-based Mode

9. Take Instance-i as a near miss (negative example) of the rule to be learned.

10. Find an explanation of why Instance-i was rejected by the user and call it Failure-Explanation-i.

Empirical Learning Mode

11. Specialize the Upper Bound as little as possible, so that not to cover Failure-Explanation-i.

    If the new Upper Bound is identical with the Lower Bound then take it as a necessary and sufficient condition of General Rule 1, show them to the user and stop, else go to step 12.

12. Specialize (if necessary) the Lower Bound as little as possible, so that not to cover Failure-Explanation-i.

13. Go to step 6.

14. Take Instance-i as a new positive example of the rule to be learned and Explanation-i as a true explanation of Instance-i.

15. Look for a maximally specific common generalization of the Lower Bound and Explanation-i. Two cases may occur:

    • if this generalization is not identical with the Upper Bound, then take it as the new Lower Bound and go to step 6;

    • if this generalization is identical with the Upper Bound, then take it as a necessary and sufficient condition of General Rule 1, show them to the user and stop.

In the following sections we shall illustrate and justify this learning method by using again Example 1 from Figure 19–5.

19.5.3 Explanation-based Mode

In its first learning step, DISCIPLE enters the explanation-based mode and tries to find an explanation (within its weak domain theory) of the validity of the solution in Figure 19–5.

We shall first define what we mean by an explanation in a weak theory and then we shall indicate a heuristic method to find such explanations.

19.5.3.1 Explanations in a Weak Theory Domain

Let 'P' be the problem to solve and 'S' a solution to this problem. As has been shown in Section 19.4, an explanation of the problem-solving episode '**solve P by S**' is a proof that 'S' solves 'P'.

In the case of a complete theory about this problem-solving episode, the learning system is able to find itself such a proof. In the case of a weak theory, however, the system is no longer able to find such a proof because it lacks the models of the actions from 'P' and 'S'. In such a case, the explanation may be regarded as being the premise of a single inference whose conclusion is '**S solves P**'.

For instance, in the context of a weak theory, a complete explanation of the problem-solving episode in Figure 19–5 would be the network from Figure 19–11. Indeed, the fact that the 'ring', the 'chassis-membrane-assembly', and the 'mowicoll' have the features in Figure 19–11 "explains" (in a weak theory) why the process of gluing the 'ring' and the 'chassis-membrane-assembly' with 'mowicoll' solves the problem of attaching them together.

19.5.3.2 A Heuristic to Find Explanations

The explanation of Example 1 consists of the leaves of the proof tree in Figure 19–11. Since such a tree cannot be built in a weak theory, DISCIPLE uses heuristics to propose plausible partial explanations to be validated by the user who may herself indicate other pieces of explanations. One heuristic is to *look for an explanation expressible in terms of the relations between the objects from the example, ignoring object features*. Therefore, to find an explanation of Example 1, DISCIPLE will look in its knowledge base for the links and for the paths (i.e., sequences of links) connecting 'ring', 'chassis-membrane-assembly', and 'mowicoll', and will propose the found connections as pieces of explanations of the Example 1. It is the user's task to validate them as true explanations:

Do the following justify your solution:
mowicoll GLUES ring? *Yes*
mowicoll GLUES chassis-membrane-assembly? *Yes*
ring PART-OF loudspeaker &
chassis-membrane-assembly PART-OF loudspeaker? *No*

All the pieces of explanations marked by a user's yes form the explanation of Example 1 (see Figure 19–15).

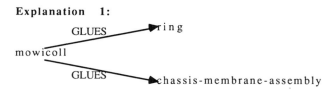

Figure 19–15:   The explanation of Example 1

Notice that this explanation is incomplete. This is partially a consequence of using heuristics, and partially a consequence of the incompleteness of the domain theory (which may not contain all the relevant object properties and relations). Nevertheless, it shows some important features of the objects, features justifying the user's solution.

This explanation will be used in the next learning mode (the analogy-based mode), which will be described in the following section. There we shall also give a justification of the heuristic presented above.

19.5.4 Analogy-based Mode

The central intuition supporting the learning by analogy paradigm is that if two entities are similar in some respects then they could be similar in other respects as well. An important result of the learning by analogy research [Bareiss and Porter 1987; Burstein, 1986; Carbonell, 1983; 1986; Chouraqui, 1982; Gentner, 1983; Kedar-Cabelli, 1985; Kodratoff, 1988; Russel, 1987; Winston, 1986] is that the analogy involves mapping some underlying causal network of relations between analogous situations. The idea is that similar causes are expected to have similar effects.

In DISCIPLE, the explanation of a problem-solving operation may be regarded as a cause for performing the operation. Therefore, two similar explanations are supposed to 'cause' similar problem-solving episodes. Moreover, the explanations are considered to be similar if they are both less general than an overgeneralized explanation that is taken as the analogy criterion.

Figure 19–16 contains an example of such an analogy. The fact that the 'mowicoll' glues both the 'ring' and the 'chassis-membrane-assembly' 'CAUSED' the reduction of the problem of attaching the 'ring' to the 'chassis-membrane-assembly' to a process of gluing them with 'mowicoll'. Because the 'neoprene' glues both the 'screening-cap' and the 'loudspeaker' we may expect (reasoning by analogy) to be able to reduce the problem of attaching the 'screening-cap' and the 'loudspeaker' to a process of gluing them with 'neoprene'.

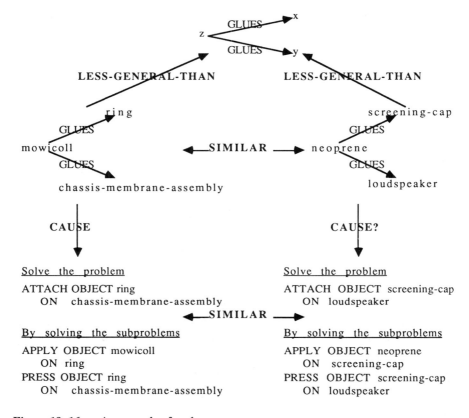

Figure 19–16:   An example of analogy

According to the structure-mapping theory of Gentner (1983), analogy usually involves mapping higher order relations (as the 'CAUSE' relation, in our case). Looking for an explanation in terms of relations between objects, DISCIPLE ensures that the 'CAUSE' relation, which it imports by analogy, is a higher order relation.

19.5.4.3 Determining a Reduced Version Space for the Rule to Be Learned

The purpose of the previous sections was to justify the following procedure for determining a reduced version space for the rule to be learned.

First of all DISCIPLE overgeneralizes Example 1 by turning all the objects into variables, thus obtaining:

General Rule 1:

solve the problem
    ATTACH OBJECT x ON y

by solving the subproblems
    APPLY OBJECT z ON x
    PRESS OBJECT x ON y

Next Explanation 1 is rewritten as a lower bound of the applicability condition of General Rule 1 (S bound in Figure 19–17). Notice that it is indeed a lower bound because it reduces General Rule 1 to Example 1, which is known to be true. Further, DISCIPLE determines an analogy criterion that will allow it to generate instances analogous to Example 1.

The analogy criterion is a generalization of Explanation 1. In the case of our example, it was obtained by simply transforming the constants of Explanation 1 into variables, or, if we consider the form of Explanation 1 in Figure 19–17, by dropping the 'ISA' predicates.

In general, *the analogy criterion should be the most general generalization of Explanation 1 that may still be accepted by the user as an explanation of General Rule1*. The analogy criterion *is taken by DISCIPLE* as an upper bound for the applicability condition of General Rule 1 (G bound in Figure 19–17). Thus, the analogy criterion, Explanation 1, and General Rule 1 define a reduced version space [Mitchell, 1978] for the rule to be learned.

IF

G:upper bound (analogy criterion)

(z GLUES x) & (z GLUES y)

S:lower bound (Explanation 1)

(x ISA ring) & (y ISA chassis-membrane-assembly) & (z ISA mowicoll)
& (z GLUES x) & (z GLUES y)

THEN
General Rule 1:
solve the problem
    ATTACH OBJECT x ON y

by solving the subproblems
    APPLY OBJECT z ON x
    PRESS OBJECT x ON y

Figure 19–17:   A reduced version space for the rule to be learned

Each rule in this space has an applicability condition that is less general than the analogy criterion and more general than Explanation 1. Therefore, it covers only instances that are analogous to Example 1.

19.5.4.4 Generation of Instances

To search the rule in the space from Figure 19–17, DISCIPLE needs positive and negative instances of it. *These instances may be provided by future problem-solving episodes or may be generated by the system itself.*

To generate an instance, DISCIPLE looks in the knowledge base for objects satisfying the analogy criterion. The objects 'screening-cap', 'loudspeaker', and 'neoprene' are such objects. DISCIPLE calls **Explanation-i** the properties of these objects that were used to prove that they satisfy the analogy criterion:

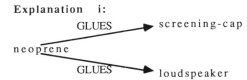

Explanation i:

It uses the found objects to generate an instance of General Rule 1 (see Figure 19–17) and asks the user to validate it (see Figure 19–18).

19.5.5 Empirical Learning Mode

The instances generated in the analogy mode are accepted or rejected by the user, being thus characterized as positive examples or as negative examples of the rule to be learned. These instances are used to search the rule in the version space from Figure 19–17.

19.5.5.1 The Use of the Positive Examples

Each positive example shows a true explanation. All these explanations are generalized [Kodratoff and Ganascia, 1986], and the obtained generalization is used as a new lower bound of the condition version space.

May I solve the problem
ATTACH OBJECT screening-cap ON loudspeaker

by solving the subproblems
APPLY OBJECT neoprene ON screening-cap
PRESS OBJECT screening-cap ON loudspeaker ? *Yes*

Figure 19–18: An instance generated by analogy with Example 1

Let us suppose, for instance, that the user accepts the decomposition in Figure 19–18. Then, Explanation-i, computed in Section 19.5.4.4, is a true explanation that may also be rewritten as a lower bound for the applicability condition of General Rule 1:

Explanation i:

(x ISA screening-cap) & (y ISA loudspeaker) & (z ISA neoprene) &
(z GLUES x) & (z GLUES y)

Therefore, DISCIPLE computes a maximally specific, common generalization of the lower bound in Figure 19–17 and of Explanation-i and takes it as a new lower bound of the condition to be learned:

IF

> **G:upper bound**
> (z GLUES x) & (z GLUES y)

> **S:lower bound**
> (x TYPE solid) & (y TYPE solid) & (z ISA adhesive) &
> (z GLUES x) & (z GLUES y)

THEN

General Rule 1:

solve the problem
> ATTACH OBJECT x ON y

by solving the subproblems
> APPLY OBJECT z ON x
> PRESS OBJECT x ON y

Notice that DISCIPLE generalized '(z ISA mowicoll)' and '(z ISA neoprene)' to '(z ISA adhesive)', by applying the well-known rule of climbing the generalization hierarchies [Michalski, 1983]. But it generalized '(x ISA ring)' and '(x ISA screening-cap)' to '(x TYPE solid)' because there is no common generalization of 'ring' and 'screening-cap', and the only relevant property common to 'ring' and 'screening-cap' is that they are both 'solid'. Another common property of 'ring' and 'screening-cap' is that they are both PART-OF 'loudspeaker'. DISCIPLE considers that this property is not relevant because it was not accepted as explanation of Example 1 (see Section 19.5.3.2).

Notice also that the new lower bound is always more specific than the upper bound because both the previous lower bound and Explanation i are less general than the upper bound. However, the generalization of the lower bound was made in the context of an incomplete knowledge. Therefore it could be an overgeneralization, to be later particularized when new knowledge becomes available.

May I solve the problem
ATTACH OBJECT screening-cap ON loudspeaker

by solving the subproblems
APPLY OBJECT scotch-tape ON screening-cap
PRESS OBJECT screening-cap ON loudspeaker? *No*

Figure 19–19: A negative example of the rule to be learned

19.5.5.2 The Use of the Negative Examples

Each negative example shows the incompleteness of Explanation 1 and of its overgeneralization (the analogy criterion). The explanation of why the instance is a negative example points to the features that were not present in Explanation 1. These new features are used to particularize both bounds of the version space.

Let us consider the objects 'screening-cap', 'loudspeaker' and 'scotch-tape' (an adhesive tape). They also satisfy the analogy criterion (the upper bound of the condition version space) but the corresponding instance is rejected by the user (see Figure 19–19).

In this case, DISCIPLE looks for an explanation of the failure because this explanation points to the important object features that were not contained in Explanation 1. The explanation is that 'scotch-tape' is not fluid (therefore, it might not be applied on a curved surface):

Failure Explanation: NOT (scotch-tape TYPE fluid)

That is, the concept represented by 'z' must be fluid. Therefore, DISCIPLE will specialize both bounds of the version space by adding the '(z TYPE fluid)':

IF

G:upper bound

(z GLUES x) & (z GLUES y) & (z TYPE fluid)

S:lower bound

(x TYPE solid) & (y TYPE solid) & (z ISA adhesive) &
(z GLUES x) & (z GLUES y) & (z TYPE fluid)

THEN

General Rule 1:

solve the problem
ATTACH OBJECT x ON y

by solving the subproblems

APPLY OBJECT z ON x

PRESS OBJECT x ON y

In another situation, failing to glue two objects whose surfaces do not fit each other, DISCIPLE discovers the condition that the objects should partially fit:

IF

G:upper bound

(z GLUES x) & (z GLUES y) & (z TYPE fluid) &
(x PARTIALLY-FITS y)

S:lower bound

(x TYPE solid) & (y TYPE solid) & (z ISA adhesive) &
(z GLUES x) & (z GLUES y) & (z TYPE fluid) &
(x PARTIALLY-FITS y)

THEN

General Rule 1:

solve the problem

ATTACH OBJECT x ON y

by solving the subproblems

APPLY OBJECT z ON x

PRESS OBJECT x ON y

The learning process decreases the distance between the two bounds of the version space. This process should, in principle, continue until the lower bound becomes identical with the upper one.

In our case, other negative examples will show that

(x TYPE solid) & (y TYPE solid) & (z ISA adhesive)

are necessary features of the objects 'x', 'y', and 'z'. Thus one learns the rule in Figure 19–6.

However, since the domain theory is weak, we should expect that this will not always happen. Therefore, we will be forced to preserve two conditions (the upper bound and the lower bound), instead of a single applicability condition. We propose to define such a case as being typical of an *uncertain explanation* (in which uncertainty is not expressed by numerical means).

19.5.5.3 Active Experimentation

In the analogy-based mode DISCIPLE may generate many instances of the rule to be learned. However, they are not equally useful for searching the version space.

Therefore, in the empirical learning mode, DISCIPLE will determine the features of the most useful instances, asking for the generation of such instances. Its strategy is to generalize the lower bound of the version space by generalizing the referred objects (i.e., 'mowicoll', 'ring', and 'chassis-membrane-assembly'). It will therefore try to climb the generalization hierarchy of these objects in such a way as to preserve consistency with the necessary condition. During this generalization process, several situations may occur:

- there are different ways to generalize;
- the generalization may cover objects that are not guaranteed to produce positive examples of the rule.

When faced with such problems, DISCIPLE will ask the user "clever" questions (as, for instance, in [Sammut and Banerji, 1986]) whose answers allow it to take the right decision. This process is illustrated in [Tecuci, 1988].

19.5.6 Developing the Domain Theory

As has been shown in Section 19.5.3.2, DISCIPLE looks for explanations in its knowledge base. Because the domain theory is weak, we may expect that it will not always contain the right pieces of explanations. In such situations the pieces of the explanation must be provided by the user.

Let us consider, for instance, that the explanation of the failure in Figure 19–19 was provided by the user. In this case the domain theory will be enriched by storing this explanation: 'NOT (scotch-tape TYPE fluid)'.

More significantly, as a consequence of updating the Lower Bound of the version space, the following relations between the objects that previously generated positive examples of the rule (and are therefore supposed to satisfy the Lower Bound) are added to the domain theory:

(mowicoll TYPE fluid) & (neoprene TYPE fluid).

19.6 LEARNING IN AN INCOMPLETE THEORY DOMAIN

19.6.1 A Sample of an Incomplete Theory

In the case of DISCIPLE, an incomplete theory of a domain may lack some object descriptions, inference rules, or action models. Also, it may contain incomplete descriptions of these.

An incomplete description of an object lacks certain properties or relations with other objects; an incomplete action model lacks some precondition predicates or some effect predicates; and an incomplete inference rule lacks some left-hand side or right-hand side predicates.

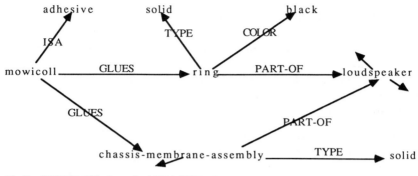

$$\forall x\ \forall y\ [(x\ \text{GLUED-ON}\ y) \Rightarrow (x\ \text{ATTACHED-ON}\ y)]$$

$$\forall x\ \forall y\ \forall z\ [(z\ \text{ISA}\ \text{adhesive})\&(z\ \text{GLUES}\ x)\&(z\ \text{GLUES}\ y)\&(z\ \text{BETWEEN}\ x\ y)$$
$$\Rightarrow (x\ \text{GLUED-ON}\ y)]$$

$$\forall x\ \forall y\ [(x\ \text{GLUES}\ y) \Rightarrow (x\ \text{ADHERENT-ON}\ y)]$$

Figure 19–20:   Incomplete descriptions of the objects from Example 1

Action	Preconditions	Effects
ATTACH OBJECT x ON y	(x TYPE solid) & (y TYPE solid)	(x ATTACHED-ON y)
APPLY OBJECT z ON x	(z ADHERENT-ON x) & (x TYPE solid)	(z APPLIED-ON x)

Figure 19–21:   Incomplete models of two actions from Example 1

A sample of an incomplete theory about Example 1 (Figure 19–5) is given in the Figures 19–20 and 19–21.

As one may notice, the explicit properties and relations of the objects 'ring', 'chassis-membrane-assembly' and 'mowicoll' are the ones considered in the case of the weak theory (see Figure 19–13).

Also notice that this incomplete theory lacks entirely the model of the action 'PRESS'. It also contains an incomplete model of the action 'APPLY', model lacking the precondition predicate '(z TYPE fluid)'.

19.6.2 General Presentation of the Learning Method

In this case, the learning method combines the two learning methods presented previously. First, the system will construct an incomplete proof of Example 1 and will generalize it, as in a complete theory. In this way, it will determine an *over-*

generalized explanation of Example 1. Then, the system will use the overgeneralized explanation as an *analogy criterion* to perform experiments and to synthesize the general rule, as in a weak theory:

1. Prove that the solution indicated by the user is indeed a solution of the problem to solve. Because the domain theory is incomplete, the system may ask the user focused questions in order to fill the possible gaps in the proof. The leaves of the proof tree represents an incomplete explanation of Example 1.

2. If the user's solution contains new actions, then use the proof found in step 1 in order to define initial version spaces for the models of these actions. As a side effect of rule learning, DISCIPLE will learn the models of these new actions.

3. Overgeneralize the proof tree found in step 1, as in a complete theory. If an action model is incompletely learned then use the upper bound of its preconditions and effects. The leaves of the overgeneralized proof tree represent an overgeneralized explanation of Example 1, being taken by DISCIPLE as an analogy criterion.

4. Formulate a reduced version space for the rule to be learned, as in a weak theory, by using the explanation found in step 1 and the overgeneralized explanation found in step 3.

5. Search the rule in the version space defined in step 4 by performing experiments, as in a weak theory. Use the overgeneralized proof determined in step 3 in order to find the explanations of the failures.

In the next section we shall illustrate this learning method.

19.6.3 Incomplete Proving of the Example

Even when the objects, the inference rules, and the actions are incompletely specified, one may be able to construct a proof tree, which lacks some parts of the complete proof tree (see Chapter 18, this volume and [Wilkins, 1988]).

When the system lacks inference rules or action models, it will try to sketch the proof tree both top-down and bottom-up, and will ask the user focused questions, in order to connect the different parts of the proof.

Using the incomplete theory about Example 1, presented in the previous section, the system may build the following proof of Example 1 (see Figure 19–22). The dotted lines from the proof tree do not result from the domain theory but are hypotheses made by the system and confirmed by the user. For instance, the system makes the hypothesis that

(mowicoll BETWEEN ring chassis-membrane-assembly)

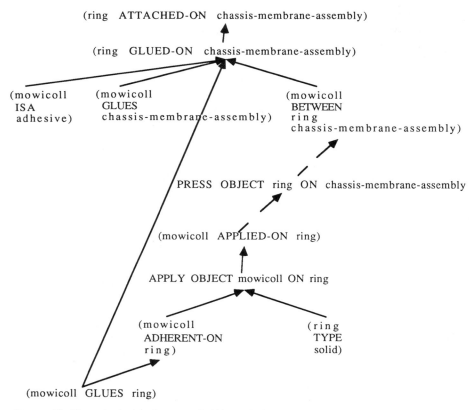

Figure 19–22:   An incomplete proof of Example 1

is an effect of the action

PRESS OBJECT ring ON chassis-membrane-assembly

from the fact that all the other left-hand side literals of the inference rule

$\forall x \, \forall y \, \forall z$ [(z ISA adhesive) & (z GLUES x) & (z GLUES y) &
(z BETWEEN x y) $\Rightarrow$ (x GLUED-ON y)]

are true in the current situation, that is

[(mowicoll ISA adhesive) & (mowicoll GLUES ring) &
(mowicoll GLUES chassis-membrane-assembly)] = TRUE

and the literal '(mowicoll BETWEEN ring chassis-membrane-assembly)' is not
known to be true.

Explanation 1:

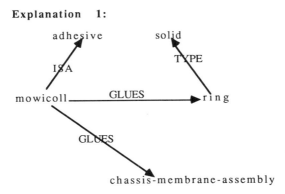

Figure 19–23:   The relevant features of Example 1, revealed by the proof tree in Figure
               19–22

Comparing the proof tree in Figure 19–22 with the complete one in Figure 19–11, one may easily notice that it lacks some leaves. Nevertheless, the leaves that are present represent some important features of the objects from Example 1; features that in the case of a weak theory would correspond to the explanation of Example 1 shown in Figure 19–23.

19.6.4 Defining Version Spaces for the Unknown Actions

The incomplete proof allows one to define initial version spaces for the models of the unknown actions used in the proof. For instance, one may define the following version space for the action 'PRESS':

Action	Preconditions	Effects
PRESS OBJECT x ON y	*upper bound:* (z APPLIED-ON x) *lower bound:* (z APPLIED-ON x) & (x ISA ring) & (y ISA chassis-membrane- assembly) & (z ISA mowicoll)	*upper bound:* (z BETWEEN x y) *lower bound:* (z BETWEEN x y) & (x ISA ring) & (y ISA chassis-membrane- assembly) & (z ISA mowicoll)

The *lower bounds* for the preconditions and effects are taken directly from the proof tree. The *upper bound* of the effects is the generalization of the lower bound (mowicoll BETWEEN ring chassis-membrane-assembly) taken from the premise of the inference rule

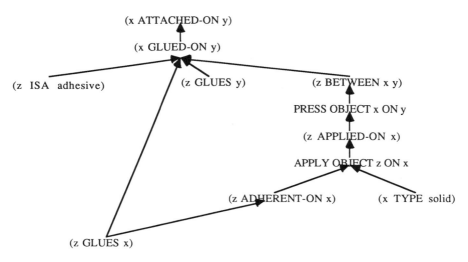

Figure 19–24:   The generalization of the proof in Figure 19–22

$\forall x \forall y \forall z [(z\ ISA\ adhesive)\ \&\ (z\ GLUES\ x)\ \&\ (z\ GLUES\ y)\ \&$
$(z\ BETWEEN\ x\ y)\ \Rightarrow (x\ GLUED\text{-}ON\ y)]$

The *upper bound* of the preconditions is the generalization of the lower bound, taken from the effects of the model of the action 'APPLY OBJECT z ON x'. During the learning of the decomposition rule in Figure 19–6, the system will also refine the model of the action 'PRESS'.

19.6.5 Generalization of the Incomplete Proof

Once the proof in Figure 19–22 is built, the system will generalize it, as in a complete theory (see Figure 19–24).

Let us notice that, for generalizing the proof, the system used the upper bounds of the preconditions and effects of the action 'PRESS'.

19.6.6 Determining a Reduced Version Space for the Rule to Be Learned

As in the case of a weak theory, the Explanation 1 in Figure 19–23 may be rewritten as a Lower Bound for the applicability condition of General Rule 1 (Figure 19–25). Also, the leaves of the generalized proof tree in Figure 19–24 provide an *overgeneralized explanation* of Example 1. This overgeneralized explanation corresponds to the *analogy criterion* from a weak theory and is taken by DISCIPLE as an Upper Bound for the applicability condition of General Rule 1 (see Figure 19–25).

IF

> **G:upper bound (analogy criterion)**
>
> (x TYPE solid) & (z ISA adhesive) & (z GLUES x) & (z GLUES y)
>
> **S:lower bound (explanation 1)**
>
> (x ISA ring) & (x TYPE solid) & (y ISA chassis-membrane-assembly) & (z ISA adhesive) & (z GLUES x) & (z GLUES y)

THEN
General Rule 1:
solve the problem
> ATTACH OBJECT x ON y

by solving the subproblems
> APPLY OBJECT z ON x
> PRESS OBJECT x ON y

Figure 19–25:   A reduced version space for the rule to be learned

Therefore, as in a weak theory, the system is able to formulate the following version space for the rule to be learned:

19.6.7 Searching the Rule in the Version Space

As soon as the version space from Figure 19–25 has been determined, rule learning will continue as in a weak theory. This time, however, the generalized proof tree in Figure 19–24 provides a focus for the process of finding the explanations of the failures. To illustrate this, let us consider again the failure in Figure 19–19.

In this case, the system generates the instance of the generalized proof in Figure 19–24, corresponding to this problem-solving episode (by replacing 'x', 'y', and 'z' with 'screening-cap', 'loudspeaker', and 'scotch-tape', respectively).

The fact that the user rejected the solution proposed by the system proves that the leaves of the instantiated tree do not imply the top of the tree (the leaf predicates are true but the top predicate is not).

This means that some action models or inference rules are faulty (incomplete, in our case). To detect them, the system follows the proof tree from bottom up, asking the user to validate each inference step. If the user says that the effect of an action or the consequent of an inference rule is not true, then the corresponding action model (inference rule) may be the incomplete one.

Therefore, in an incomplete theory, finding the explanations of the failures reduces to finding the knowledge that is lacking from the knowledge pieces. In this case, the generalized proof in Figure 19–24 plays the role of a justification structure for the rule to be learned, as in [Smith, *et al.*, 1985].

19.7 EXPERIMENTS WITH DISCIPLE

We have implemented a version of DISCIPLE in Common LISP [Steele, 1984] and we have used it to learn rules in several domains as, for instance, manufacturing, commonsense planning, chemistry, and architecture [Kodratoff and Tecuci, 1987; Tecuci and Kodratoff, 1990].

With a very poor theory of chemistry,[1] DISCIPLE was able to learn, starting from the example of the chemical reaction (NaOH + HCl → H2O + NaCl), that, in general, (Base + Acid → Water + Salt). More precisely, starting from the example

the problem
        COMBINE SUBSTANCE1 NaOH SUBSTANCE2 HCl
has the following solution
        RESULT SUBSTANCE1 H20 SUBSTANCE2 NaCl

DISCIPLE learned the following rule:

IF

G:upper bound
(b COMPOSED-OF x1) & (b COMPOSED-OF x2) &
(a COMPOSED-OF x3) & (a COMPOSED-OF x4) &
(w ISA water) & (w COMPOSED-OF x1) (COMPOSED-OF x3) &
(s ISA salt) & (s COMPOSED-OF x2) (s COMPOSED-OF x4) &
(s (COMPOSED-OF ANION-OF) a) &
(s (COMPOSED-OF CATION-OF) b))

S:lower bound
(b ISA base) & (b COMPOSED-OF x1) & (b COMPOSED-OF x2) &
(a ISA acid) & (a COMPOSED-OF x3) & (a COMPOSED-OF x4) &
(w ISA H2O) & (w COMPOSED-OF x1) & (COMPOSED-OF x3) &
(s ISA salt) & (s COMPOSED-OF x2) & (s COMPOSED-OF x4) &
(s (COMPOSED-OF ANION-OF) a) &
(s (COMPOSED-OF CATION-OF) b)) &

---

[1]This application was suggested by D. Sleeman.

predicates, constants, and variables, but no actual function evaluation is going to take place.

A semantic limitation comes from the fact that the *generality of the learned rule is limited by the generality of the overgeneralized explanation* (the analogy criterion), which may not be in the most general form. However, the rule may be further generalized, in response to a problem-solving situation in which the rule does not apply, and the user says that it should apply. In this case, the condition of the rule may be generalized to cover the new situation as well.

Also, the method of finding an explanation in a weak theory is not powerful enough. Other sources of knowledge are needed, as well as metarules for finding far off explanations. One possible extension of the current method is suggested by the way CLINT [De Raedt and Bruynooghe, 1989] changes its description language in order to be able to learn a concept. DISCIPLE might also use an ordered series of explanation schemas E1, E2, ... , En, ... First, it will be looking for an explanation of the form E1 (for instance, a path of length 1 between two concepts). If no such explanation is found, then it will be looking for an explanation of the form E2 (for instance, a path of length 2 between two concepts), and so on.

While DISCIPLE uses control knowledge in the form of metarules [Tecuci, 1988], such knowledge is not learned—it must be provided by the user. Therefore, if two experts provide different solutions to the same problem, DISCIPLE simply generates two different rules. The learning mechanisms of DISCIPLE should be used to propose explanations of this difference and find metaexplanations that can become metapreconditions on the use of the rules.

An important future direction of research consists in developing the learning methods of DISCIPLE in order to deal with other types of imperfections in the domain theory [Mitchell, Keller, and Kedar-Cabelli, 1986; Rajamoney and DeJong, 1987]. We shall consider, for instance, imperfections resulting from the fact that certain pieces of knowledge (objects, inference rules, action models) contain minor errors in their definitions in that parts of these definitions may be either more general or less general than they should be.

A weakness of all the learning apprentice systems is that they need an initial domain theory and provide no means of defining it. Although DISCIPLE facilitates this task by accepting a nonhomogeneous domain theory, the task remains difficult. A solution here is that proposed by BLIP [Morik, 1989], which is an interactive learning system mainly concerned with the construction of a domain theory as a first phase of building a knowledge-based system. Therefore, a very promising research direction seems that of building a system incorporating the capabilities of BLIP and DISCIPLE. Such a system could be an effective tool for building knowledge-based systems:

- In the first stage, the system and the user will build together an initial theory of the application domain. This theory, containing elementary knowledge about the domain (basic concepts and inference rules), will be neither complete nor entirely correct;

- In the second stage, the system and the user solve problems together and, during this cooperative problem solving, the system will learn general problem-solving rules. Since this learning takes place in the context of an imperfect domain theory, the learned rules will accumulate exceptions. These exceptions correspond in fact to lacking concepts in the domain theory. When too many exceptions are accumulated, the domain theory has to be refined. Therefore, one reenters the first stage and reformulates the domain theory to better characterize the current knowledge of the system.

There are also several *lessons* we have learned from the design of DISCIPLE. One is *to cope with the complexity of real-world applications, one should use any available learning technique*. Indeed, the different learning paradigms have many complementary prerequisites and effects. Therefore they may be synergistically combined.

Another lesson is that *full formalization of imperfect theories is short-time harmful*. Indeed, forcing the expert to completely formalize a domain theory (which may not even have such a complete theory) may result in a degradation of the knowledge he provides.

Last, we have discovered that *overgeneralization is not only harmless, but also useful and necessary when interacting with a user*, allowing the identification of features usually neglected by the expert.

ACKNOWLEDGMENTS

This work has been sponsored by PRC-GRECO "Intelligence Artificielle" and the Romanian CNST. The chapter was written while one of the authors was at LRI, on leave from his institute. His expenses were taken in charge through an agreement between the French CNRS and the Romanian Academy of Sciences. We wish to express our gratitude to all these institutions. We also wish to thank Mr. Zani Bodnaru, for his indispensable contribution as domain expert.

References

Bareiss, E. and Porter, B. 1987. PROTOS: An Exemplar-based Learning Apprentice, in Langley, P. (ed), *Proc. Fourth Int. Workshop on Machine Learning*, Irvine.

Burstein, M.H. 1986. Concept Formation by Analogical Reasoning and Debugging, in Michalski, R., Carbonell, J. and Mitchell, T. (eds), *Machine Learning: An Artificial Intelligence Approach, Volume II*, Morgan Kaufmann, pp. 351–370.

Carbonell, J. 1986. Derivational Analogy: A Theory of Reconstructive Problem Solving and Expertise Acquisition, in Michalski, R., Carbonell, J. and Mitchell, T. (eds), *Machine Learning: An Artificial Intelligence Approach, Volume II*, Morgan Kaufmann, pp. 371–392.

Carbonell, J. and Gil, Y. 1987. Learning by Experimentation, in Langley, P. (ed), *Proc. Fourth Int. Workshop on Machine Learning*, Irvine, Morgan Kaufmann.

Chouraqui, E. 1982. Construction of a Model for Reasoning by Analogy, in *Proceedings of the European Conference on Artificial Intelligence*, Orsay, France.

DeJong, G. and Mooney, R. 1986. Explanation-based Learning: An Alternative View, in *Machine Learning*, 1, pp. 145–176.

De Raedt, L. and Bruynooghe, M. 1989. Towards Friendly Concept-Learners, in *Proceedings of IJCAI-89*, Detroit, Morgan Kaufmann.

Fikes, R.E., Hart, P.E. and Nilsson, N.J. 1972. Learning and Executing Generalized Robot Plans, *Artificial Intelligence*, 3, pp. 251–288.

Gentner, D. 1983. Structure-Mapping: a Theoretical Framework for Analogy, *Cognitive Science*, 7, pp.155–170.

Kedar-Cabelli, S. 1985. Purpose-directed Analogy, in *Proceedings of the Cognitive Science Society*, pp. 150–159, Irvine.

Kodratoff, Y. 1988. *Introduction to Machine Learning*, Pitman, London. Available in the U.S. from Morgan Kaufmann.

Kodratoff, Y. and Ganascia, J-G. 1986. Improving the Generalization Step in Learning, in Michalski, R., Carbonell, J., and Mitchell, T. (eds), *Machine Learning: An Artificial Intelligence Approach, Volume II*, Morgan Kaufmann, pp. 215–244.

Kodratoff, Y. and Tecuci, G. 1987. Techniques of Design and DISCIPLE Learning Apprentice, *International Journal of Expert Systems: Research and Applications*, vol.1, no.1, pp. 39–66.

———— , 1989. The Central Role of Explanations in DISCIPLE, in Morik, K. (ed), *Knowledge Representation and Organization in Machine Learning*, Springer-Verlag, Berlin.

Michalski, R.S. 1983. A Theory and a Methodology of Inductive Learning, *Artificial Intelligence* 20, pp. 111–161.

———— , 1984. Inductive Learning as Rule-Guided Transformation of Symbolic Descriptions: A Theory and Implementation, in Biermann, A.W., Guiho, G., and

Kodratoff, Y. (eds), *Automatic Program Construction Techniques*, Macmillan Publishing Company, pp. 517–552.

———— , 1986. Understanding the Nature of Learning: Issues and Research Directions, in Michalski, R., Carbonell, J. and Mitchell, T. (eds), *Machine Learning: An Artificial Intelligence Approach, Volume II*, Morgan Kaufmann, pp. 3–25.

Mitchell, T.M. 1978. *Version Spaces: An Approach to Concept Learning*, Doctoral dissertation, Stanford University.

Mitchell, T.M., Keller, R.M., and Kedar-Cabelli, S.T. 1986. Explanation-based Generalization: A Unifying View, *Machine Learning* 1, pp. 47–80.

Mitchell, T., Mahadevan, S., and Steinberg, L. 1985. LEAP: A Learning Apprentice System for VLSI Design, *Proc. IJCAI-85*, Los Angeles, pp. 573–580.

Mooney, R. and Bennet, S. 1986. A Domain Independent Explanation Based Generalizer, in *Proceedings AAAI-86*, Philadelphia, pp. 551–555.

Morik, K. 1989. Sloppy modeling, in Morik, K. (ed), *Knowledge Representation and Organization in Machine Learning*, Springer Verlag, Berlin.

Pazzani, M.J. 1988. Integrating Explanation-based and Empirical Learning Methods in OCCAM, in Sleeman, D. (ed), *Proceedings of the Third European Working Session on Learning*, Glasgow.

Quillian, M.R. 1968. Semantic Memory, in Minsky, M., (ed), *Semantic Information Processing*, MIT Press, Cambridge, MA, pp. 227–270.

Rajamoney, S. and DeJong, G. 1987. The Classification, Detection and Handling of Imperfect Theory Problems, *Proc. IJCAI-87*, Milan, pp. 205–207.

Russel, S.J. 1987. Analogy and Single-Instance Generalization, in Langley, P. (ed) *Proc. Fourth Int. Workshop on Machine Learning*, Irvine, Morgan Kaufmann.

Sammut, C. and Banerji, R.B. 1986. Learning concepts by asking questions, in Michalski, R.S., Carbonell, J.G., Mitchell, T.M. (eds), *Machine Learning: An Artificial Intelligence Approach, Volume II*, Morgan Kaufmann, pp. 167–191.

Smith, R., Winston, H., Mitchell, T. and Buchanan, B. 1985. Representation and Use of Explicit Justifications for Knowledge Base Refinement, *Proc. IJCAI-85*, Los Angeles, Morgan Kaufmann.

Sridharan, N. and Bresina, J. 1983. *A Mechanism for the Management of Partial and Indefinite Descriptions*, Technical Report CBM-TR-134, Rutgers Univ.

Steele, G. 1984. *COMMON LISP: The Language*, Digital Press.

Tate, A. 1977. Generating Project Networks, *Proc. IJCAI-77*, Massachusetts, Morgan Kaufmann, pp. 888–893.

Tecuci, G. 1988. *DISCIPLE: A Theory, Methodology, and System for Learning Expert Knowledge*, PhD Thesis, University of Paris-Sud, 1988.

Tecuci, G. and Kodratoff, Y. 1990. How to learn it with DISCIPLE, LRI Research Report, Orsay.

Tecuci, G., Kodratoff, Y., Bodnaru, Z., and Brunet, T. 1987. DISCIPLE: An expert and learning system, Expert Systems 87, Brighton, December, 14–17, in Moralee, D.S., (ed), *Research and Development in Expert Systems IV*, Cambridge University Press.

Wilkins, D.C. 1988. Knowledge Base Refinement Using Apprenticeship Learning Techniques, *Proceedings AAAI-88*.

Winston, P.H. 1986. Learning by Augmenting Rules and Accumulating Censors, in Michalski, R.S., Carbonell, J.G., Mitchell, T.M. (eds), *Machine Learning: An Artificial Intelligence Approach, Volume II*, Morgan Kaufmann, pp. 45–61.

PART
FIVE

SUBSYMBOLIC AND HETEROGENOUS LEARNING SYSTEMS

20

CONNECTIONIST LEARNING
PROCEDURES[1]

Geoffrey E. Hinton
(University of Toronto)

Abstract

A major goal of research on networks of neuronlike processing units is to discover efficient learning procedures that allow these networks to construct complex internal representations of their environment. The learning procedures must be capable of modifying the connection strengths in such a way that internal units that are not part of the input or output come to represent important features of the task domain. Several interesting gradient-descent procedures have recently been discovered. Each connection computes the derivative, with respect to the connection strength, of a global measure of the error in the performance of the network. The strength is then adjusted in the direction that decreases the error. These relatively simple, gradient-descent learning procedures work well for small tasks, and the new challenge is to find ways of improving their convergence rate and their generalization abilities so that they can be applied to larger, more realistic tasks.

20.1 INTRODUCTION

Recent technological advances in VLSI and computer-aided design mean that it is now much easier to build massively parallel machines. This has contributed to a new wave of interest in models of computation that are inspired by neural nets rather

---

[1]This chapter appeared in Volume 40 of *Artificial Intelligence* in 1989, reprinted with permission of North-Holland Publishing. It is a revised version of Technical Report CMU-CS-87-115, which has the same title and was prepared in June 1987 while the author was at Carnegie Mellon University. The research was supported by contract N00014-86-K-00167 from the Office of Naval Research and by grant IST-8520359 from the National Science Foundation.

than the formal manipulation of symbolic expressions. To understand human abilities like perceptual interpretation, content-addressable memory, commonsense reasoning, and learning, it may be necessary to understand how computation is organized in systems, like the brain, which consist of massive numbers of richly interconnected but rather slow processing elements.

This chapter focuses on the question of how internal representations can be learned in "connectionist" networks. These are a recent subclass of neural net models that emphasize computational power rather than biological fidelity. They grew out of work on early visual processing and associative memories [Hinton and Anderson, 1981; Feldman and Ballard, 1982; Rumelhart, *et al.*, 1986]. The chapter starts by reviewing the main research issues for connectionist models and then describes some of the earlier work on learning procedures for associative memories and simple pattern recognition devices. These learning procedures cannot generate internal representations: They are limited to forming simple associations between representations that are specified externally. Recent research has led to a variety of more powerful connectionist learning procedures that can discover good internal representations, and most of the chapter is devoted to a survey of these procedures.

20.2 CONNECTIONIST MODELS

Connectionist models typically consist of many simple, neuronlike processing elements called "units" that interact using weighted connections. Each unit has a "state" or "activity level" that is determined by the input received from other units in the network. There are many possible variations within this general framework. One common, simplifying assumption is that the combined effects of the rest of the network on the jth unit are mediated by a single scalar quantity, x_j. This quantity, which is called the "total input" of unit j, is usually taken to be a *linear* function of the activity levels of the units that provide input to j:

$$x_j = -\theta_j + \sum_i y_i w_{ji}$$

(1)

where y_i is the state of the ith unit, w_{ji} is the weight on the connection from the ith to the jth unit and θ_j is the threshold of the jth unit. The threshold term can be eliminated by giving every unit an extra input connection whose activity level is fixed at 1. The weight on this special connection is the negative of the threshold. It is called the "bias," and it can be learned in just the same way as the other weights. This method of implementing thresholds will generally be assumed in the rest of this chapter. An external input vector can be supplied to the network by clamping the states of some units or by adding an input term, I_j, that contributes to the total input of some of the units. The state of a unit is typically defined to be a nonlinear function of its total input. For units with discrete states, this function typically has value 1 if the total

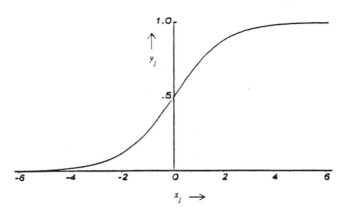

Figure 20–1: The logistic input/output function defined by equation (2). It is a smoothed version of a step function.

input is positive and value 0 (or –1) otherwise. For units with continuous states one typical nonlinear input/output function is the logistic function (as shown in Figure 20–1).

$$y_j = \frac{1}{1 + e^{-x_j}} \tag{2}$$

All the long-term knowledge in a connectionist network is encoded by where the connections are or by their weights, so learning consists of changing the weights or adding or removing connections. The short-term knowledge of the network is normally encoded by the states of the units, but some models also have fast-changing temporary weights or thresholds that can be used to encode temporary contexts or bindings [Von der Malsburg, 1981; Hinton and Plaut, 1987].

There are two major reasons for investigating connectionist networks. First, these networks resemble the brain much more closely than conventional computers do. Even though there are many detailed differences between connectionist units and real neurons, a deeper understanding of the computational properties of connectionist networks may reveal principles that apply to a whole class of devices of this kind, including the brain. Second, connectionist networks are massively parallel, so any computations that can be performed efficiently with these networks can make good use of parallel hardware.

20.3 CONNECTIONIST RESEARCH ISSUES

There are three main areas of research on connectionist networks: Search, representation, and learning. This chapter focuses on learning, but a very brief introduction to search and representation is necessary in order to understand what learning is intended to produce.

20.3.1 Search

The task of interpreting the perceptual input, or constructing a plan, or accessing an item in memory from a partial description can be viewed as a constraint-satisfaction search in which information about the current case (i.e., the perceptual input or the partial description) must be combined with knowledge of the domain to produce a solution that fits both these sources of constraint as well as possible [Ballard, Hinton, and Sejnowski, 1983]. If each unit represents a piece of a possible solution, the weights on the connections between units can encode the degree of consistency between various pieces. In interpreting an image, for example, a unit might stand for a piece of surface at a particular depth and surface orientation. Knowledge that surfaces usually vary smoothly in depth and orientation can be encoded by using positive weights between units that represent nearby pieces of surface at similar depths and similar surface orientations, and negative weights between nearby pieces of surface at very different depths or orientations. The network can perform a search for the most plausible interpretation of the input by iteratively updating the states of the units until they reach a stable state in which the pieces of the solution fit well with each other and with the input. Any one constraint can typically be overridden by combinations of other constraints and this makes the search procedure robust in the presence of noisy data, noisy hardware, or minor inconsistencies in the knowledge.

There are, of course, many complexities: Under what conditions will the network settle to a stable solution? Will this solution be the optimal one? How long will it take to settle? What is the precise relationship between weights and probabilities? These issues are examined in detail by Hummel and Zucker [1983], Hinton and Sejnowski [1983], Geman and Geman [1984], Hopfield and Tank [1985] and Marroquin [1985].

20.3.2 Representation

For tasks like low-level vision, it is usually fairly simple to decide how to use the units to represent the important features of the task domain. Even so, there are some important choices about whether to represent a physical quantity (like the depth at a point in the image) by the state of a single continuous unit, or by the activities in a set of units each of which indicates its confidence that the depth lies within a certain interval [Ballard, 1986].

The issues become much more complicated when we consider how a complex, articulated structure like a plan or the meaning of a sentence might be represented in a network of simple units. Some preliminary work has been done by Minsky [1977] and Hinton [1981] on the representation of inheritance hierarchies and the representation of framelike structures in which a whole object is composed of a number of parts each of which plays a different role within the whole. A recurring issue is the distinction between local and distributed representations. In a local representation, each concept is represented by a single unit [Barlow, 1972; Feldman, 1986]. In a distributed representation, the kinds of concepts that we have words for are represented by patterns of activity distributed over many units, and each unit takes part in many such patterns [Hinton, McClelland, and Rumelhart, 1986]. Distributed representations are usually more efficient than local ones, as well as being more damage resistant. Also, if the distributed representation allows the weights to capture important underlying regularities in the task domain, it can lead to much better generalization than a local representation [Rumelhart and McClelland, 1986; Rumelhart, Hinton, and Williams, 1986a]. However, distributed representations can make it difficult to represent several different things at the same time and so to use them effectively for representing structures that have many parts playing different roles, it may be necessary to have a separate group of units for each role so that the assignment of a filler to a role is represented by a distributed pattern of activity over a group of "role-specific" units.

Much confusion has been caused by the failure to realize that the words "local" and "distributed" refer to the *relationship* between the terms of some descriptive language and a connectionist implementation. If an entity that is described by a single term in the language is represented by a pattern of activity over many units in the connectionist system, and if each of these units is involved in representing other entities, then the representation is *distributed*. But it is always possible to invent a new descriptive language such that, relative to this language, the very same connectionist system is using *local* representations.

20.3.3 Learning

In a network that uses local representations it may be feasible to set all the weights by hand, because each weight typically corresponds to a meaningful relationship between entities in the domain. If, however, the network uses distributed representations it may be very hard to program by hand, and so a learning procedure may be essential. Some learning procedures, like the perceptron convergence procedure [Rosenblatt, 1962], are only applicable if the desired states of all the units in the network are already specified. This makes the learning task relatively easy. Other, more recent, learning procedures operate in networks that contain "hidden" units [Hinton and Sejnowski, 1986] whose desired states are not specified (either directly or indirectly) by the input or the desired output of the network. This makes learning much harder because the learning procedure must (implicitly) decide what the hidden units should represent. The learning procedure is therefore constructing new representations, and the results of learning can be viewed as a numerical solution to the problem of whether to use local or distributed representations.

Connectionist learning procedures can be divided into three broad classes: Supervised procedures, which require a teacher to specify the desired output vector; reinforcement procedures, which only require a single scalar evaluation of the output; and unsupervised procedures, which construct internal models that capture regularities in their input vectors without receiving any additional information. As we shall see, there are often ways of converting one kind of learning procedure into another.

20.4 ASSOCIATIVE MEMORIES WITHOUT HIDDEN UNITS

Several simple kinds of connectionist learning have been used extensively for storing knowledge in simple associative networks, which consist of a set of input units that are directly connected to a set of output units. Since these networks do not contain any hidden units, the difficult problem of deciding what the hidden units should represent does not arise. The aim is simply to store a set of associations between input vectors and output vectors by modifying the weights on the connections. The representation of each association is typically distributed over many connections and each connection is involved in storing many associations. This makes the network robust against minor physical damage and it also means that weights tend to capture regularities in the set of input/output pairings, so the network tends to generalize these regularities to new input vectors that it has not been trained on [Anderson and Hinton, 1981].

20.4.1 Linear Associators

In a linear associator, the state of an output unit is a linear function of the total input that it receives from the input units (see equation (1)). A simple, Hebbian procedure for storing a new association (or "case") is to increment each weight, w_{ji}, between the ith input unit and the jth output unit by the product of the states of the units

$$\Delta w_{ji} = y_i\, y_j \tag{3}$$

where y_i and y_j are the activities of an input and an output unit. After a set of associations have been stored, the weights encode the cross-correlation matrix between the input and output vectors. If the input vectors are orthogonal and have length 1, the associative memory will exhibit perfect recall. Even though each weight is involved in storing many different associations, each input vector will produce exactly the correct output vector [Kohonen, 1977].

If the input vectors are not orthogonal, the simple Hebbian storage procedure is not optimal. For a given network and a given set of associations, it may be impossible to store all the associations perfectly, but we would still like the storage procedure to produce a set of weights that minimizes some sensible measure of the differences between the desired output vectors and the vectors actually produced by the network. This "error measure" can be defined as

$$E = \frac{1}{2} \sum_{j,c} (y_{j,c} - d_{j,c})^2$$

where $y_{j,c}$ is the actual state of output unit j in input/output case c, and $d_{j,c}$ is its desired state. Kohonen [1977] shows that the weight matrix that minimizes this error measure can be computed by an iterative storage procedure that repeatedly sweeps through the whole set of associations and modifies each weight by a small amount in the direction that reduces the error measure. This is a version of the least squares learning procedure described in Section 20.5. The cost of finding an optimal set of weights (in the least squares sense of optimal) is that storage ceases to be a simple "one-shot" process. To store one new association, it is necessary to sweep through the whole set of associations many times.

20.4.2 Nonlinear Associative Nets

If we wish to store a small set of associations that have nonorthogonal input vectors, there is no simple, one-shot storage procedure for linear associative nets that guarantees perfect recall. In these circumstances, a nonlinear associative net can perform better. Willshaw [1981] describes an associative net in which both the units and the weights have just two states: 1 and 0. The weights all start at 0, and associations are stored by setting a weight to 1 if ever its input and output units are both on in any association (see Figure 20–2). To recall an association, each output unit must have its threshold dynamically set to be just less than m, the number of active input units. If the output unit should be on, the m weights coming from the active input units will have been set to 1 during storage, so the output unit is guaranteed to come on. If the output unit should be off, the probability of erroneously coming on is given by the probability that all m of the relevant weights will have been set to 1 when storing other associations. Willshaw showed that associative nets can make efficient use of the information capacity of the weights. If the number of active input units is the log of the total number of input units, the probability of incorrectly activating an output unit can be made very low even when the network is storing close to 0.69 of its information-theoretic capacity.

An associative net in which the input units are identical with the output units can be used to associate vectors with themselves. This allows the network to complete a partially specified input vector. If the input vector is a very degraded version of one of the stored vectors, it may be necessary to use an iterative retrieval process. The initial states of the units represent the partially specified vector, and the states of the units are then updated many times until they settle on one of the stored vectors. Theoretically, the network could oscillate, but Hinton [1981] and Anderson and

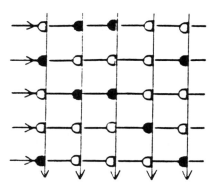

Figure 20–2:   An associative net [Willshaw, 1981]. The input vector comes in at the left
and the output vector comes out at the bottom (after thresholding). The solid
weights have value 1 and the open weights have value 0. The network is
shown after it has stored the associations $01001 \rightarrow 10001$, $10100 \rightarrow 01100$,
$00010 \rightarrow 00010$.

Mozer [1981] showed that iterative retrieval normally works well. Hopfield [1982]
showed that if the weights are symmetrical and the units are updated one at a time,
the iterative retrieval process can be viewed as a form of gradient descent in an "energy function." Hopfield nets store vectors whose components are all +1 or −1 using
the simple storage procedure described in equation (3). To retrieve a stored vector
from a partial description (which is a vector containing some 0 components), we
start the network at the state specified by the partial description and then repeatedly
update the states of units one at a time. The units can be chosen in random order or in
any other order provided no unit is ever ignored for more than a finite time. Hopfield
observed that the behavior of the network is governed by the global energy function[2]

$$E = - \sum_{i < j} s_i s_j w_{ij} + \sum_j s_j \theta_j$$

(4)

where s_i and s_j are the states of two units. Each time a unit updates its state, it adopts
the state that minimizes this energy function because the decision rule used to update
a unit is simply the derivative of the energy function. The unit adopts the state +1 if
its "energy-gap" is positive and the state −1 otherwise, where the energy gap of the
j^{th} unit, ΔE_j, is the increase in the global energy caused by changing the unit from
state +1 to state −1.

---

[2]The energy function should not be confused with the error function described earlier. Gradient descent in the energy function is performed by changing the *states* of the units, not the
weights.

$$\Delta E_j = E(s_j = -1) - E(s_j = +1) = -2\theta_j + 2\sum_i s_i w_{ij}$$

$$(5)$$

So the energy must decrease until the network settles into a local minimum of the energy function. We can therefore view the retrieval process in the following way: The weights define an "energy landscape" over global states of the network, and the stored vectors are local minima in this landscape. The retrieval process consists of moving downhill from a starting point to a nearby local minimum.

If too many vectors are stored, there may be spurious local minima caused by interactions between the stored vectors. Also, the basins of attraction around the correct minima may be long and narrow instead of round, so a downhill path from a random starting point may not lead to the nearest local minimum. These problems can be alleviated by using a process called "unlearning" [Hopfield, Feinstein, and Palmer, 1983; Crick and Mitchison, 1983].

A Hopfield net with N totally interconnected units can store about $0.15N$ random vectors.[3] This means that it is storing about 0.15 bits per weight, even though the weights are integers with $m + 1$ different values, where m is the number of vectors stored. The capacity can be increased considerably by abandoning the one-shot storage procedure and explicitly training the network on typical noisy retrieval tasks using the threshold least squares or perceptron convergence procedures described below

20.4.3 The Deficiencies of Associators without Hidden Units

If the input vectors are orthogonal, or if they are made to be close to orthogonal by using high-dimensional random vectors (as is typically done in a Hopfield net), associators with no hidden units perform well using a simple Hebbian storage procedure. If the set of input vectors satisfy the much weaker condition of being linearly independent, associators with no hidden units can learn to give the correct outputs provided an iterative learning procedure is used. Unfortunately, linear independence does not hold for most tasks that can be characterized as mapping input vectors to output vectors, because the number of relevant input vectors is typically much larger than the number of components in each input vector. The required mapping typically

---

[3] There is some confusion in the literature due to different ways of measuring storage capacity. If we insist on a fixed probability of getting *each* component of *each* vector correct, the number of vectors that can be stored is $O(N)$. If we insist on a fixed probability of getting *all* components of *all* vectors correct, the number of vectors that can be stored is $O(N/ \log N)$.

has a complicated structure that can only be expressed using multiple layers of hidden units.[4]

Consider, for example, the task of identifying an object when the input vector is an intensity array and the output vector has a separate component for each possible name. If a given type of object can be either black or white, the intensity of an individual pixel (which is what an input unit encodes) cannot provide any direct evidence for the presence or absence of an object of that type. So the object cannot be identified by using weights on direct connections from input to output units. Obviously, it is necessary to explictly extract relationships among intensity values (such as edges) before trying to identify the object. Actually, extracting edges is just a small part of the problem. If recognition is to have the generative capacity to handle novel images of familiar objects, the network must somehow encode the systematic effects of variations in lighting and viewpoint, partial occlusion by other objects, and deformations of the object itself. There is a tremendous gap between these complex regularities and the regularities that can be captured by an associative net that lacks hidden units.

20.5 SIMPLE SUPERVISED LEARNING PROCEDURES

Consider a network with input units that are directly connected to output units whose states (i.e., activity levels) are a continuous smooth function of their total input. Suppose that we want to train the network to produce particular "desired" states of the output units for each member of a set of input vectors. A measure of how poorly the network is performing with its current set of weights is:

$$E = \frac{1}{2} \sum_{j,c} (y_{j,c} - d_{j,c})^2 \tag{6}$$

where $y_{j,c}$ is the actual state of output unit j in input/output case c, and $d_{j,c}$ is its desired state.

We can minimize the error measure given in equation (6) by starting with any set of weights and repeatedly changing each weight by an amount proportional to $\partial E / \partial w$.

$$\Delta w_{ji} = -\varepsilon \frac{\partial E}{\partial w_{ji}} \tag{7}$$

---

[4] It is always possible to redefine the units and the connectivity so that multiple layers of simple units become a single layer of much more complicated units. But this redefinition does not make the problem go away.

In the limit, as ε tends to 0 and the number of updates tends to infinity, this learning procedure is guaranteed to find the set of weights that gives the least squared error. The value of $\partial E/\partial w$ is obtained by differentiating equation (6) and equation (1).

$$\frac{\partial E}{\partial w_{ji}} = \sum_{cases} \frac{\partial E}{\partial y_j} \frac{dy_j}{dx_j} \frac{\partial x_j}{\partial w_{ji}} = \sum_{cases} (y_j - d_j) \frac{dy_j}{dx_j} y_i \tag{8}$$

If the output units are linear, the term dy_j/dx_j is a constant.

The least squares learning procedure has a simple geometric interpretation. We construct a multidimensional *weight space* that has an axis for each weight and one extra axis (called *height*) that corresponds to the error measure. For each combination of weights, the network will have a certain error that can be represented by the height of a point in weight space. These points form a surface called the *error surface*. For networks with linear output units and no hidden units, the error surface always forms a bowl whose horizontal cross sections are ellipses and whose vertical cross sections are parabolas. Since the bowl only has one minimum,[5] gradient descent on the error surface is guaranteed to find it.

The error surface is actually the sum of a number of parabolic troughs, one for each training case. If the output units have a nonlinear but monotonic input/output function, each parabolic trough is deformed but no new minima are created in any one trough because the monotonic nonlinearity cannot reverse the sign of the gradient of the trough in any direction. When many deformed troughs are added together, however, it is possible to create local minima because it is possible to change the sign of the total gradient without changing the signs of any of the conflicting casewise gradients of which it is composed. But local minima cannot be created in this way if there is a set of weights that gives zero error for all training cases. If we consider moving away from this perfect point, the error must increase (or remain constant) for each individual case and so it must increase (or remain constant) for the sum of all these cases. So gradient descent is still guaranteed to work for monotonic, nonlinear input/output functions provided a perfect solution exists. However, it will be very slow at points in weight space where the gradient of the input/output function approaches zero for the output units that are in error.

The "batch" version of the least squares procedure sweeps through all the cases accumulating $\partial E/\partial w$ before changing the weights, and so it is guaranteed to move in the direction of steepest descent. The "on-line" version, which requires less memory, updates the weights after each input/output case [Widrow and Hoff, 1960].[6] This may sometimes increase the total error, E, but by making the weight changes suffi-

---

[5] This minimum may be a whole subspace.

[6] The on-line version is usually called the "Least Mean Squares" or "LMS" procedure

ciently small, the total change in the weights after a complete sweep through all the cases can be made to approximate steepest descent arbitrarily closely.

20.5.1 A Least Squares Procedure for Binary Threshold Units

Binary threshold units use a step function, so the term dy_j/dx_j is infinite at the threshold and 0 elsewhere and the least squares procedure must be modified to be applicable to these units. In the following discussion we assume that the threshold is implemented by a "bias" weight on a permanently active input line, so the unit turns on if its total input exceeds 0. The basic idea is to define an error function that is large if the total input is far from 0, and the unit is in the wrong state and is 0 when the unit is in the right state. The simplest version of this idea is to define the error of an output unit, j, for a given input case to be

$$E_{j,c}^* = \begin{cases} 0 & \text{if the output unit has the right state} \\ \frac{1}{2} x_{j,c}^2 & \text{if the output unit has the wrong state} \end{cases}$$

Unfortunately, this measure can be minimized by setting all weights and biases to 0 so that units are always exactly at their threshold [Yann Le Cun, personal communication]. To avoid this problem we can introduce a margin, m, and insist that for units that should be on, the total input is at least m; and for units that should be off, the total input is at most $-m$. The new error measure is then

$$E_{j,c}^* = \begin{cases} 0 & \text{if the output unit has the right state by at least } m \\ \frac{1}{2}(m - x_{j,c})^2 & \text{if the output unit should be on but has } x_{j,c} < m \\ \frac{1}{2}(m + x_{j,c})^2 & \text{if the output unit should be off but has } x_{j,c} > -m \end{cases}$$

The derivative of this error measure with respect to $x_{j,c}$ is

$$\frac{\partial E_{j,c}^*}{\partial x_{j,c}} = \begin{cases} 0 & \text{if the output unit has the right state by at least } m \\ x_{j,c} - m & \text{if the output unit should be on but has } x_{j,c} < m \\ x_{j,c} + m & \text{if the output unit should be off but has } x_{j,c} > -m \end{cases}$$

So the "threshold least squares procedure" becomes:

$$\Delta w_{ji} = -\varepsilon \sum_c \frac{\partial E_{j,c}^*}{\partial x_{j,c}} y_{i,c}$$

20.5.2 The Perceptron Convergence Procedure

One version of the perceptron convergence procedure is related to the on-line version of the threshold least squares procedure in the following way: The magnitude of $\partial E_{j,c}^*/\partial x_{j,c}$ is ignored, and only its sign is taken into consideration. So the weight changes are:

$$\Delta w_{ji,c} = \begin{cases} 0 & \textit{if the output unit behaves correctly by at least } m \\ +\varepsilon y_{i,c} & \textit{if the output unit should be on but has } x_{j,c} < m \\ -\varepsilon y_{i,c} & \textit{if the output unit should be off but has } x_{j,c} > -m \end{cases}$$

Because it ignores the magnitude of the error, this procedure changes weights by at least ε even when the error is very small. The finite size of the weight steps eliminates the need for a margin so the standard version of the perceptron convergence procedure does not use one.

Because it ignores the magnitude of the error this procedure does not even stochastically approximate steepest descent in E, the sum-squared error. Even with very small ε, it is quite possible for E to rise after a complete sweep through all the cases. However, each time the weights are updated, the perceptron convergence procedure is guaranteed to reduce the value of a different cost measure that is defined solely in terms of weights.

To picture the least squares procedure we introduced a space with one dimension for each weight and one extra dimension for the sum-squared error in the output vectors. To picture the perceptron convergence procedure, we do not need the extra dimension for the error. For simplicity we shall consider a network with only one output unit. Each case corresponds to a constraint hyperplane in weight space. If the weights are on one side of this hyperplane, the output unit will behave correctly and if they are on the other side it will behave incorrectly (see Figure 20–3). To behave correctly, for all cases, the weights must lie on the correct side of all the hyperplanes, so the combinations of weights that give perfect performance form a convex set. *Any set of weights in this set will be called "ideal."*

The perceptron convergence procedure considers the constraint planes one at a time. Whenever the current combination of weights is on the wrong side, it moves it perpendicularly towards the plane. This reduces the distance between the current combination of weights and *any* of the ideal combinations. So provided the weights move by less than twice the distance to the violated constraint plane, a weight update is guaranteed to reduce the measure

$$\sum_i (w_{i,actual} - w_{i,ideal})^2$$

The perceptron convergence procedure has many nice properties, but it also has some serious problems. Unlike the threshold least squares procedure, it does not necessarily settle down to a reasonable compromise when there is no set of weights that will do the job perfectly. Also, there are obvious problems in trying to generalize to more complex, multilayered nets in which the ideal combinations of weights do not form a single convex set, because the idea of moving towards *the* ideal region of weight space breaks down. It is therefore not surprising that the more sophisticated procedures required for multilayer nets are generalizations of the least squares pro-

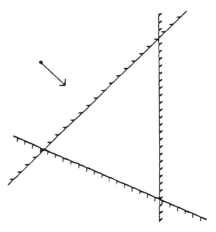

Figure 20–3:   Some hyperplanes in weight space. Each plane represents the constraint on the weights caused by a particular input/output case. If the weights lie on the correct (unshaded) side of the plane, the output unit will have the correct state for that case. Provided the weight changes are proportional to the activities of the input lines, the perceptron convergence procedure moves the weights perpendicularly towards a violated constraint plane.

cedure rather than the perceptron convergence procedure: They learn by decreasing a squared performance error, not a distance in weight space.

20.5.3 The Deficiencies of Simple Learning Procedures

The major deficiency of both the least squares and perceptron convergence procedures is that most "interesting" mappings between input and output vectors cannot be captured by any combination of weights in such simple networks, so the guarantee that the learning procedure will find the best possible combination of weights is of little value. Consider, for example, a network composed of two input units and one output unit. There is no way to set the two weights and one threshold to solve the very simple task of producing an output of 1 when the input vector is (1, 1) or (0, 0) and an output of 0 when the input vector is (1, 0) or (0, 1). Minsky and Papert [1969] give a clear analysis of the limitations on what mappings can be computed by three-layered nets. They focus on the question of what preprocessing must be done by the units in the intermediate layer to allow a task to be solved. They generally assume that the preprocessing is fixed, and so they avoid the problem of how to make the units in the intermediate layer learn useful predicates. So, from the learning perspective, their intermediate units are not true hidden units.

Another deficiency of the least squares and perceptron learning procedures is that gradient descent may be very slow if the elliptical cross section of the error surface is very elongated so that the surface forms a long ravine with steep sides and a very low gradient along the ravine. In this case, the gradient at most points in the space is almost perpendicular to the direction towards the minimum. If the coefficient ε in equation (7) is large, there are divergent oscillations across the ravine, and if it is small, the progress along the ravine is very slow. A standard method for speeding the convergence in such cases is recursive least squares [Widrow and Stearns, 1985]. Various other methods have also been suggested [Amari, 1967; Parker, 1987; Plaut and Hinton, 1987].

We now consider learning in more complex networks that contain hidden units. The next five sections describe a variety of supervised, unsupervised, and reinforcement learning procedures for these nets.

20.6 BACK-PROPAGATION: A MULTILAYER LEAST SQUARES PROCEDURE

The "back-propagation" learning procedure [Rumelhart, Hinton, and Williams, 1986a; 1986b] is a generalization of the least squares procedure that works for networks with layers of hidden units between the input and output units. These multilayer networks can compute much more complicated functions than can networks that lack hidden units, but the learning is generally much slower because it must explore the space of possible ways of using the hidden units. There are now many examples in which back-propagation constructs interesting internal representations in the hidden units, and these representations allow the network to generalize in sensible ways. Variants of the procedure were discovered independently by Werbos [1974], Le Cun [1985], and Parker [1985].

In a multilayer network it is possible, using equation (8), to compute $\partial E/\partial w_{ji}$ for *all* the weights in the network provided we can compute $\partial E/\partial y_j$ for all the units that have modifiable incoming weights. In a system that has no hidden units, this is easy because the only relevant units are the output units, and for them $\partial E/\partial y_j$ is found by differentiating the error function in equation (6). But for hidden units, $\partial E/\partial y_j$ is harder to compute. The central idea of back-propagation is that these derivatives can be computed efficiently by starting with the output layer and working backward through the layers. For each input/output case, c, we first use a forward pass, starting at the input units, to compute the activity levels of all the units in the network. Then we use a backward pass, starting at the output units, to compute $\partial E/\partial y_j$ for all the hidden units. For a hidden unit, j, in layer J the only way it can affect the error is via its effects on the units, k, in the next layer, K (assuming units in one layer only send their outputs to units in the layer above). So we have

$$\frac{\partial E}{\partial y_j} = \sum_k \frac{\partial E}{\partial y_k} \frac{dy_k}{dx_k} \frac{dx_k}{dy_j} = \sum_k \frac{\partial E}{\partial y_k} \frac{dy_k}{dx_k} w_{kj}$$

$$(9)$$

where the index c has been suppressed for clarity. So if $\partial E/\partial y_k$ is already known for all units in layer K, it is easy to compute the same quantity for units in layer J. Notice that the computation performed during the backward pass is very similar in form to the computation performed during the forward pass (though it propagates error derivatives instead of activity levels, and it is entirely linear in the error derivatives).

20.6.1 The Shape of the Error Surface

In networks without hidden units, the error surface only has one minimum (provided a perfect solution exists and the units use smooth monotonic input/output functions). With hidden units, the error surface may contain many local minima, so it is possible that steepest descent in weight space will get stuck at poor local minima. In practice, this does not seem to be a serious problem. Back-propagation has been tried for a wide variety of tasks and poor local minima are rarely encountered, provided the network contains a few more units and connections than are required for the task. One reason for this is that there are typically a very large number of qualitatively different perfect solutions, so we avoid the typical combinatorial optimization task in which one minimum is slightly better than a large number of other, widely separated minima.

In practice, the most serious problem is the speed of convergence, not the presence of nonglobal minima. This is discussed further in Section 20.12.

20.6.2 Back-Propagation for Discovering Semantic Features

To demonstrate the ability of back-propagation to discover important underlying features of a domain, Hinton [1986] used a multilayer network to learn the family relationships between 24 different people (see Figure 20–4). The information in a family tree can be represented as a set of triples of the form (person1, relationship, person2), and a network can be said to "know" these triples if it can produce the third term of any triple when given the first two terms as input.

Figure 20–5 shows the architecture of the network that was used to learn the triples. The input vector is divided into two parts, one of which specifies a person and the other a relationship (e.g., has-father). The network is trained to produce the related person as output. The input and output encodings use a different unit to represent each person and relationship, so all pairs of people are equally similar in the input and output encoding: The encodings do not give any clues about what the important features are. The architecture is designed so that all the information about an input person must be squeezed through a narrow bottleneck of six units in the first hidden layer. This forces the network to represent people using distributed patterns

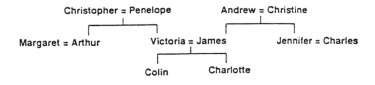

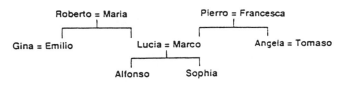

Figure 20–4: Two isomorphic family trees

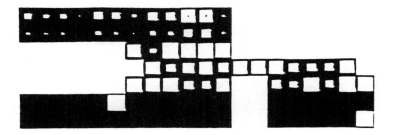

Figure 20–5: The activity levels in a five-layer network after it has learned. The bottom layer has 24 input units on the left for representing person 1 and 12 units on the right for representing the relationship. The white squares inside these two groups show the activity levels of the units. There is one active unit in the first group (representing *Colin*) and one in the second group (representing *has-aunt*). Each of the two groups of input units is totally connected to its own group of six units in the second layer. These two groups of six must learn to encode the input terms as distributed patterns of activity. The second layer is totally connected to the central layer of 12 units, and this layer is connected to the penultimate layer of six units. The activity in the penultimate layer must activate the correct output units, each of which stands for a particular *person2*. In this case, there are two correct answers (marked by black dots) because Colin has two aunts. Both the input and output units are laid out spatially with the English people in one row and the isomorphic Italians immediately below.

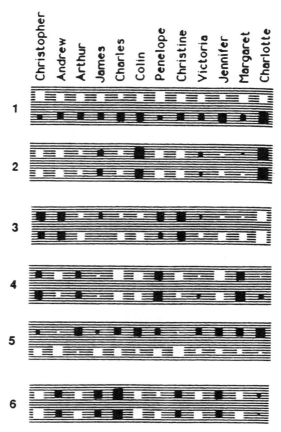

Figure 20–6: The weights from the 24 input units that represent people to the six units in the second layer that learn distributed representations of people. White rectangles stand for excitatory weights, black for inhibitory weights, and the area of the rectangle encodes the magnitude of the weight. The weights from the 12 English people are in the top row of each unit. Beneath each of these weights is the weight from the isomorphic Italian. Unit 1 learns to encode nationality, unit 2 encodes generation (using three values), and unit 4 encodes the branch of the family tree to which a person belongs. During the learning, each weight was given a tendency to decay toward 0. This tendency is balanced by the error gradient, so the final magnitude of a weight indicates how useful it is in reducing the error.

of activity in this layer. The aim of the simulation is to see if the components of these distributed patterns correspond to the important underlying features of the domain.

After prolonged training on 100 of the 104 possible relationships, the network was tested on the remaining four. It generalized correctly because during the training, it learned to represent each of the people in terms of important features such as age, nationality, and the branch of the family tree to which they belonged (see Figure 20–6), even though these "semantic" features were not at all explicit in the input or output vectors. Using these underlying features, much of the information about family relationships can be captured by a fairly small number of "microinferences" between features. For example, the father of a middle-aged person is an old person, and the father of an Italian person is an Italian person. So the features of the output person can be derived from the features of the input person and the relationship. The learning procedure can only discover these features by searching for a set of features that make it easy to express the associations. Once these features have been discovered, the *internal* representation of each person (in the first hidden layer) is a distributed pattern of activity, and similar people are represented by similar patterns. Thus the network constructs its own internal similarity metric. This is a significant advance over simulations in which good generalization is achieved because the experimenter chooses representations that already have an appropriate similarity metric.

20.6.3 Back-Propagation for Mapping Text to Speech

Back-propagation is an effective learning technique when the mapping from input vectors to output vectors contains both regularities and exceptions. For example, in mapping from a string of English letters to a string of English phonemes there are many regularities, but there are also exceptions—such as the "o" in the word "women." Sejnowski and Rosenberg [1987] have shown that a network with one hidden layer can be trained to pronounce letters surprisingly well. The input layer encodes the identity of the letter to be pronounced using a different unit for each possible letter. The input also encodes the local context, which consists of the three previous letters and three following letters in the text (spaces and punctuation are treated as special kinds of letters). This seven-letter window is moved over the text, so the mapping from text to speech is performed sequentially, one letter at a time. The output layer encodes a phoneme using 21 articulatory features and five features for stress and syllable boundaries. There are 80 hidden units, each of which receives connections from all the input units and sends connections to all the output units (see Figure 20–7). After extensive training, the network generalizes well to new examples, which demonstrates that it captures the regularities of the mapping. Its performance on new words is comparable to a conventional computer program, which uses a large number of handcrafted rules.

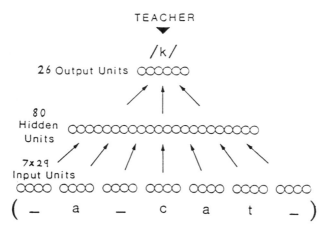

Figure 20–7: The network has 309 units and 18,629 connections. A window seven letters wide is moved over the text, and the network pronounces the middle letter. It assumes a preprocessor to identify characters, and a postprocessor to turn phonemes into sounds.

20.6.4 Back-Propagation for Phoneme Recognition

Speech recognition is a task that can be used to assess the usefulness of back-propagation for real-world signal-processing applications. The best existing techniques, such as hidden Markov models [Bahl, Jelinek, and Mercer, 1983], are significantly worse than people, and an improvement in the quality of recognition would be of great practical significance.

A subtask which is well suited to back-propagation is the bottom-up recognition of highly confusable consonants. One obvious approach is to convert the sound into a spectrogram, which is then presented as the input vector to a multilayer network whose output units represent different consonants. Unfortunately, this approach has two serious drawbacks. First, the spectrogram must have many "pixels" to give reasonable resolution in time and frequency, so each hidden unit has many incoming weights. This means that a very large number of training examples are needed to provide enough data to estimate the weights. Second, it is hard to achieve precise time-alignment of the input data, so the spatial pattern that represents a given phoneme may occur at many different positions in the spectrogram. To learn that these shifts in position do not change the identity of the phoneme requires an immense amount of training data. We already know that the task has a certain symmetry—the same sounds occurring at different times mean the same phoneme. To expedite learning and improve generalization we should build this *a priori* knowledge into the network and let it use the information in the training data to discover structure that we do not already understand.

An interesting way to build in the time symmetry is to use a multilayer, feedforward network that has connections with time delays [Tank and Hopfield, 1987]. The input units represent a single time frame from the spectrogram, and the whole spectrogram is represented by stepping it through the input units. Each hidden unit is connected to each unit in the layer below by several different connections with different time delays and different weights. So it has a limited temporal window within which it can detect temporal patterns in the activities of the units in the layer below. Since a hidden unit applies the same set of weights at different times, it inevitably produces similar responses to similar patterns that are shifted in time (see Figure 20–8).

Kevin Lang [1987] has shown that a time-delay network that is trained using a generalization of the back-propagation procedure compares favorably with hidden Markov models at the task of distinguishing the words "bee," "dee," "ee," and "vee" spoken by many different male speakers in a very noisy environment. [Waibel, et al., 1987] shows that the same network can achieve excellent speaker-dependent discrimination of the phonemes "b," "d," and "g" in varying phonetic contexts.

An interesting technical problem arises in computing the error derivatives for the output units of the time-delay network. The adaptive part of the network contains one output unit for each possible phoneme, and these units respond to the input by producing a sequence of activations. If the training data is labeled with the exact time of occurrence of each phoneme, it is possible to specify the exact time at which an output unit should be active. But in the absence of precisely time-aligned training data, it is necessary to compute error derivatives for a sequence of activations without knowing when the phoneme occurred. This can be done by using a fixed postprocessing layer to integrate the activity of each output unit over time. We interpret the instantaneous activity of an output unit as a representation of the probability that the phoneme occurred at exactly that time. So, for the phoneme that really occurred, we know that the time integral of its activity should be 1 and for the other phonemes it should be 0. So at each time, the error-derivative is simply the difference between the desired and the actual integral. After training, the network localizes phonemes in time, even though the training data contains no information about time-alignment.

20.6.5 Postprocessing the Output of a Back-Propagation Net

Many people have suggested transforming the raw input vector with a module that uses unsupervised learning before presenting it to a module that uses supervised learning. It is less obvious that a supervised module can also benefit from a nonadaptive postprocessing module. A very simple example of this kind of postprocessing occurs in the time-delay phoneme-recognition network described in Section 20.6.4.

David Rumelhart has shown that the idea of a postprocessing module can be applied even in cases where the postprocessing function is initially unknown. In try-

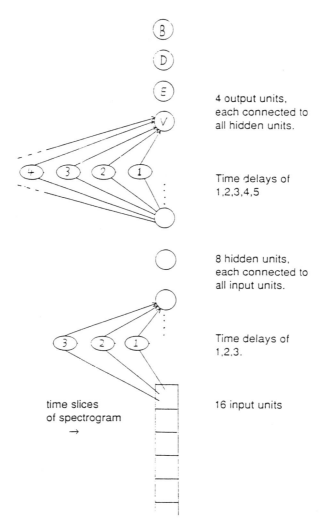

4 output units,
each connected to
all hidden units.

Time delays of
1,2,3,4,5

8 hidden units,
each connected to
all input units.

Time delays of
1,2,3.

time slices
of spectrogram
→

16 input units

Figure 20–8:   Part of the time-delay network used to recognize phonemes with variable
onset times. A unit in one layer is connected to a unit in the layer below by
several different connections that have different time delays and learn to
have different weights.

ing to imitate a sound, for example, a network might produce an output vector that
specifies how to move the speech articulators. This output vector needs to be
postprocessed to turn it into a sound, but the postprocessing is normally done by

physics. Suppose that the network does not receive any direct information about what it should do with its articulators, but it does "know" the desired sound and the actual sound, which is the transformed "image" of the output vector. If we had a postprocessing module that transformed the activations of the speech articulators into sounds, we could back-propagate through this module to compute error derivatives for the articulator activations.

Rumelhart uses an additional network (which he calls a *mental model*) that first learns to perform the postprocessing (i.e., it learns to map from output vectors to their transformed images). Once this mapping has been learned, back-propagation through the mental model can convert error derivatives for the "images" into error derivatives for the output vectors of the basic network.

20.6.6 A Reinforcement Version of Back-Propagation

Munro [1987] has shown that the idea of using a mental model can be applied even when the image of an output vector is simply a single scalar value—the reinforcement. First, the mental model learns to predict expected reinforcement from the combination of the input vector and the output vector. Then the derivative of the expected reinforcement can be back-propagated through the mental model to get the reinforcement derivatives for each component of the output vector of the basic network.

20.6.7 Iterative Back-Propagation

Rumelhart, Hinton, and Williams [1986b] show how the back-propagation procedure can be applied to iterative networks in which there are no limitations on the connectivity. A network in which the states of the units at time t determine the states of the units at time $t + 1$ is equivalent to a net which has one layer for each time slice. Each weight in the iterative network is implemented by a whole set of identical weights in the corresponding layered net, one for each time slice (see Figure 20–9). In the iterative net, the error is typically the difference between the actual and the desired final states of the network, and to compute the error derivatives it is necessary to back-propagate through time, so the history of states of each unit must be stored. Each weight will have many different error derivatives, one for each time step, and the sum of all these derivatives is used to determine the weight change.

Back-propagation in iterative nets can be used to train a network to generate sequences, or to recognize sequences, or to complete sequences. Examples are given in Rumelhart, Hinton, and Williams [1986]. Alternatively, it can be used to store a set of patterns by constructing a point attractor for each pattern. Unlike the simple storage procedure used in a Hopfield net, or the more sophisticated storage procedure used in a Boltzmann machine (see Section 20.7), back-propagation takes into

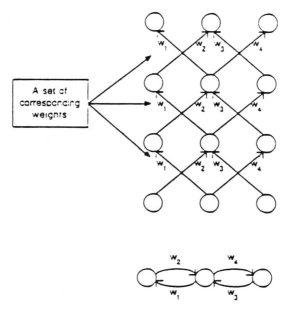

Figure 20–9:   At the bottom of the figure is a simple iterative network that is run synchronously for three iterations. At the top of the figure is the equivalent layered network.

account the path used to reach a point attractor. So it will not construct attractors that cannot be reached from the normal range of starting points on which it is trained.[7]

20.6.8 Back-Propagation as a Maximum-Likelihood Procedure

If we interpret each output vector as a specification of a conditional probability distribution over a set of output vectors given an input vector, we can interpret the back-propagation learning procedure as a method of finding weights that maximize the likelihood of generating the desired, conditional probability distributions. Two examples of this kind of interpretation will be described.

Suppose we only attach meaning to binary output vectors, and we treat a real-valued output vector as a way of specifying a probability distribution over binary

---

[7]
A back-propagation net that uses asymmetric connections (and synchronous updating) is not guaranteed to settle to a single, stable state. To encourage it to construct a point attractor, rather than a limit cycle, the point attractor can be made the desired state for the last few iterations.

vectors.[8] We imagine that a real-valued output vector is stochastically converted into a binary vector by treating the real values as the probabilities that individual components have value 1, and assuming independence between components. For simplicity, we can assume that the desired vectors used during training are binary vectors, though this is not necessary. Given a set of training cases, it can be shown that the likelihood of producing *exactly* the desired vectors is maximized when we minimize the cross-entropy, C, between the desired and actual conditional probability distributions:

$$C = -\sum_{j,c} d_{j,c} \log_2(y_{j,c}) + (1 - d_{j,c}) \log_2(1 - y_{j,c})$$

where $d_{j,c}$ is the desired probability of output unit j in case c and $y_{j,c}$ is its actual probability.

So, under this interpretation of the output vectors, we should use the cross-entropy function rather than the squared difference as our cost measure. In practice, this helps to avoid a problem caused by output units that are firmly off when they should be on (or vice versa). These units have a very small value of $\partial y/\partial x$ so they need a large value of $\partial E/\partial y$ in order to change their incoming weights by a reasonable amount. When an output unit that should have an activity level of 1 changes from a level of .0001 to a level of .001, the squared difference from 1 only changes slightly, but the cross-entropy decreases a lot. In fact, when the derivative of the cross-entropy is multiplied by the derivative of the logistic-activation function, the product is simply the difference between the desired and the actual outputs, so $\partial C_{j,c}/\partial x_{j,c}$ is just the same as for a linear output unit [Steven Nowlan, personal communication].

This way of interpreting back-propagation raises the issue of whether, under some other interpretation of the output vectors, the squared error might not be the correct measure for performing maximum-likelihood estimation. In fact, Richard Golden [1987] has shown that minimizing the squared error is equivalent to maximum-likelihood estimation if both the actual and the desired output vectors are treated as the centers of Gaussian probability density functions over the space of all real vectors. So the "correct" choice of cost function depends on the way the output vectors are most naturally interpreted.

20.6.9 Self-Supervised Back-Propagation

One drawback of the standard form of back-propagation is that it requires an external supervisor to specify the desired states of the output units (or a transformed "image" of the desired states). It can be converted into an unsupervised procedure by

---

[8] Both the examples of back-propagation described above fit this interpretation.

using the input itself to do the supervision, using a multilayer "encoder" network [Ackley, Hinton, and Sejnowski, 1985], in which the desired output vector is identical to the input vector. The network must learn to compute an approximation to the identity mapping for all the input vectors in its training set, and if the middle layer of the network contains fewer units than the input layer, the learning procedure must construct a compact, invertible code for each input vector. This code can then be used as the input to later stages of processing.

The use of self-supervised back-propagation to construct compact codes resembles the use of principal components analysis to perform dimensionality reduction, but it has the advantage that it allows the code to be a nonlinear transform of the input vector. This form of back-propagation has been used successfully to compress images [Cottrell, Munro, and Zipser, 1987] and speech waves [Elman and Zipser, 1987]. A variation of it has been used to extract the underlying degrees of freedom of simple shapes [Saund, 1986].

It is also possible to use back-propagation to predict one part of the perceptual input from other parts. For example, in predicting one patch of an image from neighboring patches it is probably helpful to use hidden units that explicitly extract edges, so this might be an unsupervised way of discovering edge detectors. In domains with sequential structure, one portion of a sequence can be used as input, and the next term in the sequence can be the desired output. This forces the network to extract features that are good predictors. If this is applied to the speech wave, the states of the hidden units will form a nonlinear predictive code. It is not yet known whether such codes are more helpful for speech recognition than are linear, predictive coefficients.

A different variation of self-supervised back-propagation is to insist that all or part of the code in the middle layer change as slowly as possible with time. This can be done by making the desired state of each of the middle units be the state it actually adopted for the previous input vector. This forces the network to use similar codes for input vectors that occur at neighboring times, which is a sensible principle if the input vectors are generated by a process whose underlying parameters change more slowly than do the input vectors themselves.

20.6.10 Deficiencies of Back-Propagation

Despite its impressive performance on relatively small problems, and its promise as a widely applicable mechanism for extracting the underlying structure of a domain, back-propagation is inadequate in its current form for larger tasks, because the learning time scales poorly. Empirically, the learning time on a serial machine is very approximately $O(N^3)$ where N is the number of weights in the network. The time for one forward and one backward pass is $O(N)$. The number of training examples is typically $O(N)$, assuming the amount of information per output vector is held constant and enough training cases are used to strain the storage capacity of the network (which is about 2 bits per weight). The number of times the weights must be updated is also approximately $O(N)$. This is an empirical observation and depends on the nature of the task.[9] On a parallel machine that used a separate processor for each connection, the time would be reduced to approximately $O(N^2)$. Back-propagation can probably be improved by using the gradient information in more sophisticated ways, but much bigger improvements are likely to result from making better use of modularity (see Section 20.12.4).

As a biological model, back-propagation is implausible. There is no evidence that synapses can be used in the reverse direction, or that neurons can propagate error derivatives backward (using a linear input/output function) as well as propagating activity levels forward using a nonlinear input/output function. One approach is to try to back-propagate the derivatives using separate circuitry that *learns* to have the same weights as the forward circuitry [Parker, 1985]. A second approach, which seems to be feasible for self-supervised back-propagation, is to use a method called *recirculation* that approximates gradient descent and is more biologically plausible [Hinton and McClelland, 1987]. At present, back-propagation should be treated as a mechanism for demonstrating the kind of learning that can be done using gradient descent, without implying that the brain does gradient descent in the same way.

20.7 BOLTZMANN MACHINES

A Boltzmann machine [Ackley, Hinton, and Sejnowski, 1985; Hinton and Sejnowski, 1986] is a generalization of a Hopfield net (see Section 20.4.2) in which the units update their states according to a *stochastic* decision rule. The units have states of 1 or 0,[10] and the probability that unit j adopts the state 1 is given by

$$p_j = \frac{1}{1 + e^{-\Delta E_j / T}} \qquad (10)$$

where $\Delta E_j = x_j$ is the total input received by the jth unit and T is the "temperature." It can be shown that if this rule is applied repeatedly to the units, the network will reach "thermal equilibrium." At thermal equilibrium the units still change state, but the *probability* of finding the network in any global state remains constant and obeys a Boltzmann distribution in which the probability ratio of any two global states depends solely on their energy difference.

---

[9] Tesauro [1987] reports a case in which the number of weight updates is roughly proportional to the number of training cases (it is actually a 4/3 power law). Judd [1987] shows that in the worst case it is exponential.

[10] A network that uses states of 1 and 0 can always be converted into an equivalent network that uses states of +1 and −1 provided the thresholds are altered appropriately.

$$\frac{P_A}{P_B} = e^{-(E_A - E_B)/T}$$

At high temperature, the network approaches equilibrium rapidly but low-energy states are not much more probable than high-energy states. At low temperature the network approaches equilibrium more slowly, but low-energy states are much more probable than high-energy states. The fastest way to approach low-temperature equilibrium is generally to start at a high temperature and to gradually reduce the temperature. This is called *simulated annealing* [Kirkpatrick, Gelatt, and Vecchi, 1983]. Simulated annealing allows Boltzmann machines to find low-energy states with high probability. If some units are clamped to represent an input vector, and if the weights in the network represent the constraints of the task domain, the network can settle on a very plausible output vector given the current weights and the current input vector.

For complex tasks there is generally no way to express the constraints by using weights on pairwise connections between the input and output units. It is necessary to use hidden units that represent higher order features of the domain. This creates a problem: Given a limited number of hidden units, what higher order features should they represent in order to approximate the required input/output mapping as closely as possible? The beauty of Boltzmann machines is that the simplicity of the Boltzmann distribution leads to a very simple learning procedure that adjusts the weights so as to use the hidden units in an optimal way.

The network is "shown" the mapping that it is required to perform by clamping an input vector on the input units and clamping the required output vector on the output units. If there are several possible output vectors for a given input vector, each of the possibilities is clamped on the output units with the appropriate frequency. The network is then annealed until it approaches thermal equilibrium at a temperature of 1. It then runs for a fixed time at equilibrium, and each connection measures the fraction of the time during which both the units it connects are active. This is repeated for all the various input/output pairs so that each connection can measure $<s_i s_j>^+$ the expected probability, averaged over all cases, that unit i and unit j are simultaneously active at thermal equilibrium when the input and output vectors are both clamped.

The network must also be run in just the same way but without clamping the output units. Again, it reaches thermal equilibrium with each input vector clamped and then runs for a fixed additional time to measure $<s_i s_j>^+$, the expected probability that both units are active at thermal equilibrium when the output vector is determined by the network. Each weight is then updated by an amount proportional to the difference between these two quantities

$$\Delta w_{ij} = \varepsilon(<s_i s_j>^+ - <s_i s_j>^-)$$

It has been shown [Ackley, Hinton, and Sejnowski, 1985] that if ε is sufficiently small, this performs gradient descent in an information-theoretic measure, G, of the difference between the behavior of the output units when they are clamped and their behavior when they are not clamped.

$$G = \sum_{\alpha,\beta} P^+(I_\alpha,O_\beta) \log \frac{P^+(O_\beta \mid I_\alpha)}{P^-(O_\beta \mid I_\alpha)} \tag{11}$$

where I_α is a state vector over the input units, O_β is a state vector over the output units, P^+ is a probability measured when both the input and output units are clamped, and P^- is a probability measured at thermal equilibrium when only the input units are clamped.

G is called the *asymmetric divergence* or *Kullback information*, and its gradient has the same form for connections between input and hidden units, connections between pairs of hidden units, connections between hidden and output units, and connections between pairs of output units. G can be viewed as the difference of two terms. One term is the cross-entropy between the "desired" conditional probability distribution that is clamped on the output units and the "actual" conditional distribution exhibited by the output units when they are not clamped. The other term is the entropy of the "desired" conditional distribution. This entropy cannot be changed by altering the weights, so minimizing G is equivalent to minimizing the cross-entropy term, which means that Boltzmann machines use the same cost function as one form of back-propagation (see Section 20.6.8).

A special case of the learning procedure is when there are no input units. It can then be viewed as an unsupervised learning procedure that learns to model a probability distribution specified by clamping vectors on the output units with the appropriate probabilities. The advantage of modeling a distribution in this way is that the network can then perform completion. When a partial vector is clamped over a subset of the output units, the network produces completions on the remaining output units. If the network has learned the training distribution perfectly, its probability of producing each completion is guaranteed to match the environmental conditional probability of this completion given the clamped partial vector.

The learning procedure can easily be generalized to networks where each term in the energy function is the product of a weight, $w_{i,j,k}, \ldots$ and an arbitrary function, $f(i,j,k, \ldots)$, of the states of a subset of the units. The network must be run so that it achieves a Boltzmann distribution in the energy function, so each unit must be able to compute how the global energy would change if it were to change state. The generalized learning procedure is simply to change the weight by an amount proportional to the difference between $<f(i,j,k, \ldots)>^+$ and $<f(i,j,k, \ldots)>^-$.

The learning procedure using simple pairwise connections has been shown to produce appropriate representations in the hidden units [Ackley, Hinton, and Sejnowski, 1985] and it has also been used for speech recognition [Prager, Harrison, and Fallside, 1986]. However, it is considerably slower than back-propagation because of the time required to reach equilibrium in large networks. Also, the process of estimating the gradient introduces several practical problems. If the network does not reach equilibrium the estimated gradient has a systematic error, and if too few samples are taken to estimate $<s_i s_j>^+$ and $<s_i s_j>^-$ accurately the estimated gradient will be extremely noisy because it is the difference of two noisy estimates. Even when the noise in the estimate of the difference has zero mean, its variance is a function of $<s_i s_j>^+$ and $<s_i s_j>^-$. When these quantities are near 0 or 1, their estimates will have much lower variance than when they are near 0.5. This nonuniformity in the variance gives the hidden units a surprisingly strong tendency to develop weights that cause them to be on all the time or off all the time. A familiar version of the same effect can be seen if sand is sprinkled on a vibrating sheet of tin. Nearly all the sand clusters at the points that vibrate the least, even though there is no bias in the direction of motion of an individual grain of sand.

One interesting feature of the Boltzmann machine is that it is relatively easy to put it directly onto a chip that has dedicated hardware for each connection and performs the annealing extremely rapidly using analog circuitry. This circuitry computes the energy gap of a unit by simply allowing the incoming charge to add itself up, and makes stochastic decisions by using physical noise. Alspector and Allen [1987] are fabricating a chip that will run about 1 million times faster than a simulation on a VAX. Such chips may make it possible to apply connectionist learning procedures to practical problems, especially if they are used in conjunction with modular approaches that allow the learning time to scale better with the size of the task.

There is another promising method that reduces the time required to compute the equilibrium distribution and eliminates the noise caused by the sampling errors in $<s_i s_j>^+$ and $<s_i s_j>^-$. Instead of directly simulating the stochastic network, it is possible to estimate its mean behavior using *mean field theory*, which replaces each stochastic binary variable by a deterministic real value that represents the expected value of the stochastic variable. Simulated annealing can then be replaced by a deterministic relaxation procedure that operates on the real-valued parameters [Hopfield and Tank, 1985] and settles to a single state that gives a crude representation of the whole equilibrium distribution. The product of the "activity levels" of two units in this settled state can be used as an approximation of $<s_i s_j>$ so a version of the Boltzmann machine learning procedure can be applied. Peterson and Anderson [1987] have shown that this works quite well.

20.7.1 Maximizing Reinforcement and Entropy in a Boltzmann Machine

The Boltzmann machine learning procedure is based on the simplicity of the expression for the derivative of the asymmetric divergence between the conditional probability distribution exhibited by the output units of a Boltzmann machine and a desired conditional probability distribution. The derivatives of certain other important measures are also very simple if the network is allowed to reach thermal equilibrium. For example, the entropy of the states of the machine is given by

$$H = -\sum_\alpha P_\alpha \log_e P_\alpha$$

where P_α is the probability of a global configuration, and H is measured in units of $\log_2 e$ bits. Its derivative is

$$\frac{\partial H}{\partial w_{ij}} = \frac{1}{T}(< Es_i s_j> - <E> <s_i s_j>) \tag{12}$$

So if each weight has access to the global energy, E, it is easy to manipulate the entropy.

It is also easy to perform gradient ascent in expected reinforcement if the network is given a global reinforcement signal, R, that depends on its state. The derivative of the expected reinforcement with respect to each weight is

$$\frac{\partial R}{\partial w_{ij}} = \frac{1}{T}(<Rs_i s_j> - <R> <s_i s_j>) \tag{13}$$

A recurrent issue in reinforcement learning procedures is how to trade-off short-term optimization of expected reinforcement against the diversity required to discover actions that have a higher reinforcement than the network's current estimate. If we use entropy as a measure of diversity, and we assume that the system tries to optimize some linear combination of the expected reinforcement and the entropy of its actions, it can be shown that its optimal strategy is to pick actions according to a Boltzmann distribution, where the expected reinforcement of a state is the analog of negative energy and the parameter that determines the relative importance of expected reinforcement, and diversity is the analog of temperature. This result follows from the fact that the Boltzmann distribution is the one which maximizes entropy (i.e., diversity) for a given expected energy (i.e., reinforcement).

This suggests a learning procedure in which the system represents the expected value of an action by its negative energy and picks actions by allowing a Boltzmann machine to reach thermal equilibrium. If the weights are updated using equations (12) and (13), the negative energies of states will tend to become proportional to their expected reinforcements, since this is the way to make the derivative of H balance the derivative of R. Once the system has learned to represent the reinforcements correctly, variations in the temperature can be used to make it more or less conservative in its choice of actions while always making the optimal trade-off between diversity and expected reinforcement. Unfortunately, this learning procedure does not make use of the most important property of Boltzmann machines—their ability to compute the quantity $<s_i s_j>$ *given* some specified state of the output units. Also, it is much harder to compute the derivative of the entropy if we are only interested in the entropy of the state vectors over the output units.

20.8 MAXIMIZING MUTUAL INFORMATION: A SEMISUPERVISED LEARNING PROCEDURE

One "semisupervised" method of training a unit is to provide it with information about what category the input vector came from but to refrain from specifying the state that the unit ought to adopt. Instead, its incoming weights are modified so as to maximize the information that the state of the unit provides about the category of the input vector. The derivative of this mutual information is relatively easy to compute and so it can be maximized by gradient ascent [Pearlmutter and Hinton, 1986]. For difficult discriminations that cannot be performed in a single step, this is a good way of producing encodings of the input vector that allow the discrimination to be made more easily. Figure 20–10 shows an example of a difficult two-way discrimination and illustrates the kinds of discriminant function that maximize the information provided by the state of the unit.

If each unit within a layer independently maximizes the mutual information between its state and the category of the input vector, many units are likely to discover similar, highly correlated features. One way to force the units to diversify is to make each unit receive its inputs from a different subset of the units in the layer below. A second method is to ignore cases in which the input vector is correctly classified by the final output units and to maximize the mutual information between the state of each intermediate unit and the category of the input *given that the input is incorrectly classified.*[11]

If the two input distributions that must be discriminated consist of examples taken from some structured domain and examples generated at random (but with the same first-order statistics as the structured domain), this semisupervised procedure will discover higher order features that characterize the structured domain and so it can be made to act like the type of unsupervised learning procedure described in Section 20.9.

20.9 UNSUPERVISED HEBBIAN LEARNING

A unit can develop selectivity to certain kinds of features in its ensemble of input vectors by using a simple weight modification procedure that depends on the

---

[11] This method of weighting the statistics by some measure of the overall error or importance of a case can often be used to allow global measures of the performance of the whole network to influence local, unsupervised learning procedures.

(a)

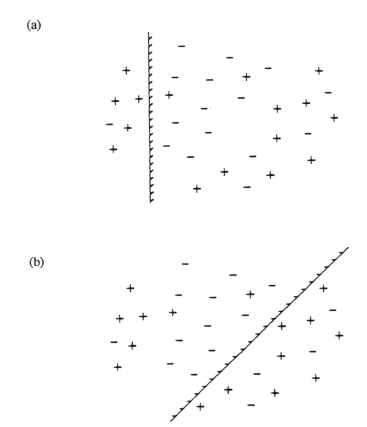

(b)

Figure 20-10:   (a) There is high mutual information between the state of a binary threshold unit that uses the hyperplane shown and the distribution (+ or −) that
the input vector came from. (b) The probability, given that the unit is on,
that the input came from the "+" distribution, is not as high using the diagonal hyperplane. However, the unit is on more often. Other things being
equal, a unit conveys most mutual information if it is on half the time.

correlation between the activity of the unit and the activity on each of its input lines.
This is called a "Hebbian" learning rule because the weight modification depends on
both presynaptic and postsynaptic activity [Hebb, 1949]. Typical examples of this
kind of learning are described by Cooper, Liberman, and Oja [1979] and by
Bienenstock, Cooper, and Munro [1982]. A criticism of early versions of this approach, from a computational point of view, was that the researchers often postulated
a simple, synaptic modification rule and then explored its consequences rather than

rigorously specifying the computational goal and then deriving the appropriate synaptic modification rule. However, an important recent development unifies these two approaches by showing that a relatively simple Hebbian rule can be viewed as the gradient of an interesting function. The function can therefore be viewed as a specification of what the learning is trying to achieve.

20.9.1 A Recent Development of Unsupervised Hebbian Learning

In a recent series of papers, Linsker has shown that with proper normalization of the weight changes, an unsupervised Hebbian learning procedure in which the weight change depends on the correlation of presynaptic and postsynaptic activity can produce a surprising number of the known properties of the receptive fields of neurons in visual cortex, including center-surround fields [Linsker, 1986a], orientation-tuned fields [Linsker, 1986b], and orientation columns [Linsker, 1986c]. The procedure operates in a multilayer network in which there is innate spatial structure so that the inputs to a unit in one layer tend to come from nearby locations in the layer below. Linsker demonstrates that the emergence of biologically suggestive, receptive fields depends on the relative values of a few generic parameters. He also shows that for each unit, the learning procedure is performing gradient ascent in a measure whose main term is the ensemble average (across all the various patterns of activity in the layer below) of:

$$\sum_{i,j} w_i s_i w_j s_j$$

where w_i and w_j are the weights on the ith and j^{th} input lines of a unit and s_i and s_j are the activities on those input lines.

It is not initially obvious why maximizing the pairwise covariances of the weighted activities produces receptive fields that are useful for visual information processing. Linsker does not discuss this question in his original three papers. However, he has shown [Linsker, 1987] that the learning procedure maximizes the variance in the activity of the postsynaptic unit subject to a "resource" constraint on overall synaptic strength. This is almost equivalent to maximizing the ratio of the postsynaptic variance to the sum of the squares of the weights, which is guaranteed to extract the first principal component (provided the units are linear). This component is the one that would minimize the sum-squared reconstruction error if we tried to reconstruct the activity vector of the presynaptic units from the activity level of the postsynaptic unit. Thus we can view Linsker's learning procedure as a way of ensuring that the activity of a unit conveys as much information as possible about its presynaptic input vector. A similar analysis can be applied to competitive learning (see Section 20.10).

20.10 COMPETITIVE LEARNING

Competitive learning is an unsupervised procedure that divides a set of input vectors into a number of disjoint clusters in such a way that the input vectors within each cluster are all similar to one another. It is called *competitive learning* because there is a set of hidden units that compete with one another to become active. There are many variations of the same basic idea, and only the simplest version is described here. When an input vector is presented to the network, the hidden unit that receives the greatest total input wins the competition and turns on with an activity level of 1. All the other hidden units turn off. The winning unit then adds a small fraction of the current input vector to its weight vector. So, in future, it will receive even more total input from this input vector. To prevent the same hidden unit from being the most active in all cases, it is necessary to impose a constraint on each weight vector that keeps the sum of the weights (or the sum of their squares) constant. So when a hidden unit becomes more sensitive to one input vector it becomes less sensitive to other input vectors.

Rumelhart and Zipser [1985] present a simple geometrical model of competitive learning. If each input vector has three components and is of unit length it can be represented by a point on the surface of the unit sphere. If the weight vectors of the hidden units are also constrained to be of unit length, they too can be represented by points on the unit sphere as shown in Figure 20–11. The learning procedure is equivalent to finding the weight vector that is closest to the current input vector, and moving it closer still by an amount that is proportional to the distance. If the weight changes are sufficiently small, this process will stabilize when each weight vector is at the center of gravity of a cluster of input vectors.

We can think of the network as performing the following task: Represent the current input vector, $\mathbf{y}_c$, as accurately as possible by using a single, active, hidden unit. The representation is simply the weight vector, $\mathbf{w}_c$, of the hidden unit which is active in case c. If the weight changes are sufficiently small, this version of competitive learning performs steepest descent in a measure of the sum-squared inaccuracy of the representation. The solutions it finds are minima of the function

$$E = \frac{1}{2} \sum_c (w_c - y_c)^2$$

Although they use the geometrical analogy described above, Rumelhart and Zipser actually use a slightly different learning rule, which cannot be interpreted as performing steepest descent in such a simple error function.

There are many variations of competitive learning in the literature [Von der Malsburg, 1973; Fukushima, 1975; Grossberg, 1976; Amari, 1983], and there is not

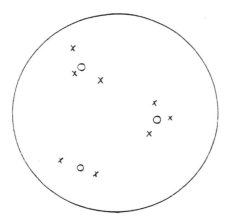

Figure 20–11:   The input vectors are represented by points marked "x" on the surface of a
sphere. The weight vectors of the hidden units are represented by points
marked "o." After competitive learning, each weight vector will be close to
the center of gravity of a cluster of input vectors.

space here to review them all. A model with similarities to competitive learning has
been used by Willshaw and Von der Malsburg [1979] to explain the formation of
topographic maps between the retina and the tectum. Recently, it has been shown
that a variation of this model can be interpreted as performing steepest descent in an
error function and can be applied to a range of optimization problems that involve
topographic mappings between geometrical structures [Durbin and Willshaw, 1987].

One major theme has been to show that competitive learning can produce topographic maps [Kohonen, 1982]. The hidden units are laid out in a spatial structure
(usually two-dimensional) and instead of just updating the weight vector of the hidden unit that receives the greatest total input, the procedure also updates the weight
vectors of adjacent hidden units. This encourages adjacent units to respond to similar
input vectors, and it can be viewed as a way of performing gradient descent in a cost
function that has two terms. The first term measures how inaccurately the weight
vector of the most active hidden unit represents the input vector. The second term
measures the dissimilarity between the input vectors that are represented by adjacent
hidden units. Kohonen has shown that this version of competitive learning performs
dimensionality reduction, so that surplus degrees of freedom are removed from the
input vector, and it is represented accurately by a point in a lower dimensional space
[Kohonen, 1982]. It is not clear how this compares in efficiency with self-supervised
back-propagation (see Section 20.6.9) for dimensionality reduction.

Fukushima and Miyake [1982] have demonstrated that a version of competitive learning can be used to allow a multilayer network to recognize simple two-

dimensional shapes in a number of different positions. After learning, the network can recognize a familiar shape in a novel position. The ability to generalize across position depends on using a network in which the layers of units that learn are interleaved with layers of nonlearning units prewired to generalize across position. Thus, the network does not truly learn translation invariance. By contrast, it is possible to design a back-propagation network that starts with no knowledge of the effects of translation and no knowledge of which input units are adjacent in the image. After sufficient experience, the network can correctly identify familiar, simple shapes in novel positions [Hinton, 1987c].

20.10.1 The Relationship Between Competitive Learning and Back-Propagation

Because it is performing gradient descent in a measure of how accurately the input vector could be reconstructed, competitive learning has a close relationship to self-supervised back-propagation. Consider a three-layer encoder network in which the desired states of the output units are the same as the actual states of the input units. Suppose that each weight from an input unit to a hidden unit is constrained to be identical to the weight from that hidden unit to the corresponding output unit. Suppose, also, that the output units are linear and the hidden units, instead of using the usual nonlinear input/output function, use the same "winner-take-all" nonlinearity as is used in competitive learning. So only one hidden unit will be active at a time, and the actual states of the output units will equal the weights of the active hidden unit. This makes it easy to compute the error derivatives of the weights from the hidden units to the output units. For weights from the active hidden unit, the derivatives are simply proportional to the difference between the actual and desired outputs (which equals the difference between the weight and the corresponding component of the input vector). For weights from inactive, hidden units the error derivatives are all 0. So gradient descent can be performed by making the weights of the active hidden unit regress towards the input vector, which is precisely what the competitive learning rule does.

Normally, back-propagation is needed in order to compute the error derivatives of the weights from the input units to the hidden units, but the winner-take-all nonlinearity makes back-propagation unnecessary in this network because all these derivatives are equal to 0. So long as the same hidden unit wins the competition, its activity level is not changed by changing its input weights. At the point where a small change in the weights would change the winner from one hidden unit to another, both hidden units fit the input vector equally well, so changing winners does not alter the total error in the output (even though it may change the output vector a lot). Because the error derivatives are so simple, we can still do the learning if we omit the output units altogether. This removes the output weights, and so we no longer need to constrain the input and output weights of a hidden unit to be identical.

Thus the simplified version of competitive learning is a degenerate case of self-supervised back-propagation.

It would be interesting if a mechanism as simple as competitive learning could be used to implement gradient descent in networks that allow the m most activated, hidden units to become fully active (where $m > 1$). This would allow the network to create more complex, distributed representations of the input vectors. Unfortunately the implementation is not nearly as simple because it is no longer possible to omit the output layer. The output units are needed to combine the effects of all the active hidden units and compare the combined effect with the input vector in order to compute the error derivatives of the output weights. Also, at the point at which one hidden unit ceases to be active and another becomes active, there may be a large change in the total error, so at this point there are infinite error derivatives for the weights from the input to the hidden units. It thus appears that the simplicity of the mechanism required for competitive learning is crucially dependent on the fact that only one hidden unit within a group is active.

20.11 REINFORCEMENT LEARNING PROCEDURES

There is a large and complex literature on reinforcement learning procedures, which is beyond the scope of this chapter. The main aim of this section is to give an informal description of a few of the recent ideas in the field that reveals their relationships to other types of connectionist learning.

A central idea in many reinforcement learning procedures is that we can assign credit to a local decision by *measuring* how it correlates with the global reinforcement signal. Various values are tried for each local variable (such as a weight or a state), and these variations are correlated with variations in the global reinforcement signal. Normally, the local variations are the result of independent stochastic processes, so if enough samples are taken, each local variable can average away the noise caused by the variation in the other variables to reveal its own effect on the global reinforcement signal (given the current average behavior of the other variables). The network can then perform gradient ascent in the expected reinforcement by altering the probability distribution of the value of each local variable in the direction that increases the expected reinforcement. If the probability distributions are altered after each trial, the network performs a stochastic version of gradient ascent.

The main advantage of reinforcement learning is that it is easy to implement because, unlike back-propagation, which *computes* the effect of changing a local variable, the "credit assignment" does not require any special apparatus for *computing* derivatives. So reinforcement learning can be used in complex systems in which it would be very hard to analytically compute reinforcement derivatives. The main disadvantage of reinforcement learning is that it is very inefficient when there are more than a few local variables. Even in the trivial case when all the local variables contribute independently to the global reinforcement signal, $O(NM)$ trials are required to allow the measured effects of each of the M possible values of a variable to achieve a reasonable signal-to-noise ratio by averaging away the noise caused by the N other variables. So reinforcement learning is very inefficient for large systems unless they are divided into smaller modules. It is as if each person in the United States tried to decide whether he or she had done a useful day's work by observing the gross national product on a day-by-day basis.

A second disadvantage is that gradient ascent may get stuck in local optima. As a network concentrates more and more of its trials on combinations of values that give the highest expected reinforcement, it gets less and less information about the reinforcements caused by other combinations of values.

20.11.1 Delayed Reinforcement

In many real systems, there is a delay between an action and the resultant reinforcement, so in addition to the normal problem of deciding how to assign credit to decisions about hidden variables, there is a temporal credit assignment problem [Sutton, 1984]. If, for example, a person wants to know how their behavior affects the gross national product, he needs to know whether to correlate today's GNP with what he did yesterday or with what he did five years ago. In the iterative version of back-propagation (Section 20.6.7), temporal credit assignment is performed by explicitly computing the effect of each activity level on the eventual outcome. In reinforcement learning procedures, temporal credit assignment is typically performed by learning to associate "secondary" reinforcement values with the states that are intermediate in time between the action and the external reinforcement. One important idea is to make the reinforcement value of an intermediate state regress towards the weighted average of the reinforcement values of its successors, where the weightings reflect the conditional probabilities of the successors. In the limit, this causes the reinforcement value of each state to be equal to the expected reinforcement of its successor, and hence equal to the expected final reinforcement.[12] Sutton [1987] explains why, in a stochastic system, it is typically more efficient to regress towards the reinforcement value of the next state rather than the reinforcement value of the final outcome. Barto, Sutton, and Anderson [1983] have demonstrated the usefulness of this type of procedure for learning with delayed reinforcement.

---

[12]There may also be a "tax" imposed for failing to achieve the external reinforcement quickly. This can be implemented by reducing the reinforcement value each time it is regressed to an earlier state.

20.11.2 The A_{R-P} Procedure

One obvious way of mapping results from learning automata theory onto connectionist networks is to treat each unit as an automaton and to treat the states it adopts as its actions. Barto and Anandan [1985] describe a learning procedure of this kind called *Associative Reward-Penalty* or A_{R-P}, which uses stochastic units like those in a Boltzmann machine (see equation (10)). They prove that if the input vectors are linearly independent and the network only contains one unit, A_{R-P} finds the optimal values of the weights. They also show empirically that if the same procedure is applied in a network of such units, the hidden units develop useful representations. Williams [1986] has shown that a limiting case of the A_{R-P} procedure performs stochastic gradient ascent in expected reinforcement.

20.11.3 Achieving Global Optimality by Reinforcement Learning

Thatachar and Sastry [1985] use a different mapping between automata and connectionist networks. Each *connection* is treated as an automaton, and the weight values that it takes on are its actions. On each trial, each connection chooses a weight (from a discrete set of alternatives), and then the network maps an input vector into an output vector and receives positive reinforcement if the output is correct. They present a learning procedure for updating the probabilities of choosing particular weight values. If the probabilities are changed slowly enough, the procedure is guaranteed to converge on the globally optimal combination of weights, even if the network has hidden layers. Unfortunately their procedure requires exponential space, because it involves storing and updating a table of estimated expected reinforcements that contains one entry for every combination of weights.

20.11.4 The Relative Payoff Procedure

If we are content to reach a local optimum, it is possible to use a very simple learning procedure that uses yet another way of mapping automata onto connectionist networks. Each connection is treated as a stochastic switch that has a certain probability of being closed at any moment [Minsky, 1954]. If the switch is open, the "postsynaptic" unit receives an input of 0 along that connection, but if the switch is closed it transmits the state of the "presynaptic" unit. A real synapse can be modeled as a set of these stochastic switches arranged in parallel. Each unit computes some fixed function of the vector of inputs that it receives on its incoming connections. Learning involves altering the switch probabilities to maximize the expected reinforcement signal.

A learning procedure called L_{R-I} can be applied in such networks. It is only guaranteed to find a local optimum of the expected reinforcement, but it is very simple to implement. A "trial" consists of four stages:

1. Set the switch configuration. For each switch in the network, decide whether it is open or closed on this trial using the current switch probability. The decisions are made independently for all the switches.

2. Run the network with this switch configuration. There are no constraints on the connectivity so cycles are allowed, and the units can also receive external inputs at any time. The constraint on the external inputs is that the probability distribution over patterns of external input must be stationary.

3. Compute the reinforcement signal. This can be any nonnegative, stationary function of the behavior of the network and of the external input it received during the trial.

4. Update the switch probabilities. For each switch that was closed during the trial, we increment its probability by $\varepsilon R(1 - p)$, where R is the reinforcement produced by the trial, p is the switch probability and ε is a small coefficient. For each switch that was open, we decrement its probability by εRp.

If ε is sufficiently small this procedure stochastically approximates hill climbing in expected reinforcement. The "batch" version of the procedure involves observing the reinforcement signal over a large number of trials before updating the switch probabilities. If a sufficient number of trials is observed, the following "relative payoff" update procedure always increases expected reinforcement (or leaves it unchanged): Change the switch probability to be equal to the fraction of the total reinforcement received when the switch was closed. This can cause large changes in the probabilities, and I know of no proof that it hill climbs in expected reinforcement, but in practice it always works. The direction of the jump in switch-probability space caused by the batch version of the procedure is the same as the expected direction of the small change in switch probabilities caused by the "on-line" version.

A variation of the relative payoff procedure can be used if the goal is to make the "responses" of a network match some desired probability distribution rather than maximize expected reinforcement. We simply define the reinforcement signal to be the desired probability of a response divided by the network's current probability of producing that response. If a sufficient number of trials are made before updating the switch probabilities, it can be shown [Larry Gillick and Jim Baker, personal communication] that this procedure is guaranteed to decrease an information-theoretic measure of the difference between the desired probability distribution over responses and the actual probability distribution. The measure is actually the G measure described in equation (11) and the proof is an adaptation of the proof of the EM procedure [Dempster, Laird, and Rubin, 1976].

20.11.5 Genetic Algorithms

Holland and his coworkers [Holland, 1975; Davis, 1987] have investigated a class of learning procedures which they call *genetic algorithms*, because they are explicitly inspired by an analogy with evolution. Genetic algorithms operate on a population of individuals to produce a better-adapted population. In the simplest case, each individual member of the population is a binary vector, and the two possible values of each component are analogous to two alternative versions (alleles) of a gene. There is a fitness function that assigns a real-valued fitness to each individual, and the aim of the "learning" is to raise the average fitness of the population. New individuals are produced by choosing two existing individuals as "parents" (with a bias toward individuals of higher than average fitness) and copying some component values from one parent and some from the other. Holland [1975] has shown that for a large class of fitness functions, this is an effective way of discovering individuals that have high fitness.

20.11.6 Genetic Learning and the Relative Payoff Rule

If an entire generation of individuals is simultaneously replaced by a generation of their offspring, genetic learning has a close relationship to the batch form of the L_{R-I} procedure described in Section 20.11.4. This is most easily understood by starting with a particularly simple version of genetic learning in which every individual in generation $t + 1$ has many different parents in generation t. Candidate individuals for generation $t + 1$ are generated from the existing individuals in generation t in the following way: To decide the value of the ith component of a candidate, we randomly choose one of the individuals in generation t and copy the value of its ith component. So the probability that the ith component of a candidate has a particular value is simply the relative frequency of that value in generation t. A selection process then operates on the candidates: Some are kept to form generation $t + 1$, and others are discarded. The fitness of a candidate is simply the probability that it is not discarded by the selection process. Candidates that are kept can be considered to have received a reinforcement of 1 and candidates that are discarded receive a reinforcement of 0. After selection, the probability that the ith component has a particular value is equal to the fraction of the successful candidates that have that value. This is exactly the relative payoff rule described in Section 20.11.4. The probabilities it operates on are the relative frequencies of alleles in the population instead of switch probabilities.

If the value of every component is determined by an independently chosen parent, information about the correlations between the values of different components is lost when generation $t + 1$ is produced from generation t. If, however, we use just two parents we maximize the tendency for the pairwise and higher order correlations to be preserved. This tendency is further increased if components whose correlations are important are near one another and the values of nearby components are normally taken from the same parent. So a population of individuals can effectively represent the probabilities of small combinations of component values as well as the probabilities of individual values. Genetic learning works well when the fitness of an individual is determined by these small combinations, which Holland calls *critical schemas*.

20.11.7 Iterated Genetic Hill Climbing

It is possible to combine genetic learning with gradient descent (or *hill climbing*) to get a hybrid learning procedure called *iterated genetic hill climbing* or *IGH* that works better than either learning procedure alone [Brady, 1985; Ackley, 1987]. IGH is as a form of multiple-restart hill climbing in which the starting points, instead of being chosen at random, are chosen by "mating" previously discovered local optima. Alternatively, it can be viewed as genetic learning in which each new individual is allowed to perform hill climbing in the fitness function before being evaluated and added to the population. Ackley [1987] shows that a stochastic variation of IGH can be implemented in a connectionist network that is trying to learn which output vector produces a high enough payoff to satisfy some external criterion.

20.12 DISCUSSION

This review has focused on a small number of recent connectionist learning procedures. There are many other interesting procedures that have been omitted [Feldman, 1982; Grossberg, 1980; Volper and Hampson, 1986; Hampson and Volper, 1987; Hogg and Huberman, 1984; Kerszberg and Bergman, 1986; Edelman and Reeke, 1982]. In particular, there has been no discussion of a large class of procedures that dynamically allocate new units instead of simply adjusting the weights in a fixed architecture. Rather than attempting to cover all of these, I conclude by discussing two major problems that plague most of the procedures I have described.

20.12.1 Generalization

A major goal of connectionist learning is to produce networks that generalize correctly to new cases after training on a sufficiently large set of typical cases from some domain. In much of the research, there is no formal definition of what it means to generalize correctly. The network is trained on examples from a domain that the experimenter understands (like the family relationships domain described in Section 20.6), and it is judged to generalize correctly if its generalizations agree with those of the experimenter. This is sufficient as an informal demonstration that the network can indeed perform nontrivial generalization, but it gives little insight into the reasons the generalizations of the network and the experimenter agree, and so it does not allow predictions to be made about when networks will generalize correctly and when they will fail.

What is needed is a formal theory of what it means to generalize correctly. One approach that has been used in studying the induction of grammars is to define a hypothesis space of possible grammars, and to show that with enough training cases the system will converge on the correct grammar with probability 1 [Angluin and Smith, 1984]. Valiant [1984] has recently introduced a rather more subtle criterion of success in order to distinguish classes of Boolean function that can be induced from examples in polynomial time from classes that require exponential time. He assumes that the hypothesis space is known in advance. He allows the training cases to be selected according to *any* stationary distribution but insists that the same distribution be used to generate the test cases. The induced function is considered to be good enough if it differs from the true function on less than a small fraction, $1/h$, of the test cases. A class of Boolean functions is considered to be learnable in polynomial time if, for any choice of h, there is a probability of at least $(1 - 1/h)$ that the induced function is good enough after a number of training examples that is polynomial in both h and the number of arguments of the Boolean function. Using this definition, Valiant has succeeded in showing that several interesting subclasses of Boolean function are learnable in polynomial time. Our understanding of other connectionist learning procedures would be considerably improved if we could derive similar results that were as robust against variations in the distribution of the training examples.

The work on inducing grammars or Boolean functions may not provide an appropriate framework for studying systems that learn inherently stochastic functions, but the general idea of starting with a hypothesis space of possible functions carries over. A widely used statistical approach involves maximizing the *a posteriori* likelihood of the model (i.e., the function) given the data. If the data really is generated by a function in the hypothesis space, and if the amount of information in the training data greatly exceeds the amount of information required to specify a point in the hypothesis space, the maximum-likelihood function is very probably the correct one, so the network will then generalize correctly. Some connectionist learning schemes (e.g., the Boltzmann machine learning procedure) can be made to fit this approach exactly. If a Boltzmann machine is trained with much more data than there are weights in the machine, and if it really does find the global minimum of G, and if the correct answer lies in the hypothesis space (which is defined by the architecture of the machine),[13] then there is every reason to suppose that it will generalize correctly, even if it has only been trained on a small fraction of the *possible* cases. Unfortunately, this kind of guarantee is of little use for practical problems where we usually know in advance that the "true" model does not lie in the hypothesis space of the network. What needs to be shown is that the best available point within the hypothe-

---

[13] One popular idea is that evolution implicitly chooses an appropriate hypothesis space by constraining the architecture of the network and learning then identifies the most likely hypothesis within this space. How evolution arrives at sensible hypothesis spaces in reasonable time is usually unspecified. The evolutionary search for good architectures may actually be guided by learning [Hinton and Nowlan, 1987].

sis space (even though it is not a perfect model) will also generalize well to test cases.

A simple thought experiment shows that the "correct" generalization from a set of training cases, however it is defined, must depend on how the input and output vectors are encoded. Consider a mapping, M_I, from entire input vectors onto entire input vectors and a mapping, M_O, from entire output vectors onto entire output vectors. If we introduce a precoding stage that uses M_I and a postcoding stage that uses M_O, we can convert a network that generalizes in one way into a network that generalizes in any other way we choose simply by choosing M_I and M_O appropriately.

20.12.2 Practical Methods of Improving Generalization

One very useful method of improving the generalization of many connectionist learning procedures is to introduce an extra term into the error function. This term penalizes large weights, and it can be viewed as a way of building in an *a priori* bias in favor of simple models (i.e., models in which there are not too many strong interactions between the variables). If the extra term is the sum of the squares of the weights, its derivative corresponds to "weight decay"—each weight continually decays toward 0 by an amount proportional to its magnitude. When the learning has equilibrated, the magnitude of a weight is equal to its error derivative because this error derivative balances the weight decay. This often makes it easier to interpret the weights. Weight decay tends to prevent a network from using table lookup and forces it to discover regularities in the training data. In a simple linear network without hidden units, weight decay can be used to find the weight matrix that minimizes the effect of adding zero-mean, uncorrelated noise to the input units [Le Cun, 1987].

Another useful method is to impose equality constraints between weights that encode symmetries in the task. In solving any practical problem, it is wasteful to make the network learn information that is known in advance. If possible, this information should be encoded by the architecture or the initial weights so that the training data can be used to learn aspects of the task that we do not already know how to model.

20.12.3 The Speed of Learning

Most existing connectionist learning procedures are slow, particularly procedures that construct complicated internal representations. One way to speed them up is to use optimization methods such as recursive least squares that converge faster. If the second derivatives can be computed or estimated, they can be used to pick a direction for the weight change vector that yields faster convergence than the direction of steepest descent [Parker, 1987]. It remains to be seen how well such methods work for the error surfaces generated by multilayer networks learning complex tasks.

A second method of speeding up learning is to use dedicated hardware for each connection and to map the inner-loop operations into analog instead of digital hardware. As Alspector and Allen [1987] have demonstrated, the speed of one particular learning procedure can be increased by a factor of about one million if we combine these techniques. This significantly increases our ability to explore the behavior of relatively small systems, but it is not a panacea. By using silicon in a different way we typically gain a large but constant factor (optical techniques may eventually yield a *huge* constant factor), and by dedicating a processor to each of the N connections we gain at most a factor of N in time at the cost of at least a factor of N in space. For a learning procedure with a time complexity of, say, $O(N \log N)$ a speedup of N makes a very big difference. For a procedure with a complexity of, say, $O(N^3)$ alternative technologies and parallelism will help significantly for small systems, but not for large ones.[14]

20.12.4 Hardware Modularity

One of the best and most common ways of fighting complexity is to introduce a modular, hierarchical structure in which different modules are only loosely coupled [Simon, 1969]. Pearl [1986] has shown that if the interactions between a set of probabilistic variables are constrained to form a tree structure, there are efficient parallel methods for estimating the interactions between "hidden" variables. The leaves of the tree are the observables, and the higher level nodes are hidden. The probability distribution for each variable is constrained by the values of its immediate parents in the tree. Pearl shows that these conditional probabilities can be recovered in time $O(N \log N)$ from the pairwise correlations between the values of the leaves of the tree. Remarkably, it is also possible to recover the tree structure itself in the same time.

Self-supervised back-propagation (see Section 20.6.9) was originally designed to allow efficient bottom-up learning in domains where there is hierarchical modular structure. Consider, for example, an ensemble of input vectors that are generated in the following modular way: Each module has a few high-level variables whose values help to constrain the values of a larger number of low-level variables. The low-level variables of each module are partitioned into several sets, and each set is identified with the high-level variables of a lower module, as shown in Figure 20–12.

Now suppose that we treat the values of all the low-level variables of the leaf modules as a single input vector. Given a sufficiently large ensemble of input vectors and an "innate" knowledge of the architecture of the generator, it should be possible to recover the underlying structure by using self-supervised back-propagation to learn compact codes for the low-level variables of each leaf module. It is possible to

---

[14]Tsotsos [1987] makes similar arguments in a discussion of the space-complexity of vision.

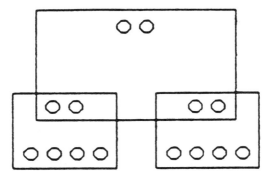

Figure 20–12:   The lower level variables of a high-level module are the higher level variables of several low-level modules.

learn codes for all the lowest level modules in parallel. Once this has been done, the network can learn codes at the next level up the hierarchy. The time taken to learn the whole hierarchical structure (given parallel hardware) is just proportional to the depth of the tree and hence it is $O(\log N)$ where N is the size of the input vector. An improvement on this strictly bottom-up scheme is described by Ballard [1987]. He shows why it is helpful to allow top-down influences from more abstract representations to less abstract ones, and he presents a working simulation.

20.12.5 Other Types of Modularity

There are several other helpful types of modularity that do not necessarily map so directly onto modular hardware but are nevertheless important for fast learning and good generalization. Consider a system that solves hard problems by creating its own subgoals. Once a subgoal has been created, the system can learn how best to satisfy it, and this learning can be useful on other occasions even if it was a mistake to create that subgoal on this particular occasion. So the assignment of credit to the decision to create a subgoal can be decoupled from the assignment of credit to the actions taken to achieve the subgoal. Since the ability to achieve the subgoals can be learned separately from the knowledge about when they are appropriate, a system can use achievable subgoals as building blocks for more complex procedures. This avoids the problem of learning the complex procedures from scratch. It may also constrain the way in which the complex procedures will be generalized to new cases, because the knowledge about how to achieve each subgoal may already include knowledge about how to cope with variations. By using subgoals we can increase modularity and improve generalization even in systems that use the very same hardware for solving the subgoal as was used for solving the higher level goal. Using subgoals, it may even be possible to develop reasonable, fast reinforcement learning procedures for large systems.

There is another type of relationship between easy and hard tasks that can facilitate learning. Sometimes a hard task can be decomposed into a set of easier constituents, but other times a hard task may just be a version of an easier task that requires finer discrimination. For example, throwing a ball in the general direction of another person is much easier than throwing it through a hoop, and a good way to train a system to throw it through a hoop is to start by training it to throw it in the right, general direction. This relation between easy and hard tasks is used extensively in "shaping" the behavior of animals and should also be useful for connectionist networks (particularly those that use reinforcement learning). It resembles the use of multiresolution techniques to speed up search in computer vision [Terzopoulos, 1984]. Having learned the coarse task, the weights should be close to a point in weight space where minor adjustments can tune them to perform the finer task.

One application where this technique should be helpful is in learning filters that discriminate between very similar sounds. The approximate shapes of the filters can be learned using spectrograms that have low resolution in time and frequency, and then the resolution can be increased to allow the filters to resolve fine details. By introducing a "regularization" term that penalizes filters that have very different weights for adjacent cells in the high-resolution spectrogram, it may be possible to allow filters to "attend" to fine detail when necessary without incurring the cost of estimating all the weights from scratch. The regularization term encodes prior knowledge that good filters should generally be smooth, and so it reduces the amount of information that must be extracted from the training data.

20.12.6 Conclusion

There are now many different connectionist learning procedures that can construct appropriate internal representations in small domains, and it is likely that many more variations will be discovered in the next few years. Major new advances can be expected on a number of fronts: Techniques for making the learning time scale better may be developed; attempts to apply connectionist procedures to difficult tasks like speech recognition may actually succeed; new technologies may make it possible to simulate much larger networks; and finally the computational insights gained from studying connectionist systems may prove useful in interpreting the behavior of real neural networks.

ACKNOWLEDGMENTS

I thank David Ackley, Joshua Alspector, Jim Baker, Dana Ballard, Andrew Barto, John Bridle, Yann Le Cun, Mark Derthick, Larry Gillick, Ralph Linsker, Steve Nowlan, David Plaut, David Rumelhart, Terry Sejnowski, John Tsotsos, and members of the Carnegie Mellon Boltzmann group for helpful comments.

References

Ackley, D.H. 1987. *Stochastic Iterated Genetic Hill-climbing*, PhD Thesis, Carnegie Mellon University, Pittsburgh PA.

Ackley, D.H. and Hinton, G.E. and Sejnowski, T.J. 1985. A Learning Algorithm for Boltzmann Machines, *Cognitive Science*, vol. 9, pp. 147–169.

Alspector, J. and Allen, R.B. 1987. A Neuromorphic VLSI Learning System, edited by P. Loseleben, *Advanced Research in VLSI: Proceedings of the 1987 Stanford Conference*, Cambridge, MA, MIT Press.

Amari, S-I. 1967. A theory of adaptive pattern classifiers, *IEEE Transactions on Electronic Computers*, vol. EC-16, pp. 299–307.

——— , 1983. Field theory of self-organizing neural nets, *IEEE Transactions on Systems, Man, and Cybernetics*, vol. SMC-13, pp. 741–748.

Anderson, J.A. and Hinton, G.E. 1981, Models of information processing in the brain, edited by G.E. Hinton and J.A. Anderson, *Parallel Models of Associative Memory*, Hillsdale, NJ, Erlbaum.

Anderson, J.A. and Mozer, M.C. 1981. Categorization and selective neurons, edited by G.E. Hinton and J.A. Anderson, *Parallel Models of Associative Memory*, Hillsdale, NJ, Erlbaum.

Angluin, D. and Smith, C.H. 1983. Inductive inference: Theory and methods, *Computing Surveys*, vol. 15, pp. 237–269.

Bahl, L.R., Jelinek, F., and Mercer, R.L. 1983. A maximum likelihood approach to continuous speech recognition, *IEEE Transactions on Pattern Analysis and Machine Intelligence*, vol. PAMI-5, pp. 179–190.

Ballard, D.H. 1986. Cortical connections and parallel processing: Structure and function, *The Behavioral and Brain Sciences*, vol. 9, pp. 67–120.

——— , 1987. Modular learning in neural networks, *Proceeding of the Sixth National Conference on Artificial Intelligence*, American Association for Artificial Intelligence, Seattle, WA, pp. 279–284.

Ballard, D.H., Hinton, G.E., and Sejnowski, T.J. 1983, Parallel visual computation, *Nature*, vol. 306, pp. 21–26.

Barlow, H.B. 1985. Cognitronics: Methods for Acquiring and Holding Cognitive Knowledge, Physiology Laboratory, Cambridge University, Unpublished manuscript.

————, 1972. Single units and sensation: A neuron doctrine for perceptual psychology?, *Perception*, vol. 1, pp. 371–394.

Barto, A.G. and Anandan, P. 1985. Pattern recognizing stochastic learning automata, *IEEE Transactions on Systems, Man and Cybernetics*, vol. 15, pp. 360–375.

Barto, A.G., Sutton, R.S., and Anderson, C.W. 1983. Neuronlike elements that solve difficult learning control problems, *IEEE Transactions on Systems, Man, and Cybernetics*.

Bienenstock, E.L., Cooper, L.N., and Munro, P.W. 1982. Theory for the development of neuron selectivity: Orientation specificity and binocular interaction in visual cortex, *Journal of Neuroscience*, vol. 2, pp. 32–48.

Brady, R.M. 1985. Optimization strategies gleaned from biological evolution, *Nature*, vol. 317, pp. 804–806.

Cooper, L.N., Liberman, F., and Oja, E. 1979. A theory for the acquisition and loss of neuron specificity in visual cortex, *Biological Cybernetics*, vol. 33, pp. 9–28.

Cottrell, G.W., Munro, P., and Zipser, D. 1987. Learning internal representations from gray-scale images: an example of extensional programming, *Proceeding of the Ninth Annual Conference of the Cognitive Science Society*, pp. 461–473, Seattle, WA.

Crick, F. and Mitchison, G. 1983. The function of dream sleep, *Nature*, vol. 304, pp. 111–114.

Davis, L. (ed). 1987. *Genetic Algorithms and Simulated Annealing*, London, Pitman and San Mateo, Morgan Kaufmann.

Dempster, A.P., Laird, N.M., and Rubin, D.B. 1976. Maximum likelihood from incomplete data via the EM algorithm, *Proceedings of the Royal Statistical Society*, pp. 1–38.

Durbin, R. and Willshaw, D. 1987. The elastic net method: An analogue approach to the travelling salesman problem, *Nature*, vol. 326, pp. 689–691.

Edelman, G.M. and Reeke, G.N. 1982. Selective networks capable of representative transformations, limited generalizations, and associative memory, *Proceedings of the National Academy of Sciences U.S.A.*, vol. 79, pp. 2091–2095.

Elman, J.L. and Zipser, D. 1987. *Discovering the Hidden Structure of Speech*, Institute for Cognitive Science, University of California, San Diego., Technical Report No. 8701.

Feldman, J.A. 1986. Neural representation of conceptual knowledge, Technical Report TR189, Department of Computer Science, University of Rochester, Rochester, NY.

———, 1982. Dynamic connections in neural networks, *Biological Cybernetics*, vol. 46, pp. 27–39.

Feldman, J.A. and Ballard, D.H. 1982. Connectionist models and their properties, *Cognitive Science*, vol. 6, pp. 205–254.

Fukushima, K. 1975. Cognitron: A self-organizing multilayered neural network, *Biological Cybernetics*, vol. 20, pp. 121–136.

Fukushima, K. and Miyake, S. 1982. Neocognitron: A new algorithm for pattern recognition tolerant of deformations and shifts in position, *Pattern Recognition*, vol. 15, pp. 455–469.

Geman, S. and Geman, D. 1984. Stochastic relaxation, gibbs distributions, and the bayesian restoration of images, *IEEE Transactions on Pattern Analysis and Machine Intelligence*, vol. PAMI-6, pp. 721–741.

Golden, R.M. 1987. A Unified Framework for Connectionist Systems, Manuscript, Learning Research and Development Center, University of Pittsburgh.

Grefenstette, J.J. 1985. *Proceedings of an International Conference on Genetic Algorithms and Their Applications*, Carnegie Mellon University, Pittsburgh, PA.

Grossberg, S. 1976. Adaptive pattern classification and universal recoding, i: parallel development and coding of neural feature detectors, *Biological Cybernetics*, vol. 23, pp. 121–134.

———, 1980. How does the brain build a cognitive code?, *Psychological Review*, vol. 87, pp. 1–51.

Hampson, S.E. and Volper, D.J. 1987. Disjunctive models of Boolean category learning, *Biological Cybernetics*, vol. 55, pp. 1–17.

Harth, E., Pandya, A.S., and Unnikrishnan, K.P. 1986. Perception as an optimization process, *Proc. IEEE Computer Society Conf. on Computer Vision and Pattern Recognition*, Miami, FL.

Hebb, D.O. 1949. *The Organization of Behavior*, Wiley, NY.

Hinton, G.E. 1981. Implementing semantic networks in parallel hardware, edited by G.E. Hinton and J.A. Anderson, *Parallel Models of Associative Memory*, Hillsdale, NJ, Erlbaum.

————, 1986. Learning distributed representations of concepts, *Proc. Eighth Annual Conference of the Cognitive Science Society*, Amherst, MA.

————, 1987. Learning translation invariant recognition in a massively parallel network, *Parallel Architectures and Languages Europe, Volume I*, Springer-Verlag, Lecture Notes in Computer Science, Berlin, pp. 1–14.

Hinton, G.E. and Anderson, J.A. (eds). 1981. *Parallel models of associative memory*, Hillsdale, NJ, Erlbaum.

Hinton, G.E. and McClelland, J.L. 1987. Learning Representations by Recirculation, Carnegie Mellon University, Pittsburgh, PA, Manuscript in preparation.

Hinton, G.E. and Nowlan, S.J. 1987. How Learning Can Guide Evolution, *Complex Systems*, Volume 1, pp. 495–502.

Hinton, G.E. and Plaut, D.C. 1987. Using Fast Weights to Deblur Old Memories, *Proc. Ninth Annual Conference of the Cognitive Science Society*, Seattle, WA, Erlbaum.

Hinton, G.E. and Sejnowski, T.J. 1986. Learning and Relearning in Boltzmann Machines, edited by D.E. Rumelhart and J.L. McClelland and the PDP Research Group, *Parallel Distributed Processing: Explorations in the Microstructure of Cognition, Volume I Foundations*, Cambridge, MA, MIT Press.

————, 1983. Optimal Perceptual Inference, *Proceedings of the IEEE conference on Computer Vision and Pattern Recognition*, IEEE Computer Society, Washington, DC, pp. 448–453.

Hinton, G.E., McClelland, J.L., and Rumelhart, D.E. 1986. Distributed representations, edited by D.E. Rumelhart and J.L. McClelland and the PDP Research Group, *Parallel Distributed Processing: Explorations in the Microstructure of Cognition, Volume I: Foundations*, Cambridge, MA, MIT Press.

Hogg, T. and Huberman, B.A. 1984. Understanding biological computation: Reliable learning and recognition, *Proceedings of the National Academy of Sciences U.S.A.*, vol. 81, pp. 6871–6875.

Holland, J.H. 1975. *Adaptation in Natural and Artificial Systems*, University of Michigan Press.

Hopfield, J.J. 1982. Neural networks and physical systems with emergent collective computational abilities, *Proceedings of the National Academy of Sciences U.S.A.*, vol. 79, pp. 2554–2558.

Hopfield, J.J. and Tank, D.W. 1985. "Neural" computation of decisions in optimization problems, *Biological Cybernetics*, vol. 52, pp. 141–152.

Hopfield, J.J., Feinstein, D.I., and Palmer, R.G. 1983. "Unlearning" has a stabilizing effect in collective memories, *Nature*, vol. 304.

Hummel, R.A. and Zucker, S.W. 1983. On the foundations of relaxation labeling processes, *IEEE Transactions on Pattern Analysis and Machine Intelligence*, vol. PAMI-5, pp. 267–287.

Judd, J.S. 1987. *Complexity of Connectionist Learning with Various Node Functions*, COINS Technical Report 87–60, University of Amherst, Amherst, MA.

Kerszberg, M. and Bergman, A. 1986. The evolution of data processing abilities in competing automata, *Proc. Computer Simulation in Brain Science*, Copenhagen, Denmark.

Kirkpatrick, S., Gelatt, C.D., and Vecchi, M.P. 1983. Optimization by simulated annealing, *Science*, vol. 220, pp. 671–680.

Kohonen, T. 1977. *Associative Memory: A System-theoretical Approach*, Berlin, Springer.

——— , 1982. Clustering, taxonomy, and topological maps of patterns, edited by M. Lang, *Proceedings of the Sixth International Conference on Pattern Recognition*, Silver Spring, MD, IEEE Computer Society Press.

——— , 1984. *Self-Organization and Associative Memory* (second edition), Springer-Verlag, NY.

Lang, K.J. 1987. Connectionist speech recognition, Thesis proposal, Carnegie Mellon University, Pittsburgh, PA.

Le Cun, Y. 1985. A learning scheme for asymmetric threshold networks, *Proceedings of Cognitiva 85*, Paris, France, pp. 599–604.

——— , 1987. *Modèles Connexionnistes de l'Apprentissage*, Paris, France, Universitè Pierre et Marie Curie.

Linsker, R. 1986a. From basic network principles to neural architecture: Emergence of spatial opponent cells, *Proceedings of the National Academy of Sciences U.S.A.*, vol. 83, pp. 7508–7512.

——— , 1986b. From basic network principles to neural architecture: Emergence of orientation-selective cells, *Proceedings of the National Academy of Sciences U.S.A.*, vol. 83, pp. 8390–8394.

——— , 1986c. From basic network principles to neural architecture: Emergence of orientation columns, *Proceedings of the National Academy of Sciences U.S.A.*, vol. 83, pp. 8779–8783.

——— , 1987. Development of feature-analyzing cells and their columnar organization in a layered self-adaptive network, *Computer Simulation in Brain Science*, edited by R. Cotterill, Cambridge University Press.

Marroquin, J.L. 1985. *Probabilistic Solution of Inverse Problems*, MIT.

Minsky, M.L. 1954. Theory of neural-analog reinforcement systems and its application to the brain-model problem, PhD Dissertation, Princeton University.

——— , 1977. Plain talk about neurodevelopmental epistemology, *Fifth International Joint Conference on Artificial Intelligence*, Vol 2, pp. 1083–1092.

Minsky, M.L. and Papert, S. 1969. *Perceptrons*, Cambridge, MA, MIT Press.

Munro, P.W. 1987. A dual back-propagation scheme for scalar reinforcement learning, *Proceeding of the Ninth Annual Conference of the Cognitive Science Society*, Seattle, WA.

Natarajan, B.K. 1987. Learning functions from examples, Manuscript, The Robotics Institute, Carnegie Mellon University, Pittsburgh, PA.

Parker, D.B. 1985. *Learning-logic*, Sloan School of Management, Massachusetts Institute of Technology, Cambridge, MA, Technical Report TR-47, April, 1985.

——— , 1987. *Second order back-propagation: An optimal adaptive algorithm for any adaptive network*, Unpublished manuscript.

Pearl, J. 1986. Fusion, propagation, and structuring in belief networks, *Artificial Intelligence*, vol. 29, pp. 241–288.

Pearlmutter, B.A. and Hinton, G.E. 1986. G-Maximization: An unsupervised learning procedure for discovering regularities, edited by J. S. Denker, *Neural Networks for Computing: American Institute of Physics Conference Proceedings 151*, pp. 333–338.

Peterson, C. and Anderson, J.R. 1987. *A Mean Field Theory Learning Algorithm for Neural Networks*, MCC Technical Report E1–259–87, Microelectronics and Computer Technology Corporation.

Plaut, D.C. and Hinton, G.E. 1987. Learning sets of filters using back-propagation, *Computer Speech and Language*, vol. 2.

Prager, R. and Harrison, T.D. and Fallside, F. 1986. Boltzmann machines for speech recognition, *Computer Speech and Language*, vol. 1, pp. 1–20.

Rosenblatt, F. 1962. *Principles of Neurodynamics*, New York, Spartan Books.

Rumelhart, D.E. and Zipser, D. 1985. Competitive learning, *Cognitive Science*, vol. 9, pp. 75–112.

Rumelhart, D.E. and McClelland, J.L. 1986. On the acquisition of the past tense in English, edited by McClelland, J.L. and Rumelhart, D.E., *Parallel Distributed Processing: Explorations in the Microstructure of Cognition, Volume 2: Applications*, Cambridge, MA, MIT Press.

Rumelhart, D.E., Hinton, G.E., and Williams, R.J. 1986a. Learning internal representations by error propagation, edited by D.E. Rumelhart and J.L. McClelland and the PDP Research Group, *Parallel Distributed Processing: Explorations in the Microstructure of Cognition. Volume I Foundations*, Cambridge, MA, MIT Press.

———, 1986b. Learning internal representations by back-propagating errors, *Nature*, pp. 533–536, vol. 323.

Saund, E. 1986. Abstraction and representation of continuous variables in connectionist networks, *Proceedings of the Fifth National Conference on Artificial Intelligence*, San Mateo, CA, Morgan Kaufmann, pp. 638–644.

Sejnowski, T.J. and Rosenberg, C.R. 1987. Parallel networks that learn to pronounce English text, *Complex Systems*, vol. 1, pp. 145–168.

Simon, H.A. 1969. *The Sciences of the Artificial*, Cambridge, MA, MIT Press.

Sutton, R.S. 1987. *Learning to predict by the method of temporal differences*, GTE Laboratories technical report TR87–509.1, Waltham, MA.

———, 1984. *Temporal credit assignment in reinforcement learning*, University of Massachusetts, Amherst, MA, COINS Technical Report 84–02, Feb, 1984.

Tank, D.W. and Hopfield, J.J. 1987. Neural Computation by Concentrating Information in Time, *Proceedings of the National Academy of Sciences*, U.S.A., vol. 84, pp. 1896–1900.

Terzopoulos, D. 1984. *Multiresolution computation of visible surface representations*, PhD Dissertation, Department of Electrical Engineering and Computer Science, Massachusetts Institute of Technology, Cambridge, MA.

Tesauro, G. 1987. Scaling relationships in back-propagation learning: dependence on training set size, *Complex Systems*, vol. 2, pp. 367–372.

Thatachar, M.A.L and Sastry, P.S. 1985. *Learning optimal discriminant functions through a cooperative game of automata*, Technical Report EE/64/1985, Department of Electrical Engineering, Indian Institute of Science, Bangalore-560012, India.

Tsotsos, J.K. 1987. A "complexity level" analysis of vision, *Proc. First International Conference on Computer Vision*, London, England, pp. 346–355.

Valiant, L.G. 1984. A theory of the learnable, *Communications of the ACM*, vol. 27, pp. 1134–1142.

Volper, D.J. and Hampson, S.E. 1986. Connectionist models of Boolean category representation, *Biological Cybernetics*, vol. 54, pp. 393–406

Von der Malsburg, C. 1973. Self-organization of orientation sensitive cells in striate cortex, *Kybernetik*, vol. 14, pp. 85–100.

———— , 1981. *The Correlation Theory of Brain Function*, Internal Report 81–2, Department of Neurobiology, Max Planck Institute for Biophysical Chemistry, Gottingen, FRG.

Waibel, A., Hanazawa, T., Hinton, G., Shikano, K., and Lang, K. 1987. *Phoneme Recognition Using Time-Delay Neural Networks*, Technical Report TR-1-0006, ATR Interpreting Telephony Research Laboratories, Japan.

Weisbuch, G. and Fogelman-Soulie, F. 1985. Scaling Laws for the Attractors of Hopfield Networks, *Journal of Physics Letters*, vol. 46, pp. 623–630.

Werbos, P.J. 1974. *Beyond Regression: New Tools for Prediction and Analysis in the Behavioral Sciences*, PhD Thesis, Harvard University, Cambridge, MA.

Widrow, B. and Hoff, M.E. 1960. Adaptive switching circuits, *IRE WESCON Conv. Record*, Part 4, pp. 96–104.

Widrow, B. and Stearns, S.D. 1985. *Adaptive Signal Processing*, Englewood Cliffs, NJ, Prentice-Hall.

Williams, R.J. 1986. *Reinforcement learning in connectionist networks: A mathematical analysis*, Technical Report, Institute for Cognitive Science, University of California San Diego, La Jolla, CA.

Willshaw, D.J. and Von der Malsburg, C. 1979. A marker induction mechanism for the establishment of ordered neural mapping: Its application to the retino-tectal connections, *Philosophical Transactions of the Royal Society*, London, vol. 287, pp. 203–243.

Willshaw, D. 1981. Holography, associative memory, and inductive generalization, edited by G.E. Hinton and J.A. Anderson, *Parallel Models of Associative Memory*, Hillsdale, NJ, Erlbaum.

21

GENETIC-ALGORITHM-BASED LEARNING

Kenneth De Jong
(George Mason University)

Abstract

This chapter describes a subarea of machine learning that is actively exploring the use of genetic algorithms as the key element in the design of robust learning strategies. After characterizing the kinds of learning problems motivating this approach, a brief overview of genetic algorithms is presented. Three major approaches to using genetic algorithms for machine learning are described, and an example of their use in learning entire task programs is given. Finally, an assessment of the strengths and weaknesses of this approach to machine learning is provided.

21.1 INTRODUCTION

The explosive growth of interest in machine learning has lead to a rich diversity of approaches to the design of learning systems. One of the consequences of this diversity is the formation of subgroups that share common interests such as similarity-based learning, explanation-based learning, neural net learning, and so on. The advantage of such groups is the ability to focus intensively on a highly specialized set of issues and make considerable progress in understanding machine learning in that context. The primary danger of such groups is that the high degree of specialization can lead easily to a state in which communicating ideas and results among subgroups is difficult.

One of the goals of this book (and the two preceding volumes) is to provide cogent descriptions of specialty areas in machine learning in terms that "outsiders" can understand and assess the strengths and limitations of a particular approach. This chapter attempts to achieve that goal for an active subgroup concerned with machine learning from an *adaptive systems* perspective as initially proposed by [Holland, 1975], and with a special interest in the use of *genetic algorithms* as a key element in the design of learning strategies. In keeping with present convention, this approach will be referred to as Genetic-Algorithm-based Learning (GABL).

21.1 AN ADAPTIVE SYSTEMS PERSPECTIVE

The casual and imprecise usage of the term "learning" in everyday life seems to confound attempts to provide a succinct, all-inclusive definition for it. Faced with this difficulty, the operational workaround of the machine learning research community has been to focus on *useful and interesting aspects* of learning without concern for capturing all facets. From an adaptive systems perspective, that focus is on *systems that are capable of making changes to themselves over time with the goal of improving their performance on the tasks confronting them in a particular environment.*

This view reflects several biases of the adaptive systems community. Note first the *performance-oriented* nature of the definition. There is much less emphasis on evaluating learning in terms of changes to internal structures and much more emphasis on evaluating learning in terms of changes in performance over time. This focus on performance is in some sense a pragmatic reflection of our own difficulty in dealing with complex problems. It is generally beyond our current abilities to characterize the behavior of a system of any complexity by means of a static analysis of its internal structure regardless of whether the system was built by hand or constructed using some automated (learning) techniques. Although we can develop a set of tools capable of catching syntactic and simple semantic problems via a static analysis of the system, this is invariably complemented by the development of an extensive "test suite" of problems for empirical validation.

This is closely related to another issue: *When does learning stop?* The answer from an adaptive systems perspective is: *Never!* Consider the construction of a self-improving diagnostic expert system from this perspective. If such a system is designed to continue learning "in the field," there is less concern about anticipating (and validating) all possible situations *before* the system is released. A strong motivation for this point of view comes from the observation that the world (environment) in which such systems perform is *itself* very seldom static. Designing systems to adapt to such environmental changes rather than requiring manual intervention would seem preferable.

A second bias reflected in the definition of learning given above is the emphasis on *self-modification.* The mental image of an adaptive system is that of a "black box" whose internal state is not directly accessible to anything in its environment, including teachers. Advice or any other form of feedback is presented in terms of an interface language, which must be interpreted and integrated internally by the adaptive system itself.

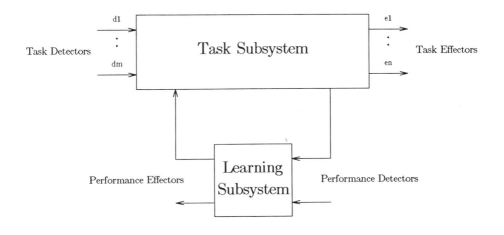

Figure 21–1:   Model of an adaptive system

If one attempts to formalize these ideas, the adaptive system model that generally emerges is an abstraction of an autonomous robot equipped with a fixed set of detectors (sensors) and effectors (operators) presumed to be useful primitives for improving performance in the task domain defined by the environment. As has been the case in other machine learning areas, it is useful (as illustrated in Figure 21–1) to separate out the problem-solving component (whose performance is to be improved) from the learning component, which is charged with finding ways of improving the performance of the problem solver. Notice that both components have detectors and effectors appropriate to their roles.

Since the goal of the learning subsystem is to improve the performance of the problem-solving component, its detectors must provide a means for measuring changes in performance over time. This is typically formalized by breaking performance into two components: internal measurements relating to resources used within the robot to accomplish the task, and external measurements involving task-related aspects such as the number of correct classifications, the final score of a game, etc. Similarly, the effectors of the learning component are separated into internal effectors for making changes to the task subsystem to improve performance and external effectors capable of making changes to the environment needed to activate further evaluation of the task subsystem.

As an example of such an adaptive system, one might consider a rule-based diagnostic expert system as the task subsystem augmented with a learning subsystem that *continually* monitors the performance of the expert system, making changes (when appropriate) to the rule base in an attempt to improve diagnostic performance.

An obvious and important issue is the extent to which domain-specific knowledge must be used in the construction of learning algorithms capable of effecting significant performance improvements. One can easily imagine the two extremes that occur in most areas of AI: very general methods, which have a wide range of applicability but are weak in the sense that they exhibit intolerably slow rates of learning; and very problem-specific techniques, which are capable of achieving highly efficient learning but have little use in other problem domains. The remainder of this chapter will be devoted to exploring a family of learning techniques that fall somewhere in between these two extremes. The power of these learning strategies comes from the use of an intriguing class of adaptive search techniques called *genetic algorithms*, which have been studied since the early 1970s. Section 21.3 provides a brief overview of genetic algorithms and can be skipped by an already informed reader.

21.3 A BRIEF OVERVIEW OF GENETIC ALGORITHMS

Many AI problems can be viewed as searching a space of legal alternatives for the best solution one can find within reasonable time and space limitations. Path planning in robotics and move selection in board games are familiar examples. What is required for such problems are techniques for rapid location of high-quality solutions in search spaces of sufficient size and complexity to rule out any guarantees of optimality. When sufficient knowledge about such search spaces is available *a priori*, one can usually exploit that knowledge to develop problem-specific strategies capable of rapidly locating "satisficing" solutions. If, however, such *a priori* knowledge is unavailable, acceptable solutions are typically only achieved by *dynamically* accumulating information about the problem and using that knowledge to control the search process. Problems of this character are not hard to find. Robot path planning in an unstructured environment and games whose strategies involve identifying and exploiting the characteristics of an opponent are excellent examples. Inferring an acceptable set of classification rules from training examples without a significant amount of domain knowledge is a familiar example from classical machine learning problems.

Problems of this type, which require exploitation of dynamically accumulating knowledge to control the search process, are called *adaptive search problems*. Genetic algorithms are of considerable interest in this context because they represent a reasonably general, yet efficient, family of adaptive search techniques that produce acceptable performance over a broad class of problems.

21.3.1 Adaptive Search Techniques

To motivate the discussion of genetic algorithms, consider for a moment several other strategies one might employ in dealing with combinatorially explosive search spaces about which little can be assumed to be known *a priori*. One approach might be to employ some form of random search. This can be effective if the search space is reasonably dense with acceptable solutions, so that the probability of finding one is reasonably high. However, in most cases such approaches fail to generate acceptable solutions in a reasonable amount of time because they make no use of the accumulating information about the search space to increase the probability of finding acceptable solutions.

An alternative approach is to use some form of hill climbing in which better solutions are found by exploring only those solutions that are "adjacent" to the best found so far. Techniques of this type work well on search spaces with relatively few hills, but they frequently get "stuck" on local peaks that are still below an acceptable level of performance.

One way of attempting to avoid some of these problems is to combine these two strategies in creative ways, such as including some random samples in addition to adjacent points while hill climbing, or restarting hill climbing from a randomly selected point when it appears to be stuck on a local peak. Although such variations frequently improve the robustness of an adaptive search strategy, they still can generate unacceptable performance because of their inability to exploit accumulating *global* information about the search space.

Statistical sampling techniques are typical alternative approaches which emphasize the accumulation and exploitation of more global information. Generally they operate by dividing the space into regions to be sampled. After sufficient sampling, most regions are discarded as unlikely to produce acceptable solutions, and the remaining regions are subdivided for further sampling, resulting in further discarding of regions, and so on. Such strategies are usually successful when the space to be searched can be divided into a reasonable number of useful subregions. They are much less effective when little is known about the appropriate granularity of the subregions, or when the required granularity is so fine that the cost of accumulating the necessary statistics for, say, 100,000 subregions is unacceptable.

Genetic algorithms, introduced initially by Holland [1975], provide an alternative approach to adaptive search problems that has proven to be a robust and effective strategy over a broad range of problems. The power of genetic algorithms comes from the fact that they blend in a natural way elements of random search, hill climbing, and sampling with a fourth important idea: *competition*.

21.3.2 The Anatomy of a Genetic Algorithm

Genetic algorithms (GAs) derive their name from the fact that they are loosely based on models drawn from the area of population genetics. These models were developed to explain how the genetic material in a population of individuals changes over time. The basic elements of these models consisted of: (1) a Darwinian notion of "fitness," which governed the extent to which an individual could influence future generations; (2) the notion of "mating" to produce offspring for the next generation; and (3) the notion of genetic operators, which determine the genetic makeup of offspring from the genetic material of the parents.

These ideas can be used as components of an adaptive search procedure in the following way. Consider each point in the space to be searched as a legal instance of genetic material. Assume that for each such point, a fitness measure can be invoked to assess the quality of the solution it represents. Adaptive searching of the solution space is then achieved by simulating the dynamics of population development as illustrated in Figure 21–2.

The process begins by randomly generating an initial population $M(0)$ of (typically 50–100) individuals whose genetic material represents sample points in the solution space. Each individual m in the population is evaluated by invoking the fitness function **u** to measure the quality of the solution that individual represents. A selection probability distribution **p** is then defined over the current population $M(t)$ as follows: for each individual m in $M(t)$, let

$$p(m) = \frac{u(m)}{\sum_j (m_j)}.$$

Intuitively, this defines a probability distribution in which an individual's chance of being selected, **p**(m), is proportional to its observed fitness **u**(m). Finally, the next generation $M(t + 1)$ is produced by selecting individuals *via the selection probabilities* to produce offspring via genetic operators.

To get a feeling for how GAs work, note that the selection probabilities are defined in such a way that the expected number of offspring produced by an individual is proportional to its associated performance (fitness) value. This can be seen by considering the process of selecting individuals for reproduction as N samples from $M(t)$ with replacement using the selection probabilities. The expected number of offspring from individual mi is given by

$$O(mi) = N * p(m_i) = N * \frac{u(m_i)}{\sum_j u(m_j)} = \frac{u(m_i)}{\frac{1}{N} * \sum_j u(m_j)}$$

which indicates that individuals with average performance ratings produce on the average one offspring, while better individuals produce more than one and below-average individuals less than one. Hence, with no other mechanism for adaptation, reproduction proportional to performance results in a sequence of generations $M(t)$ in which the best individual in $M(0)$ takes over a larger and larger proportion of the population.

However, in nature as well as in these artificial systems, offspring are almost never exact duplicates of a parent. It is the role of genetic operators to exploit the

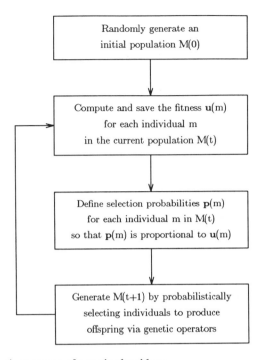

Figure 21–2: Basic structure of genetic algorithms

selection process by producing new individuals with high-performance expectations. The choice of operators is motivated by the primary mechanisms of nature: crossover, mutation, and inversion.

In order to understand how these genetic operators produce high-quality offspring, we need to discuss briefly how points in the solution space S are represented internally as genetic material. The simplest genetic algorithms represent a point in S as a single string of length L taken from some alphabet of symbols. Hence a particular solution s_i in S is represented internally as an individual $m_j = g_{j1}g_{j2} \ldots g_{jL}$ where the symbols g_{jk} play the role of genes. With this simple representation two basic genetic operators are used: crossover and mutation. The crossover operation works as follows. Whenever an individual m_i is selected from the current population M(t) to undergo reproduction, a mate m_j is also selected from M(t). Their offspring m_k is produced by concatenating segments of m_i with segments from m_j. The segments are defined by selecting at random a small number (typically 1 or 2) of crossover points from the L – 1 possible crossover points. Figure 21–3 illustrates how an offspring might be generated using two crossover points.

$m_i = ABCDEFGH$

$\Rightarrow \qquad m_k = ABCdefGH \qquad$ via crossover

$m_j = abcdefgh$

$m_k = ABCdefGH \qquad \Rightarrow \qquad m_l = AyCdefGH \qquad$ via mutation

Figure 21–3:   Simple crossover and mutation operators

Thus, the strategy employed by crossover is to construct new individuals from existing high-performance individuals by recombining subcomponents. Notice, however, that crossover will explore only those subspaces of the search space S which are already represented in M(t). If, for example, every individual in M(t) contains an N in the first gene position, crossover will never generate a new individual with an M (or any other legal gene value) in that position. A subspace may not be represented in M(t) for several reasons. It may have been deleted by selection due to associated poor performance. It may also be missing because of the limited size of M(t). In the basic GAs this problem is resolved via the second genetic operator: *mutation.*

The mutation operator generates a new individual by independently modifying one or more of the gene values of an existing individual as illustrated in Figure 21–3. In nature as well as these artificial systems, the probability of a gene undergoing a mutation is less than .001, suggesting that it is not a primary genetic operator. Rather, it serves to guarantee that the probability of searching a particular subspace of S is never zero.

21.3.3 An Analysis of Genetic Algorithms

The behavior of GAs has been formally analyzed in a variety of ways (see, for example, [Holland, 1975; De Jong, 1975; or Bethke, 1980]). The intent here is to provide the reader with a brief, intuitive idea of how GAs adaptively search large, complex spaces in a relatively efficient manner.

A good way to get a feeling for the dynamics of the search process is to focus attention on certain groups of hyperplanes defined over the internal string representation of the search space. For simplicity of notation, assume that each point S is uniquely represented by a binary string of length L. Let 0 # # ... # denote the set of points in S whose binary string representation begins with a 0. Since we are focusing on only one position in the string (in this case the first position), 0 # # ... # is called a first-order hyperplane, and it contains exactly one-half of the points in S. The hyperplane 1 # # ... # contains the remaining points; and together, they define a first-order *partition* of S. Of course, we could just as well have focused on any other position on the string and derived another first-order partition of S (for example, # 0 # ... # and # 1 # ... #). Similarly, one can study second-order partitions of S by fixing two of the string positions such as {00 # ... #, 01 # ... #, 10 # ... #, 11 # ... #}. In general, if the binary strings are of length L, there are

$$\binom{L}{N}$$

distinct Nth-order partitions of S.

The characterization of GAs can now be intuitively stated as follows: For any reasonably low-order hyperplane partition of S, GAs use their population M(t) of samples from S to bias subsequent search toward hyperplanes in the partition with higher expected payoff in terms of the fitness measure **u**. The power of this approach (this heuristic, if you like) is that this dynamic shifting of search occurs *simultaneously* in all low-order hyperplane partitions of S. As the search proceeds, the population M(t) reflects this bias in the sense that members of M(t) increasingly share common substrings. This growing homogeneity of M(t) indicates a reduction in the scope of the search (a focus of attention) toward high-payoff hyperplanes. As this homogeneity increases, certain positions on the strings become fixed throughout the entire population M(t). This has the effect of reducing higher order partitions into lower order ones which, in turn, are now subject to the same payoff bias, resulting in a further reduction in the scope of the search, and so on.

The overall effect is to produce a search technique which rapidly adapts to the characteristics of S as defined by **u** in order to home-in on high-performance objects in S. Figure 21–4 provides a simple way to visualize this adaptive search strategy on a solution space S whose performance measure **u** defines hilly surface over S.

The important point here is that GAs make no *a priori* assumptions about the characteristics of this surface. Rather, the initial population consists of a random sample of solution points in S. Using the performance feedback provided by **u**, subsequent generations "home-in" on the high-performance regions of S.

Note that, although our discussion here has been confined to simple, fixed-length string representations of the solution space and to the simplest forms of genetic operators, similar analyses have been done for other genetic operators and more complex representations of S. These characterizations of GAs are supported by a large body of experimental work in which GAs have been applied to a broad range of problems including difficult global function optimization problems, NP-hard problems, and model-fitting problems. An excellent coverage of these activities is provided in the proceedings of the Genetic Algorithms Conferences [Grefenstette, 1985; 1987; and Schaffer, 1989]. However, our interest here is in exploring how GAs can be used to design systems that learn. The remainder of the chapter addresses this issue.

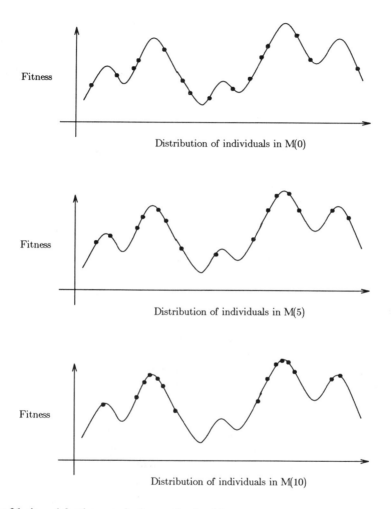

Figure 21–4: Adaptive search via genetic algorithms

21.4 USING GAs FOR MACHINE LEARNING

We can begin to conceptualize how one might exploit the power of GAs in a learning system by referring back to the architecture of an adaptive system illustrated in Figure 21–1. By clearly separating out the task component from the learning component, one can focus on the ways in which the learning component can effect changes in the behavior of the task subsystem to improve performance over time.

In considering what kinds of changes might be made to the task component, there are a variety of strategies for increasing sophistication and complexity. The simplest and most straightforward approach is to have GAs make changes to a set of parameters that control the behavior of a predeveloped, parameterized task program. A second and more interesting approach is to make changes to more complex data structures, such as "agendas," which control the behavior of the task subsystem. A third, intriguing but difficult approach is to make changes to the task program itself. Each of these possibilities is explored in more detail in the following sections.

21.4.1 Changing Parameters

The primary advantage of this approach to effecting behavioral changes is that it immediately places us on the familiar terrain of parameter optimization problems for which there is considerable understanding and guidance, and for which the simplest forms of GAs can be used. At first glance, it is easy to discard this approach as trivial and not at all representative of what is meant by "learning." But note that significant behavioral changes can be achieved within this simple framework. Samuel's checker player is a striking example of the power of such an approach. If one views the adjustable weights and thresholds as parameters of a structurally fixed neural network, then much of the neural net learning research also falls into this category.

So, how does one use GAs to quickly and efficiently search parameter spaces for combinations of parameters that improve the performance of the task subsystem? The simplest and most intuitive approach is to think of the parameters as genes and the genetic material of individuals as a fixed-length string of genes, one for each parameter. Then crossover generates new parameter combinations from existing good combinations in the current database (population) and mutation provides new parameter values.

There is a good deal of experimental and theoretical evidence to support the surprising rate at which GAs can home-in on high-performance parameter combinations (see, for example, [De Jong, 1975; Brindle, 1980; or Grefenstette, 1985a]). Typically, even for large search spaces (e.g., 10^{30} points), acceptable combinations are being found after only 10 simulated generations. To be fair, however, there are several issues that can catch a GA practitioner off-guard when attacking a particular parameter modification problem.

The first issue has to do with the number of distinct values genes can have. With population sizes generally in the 50 to 100 range, a given population can usually represent only a small fraction of the possible gene values. Since the only way of generating new gene values is via mutation, one can be faced with the following dilemma: If the mutation rate is too low, there can be insufficient global sampling to prevent premature convergence to local peaks. However, by significantly increasing the rate of mutation one reverts to a form of random search, which decreases the probability that new individuals will have high performance. Fortunately, this problem has both a theoretical and a practical solution, although it is not usually obvious to the casual reader.

Holland [1975] has provided an analysis of GAs which suggests that they are most effective when the number of values a gene can take on is small and that binary (two-valued) genes are in some sense optimal for GA-style adaptive search. This theoretical result translates rather naturally into what has now become standard practice in the GA community. Rather than representing a 20-parameter problem internally as strings of 20 genes (with each gene taking on many values), a binary string representation is chosen in which parameters are represented as *groups* of binary-valued genes. Although the two spaces are equivalent in that they both represent the same parameter space, GAs perform significantly better on the binary representation because, in addition to mutation, crossover is now generating new parameter values each time it combines part of a parameter's bits from one parent with those of another.

The easiest way to illustrate this point is to imagine the extreme case of a system in which there is only one parameter to be adjusted, but that parameter can take on 2^{30} distinct values. Representing this problem internally as a 1-gene problem renders crossover useless and leaves mutation as the only mechanism for generating new individuals. However, by choosing a 30-gene binary representation, crossover plays an active and crucial role in generating new parameter values with high-performance expectations.

A second issue that arises in this context is that of convergence to a global optimum. Can we guarantee or expect with high probability that GAs will find the undisputed best combination of parameter settings for a particular problem? The answer is "yes and no"! One can show theoretically that every point in the search space has a nonzero probability of being sampled. However, for most problems of interest, the search space is so large as to make it impractical to wait long enough for guaranteed global optima. A much better way to view GAs is as a powerful sampling heuristic that can rapidly find high-quality solutions in large complex spaces.

In summary, one effective approach to machine learning is to restrict the kinds of changes that the learning component can make to a task program to that of parameter modification, and use GAs to quickly locate useful combinations of parameter values. The interested reader can see [De Jong, 1980] or [Grefenstette, 1985a] for more detailed examples of this approach.

21.4.2 Changing Data Structures

However, there are many problems for which such a simple approach is inappropriate in the sense that "more significant" structural changes to task programs seem to be required. Frequently in these situations a more complex data structure is intimately involved in controlling the behavior of the task, and so the most natural approach is to have GAs make changes to these key structures. A good example of problems of this type occur when the task systems, whose behavior is to be modified, are designed with top-level "agenda" control mechanisms. Task programs for traveling salesman problems, bin packing, and scheduling problems are frequently organized in this manner as are systems driven by decision trees. In this context GAs are expected to select data structures to be tested, evaluated, and subsequently used to fabricate better ones.

This approach at first glance may not seem to introduce any difficulties as far as using GAs, since it is usually not hard to "linearize" these data structures, map them into a string representation that can be manipulated by GAs, and then reverse the process to produce new data structures for evaluation. However, there are some issues here with which the designer of a learning system must be familiar in order to make effective use of GAs.

Just as we saw in the previous section on searching parameter spaces, these issues center around the way in which the space (in this case, a space of data structures) to be searched is represented internally for manipulation by GAs. It is not difficult to invent internal string representations for agendas and other complex data structures that have the following property: Almost every new structure produced by the standard crossover and mutation operators is an internal representation of an *illegal* data structure!

My favorite example of this is to consider how one might use GAs to quickly find good agendas (tours) for a traveling salesman who needs to visit each of N cities exactly once, minimizing the distance traveled. The most straightforward approach would be to internally represent a tour as N genes and the value of each gene is the name of the next city to be visited. Notice, however, that using the standard crossover and mutation operators, GAs will explore the space of all *combinations* of city names when, in fact, it is the space of all *permutations* which is of interest. The obvious problem is that as N increases, the space of permutations is a vanishingly small subset of the space of combinations, and the powerful GA sampling heuristic has been rendered impotent by a poor choice of representation.

Fortunately, a sensitivity to this issue is usually sufficient to avoid it in one of several ways. One approach is to design an alternative representation for the same space for which the traditional genetic operators are appropriate. This has been done for a variety of problems of this type including the traveling salesman problem (see, for example, [Grefenstette, 1985b; Goldberg, 1985b; or Davis, 1985]).

An equally useful alternative is to select different genetic operators that are more appropriate to "natural representations." For example, in the case of traveling salesman problems, a genetic-like inversion operator (which can be viewed as a particular kind of permutation operator) is clearly a more "natural" operator. Similarly, representation-sensitive crossover and mutation operators can be defined to ensure offspring representing legal points in the solution space.

The key point to be made here is that there is nothing sacred about the traditional string-oriented genetic operators. The mathematical analysis of GAs indicates that they work best when the internal representation encourages the emergence of useful building blocks that can be subsequently combined with others to produce improved performance. String representations are just one of many ways of achieving this.

21.4.3 Changing Executable Code

Perhaps by now the reader is ready to reply that neither of the approaches just discussed "really" involves learning. Rather, the reader has in mind the ability to effect behavioral changes in the task system by making changes to the task program itself. I'm not sure that there is anything fundamentally different between interpreting an agenda and executing a Pascal program. However, I think that most everyone will agree that, in general, program spaces are very large and complex. In any case, there is good deal of interest in designing systems that learn at this level. The remainder of the chapter will discuss how GAs are used in such systems.

21.4.3.1 Choosing a Programming Language

It is quite reasonable to view programs written in conventional languages like FORTRAN and Pascal (or even less conventional languages like LISP and PROLOG) as linear strings of symbols. This is certainly the way they are treated by editors and compilers in current program-development environments. However, it is also quite obvious that this "natural" representation is a disastrous one as far as traditional GAs are concerned, since standard operators like crossover and mutation seldom produce syntactically correct programs and, of those, even fewer that are semantically correct.

One alternative is to attempt to devise new, language-specific, "genetic" operators that preserve at least the syntactic (and hopefully, the semantic) integrity of the programs being manipulated. Unfortunately, the complexity of both the syntax and semantics of traditional languages makes it difficult to develop such operators. An obvious next step would be to focus on less traditional languages, such as "pure" LISP, whose syntax and semantics are much simpler, leaving open the hope of developing reasonable genetic operators with the required properties. There have been a number of activities in this area (see, for example, [Fujiko, 1987] or [Koza, 1989]).

However, there is at least one important feature that "pure" LISP shares with other more traditional languages: They are all procedural in nature. As a consequence most reasonable representations have the kinds of properties that cause considerable difficulty in GA applications. The two most obvious representation problems are order dependencies (interchanging two lines of code can render a program meaningless) and context-sensitive interpretations (the entire meaning of a section of code can be changed by minor changes to preceding code, such as the insertion or deletion of a punctuation symbol). A more detailed discussion of these representation problems is presented in [De Jong, 1985].

These issues are not new and were anticipated by Holland to the extent that he proposed a family of languages called *classifier languages*, which were designed to overcome the kinds of problems being raised here [Holland, 1975]. What is perhaps a bit surprising is that these classifier languages are members of a broader class of languages that continues to reassert its usefulness across a broad range of activities (from compiler design to expert systems); namely, production systems (PSs) or rule-based systems. As a consequence, a good deal of time and effort has gone into studying this class of languages as a suitable language for use in evolving task programs with GAs.

21.4.3.2 Learning PS Programs

One of the reasons that production systems have been and continue to be a favorite programming paradigm in both the expert system and machine learning communities is that PSs provide a representation of knowledge that can *simultaneously* support two kinds of activities: 1) treating knowledge as data to be manipulated as part of a knowledge acquisition and refinement process, and 2) treating knowledge as an "executable" entity to be used to perform a particular task (see, for example, [Newell, 1977; Buchanan, 1978; or Hedrick, 1976]). This is particularly true of the "data-driven" forms of PSs (such as OPS5) in which the production rules that make up a PS program are treated as an unordered set of rules whose "left-hand sides" are all independently and in parallel monitoring changes in "the environment."

It should be obvious that this same programming paradigm offers significant advantages for GA applications and, in fact, has precisely the same characteristics as Holland's early classifier languages. If we focus then on PSs whose programs consist of unordered collections (sets) of rules, we can then ask how GAs can be used to search the space of PS programs for useful rulesets.

To anyone who has read Holland's book [Holland, 1975], the most obvious and "natural" way to proceed is to represent an entire ruleset as a string (individual), maintain a population of candidate rulesets, and use selection and genetic operators to produce new generations of rulesets. Historically, this was the approach taken by De Jong and his students while at the University of Pittsburgh (see, for example, [Smith, 1980 or 1983]) and has been dubbed "the Pitt approach."

However, during that same time, Holland developed a model of cognition (*classifier systems*) in which each member of the population represents a rule, and the entire population corresponds to a single ruleset (see, for example, [Holland, 1978] and [Booker, 1982]). This quickly became known as "the Michigan approach" and initiated a continuing (friendly, but provocative) series of discussions concerning the strengths and weaknesses of the two approaches.

21.4.3.2.1 The Pitt Approach

If we adopt the view that each individual in a GA population represents an *entire* PS program, there are several issues that must be addressed. The first is the (by now familiar) choice of representation. The most immediate "natural" representation that comes to mind is to regard individual rules as genes, and entire programs as strings of these genes. Then, crossover serves to provide new combinations of rules and mutation provides new rules. Notice, however, that we have chosen a representation in which genes can take on many values. As discussed in the previous section on parameter modification, this can result in premature convergence when population sizes are typically 50 to 100. Since individuals represent entire PS programs, it is unlikely that one can afford to increase significantly the size of the population. Nor, as we have seen, does it help to increase the rate of mutation. Rather, we need to move toward an internal, binary representation of the space of PS programs so that crossover is also involved in constructing new rules from parts of existing rules.

If we go directly to a binary representation, we must now exercise care that crossover and mutation are appropriate operators in the sense in that they produce new high-potential individuals from existing ones. The simplest way to guarantee this is to assume that all rules have a fixed-length, fixed-field format. Although this may seem restrictive in comparison with the flexibility and variability of OPS5 or MYCIN rules, it has proven to be quite adequate when working at a lower sensory level. At this level, one typically has a fixed number of detectors and effectors, so that condition-action rules quite naturally take the form of a fixed number of detector patterns to be matched together with the appropriate action. Many of the successful classifier systems make this assumption (see, for example, [Wilson, 1985] or [Goldberg, 1985a; 1989]).

It is not difficult, however, to relax this assumption and allow more flexible rulesets without subverting the power of the genetic operators. This is achieved by making the operators "representation sensitive" in the sense that they no longer make arbitrary changes to linear bit strings. Rather, the internal representation is extended to provide "punctuation marks" so that meaningful changes are made. For example, if the crossover operator chooses to break parent 1 on a rule boundary, it also breaks parent 2 on a rule boundary, and so on. This is the approach used successfully on the LS systems of Smith [1983] and Schaffer [1985].

A second representation-related issue that arises in the Pitt approach has to do with the number of rules in a ruleset. If we think of rulesets as programs or knowledge bases, it seems rather silly and artificial to demand that all rulesets be the same size. Historically, however, all of the analytical results and most of the experimental work was done with GAs that maintained populations of fixed-length strings.

One can adopt the same view using the Pitt approach and require all rulesets (strings) to be the same fixed length. The justification is usually in terms of the advantages of having redundant copies of rules and having "workspace" within a ruleset for new, experimental building blocks without having to necessarily replace existing ones. However, Smith [1980] was able to show that the formal results could indeed be extended to variable-length strings. He complemented those results with a GA implementation that maintained a population of variable-length strings and efficiently generated variable-length rulesets for a variety of tasks. One of the interesting side issues of this work was the effectiveness of providing via feedback an "incentive" to keep down the size of the rulesets by including a "bonus" for achieving the same level of performance with a shorter string.

With these issues resolved, GAs have been shown to be surprisingly effective in producing nontrivial rulesets for such diverse tasks as solving maze problems, playing poker, and gait classification. The interested reader can see, for example, [Smith, 1983] or [Schaffer, 1985] for more details.

21.4.3.2.2 The Michigan Approach

A quite different approach to learning PS programs was developed by Holland and his colleagues while working on computational models of cognition. In this context, it seemed natural to view the knowledge (experience) of a particular person (cognitive entity) as a collection of rules that are modified over time via interaction with one's environment. Unlike genetic material, this kind of knowledge doesn't evolve over generations via selection and mating. Rather, it accumulates "in real time" as individuals struggle to cope with their environment. Out of this perspective came a family of cognitive models called *classifier systems* in which *rules* rather than *rulesets* are the internal entities manipulated by GAs. There are excellent descriptions of this approach in *Machine Learning, Volume II* [Holland, 1986] and in Goldberg's recent book [Goldberg, 1989]. Wilson and Goldberg [Wilson, 1989] also provide an excellent critical review of the classifier approach. So, the details of classifier systems need not be repeated here. Instead, I want to focus on how these two approaches differ.

I think it is fair to say that most people who encounter classifier systems *after* becoming familiar with the traditional GA literature are somewhat surprised at the emergence of the rather elaborate "bucket brigade" mechanism to deal with apportionment of credit issues. In the traditional genetic view, apportionment of credit is handled via the emergence of "coadapted" sets of gene values in the population. The idea is that combinations of gene values that work well together have a higher than average likelihood of being represented in subsequent generations. As the frequency of a particular combination increases, it is also less likely that this set will be broken up via crossover since it is clearly the case that, if both parents have a coadapted set, so will any offspring produced by crossover. Intuitively, these initially emerging coadapted sets get combined with other sets, forming larger sets with improved performance, which replace inferior ones, and so on.

If we now reinterpret these ideas in the context of PS programs, the process of interest is the emergence of coadapted sets of *rules*. Because the Pitt approach maps *entire* PS programs into strings, one gets this coadaptation mechanism "for free." One can observe over time the emergence in the population of above-average rulesets, which combine with other sets of rules to form larger rulesets with improved performance. Because in classifier systems the population represents a single PS program, coadapted sets of rules must emerge from some other mechanism, namely the bucket brigade.

Which approach is better in the sense of being more effective in evolving PS programs? It is too early to tell what the answer might be or even if the question is a valid one. There are equally impressive examples of classifier systems that have solved problems involving the regulation of gas flow through pipe lines [Goldberg, 1985a; 1989], controlling vision systems [Wilson, 1985], and inferring Boolean functions [Wilson, 1987]. The current popular view is that the classifier approach will prove to be most useful in on-line, real-time environments in which radical changes in behavior cannot be tolerated; whereas the Pitt approach will be useful with off-line environments in which more leisurely exploration and more radical behavioral changes are acceptable.

What I find exciting and provocative is that there are some recent developments suggesting that it might be possible to combine the two approaches in powerful and interesting ways [Grefenstette, 1988; 1989].

21.4.3.3 PS Architecture Issues

So far we have been focusing on representation issues in an attempt to understand how GAs can be used to learn PS programs. The only constraint on production system architectures that has emerged so far is the observation that GAs are much more effective on PS programs that consist of unordered rules. In this section, I will attempt to summarize any other implications that the use of GAs might have on PS architectural decisions.

21.4.3.3.1 The Left-Hand Side of Rules

Many of the rule-based expert system paradigms (e.g., MYCIN-like shells) and most traditional programming languages provide an IF-THEN format in which the left-hand side is a Boolean expression to be evaluated. This Boolean sublanguage can itself become quite complex syntactically and can raise many of the representation issues discussed earlier. In particular, variable-length expressions, varying types of operators and operands, and function invocations make it difficult to choose a representation in which the traditional string-oriented genetic operators are useful. However, genetic operators that "know about" the syntax of the Boolean sublanguage can be developed and have been shown to be effective in producing high-level (symbolic) rulesets. The Samuel system [Grefenstette, 1989] is an excellent example of this approach.

An alternative approach used in languages like OPS5 and SNOBOL is to express the "conditions" of the left-hand side as patterns to be matched. Unfortunately, the pattern language used can easily be as complex as Boolean expressions and in many cases more complex because of the additional need to "save" objects being matched for later use in the pattern or on the right-hand side.

As we have seen, the GA implementor must temper the style and complexity of the left-hand side with the need for an effective internal representation. As a consequence, most implementations have followed Holland's lead and have chosen the simple {0, 1, #} fixed-length pattern language, which permits a relatively direct application of traditional genetic operators. Combined with internal working memory, such languages can be shown to be computationally complete. However, this choice is not without problems. The rigid fixed-length nature of the patterns can lead to very complex and "creative" representations of the objects to be matched. Simple relationships like "speed > 200" may require multiple rule firings and internal memory in order to be correctly evaluated. As discussed earlier, some of this rigidity can be alleviated by the use of context-sensitive genetic operators [Smith, 1983]. However, finding a more pleasing compromise between simplicity and expressive power of the left-hand sides of rules is an active and open area of research.

A favorite cognitive motivation for preferring pattern matching over Boolean expressions is the feeling that "partial matching" is one of the powerful mechanisms that humans use to deal with the enormous variety of everyday life. The observation is that we are seldom in precisely the same situation twice, but we manage to function reasonably well by noting a given situation's similarity to previous experience.

This has led to some interesting discussions as to how "similarity" can be captured computationally in a natural and efficient way. Holland and other advocates of the {0, 1, #} paradigm argue that this is precisely the role that the "#" plays as patterns evolve to their appropriate level of generality. Booker and others have felt that requiring perfect matches *even* with the {0, 1, #} pattern language is still too strong and rigid a requirement, particularly as the length of the left-hand side pattern increases. They feel that the pattern matcher should return a "match score" indicating how close the pattern came to matching, rather than returning simply success or failure. An important issue here that needs to be understood better is how one computes match scores in a reasonably general, but computationally efficient manner. The interested reader can see [Booker, 1985] for more details.

21.4.3.3.2 Working Memory

Another PS architectural issue revolves around the decision whether to use "stimulus-response" production systems in which left-hand sides only "attend to" external events and right-hand sides consist only of invocations of external "effectors," or whether to use the more general OPS5 model in which rules can also attend to and make changes to an internal working memory.

Arguments in favor of the latter approach involve the observation that the addition of working memory provides a more powerful computational engine, which is frequently required with fixed-length rule formats. The strength of this argument can be weakened somewhat by noting that in some cases the external environment *itself* can be used as working memory.

Arguments against including working memory generally fall along the lines of: (1) the application doesn't need the additional generality and complexity; (2) concerns about how one bounds the number of internal actions before generating the next external action (i.e., the halting problem); or (3) pointing out that most of the more traditional machine learning work in this area (e.g., [Michalski, 1983]) has focused on stimulus-response models.

Most of the implementations of working memory provide a restricted form of internal memory, namely, a fixed-format, bounded-capacity message list [Holland, 1978; Booker, 1982]. However, it's clear that there are plenty of uses for both architectures. The important point here is that this choice is not imposed on us by GAs.

21.4.3.3.3 Parallelism

Another side benefit of PSs with working memory is that they can be easily extended to allow parallel rule firings. In principle, the only time conflict resolution (serialization) needs to occur is when an "external effector" is to be activated. Hence, permitting parallel firing of rules invoking internal actions is a natural way to extend PS architectures in order to exploit the power of parallelism. Whether this power is appropriate for a particular application is of course up to the implementor. An excellent example of a parallel implementation can be found in [Robertson, 1988; 1989].

21.4.3.4 The Role of Feedback

So far, in attempting to understand how GAs can be used to learn PS programs, we have discussed how PS programs can be represented and what kinds of PS architectures can be used to exploit the power of GAs. In this section we focus on a third issue: the role of feedback.

Recall that the intuitive view of how GAs search large, complex spaces is via a sampling strategy that is adaptive in the sense that feedback from current samples is used to bias subsequent sampling into regions with high expected performance. This means that, even though we have chosen a good representation and have selected an appropriate PS architecture, the effectiveness of GAs in learning PS programs will also depend on the usefulness of the information obtained via feedback. Since the designer typically has a good deal of freedom here, it is important that the feedback mechanism be chosen to facilitate this adaptive search strategy.

Fortunately, there is a family of feedback mechanisms which is both simple to use and which experience has shown to be very effective: *payoff functions*. This form of feedback uses a classical "reward-and-punishment" scheme in which performance evaluation is expressed in terms of a payoff value. GAs can use this information (almost) directly to bias the selection of parents used to produce new samples (offspring). Of course, not all payoff functions are equally useful in this role. It is important that the function chosen provide useful information early in the search process to help focus the search. For example, a payoff function that is zero almost everywhere provides almost no information for reducing the scope of search process.

The way in which payoff is obtained differs somewhat depending on whether one is using the Pitt or the Michigan approach. In classifier systems the bucket brigade mechanism stands ready to distribute payoff to those *rules* that are deemed responsible for achieving that payoff. Because payoff is the currency of the bucket brigade economy, it is important to design a feedback mechanism that provides a relatively steady flow of payoff rather than one in which there are long "dry spells." Wilson's "animat" environment is an excellent example of this style of payoff [Wilson, 1985].

The situation is somewhat different in the Pitt approach in that the usual view of evaluation consists of injecting the PS program defined by a particular individual into the task subsystem and evaluating how well that program *as a whole* performed. This view can lead to some interesting considerations such as whether to reward programs that perform tasks as well as others but use less space (rules) or time (rule firings). Smith [1980] found it quite useful to break up the payoff function into two components: a task-specific evaluation and a task-independent measure of the program itself. Although these two components were combined into a single payoff value, work by Schaffer [1985] suggests that it might be more effective to use a vector-valued payoff function in situations such as this.

There is still a good deal to be learned about the role of feedback from both an analytical and an empirical point of view. Bethke [1980] has used Walsh transforms as the basis for a formal understanding of the kind of feedback information best suited for GA-style adaptive search. Recent experimental work suggests that it may be possible to combine aspects of both the Michigan and Pitt approaches via a multilevel credit assignment strategy, which assigns payoff to rulesets as well as individual rules [Grefenstette, 1988; 1989]. This is an interesting idea that will generate a good deal of discussion and merits further attention.

21.4.3.5 The Use of Domain Knowledge

It is conventional to view GAs as "weak" search methods in the sense that they can be applied without requiring any knowledge of the space being searched. However, a more accurate view is that, although no domain knowledge is required, there are ample opportunities to exploit domain knowledge if it is available. We have already seen a few examples of how domain knowledge can be used. As designers, we select the space to be searched and the internal representation to be used by GAs. As discussed in the previous sections, such decisions require knowledge about both the problem domain and the characteristics of GAs. Closely related to representation decisions is the choice of genetic operators to be used. As we have seen, a good deal of domain knowledge can go into the selection of effective operators. Grefenstette [1987b] has an excellent discussion of this.

A more direct example of the use of domain knowledge involves the choice of the initial population used to start the search process. Although we have described this as a "random" initial population, there is no reason to start with a "blank slate" if there is *a priori* information available that permits the seeding of the initial population with individuals known to have certain kinds or levels of performance.

A third and perhaps the most obvious way of exploiting domain knowledge is by means of the feedback mechanism. As we have seen, the effectiveness of GAs depends on the usefulness of the feedback information provided. Even the simplest form of feedback, namely payoff-only systems, can and frequently does use domain knowledge to design an effective payoff function. More elaborate forms of feedback such as the vector-valued strategies and multilevel feedback mechanisms discussed above provide additional opportunities to incorporate domain-specific knowledge.

In practice, then, we see a variety of scenarios ranging from the use of "vanilla" GAs, with little or no domain-specific modifications, to highly creative applications, in which a good deal of domain knowledge has been used.

21.5 AN EXAMPLE: THE LS-1 FAMILY

In the previous section we described three broad classes of techniques for designing genetic-algorithm-based learning (GABL) systems. A common theme throughout that discussion was the representation issue: choosing a representation of the space to be searched that is both natural to the application and appropriate for GAs. In this section, we illustrate these ideas by presenting in more detail one particular family of GABL systems, the LS-1 family [Smith, 1980; 1983], which has been successfully applied to a wide variety of task domains.

LS-1 systems are designed to allow entire task programs to be learned. An LS-1 system consists of three basic components: a task subsystem, a critic, and a learning subsystem. The task subsystem is equipped with a fixed set of detectors (sensors) and effectors (actions) assumed to be useful for the task to be learned. Task programs consist of production rules whose left-hand sides represent patterns to be matched against the current contents of working memory and the current external detector values. The right-hand sides specify one of two types of actions to be taken: changes to working memory or activating an external effector. An execution cycle consists of firing *in parallel all* rules whose left-hand side matches something in working memory. Conflict resolution is only performed when, on a given execution cycle, more than one request is made to activate an external effector. Conceptually, task programs have a strong OPS5-like flavor (unordered, forward chaining, pattern matching) without the restriction that only one rule can fire each cycle.

If we want to use GAs to evolve these rule-based task programs, we must choose an internal representation of the space to be searched. LS-1 uses the Pitt approach in which each individual in a GA population represents an entire task program and, hence, a given population represents (typically 50–100) competing task programs. Each task program is submitted to the critic subsystem which, in turn, injects the task program into the task subsystem and evaluates the "fitness" of the task program by observing its behavior on a series of tasks. After the entire population of task programs has been evaluated, a new generation of task programs is created by probabilistically selecting parents on the basis of fitness, and using crossover, inversion, and mutation to produce offspring that are "interesting" variants of their parents.

As discussed in the previous section, there are two ways of guaranteeing that the genetic operators produce viable offspring: (1) by building specific language and domain knowledge into the operators so that crossover, mutation, and inversion produce only syntactically and semantically correct rulesets; or (2) restricting the language so that the standard operators preserve syntactic and semantic integrity. LS-1 adopts the latter strategy, preferring to buy more domain independence at the cost of a less flexible language. It achieves this by requiring that every rule have an identical, fixed-length format as follows:

$$pd1 \ pd2 \ ... \ pdn \ pw1 \ pw2 \ ... \ pwm \rightarrow some\_action$$

where the pdi represent patterns to be matched against the n external detector values, and the pwj represent m patterns to be matched against the contents of working memory. LS-1 uses Holland's $\{0, 1, \#\}$ pattern language, so that the length of a particular pattern is determined by the binary representation of the objects to be matched. So, for example, the following rules:

	pd1	pd2	pw1	action
R1:	00#	#111##	1#1#01##→	010
R2: 1	## 0011	# ##110##0→		110

might represent a situation in which the first pattern of each matches a 3-bit detector, the second pattern matches a 5-bit detector, the third pattern matches 8-bit working memory cells, and the right-hand side selects one of eight possible actions.

A ruleset is therefore represented internally as a variable-length string of fixed-length rules. The important point is that the standard crossover and mutation operators always produce viable offspring. If we restrict inversion to occur only at rule boundaries, the same is is true for it.

So, how does one apply LS-1 to a particular task domain? First, the number and sizes of each external detector must be chosen (analogous to selecting feature vectors) and the set of legal operations (effectors) must be specified. Second, the number of internal detectors and actions on working memory must be specified (no internal activity corresponds to a stimulus-response system). Finally, a domain-specific critic must be developed to provide fitness feedback for each ruleset generated during the learning process.

What is surprising is that, even though LS-1 assumes a fairly rigid rule format, there is considerable empirical evidence of its robustness in rapidly generating high-performance rulesets (task programs) for problem domains as diverse as maze puzzles, poker playing, human gait classification, VLSI layout problems, and network scheduling.

21.6 SUMMARY AND CONCLUSIONS

The goal of this chapter has been to understand how GAs might be used to design systems capable of learning. The approach has been to visualize learning systems as consisting of two components: a task subsystem, whose behavior is to be modified over time via learning; and a learning subsystem, whose job is to observe the task subsystem over time and effect the desired behavioral changes. This perspective focuses attention on the kinds of *structural* changes a learning subsystem might possibly make to a task subsystem in order to effect *behavioral* changes. Three classes of structural changes of increasing complexity were identified: parameter modification, data structure manipulation, and changes to executable code.

Having characterized learning in this way, we can restate the problem as one of searching the space of legal structural changes for instances that achieve the desired behavioral changes. In domains for which there is a strong theory to guide this search, it would be silly not to exploit such knowledge. However, there are many domains in which uncertainty and ignorance preclude such approaches and require learning algorithms to discover (infer) the important characteristics of these search spaces *while* the search is in progress. This is the context in which GAs are most effective. Without requiring a significant amount of domain knowledge, GAs have been used to rapidly search spaces from each of the categories listed above.

At the same time it is important to understand the limitations of such an approach. In most cases several thousand samples must be taken from the search space before high-quality solutions are found. Clearly, there are many domains in which such a large number of samples is out of the question. At the same time, generating several thousand examples can frequently involve much less effort than building "by hand" a sufficiently strong domain theory. It is also true that choosing a good internal representation for the search space to tends to be a more difficult task as the complexity of the search space increases, thus reducing the effectiveness of GAs. Finally, even with a good internal representation, care must be taken to provide an effective feedback mechanism. If, for example, the only feedback about a task program is "yes, it works" or "no, it fails," there is no information about the quality of partial solutions on which GAs depend to construct new trial solutions.

Hence, GABL should be viewed as another tool for the designer of learning systems, which, like other more familiar tools such as similarity-based techniques and explanation-based approaches, is not the answer to all learning problems but provides an effective strategy for specific kinds of situations.

References

Bethke, A. 1980. *Genetic Algorithms as Function Optimizers*, Doctoral Thesis, CCS Department, University of Michigan, Ann Arbor, MI.

Booker, L.B. 1982. *Intelligent Behavior as an Adaptation to the Task Environment.* Doctoral Thesis, CCS Department, University of Michigan, Ann Arbor, MI.

————, 1985. Improving the Performance of Genetic Algorithms in Classifier Systems. *Proc. First Int'l Conference on Genetic Algorithms and Their Applications* (pp. 80–92). Pittsburgh, PA.

Brindle, A. 1980. *Genetic Algorithms for Function Optimization*, Doctoral Thesis, Department of Computing Science, University of Alberta, Alberta, Canada.

Buchanan, B. and Mitchell, T.M. 1978. Model-directed Learning of Production Rules. *Pattern-directed Inference Systems*, Waterman, D. and Hayes-Roth, F. (Eds.), Academic Press.

Davis, L.D. 1985. Job Shop Scheduling Using Genetic Algorithms. *Proc. First Int'l Conference on Genetic Algorithms and Their Applications* (pp. 136–140). Pittsburgh, PA.

De Jong, K. 1975. *An Analysis of the Behavior of a Class of Genetic Adaptive Systems.* Doctoral Thesis, CCS Department, University of Michigan, Ann Arbor, MI.

————, 1980. Adaptive System Design: A Genetic Approach. *IEEE Trans. on Systems, Man, and Cybernetics* (pp. 556–574), Vol. 10, #9.

————, 1985. Genetic Algorithms: A 10 Year Perspective. *Proc. First Int'l Conference on Genetic Algorithms and Their Applications* (pp. 169–177). Pittsburgh, PA.

———— , 1987. On Using Genetic Algorithms to Search Program Spaces. *Proc. Second Int' l Conference on Genetic Algorithms and Their Applications* (pp. 169–177). Cambridge, MA.

Fujiko, C. and Dickinson, J. 1987. Using the Genetic Algorithm to Generate LISP Code to Solve the Prisoner's Dilemma. *Proc. Second Int' l Conference on Genetic Algorithms and Their Applications* (pp. 236–240). Cambridge, MA.

Goldberg, D. 1985a. Genetic Algorithms and Rule Learning in Dynamic System Control. *Proc. First Int' l Conference on Genetic Algorithms and Their Applications* (pp. 8–15). Pittsburgh, PA.

Goldberg, D. and Lingle, R. 1985b. Alleles, Loci, and the Traveling Salesman Problem. *Proc. First Int' l Conference on Genetic Algorithms and Their Applications* (pp. 154–159). Pittsburgh, PA.

Goldberg, D. 1989. *Genetic Algorithms in Search, Optimization, and Machine Learning*. Addison-Wesley Publishing.

Grefenstette, J. 1985a. Optimization of Control Parameters for Genetic Algorithms. *IEEE Trans. on Systems, Man, and Cybernetics* (pp. 122–128), Vol. 16, #1.

Grefenstette, J., Gopal, R., Rosmita, B., and Van Gucht, D. 1985b. Genetic Algorithms for the Traveling Salesman Problem. *Proc. First Int' l Conference on Genetic Algorithms and Their Applications* (pp. 160–168). Pittsburgh, PA. Lawrence Erlbaum Publishers.

Grefenstette, J. 1987a. Multilevel Credit Assignment in a Genetic Learning System. *Proc. Second Int' l Conference on Genetic Algorithms and Their Applications* (pp. 202–209). Cambridge, MA. Lawrence Erlbaum Publishers.

———— , 1987b. Incorporating problems specific knowledge into Genetic Algorithms. *Genetic Algorithms and Simulated Annealing*. D. Davis (Ed.). Pitman Series on AI.

———— , 1988. Credit Assignment in Rule Discovery Systems. *Machine Learning Journal* (pp. 225–246), Volume 3, numbers 2/3, Kluwer Academic Publishers.

———— , 1989. A System for Learning Control Strategies with Genetic Algorithms. *Proc. Third International Conference on Genetic Algorithms* (pp. 183–90). Fairfax, VA. Morgan Kaufmann Publishers.

Hedrick, C.L. 1976. Learning Production Systems from Examples. *Artificial Intelligence*, Vol. 7.

Holland, J.H. 1975. *Adaptation in Natural and Artificial Systems*. University of Michigan Press, Ann Arbor, MI.

Holland, J.H., Reitman, J. 1978. Cognitive Systems Based on Adaptive Algorithms. *Pattern-directed Inference Systems.* Waterman, D. and Hayes-Roth, F. (Eds.), Academic Press.

Holland, J.H. 1986. Escaping Brittleness: The Possibilities of General-Purpose Learning Algorithms Applied to Parallel Rule-based Systems. *Machine Learning: An Artificial Intelligence Approach, Volume II.* Michalski, R.S., Carbonell, J.G., and Mitchell, T.M. (Eds.). Morgan Kaufman Publishers.

Holland, J.H., Holyoke, K., Hisbett, R., and Thagard, P. 1986. *Induction: Processes of Inference, Learning, and Discovery.* MIT Press. Cambridge, MA.

Koza, J. 1989. Hierarchical Genetic Algorithms Operating on Populations of Computer Programs. *Proc. 11th Int'l Joint Conference on AI.* Detroit, MI.

Michalski, R. 1983. A Theory and Methodology of Inductive Learning. *Machine Learning: An Artificial Intelligence Approach.* Michalski, R.S., Carbonell, J.G., and Mitchell, T.M. (Eds.). Morgan Kaufmann Publishers.

Newell, A. 1977. Knowledge Representation Aspects of Production Systems. *Proc. fifth IJCAI* (pp. 430–437). Cambridge, MA,

Robertson, G. 1988. Parallel Implementation of Genetic Algorithms in a Classifier System. *Genetic Algorithms and Simulated Annealing.* D. Davis (Ed.). Pitman Series on AI.

Robertson, G. and Riolo, R. 1989. A Tale of Two Classifier Systems. *Machine Learning Journal* (pp. 139–160), Volume 3, numbers 2/3, Kluwer Academic Publishers.

Schaffer, D. 1985. Multiple Objective Optimization with Vector Evaluated Genetic Algorithms. *Proc. First Int'l Conference on Genetic Algorithms and Their Applications* (pp. 93–100). Pittsburgh, PA.

———, 1989. Editor, *Proc. Third International Conference on Genetic Algorithms.* Morgan Kaufmann Publishers.

Smith, S.F. 1980. *A Learning System Based on Genetic Adaptive Algorithms.* Doctoral Thesis, Department of Computer Science, University of Pittsburgh, Pittsburgh, PA.

———, 1983. Flexible Learning of Problem Solving Heuristics Through Adaptive Search. *Proc. Eighth IJCAI* (pp. 422–425), Karlsruhe, Germany.

Wilson, S. 1985. Knowledge Growth in an Artificial Animal. *Proc. First Int'l Conference on Genetic Algorithms and Their Applications* (pp. 16–23). Pittsburgh, PA.

———— , 1987. Quasi-Darwinian Learning in a Classifier System (pp. 59–65). *Proc. Fourth Intl. Workshop on Machine Learning.* Irvine, CA.

Wilson, S. and Goldberg, D. 1989. A Critical Review of Classifier Systems *Proc. Third International Conference on Genetic Algorithms* (pp. 244–255). Fairfax, VA. Morgan Kaufmann Publishers.

PART
SIX

FORMAL ANALYSIS

22

APPLYING VALIANT'S
LEARNING FRAMEWORK TO
AI CONCEPT-LEARNING PROBLEMS

David Haussler
(University of California, Santa Cruz)

Abstract

We present an overview of some recent theoretical results in the learning framework introduced by Valiant in [Valiant, 1984] and further developed in [Valiant 1985; Blumer, *et al.*, 1987; 1989; Pitt and Valiant, 1988; Haussler, 1988; Angluin and Laird, 1988; Angluin, 1988; Rivest, 1987; Haussler, 1989; Kearns, *et al.*, 1987a; 1987b]. Our focus is on applications to AI problems of learning from examples as given in [Haussler, 1988; 1989] and [Kearns, *et al.*, 1987a; 1987b], along with a comparison to the work of Mitchell on version spaces [Mitchell, 1982]. We discuss learning problems for both attribute-based and structural domains. This is a revised and expanded version of [Haussler, 1987].

22.1 INTRODUCTION

For the last few decades the bulk of the work in machine learning has been quite strongly divided into three areas, which we will call *pattern recognition* (e.g., [Duda and Hart, 1973]), *AI/cognitive science machine learning* (e.g., [Michalski, Carbonell, and Mitchell, 1983; 1986], and *theory of inductive inference* (e.g., [Angluin and Smith, 1983]. Since researchers in each of these distinct areas also tend to have fairly distinct goals in mind, it is entirely appropriate that they have developed their own methodologies and terminology. However, this has on occasion prevented some potentially valuable cross-fertilization of ideas. A new machine learning framework introduced by Valiant [Valiant, 1984] incorporates elements from each of these areas and may provide a useful vehicle for such cross-fertilization in the near future. Here we describe that framework in the terminology of the empirical AI/cognitive science work on learning from examples and summarize some of the recent results obtained within it. For a more complete picture of recent work in this area, the reader is referred to [Haussler and Pitt, 1988] and [Rivest, *et al.*, 1989].

The Valiant framework differs from other AI frameworks for learning from examples in that it does not demand that the hypothesis produced by the learning algorithm be exactly correct, only that it be approximately correct with high probability. In other words, a successful learning algorithm is defined as an algorithm that, given enough randomly chosen examples of an unknown target concept, produces, with high probability, a hypothesis that is a good approximation of the target concept. Performance is measured in terms of the number of examples needed and the computational effort required to produce the hypothesis.

The important feature of the Valiant framework is that, at least in principle, it allows us to give a meaningful quantitative analysis of the performance of symbolic AI learning algorithms, akin to the rigorous analysis given for some of the numerical methods of pattern recognition. Moreover, while this analysis is based on probability theory, and hence requires certain probabilistic assumptions about the way that examples are generated and the way that successful learning is defined, the model is distribution-free—which means that the results will hold for any probability distribution that governs the generation of examples. Hence, it can be expected that performance bounds derived from this theory will hold in a wide variety of real-world learning situations.

Mitchell's work on version spaces [Mitchell, 1982] provides an important bridge between the AI work in learning from examples and the Valiant framework. We will begin by describing the basic framework of learning from examples common to both the AI work and the Valiant-style work, then take a look at Mitchell's notion of version spaces, and from there go on to the Valiant framework. Along this path from Mitchell to Valiant we will also see how demands for computational efficiency necessitated by larger learning problems lead us away from the more comprehensive, exact learning algorithms, such as Mitchell's candidate-elimination algorithm, to simpler algorithms that achieve weaker, approximate learning goals.

22.2 INSTANCE SPACES AND HYPOTHESIS SPACES

Examples used for learning will be drawn from a fixed *instance space* X. For our present purposes we will assume that X is finite or countably infinite, although X can also be taken to be a (uncountably infinite) finite-dimensional Euclidean space [Blumer, *et al.*, 1989]. The nature of X is determined by the description language that we use to define the domain in which learning takes place. The simplest case is an attribute-based domain, in which each instance in X is characterized by the values of a finite set of finitely valued attributes (see e.g., [Quinlan, 1986; Michalski, *et al.*, 1986; Haussler, 1988]). For example, if the description language consists of the attributes **color, shape** and **size**, with values *red* and *blue* for **color**; *square, hexagon, triangle, circle*, and *crescent* for **shape**; and *small, medium*, and *large* for **size**, then the instance space X is the set of all 30 3-tuples that can be formed by choosing one value for each of these attributes.

More complex instance spaces arise in structural learning domains like the blocks world [Winston, 1975; Vere, 1975; Hayes-Roth and McDermott, 1978; Dietterich and Michalski, 1983; Kodratoff and Ganascia, 1986; Sammut and Banerji, 1986; Haussler, 1989]. Here each instance is composed of many objects, each of which is described by a tuple of values for attributes, and every pair of which is related by one or more binary relations. For example, each instance might be a blocks-world scene composed of individual blocks with attributes **color, shape**, and **size**, and binary relations like **bigger_than** holding between certain pairs of blocks. Binary relations can also be defined like attributes to take on several possible values, not just *true* and *false*. For example, the binary relation **rel_pos** (relative position) may take the values *left_of, right_of, on_top_of*, or *under*. In this case each instance in X can be viewed as a directed graph with nodes representing objects, labeled by tuples of attribute values, and edges representing binary relations between objects, labeled with tuples giving the values of these relations. If we restrict the maximum number of objects per instance to some fixed number k then X is the finite set of all such labeled graphs with at most k nodes, otherwise X is countably infinite and includes arbitrarily large graphs.

Given an instance space X, a *concept* is defined as an arbitrary subset of X. This is the classical extensional view of a concept. In practice, learning algorithms often restrict themselves to concepts that can be represented within some limited concept-description language defined on X, an intensional view of concepts. We say that such algorithms use a restricted *hypothesis space H*, defined as the set of all concepts on the instance space that can be represented in the given concept-description language. The use of a restricted hypothesis space is called an *inductive bias* [Mitchell, 1980; Utgoff, 1986].[1]

In an attribute-based instance space, the simplest inductive bias is a restriction to a concept-description language that only allows atomic formulae (*atoms*) of the form **attribute** = *value* (e.g., **color** = *red*) joined by conjunctions (e.g., (**color** = *red*) and (**shape** = *square*)). The set of concepts that can be represented in this way is severely limited since one can only generalize from single instances by dropping terms from their full conjunctive descriptions. To enrich this description language it is typical to define certain additional abstract (unobservable) values for an attribute;

---

[1] Other forms of inductive bias are also identified in these papers.

e.g., we might add the values *polygon*, *nonpolygon*, and *any_shape* to the attribute **shape** introduced above, giving it a hierarchical value structure. We can also impose a linear order on the existing (observable) values of the attribute. In the former case we call the resulting attribute a *tree-structured* attribute and in the latter a *linear* attribute [Michalski, 1983]. These enrichments are then incorporated into the language by allowing atoms of the form **attribute** = *abstract_value* for tree structured attributes and *value*$_1$ ≤ **attribute** ≤ *value*$_2$ for linear attributes (e.g., allowing concepts like (**shape** = *polygon*) and (*small* ≤ **size** ≤ *medium*)). The class of concepts that can be represented by conjunctions in this enriched language will be called *pure conjunctive concepts*.

Other restricted hypothesis spaces on attribute-based domains can be defined by restricting *H* to include only concepts given by atoms as above linked by disjunctions (*pure disjunctive concepts*) or mixing conjunction and disjunction in a limited way as in the

- *k-DNF concepts*: arbitrary disjunctions of pure conjunctive concepts, with each pure conjunctive concept using at most *k* atoms;
- *k-term DNF concepts*: disjunctions of at most *k* pure conjunctive concepts, each using an unlimited number of atoms;
- *k-CNF concepts*: arbitrary conjunctions of pure disjunctive concepts, with each pure disjunctive concept using at most *k* atoms; and
- *k-clause CNF concepts*: conjunctions of at most *k* pure disjunctive concepts, each using an unlimited number of atoms.[2]

Note that the pure conjunctive concepts are just the 1-CNF concepts, or equivalently the 1-term DNF concepts, and the pure disjunctive concepts are the 1-DNF concepts, or equivalently the 1-clause CNF concepts. Restricted hypothesis spaces that only allow conjunction and "internal" disjunction (i.e., atoms such as **shape** = *polygon or circle*) have also been defined [Michalski, 1983; Haussler, 1988]. We call these *internal disjunctive concepts*.

In structural domains the natural analog of pure conjunctive concepts is the class of *existential conjunctive concepts*, defined by expressions of the form

$$\exists^* \; x_1, \ldots, x_r : f_1 \; \text{and} \; f_2 \; \text{and} \; \cdots \; \text{and} \; f_s,$$

where each x_j, $1 \leq j \leq r$, is a variable, and each f_i, $1 \leq i \leq s$ is an atom of the type, described above, except that it also involves either a single variable (if it is describing the value of an attribute) or a pair of distinct variables (if it is describing a rela-

---

[2] These definitions are given in [Pitt and Valiant, 1988] for instance spaces of Boolean attributes, but they extend naturally to instance spaces with tree-structured and linear attributes.

tionship between two objects). As an example we might represent the concept "any scene that contains a polygon on top of a square" as

$\exists^* x_1, x_2 :$ (**shape** (x_1)) = *polygon* and
(**shape** (x_2) = *square*) and (**rel_pos** (x_1, x_2) = *on_top_of*)

This expression may be read "there exist distinct objects x_1 and x_2 such that the shape of x_1 is *polygon*, the shape of x_2 is *square*, and the relative position of x_1 to x_2 is *on_top_of*." Because we insist that each variable correspond to a distinct object, we use the quantifier $\exists^*$, thus avoiding confusion with the quantifier $\exists$; which, under the standard interpretation, would permit many-one bindings between variables and objects.

Subclasses of the class of all existential conjunctive concepts can be defined by restricting the number of distinct variables that can appear in the expression to k. We call these concepts *k-variable existential conjunctive concepts*.

For our present purposes, whenever we are working with the restricted hypothesis space of k-variable existential conjunctive concepts, we will also assume that the maximum number of objects per instance in the instance space is k.

Clearly many other types of hypothesis spaces are also reasonable for structural domains. For example, we could use the standard existential operator, or we could use—in place of pure conjunctive concepts—any of the other attribute-based concept types listed above for the body of the expression.

22.3 VERSION SPACES AND HYPOTHESIS FINDERS [3]

Given an instance space X and a hypothesis space H over X, the basic framework for learning from examples can be described as follows. For any concept on X we say that instances in X that are contained in this concept are *positive examples* of the concept and instances not contained in the concept are *negative examples*. The basic technique used in learning from examples is to take a *sample* consisting of a sequence of positive and negative examples of an unknown *target concept* on X and produce a hypothesis in H that is *consistent* with the sample, in the sense that it contains all positive examples and no negative examples.[4] Of course, if the target concept is not in the hypothesis space H, this may be impossible. The problem of deciding if there is a hypothesis in H that is consistent with a sample, and if so producing one, will be called the *hypothesis-finding problem*.

---

[3] These are called recognition algorithms in [Haussler, 1989].

[4] Here we disregard the important issue of noise (incorrect classification) within the sample and the possibility of querying a "teacher" of the concept on specifically constructed examples.

We are not interested in just solving the hypothesis-finding problem for a single hypothesis space H (e.g., the set of pure conjunctive concepts on a particular instance space X); instead, we seek a general algorithm that works for any hypothesis space of a given type (e.g., any pure conjunctive hypothesis space). Let **H** denote a *class* of hypothesis spaces of a given type, e.g., the class of all hypothesis spaces of pure conjunctive concepts, over all instance spaces defined by tree-structured and linear attributes. We assume that **H** has the property that given any instance space X, there is a unique hypothesis space H_X in **H** for X. For example, if **H** is the class of pure conjunctive hypothesis spaces, then once we have defined the attributes that determine the instance space X, then this also determines a particular $H_X \in$ **H**: H_X is the class of pure conjunctive concepts over these attributes. A *hypothesis finder* for **H** is an algorithm that takes a description of an instance space X and a sample of an arbitrary unknown target concept on X and produces a hypothesis in H_X that is consistent with the sample if one exists, or else indicates that no hypothesis in H_X is consistent with the sample.

Mitchell's version-space framework and candidate-elimination algorithm ([Mitchell, 1982]; see also [Cohen and Feigenbaum, 1982]) provide one way to construct a hypothesis finder for any given class of hypothesis spaces **H**. We define the *version space* of a sample Q with respect to a hypothesis space $H \in$ **H** as the set of all hypotheses in H that are consistent with Q. The *candidate-elimination algorithm* computes the version space of a sample Q incrementally as follows.

The algorithm begins by reading in the attributes that determine the instance space X, and thus the hypothesis space H_X. Initially the version space is the entire hypothesis space H_X. As each example in Q is examined, hypotheses that are inconsistent with this example are eliminated from the version space, and thus the version space shrinks. After all examples in Q have been examined, the remaining set of hypotheses forms the version space of Q.

The candidate-elimination algorithm takes advantage of the natural partial order of increasing *generality* on the hypotheses in the version space. From the extensional viewpoint, this is just the partial order of set containment among the hypotheses. With respect to this partial order, the candidate-elimination algorithm keeps track only of the set of maximal elements of the version space (the set G) and the set of minimal elements of the version space (the set S), updating these sets directly as each new example is examined. Thus after all examples of Q have been examined, S is the set of maximally specific hypotheses in H_X consistent with Q, and G is the set of maximally general hypotheses consistent with Q. If either of these sets becomes empty during processing, then the version space of Q must be empty and so the algorithm stops, reporting that no hypothesis in H_X is consistent with Q. Otherwise, after all examples have been examined, any hypothesis in either S or G, or between a hypothesis in S and a hypothesis in G in the partial order, can be given as a consistent hypothesis. In this sense the candidate-elimination algorithm yields a hypothesis finder for **H**. In fact, it yields much more, since it allows us to generate all consistent hypotheses, and thus to detect when more than one consistent hypothesis remains, which is useful for exact learning.

The drawback of the candidate-elimination algorithm as a hypothesis finder is lack of computational efficiency. We say that a hypothesis finder is *polynomial* if it runs in time polynomial in the length of its input; i.e., polynomial in both the number of examples in the sample (the *size* of the sample) and the parameters defining the complexity of the instance space (the number of attributes, number of values per attribute, and in structural domains the number of binary relations and the number of objects per example). The candidate-elimination algorithm is not a polynomial hypothesis finder unless S and G can be updated efficiently, which requires at the very least that they do not become too large as examples are added to Q. Unfortunately, it can be shown that for each of the classes of hypothesis spaces listed above, the size of either S, G, or both S and G can be exponential in the number of examples in Q and the number of attributes used to define X. Specifically,

i.   the size of G can be exponential when H_X is the space of pure conjunctive concepts on X (and hence also for internal disjunctive and k-CNF concepts, $k > 1$) [Haussler, 1988];

ii. the size of S can be exponential when H_X is the space of pure disjunctive concepts on X (and hence also for k-DNF concepts, $k > 1$) (this is just the dual version of the example given in [Haussler, 1988]); and

iii. the sizes of both S and G can be exponential when H_X is the space of 2-term DNF, 2-clause CNF or 2-variable existential conjunctive concepts on X (and hence also for $k > 2$) [Haussler, 1989]. (The 2-term DNF and 2-clause CNF results can be derived in a similar fashion from the construction in theorem 3.2 of [Pitt and Valiant, 1988]).

For cases (i) and (ii) where only one of the sets S or G can be exponential, it turns out that the other set (i.e., the set S for the hypothesis space of pure conjunctive concepts and relatives, and the set G for the space of pure disjunctive concepts and relatives) never has more than one element. This means that there is still the possibility of an efficient, "one-sided" candidate-elimination algorithm that maintains only this one hypothesis. This algorithm exists in each case and is a polynomial hypothesis finder for **H**. For the case when **H** is the class of pure conjunctive hypothesis spaces it is the following algorithm (called the *classical algorithm* in [Haussler, 1988]):

Algorithm 1 (One-sided algorithm for pure conjunctive concepts)

0.   Read in the attributes and their values, then begin with the examples.

1.   For each negative example do nothing but save it in a list.

2. When the first positive example arrives, initialize S to be the hypothesis that consists of only this example; i.e., the complete conjunctive description of this example using all attributes.

3. For each new positive example after the first, take the hypothesis in S and generalize it as little as possible so as to include the new example. (This is done by generalizing the atoms for each attribute: for a linear attribute by expanding the interval of values minimally to include the new value and for a tree-structured attribute by "climbing" the tree of abstract values as little as possible to include the new value (see [Michalski, 1983; Bundy, *et al.*, 1985]).)

4. After all examples have been input, go through the list of negative examples and check if any are included in the hypothesis in S. If not then return this hypothesis, else declare that no pure conjunctive hypothesis is consistent with the sample (i.e., the version space is empty).

While this algorithm is not really incremental in the way it handles negative examples, it does run in polynomial time for instance spaces with a large number of attributes, whereas the full candidate elimination algorithm does not. Similar "one-sided," candidate-elimination algorithms exist for pure disjunctive, internal disjunctive, k-DNF, and k-CNF concepts [Valiant, 1984; 1985; Haussler, 1988]. It should be noted that these algorithms for k-DNF and k-CNF concepts are polynomial only for a fixed k. As k grows large, they rapidly become impractical.

The situation for the hypothesis spaces of 2-term DNF, 2-clause CNF and 2-variable existential conjunctive concepts is entirely different. In each case it is NP-complete to determine if there is a hypothesis in the space that is consistent with a given sample. This is demonstrated for 2-term DNF and 2-clause CNF in [Pitt and Valiant, 1988] and for 2-variable existential conjunctive concepts in [Haussler, 1989]. Hence, we do not expect these classes of hypothesis spaces to have polynomial hypothesis finders.

In summary, we have

Theorem 1 If **H** is the class of pure conjunctive, pure disjunctive, internal disjunctive, k-CNF, or k-DNF hypothesis spaces for any fixed $k \geq 2$, then **H** has a polynomial hypothesis finder. If **H** is the class of k-term DNF, k-clause CNF or k-variable existential conjunctive hypothesis spaces for any fixed $k \geq 2$, then the hypothesis finding problem for **H** is NP-hard.

22.4 LEARNING ALGORITHMS IN THE SENSE OF VALIANT

A hypothesis finder is not what one usually thinks of when one thinks of learning from examples. Given examples of an unknown target concept, we are not so much concerned with finding a hypothesis in some hypothesis space H that is consistent with these examples, but rather with finding a hypothesis that is in some sense "close" to the target concept. Furthermore, if the target concept is in the hypothesis space H, we would like the hypothesis we choose from H to get arbitrarily close to the target concept as more examples are processed. This is an intuitive notion of *convergence* for learning algorithms.

We can formalize the notion of closeness by assuming that examples are drawn at random from the instance space, using some probability distribution on this space,[5] and letting the *error* of a hypothesis be the probability that it will disagree with the target concept on a given randomly drawn example. If X is finite and all instances are equally likely, the error is simply the fraction of all instances on which the hypothesis and target concept disagree. If, as is the typical case, some instances are more likely than others, the error still measures the *expected performance* of the hypothesis as the fraction of randomly drawn examples we expect the hypothesis and target concept to disagree on.

Given this notion of error, we can then formalize the notion of an algorithm that "converges" to the target concept as follows. We define a *learning algorithm* for a class of hypothesis spaces **H** as an algorithm that takes as input a description of an instance space X and a sample of some unknown target concept contained in X, outputs a hypothesis in H_X, and has the following additional property: For any instance space X, probability distribution on X and target concept in H_X, given a large enough random sample of the target concept, the algorithm produces, with arbitrarily high probability, a hypothesis with arbitrarily small error.[6] This last requirement is formalized by defining an *error parameter* ε and a *confidence parameter* δ, and insisting that for all ε and δ, $0 < \varepsilon$, $\delta < 1$, there be a sample size such that the algorithm produces, with probability at least $1 - \delta$, a hypothesis with error at most ε. Note that we require convergence for any probability distribution on the instance space, hence this framework corresponds most closely to the distribution-free, nonparametric models in pattern recognition [Duda and Hart, 1973].

Of course we are also concerned with the sample size and the computation time required for convergence. We can take care of the computation time by considering only polynomial algorithms; i.e., algorithms that produce their hypotheses in time polynomial in the size of the sample and the parameters of the instance space (num-

---

[5] We use a simplified version of the probabilistic model of [Valiant, 1984] in which there is only one probability distribution on the instance space, regardless of the target concept, instead of having two distributions defined for each target concept, one for the instances that are positive examples of the target and one for the negative examples. This simplification does not significantly alter the notion of polynomial learnability [Haussler, *et al.*, in press].

[6] In contrast with [Haussler, 1987b], we do not require that a learning algorithm always produce a hypothesis that is consistent with the sample.

ber of attributes, etc.). As for the sample size, we expect that more examples will be required for learning if we

i.   demand more accuracy of the hypothesis (i.e., decrease the error parameter ε);

ii. demand a given accuracy with higher confidence (i.e., decrease the confidence parameter δ);

iii. increase the complexity of the instance space; or

iv. increase the complexity of the target concept we are trying to learn.

To compare and analyze sample sizes required by different learning algorithms in any given domain, we need to specify how we measure the complexity of the instance space and target concept. Unfortunately, this is somewhat domain-dependent, since the relevant parameters of the instance space (e.g., number of attributes, number of values per attribute, etc.) and of the target concept (e.g., number of terms and number of atoms per term for DNF) vary from one learning problem to another.

In practice, one would like to define separate parameters (i.e., complexity functions) for each of the relevant aspects of the instance space and target concept for each type of learning problem. One could then study how the sample size depends on each of these aspects, both separately and in various combinations. However, for simplicity, in this chapter we will define only one instance-space complexity function and one target-concept complexity function.

For an instance space X in an attribute-based domain, we take *complexity*(X) to be the number of attributes that define X; in a structural domain with a fixed maximum number of objects per scene, *complexity*(X) is the total number of attributes and binary relations that define the instance space X. These definitions are chosen for convenience. We do not include the number of values per attribute or binary relation in our complexity measure because, as we will see below, the sample size required by the learning algorithms we discuss can be upper-bounded independent of these quantities.

For each of the types of concept introduced in Section 22.2 we take *complexity* (c) to be the number of atoms in the smallest description of c, except in the case of internal disjunctive concepts, where *complexity*(c) is taken to be the total number of values or value ranges (for linear attributes) in all internal disjunctions of c combined. Ignoring small constant and logarithmic factors, this measurement of complexity corresponds roughly to the number of symbols in the smallest description of c in the concept description language associated with **H**.

Returning now to our formulation of an efficient learning algorithm, what we want is that the sample size required for learning does not grow too rapidly if we do any of the things listed in (i)–(iv) above. Specifically, we want the sample size required to get a hypothesis in H_X of error at most ε with probability at least $1 - \delta$ for any target concept $c \in H_X$ to grow only polynomially in

$$\frac{1}{\varepsilon}, \frac{1}{\delta},$$

complexity(X), and *complexity*(c). As above, the sample size required should grow by a fixed polynomial, independent of the probability distribution on X that governs the generation of examples. If a learning algorithm satisfies these requirements and also runs in polynomial time then it is a polynomial learning algorithm for **H**. Formally, an algorithm A is a polynomial learning algorithm for **H** if it

   i. takes as input a description of an instance space X and a sample and outputs a hypothesis in H_X;

  ii. runs in time polynomial in the length of its input; and

 iii. for all $0 < \varepsilon, \delta < 1$ and $n, s \geq 1$ there exists a sample size S_A (ε,δ,n,s), polynomial in

$$\frac{1}{\varepsilon}, \frac{1}{\delta},$$

n, and s such that for all domains X of complexity n, all probability distributions P on X and all target concepts $c \in H_X$ of complexity at most s, given a random sample of c of size S_A (ε,δ,n,s) drawn independently according to P, A produces a hypothesis in H_X that, with probability at least $1 - \delta$, has error at most ε.

The smallest such sample size S_A (ε,δ,n,s) is called the *sample complexity* of A. We say the class of hypothesis spaces **H** is *polynomially learnable (from random examples)* if there is a polynomial learning algorithm for **H**.[7]

    To illustrate the notion of polynomial learnability, we quote the following result from [Haussler, 1988] on the sample complexity of the learning algorithm for pure conjunctive concepts given in the previous section (algorithm 1).

Proposition 1 Let n denote the number of attributes in the instance space, ε denote the error parameter, and δ the confidence parameter. Then the sample complexity of algorithm 1 is

$$O\left(\frac{n}{\varepsilon} \log \frac{n}{\varepsilon\delta}\right),$$

i.e., there exists a constant c_0 such that for any instance space X defined by n attributes, each tree-structured or linear, any pure conjunctive target concept $c \subseteq X$, any probability distribution P on X and any $0 < \varepsilon, \delta < 1$, given a random sample of c of size

---

[7] The close relationship between this notion of polynomially learnable and the notion of learnable in [Pitt and Valiant, 1988; Kearns, *et al.*, 1987a; 1987b] is discussed in [Haussler, *et al.*, in press].

$$c_0 \frac{n}{\varepsilon} \log \frac{n}{\varepsilon\delta},$$

algorithm 1 produces a hypothesis that, with probability at least $1 - \delta$, has error at most ε.

This result shows that the sample complexity of algorithm 1 is polynomial in all the required quantities, namely

$$\frac{1}{\varepsilon}, \frac{1}{\delta},$$

the complexity of the instance space, and the complexity of the target concept. In fact, the sample complexity is bounded independently of the latter quantity. Since algorithm 1 runs in polynomial time, it follows that it is a polynomial learning algorithm for the class **H** of pure conjunctive hypothesis spaces, and hence this class is polynomially learnable from random examples. Notice also that algorithm 1 uses only the positive examples to form its hypothesis, saving the negative examples just to check if the version space of pure conjunctive concepts is empty, a situation that can never occur if the target concept is pure conjunctive. Hence, using the above result for algorithm 1, we can make the stronger claim that **H** is in fact polynomially learnable from random *positive* examples alone (see [Kearns, *et al.*, 1987a; 1987b] for a precise definition).

In the following section we will briefly discuss how proposition 1 is obtained, and indicate how similar results may be obtained for the other classes listed in theorem 1 above. Before doing so however, we note that we can get a better sample complexity for learning pure conjunctive concepts by an algorithm that uses both positive and negative examples to form its hypothesis. The basic idea is simple: Instead of producing the most specific hypothesis that is consistent with the examples as in algorithm 1, try to produce the simplest hypothesis that is consistent. For example, if all positive examples are red squares and all negative examples are either red circles or blue circles, then form the hypothesis **shape** = *square* instead of the hypothesis (**shape** = *square*) and (**color** = *red*).

One way to implement this idea is to first form the most specific hypothesis that is consistent with the positive examples as described in the steps 0 to 3 of algorithm 1, and then simplify it as much as possible by deleting atoms (e.g., **color** = *red*), taking care not to include negative examples. (By deleting atoms we only generalize, hence we needn't worry about the positive examples, they remain included in the hypothesis). Unfortunately, there may be many possible ways to simplify this hypothesis, and it is NP-hard to find a simplification that is still consistent with the negative examples and has the fewest atoms left [Haussler, 1988]. We can avoid this problem by working "bottom up," i.e., deciding which atoms to save instead of deciding which to delete, using a greedy heuristic ([Blumer, *et al.*, 1989; Haussler, 1988] see also the related heuristics used in [Michalski, 1983]). A greedy method for simplification can in fact be applied any time we have a pure conjunctive hypothesis that is consistent with a set of negative examples.

Greedy Method for Simplification

0. Start with any pure conjunctive hypothesis *h* and any set *N* of negative examples, none of which are included in *h*. Initialize the set *S* of "useful" atoms to empty.

1. While *N* is not empty:

    A. Find the atom of *h* that excludes the most negative examples in *N* (e.g., **shape** = *square* excludes all negative examples that aren't squares).

    B. Add this atom to *S* and delete from *N* all negative examples that it excludes.

2. Return the conjunction of all the atoms in *S*.

It is clear that the hypothesis returned will still be consistent with the negative examples in *N*, and since it is equal to or more general than the original hypothesis *h*, it will also still be consistent with any positive examples of *h*.

Now let algorithm 2 be the variant of algorithm 1 obtained by applying the greedy method for simplification to the hypothesis before it is returned. We have the following:

Proposition 2 [Haussler, 1988] Let $n \geq 2$ denote the number of attributes in the instance space, *s* denote the complexity of the target concept, ε denote the error parameter, and δ the confidence parameter. Then the sample complexity of algorithm 2 is

$$O\left(\frac{s\log n}{\varepsilon}\left(\log\frac{s\log n}{\varepsilon\delta}\right)^2\right).$$

Since it depends only logarithmically on the number of attributes, this bound on the sample complexity is significantly better than that of proposition 1 when the number of attributes is large, and the complexity of the target concept is small. This is a typical case in practice, where there are often very many attributes defined for an instance, but only few are relevant in any one learning task (see also [Littlestone, 1988]).

22.5 PERFORMANCE ANALYSIS

In this section we outline a technique for obtaining upper bounds on the sample complexities of learning algorithms derived from the results of Vapnik and Chervonenkis ([1971]; see also, [Pearl, 1978; Vapnik, 1982; Haussler and Welzl, 1987; Blumer, *et al.*, 1989; Haussler, 1988]).

Let X be an instance space and H be a hypothesis space defined on X. Let I be a finite set of instances in X. For a given hypothesis $h \in H$, label I so that it becomes a sample of h; i.e., label all the instances of I contained in h with "+" and the others with "–". This labeling defines a partition of I into two distinct, disjoint subsets. We will call this (labeled) partition the *dichotomy of I induced by h* ([Cover, 1965] see also [Rendell, 1986]). $\Pi_H (I)$ denotes the set of all dichotomies of I induced by hypotheses in H, i.e., the set of all ways the instances in I can be labeled with "+" and "–" so as to be consistent with at least one hypothesis in H. For any integer m,

$$1 \le m \le |X|, \Pi_H(m) = \max \{|\Pi_H (I)| : I \subseteq X \text{ and } |I| = m\}$$

where |.| denotes the cardinality of a set. Hence $\Pi_H(m)$ is the maximum number of dichotomies induced by hypotheses in H on any set of m instances.

Our technique for bounding sample complexities involves obtaining an upper bound on $\Pi_H(m)$ for a given hypothesis space H. As an example, consider an instance space X defined by one linear attribute *height*, taking integer values from 1 to q, and the hypothesis space H of all possible height intervals; i.e., all hypotheses of the form $a \le height \le b$ where $1 \le a \le b \le q$. Instances in X are simply height values between 1 and q, so $|X| = q$. If I consists of $2 \le m < q$ distinct instances $x_1, \ldots, x_m$, linearly ordered by height, then there are

$$\binom{m}{2} + m + 1$$

ways that we can label the instances in I so as to be consistent with a hypothesis in H. This is because to be consistent with some hypothesis in H, it must either be the case that all instances are labeled "–", or there must be some i and j, $1 \le i \le j \le m$ such that all of the instances $x_i, \ldots, x_j$ are labeled "+" and the other instances "–". There are

$$\binom{m}{2} + m$$

ways to choose such i and j, and 1 way to choose all "–". Since

$$\binom{m}{2} + m + 1 \le m^2$$

for all $m \ge 2$, m^2 is an upper bound on $\Pi_H(m)$.

By a similar argument, we can show that if X is an instance space defined by n attributes, each linear or tree-structured, and H is the hypothesis space of all pure conjunctive hypotheses over X, then $\Pi_H(m) \le m^{2n}$ for all $m \ge 2$. This result, along with a variety of other bounds on $\Pi_H(m)$ for various hypothesis spaces, is given in the appendix.

There are two trivial upper bounds on $\Pi_H(m)$ that hold for any H. First, since there are only 2^m distinct labelings of m points with "+" and "–", $\Pi_H(m) \le 2^m$. This bound is achieved in the cases $m = 1$ and $m = 2$ in the "height" example above. The largest m such that $\Pi_H(m) = 2^m$ has a special significance in this context, and is called the *Vapnik-Chervonenkis (VC) dimension of H* ([Haussler and Welzl, 1987];

see also [Vapnik, 1982], where it is called the *capacity*, following [Cover, 1965]). It can be shown that if the VC dimension of H is d, where $d \geq 2$, then $\Pi_H(m) \leq m^d$ for all $m \geq d$ [Vapnik, 1982]. The above example illustrates this result for the case $d = 2$. Calculating the VC dimension of H can be a clean way to bound the growth of $\Pi_H(m)$.

For the second trivial bound, note that each distinct dichotomy in $\Pi_H(I)$ must be induced by a distinct hypothesis in H, so $\Pi_H(m) \leq |H|$, independently of m.

$\Pi_H(m)$ is a rough measure of the "expressiveness" or "richness" of the concept-description language that defines, and hence limits, the hypothesis space H. We have referred to this as *inductive bias*. The more expressive the concept-description language, the weaker the inductive bias. In many cases the essential quantitative aspects of this bias are given by the asymptotic behavior of $\Pi_H(m)$ as m grows, which can be summarized as a single integer exponent: the VC dimension of H [Haussler, 1988]. In other cases the cardinality of H is a more appropriate measure of bias. The significance of both these measurements is highlighted in the following theorem from [Blumer, *et al.*, 1989], derived from results in [Vapnik, 1982].

Theorem 2 Let X be an instance space, H be a hypothesis space over X, P be a probability distribution on X and c be a target concept contained in X. Then for any ε, $0 < \varepsilon < 1$, given m independent random examples of c drawn according to P, the probability that there exists a hypothesis in H that is consistent with all of these examples and has error greater than ε is at most

$$2\Pi_H (2m)\, 2^{-\varepsilon m/2} .$$

The intuitive content of this theorem can be obtained by mentally placing the target concept c in the hypothesis space H and imagining a "ball of radius ε" around c consisting of all the hypotheses in H that have error at most ε with respect to c and a given probability distribution P on the instance space. The theorem then says that if the richness of the concept description language of H is sufficiently limited (i.e., if $\Pi_H(2m)$ grows more slowly than $2^{-\varepsilon m/2}$), then for large enough samples, the probability that any hypothesis in H consistent with the sample lies outside this ball of radius ε is extremely small. In other words, with overwhelming probability, the entire version space collapses to the extent that it is entirely contained within this ball of radius ε. Moreover, this occurs independent of the specific probability distribution P.

To apply theorem 2, given a confidence parameter δ between 0 and 1 we need only find a sample size m such that

$$2\Pi_H (2m)\, 2^{-\varepsilon m/2} \leq \delta \tag{1}$$

and then we can assert that for a random sample of size m, with probability at least 1 $- \delta$ *every* hypothesis in H that is consistent with the sample has error at most ε.

So long as $\Pi_H(m)$ does not grow too rapidly with m, this provides a useful tool for obtaining upper bounds on sample complexities of learning algorithms. Our only requirement is that the algorithm always produce a consistent hypothesis in the hypothesis space H whenever the sample allows it. This guarantees that the algorithm produces a consistent hypothesis in H whenever the target concept is in H. Then, if H is sufficiently biased so that $\Pi_H(m)$ grows slowly, using theorem 2 we can assert that this hypothesis has small error with high probability even for relatively small sample sizes. Results obtained by "solving" equation (1) for m for some typical forms of $\Pi_H(m)$ are given in the following lemma (see also [Blumer, *et al.*, 1989]). A sketch of the proof is given at the end of the appendix.

Lemma 1

i.   If there exists a constant $a \geq 1$ such that $\Pi_H(m) \leq a$ for all m then equation (1) is satisfied for

$$m = \frac{2}{\varepsilon} \log \frac{2a}{\delta},$$

hence equation (1) is satisfied for some m that is

$$O\left(\frac{1}{\varepsilon} \log \frac{a}{\delta}\right),$$

ii. If there exist constants $a, d \geq 1$ such that $\Pi_H(m) \leq am^d$ for all m then equation (1) is satisfied for some m that is

$$O\left(\frac{1}{\varepsilon} \log \frac{a}{\delta} + \frac{d}{\varepsilon} \log \frac{d}{\varepsilon}\right),$$

which is

$$O\left(\frac{d}{\varepsilon} \log \frac{ad}{\varepsilon\delta}\right).$$

iii. If there exist constants $a, b, d \geq 1$ such that $\Pi_H(m) \leq a(bm)^{d\log m}$ for all m then equation (1) is satisfied for some m that is

$$O\left(\frac{1}{\varepsilon} \log \frac{a}{\delta} + \frac{d\log b}{\varepsilon} \log \frac{d\log b}{\varepsilon} + \frac{d}{\varepsilon}(\log\frac{d}{\varepsilon})^2\right),$$

which is

$$O\left(\frac{d(\log b + 1)}{\varepsilon}\left(\log \frac{ad(\log b + 1)}{\varepsilon\delta}\right)^2\right).$$

The result given in proposition 1 above is derived from theorem 2 and lemma 1 using the result quoted above that $\Pi_H(m) \leq m^{2n}$ when H is the class of pure conjunctive concepts on an instance space defined by n attributes, each tree-structured or linear (lemma 3, appendix). We simply use lemma 1, part (ii) with $a = 1$ and $d = 2n$. (The constant factor of 2 is ignored in the final asymptotic bound.) Essentially, the result follows from the fact that H is strongly biased, as measured by $\Pi_H(m)$, and the fact that algorithm 1 always produces a consistent hypothesis. Hence, it actually follows that any polynomial hypothesis finder for pure conjunctive concepts is a polynomial learning algorithm and has a sample complexity that is at least this good.

A similar, but slightly more involved, argument can be used to derive proposition 2 using theorem 2 and part (iii) of lemma 1. The trick here is to bound $\Pi_H(m)$ for the hypothesis space H restricted to the relatively small subspace of pure conjunctive concepts that is used by the greedy algorithm (algorithm 2) when it produces a hypothesis that is consistent with m examples of some pure, conjunctive target concept with at most s atoms. Using standard bounds on the performance of the greedy heuristic, it can be shown that this hypothesis space H includes only pure conjunctive concepts with at most $s \ln m + 1$ atoms, and then from lemma 4, part (i) (given in the appendix) it follows that

$$\Pi_H(m) \leq (\sqrt{nm})^{2s \ln m + 2},$$

giving the desired bounds using the last approximation of part (iii). Details are given in [Haussler, 1988].

Part (i) of lemma 1 is useful when H is so small that the trivial bound of

$$\Pi_H(m) \leq |H|$$

is good enough (see also [Blumer, et al., 1989]). This often occurs when we restrict ourselves to Boolean attributes. For example, if H is the hypothesis space of all k-DNF (or k-CNF) concepts over an instance space defined by n Boolean attributes, then $|H| \leq 2^{(2n)^k}$ (lemma 2, appendix). Setting a to this value and using part (i) of lemma 1 shows that equation (1) is satisfied for a sample size m that is

$$O\left(\frac{1}{\varepsilon} \log \frac{2^{(2n)^k}}{\delta}\right),$$

i.e.,

$$O\left(\frac{1}{\varepsilon}\left((2n)^k + \log\frac{1}{\delta}\right)\right).$$

As above, it then follows from theorem 2 that any polynomial hypothesis finder for k-DNF (or k-CNF) concepts on Boolean attributes is a polynomial learning algorithm for fixed k and has a sample complexity at least this good.

A better sample complexity can be obtained by generalizing the greedy method of algorithm 2 to handle k-CNF (or in the dual form k-DNF) hypotheses. This algorithm is described and analyzed in [Haussler, 1988] for the general case of k-DNF concepts on tree-structured and linear attributes. By using the greedy method, the dependence of the sample complexity on the number n of attributes is reduced from n^k to logarithmic in n. This paper also gives a polynomial learning algorithm for internal disjunctive concepts, based on a form of greedy algorithm as well. Putting all these results together, we have

Theorem 3 If **H** is the class of pure conjunctive, pure disjunctive, internal disjunctive, k-CNF, or k-DNF hypothesis spaces for any fixed $k \geq 2$, then **H** is polynomially learnable.

We believe that this result is of practical significance. However, the upper bounds given above on the sample sizes needed are still too crude to be directly useful in practice.

22.6 FURTHER RESULTS

In Section 22.2 we introduced six basic classes of hypothesis spaces: internal disjunctive, k-CNF, k-DNF, k-term DNF, k-clause CNF, and k-variable existential conjunctive. (Here we include pure conjunctive as 1-CNF and pure disjunctive as 1-DNF). In Section 22.3 we saw that the first three of these have polynomial hypothesis finders and, for $k \geq 2$, the last three do not, given that $P \neq NP$. Finally, we have seen that these first three classes not only have polynomial hypothesis finders, but they are polynomially learnable from random examples.

It turns out that it is unlikely that any of these last three classes are polynomially learnable from random examples in the sense that we have defined. This follows from the results in [Pitt and Valiant, 1988], which essentially show how to construct a randomized polynomial time hypothesis finder for **H** given a polynomial learning algorithm for **H** (see [Blumer, *et al.*, 1989]). Since it is thought unlikely that NP-hard problems can be solved by randomized polynomial time algorithms, just as it is thought unlikely that $P = NP$, this gives evidence that these classes are not polynomially learnable.

However, there is another sense in which these classes *are* polynomially learnable from random examples. We just need to allow for the possibility that concepts represented in one concept-description language could be learned by forming hypotheses in a different, richer concept-description language. This amounts to using a richer hypothesis space than is strictly necessary to represent the type of target concept being learned. The advantage of this is that the richer hypothesis space may be easier to search, so that it becomes easier to find a consistent hypothesis. The disadvantage is that the bias is weakened, so that it is likely that more examples will be required for convergence.

Results in [Pitt and Valiant, 1988] for Boolean k-term DNF and k-clause CNF show that k-term DNF concepts can be represented as k-CNF concepts, and k-clause CNF concepts can be represented as k-DNF concepts. These results hold for tree-structured and linear attributes as well. Using these ideas, it can be shown that k-variable existential conjunctive concepts can be represented as $k!$-CNF concepts over an appropriate attribute-based instance space. Hence, in each of these three cases we can find a richer hypothesis space that is polynomially learnable (for fixed k) from which to draw our hypotheses. This can be used to show that in fact all six classes of hypothesis space are polynomially learnable from random examples in the broadest sense. Rivest [1987] takes the Boolean results even further by exhibiting a class of Boolean concepts defined by a type of production rule that is polynomially learnable from random examples and generalizes both k-DNF and k-CNF (and hence k-term DNF and k-clause CNF as well by the Pitt and Valiant result). This learnability result can be established like those above, by counting the number of distinct concepts and then applying theorem 2 and lemma 1, part (i). However, because the best known learning algorithms for k-DNF and k-CNF, including Rivest's algorithm, are still impractical for large k, the learning algorithms that use this change of representation trick will also be impractical for large k, especially the one that learns k-variable existential conjunctive concepts with $k!$-CNF hypotheses.

There is another approach to learning these other three types of concepts that may prove more fruitful. This is to allow the learning algorithm to make certain types of queries about the target concept during learning, in addition to having a source of random examples [Valiant, 1984; Angluin, 1987a; 1987b; 1988]. The simplest type of query is a *membership query*, in which the learning algorithm constructs an instance and asks if it is an instance of the target concept or not (e.g., [Sammut and Banerji, 1986]). A related query is a *subset query*, in which the learning algorithm constructs a hypothesis and asks if this hypothesis is contained in (i.e., a specialization of) the target concept. In the Boolean case, Angluin has shown that k-term DNF concepts are polynomially learnable from random examples and membership queries ([Angluin, 1987b]; see also [Angluin, 1988]). This algorithm is practical even for large k when the concepts are monotone (i.e., their expressions contain no negated literals; see also [Valiant, 1984]). These results also hold for k-clause CNF. To our knowledge, they have not been extended to linear and tree-structured attributes. An algorithm to learn k-variable existential conjunctive concepts using queries is given in [Haussler, 1989].

One impetus for research in this direction is the observation that the only impediment to learning from random examples in these cases is the computational complexity of producing a consistent hypothesis. In particular, by using theorem 2 in conjunction with lemmas 1 to 5 as illustrated above, we can show that for any of the hypothesis spaces of k-term DNF, k-clause CNF, or k-variable existential conjunctive concepts, given a reasonable-size random sample, *any* hypothesis that is consistent with the sample will have small error with high probability. Since it doesn't matter how we come up with this hypothesis, we are free to explore any means we wish to make this computational task easier. One appealing approach is to use queries to help reduce the number of the alternatives encountered in the search for a consistent hypothesis. Certainly there are also other approaches.

22.7 CONCLUSION

We have explored some of the possibilities inherent in the probabilistic learning framework proposed by Valiant, and compared this framework to the version-space model of Mitchell. We have seen that by weakening the performance criterion for learning by demanding only that we produce a good approximation to the target concept with high probability, but strengthening it by demanding computational efficiency, we can exhibit a variety of simple and provably efficient learning algorithms that will scale up gracefully as the complexity of the instance space and the target concept increase. Further, we have provided a general mechanism for obtaining probabilistic convergence results for learning algorithms that requires only that the hypotheses they produce be consistent with the sample, and that the hypothesis space be reasonably biased in the sense that the number of distinct dichotomies induced by its hypotheses does not grow too fast with the number of instances.

There are a number of important performance issues that we have not dealt with. One is the possibility of errors or noise in the sample data. A more general form of theorem 2, one that tolerates some degree of misclassification in the hypothesis, is given in [Blumer, *et al.*, 1989] (see also [Haussler, 1989]) and is also based on results from [Vapnik, 1982]. This result is useful for obtaining convergence results when there is a possibility of noise in the sample. More extensive treatments of this issue are given in [Laird, 1987; Angluin and Laird, 1988; Kearns and Li, 1987]; see also [Valiant, 1985].

Another issue is whether the learning algorithm is incremental or not. Results in [Littlestone, 1988] show that in the case of k-DNF and k-CNF concepts on a Boolean domain, the inherently nonincremental method of learning using the greedy heuristic for simplification can be replaced by a connectionist-like mechanism of maintaining and updating real-valued weights associated with the terms that are candidates for being in the hypothesis (see also [Schlimmer, 1987] for another algorithm of this type). This gives an incremental algorithm that has performance comparable to the nonincremental greedy technique. Moreover, the methods employed in obtaining this performance bound are quite unlike those we have presented here. Both the issue of noise and the issue of incremental learning are certain to figure prominently in future work within the Valiant framework.

ACKNOWLEDGMENTS

I would like to thank Nick Littlestone for suggesting that to obtain better bounds one should look directly at $\prod_H(m)$ rather than just at the VC dimension of H. I also thank Lenny Pitt and Doug Fisher for several useful suggestions concerning the content of this paper. The author gratefully acknowledges the support of ONR grant N00014-86-K-0454.

APPENDIX   COMPUTING UPPER BOUNDS ON $\Pi_H(m)$

In order to apply theorem 2, one has to obtain an upper bound on the function $\Pi_H(m)$ for the hypothesis space H used by a particular learning algorithm. Here we outline a few tricks for doing this.

The simplest method is to calculate a bound on the cardinality of H itself. As mentioned above, this is an upper bound on $\Pi_H(m)$ for all m. This technique works quite well when the number of values per attribute is fixed at some small number; e.g., for Boolean attributes. We give two examples.

Lemma 2

  i. Let H be the hypothesis space of all k-DNF (k-CNF) concepts on an instance space defined by n Boolean attributes. Then $|H| \leq 2^{(2n)^k}$.

  ii. Let H be the hypothesis space of all k-term DNF (k-clause CNF) concepts on an instance space defined by n Boolean attributes. Then $|H| \leq 3^{kn}$.

Proof   For part (i), we begin with a crude upper bound on the number of distinct terms over n Boolean variables that can be formed by the conjunction of up to k atoms. In the Boolean case, each atom corresponds to a *literal*; i.e., a variable or its negation. There are $2n$ such literals, and each term is formed by choosing up to k out of these $2n$ and conjoining them. Hence the number of possible (nonempty) terms is at most

$$\sum_{i=1}^{k} \binom{2n}{i} \leq (2n)^k.$$

(Here we disregard the fact that all terms that contain both a variable and its negation are equivalent.) A k-DNF expression is formed by choosing a subset of these terms and taking their disjunction. Hence there are at most

$$2^{(2n)^k}$$

distinct k-DNF expressions. Clearly the same bound holds for k-CNF by a similar argument.

For part (ii), note that the total number of essentially distinct (nonempty) terms of arbitrary length over n Boolean variables is 3^n. (Here we do regard two terms to be equivalent if they each contain a variable and its negation.) This is because in each term that does not include both a variable and its negation, for each variable we can either include it, include its negation, or not include it at all. Excluding the empty term, this gives $3^n - 1$ possibilities. Since all other terms are equivalent, we only count them once, giving a total of 3^n. It follows that the number of distinct (non-empty) k-term DNF expressions is at most

$$\sum_{i=1}^{k} \binom{3^n}{i} \le (3^n)^k = 3^{kn}.$$

Again, essentially the same argument works for k-clause CNF.

These bounds can be used to derive bounds on the sample complexity of learning algorithms for these types of expressions as illustrated in Section 22.5.

If the number of values per attribute is unknown, or is fixed but very large, then it is usually better to use techniques like those illustrated in the "height" example of Section 22.5 to bound $\Pi_H(m)$ as a function of m. In some cases this method is significantly better even for Boolean attributes (see [Blumer, et al., 1989]). We give two further examples of this method.

Lemma 3 Let X be an instance space defined by n attributes, each tree-structured or linear.

   i. If H is the hypothesis space of all pure conjunctive concepts on X then $\Pi_H(m) \le m^{2n}$ for all $m \ge 2$.

   ii. If H is the hypothesis space of all k-term DNF concepts on X then $\Pi_H(m) \le m^{2kn}$ for all $m \ge 2$.

Proof For part (i), first note that we can assume that each hypothesis $h \in H$ contains exactly one atom for each of the n attributes. This is because the conjunction of two atoms, both involving the same attribute A can always be replaced by a single atom on A whose value range is the intersection of the ranges of the original atoms (e.g., "$(3 \le \text{size} \le 7)$ and $(5 \le \text{size} \le 9)$" can be replaced by "$(5 \le \text{size} \le 7)$"), and because we can always add a "dummy atom" (i.e., *smallestsize* $\le$ **size** $\le$ *largestsize*) for any attribute that does not already appear in some atom.

Now let $I = \{x_1, \dots, x_m\}$ be a set of m instances in X. By the argument given in the "height" example in Section 22.5 above, for any atom involving a linear attribute A, when $m \ge 2$ there are at most

$$\binom{m}{2} + m + 1 \le m^2$$

ways this atom can induce a dichotomy on the set I by partitioning it into those x_i's whose values on A satisfy the atom and those whose values do not. Since the leaves of any tree can be ordered so that the set of leaves of the subtree defined by any internal node forms an interval of this ordering, this result also holds for tree-structured attributes. (A tighter bound of at most $2m$ dichotomies can also be derived for the tree-structured case).

Finally, since the dichotomy of I induced by a conjunction of atoms is entirely determined by the dichotomies induced by the individual atoms, the number of distinct dichotomies of I induced by hypotheses $h \in H$ is at most $(m^2)^n = m^{2n}$. This establishes part (i). Part (ii) follows easily from part (i), since the dichotomies induced by a k-DNF expression are determined by the dichotomies induced by each of its terms, and hence there are at most $(m^{2n})^k = m^{2kn}$ such dichotomies.

The method used in the above lemma cannot be usefully applied in the case of pure disjunctive concepts. This is because the "normal form" of one atom per attribute used in the first part of the proof is not valid for pure disjunctive concepts. In fact, the number of dichotomies of a set of m instances induced by the class of pure disjunctive hypotheses can be a high as 2^m for any m: We just take a set of instances for which some attribute has a distinct value in each instance. Any subset of these instances can be specified by a disjunction of atoms for this attribute that each include only one instance. This implies that the only bound on $\Pi_H(m)$ in this case is the trivial bound of 2^m. (Note however that this cannot occur if we restrict the number of values per attribute.) This also implies that we cannot get nontrivial bounds on $\Pi_H(m)$ for an arbitrary number of values per attribute when H is the space of internal disjunctive, k-DNF or k-clause CNF concepts either.

However, we can obtain useful bounds on $\Pi_H(m)$ for these classes if we restrict the complexity of the hypotheses we allow; e.g., by putting a limit on the total number of atoms in the expression. For k-DNF this can be accomplished by limiting the number of terms. We have the following results.

Lemma 4 Let X be an instance space defined by n attributes, each tree-structured or linear.

i. If H is the hypothesis space of all pure conjunctive (or pure disjunctive) concepts on X that contain at most s atoms then $\Pi_H(m) \leq n^s m^{2s}$ for all $m \geq 2$.

ii. If H is the hypothesis space of all internal disjunctive concepts on X of complexity at most s (i.e., with at most s occurrences of values or value ranges in all atoms combined) then $\Pi_H(m) \leq n^s m^{2s}$ for all $m \geq 2$.

iii. If H is the hypothesis space of all k-DNF concepts on X with at most s terms (or k-CNF concepts with at most s clauses) then $\Pi_H(m) \leq n^{ks} m^{2ks}$ for all $m \geq 2$.

Proof For part (i), by adding "dummy atoms" as in the previous proof, we can, without loss of generality, assume that the hypotheses in H have exactly s atoms. Furthermore, by that same argument, for each attribute, the atoms associated with that attribute are capable of inducing at most m^2 dichotomies on a set of m instances. Since for each of the s atoms there are n ways to assign it an attribute and at most m^2

ways to choose the dichotomy induced by its value range given its assigned attribute, this gives a bound of $(nm^2)^s = n^s m^{2s}$ on the total number of distinct dichotomies.

Clearly the same argument works for pure disjunctive concepts. (We have not used the fact that each attribute need only appear once, which is the only part of the previous proof that does not generalize to pure disjunctive expressions.) This verifies part (i).

The same argument also works for internal disjunctive concepts. Once we have assigned attributes to atoms, we can collect all the atoms that share a common attribute together to form one internal disjunction of values on that attribute and then form the conjunction of these. This determines an internal disjunctive expression of complexity s, and every internal disjunctive expression of complexity s can be formed in this way. This verifies part (ii).

For part (iii), note that by part (i) the number of dichotomies induced by a single term of a k-DNF is at most $n^k m^{2k}$. Since the dichotomies induced by a k-DNF expression are determined by the dichotomies induced by each of its terms, there are at most $(n^k m^{2k})^s = n^{ks} m^{2ks}$ dichotomies induced by k-DNF expressions with at most s terms. Clearly the same argument works for k-CNF.

The above results can also be extended to structural domains.

Lemma 5 Let X be a structural instance space defined by a total of n attributes and binary relations with a limit of at most k objects per scene.

  i. If H is the hypothesis space of all k-variable existential conjunctive concepts on X then $\Pi_H(m) \leq 2(k^2 m)^{2k^2 n}$.

 ii. If H is the hypothesis space of all k-variable existential conjunctive concepts on X with at most s atoms then $\Pi_H(m) \leq k^{6s+1} n^s m^{2s}$.

Proof These results can be established by an extension of the method used in the previous two lemmas. Details are given in [Haussler, 1987a].

As promised in Section 22.5, we conclude with the following proof.

Proof of Lemma 1

Part (i) follows directly by substituting a for $\Pi_H(2m)$ and

$$\frac{2}{\varepsilon} \log \frac{2a}{\delta}$$

for m in equation (1).

For part (ii) we will show that

$$2a(2m)^d 2^{\frac{-\varepsilon m}{2}} \leq \delta$$

for

$$m = \max\left(\frac{4}{\varepsilon} \log \frac{2a}{\delta}, \frac{8d}{\varepsilon} \log \frac{16d}{\varepsilon}\right).$$

Since this value of m is

$$O\left(\frac{1}{\varepsilon} \log \frac{a}{\delta} + \frac{d}{\varepsilon} \log \frac{d}{\varepsilon}\right),$$

the result follows.

Taking logarithms and rearranging, our problem reduces to showing that

$$\frac{em}{2} \geq d\log(2m) + \log \frac{2a}{\delta}$$

for m as above. Rewrite

$$\frac{\varepsilon m}{2} \text{ as } \frac{\varepsilon m}{4} + \frac{\varepsilon m}{4}.$$

Since

$$\frac{\varepsilon m}{4} \geq \log \frac{2a}{\delta}$$

by the first bound on m, it suffices to show that

$$\frac{\varepsilon m}{4} \geq d \log(2m)$$

using the second bound. Substituting this second bound on m into this equation and reducing yields the equation

$$16\frac{d}{\varepsilon} \geq \log \frac{16d}{\varepsilon}.$$

Since

$$\varepsilon \leq 1 \text{ and } d \geq 1, \frac{16d}{\varepsilon} \geq 16.$$

Since $x \geq \log x$ for all $x \geq 4$, the result follows.

For part (iii) we will show that

$$2a(2bm)^{d\log(2m)} 2^{\frac{-\varepsilon m}{2}} \leq \delta$$

for

$$m = \max\left(\frac{4}{\varepsilon} \log \frac{2a}{\delta}, \frac{16d\log(2b)}{\varepsilon} \log \frac{32d\log(2b)}{\varepsilon}, \frac{128d}{\varepsilon}\left(\log\frac{128d}{\varepsilon}\right)^2\right).$$

Since the latter quantity is

$$O\left(\frac{1}{\varepsilon}\log\frac{a}{\delta} + \frac{d\log b}{\varepsilon}\log\frac{d\log b}{\varepsilon} + \frac{d}{\varepsilon}\left(\log\frac{d}{\varepsilon}\right)^2\right),$$

the result follows.

Proceeding as we did in the previous case, using the first bound in the formula for m we can reduce the problem to showing that

$$\frac{\varepsilon m}{4} \geq d\log(2m)\log(2bm).$$

We do this by showing that

$$\frac{\varepsilon m}{8} \geq d\log(2b)\log(2m) \text{ and } \frac{\varepsilon m}{8} \geq d(\log(2m))^2$$

using the second and third bounds on m, respectively. The calculations are similar to those of the previous case.

References

Angluin, D. 1988. Queries and concept learning. *Machine Learning*, 2:319–342.

———— , 1987a. On the complexity of minimum inference of regular sets. *Information and Control*, 39:337–350.

———— , 1987b. *Learning k-Term DNF Formulas Using Queries and Counterexamples,* (Technical Report YALEU/DCS/RR-559). Yale University.

Angluin, D. and Laird, P. 1988. Learning from noisy examples. *Machine Learning*, 2:343–370.

Angluin, D. and Smith, C. 1983. Inductive inference: Theory and methods. *ACM Comp. Surveys*, 15 (3), 237–270.

Blumer, A., Ehrenfeucht, A., Haussler, D., and Warmuth, M.K. 1989. Learnability and the Vapnik-Chervonenkis dimension. *JACM*, 36(4):929–965.

———— , 1987. Occam's Razor. *Inf. Proc. Let.* 24, 377–380.

Bundy, A., Silver, B., and Plummer, D. 1985. An analytical comparison of some rule-learning programs. *Artificial Intelligence*, 27, 137–181.

Cohen, P. and Feigenbaum, E. 1982. *Handbook of Artificial Intelligence*, Vol. III, Addison-Wesley.

Cover, T. 1965. Geometrical and statistical properties of systems of linear inequalities with applications to pattern recognition. *IEEE Trans. Elect. Comp.*, 14, 326–334.

Dietterich, T.G. and Michalski, R.S. 1983. A comparative review of selected methods from learning from examples. *Machine Learning: An Artificial Intelligence Approach*. Morgan Kaufmann, San Mateo, CA.

Duda, R. and Hart, P. 1973. *Pattern Classification and Scene Analysis*. Wiley.

Haussler, D. 1987. Bias, version spaces and Valiant's learning framework. *Proc. 4th Int. Workshop on Machine Learning*, Morgan Kaufmann, San Mateo, CA, 324–336.

———— , 1988. Quantifying inductive Bias: AI learning algorithms and Valiant's learning framework. *Artificial Intelligence*, 36:177–221.

———— , 1989. Learning conjunctive concepts in structural domains. *Machine Learning*, 4:7–40.

Haussler, D. and Pitt, L. (Eds.). 1988. *Proceedings of the 1988 Workshop on Computational Learning Theory*. Morgan Kaufmann, San Mateo, CA.

Haussler, D. and Welzl, E. 1987. Epsilon-nets and simplex range queries. *Discrete and Comp. Geometry*, 2, 127–151.

Haussler, D., Kearns, M., Littlestone, N.. and Warmuth, M.K., in press. "Equivalence of models for polynomial learnability," to appear in *Information and Computation*.

Hayes-Roth, F. and McDermott, J. 1978. An interference matching technique for inducing abstractions. *CACM*, 21, (5), 401–410.

Kearns, M. and Li, M. 1987. Learning in the presence of malicious errors. (Tech. Rep. TR-03-87), Aiken Computation Laboratory, Harvard.

Kearns, M., Li, M., Pitt, L., and Valiant, L. 1987a. On the learnability of Boolean Formulae. *Proc. 19th ACM Sym. on Theory of Computation.*

———— , 1987b. Recent results on Boolean concept learning. *Proc. 4th Int. Workshop on Machine Learning*, Morgan Kaufmann, San Mateo, CA, 337–352.

Kodratoff, Y. and Ganascia, J. 1986. Improving the generalization step in learning. In Michalski, R., Carbonell, J., and Mitchell, T. (Eds.), *Machine Learning: An Artificial Intelligence Approach, Volume II*, 215–244. San Mateo, CA: Morgan Kaufmann.

Laird, P.D. 1987. "Learning form good data and bad," Tech. Rep. YALEU/DCS/TR-551, Yale Univ., New Haven, CT.

Littlestone, N. 1988. "Learning quickly when irrelevant attributes abound: A new linear-threshold algorithm," *Machine Learning*, 2:285–318.

Michalski, R.S. 1983. A theory and methodology of inductive learning. In R. Michalski, J. Carbonell, and T. Mitchell (Eds.), *Machine Learning: An Artificial Intelligence Approach, Volume II,* 215–244. San Mateo, CA: Morgan Kaufmann.

Michalski, R., Carbonell, J., and Mitchell, T. (Eds.). 1983. *Machine Learning: An Artificial Intelligence Approach.* Morgan Kaufmann, San Mateo, CA.

——— , 1986. *Machine Learning: An Artificial Intelligence Approach, Volume II.* Morgan Kaufmann, San Mateo, CA.

Mitchell, T.M. 1980. *The Need for Biases in Learning Generalizations* (Technical Report CBM-TR-117). Department of Computer Science, Rutgers University, New Brunswick, NJ.

——— , 1982. Generalization as search. *Artificial Intelligence*, 18, 203–226.

Michalski, R., Mozetic, I., Hong, J., and Lavrac, N. 1986. *The AQ15 Inductive Learning System: An Overview and Experiments* (Technical Report UIUCDCS-R-86-1260). Department of Computer Science, University of Illinois at Urbana, IL.

Pearl, J. 1978. On the connection between the complexity and credibility of inferred models. *Int. J. Gen. Sys., 4,* 255–264.

Pitt, L. and Valiant, L.G. 1988. Computational limitations on learning from examples. *JACM*, 35(4):965–984.

Quinlan, J.R. 1986. Induction of decision trees. *Machine Learning*, 1(1), 81–106.

Rendell, L. 1986. A general framework for induction and a study of selective induction. *Machine Learning*, 1(2), 177–226.

Rivest, R. 1987. Learning decision-lists. *Machine Learning*, 2(3):229–246.

Rivest, R., Haussler, D., and Warmuth, M.K. (Eds.). 1989. *Proceedings of the 1989 Workshop on Computational Learning Theory.* Morgan Kaufmann, San Mateo.

Sammut, C. and Banerji, R. 1986. Learning concepts by asking questions. In *Machine Learning: An Artificial Intelligence Approach, Volume II*, R. Michalski, J. Carbonell and T. Mitchell, (Eds.). Morgan Kaufmann, San Mateo, CA.

Schlimmer, J.C. 1987. Incremental adjustment of representations for learning, *Proc. 4th Int. Workshop on Machine Learning*, Morgan Kaufmann, 79–90.

Utgoff, P. 1986. Shift of bias for inductive concept learning. In *Machine Learning: An Artificial Intelligence Approach, Volume II*. R. Michalski, J. Carbonell and T. Mitchell, (Eds.). Morgan Kaufmann, San Mateo, CA.

Valiant, L.G. 1984. A theory of the learnable. *Comm. ACM*, 27 (11), 1134–1142.

———— , 1985. Learning disjunctions of conjunctions. *Proc. 9th IJCAI* (vol. 1, pp. 560–566). Los Angeles, CA.

Vapnik, V.N. 1982. Estimation of Dependences Based on Empirical Data, Springer Verlag, New York.

Vapnik, V.N., and Chervonenkis, A.Ya. 1971. On the uniform convergence of relative frequencies of events to their probabilities. *Th. Prob. and its Appl.*, 16(2), 264–280.

Vere, S.A. 1975. Induction of concepts in the predicate calculus. *Proc. 4th IJCAI* (pp. 281–287). Tbilisi, USSR.

Winston, P. 1975. Learning structural descriptions from examples. *The Psychology of Computer Vision*, McGraw-Hill, New York.

23

A NEW APPROACH
TO UNSUPERVISED LEARNING
IN DETERMINISTIC ENVIRONMENTS

Ronald L. Rivest
Robert E. Schapire
(MIT Laboratory for Computer Science)

Abstract

We present a new approach to the problem of inferring the structure of a deterministic finite-state environment by experimentation. The learner is presumed to have no *a priori* knowledge of the environment other than knowing how to perform a set of basic actions and knowing what elementary sensations are possible. The actions affect the state of the environment and the sensations of the learner according to deterministic rules that are to be learned. The goal of the learner is to construct a perfect model of his environment—one that enables him to predict perfectly the result of any proposed sequence of actions.

Our approach is based on the notion of a "test": a sequence of actions followed by a predicted sensation. The value (true or false) of a test at the current state can be easily determined by executing it. We define two tests to be "equivalent" if they have the same value at any global state. Our procedure uses systematic experimentation to discover the equivalence relation on tests determined by the environment, and produces a set of "canonical" tests.

The equivalence classes produced correspond in many cases to a natural decomposition of the structure of the environment; one may say that our procedure discovers the appropriate set of "hidden state variables" useful for describing the environment.

Our procedure has been implemented and appears to be remarkably effective in practice. For example, it has successfully inferred, in a few minutes each, the struc-

ture of Rubik's Cube (over 10^{19} global states) and a simple "grid world" environment (over 10^{11} global states); these examples are many orders of magnitude larger
than what was possible with previous techniques.

23.1 INTRODUCTION

23.1.1 Unsupervised Learning of Environments

We address the learning problem faced by a robot in an unknown environment.
The robot and the environment form an interacting system (see Figure 23–1): The
actions chosen by the robot are inputs to the environment, causing it to change state,
and the state of the environment determines the sensations experienced by the robot.

A newly created robot may have little built-in knowledge of its environment.
(To coin a term, we use "newbot" to denote a newly created robot with little or no
experience and knowledge about its environment; the term "robot" is generic.) In our
case we assume that a newbot knows how to perform basic actions and can experience elementary sensations, but no more.

At each point in time the environment is in some (global) *state*; we denote the
set of all possible such states by Q. In this paper we assume that Q is finite.

We also assume that the set B of *basic actions* is a finite, relatively small set.

If the robot performs a basic action $a \in B$ the environment makes a transition
from its current state q to a new state $q' = \delta(q,a)$; here δ is the (deterministic) transition function for the environment.

For convenience, we define the set A to be the set of all *actions*; where an action is defined to be a sequence of zero or more basic actions. We similarly extend

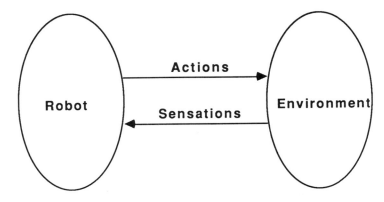

Figure 23–1:   The robot-environment system

the interpretation of δ so that δ(q,a) is the environmental state resulting from executing the action a (i.e., executing the basic actions of a in sequence).

We assume that the robot has a finite set S of *senses*. Think of a *sense* as a sense modality, such as vision, hearing, touch, etc. Each sense has a corresponding sensor which "reads" or "senses" the value of that sense. We call the values returned by the sensor *sensations*. We let V denote the set of all possible sensations and assume that different sensors cannot return the same sensation. As an example, one sensation might be "a tone of 1000 hertz"; another might be "a temperature of 68 degrees." These would be returned by audio and temperature sensors, respectively. (Note that if we wish to model the perception of several tones of different frequencies simultaneously, we would call each such tone a "sense," which returned a sensation of "present" or "absent.") In what follows we will regard each sensation as a binary predicate of the current environment, although in practice (as in some of our implementation examples) the more general notion of a sense may be useful.

Abstractly, the situation a newbot faces is exemplified in Figure 23–2; the newbot has one button to push for each basic action $a \in B$, and one light for each sensation $v \in V$. At each moment a subset of the lights will be on, indicating which sensations obtain in the current global state.

The goal of the newbot is to learn enough about its environment to build a perfect model of it. We say that a robot has a *perfect model* of its environment if it can predict perfectly what sensations would result from any desired sequence of basic actions. Having a perfect model is clearly useful for planning, although we do not address planning in this paper.

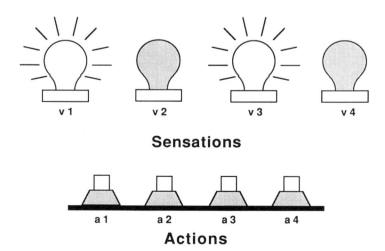

Sensations

Actions

Figure 23–2:   The buttons and lights model

We would like to point out one realistic feature of our model: There is typically no "reset" or "undo" buttons available to the robot—the actions of the robot have a cumulative effect on the global state.

Also, there is no teacher. The robot is engaged in unsupervised learning.

Finally, we note that while the robot may indeed converge on a perfect model of its environment, it might never be certain that its model is perfect—the fact that the model has been predicting perfectly for a while is no guarantee that it will continue to do so. Of course, this is the standard problem with induction.

23.1.2 An Example: The Little Prince's Planet

As a concrete example, consider a newbot just delivered to the "Little Prince" [Saint-Exupèry, 1943] on his home planet (an asteroid, really). This planet has a rose and a volcano, which the newbot can see when it is next to them; the available sense values are v = "See Volcano" and r = "See Rose." The planet is very small—it takes only four steps to go all the way around it. The basic actions available to the newbot are f = "Step Forward," b = "Step Backward," and t = "Turn Around." See Figure 23-3. In the state shown, the robot has no sensations, but it will see the volcano if it takes a step forward, and will see the rose if it takes a step backwards (or turns around and takes a step forwards). There are eight (global) states: the robot can be facing clockwise or counterclockwise, and can be in one of four positions. By symmetry of the north and south poles, however, there are only four states in a reduced sense.

23.1.3 Previous Work

Our learning problem can be viewed as the problem of inferring a finite automaton from its input/output behavior. Angluin and Smith [1983] give an excellent overview of the field of inductive inference, including a discussion of this problem. The following previous works were particularly inspirational to us.

- Gold [1972] gives an algorithm for inferring a machine from a sample of its input/output behavior. Angluin [1986] elaborates this algorithm to show how to infer an automaton using active experimentation with the automaton, and a "teacher" who can provide counterexamples to incorrect conjectures.
- Angluin [1978] and Gold [1978] prove that finding an automaton of n states or less agreeing with a given sample of input/output pairs is NP-complete. (We note that the concern here is with the number of states in the inferred automaton, and that the data is *given*—the inference algorithm does not have access to the automaton.)
- Angluin [1982] shows how to infer a special class of finite-state automata, called *k-reversible* automata, from a sample of its input/output behavior.

Figure 23–3:   The Little Prince's planet

23.2 OUR INFERENCE PROCEDURES

23.2.1 Tests

The notion of a *test* is essential to the development of our work: A *test* is an element of $T = AV = B^*V$; that is, a (possibly empty) sequence of actions $a \in A$ followed by a (predicted) sensation $v \in V$. We say that a test $t = av$ *holds* or *is true* at a given state q if sensation v obtains in the state qa reached by executing action (sequence) $a \in A$ starting in state q. We denote the value (**true** or **false**) of test t in state q as qt.

For example, for the state shown in Figure 23–3, the test fv is true: if the robot steps forward he will see the volcano. Similarly, the test $btffv$ is true, while the tests r, $bbtv$, and bv are false.

(In some of our procedures, we generalize the notion of a "test" to include sequences of the form AS: a sequence $a \in A$ of actions followed by a sense $s \in S$. In this case the value of a test $t = as$ at a given state q (which we denote qt) is not **true** or **false**, but rather the element of V that the selected sensor s yields in the state qa. This "extended test" variation does not affect our theory very much, but does provide some practical benefits in certain cases.)

There is an infinity of tests in $T = AV$; to say that the robot has a perfect model of its environment is to say that it knows the value of each test in T—that is, it knows what sensations would result from any sequence of actions. How can this knowledge be obtained and represented?

23.2.2 Equivalence of Tests

We say that tests t and t' are *equivalent*, denoted $t \equiv t'$, if they yield the same result from any state: $(\forall q \in Q)(qt = qt')$.

We observe that if the number of global states $|Q|$ is finite, then the number of equivalence classes of tests is also finite. This number, which we call the *diversity* of the environment and denote by D, is at most $2^{|Q|}$, and may be as small as $\log_2(|Q|)$. (Proofs omitted; see [Rivest and Schapire, 1987].) We have discovered that for many "natural" environments the diversity is actually much smaller than the number of states. Our aim is thus to design representations and procedures whose cost is polynomial in the diversity, rather than in the size of the environment.

For the environment of asteroid B-612 (see Figure 23–3) there are four equivalence classes of tests:

- $v \equiv tv \equiv ffr \equiv fbv \equiv ftfv \equiv \ldots$
- $r \equiv tr \equiv ffv \equiv fbr \equiv ftfr \equiv \ldots$
- $fv \equiv tfr \equiv br \equiv tbv \equiv \ldots$
- $fr \equiv tfv \equiv bv \equiv tbr \equiv \ldots$

We can thus select as "canonical" the tests

1. v: do you see a volcano?,
2. r: do you see a rose?,
3. fv: if you step forward will you see a volcano?, and
4. fr: if you step forward will you see a rose?

Any other test will be equivalent to one of these; thus, knowing the values of these four tests is sufficient to predict the value of any other test. Knowing the values of these tests determines what the global state is, as far as possible. (In this world none of the available tests allow you to tell if you are at the north or the south pole.)

Although this example is very simple, we see that the equivalence classes correspond to the natural state decomposition; it is important to know if you are at the rose or at the volcano, and (if not) whether you are facing the rose or the volcano.

A nice feature of this approach is that it allows the robot to create a model that consists of *independent* parts, which are *independently testable*. (This is reminiscent of Shapiro's [1981] work.) In our case, the independent parts are elementary statements of equivalence between two specified tests.

Let $<<$ denote the ordering relation between tests defined as follows: we say $t << t'$ if t is shorter than t' or if they are of the same length but t precedes t' in the usual alphabetic ordering (using some standard ordering of the symbols in B and V).

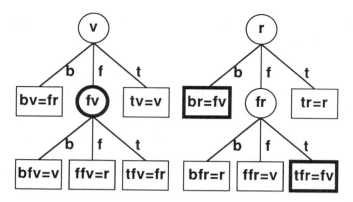

Figure 23–4:   The forest of tests

Let $\langle t \rangle$ denote the least (in the sense of $<<$ test in the equivalence class containing test t; we say that $\langle t \rangle$ is the "canonical" test in its class. For example, $\langle \mathtt{ffr} \rangle = v$.

Using this ordering of tests and definition of canonical, it is easy to prove that if t is canonical, then so is any nonempty suffix of t. Putting it another way, if t is *non*canonical then so is xt, for any sequence of actions $x \in A$. (Note that if $t \equiv \langle t \rangle$ then $xt \equiv x\langle t \rangle$.)

If $t = at'$ is noncanonical (where $a \in B$), but t' is canonical, we say that t is *square*; square tests are the minimal noncanonical tests. Each square test will be equivalent to some canonical test; discovering the set of canonical tests and the square-canonical equivalences is the goal of our inference procedure.

It is convenient to draw the set of canonical and square tests in the form of a forest, as illustrated in Figure 23–4. There are as many trees as elementary sensations (each sensation is the root of a tree), and the children of a test t are tests of the form at for $a \in B$. The square tests form the leaves of the tree, and arrows (omitted from the figure) may connect a leaf t with its canonical form $\langle t \rangle$.

As another means of representing the test classes, we may build a graph, as in Figure 23–5, in which each vertex is a canonical test, and an edge labeled $a \in B$ is directed from $\langle t \rangle$ to $\langle t' \rangle$ if $t \equiv at'$. We call this the *update graph* of the environment. The update graph may alternatively be derived from the forest of tests described above by directing each tree edge up and merging each square test with its equivalent canonical test.

We associate with each vertex $\langle t \rangle$ its value in the current state q. When action a is executed, the value of each vertex is passed along each outgoing edge labeled a yielding the new value of each test in state qa.

Similarly, in the forest of tests, we again associate with each test its current value. Under action a, the new value of each canonical test is received from below

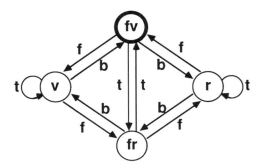

Figure 23–5:   The update graph

along branch a, while each square is assigned the new value of its equivalent canonical test.

In both Figures 23–4 and 23–5, the borders of the square and canonical tests which are **true** in the current state depicted in Figure 23–3 have been darkened.

23.2.3 Simulation and Prediction

The following theorem states that to have a perfect model (in the sense of being able to correctly predict the results of any sequence of actions), it suffices to know the canonical tests, their current values, and the relationship between the square tests and the canonical tests.

Theorem 1   To simulate an environment it suffices to know:

1. The set of canonical tests.
2. The value qt of each canonical test t at the current state q.
3. For each square test s in S, the test $\langle s \rangle$.

Proof Suppose a transition is made from state q to state qa, for some $a \in B$. We need to compute $(qa)t = q(at)$ for each canonical test t. However, the test at is either canonical or square, so that in either case the canonical test $u = \langle at \rangle$ is known. By assumption, we know qu; this is the desired value of $(qa)t$.

23.2.4 A Simple Inference Procedure

The simplest version of our inference procedure can be described as follows, using a subroutine (not described here) for determining if two tests are equivalent:

1. Begin with W (the set of tests to be examined) equal to V (the set of elementary sensations), and C (the set of tests known to be canonical) and SQ (the set of tests known to be square) equal to the empty set.

2. If W is empty, stop. Otherwise remove from W the least test t (under the ordering $\ll$).

3. If t is equivalent to any test $u \in C$, place t in SQ, record that $\langle t \rangle = u$, and return to step 2.

4. Otherwise, add t to C, for each $a \in B$ place the test at in W, and return to step 2.

When this program terminates, it has gathered all of the information needed for the simulation theorem; it has a "perfect" model.

We claim that the number of equivalence tests performed by this algorithm in step 3 is polynomial in the diversity D of the environment. More specifically, it is at most $D \cdot (D + D \cdot |B|)$. (Note that C can contain at most D tests, and no more than D canonical and $D \cdot |B|$ square tests can be added and extracted from W; as each test is removed from W, it may be compared in step 3 to all the tests in C.)

23.2.5 Determining Equivalence of Tests

Now for the final step: How can we tell if two tests are equivalent? The key difficulty here is that we have no "undo" operator, so that we can't check whether $qt = qt'$ by executing test t, backing up to state q, and then executing test t'. We need to know whether qt is **true** or **false** *without actually executing it*, so we can execute t' instead.

To do this, we repeatedly execute the test t until the results become periodic and predictable. Then we can execute t' from a state q where we know qt without executing test t. (It is not too difficult to prove using the update graph that the period of the results of test t is at most the diversity D of the environment.)

If we discover that $qt \neq qt'$, we conclude that $t \not\equiv t'$; otherwise we repeat the procedure until we are confident that $t \equiv t'$. The end result is a conclusion that either $t \equiv t'$ or $t \not\equiv t'$. (The repetitions make use of randomization to increase our confidence—for example, a random walk may be taken between each execution of the procedure, hopefully to bring the environment into a random starting state from which the procedure will have a chance of distinguishing t and t', if inequivalent. Additionally, a random sequence x may be chosen, and the tests xt and xt' compared for equivalence in the manner described above; with a lucky choice of x, it may be relatively easy to show $xt \not\equiv xt'$, which implies $t \not\equiv t'$.)

(A fine point: in order to be sure that the algorithm has discovered the correct period for t, it must either be given an upper bound on the diversity D of the environment, or it must repeatedly try out increasingly larger upper bounds, say $2, 4, 8, \dots$.)

23.2.6 Extensions and Variations

By exploiting a few simple observations, the efficiency of this basic algorithm can be improved by several orders of magnitude.

The first observation is that the values of some pairs of tests can be compared directly without any need of repeating one test until its values become periodic. We call such pairs *compatible* and say that two tests $t = av$ and $t' = a'v'$ are compatible if a is a prefix of a' or a' is a prefix of a. In the Little Prince example, the test fv is compatible with fbr because we can in a single sequence of actions and senses determine the values of both. In particular, we can move forward, test if we are at the volcano (this gives us the value of fv), and then move back and test if we are seeing the rose (this gives us the value of fbr).

Some experiments comparing two incompatible tests can be transformed into ones in which the tests are compatible, using knowledge already attained. Suppose the Little Prince has already learned that $ffffr \equiv r$, and that he now wishes to compare fr to tv. Their equivalence would imply that $ffftv \equiv ffffr \equiv r$. Thus, if the easy experiment of the compatibles r and $ffftv$ turns out negative, the Little Prince may conclude that $fr \not\equiv tv$.

For the special class of *permutation environments*, the equivalence of the derived compatible pair of tests is not only necessary but sufficient to the equivalence of the original incompatible pair. Conceptually, these are environments in which no information is ever lost: Every action can be reversed by some other fixed sequence of actions. The Little Prince's planet is an example of a permutation environment, as is the Rubik's Cube example described below. Thus, it is never necessary to test for periodicity for this class of environments.

We have been able to prove that our algorithm is correct with high probability for this special case, and have determined the number of experiments and the sort of randomization needed to conclude the equivalence of two tests with arbitrarily strong confidence. More precisely, we have proved that, given an error tolerance parameter $\varepsilon > 0$, and a permutation environment with diversity D and basic actions B, our algorithm correctly infers a perfect model of the environment with probability at least $1 - \varepsilon$ in time polynomial in D, $|B|$ and $\log(\frac{1}{\varepsilon})$ [Rivest and Schapire, 1987].

In many instances, whole sets of tests can be compared against one another in a single experiment. Suppose as above that the Little Prince has learned that fr has period four (i.e., $ffffr \equiv r$)and that the test bv does as well. He knows that the tests r, fr, ffr and $fffr$ are distinct, as are v, bv, bbv and $bbbv$. To compare each test in the first set against each in the other would require 16 experiments. To compare one such pair $f^n r$ and $b^m v$, the Little Prince could derive and test the compatible pair r and $f^{4-n}b^m v$ or the pair v and $b^{4-m}f^n r$, as described above. The important observation is that all of these pairs can be tested with a single experiment, namely the sequence of actions and senses $rfrfrfrfvbvbvbvbv$. The reader can verify that all 16 experiments are contained in this one, a tremendous savings for the newbot. (This technique generalizes to tests involving action sequences of length greater than one.)

Unlike the original algorithm, for these variations the conclusions drawn from an experiment depend on knowledge derived from other tests. Thus, our assertion that two tests can be compared in an experiment independent of all others has been compromised, in return for enhanced efficiency. The price we pay is a greater vulnerability to error: One mistake can snowball into an avalanche of wrong conclusions.

23.3 EXPERIMENTAL RESULTS

We present in this section three of the other toy environments we have used to test our algorithm, and how our implementations performed in each instance.

In the Grid World (Figure 23–6), the newbot finds itself on a 5 × 5 grid with wraparound, each tile of which is colored either red, green, or blue. The newbot can see only the color of the tile it is facing, so it has one sensation for each of the colors. Its basic actions allow it to paint the square it is facing any of the three colors, to turn left or right, or to step ahead one tile. Stepping ahead causes the color of the tile it moves to to replace that of the one it previously occupied. Because there is no way of recovering the color overwritten by one of the painting actions, the Grid World is not a permutation environment.

In the second microworld, the newbot can fiddle with the controls of a car radio (see Figure 23–7) and can detect what kind of music is being played. There are three distinctive stations which define V: rock, classical, and news. The newbot can use the auto-tune to dial the next station to the left or right (with wraparound), or can

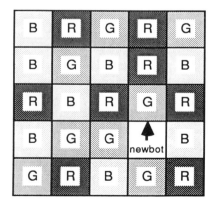

Figure 23–6:   The 5 × 5 Grid World

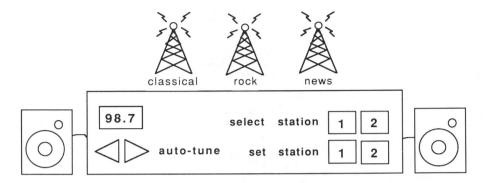

Figure 23–7:   The Car Radio World

select one of the two programmed stations, or can set one of these two program buttons to the current station.

The last environment is based on "Rubik's Cube" (see Figure 23–8). The newbot is allowed to see only three of the 54 tiles: a corner tile, an edge tile, and a center tile, all on the front face. Each of these three senses can indicate any one of six colors. The newbot may rotate the front face, and may turn the whole cube about the x and y axes. (By reorienting the cube the newbot can thus turn and view any of the six faces.)

Table 23–1 summarizes how our procedures handled these environments. The most complicated environment (Rubik's Cube) took approximately two minutes of CPU time to master—we consider this very encouraging.

The Rubik's Cube and Little Prince worlds were explored with an implementation (version "P"), which exploits the special properties of permutation environments, but only compares one pair of tests at a time. All worlds were explored as well by version "M," which tries to compare many tests against many other tests in a single experiment. The run times given are in seconds. The last three columns give the number of basic actions taken by the robot, the number of sense values asked for, and the number of experiments performed. (An experiment is defined loosely as a sequence of actions and senses from which the robot deduces a conclusion about equivalence between tests. Information about several tests may be obtained in a single experiment, and the same sequence of actions and senses may be repeated several times, each repetition counting as one experiment.) Except for the Little Prince world, we take a test to be of the form AS as described in Section 23.2.1. These implementations were done in C on a DEC MicroVAX II workstation.

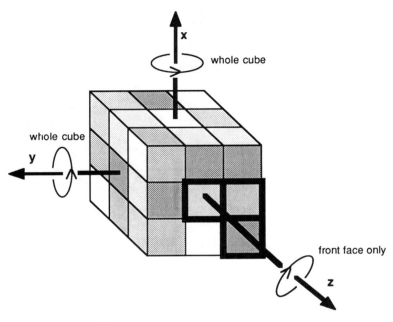

Figure 23–8:   The Rubik's Cube World

Table 23–1:   Experimental results

Environment	Diver-sity	Global states	|B|	|V|	Version	Time	Moves	Sense	Experi-ments
Little Prince	4	4	3	2	P	0.1	303	102	51
					M	0.2	900	622	50
Car Radio	9	27	6	3	M	3.7	27,695	9,557	1,146
Grid World	27	$\approx 10^{11}$	6	3	M	90.4	583,195	123,371	9,403
Rubik's Cube	54	$\approx 10^{19}$	3	18	P	126.3	58,311	4,592	2,296
					M	401.3	188,405	79,008	2,874

23.4 CONCLUSIONS AND OPEN PROBLEMS

We have presented a new technique for inferring a deterministic finite-state environment by experimentation. This technique can be highly effective when the environment is very regular.

One outstanding and rather unique characteristic of our technique is its ability to create "hidden state variables" in order to describe the environment. Each equivalence class of tests forms such a "hidden state variable," and our method in many cases will identify just the right set of such variables for the most economical description of the environment.

However, the work presented here is merely a first step, and it has many significant limitations. The following ones are probably most significant; further research is needed to see how best to overcome these difficulties.

- *Anisotropy:* Consider a 5 × 6 Grid World instead of the 5 × 5 Grid World. The hidden state variable indicating which axis the robot is oriented along is *not* an equivalence class of tests, and this world is not well handled with our technique.
- *Actions with probabilistic effects:* Consider a "spin" action in the Grid World, which leaves the robot facing in a random direction.
- *Actions with conditional effects:* Consider a Grid World with boundaries, so that the "step ahead" action has no effect *if* the robot is facing and up against the boundary.
- *Dependence on global state variables:* An "on-off" switch in the Car Radio World is not handled very well. (This is essentially the same as the "anisotropy" problem.)
- *Difficult to reach states:* If a long, complicated sequence of actions is required to get the environment into a state needed to learn something, then our method of "random walks" is unlikely to work efficiently, and the careful planning of experiments is required. (We have recent work in this regard.)

ACKNOWLEDGMENTS

This chapter was prepared with support from NSF grant DCR-8607494, ARO Grant DAAL03-86-K-0171, and a grant from the Siemens Corporation.

References

Angluin, D. 1978. On the complexity of minimum inference of regular sets. *Information and Control,* 39, 337–350.

———— , 1982. Inference of reversible languages. *Journal of the ACM,* 29(3), 741–765.

———— , 1986. *Learning regular sets from queries and counterexamples* (Technical Report YALEU/DCS/TR-464). New Haven, CT: Yale University, Department of Computer Science.

Angluin, D. and Smith, C.H. 1983. Inductive inference: Theory and methods. *Computing Surveys,* 15(3), 237–269.

Gold, E.M. 1972. System identification via state characterization. *Automatica,* 8, 621–636.

———— , 1978. Complexity of automaton identification from given data. *Information and Control,* 37, 302–320.

Rivest, R.L., and Schapire, R.E. 1987. Diversity-based inference of finite automata. *Proceedings 28th IEEE Foundations of Computer Science Conference.* To appear.

de Saint-Exupèry, A. 1943. *The Little Prince.* New York, NY: Harcourt, Brace and World.

Shapiro, E.Y. 1981. *Inductive inference of theories from facts* (Research Report 192). New Haven, CT: Yale University, Department of Computer Science.

BIBLIOGRAPHY OF RECENT
MACHINE LEARNING RESEARCH
1985–1989

Pawel A. Stefanski
Janusz Wnek
Jianping Zhang
(George Mason University)

INTRODUCTION

This bibliography is intended to be a useful reference for researchers, students, and any other readers interested in the field of machine learning. It is a continuation of the bibliographies provided in *Machine Learning: An Artificial Intelligence Approach, Volume I* and *Volume II* (edited by Michalski, Carbonell, and Mitchell) published in 1983 and 1986, respectively. Volume I (ML1) covered the period from the beginning of the field until 1982, and the bibliography contained 572 entries. Volume II (ML2) covered the period from 1983 to 1984, and its bibliography contained 312 entries.

This bibliography covers the period 1985 to 1989 and contains 1095 entries. This increased number of publications reflects the very rapid growth of the field in recent years. In selecting items for the bibliography we primarily emphasized research in machine learning from the artificial intelligence perspective, although some relevant contributions from related disciplines, such as psychology, cognitive science, philosophy and mathematics are also included. The selection is representative rather than exhaustive, with better representation of research done in Europe. In contrast to bibliographies in ML1 and ML2, the current bibliography also includes a substantial number of references on connectionist methods and the computational theory of learning, two areas that have been rapidly growing in recent years. To round out the bibliography, several classics in machine learning and a few selected overviews and background materials published before 1985 have been included. We restricted ourselves specifically to publications in English, due to their greater availability throughout the world. In a few cases where publications are also available in another language we indicated this in the annotation.

To help the reader locate publications of interest, each of the entries has been assigned one or more categories from 17 categories reflecting the type of article and/or research methodology used. All entries were sorted in lexicographic order, where the key is defined as the concatenation of the last name and initials of the first author, the year of publication and when applicable, the last names and initials of other authors.

In preparing this bibliography we thoroughly examined the following sources:

- *Machine Learning* journal 1986–1989
- Proceedings of the International Machine Learning Workshops: Skytop 1985, Irvine 1987, Ann Arbor 1988, Ithaca 1989
- Proceedings of IJCAI: Los Angeles 1985, Milan, Italy 1987, Detroit 1989
- Proceedings of AAAI: Philadelphia 1986, Seattle 1987, Saint Paul 1988
- Proceedings of the European Conference on Artificial Intelligence (ECAI): Brighton, England 1986; Munich, W. Germany 1988
- Proceedings of the European Working Session on Learning (EWSL): Bled, Yugoslavia 1987; Glasgow, Scotland 1988; Montpellier, France 1989
- *Proceedings of the 1988 AAAI Symposium on Explanation-based Learning*
- Proceedings of the International Conference on Genetic Algorithms: Pittsburgh 1985; Cambridge 1987; Fairfax 1989
- Proceedings of the Annual Workshop on Computational Learning Theory (COLT): Pittsburgh 1988; Santa Cruz 1989
- *Proceedings of the ONR Workshop on Knowledge Acquisition*, Arlington 1989
- *Proceedings of the IEEE International Workshop on Tools for AI*, Fairfax 1989
- *Artificial Intelligence* journal 1985–1988
- *AI Magazine* 1985–1989

We also searched through other relevant periodicals and publications, but covered them only partially. Among them are:

- *Proceedings of the Workshop on Knowledge Discovery in Databases*, Detroit 1989
- *Proceedings of the First International Conference on Principles of Knowledge Representation and Reasoning*, Toronto, Canada 1989

- Proceedings of International Symposiums on Methodologies for Intelligent Systems, 1986; 1987; 1988; 1989.
- *Proceedings of the International Workshop on Machine Learning, Meta-Reasoning and Logics*, Sesimbra, Portugal 1988
- Proceedings of the First, Second, and Third Workshops on Knowledge Acquisition for Knowledge-based Systems
- *Proceedings of the Fourth IEEE Conference on Artificial Intelligence Applications*, San Diego, 1988
- *Proceedings of the 1988 Connectionist Models Summer School*, Pittsburgh 1988
- *Proceedings of the Workshop on Knowledge Compilation*, Corvalis, Oregon 1986
- *IEEE Transactions on Pattern Analysis and Machine Intelligence* 1985–1989
- *IEEE Transactions on Systems, Man and Cybernetics* 1985–1989
- *IEEE Expert* 1985–1989
- *Proceedings of the 1986 IEEE International Conference on Systems, Man and Cybernetics*
- *Proceedings of the 1988 IEEE International Symposium on Intelligent Control*
- *International Journal for Man-Machine Studies*
- Proceedings of the Conferences of the Cognitive Science Society
- *ACM Sigart Newsletter*
- *ACM Computing Surveys*
- *Neural Network Journal*
- *Knowledge Acquisition Journal*

ACKNOWLEDGMENTS

The authors gratefully acknowledge several individuals who helped prepare this bibliography. In particular, thanks go to Ryszard S. Michalski, who guided us throughout the whole process, helped to construct the list of categories used in this classification, and carefully reviewed the final outcome. We are also very grateful to Yves Kodratoff and Katharina Morik for providing us with extensive lists of European publications. Despite all efforts, some references may have been overlooked, and the editors apologize in advance to the authors of these works, as well as to the readers, for any omissions or errors.

This work was done in the Center for Artificial Intelligence at George Mason University. Research in the Center for Artificial Intelligence is supported in part by the Defense Advanced Research Projects Agency under a grant, administered by the Office of Naval Research, No. N00014–87-K-0874, in part by the Office of Naval Research under grant No. N00014–88-K-0226, and in part by the Office of Naval Research under grant No. N00014–88-K-0397.

EXPLANATION OF THE CATEGORIES

Following the style introduced in ML1 and ML2, we have categorized all publications with respect to the topic, research paradigm and type of publication. To accommodate the changes and the growth of the field, we have modified and expanded the classification schemas used in ML1 and ML2. Each publication is marked with a label, denoting the categories it belongs to. We also provide the cross reference to each category to identify publications belonging to the category of interest. Below are the labels, names of the associated categories, and a brief explanations of the categories.

a   Analogical and case-based learning systems

Publications on methods that employ analogy to known problem solutions, concepts, or past cases.

b   Background material, overviews, and conference proceedings

Foundational sources and introductory material to the fields of artificial intelligence and machine learning. Also included are proceedings of the major AI-related conferences.

c   Conceptual clustering

Publications concerned with organizing a set of observations into a hierarchy of meaningful categories. Each category is associated with a simple descriptive concept.

d   Discovery systems

Publications on methods and systems that explore given domains, in either a passive or an active way, trying to develop empirical laws and theories about it. Conceptual clustering can be viewed as one of the forms of discovery, as can be any form of unsupervised learning.

e   Experimental applications and comparisons

Publications concerning applications of learning methods to artificial or real-world problems, as well as reviews and experimental comparisons of different learning systems.

g   **Genetic algorithms and classifier systems**

Publications describing methods based on the idea of probabilistic search through large spaces involving states that can be represented as strings in some language.

i   **Integrated learning systems**

Publications on systems combining two or more learning strategies or paradigms.

k   **Knowledge acquisition for expert systems and learning apprentice systems**

Publications on methods or systems that acquire and improve knowledge through an interaction with a human expert, during the particular problem solving task.

l   **Learning in control systems**

Publications about methods or systems developed for learning in complex, real-time systems, controlling various physical devices.

m   **Cognitive modeling of learning and reasoning**

Research in this category is based on investigations of human methods of learning and reasoning. Primary effort is to build computational models of these processes and eventually apply them to some practical tasks.

n   **Neural nets and connectionist systems**

These publications describe a broad class of methods using algorithms for training a network to respond correctly to a set of examples, by appropriately modifying its connection weights.

p   **Problem solving and planning with learning capabilities**

Publications in this category describe systems for learning domain and control knowledge through observing their own performance on subsequent tasks. Some of these methods are closely related to learning apprentice systems.

r   **Prediction and discovery of patterns in sequences and processes**

Publications about methods or systems dealing with prediction of sequences or time-dependent processes.

s   **Symbolic empirical learning from examples**

Research methods in this category use examples in order to learn new concepts or solve problems. They use symbolic representation, easily comprehensible to humans: rules, decision trees, frames, scripts, semantic networks, or some form of logic.

t   **Theoretical analysis**

This category includes research concerned with theoretical analysis of formalized, abstract learning systems.

v   **Constructive induction, abduction or knowledge representation shift**

Publications on inductive learning methods that utilize background knowledge to create knowledge represented at a higher level of abstraction (e.g., causal knowledge) and/or in a different form than the original input information.

x   **Explanation-based learning and other analytic methods**

Publications in this category describe methods that rely heavily on preexisting knowledge in order to learn/improve the quality of possessed knowledge.

The list of publications follows. Next to each reference in the left margin are the code letters of the categories to which the reference belongs. This list is supplemented with the cross reference, where numbers of references belonging to this category are listed under each category name.

CROSS-REFERENCE OF THE CATEGORIES

a   **Analogical and case-based learning systems**

[5], [6], [7], [11], [22], [32], [33], [34], [36], [37], [41], [42], [43], [44], [46], [47], [100], [101], [102], [115], [120], [121], [158], [180], [181], [202], [204], [206], [244], [245], [246], [247], [248], [342], [343], [359], [363], [364], [365], [367], [368], [406], [421], [450], [454], [455], [458], [459], [461], [472], [473], [503], [506], [508], [558], [559], [560], [603], [684], [731], [732], [771], [774], [798], [799], [827], [830], [844], [868], [871], [887], [924], [948], [951], [991], [997], [1025], [1026], [1027], [1036], [1088]

b   **Background material and overviews**

[20], [27], [49], [78], [87], [92], [99], [123], [124], [141], [162], [163], [167], [182], [187], [191], [193], [236], [255], [276], [289], [298], [306], [320], [333], [405], [406], [412], [413], [435], [444], [474], [489], [492], [494], [528], [530], [531], [534], [562], [581], [611], [614], [619], [626], [627], [628], [629], [630], [631], [634], [636], [637], [638], [645], [646], [647], [651], [661], [663], [664], [677], [680], [698], [709], [742], [759], [760], [776], [781], [782], [783], [784], [785], [786], [787], [788], [789], [790], [791], [792], [793], [794], [795], [796], [797], [798], [799], [800], [801], [802], [803], [804], [805], [806], [807], [856], [866], [886], [888], [923], [952], [955], [967], [969], [1032], [1052], [1077]

c   **Conceptual clustering**

[148], [174], [186], [189], [256], [257], [258], [259], [260], [261], [263], [264], [284], [307], [308], [351], [354], [355], [369], [373], [374], [375], [453], [543], [549], [550], [604], [633], [638], [678], [710], [738], [770], [805], [902], [903], [935], [963], [964], [994], [1073], [1075], [1081]

d   **Discovery systems**

[9], [13], [122], [126], [153], [185], [220], [221], [239], [246], [249], [250], [335], [353], [407], [408], [409], [412], [418], [423], [426], [427], [428], [434], [436], [446], [452], [453], [468], [469], [477], [496], [497], [498], [499], [501], [514], [524], [527], [529], [530], [533], [534], [535], [536], [578], [579], [685], [708], [711], [712], [713], [730], [758], [778], [822], [846], [848], [852], [853], [854], [855], [882], [883], [897], [937], [938], [940], [941], [949], [950], [960], [1017], [1038], [1065], [1068], [1069], [1070], [1089], [1091], [1092], [1093], [1094], [1095]

e   **Experimental applications and comparisons**

[9], [12], [80], [84], [100], [101], [110], [111], [139], [174], [199], [200], [232], [233], [236], [237], [240], [265], [266], [283], [290], [326], [359], [385], [393], [394], [396], [425], [439], [453], [473], [475], [492], [494], [529], [537], [538], [558], [578], [579], [588], [605], [627], [649], [650], [662], [665], [676], [677], [681], [693], [704], [733], [738], [740], [744], [764], [773], [797], [817], [839], [857], [862], [878], [889], [956], [960], [991], [995], [1016], [1035], [1054], [1067], [1074]

g   **Genetic algorithms and classifier systems**

[2], [54], [88], [89], [90], [129], [130], [131], [166], [182], [184], [192], [193], [195], [196], [267], [272], [321], [322], [323], [334], [336], [337], [338], [339], [341], [397], [410], [411], [412], [413], [509], [515], [567], [667], [727], [783], [790], [803], [817], [832], [842], [843], [849], [850], [851], [879], [884], [885], [918], [922], [1013], [1048], [1049], [1050], [1051], [1085], [1086], [1087], [1088]

i   **Integrated learning systems**

[10], [48], [63], [64], [70], [71], [73], [128], [176], [177], [178], [214], [217], [224], [225], [251], [282], [356], [401], [424], [448], [451], [481], [482], [487], [495], [502], [512], [539], [546], [547], [549], [550], [552], [600], [617], [618], [639], [641], [643], [675], [679], [711], [715], [746], [747], [749], [752], [754], [755], [756], [757], [830], [880], [914], [933], [945], [949], [966], [974], [986], [1040], [1041], [1046], [1058], [1061], [1066], [1075], [1083]

k   **Knowledge acquisition for expert systems and learning apprentice systems**

[41], [42], [44], [45], [46], [51], [84], [91], [92], [94], [95], [108], [109], [110], [138], [156], [161], [173], [183], [201], [203], [211], [212], [241], [242], [254], [281], [288], [296], [311], [312], [314], [315], [316], [317], [318], [327], [348], [349], [350], [372], [393], [395], [404], [419], [441], [442], [443], [449], [452], [467], [478], [479], [487], [538], [561], [562], [564], [584], [593], [594], [595], [613], [620], [662], [665], [677], [695], [696], [697], [718], [725], [728], [739], [768], [771], [774], [777], [822], [827], [855], [861], [872], [896], [908], [920], [924], [941], [943], [946], [953], [986], [987], [992], [993], [996], [1009], [1010], [1011], [1012], [1020], [1034], [1042], [1043], [1044], [1045], [1046], [1047], [1066], [1076]

l   **Learning in control systems**

[52], [98], [171], [209], [252], [277], [278], [283], [293], [321], [322], [340], [440], [500], [704], [708], [797], [875], [877], [878], [1039], [1082]

m   **Cognitive modeling of learning and reasoning**

[8], [15], [22], [34], [87], [119], [167], [168], [221], [222], [227], [244], [262], [275], [298], [319], [404], [406], [435], [520], [540], [545], [547], [576], [598], [603], [607], [611], [614], [624], [644], [651], [693], [747], [750], [751], [752], [844], [858], [859], [866], [916], [947], [962], [967], [979], [980], [981], [1060], [1078], [1079], [1080]

n   **Neural nets and connectionist systems**

[3], [12], [17], [18], [19], [20], [38], [50], [81], [82], [179], [189], [200], [213], [214], [265], [266], [273], [370], [371], [386], [398], [399], [432], [438], [451], [505], [525], [553], [580], [581], [583], [608], [614], [624], [667], [676], [699], [727], [751], [805], [821], [866], [915], [917], [933], [970], [971], [972], [982], [988], [989], [1007], [1008], [1024], [1029], [1031], [1035], [1057], [1082]

p   **Problem solving and planning with learning capabilities**

[11], [14], [17], [53], [57], [58], [60], [61], [79], [85], [120], [121], [122], [125], [140], [142], [146], [152], [169], [170], [172], [188], [199], [206], [220], [269], [309], [324], [340], [360], [361], [363], [364], [367], [368], [369], [420], [426], [437], [439], [480], [481], [483], [484], [503], [507], [510], [518], [519], [521], [522], [554], [555], [559], [563], [584], [585], [612], [615], [616], [618], [652], [655], [656], [660], [666], [672], [673], [682], [683], [685], [695], [724], [726], [775], [779], [808], [863], [864], [905], [906], [907], [908], [910], [919], [932], [936], [939], [948], [954], [961], [962], [977], [981], [984], [990], [1015], [1018], [1033], [1056], [1072], [1073], [1076]

r   **Prediction and discovery of patterns in sequences and processes**

[207], [216], [436], [453], [640], [973], [1081]

s   Symbolic empirical learning from examples

[24], [25], [30], [35], [39], [51], [63], [64], [65], [66], [67], [68], [69],
[72], [74], [75], [76], [83], [87], [91], [94], [103], [108], [109], [111],
[112], [113], [114], [117], [127], [133], [134], [135], [136], [137], [138],
[139], [143], [144], [145], [146], [147], [149], [154], [157], [158], [159],
[160], [176], [177], [185], [194], [197], [198], [199], [205], [217], [218],
[224], [226], [228], [230], [231], [237], [238], [253], [263], [265], [266],
[268], [270], [279], [280], [286], [287], [290], [291], [292], [294], [295],
[302], [304], [305], [310], [325], [328], [329], [330], [331], [332], [346],
[347], [351], [376], [377], [378], [380], [384], [387], [388], [389], [390],
[412], [414], [416], [417], [418], [429], [430], [439], [453], [456], [471],
[485], [490], [491], [493], [504], [505], [511], [523], [532], [537], [539],
[544], [546], [548], [551], [556], [557], [569], [570], [572], [573], [576],
[584], [588], [589], [590], [591], [592], [596], [597], [601], [606], [621],
[625], [632], [635], [637], [642], [649], [650], [676], [677], [686], [687],
[688], [689], [693], [694], [703], [705], [706], [707], [714], [716], [728],
[734], [735], [736], [737], [740], [743], [754], [755], [757], [762], [763],
[764], [765], [766], [767], [769], [772], [805], [810], [812], [813], [814],
[815], [816], [817], [818], [819], [820], [828], [829], [831], [832], [833],
[834], [835], [836], [837], [838], [840], [845], [847], [862], [865], [867],
[869], [870], [871], [874], [875], [876], [877], [889], [891], [892], [893],
[894], [898], [899], [900], [901], [921], [936], [956], [957], [958], [965],
[978], [982], [983], [990], [993], [1000], [1001], [1002], [1004], [1005],
[1006], [1011], [1015], [1016], [1020], [1025], [1026], [1027], [1033],
[1037], [1047], [1053], [1062], [1066], [1067], [1074], [1084]

t   Theoretical analysis

[1], [15], [16], [23], [24], [25], [26], [27], [28], [29], [31], [40], [55], [56],
[72], [80], [82], [86], [96], [97], [111], [112], [132], [137], [149], [175],
[197], [207], [215], [218], [230], [231], [243], [263], [271], [274], [285],
[286], [297], [299], [300], [301], [304], [344], [376], [377], [378], [379],
[380], [381], [382], [383], [384], [388], [390], [391], [392], [410], [415],
[430], [431], [433], [438], [440], [454], [456], [457], [469], [470], [476],
[486], [516], [517], [524], [529], [532], [565], [566], [568], [571], [574],
[575], [586], [602], [609], [647], [648], [657], [680], [700], [701], [702],
[717], [718], [729], [741], [761], [762], [769], [770], [772], [796], [804],
[805], [821], [833], [834], [838], [846], [848], [857], [859], [867], [869],
[870], [873], [921], [942], [968], [992], [995], [1006], [1007], [1008],
[1014], [1019], [1021], [1022], [1023], [1036], [1064], [1071], [1095]

v   **Constructive induction, abduction or knowledge**
        representation shift

        [39], [118], [154], [202], [204], [205], [224], [225], [268], [295], [332],
        [346], [493], [499], [502], [526], [569], [570], [582], [609], [610], [622],
        [623], [666], [688], [689], [690], [691], [692], [734], [735], [833], [834],
        [836], [837], [838], [839], [841], [881], [890], [891], [892], [893], [894],
        [895], [985], [998], [999], [1001], [1030], [1059], [1063], [1065], [1066]

x   **Explanation-based learning and other analytic methods**

        [4], [8], [13], [14], [21], [43], [47], [57], [58], [59], [60], [61], [62], [63],
        [64], [77], [78], [93], [95], [104], [105], [106], [107], [116], [142], [150],
        [151], [152], [155], [164], [165], [169], [176], [177], [190], [191], [208],
        [209], [210], [217], [219], [223], [229], [232], [233], [234], [235], [236],
        [249], [270], [303], [309], [313], [315], [316], [326], [344], [345], [352],
        [357], [358], [362], [363], [364], [366], [400], [401], [402], [403], [422],
        [423], [445], [447], [459], [460], [462], [463], [464], [465], [466], [468],
        [488], [493], [513], [519], [522], [541], [542], [563], [577], [582], [585],
        [586], [587], [599], [612], [639], [653], [654], [655], [656], [657], [658],
        [659], [660], [663], [665], [668], [669], [670], [671], [672], [673], [674],
        [681], [682], [719], [720], [721], [722], [723], [724], [725], [745], [746],
        [748], [749], [750], [753], [754], [755], [756], [757], [773], [779], [780],
        [795], [808], [809], [811], [823], [824], [825], [826], [830], [857], [860],
        [896], [904], [905], [906], [907], [908], [909], [910], [911], [912], [913],
        [925], [926], [927], [928], [929], [930], [931], [932], [934], [944], [945],
        [953], [959], [968], [974], [975], [976], [977], [981], [984], [1003],
        [1012], [1014], [1028], [1055], [1072], [1090]

REFERENCES

t   [1]   Abe, N., "Polynomial Learnability of Semilinear Sets, "
                Proceedings of the 1989 Workshop on Computational Learning
                Theory COLT '89, pp. 25–41, University of California, Santa
                Cruz, 1989.

g   [2]   Ackley, D.H., "Stochastic Iterated Genetic Hillclimbing," Thesis,
                Computer Science Dept. Carnegie-Mellon University, 1987.

n   [3]   Ackley, D.H., Hinton, G.E, and Sejnowski, T.J., "A Learning
                Algorithm for Boltzmann Machines," Cognitive Science, Vol. 9,
                pp. 147–169, 1987.

x   [4]   **Acosta, R.D., and Huhns, M.N.,** "Alternative Explanation
           Structures for Explanation-Based Learning," MCC Technical
           Report ACA/AI-CAD-079-88, Microelectronics and Comp. Tech.
           Corp., Austin, TX, 1988.

a   [5]   **Agnar, A.,** "Towards Robust Expert Systems that Learn from
           Experience—An Architectural Framework," Proceedings of the
           3rd European Workshop on Knowledge Acquisition for
           Knowledge-Based Systems, pp. 311–326, 1989.

a   [6]   **Aha, D.W.,** "Incremental, Instance-Based Learning of
           Independent and Graded Concept Descriptions," Proceedings of
           the 6th International Workshop on Machine Learning, pp.
           387–391, Ithaca, NY, 1989.

a   [7]   **Aha, D.W., and Kibler, D.,** "Noise-Tolerant Instance-Based
           Learning Algorithms," Proceedings of IJCAI-89, pp. 794–799,
           Detroit, MI, 1989.

mx   [8]   **Ahn, W., Mooney, R., Brewer, W., and DeJong, G.F.,** "Schema
           Acquisition from One Example: Psychological Evidence for
           Explanation-Based Learning," CSL Technical Report, University
           of Illinois at Urbana-Champaign, 1987.

de   [9]   **Ai, C.S., Blower, P., and Ledwith, P.,** "Discovering Reaction
           Information from Chemical Abstracts," Proceedings of IJCAI-89
           Workshop on Knowledge Discovery in Databases, pp. 1–3,
           Detroit, MI, 1989.

i   [10] **Ali, K.M.,** "Augmenting Domain Theory for Explanation-Based
           Generalization," Proceedings of the 6th International Workshop on
           Machine Learning, pp. 40–42, Ithaca, NY, 1989.

ap   [11] **Allen, J.A., and Langley, P.W.,** "Using Concept Hierarchies to
           Organize Plan Knowledge," Proceedings of the 6th International
           Workshop on Machine Learning, pp. 229–231, Ithaca, NY, 1989.

en   [12] **Alspector, J., and Allen, R.B.,** "A Neuromorphic VLSI Learning
           System," Technical Report, Bell Communications Research, 1987.

dx   [13] **Amarel, S.,** "Program Synthesis as a Theory Formation Task:
           Problem Representations and Solution Methods," Machine
           Learning: An Artificial Intelligence Approach, Volume II, Morgan
           Kaufmann, San Mateo, CA, R.S. Michalski, J.G. Carbonell and
           T.M. Mitchell (Eds.), pp. 499–570, 1986.

px   [14] **Ammon, K.,** "The Automatic Acquisition of Proof Methods,"
           Proceedings of AAAI-88, pp. 558–563, Saint Paul, MN, 1988.

mt   [15]   **Amsterdam, J.,** "Some Philosophical Problems with Formal Learning Theory, " Proceedings of AAAI-88, pp. 580–584, Saint Paul, MN, 1988.

t   [16]   **Amsterdam, J.,** "Extending the Valiant Learning Model," Proceedings of the 5th International Conference on Machine Learning, pp. 381–394, Ann Arbor, MI, 1988.

np   [17]   **Anderson, C.W.,** "Learning and Problem Solving with Multilayer Connectionist System," Thesis, Computer Science Dept. University of Massachusetts, 1986.

n   [18]   **Anderson, C.W.,** "Strategy Learning with Multilayer Connectionist Representations," Proceedings of the 4th International Machine Learning Workshop, pp. 103–114, University of California, Irvine, 1987.

n   [19]   **Anderson, C.W.,** "Tower of Hanoi with Connectionist Networks: Learning New Features," Proceedings of the 6th International Workshop on Machine Learning, pp. 345–349, Ithaca, NY, 1989.

bn   [20]   **Anderson, J.A., and Rosenfeld, E.,** "Neurocomputing: Foundations of Research," The MIT Press, 1988.

x   [21]   **Anderson, J.R.,** "Knowledge Compilation: The General Learning Mechanism," Machine Learning: An Artificial Intelligence Approach, Volume II, Morgan Kaufmann, San Mateo, CA, R.S. Michalski, J.G. Carbonell and T.M. Mitchell (Eds.), pp. 289–310, 1986.

am   [22]   **Anderson, J.R.,** "Causal Analysis and Inductive Learning," Proceedings of the 4th International Machine Learning Workshop, pp. 288–299, University of California, Irvine, 1987.

t   [23]   **Angluin, D.,** "Learning Regular Sets from Queries and Counter-Examples," Technical Report YALEU/DCS/TR-464, Yale University, 1986.

st   [24]   **Angluin, D.,** "Types of Queries for Concept Learning," Technical Report YALEU/DCS/TR-479, Yale University, 1986.

st   [25]   **Angluin, D.,** "Queries and Concept Learning," Machine Learning, Vol. 2, No. 4, 1987.

t   [26]   **Angluin, D., and Laird, P.D.,** "Learning from Noisy Examples," Machine Learning, Vol. 2, No. 4, 1987.

bt   [27]   **Angluin, D., and Smith, C.H.,** "Inductive Inference," Encyclopedia of Artificial Intelligence, John Wiley & Sons, S.C. Shapiro (Ed.), pp. 409–418, 1987.

t   [28]   **Angluin, D.,** "Learning with Hints," Proceedings of the 1988 Workshop on Computational Learning Theory COLT '88, pp. 167–181, MIT, 1988.

t   [29]   **Angluin, D.,** "Equivalence Queries and Approximate Fingerprints," Proceedings of the 1989 Workshop on Computational Learning Theory COLT '89, pp. 134–145, University of California, Santa Cruz, 1989.

s   [30]   **Arbab, B., and Michie, D.,** "Generating Rules from Examples," Proceedings of IJCAI-85, pp. 631–633, Los Angeles, CA, 1985.

t   [31]   **Arikawa, S., Shinohara, T., and Yamamoto, A.,** "Elementary Formal System as a Unifying Framework for Language Learning," Proceedings of the 1989 Workshop on Computational Learning Theory COLT '89, pp. 312–327, University of California, Santa Cruz, 1989.

a   [32]   **Ashley, K.D.,** "Modeling Legal Argument: Reasoning with Cases and Hypotheticals," Thesis, University of Massachusetts, 1988.

a   [33]   **Ashley, K.D., and Rissland, E.L.,** "Compare and Contrast, A Test of Expertise," Proceedings of the Case-Based Reasoning Workshop, pp. 31–36, 1988.

am   [34]   **Ashley, K.D.,** "Defining Salience in Case-Based Arguments," Proceedings of IJCAI-89, pp. 537–542, Detroit, MI, 1989.

s   [35]   **Baim, P.W.,** "A Method for Attribute Selection in Inductive Learning Systems," IEEE Transactions on Pattern Analysis and Machine Intelligence, Vol. PAMI-10, No. 6, pp. 888–896, 1988.

a   [36]   **Bain, W.M.,** "A Case-Based Reasoning System for Subjective Assessment," Proceedings of AAAI-86, pp. 523–527, Philadelphia, PA, 1986.

a   [37]   **Bain, W.M.,** "Case-Based Reasoning: A Computer Model of Subjective Assessment," Thesis, Yale University, 1986.

n   [38]   **Ballard, D.H.,** "Modular Learning in Neural Networks," Proceedings of AAAI-87, pp. 279–284, Seattle, WA, 1987.

sv   [39]   **Banerji, R.B.,** "Learning in the Limit in a Growing Language," Proceedings of IJCAI-87, pp. 280–282, Milan, Italy, 1987.

t   [40]   **Banerji, R.B.,** "Learning Theories in a Subset of a Polyadic Logic," Proceedings of the 1988 Workshop on Computational Learning Theory COLT '88, pp. 267–277, MIT, 1988.

ak [41] **Bareiss, E.R., and Porter, B.W.,** "Protos: An Exemplar-Based Learning Apprentice," Proceedings of the 4th International Machine Learning Workshop, pp. 12–23, University of California, Irvine, 1987.

ak [42] **Bareiss, E.R.,** "Protos: A Unified Approach to Concept Representation, Classification, and Learning," Computer Science Dept. Vanderbilt University, Thesis, No. CS-88–10, Nashville, TN, 1988.

ax [43] **Bareiss, E.R., Banting, K., and Porter, B.W.,** "The Role of Explanation-Based Indexing of Cases," Proceedings of the Case-Based Reasoning Workshop at AAAI-88, Saint Paul, MN, 1988.

ak [44] **Bareiss, E.R.,** "Exemplar-Based Knowledge Acquisition: A Unified Approach to Concept Representation, Classification, and Learning," Academic Press, Perspectives in AI, 1989.

k   [45] **Bareiss, E.R., Porter, B.W., and Murray, K.S.,** "Supporting Start-to-Finish Development of Knowledge Bases," Machine Learning, Vol. 4, No. 3/4, 1989.

ak [46] **Bareiss, E.R., Porter, B.W., and Wier, C.C.,** "Protos: An Exemplar-Based Learning Apprentice," Machine Learning: An Artificial Intelligence Approach, Volume III, Morgan Kaufmann, San Mateo, CA,   Kodratoff, Y. and Michalski, R.S. (Eds.), Ch. 4, 1990.

ax [47] **Barletta, R., and Mark, W.,** "Explanation-Based Indexing of Cases," Proceedings of AAAI-88, pp. 541–546, Saint Paul, MN, 1988.

i   [48] **Barletta, R., and Kerber, R.,** "Improving Explanation-Based Indexing with Empirical Learning," Proceedings of the 6th International Workshop on Machine Learning, pp. 84–86, Ithaca, NY, 1989.

b   [49] **Barr, A., and Feigenbaum, E.A.,** "The Handbook of Artificial Intelligence: Volume I and II," Addison-Wesley, 1981.

n   [50] **Barto, A.G., and Anderson, C.W.,** "Structural Learning in Connectionist Systems," Proceedings of the 7th Conference of the Cognitive Science Society, pp. 43–53, 1985.

ks   [51]   **Baskin, A.B., and Michalski, R.S.,** "An Integrated Approach to
                the Construction of Knowledge-Based Systems: Experience with
                Advise and Related Programs," Topics in Expert System Design,
                North-Holland, Amsterdam, G. Guida and C. Tasso (Eds.), pp.
                111–143, 1989.

l   [52]   **Basser, T.,** "Modelling of Skilled Behaviour and Learning,"
                Proceedings of the IEEE International Conference on Systems,
                Man, and Cybernetics, pp. 272–276, Atlanta, GA, 1986.

p   [53]   **Basye, K., Dean, T., and Vitter, J.S.,** "Coping with Uncertainty
                in Map Learning," Proceedings of IJCAI-89, pp. 663–668, Detroit,
                MI, 1989.

g   [54]   **Belew, R.K., and Forrest, S.,** "Learning and Programming in
                Classifier Systems," Machine Learning, Vol. 3, No. 2/3, pp.
                193–224, 1988.

t   [55]   **Ben-David, S., Benedek, G.M., and Mansour, Y.,** "A
                Parametrization Scheme for Classifying Models of Learnability,"
                Proceedings of the 1989 Workshop on Computational Learning
                Theory COLT '89, pp. 285–302, University of California, Santa
                Cruz, 1989.

t   [56]   **Benedek, G.M., and Itai, A.,** "Learnability by Fixed
                Distributions," Proceedings of the 1988 Workshop on
                Computational Learning Theory COLT '88, pp. 81–90, MIT, 1988.

px   [57]   **Benjamin, D.P.,** "Learning Strategies by Reasoning about Rules,"
                Proceedings of IJCAI-87, pp. 256–259, Milan, Italy, 1987.

px   [58]   **Benjamin, D.P.,** "Learning Search Control Knowledge Within a
                Metalevel Representation," Proceedings of 1988 Symposium on
                Explanation-Based Learning, pp. 175–179, Stanford, 1988.

x   [59]   **Bennett, S.W.,** "Approximation in Mathematical Domains,"
                Proceedings of IJCAI-87, pp. 239–241, Milan, Italy, 1987.

px   [60]   **Bennett, S.W.,** "Real-World EBL: Learning Error Tolerant Plans
                in the Robotics Domain," Proceedings of 1988 Symposium on
                Explanation-Based Learning, pp. 122–126, Stanford, 1988.

px   [61]   **Bennett, S.W.,** "Learning Approximate Plans for Use in the Real
                World," Proceedings of the 6th International Workshop on
                Machine Learning, pp. 224–228, Ithaca, NY, 1989.

x   [62]   **Bennett, S.W., and DeJong, G.F.,** "Learning to Plan in Uncertain
                and Continuous Domains," Proceedings of Office of Naval
                Research Workshop on Knowledge Acquisition, A.L. Meyrowitz
                (Ed.), Arlington, VA, 1989.

isx   [63]   **Bergadano, F., and Giordana, A.,** "A Knowledge Intensive
             Approach to Concept Induction," Proceedings of the 5th
             International Conference on Machine Learning, pp. 305–317, Ann
             Arbor, MI, 1988.

isx   [64]   **Bergadano, F., Giordana, A., and Saitta, L.,** "Concept
             Acquisition in an Integrated EBL and SBL Environment,"
             Proceedings of ECAI-88, pp. 363–368, Munich, W. Germany,
             1988.

s   [65]   **Bergadano, F., Matwin, S., Michalski, R.S., Zhang, J.,**
             "Measuring Quality of Concept Descriptions," Proceedings of
             EWSL-88, pp. 1–14, Glasgow, Scotland, 1988.

s   [66]   **Bergadano, F., Matwin, S., Michalski, R.S., Zhang, J.,**
             "Representing and Acquiring Imprecise and Context-Dependent
             Concepts in Knowledge-Based Systems," Proceedings of the 3rd
             International Symposium on Methodologies for Intelligent
             Systems, Torino, Italy, 1988.

s   [67]   **Bergadano, F., Matwin, S., Michalski, R.S., and Zhang, J.,**
             "Learning Flexible Concept Descriptions Using a Two-Tiered
             Knowledge Representation: Ideas and a Method," AI Center,
             George Mason University, No. MLI-88–4, 1988.

s   [68]   **Bergadano, F., Matwin, S., Michalski, R.S., and Zhang, J.,**
             "Learning Flexible Concept Descriptions Using a Two-Tiered
             Knowledge Representation: Implementation and experiments," AI
             Center, George Mason University, No. MLI-88–5, 1988.

s   [69]   **Bergadano, F., Brancadori, F., Giordana, A., and Saitta, L.,** "A
             System that Learns Diagnostic Knowledge in a Database
             Framework," Proceedings of IJCAI-89 Workshop on Knowledge
             Discovery in Databases, pp. 4–15, Detroit, MI, 1989.

i   [70]   **Bergadano, A., Giordana, A., and Ponsero, S.,** "Deduction in
             Top-Down Inductive Learning," Proceedings of the 6th
             International Workshop on Machine Learning, pp. 23–25, Ithaca,
             NY, 1989.

i   [71]   **Bergadano, F., and Ponsero, S.,** "Integrating Empirical and
             Analytic Learning in Concept Acquisition," Proceedings of the 4th
             International Symposium on Methodologies for Intelligent
             Systems, pp. 273–280, 1989.

st   [72]   **Bergadano, F., and Saitta, L.,** "On the Error Probability of
             Boolean Concept Descriptions," Proceedings of EWSL-89,
             Montpellier, France, 1989.

i   [73]   **Bergadano, F., and Giordana, A.,** "Guiding Induction with
             Domain Theories," Machine Learning: An Artificial Intelligence
             Approach, Volume III, Morgan Kaufmann, San Mateo, CA,
             Kodratoff, Y. and Michalski, R.S. (Eds.), Ch. 17, 1990.

s   [74]   **Berwick, R.C.,** "Learning from Positive-Only Examples: The
             Subset Principle and Three Case Studies," Machine Learning: An
             Artificial Intelligence Approach, Volume II, Morgan Kaufmann,
             San Mateo, CA, R.S. Michalski, J.G. Carbonell and T.M. Mitchell
             (Eds.), pp. 625–646, 1986.

s   [75]   **Berwick, R.C., and Pilato, S.,** "Learning Syntax by Automata
             Induction," Machine Learning, Vol. 2, No. 1, pp. 9–38, 1987.

s   [76]   **Berzuini, C.,** "Combining Symbolic Learning Techniques and
             Statistical Regression Analysis," Proceedings of AAAI-88, pp.
             612–617, Saint Paul, MN, 1988.

x   [77]   **Bhatnager, N.,** "A Correctness Proof of Explanation-Based
             Generalization as Resolution Theorem Proving," Proceedings of
             1988 Symposium on Explanation-Based Learning, pp. 220–225,
             Stanford, 1988.

bx   [78]   **Biermann, A.W., Guiho, G., and Kodratoff, Y.,** "Automatic
             Program Construction Techniques," Macmillan Publishing
             Company, 1984.

p   [79]   **Birnbaum, L., Collins, G., and Krulwich, B.,** "Issues in the
             Justification-Based Diagnosis of Planning Failures," Proceedings
             of the 6th International Workshop on Machine Learning, pp.
             194–196, Ithaca, NY, 1989.

et   [80]   **Bisson, G., and Laublet, P.,** "A Functional Model to Evaluate
             Learning System," Proceedings of EWSL-89, Montpellier, France,
             1989.

n   [81]   **Blelloch, G., and Rosenberg, C.R.,** "Network Learning on the
             Connection Machine," Proceedings of IJCAI-87, pp. 323–326,
             Milan, Italy, 1987.

nt   [82]   **Blum, A., and Rivest, R.L.,** "Training a 3-Node Neural Network
             is NP-Complete," Proceedings of the 1988 Workshop on
             Computational Learning Theory COLT '88, pp. 9–18, MIT, 1988.

s   [83]   **Blythe, J.,** "Constraining Search in a Hierarchical Discriminative
             Learning System," Proceedings of ECAI-88, pp. 378–383,
             Munich, W. Germany, 1988.

ek [84] Blythe, J., et al., "Knowledge Acquisition by Machine Learning: the INSTIL Project," Esprit88: Putting the Technology to Use, North-Holland, Amsterdam, pp. 769–779, 1988.

p [85] Blythe, J., and Mitchell, T.M., "On Becoming Reactive," Proceedings of the 6th International Workshop on Machine Learning, pp. 255–258, Ithaca, NY, 1989.

t [86] Board, R, and Pitt, L., "Semi-Supervised Learning," Machine Learning, Vol. 4, No. 1, 1989.

bms [87] Bolc, L., "Computational Models of Learning," Springer-Verlag, Symbolic Computation: Artificial Intelligence, Berlin Heidelberg, 1987.

g [88] Booker, L.B., "Improving the Performance of Genetic Algorithms in Classifier Systems," Genetic Algorithms and Simulated Annealing, Pittman Press, D. Davis (Ed.), pp. 69–81, 1987.

g [89] Booker, L.B., "Classifier Systems that Learn Internal World Models," Machine Learning, Vol. 3, No. 2/3, pp. 161–192, 1988.

g [90] Booker, L.B., Goldberg, D.E., and Holland, J.H., "Classifier Systems and Genetic Algorithms," Artificial Intelligence, Vol. 40, pp. 235–282, 1989.

ks [91] Boose, J.H., and Bradshaw, J.M., "Expertise Transfer and Complex Problems Using AQUINAS as a Knowledge Acquisition Workbench for Expert Systems," Proceedings of the Knowledge Acquisition for Knowledge-Based Systems Workshop, Banff, Canada, 1987.

bk [92] Boose, J.H., and Gaines, B.R., "Knowledge Acquisition for Knowledge-Based Systems: Notes on the State of the Art," Machine Learning, Vol. 4, No. 2, 1989.

x [93] Boswell, R.A., "Analytic Goal-Regression: Problems, Solutions, and Enhancements," Proceedings of ECAI-86, Brighton, England, 1986.

ks [94] Botta, M., and Saitta, L., "Improving Knowledge Based System Performance by Experience," Proceedings of EWSL-88, pp. 15–24, Glasgow, Scotland, 1988.

kx [95] Botta, M., Giordana, A., and Saitta, L., "Use of Deep Theory to Refine a Knowledge Base," Proceedings of EWSL-89, Montpellier, France, 1989.

t [96] Boucheron, S., and Sallantin, J., "Learnability in the Presence of Noise," Proceedings of EWSL-88, pp. 25–36, Glasgow, Scotland, 1988.

t   [97]   **Boucheron, S., and Sallantin, J.,** "Some Remarks About
               Space-Comlexity of Learning, and Circuit Complexity of
               Recognizing," Proceedings of the 1988 Workshop on
               Computational Learning Theory COLT '88, pp. 125–138, MIT,
               1988.

l   [98]   **Bourbakis, N.G.,** "A Learning Algorithmic Scheme for Collision
               Free Robot Navigation," Proceedings of IEEE International
               Symposium on Intelligent Control, 1988.

b   [99]   **Brachman, R.J., and Levesque, H.J.,** "Readings in Knowledge
               Representation," Morgan Kaufmann, 1985.

ae   [100]   **Bradshaw, G.L.,** "Learning to Recognize Speech Sounds: A
               Theory and Model," Thesis, Department of Psychology,
               Carnegie-Mellon Univ., 1985.

ae   [101]   **Bradshaw, G.L.,** "Learning about Speech Sounds: The NEXUS
               Project," Proceedings of the 4th International Machine Learning
               Workshop, pp. 1–11, University of California, Irvine, 1987.

a   [102]   **Branting, L.K.,** "The Role of Explanation in Reasoning from
               Legal Precedents," Proceedings of the Case-Based Reasoning
               Workshop, pp. 94–103, 1988.

s   [103]   **Bratko, I., and Kononenko, I.,** "Learning Diagnostic Rules from
               Incomplete and Noisy Data," Interactions in Artificial Intelligence
               and Statistical Method, London, England, B. Phelps (Ed.), pp.
               142, 1986.

x   [104]   **Braudaway W., and Tong C.,** "Automated Synthesis of
               Constrained Generators," Proceedings of IJCAI-89, pp. 583–589,
               Detroit, MI, 1989.

x   [105]   **Braverman, M.S., and Russell, S.J.,** "Explanation-Based
               Learning in Complex Domains," Proceedings of 1988 Symposium
               on Explanation-Based Learning, pp. 90–94, Stanford, 1988.

x   [106]   **Braverman, M.S., and Russell, S.J.,** "IMEX: Overcoming
               Intractability in Explanation-Based Learning," Proceedings of
               AAAI-88, pp. 575–579, Saint Paul, MN, 1988.

x   [107]   **Braverman, M.S., and Russell, S.J.,** "Boundaries of
               Operationality," Proceedings of the 5th International Conference
               on Machine Learning, pp. 221–234, Ann Arbor, MI, 1988.

ks   [108]   **Brazdil, P.B.,** "Knowledge States and Meta-Knowledge
               Maintenance," Proceedings of EWSL-87, pp. 138–146, Bled,
               Yugoslavia, 1987.

ks   [109]   **Buchanan, B.G., Sullivan, J., Cheng, T.P., and Clearwater, S.H.,** "Simulation-Assisted Inductive Learning," Proceedings of AAAI-88, pp. 552–557, Saint Paul, MN, 1988.

ek   [110]   **Buchanan, B.G.,** "Can Machine Learning Offer Anything to Expert Systems?," Machine Learning, Vol. 4, No. 3/4, 1989.

est   [111]   **Bundy, A., Silver, B., and Plummer, D.,** "An Analytical Comparison of Some Rule-Learning Programs," Artificial Intelligence, Vol. 27, No. 2, pp. 137–181, 1985.

st   [112]   **Buntine, W.,** "Generalized Subsumption and Its Applications to Induction and Redundancy," Artificial Intelligence, Vol. 36, pp. 149–176, (earlier version published in proceedings of ECAI-86), 1988.

s   [113]   **Buntine, W.,** "Learning Classification Rules Using Bayes," Proceedings of the 6th International Workshop on Machine Learning, pp. 94–98, Ithaca, NY, 1989.

s   [114]   **Buntine, W.,** "Stratifying Samples to Improve Learning," Proceedings of IJCAI-89 Workshop on Knowledge Discovery in Databases, pp. 16–25, Detroit, MI, 1989.

a   [115]   **Burstein, M.H.,** "Concept Formation by Incremental Analogical Reasoning and Debugging," Machine Learning: An Artificial Intelligence Approach, Volume II, Morgan Kaufmann, San Mateo, CA, R.S. Michalski, J.G. Carbonell and T.M. Mitchell (Eds.), pp. 351–370, 1986.

x   [116]   **Bylander, T., and Weintraub, M.A.,** "A Corrective Learning Procedure Using Different Explanatory Types," Proceedings of 1988 Symposium on Explanation-Based Learning, pp. 27–30, Stanford, 1988.

s   [117]   **Cai, Y., Cercone, N., and Han, J.,** "Attribute-Oriented Induction in Relational Databases," Proceedings of IJCAI-89 Workshop on Knowledge Discovery in Databases, pp. 26–36, Detroit, MI, 1989.

v   [118]   **Callan, J.P.,** "Knowledge-Based Feature Generation," Proceedings of the 6th International Workshop on Machine Learning, pp. 441–443, Ithaca, NY, 1989.

m   [119]   **Carbonell, J.G., and Hood. G.,** "The World Modeler's Project: Objectives and Simulator Architecture," Proceedings of the 3rd International Machine Learning Workshop, pp. 14–16, Skytop, PA, 1985.

ap   [120]   **Carbonell, J.G.,** "Analogical Reasoning in Planning and Decision
              Making," Proceedings of the 1st International Symposium on
              Methodologies for Intelligent Systems, pp. 288, Knoxville, TN,
              1986.

ap   [121]   **Carbonell, J.G.,** "Derivational Analogy: A Theory of
              Reconstructive Problem Solving and Expertise Acquisition,"
              Machine Learning: An Artificial Intelligence Approach, Volume II,
              Morgan Kaufmann, San Mateo, CA, R.S. Michalski, J.G.
              Carbonell and T.M. Mitchell (Eds.), pp. 371–392, 1986.

dp   [122]   **Carbonell, J.G., and Gil, Y.,** "Learning by Experimentation,"
              Proceedings of the 4th International Machine Learning Workshop,
              pp. 256–266, University of California, Irvine, 1987.

b   [123]   **Carbonell, J.G., and Langley, P.W.,** "Machine Learning,"
              Encyclopedia of Artificial Intelligence, John Wiley & Sons, S.C.
              Shapiro (Ed.), pp. 464–488, 1987.

b   [124]   **Carbonell, J.G.,** "Introduction: Paradigms for Machine
              Learning," Artificial Intelligence, Vol. 40, pp. 1–9, 1989.

p   [125]   **Carbonell, J.G.,** "Hierarchical and Multi-Agent Planning in
              PRODIGY," Proceedings of Office of Naval Research Workshop
              on Knowledge Acquisition, A.L. Meyrowitz (Ed.), Arlington, VA,
              1989.

d   [126]   **Carbonell, J.G., and Gil, Y.,** "Learning by Experimentation: The
              Operator Refinement Method," Machine Learning: An Artificial
              Intelligence Approach, Volume III, Morgan Kaufmann, San
              Mateo, CA, Kodratoff, Y. and Michalski, R.S. (Eds.), Ch. 7, 1990.

s   [127]   **Carlos, G.J., and Alcaraz, R.F.,** "A Learning System for
              INFERNO Inference Networks," Proceedings of the 3rd European
              Workshop on Knowledge Acquisition for Knowledge-Based
              Systems, pp. 365–379, 1989.

i   [128]   **Carpineto, C.,** "An Approach Based on Integrated Learning to
              Generating Stories from Stories," Proceedings of the 5th
              International Conference on Machine Learning, pp. 298–304, Ann
              Arbor, MI, 1988.

g   [129]   **Caruana, R.A., and Schaffer, J.D.,** "Representation and Hidden
              Bias: Gray vs. Binary Coding for Genetic Algorithms,"
              Proceedings of the 5th International Conference on Machine
              Learning, pp. 153–161, Ann Arbor, MI, 1988.

g　　[130]　**Caruana, R.A., Eshelman, L.J., and Schaffer, J.D.,** "Representation and Hidden Bias II: Eliminating Defining Length Bias in Genetic Search via Shuffle Crossover," Proceedings of IJCAI-89, pp. 750–755, Detroit, MI, 1989.

g　　[131]　**Caruana, R.A., Schaffer, J.D., and Eshelman, L.J.,** "Using Multiple Representations to Improve Inductive Bias: Gray and Binary Coding for Genetic Algorithms," Proceedings of the 6th International Workshop on Machine Learning, pp. 375–378, Ithaca, NY, 1989.

t　　[132]　**Case, J.,** "The Power of Vacillation," Proceedings of the 1988 Workshop on Computational Learning Theory COLT '88, pp. 196–205, MIT, 1988.

s　　[133]　**Cestnik, B., and Kononenko, I.,** "ASSISTANT86: A Knowledge-Elicitation Tool for Sophisticated Users," Proceedings of EWSL-87, pp. 31–45, Bled, Yugoslavia, 1987.

s　　[134]　**Cestnik, B., and Bratko, I.,** "Learning Redundant Rules in Noisy Domains," Proceedings of ECAI-88, pp. 348–350, Munich, W.Germany, 1988.

s　　[135]　**Chan, C.C., and Grzymala-Busse, J.W.,** "Rough-Set Boundaries as a Tool for Learning Rules from Examples," Proceedings of the 4th International Symposium on Methodologies for Intelligent Systems, pp. 281–288, 1989.

s　　[136]　**Chan, K.C., and Wong, A.K.,** "Automatic Construction of Expert Systems from Data: A Statistical Approach," Proceedings of IJCAI-89 Workshop on Knowledge Discovery in Databases, pp. 37–48, Detroit, MI, 1989.

st　　[137]　**Chan, P.K.,** "Inductive Learning with BCT," Proceedings of the 6th International Workshop on Machine Learning, pp. 104–108, Ithaca, NY, 1989.

ks　　[138]　**Chandrasekaran, B.,** "Task-Structures, Knowledge Acquisition and Learning," Machine Learning, Vol. 4, No. 3/4, 1989.

es　　[139]　**Channic, T.,** "TEXPERT: An Application of Machine Learning to Texture Recognition," AI Center, George Mason University, No. MLI-89–17, 1989.

p　　[140]　**Chapman, D.,** "Planning for Conjunctive Goals," Artificial Intelligence, Vol. 32, 1987.

b　　[141]　**Charniak, E., and McDermott, D.,** "Introduction to Artificial Intelligence," Addison-Wesley, 1985.

px   [142] Chase, M.P., Zweben, M., Piazza, R.L., Burger, J.D., Maglio,
             P.P., and Hirsh, H., "Approximating Learned Search Control
             Knowledge," Proceedings of the 6th International Workshop on
             Machine Learning, pp. 21–220, Ithaca, NY, 1989.

s   [143] Cheeseman, P., Kelly, J., Self, M., Stutz, J., Taylor, W., and
             Freeman, D., "Bayesian Classification," Proceedings of
             AAAI-88, pp. 607–611, Saint Paul, MN, 1988.

s   [144] Cheeseman, P., Kelly, J., Self, M., Stutz, J., Taylor, W., and
             Freeman, D., "AutoClass: A Bayesian Classification System,"
             Proceedings of the 5th International Conference on Machine
             Learning, pp. 54–64, Ann Arbor, MI, 1988.

s   [145] Chen, M.C., and McNamee, L., "Summary Data Estimation
             using Decision Trees," Proceedings of IJCAI-89 Workshop on
             Knowledge Discovery in Databases, pp. 49–56, Detroit, MI, 1989.

ps   [146] Cheng, C., and Carbonell, J.G., "The FERMI System: Inducing
             Iterative Macro-Operators from Experience," Proceedings of
             AAAI-86, pp. 490–495, Philadelphia, PA, 1986.

s   [147] Cheng, J., Fayyad, U.M., Irani, K.B., and Qian, Z., "Improved
             Decision Trees: A Generalized Version of ID3," Proceedings of
             the 5th International Conference on Machine Learning, pp.
             100–106, Ann Arbor, MI, 1988.

c   [148] Cheng, Y. and Fu, K., "Conceptual Clustering in Knowledge
             Organization," IEEE Transactions on Pattern Analysis and
             Machine Intelligence, Vol. PAMI-7, No. 5, pp. 592–598, 1985.

st   [149] Cherniavsky, J.C., Velauthapillai, M., and Statman, R.,
             "Inductive Inference: An Abstract Approach," Proceedings of the
             1988 Workshop on Computational Learning Theory COLT '88,
             pp. 251–266, MIT, 1988.

x   [150] Chien, S.A., "A Framework for Explanation-Based Refinement,"
             Proceedings of 1988 Symposium on Explanation-Based Learning,
             pp. 137–141, Stanford, 1988.

x   [151] Chien, S.A., "Using and Refining Simplifications:
             Explanation-Based Learning of Plans in Intractable Domains,"
             Proceedings of IJCAI-89, pp. 590–595, Detroit, MI, 1989.

px   [152] Chien, S.A., "Learning by Analyzing Fortuitous Occurrences,"
             Proceedings of the 6th International Workshop on Machine
             Learning, pp. 249–251, Ithaca, NY, 1989.

d [153] **Chiu, D.K., and Wong, A.K.,** "Discretization, Event-Covering, Data Synthesis and Information," Proceedings of IJCAI-89 Workshop on Knowledge Discovery in Databases, pp. 57–70, Detroit, MI, 1989.

sv [154] **Chrisman, L.,** "Evaluating Bias During Pac-Learning," Proceedings of the 6th International Workshop on Machine Learning, pp. 469–471, Ithaca, NY, 1989.

x [155] **Clancey, W.J.,** "Detecting and Coping with Failure," Proceedings of 1988 Symposium on Explanation-Based Learning, pp. 22–26, Stanford, 1988.

k [156] **Clancey, W.J.,** "The Knowledge Level Reinterpreted: Modeling How Systems Interact," Machine Learning, Vol. 4, No. 3/4, 1989.

s [157] **Clark, P., and Niblett, T.,** "Induction in Noisy Domains," Proceedings of EWSL-87, pp. 11–30, Bled, Yugoslavia, 1987.

as [158] **Clark, P.,** "Representing Arguments as Background Knowledge for Constraining Generalization," Proceedings of EWSL-88, pp. 37–44, Glasgow, Scotland, 1988.

s [159] **Clark, P., and Niblett, T.,** "The CN2 Induction Algorithm," Machine Learning, Vol. 3, No. 4, pp. 261–284, 1989.

s [160] **Clearwater, S.H., Cheng, T.P., Hirsh, H., and Buchanan, B.G.,** "Incremental Batch Learning," Proceedings of the 6th International Workshop on Machine Learning, pp. 366–370, Ithaca, NY, 1989.

k [161] **Cleynenbreugel, J.V., Suetens, P., and Oosterlink, A.,** "Tapping GIS-Related Knowledge Sources to Delineate Road Structures on Satellite Imagery," Proceedings of IJCAI-89 Workshop on Knowledge Discovery in Databases, pp. 71–80, Detroit, MI, 1989.

b [162] **Cohen, P.R., and Feigenbaum, E.A.,** "The Handbook of Artificial Intelligence: Volume III," Addison-Wesley, 1981.

b [163] **Cohen, P.R.,** "Heuristic Reasoning about Uncertainty: An AI Approach," Pitman, London, and Morgan Kaufmann, San Mateo, CA, 1985.

x [164] **Cohen, W.,** "Generalizing Number and Learning from Multiple Examples in Explanation Based Learning," Proceedings of the 5th International Conference on Machine Learning, pp. 256–269, Ann Arbor, MI, 1988.

x [165] **Cohen, W., Mostow, J., and Borgida, A.,** "Generalizing Number in Explanation-Based Learning," Proceedings of 1988 Symposium on Explanation-Based Learning, pp. 68–72, Stanford, 1988.

g   [166] **Cohoon, J.P., Martin, W.N., and Richards, D.,** "Punctuated
               Equilibria: A Paradigm for Probabilistic Search," Proceedings of
               Office of Naval Research Workshop on Knowledge Acquisition,
               A.L. Meyrowitz (Ed.), Arlington, VA, 1989.

bm   [167] **Collins, A., and Smith, E.E.,** "Readings in Cognitive Science: A
               Perspective from Psychology and Artificial Intelligence," Morgan
               Kaufmann, 1988.

m   [168] **Collins, A., and Michalski, R.S.,** "The Logic of Plausible
               Reasoning: A Core Theory," Cognitive Science, Vol. 13, No. 2,
               1989.

px   [169] **Collins, G., and Birnbaum, L.,** "An Explanation-Based
               Approach to the Transfer of Planning Knowledge Across
               Domains," Proceedings of 1988 Symposium on
               Explanation-Based Learning, pp. 107–111, Stanford, 1988.

p   [170] **Collins, G., Birnbaum, L., and Krulwich, B.,** "An Adaptive
               Model of Decision-Making in Planning," Proceedings of
               IJCAI-89, pp. 511–516, Detroit, MI, 1989.

l   [171] **Connell, M.E., and Utgoff, P.E.,** "Learning to Control Dynamic
               Physical Systems," Proceedings of AAAI-87, pp. 456–460,
               Seattle, WA, 1987.

p   [172] **Converse, T., Hammond, K.J., and Marks, M.,** "Learning from
               Opportunity," Proceedings of the 6th International Workshop on
               Machine Learning, pp. 246–248, Ithaca, NY, 1989.

k   [173] **Cornuejols, A.,** "An Exploration into Incremental Learning: The
               INFLUENCE System," Proceedings of the 6th International
               Workshop on Machine Learning, pp. 383–386, Ithaca, NY, 1989.

ce   [174] **Dale, M.B.,** "On the Comparison of Conceptual Clustering and
               Numerical Taxonomy," IEEE Transactions of Pattern Analysis and
               Machine Intelligence, Vol. PAMI-7, No. 1, pp. 241–244, 1985.

t   [175] **Daley, R.,** "Transformation of Probabilistic Learning Strategies
               into Deterministic," Proceedings of the 1988 Workshop on
               Computational Learning Theory COLT '88, pp. 220–226, MIT,
               1988.

isx   [176] **Danyluk, A.P.,** "The Use of Explanations for Similarity-Based
               Learning," Proceedings of IJCAI-87, pp. 274–276, Milan, Italy,
               1987.

isx   [177] **Danyluk, A.P.,** "Integrated Learning is a Two-Way Street,"
               Proceedings of 1988 Symposium on Explanation-Based Learning,
               pp. 36–40, Stanford, 1988.

i   [178] **Danyluk, A.P.,** "Finding New Rules for Incomplete Theories: Explicit Biases for Induction with Contextual Information," Proceedings of the 6th International Workshop on Machine Learning, pp. 34–36, Ithaca, NY, 1989.

n   [179] **DARPA,** "Neural Network Study, October 1987–February 1988", AFCEA International Press, November, 1988, .

a   [180] **Davies, T.R.,** "Analogy," Informal Note CSLI-IN-85-4, CSLI, Stanford University, 1985.

a   [181] **Davies, T.R., and Russell, S.J.,** "A Logical Approach to Reasoning by Analogy," Proceedings of IJCAI-87, pp. 264–270, Milan, Italy, 1987.

bg   [182] **Davis, D.,** "Genetic Algorithms and Simulated Annealing," Pitman, London and Morgan Kaufmann, San Mateo, CA, 1987.

k   [183] **Davis, E.,** "Representing and Acquiring Geographic Knowledge," Pitman, London and Morgan Kaufmann, Research Notes in Artificial Intelligence, San Mateo, CA, 1987.

g   [184] **Davis, L., and Young, D.K.,** "Classifier Systems with Hamming Weights," Proceedings of the 5th International Conference on Machine Learning, pp. 162–173, Ann Arbor, MI, 1988.

ds   [185] **Decaestecker, C.,** "Incremental Concept Formation with Attribute Selection," Proceedings of EWSL-89, Montpellier, France, 1989.

c   [186] **Decaestecker, C.,** "Incremental Concept Formation via a Suitability Criterion," Proceedings of the Conference on Data Analysis, Learning Symbolic and Numeric Knowledge, pp. 435–442, INRIA, Antibes, 1989.

b   [187] **Defays, D.,** "Statistics and Artificial Intelligence," Proceedings of the Conference on Data Analysis, Learning Symbolic and Numeric Knowledge, pp. 381–388, INRIA, Antibes, 1989.

p   [188] **DeFigureiredo, R.J.P. and Wang, K.H.,** "An Evolving Frame Approach to Learning with Application to Adaptive Navigation," Proceedings of the IEEE International Conference on Systems, Man, and Cybernetics, pp. 51–54, Atlanta, GA, 1986.

cn   [189] **DeGaris, H.,** "COMPO: Conceptual Clustering with Connectionist Competitive Learning," Proceeding of the 1st IEE International Conference on Neural Networks, London, England, 1989.

x   [190]   DeJong, G.F., "An Approach to Learning from Observation,"
                 Machine Learning: An Artificial Intelligence Approach, Volume II,
                 Morgan Kaufmann, San Mateo, CA, R.S. Michalski, J.G.
                 Carbonell and T.M. Mitchell (Eds.), pp. 571–590, 1986.

bx   [191]   DeJong, G.F., and Mooney, R., "Explanation-Based Learning: An
                 Alternative View," Machine Learning, Vol. 1, No. 2, pp. 145–176,
                 1986.

g   [192]   De Jong, K.A., "On Using Genetic Algorithms to Search Program
                 Spaces," Proceedings of the 2nd International Conference on
                 Genetic Algorithms, pp. 210–216, Cambridge, MA, 1987.

bg   [193]   De Jong, K.A., "Learning with Genetic Algorithms: An
                 Overview," Machine Learning, Vol. 3, No. 2/3, pp. 121–138, 1988.

s   [194]   De Jong, K.A., and Schultz, A.C., "Using Experience-Based
                 Learning in Game Playing," Proceedings of the 5th International
                 Conference on Machine Learning, pp. 284–290, Ann Arbor, MI,
                 1988.

g   [195]   De Jong, K.A., and Spears, W., "Using Genetic Algorithms to
                 Solve NP-Complete Problems," Proceedings of the 3rd
                 International Conference on Genetic Algorithms and their
                 Applications, Fairfax, VA, 1989.

g   [196]   De Jong, K.A., "Genetic-Algorithm-based Learning," Machine
                 Learning: An Artificial Intelligence Approach, Volume III, Morgan
                 Kaufmann, San Mateo, CA, Kodratoff, Y. and Michalski, R.S.
                 (Eds.), Ch. 21, 1990.

st   [197]   Delgrande, J.P., "A Formal Approach to Learning from
                 Examples," Proceedings of IJCAI-87, pp. 315–322, Milan, Italy,
                 1987.

s   [198]   DeMantaras, R.L., "ID3 Revisited: A Distance-Based Criterion
                 for Attribute Selection," Proceedings of the 4th International
                 Symposium on Methodologies for Intelligent Systems, pp.
                 342–450, 1989.

eps   [199]   DeMori, R., Lam, L., and Gilloux, M., "Learning and Plan
                 Refinement in a Knowledge-Based System for Automatic Speech
                 Recognition," IEEE Transactions on Pattern Analysis and Machine
                 Intelligence, Vol. PAMI-9, No. 2, pp. 289, 1987.

en   [200]   DeMori, R., Bengio, Y., and Cosi, P., "On the Generalization
                 Capability of Multi-Layered Networks in the Extraction of Speech
                 Properties," Proceedings of IJCAI-89, pp. 1531–1536, Detroit, MI,
                 1989.

k   [201]   **DeRaedt, L., and Bruynooghe, M.,** "On Interactive Concept-Learning and Assimilation," Proceedings of EWSL-88, pp. 167–176, Glasgow, Scotland, 1988.

av   [202]   **DeRaedt, L.,** "Constructive Induction By Analogy: How to Learn," Proceedings of EWSL-89, Montpellier, France, 1989.

k   [203]   **DeRaedt, L., and Bruynooghe, M.,** "Towards Friendly Concept-Learners," Proceedings of IJCAI-89, pp. 849–854, Detroit, MI, 1989.

av   [204]   **DeRaedt, L., and Bruynooghe, M.,** "Constructive Induction by Analogy," Proceedings of the 6th International Workshop on Machine Learning, pp. 476–477, Ithaca, NY, 1989.

sv   [205]   **DeRaedt, L., and Maurice, B.,** "On Explanation and Bias in Inductive Concept-Learning," Proceedings of the 3rd European Workshop on Knowledge Acquisition for Knowledge-Based Systems, pp. 338–353, 1989.

ap   [206]   **Dershowitz, N.,** "Programming by Analogy," Machine Learning: An Artificial Intelligence Approach, Volume II, Morgan Kaufmann, Los Altos, CA, R.S. Michalski, J.G. Carbonell and T.M. Mitchell (Eds.), pp. 395–424, 1986.

rt   [207]   **DeSantis, A., Markowsky, G., and Wegman, M.N.,** "Learning Probabilistic Prediction Functions," Proceedings of the 1988 Workshop on Computational Learning Theory COLT '88, pp. 312–327, MIT, 1988.

x   [208]   **Desimone, R.V.,** "Explanation-Based Learning of Proof Plans," Proceedings of EWSL-86, Orsay, France, 1986.

lx   [209]   **Desimone, R.V.,** "Learning Control Knowledge within an Explanation-Based Learning Framework," Proceedings of EWSL-87, pp. 107–120, Bled, Yugoslavia, 1987.

x   [210]   **DeSigueira, J.L.N., and Puget, J.-F.,** "Explanation-Based Generalization of Failures," Proceedings of ECAI-88, pp. 339–344, Munich, W.Germany, 1988.

k   [211]   **Diederich, J.,** "Knowledge-Based Knowledge Elicitation," Proceedings of IJCAI-87, pp. 201–204, Milan, Italy, 1987.

k   [212]   **Diederich, J., Ruhmann, I., and May, M.,** "KRITON: A Knowledge Acquisition Tool for Expert Systems," Proceedings of the Knowledge Acquisition for Knowledge-Based Systems Workshop, Banff, Canada, 1987.

n   [213]   **Diederich, J.,** "Connectionist Recruitment Learning," Proceedings of ECAI-88, pp. 351–356, Munich, W.Germany, 1988.

in   [214] **Diederich, J.,** "'Learning by Instruction' in Connectionist
               Systems," Proceedings of the 6th International Workshop on
               Machine Learning, pp. 66–68, Ithaca, NY, 1989.

t   [215] **Dietterich, T.G.,** "Learning at the Knowledge Level," Machine
               Learning, Vol. 1, No. 3, pp. 287–316, 1986.

r   [216] **Dietterich, T.G., and Michalski, R.S.,** "Learning to Predict
               Sequences," Machine Learning: An Artificial Intelligence
               Approach, Volume II, Morgan Kaufmann, San Mateo, CA, R.S.
               Michalski, J.G. Carbonell and T.M. Mitchell (Eds.), pp. 63–106,
               1986.

isx   [217] **Dietterich, T.G., and Flann, N.S.,** "An Inductive Approach to
               Solving the Imperfect Theory Problem," Proceedings of 1988
               Symposium on Explanation-Based Learning, pp. 42–46, Stanford,
               1988.

st   [218] **Dietterich, T.G.,** "Limitations on Inductive Learning,"
               Proceedings of the 6th International Workshop on Machine
               Learning, pp. 124–128, Ithaca, NY, 1989.

x   [219] **Dietzen, S., and Pfenning, F.,** "Higher-Order and Modal Logic as
               a Framework for Explanation-Based Generalization," Proceedings
               of the 6th International Workshop on Machine Learning, pp.
               447–449, Ithaca, NY, 1989.

dp   [220] **Dolan, C., and Dyer, M.,** "Learning Planning Heuristics through
               Observation," Proceedings of IJCAI-85, pp. 600–602, Los
               Angeles, CA, 1985.

dm   [221] **Dontas, K.J.,** "APPLAUSE: An Implementation of
               Collins-Michalski Theory of Plausible Reasoning," AI Center,
               George Mason University, No. MLI-88-29, 1988.

m   [222] **Dontas, K.J., and Zemankova, M.,** "APPLAUSE: An
               Experimental Plausible Reasoning System," Proceedings of the
               3rd International Symposium on Methodologies for Intelligent
               Systems, North-Holland, pp. 29–39, Torino, Italy, 1988.

x   [223] **Doyle, R.J.,** "Constructing and Refining Causal Explanations
               From an Inconsistent Domain Theory," Proceedings of AAAI-86,
               pp. 538–544, Philadelphia, PA, 1986.

isv   [224] **Drastal, G., Czako, G., and Raatz, S.,** "Induction in an
               Abstraction Space: A Form of Constructive Induction,"
               Proceedings of IJCAI-89, pp. 707–712, Detroit, MI, 1989.

iv [225] **Drastal, G., Meunier, R., and Raatz, S.,** "Error Correction in Constructive Induction," Proceedings of the 6th International Workshop on Machine Learning, pp. 80–83, Ithaca, NY, 1989.

s [226] **Drastal, G., Raatz, S., and Meunier, R.,** "Correcting Feature Noise in Disjunctive Concept Learning," Proceedings of EWSL-89, Montpellier, France, 1989.

m [227] **Drescher, G.L.,** "A Mechanism for Early Piagetian Learning," Proceedings of AAAI-87, pp. 290–294, Seattle, WA, 1987.

s [228] **Dupas, R., and Millot, P.,** "A Learning Expert System for Preventive Maintenance," Proceedings of the 3rd European Workshop on Knowledge Acquisition for Knowledge-Based Systems, pp. 354–364, 1989.

x [229] **Duval, B., and Kodratoff, Y.,** "A Tool for the Management of Incomplete Theories: Reasoning about Explanations," Machine Learning, Meta-Reasoning, Logic, Pitman, P.B. Brazdil (Ed.), 1989.

st [230] **Ehrenfeucht, A., and Haussler, D.,** "Learning Decision Trees from Random Examples," Proceedings of the 1988 Workshop on Computational Learning Theory COLT '88, pp. 182–193, MIT, 1988.

st [231] **Ehrenfeucht, A., Haussler, D., Kearns, M., and Valiant, L.,** "A General Lower Bound on the Number of Examples Needed for Learning," Proceedings of the 1988 Workshop on Computational Learning Theory COLT '88, pp. 139–154, MIT, 1988.

ex [232] **Ellman, T.,** "Explanation-Based Learning in Logic Circuit Design," Proceedings of the 3rd International Machine Learning Workshop, pp. 35–37, Skytop, PA, 1985.

ex [233] **Ellman, T.,** "Generalizing Logic Circuit Designs by Analyzing Proofs of Correctness," Proceedings of IJCAI-85, Los Angeles, CA, 1985.

x [234] **Ellman, T.,** "Explanation-Directed Search for Simplifying Assumptions," Proceedings of 1988 Symposium on Explanation-Based Learning, pp. 95–99, Stanford, 1988.

x [235] **Ellman, T.,** "Approximate Theory Formation: An Explanation-Based Approach," Proceedings of AAAI-88, pp. 570–574, Saint Paul, MN, 1988.

bex [236] **Ellman, T.,** "Explanation-Based Learning: A Survey of Programs and Perspectives," ACM Computing Surveys, Vol. 21, No. 2, pp. 163–222, June, 1989.

es [237] Elomaa, T., and Holsti, N., "An Experimental Comparison of Inducing Decision Trees and Lists in Noisy Domains," Proceedings of EWSL-89, Montpellier, France, 1989.

s [238] Emde, W., "Non-Cumulative Learning in METAXA.3," Proceedings of IJCAI-87, pp. 208–210, Milan, Italy, 1987.

d [239] Epstein, S., "On the Discovery of Mathematical Theorems," Proceedings of IJCAI-87, pp. 194–197, Milan, Italy, 1987.

e [240] Erickson, M.D. and Zytkow, J.M., "Utilizing Experience for Improving the Tactical Manager," Proceedings of the 5th International Conference on Machine Learning, pp. 444–450, Ann Arbor, MI, 1988.

k [241] Eshelman, L. and McDermott, J., "MOLE: A Knowledge Acquisition Tool that Uses Its Head," Proceedings of AAAI-86, Philadelphia, PA, 1986.

k [242] Eshelman, L., Ehret, D., McDermott, J. and Tan, M., "MOLE: A Tenacious Knowledge Acquisition Tool," Proceedings of the Knowledge Acquisition for Knowledge-Based Systems Workshop, Banff, Canada, 1987.

t [243] Etzioni, O., "Hypothesis Filtering: A Practical Approach to Reliable Learning," Proceedings of the 5th International Conference on Machine Learning, pp. 416–429, Ann Arbor, MI, 1988.

am [244] Falkenhainer, B.C., Forbus, K.D., and Gentner, D., "The Structure-Mapping Engine," Proceedings of AAAI-86, pp. 272–277, Philadelphia, PA, 1986.

a [245] Falkenhainer, B.C., "An Examination of the Third Stage in the Analogy Process: Verification-Based Analogical Learning," Proceedings of IJCAI-87, pp. 260–263, Milan, Italy, 1987.

ad [246] Falkenhainer, B.C., "Scientific Theory Formation Through Analogical Inference," Proceedings of the 4th International Machine Learning Workshop, pp. 218–229, University of California, Irvine, 1987.

a [247] Falkenhainer, B.C., "The Utility of Difference-Based Reasoning," Proceedings of AAAI-88, pp. 530–535, Saint Paul, MN, 1988.

a [248] Falkenhainer, B.C., "Learning from Physical Analogies: A Study in Analogy and the Explanation Process," Thesis, University of Illinois at Urbana-Champaign, December, 1988.

dx [249] **Falkenhainer, B.C., and Rajamoney, S.,** "The Interdependences of Theory Formation, Revision, and Experimentation," Proceedings of the 5th International Conference on Machine Learning, pp. 353–366, Ann Arbor, MI, 1988.

d [250] **Falkenhainer, B.C., and Michalski, R.S.,** "Integrating Quantitative and Qualitative Discovery in the ABACUS System," Machine Learning: An Artificial Intelligence Approach, Volume III, Morgan Kaufmann, San Mateo, CA, Kodratoff, Y. and Michalski, R.S. (Eds.), Ch. 6, (earlier version published in Machine Learning Journal, Vol.1, No.4, 1986), 1990.

i [251] **Fawcett, T.E.,** "Learning form Plausible Explanations," Proceedings of the 6th International Workshop on Machine Learning, pp. 37–39, Ithaca, NY, 1989.

l [252] **Fayyad, U.A., VanVoorhis, K.E. and Wiesmeyer, M.D.,** "Learning Control Information In Rule-Based Systems: A Weak Method," Proceedings of the 4th IEEE International Conference on Artificial Intelligence Applications, pp. 188–193, San Diego, CA, 1988.

s [253] **Fayyad, U.A., and Irani, K.,** "Relating Performance Measures for Decision Trees: What Should We Minimize in a Decision Tree?," Proceedings of IJCAI-89 Workshop on Knowledge Discovery in Databases, pp. 81–93, Detroit, MI, 1989.

k [254] **Fertig, S., and Gelernter, D.,** "Experiments with a Database-Driven Expert System," Proceedings of IJCAI-89 Workshop on Knowledge Discovery in Databases, pp. 94–98, Detroit, MI, 1989.

b [255] **Firebaugh, M.W.,** "Artificial Intelligence: A Knowledge-Based Approach," Boyd and Fraser, Boston, 1988.

c [256] **Fisher, D.H.,** "A Proposed Method of Conceptual Clustering for Structured and Decomposable Objects," Proceedings of the 3rd International Machine Learning Workshop, pp. 38–40, Skytop, PA, 1985.

c [257] **Fisher, D.H., and Langley, P.W.,** "Approaches to Conceptual Clustering," Proceedings of IJCAI-85, pp. 691–697, Los Angeles, CA, 1985.

c [258] **Fisher, D.H., and Langley, P.W.,** "Methods of Conceptual Clustering and their Relation to Numerical Taxonomy," Technical Report 85–26, University of California, Irvine, 1985.

c   [259]   **Fisher, D.H.,** "Improving Inference Through Conceptual
                Clustering," Proceedings of AAAI-87, pp. 461–465, Seattle, WA,
                1987.

c   [260]   **Fisher, D.H.,** "Knowledge Acquisition Via Incremental
                Conceptual Clustering," Machine Learning, Vol. 2, No. 2, pp.
                139–172, 1987.

c   [261]   **Fisher, D.H.,** "Conceptual Clustering, Learning from Examples,
                and Inference," Proceedings of the 4th International Machine
                Learning Workshop, pp. 38–49, University of California, Irvine,
                1987.

m   [262]   **Fisher, D.H.,** "A Computational Account of Basic Level and
                Typicality," Proceedings of AAAI-88, pp. 233–238, Saint Paul,
                MN, 1988.

cst   [263]   **Fisher, D.H., and Schlimmer, J.C.,** "Concept Simplification and
                Prediction Accuracy," Proceedings of the 5th International
                Conference on Machine Learning, pp. 22–28, Ann Arbor, MI,
                1988.

c   [264]   **Fisher, D.H.,** "Noise-Tolerant Conceptual Clustering,"
                Proceedings of IJCAI-89, pp. 825–830, Detroit, MI, 1989.

ens   [265]   **Fisher, D.H., and McKusick, K.B.,** "An Empirical Comparison
                of ID3 and Backpropagation," Proceedings of IJCAI-89, pp.
                788–793, Detroit, MI, 1989.

ens   [266]   **Fisher, D.H., McKusick, K., Mooney, R., Shavlik, J.W., and
                Towell, G.,** "Processing Issues in Comparisons of Symbolic and
                Connectionism Learning Systems," Proceedings of the 6th
                International Workshop on Machine Learning, pp. 169–173,
                Ithaca, NY, 1989.

g   [267]   **Fitzpatrick, J.M., and Grefenstette, J.J.,** "Genetic Algorithms in
                Noisy Environments," Machine Learning, Vol. 3, No. 2/3, pp.
                101–121, 1988.

sv   [268]   **Flann, N.S. and Dietterich, T.G.,** "Selecting Appropriate
                Representations for Learning from Examples," Proceedings of
                AAAI-86, pp. 460–466, Philadelphia, PA, 1986.

p   [269]   **Flann, N.S.,** "Learning Appropriate Abstractions for Planning in
                Formation Problems," Proceedings of the 6th International
                Workshop on Machine Learning, pp. 235–239, Ithaca, NY, 1989.

sx   [270]   **Flann, N.S., and Dietterich, T.G.,** "A Study of
                Explanation-Based Methods for Inductive Learning," Machine
                Learning, Vol. 4, No. 2, 1989.

t   [271]   **Floyd, S.,** "Space-Bounded Learning and the
                Vapnik-Chervonenkis Dimension," Proceedings of the 1989
                Workshop on Computational Learning Theory COLT '89, pp.
                349–364, University of California, Santa Cruz, 1989.

g   [272]   **Fogarty, T.C.,** "An Incremental Genetic Algorithm for Real-Time
                Learning," Proceedings of the 6th International Workshop on
                Machine Learning, pp. 416–419, Ithaca, NY, 1989.

n   [273]   **Fogelman-Soulie, F.,** "Generalization Processes in Network
                Learning," unpublished manuscript.

t   [274]   **Forbus, K.D.,** "Qualitative Process Theory," Qualitative
                Reasoning About Physical Systems, MIT Press, Cambridge, MA,
                D.G. Bobrow (Ed.), 1985.

m   [275]   **Forbus, K.D., and Gentner, D.,** "Learning Physical Domains:
                Toward a Theoretical Framework," Machine Learning: An
                Artificial Intelligence Approach, Volume II, Morgan Kaufmann,
                San Mateo, CA, R.S. Michalski, J.G. Carbonell and T.M. Mitchell
                (Eds.), pp. 311–348, 1986.

b   [276]   **Forsyth, R., and Rada, R.,** "Machine Learning: Applications in
                Expert Systems and Information Retrieval," Ellis Horwood Series
                in AI, 1986.

l   [277]   **Franklin, J.A.,** "Learning Control in a Robotic System,"
                Proceedings of the IEEE International Conference on Systems,
                Man, and Cybernetics, pp. 466–471, Alexandria, VA, 1987.

l   [278]   **Franklin, J.A.,** "Learning Control of a One Line Robot Arm,"
                ECE Technical Report CCS-87–101, University of Massachusetts
                at Amherst, 1987.

s   [279]   **Frawley, W.J.,** "Entropy-Based Decision Tree Induction from
                Large Numbers of Examples," Technical Note TN 87-506.1, GTE
                Laboratories, 1987.

s   [280]   **Frawley, W.J.,** "Using Functions to Encode Domain and
                Contextual Knowledge in Statistical Induction," Proceedings of
                IJCAI-89 Workshop on Knowledge Discovery in Databases, pp.
                99–108, Detroit, MI, 1989.

k   [281]   **Freiling, M.J., and Jacobson, C.E.,** "A New Look at Inference
                Engine Synthesis," An International Journal of Knowledge
                Acquisition for Knowledge-Based Systems, Vol. 1, No. 3, pp.
                235–254.

i   [282] **Friedrich, G., and Nejdl, W.,** "Using Domain Knowledge to
               Improve Inductive Learning Algorithms for Diagnosis,"
               Proceedings of the 6th International Workshop on Machine
               Learning, pp. 75–77, Ithaca, NY, 1989.

el   [283] **Fu, K.S.,** "Learning Control Systems-Review and Outlook," IEEE
               Transactions On Pattern Analysis and Machine Intelligence, Vol.
               PAMI-8, No. 3, pp. 327, 1986.

c   [284] **Fu, L., and Buchanan, B.G.,** "Learning Intermediate Concepts in
               Constructing a Hierarchical Knowledge Base," Proceedings of
               IJCAI-85, pp. 659–666, Los Angeles, CA, 1985.

t   [285] **Fulk, M., and Jain, S.,** "Learning in the Presence of Inaccurate
               Information," Proceedings of the 1989 Workshop on
               Computational Learning Theory COLT '89, pp. 175–188,
               University of California, Santa Cruz, 1989.

st   [286] **Gaines, B.R.,** "An Ounce of Knowledge is Worth a Ton of Data:
               Quantitative Studies of the Trade-Off Between Expertise and Data
               Based on Statistically Well-Founded Empirical Induction,"
               Proceedings of the 6th International Workshop on Machine
               Learning, pp. 156–159, Ithaca, NY, 1989.

s   [287] **Gaines, B.R.,** "Extracting Knowledge from Data," Proceedings of
               IJCAI-89 Workshop on Knowledge Discovery in Databases, pp.
               109–116, Detroit, MI, 1989.

k   [288] **Gaines, B.R., and Shaw, L.G.,** "Comparing the Conceptual
               Systems of Experts," Proceedings of IJCAI-89, pp. 633–638,
               Detroit, MI, 1989.

b   [289] **Gale, W.A.,** "AI and Statistics," Addison-Wesley, Reading, MA,
               1986.

es   [290] **Gams, M., and Lavrac, N.,** "Review of Five Empirical Learning
               Systems Within a Proposed Schema," Proceedings of EWSL-87,
               pp. 46–66, Bled, Yugoslavia, 1987.

s   [291] **Gams, M.,** "New Measurements Highlight the Importance of
               Redundant Knowledge," Proceedings of EWSL-89, Montpellier,
               France, 1989.

s   [292] **Gams, M., and Karalic, A.,** "New Empirical Learning
               Mechanisms Perform Significantly Better in Real Life Domains,"
               Proceedings of the 6th International Workshop on Machine
               Learning, pp. 99–103, Ithaca, NY, 1989.

l   [293] **Ganascia, J.G.,** "Learning with Hilbert Cubes," Proceedings of
               EWSL-87, pp. 158–171, Bled, Yugoslavia, 1987.

s   [294]   **Ganascia, J.G.,** "CHARADE: A Rule System Learning System,"
                Proceedings of IJCAI-87, pp. 345–347, Milan, Italy, 1987.

sv   [295]   **Ganascia, J.G.,** "Improvement and Refinement of the Learning
                Bias Semantic," Proceedings of ECAI-88, pp. 384–389, Munich,
                W.Germany, 1988.

k   [296]   **Ganascia, J.G.,** "Automatic Knowledge Bases Construction,"
                Proceedings of the Conference on Data Analysis, Learning
                Symbolic and Numeric Knowledge, pp. 399–406, INRIA, Antibes,
                1989.

t   [297]   **Gao, Q., and Li, M.,** "The Minimum Description Length
                Principle and Its Application to line Learning of Handprinted
                Characters," Proceedings of IJCAI-89, pp. 843–848, Detroit, MI,
                1989.

bm   [298]   **Gardner, H.,** "The Mind's New Science: A History of the
                Cognitive Revolution," Basic Books, 1985.

t   [299]   **Gasarch, W.I., Sitaraman, R.K., Smith, C.H., and
                Velauthapillai, M.,** "Learning Programs with an Easy to Calculate
                Set of Errors," Proceedings of the 1988 Workshop on
                Computational Learning Theory COLT '88, pp. 242–250, MIT,
                1988.

t   [300]   **Gasarch, W.I., and Smith, C.H.,** "Learning via Queries,"
                Proceedings of the 1988 Workshop on Computational Learning
                Theory COLT '88, pp. 227–241, MIT, 1988.

t   [301]   **Gasarch, W.I., and Pleszkoch, M.B.,** "Learning Via Queries to
                an Oracle," Proceedings of the 1989 Workshop on Computational
                Learning Theory COLT '89, pp. 214–229, University of
                California, Santa Cruz, 1989.

s   [302]   **Gascuel, O., and Danchin, A.,** "Data Analysis using a Learning
                Program, A Case Study—An Application of PLAGE to a
                Biological Sequence Analysis," Proceedings of ECAI-88, pp.
                390–395, Munich, W.Germany, 1988.

x   [303]   **Gascuel, O.,** "A Conceptual Regression Method," Proceedings of
                EWSL-89, Montpellier, France, 1989.

st   [304]   **Gascuel, O.,** "Inductive Learning, Numerical Criteria and
                Combinatorial Optimization: Some Results," Proceedings of the
                Conference on Data Analysis, Learning Symbolic and Numeric
                Knowledge, pp. 417–424, INRIA, Antibes, 1989.

s   [305] **Gemello, R., and Mana, F.,** "An Integrated Characterization and Discrimination Scheme to Improve Learning Efficiency in Large Data Sets," Proceedings of IJCAI-89, pp. 719–724, Detroit, MI, 1989.

b   [306] **Genesereth, M.R., and Nilsson, N.J.,** "Logical Foundations of Artificial Intelligence," Morgan Kaufmann, 1987.

c   [307] **Gennari, J.H.,** "Focused Concept Formation," Proceedings of the 6th International Workshop on Machine Learning, pp. 379–382, Ithaca, NY, 1989.

c   [308] **Gennari, J.H., Langley, P.W., and Fisher, D.H.,** "Model of Incremental Concept Formation," Artificial Intelligence, Vol. 40, pp. 11–61, 1989.

px   [309] **Gervasio, M.T., and DeJong, G.F.,** "Explanation-Based Learning of Reactive Operators," Proceedings of the 6th International Workshop on Machine Learning, pp. 252–254, Ithaca, NY, 1989.

s   [310] **Giannetti, A., and Lucchelli, M.,** "PINOCCHIO: An Automatic Concept Learning System," Proceedings of EWSL-89, Montpellier, France, 1989.

k   [311] **Ginsberg, A., Weiss, S., and Politakis, P.,** "SEEK2: A Generalized Approach to Automatic Knowledge Base Refinement," Proceedings of IJCAI-85, pp. 367–374, Los Angeles, CA, 1985.

k   [312] **Ginsberg, A.,** "A Metalinguistic Approach to the Construction of Knowledge Base Refinement Systems," Proceedings of AAAI-86, pp. 436–441, Philadelphia, PA, 1986.

x   [313] **Ginsberg, A.,** "Theory Reduction: Operationalization as a Prelude to Learning," Proceedings of 1988 Symposium on Explanation-Based Learning, pp. 143–147, Stanford, 1988.

k   [314] **Ginsberg, A.,** "Knowledge-Based Reduction: A New Approach to Checking Knowledge Bases for Inconsistency and Redundancy," Proceedings of AAAI-88, pp. 585–589, Saint Paul, MN, 1988.

kx   [315] **Ginsberg, A.,** "Theory Revision via Prior Operationalization," Proceedings of AAAI-88, pp. 590–595, Saint Paul, MN, 1988.

kx   [316] **Ginsberg, A.,** "Automatic Refinement of Expert System Knowledge Bases," Pitman, London, and Morgan Kaufmann, San Mateo, CA, Research Notes in Artificial Intelligence, 1988.

k   [317] **Ginsberg, A., Weiss, S.M., and Politakis, P.,** "Automatic Knowledge Base Refinement for Classification Systems," Artificial Intelligence, Vol. 35, pp. 197–226, 1988.

k   [318]   **Ginsberg, A.,** "Knowledge Base Refinement and Theory Revision," Proceedings of the 6th International Workshop on Machine Learning, pp. 260–265, Ithaca, NY, 1989.

m   [319]   **Gluck, M. and Corter, J.,** "Information, Uncertainty and the Utility of Categories," Proceedings of the 7th Conference of the Cognitive Science Society, pp. 283–287, Irvine, CA, 1985.

b   [320]   **Glymour, C., Scheins, R., Spirites, P., and Kelly, K.,** "Discovering Causal Structure," Academic Press, 1987.

gl   [321]   **Goldberg, D.E.,** "Dynamic System Control Using Rule Learning and Genetic Algorithms," Proceedings of IJCAI-85, pp. 588–592, Los Angeles, 1985.

gl   [322]   **Goldberg, D.E.,** "Genetic Algorithms and Rule Learning in Dynamic System Control," Proceedings of the 1st International Conference on Genetic Algorithms, pp. 8–15, Pittsburgh, PA, 1985.

g   [323]   **Goldberg, D.E.,** "Genetic Algorithms in Search, Optimization, and Machine learning," Addison-Wesley, 1989.

p   [324]   **Golding, A., Rosenbloom, P. S. and Laird, J.E.,** "Learning General Search Control from Outside Guidance," Proceedings of IJCAI-87, pp. 334–337, Milan, Italy, 1987.

s   [325]   **Golmard, J., and Mallet, A.,** "Learning Probabilities in Causal Trees from Incomplete Databases," Proceedings of IJCAI-89 Workshop on Knowledge Discovery in Databases, pp. 117–126, Detroit, MI, 1989.

ex   [326]   **Gomez, F., and Segami, C.,** "Finding and Learning Explanatory Connections from Scientific Texts," Proceedings of IEEE International Workshop on Tools for Artificial Intelligence, pp. 85–90, Fairfax, VA, 1989.

k   [327]   **Gonzalez, A., Myler, H., Towhidneja, M., McKenzie, F., and Kladke, R.,** "Automated Knowledge Generation From a CAD Database," Proceedings of IJCAI-89 Workshop on Knowledge Discovery in Databases, pp. 127–138, Detroit, MI, 1989.

s   [328]   **Goodman, R.M., and Smyth, P.,** "Information-Theoretic Rule Induction," Proceedings of ECAI-88, pp. 357–362, Munich, W.Germany, 1988.

s   [329]   **Goodman, R.M., and Smyth, P.,** "The Induction of Probabilistic Rule Sets—The ITRULE Algorithm," Proceedings of the 6th International Workshop on Machine Learning, pp. 129–132, Ithaca, NY, 1989.

s [330] **Goodman, R.M., and Smyth, P.,** "The ITRULE Algorithm for Rule Induction," Proceedings of IJCAI-89 Workshop on Knowledge Discovery in Databases, pp. 139–146, Detroit, MI, 1989.

s [331] **Gordon, D.,** "Screening Hypotheses with Explicit Bias," Proceedings of the 6th International Workshop on Machine Learning, pp. 499–500, Ithaca, NY, 1989.

sv [332] **Granger, R., and Schlimmer, J.,** "Combining Numeric and Symbolic Learning Techniques," Proceedings of the 3rd International Machine Learning Workshop, Skytop, PA, 1985.

b [333] **Graubard, S.R.,** "The Artificial Intelligence Debate: False Starts, Real Foundations," The MIT Press, 1989.

g [334] **Green, D.P., and Smith, S.F.,** "A Genetic System for Learning Models of Consumer Choice," Proceedings of the 2nd International Conference on Genetic Algorithms, pp. 217–223, Cambridge, MA, 1987.

d [335] **Greene, G.H.,** "The ABACUS.2 System for Quantitative Discovery: Using Dependencies to Discover Non-Linear Terms," George Mason University, Reports of Machine Learning and Inference Laboratory, No. MLI-88–5, 1988.

g [336] **Grefenstette, J.J., and Pettey, C.,** "Approaches to Machine Learning with Genetic Algorithms," Proceedings of the IEEE International Conference on Systems, Man, and Cybernetics, pp. 55–60, Atlanta, GA, 1986.

g [337] **Grefenstette, J.J.,** "Multilevel Credit Assignment in a Genetic Learning System," Proceedings of the 2nd International Conference on Genetic Algorithms, pp. 202–209, Cambridge, MA., 1987.

g [338] **Grefenstette, J.J.,** "Optimization of Control Parameters for Genetic Algorithms," IEEE Transactions on Systems, Man, and Cybernetics, Vol. SMC-16, No. 1, pp. 122–128, 1987.

g [339] **Grefenstette, J.J.,** "Credit Assignment in Genetic Learning Systems," Proceedings of AAAI-88, pp. 596–600, Saint Paul, MN, 1988.

lp [340] **Grefenstette, J.J.,** "Incremental Learning of Control Strategies with Genetic Algorithms," Proceedings of the 6th International Workshop on Machine Learning, pp. 340–344, Ithaca, NY, 1989.

g [341] **Grefenstette, J.J., Cobb, H.G., Gordon, D.F., Ramsey, C.L., and Schultz, A.C.,** "Competition-Based Learning in SAMUEL," Proceedings of Office of Naval Research Workshop on Knowledge Acquisition, A.L. Meyrowitz (Ed.), Arlington, VA, 1989.

a [342] **Greiner, R.,** "Learning by Understanding Analogies," Thesis, Computer Science Dept., Stanford University, 1985.

a [343] **Greiner, R.,** "Learning by Understanding Analogies," Artificial Intelligence, Vol. 35, No. 1, pp. 81–125, 1988.

tx [344] **Greiner, R.,** "Towards a Formal Analysis of EBL," Proceedings of the 6th International Workshop on Machine Learning, pp. 450–453, Ithaca, NY, 1989.

x [345] **Greiner, R., and Likuski, J.,** "Incorporating Redundant Learning Rules: A Preliminary Formal Analysis of EBL," Proceedings of IJCAI-89, pp. 744–749, Detroit, MI, 1989.

sv [346] **Grosof, B.N., and Russell, S.J.,** "Declarative Bias for Structural Domains," Proceedings of the 6th International Workshop on Machine Learning, pp. 480–482, Ithaca, NY, 1989.

s [347] **Gross, K.P.,** "Incremental Multiple Concept Learning Using Experiments," Proceedings of the 5th International Conference on Machine Learning, pp. 65–72, Ann Arbor, MI, 1988.

k [348] **Gruber, T.R.,** "A Method for Acquiring Strategic Knowledge," An International Journal of Knowledge Acquisition for Knowledge-Based Systems, Vol. 1, No. 3, pp. 255–278, .

k [349] **Gruber, T.R.,** "Automated Knowledge Acquisition for Strategic Knowledge," Machine Learning, Vol. 4, No. 3/4, 1989.

k [350] **Gruber, T.R.,** "The Acquisition of Strategic Knowledge," Academic Press, Perspectives in AI, 1989.

cs [351] **Guenoche, A.,** "Generalization and Conceptual Classification: Indices and Algorithm," Proceedings of the Conference on Data Analysis, Learning Symbolic and Numeric Knowledge, pp. 503–510, INRIA, Antibes, 1989.

x [352] **Gupta, A.,** "Significance of the Explanation Language in EBL," Proceedings of 1988 Symposium on Explanation-Based Learning, pp. 73–77, Stanford, 1988.

d [353] **Haase, K.W. Jr.,** "Discovery Systems," Proceedings of ECAI-86, pp. 546–555, Brighton, England, 1986.

c   [354] **Hadzikadic, M.,** "Prototypes and Similarity in Incremental
             Conceptual Clustering Systems," Proceedings of the 4th
             International Symposium on Methodologies for Intelligent
             Systems, pp. 289–296, 1989.

c   [355] **Hadzikadic, M., and Yun, D.Y.Y.,** "Concept Formulation by
             Incremental Conceptual Clustering," Proceedings of IJCAI-89, pp.
             831–836, Detroit, MI, 1989.

i   [356] **Haines, D.,** "Explanation Based Learning as Constrained Search,"
             Proceedings of the 6th International Workshop on Machine
             Learning, pp. 43–45, Ithaca, NY, 1989.

x   [357] **Hall, R.J.,** "Learning by Failing to Explain," Proceedings of
             AAAI-86, pp. 568–572, Philadelphia, PA, 1986.

x   [358] **Hall, R.J.,** "Learning by Failing to Explain: Using Partial
             Explanations to Learn in Incomplete or Intractable Domains,"
             Machine Learning, Vol. 3, No. 1, pp. 45–78, 1988.

ae   [359] **Hall, R.P.,** "Computational Approaches to Analogical Reasoning:
             A Comparative Analysis," Artificial Intelligence, Vol. 39, pp.
             39–120, 1989.

p   [360] **Hamakawa, R.,** "One General Navigation Strategy for Intelligent
             Mobile Robots," Proceedings of the Conference on Intelligent
             Autonomous Systems, Amsterdam, Netherlands, 1989.

p   [361] **Hamakawa, R., and Miyashita, Y.,** "Self-Adaptation Methods in
             an Intelligent User Interface," Proceedings of the 3rd International
             Conference on Human-Computer Interaction, Boston, MA, 1989.

x   [362] **Hammond, K.J.,** "Learning to Anticipate and Avoid Planning
             Problems through the Explanation of Failures," Proceedings of
             AAAI-86, pp. 556–560, Philadelphia, PA, 1986.

apx   [363] **Hammond, K.J.,** "Learning and Reusing Explanations,"
             Proceedings of the 4th International Machine Learning Workshop,
             pp. 141–147, University of California, Irvine, 1987.

apx   [364] **Hammond, K.J.,** "Explaining and Repairing Plans that Fail,"
             Proceedings of IJCAI-87, pp. 109–114, Milan, Italy, 1987.

a   [365] **Hammond, K.J., Converse, T., and Marks, M.,** "Learning from
             Opportunities: Storing and Reusing Execution-Time
             Optimizations," Proceedings of AAAI-88, pp. 536–540, Saint
             Paul, MN, 1988.

x   [366] **Hammond, K.J., and Hurwitz, N.,** "Extracting Diagnostic
             Features from Explanations," Proceedings of 1988 Symposium on
             Explanation-Based Learning, pp. 31–35, Stanford, 1988.

ap [367] Hammond, K.J., "Opportunistic Memory," Proceedings of IJCAI-89, pp. 504–510, Detroit, MI, 1989.

ap [368] Hammond, K.J., "Viewing Planning as a Memory Task," Academic Press, Perspectives in AI, 1989.

cp [369] Hammond, K.J., and Seifert, C., "Learning from Opportunity," Proceedings of Office of Naval Research Workshop on Knowledge Acquisition, A.L. Meyrowitz (Ed.), Arlington, VA, 1989.

n [370] Hampson, S.E., and Volper, D.J., "Linear Function Neurons: Structure and Training," Biological Cybernetics, Vol. 53, pp. 203–217, 1986.

n [371] Hampson, S.E., and Volper, D.J., "Disjunction Models of Boolean Category Learning," Biological Cybernetics, Vol. 56, pp. 121–137, 1987.

k [372] Handa, K, and Ishizaki, S., "Acquiring Knowledge about a Relation between Concepts," Proceedings of the 3rd European Workshop on Knowledge Acquisition for Knowledge-Based Systems, pp. 380–390, 1989.

c [373] Hanson, S.J., and Bauer, M., "Conceptual Clustering, Semantic Organization and Polymorphy," Uncertainty in Artificial Intelligence, North Holland, L.N. Kanal and D. Lemmer (Eds.), 1986.

c [374] Hanson, S.J., and Bauer, M., "Conceptual Clustering, Categorisation, and Polymorphy," Machine Learning, Vol. 3, No. 4, pp. 343–372, 1989.

c [375] Hanson, S.J., "Conceptual Clustering and Categorization: Bridging the Gap between Induction and Causal Models," Machine Learning: An Artificial Intelligence Approach, Volume III, Morgan Kaufmann, San Mateo, CA, Kodratoff, Y. and Michalski, R.S. (Eds.), Ch. 9, 1990.

st [376] Haussler, D., "Quantifying the Inductive Bias in Concept Learning," Proceedings of AAAI-86, pp. 485–489, Philadelphia, PA, 1986.

st [377] Haussler, D., "Bias, Version Spaces and Valiant's Learning Framework," Proceedings of the 4th International Machine Learning Workshop, pp. 324–336, University of California, Irvine, 1987.

st   [378]   **Haussler, D.,** "Learning Conjunctive Concepts in Structural
               Domains," Proceedings of AAAI-87, pp. 466–470, Seattle, WA,
               1987.

t   [379]   **Haussler, D.,** "New Theoretical Directions in Machine Learning,"
               Machine Learning, Vol. 2, No. 4, 1988.

st   [380]   **Haussler, D.,** "Quantifying Inductive Bias: AI Learning
               Algorithms and Valiant's Learning Framework," Artificial
               Intelligence, Vol. 36, pp. 177–221, 1988.

t   [381]   **Haussler, D., Kearns, M., Littlestone, N., and Warmuth M.K.,**
               "Equivalence of Models for Polynomial Learnability,"
               Proceedings of the 1988 Workshop on Computational Learning
               Theory COLT '88, pp. 42–55, MIT, 1988.

t   [382]   **Haussler, D.,** "Learning Conjunctive Concepts in Structural
               Domains," Machine Learning, Vol. 4, No. 1, 1989.

t   [383]   **Haussler, D., and Warmuth, M.K.,** "Analyzing the Performance
               of Learning Algorithms," Proceedings of Office of Naval Research
               Workshop on Knowledge Acquisition, A.L. Meyrowitz (Ed.),
               Arlington, VA, 1989.

st   [384]   **Haussler, D.,** "Applying Valiant's Learning Framework to AI
               Concept-Learning Problems," Machine Learning: An Artificial
               Intelligence Approach, Volume III, Morgan Kaufmann, San
               Mateo, CA, Kodratoff, Y. and Michalski, R.S. (Eds.), Ch. 22, 1990.

e   [385]   **Hecht, A., and Meunier, R.,** "Learning Rules for Fault Diagnosis
               in Power Distribution Systems," Proceedings of EWSL-89,
               Montpellier, France, 1989.

n   [386]   **Hecht-Nielsen, et al.,** "Proceedings of the International Joint
               Conference on Neural Networks (two volumes)," IEEE TAB
               Neural Network Committee, 1989.

s   [387]   **Heeffer, A.,** "Validating Concepts from Automated Acquisition
               Systems," Proceedings of IJCAI-85, pp. 613–615, Los Angeles,
               CA, 1985.

st   [388]   **Helft, N.,** "Inductive Generalization: A Logical Framework,"
               Proceedings of EWSL-87, pp. 149–157, Bled, Yugoslavia, 1987.

s   [389]   **Helft, N.,** "Learning Systems of First-Order Rules," Proceedings
               of the 5th International Conference on Machine Learning, pp.
               395–401, Ann Arbor, MI, 1988.

st   [390] **Helft, N.,** "Induction as Nonmonotonic Inference," Proceedings of
               the 1st International Conference on Principles of Knowledge
               Representation and Reasoning, pp. 149–156, Toronto, Canada,
               1989.

t   [391] **Hellerstein, L., and Karpinski, M.,** "Learning Read-Once
               Formulas Using Membership Queries," Proceedings of the 1989
               Workshop on Computational Learning Theory COLT '89, pp.
               146–161, University of California, Santa Cruz, 1989.

t   [392] **Helmbold, D., Sloan, R., and Warmuth, M.K.,** "Learning
               Nested Differences of Intersection-Closed Concept Classes,"
               Proceedings of the 1989 Workshop on Computational Learning
               Theory COLT '89, pp. 41–56, University of California, Santa
               Cruz, 1989.

ek   [393] **Henrion, M., and Cooley, D. R.,** "An Experimental Comparison
               of Knowledge Engineering for Expert Systems and Decision
               Analysis," Proceedings of AAAI-87, pp. 471–476, Seattle, WA,
               1987.

e   [394] **Herrman, J.,** "A Machine Learning Approach to Estimation for
               IC Design," Proceedings of ECAI-88, pp. 345–347, Munich,
               W.Germany, 1988.

k   [395] **Herrmann, J., and Beckmann, R.,** "MALEFIZ—A Learning
               Apprentice System that Acquires Geometrical Knowledge about a
               Complex Design Task," Proceedings of the 3rd European
               Workshop on Knowledge Acquisition for Knowledge-Based
               Systems, pp. 391–405, 1989.

e   [396] **Hill, W.L.,** "Machine Learning for Software Reuse," Proceedings
               of IJCAI-87, pp. 338–344, Milan, Italy, 1987.

g   [397] **Hilliard, M.R., Liepins, G., Rangarajan, G., and Palmer, M.,**
               "Learning Decision Rules for Scheduling Problems: A Classifier
               Hybrid Approach," Proceedings of the 6th International Workshop
               on Machine Learning, pp. 188–190, Ithaca, NY, 1989.

n   [398] **Hinton, G.E.,** "Connectionist Learning Procedures," Artificial
               Intelligence, Vol. 40, pp. 185–234, 1989.

n   [399] **Hinton, G.E.,** "Connectionist Learning Procedures," Machine
               Learning: An Artificial Intelligence Approach, Volume III, Morgan
               Kaufmann, San Mateo, CA, Kodratoff, Y. and Michalski, R.S.
               (Eds.), Ch. 20, 1990.

x   [400] **Hirsh, H.,** "Explanation-Based Generalization in a Logic Programming Environment," Proceedings of IJCAI-87, pp. 221–227, Milan, Italy, 1987.

ix   [401] **Hirsh, H.,** "Empirical Techniques for Repairing Imperfect Theories," Proceedings of 1988 Symposium on Explanation-Based Learning, pp. 57–61, Stanford, 1988.

x   [402] **Hirsh, H.,** "Reasoning about Operationality for Explanation-Based Learning," Proceedings of the 5th International Conference on Machine Learning, pp. 214–220, Ann Arbor, MI, 1988.

x   [403] **Hirsh, H.,** "Conditional Operationality and Explanation-based Generalization," Machine Learning: An Artificial Intelligence Approach, Volume III, Morgan Kaufmann, San Mateo, CA, Kodratoff, Y. and Michalski, R.S. (Eds.), Ch. 14, 1990.

km   [404] **Hoffman, R.R.,** "The Problem of Extracting the Knowledge of Experts from the Perspective of Experimental Psychology," AI Magazine, Vol. 8, No. 2, 1987.

b   [405] **Hofstadter, D.R.,** "Metamagical Themas: Questing for the Essence of Mind and Pattern," Basic Books, New York, 1985.

abm   [406] **Hofstadter, D.R.,** "Analogies and Roles in Human and Machine Thinking," Metamagical Themes, Basic Books, New York, 1985.

d   [407] **Holder, L.B.,** "Discovering Substructure In Examples," University of Illinois at Urbana-Champaign, Report of Coordinated Science Laboratory , No. UILU-ENG-88–2223, May, 1988.

d   [408] **Holder, L.B.,** "Substructure Discovery in SUBDUE," University of Illinois at Urbana-Champaign, Report of Coordinated Science Laboratory , No. UILU-ENG-88–2220, May, 1988.

d   [409] **Holder, L.B.,** "Empirical Substructure Discovery," Proceedings of the 6th International Workshop on Machine Learning, pp. 133–136, Ithaca, NY, 1989.

gt   [410] **Holland, J.H.,** "Properties of the Bucket Brigade Algorithm," Proceedings of the 1st International Conference on Genetic Algorithms, pp. 1–7, Pittsburgh, PA, 1985.

g   [411] **Holland, J.H.,** "Escaping Brittleness: The Possibilities of General Purpose Learning Algorithms Applied to Parallel Rule-Based Systems," Machine Learning: An Artificial Intelligence Approach, Volume II, Morgan Kaufmann, San Mateo, CA, R.S. Michalski, J.G. Carbonell and T.M. Mitchell (Eds.), pp. 593–624, 1986.

bdgs [412] **Holland, J.H., Holyoak, K., Nisbett, R., and Thagard, P.,**
             "Induction: Processes of Inference, Learning and Discovery," MIT
             Press, Cambridge, MA, 1986.

bg   [413] **Holland, J.H.,** "Genetic Algorithms and Classifier Systems:
             Foundations and Future Directions," Proceedings of the 2nd
             International Conference on Genetic Algorithms, pp. 82–89,
             Cambridge, MA, 1987.

s   [414] **Holte, R.C., Acker, L.E., and Porter, B.W.,** "Concept Learning
             and the Problem of Small Disjuncts," Proceedings of IJCAI-89,
             pp. 813–818, Detroit, MI, 1989.

t   [415] **Holte, R.C., and Zimmer, R.M.,** "A Mathematical Framework
             for Studying Representation," Proceedings of the 6th International
             Workshop on Machine Learning, pp. 454–456, Ithaca, NY, 1989.

s   [416] **Hong, J., Mozetic, I., and Michalski, R. S.,** "AQ15: Incremental
             Learning of Attribute-Based Descriptions from Examples, the
             Method and User's Guide," Report ISG 86–5,
             UIUCDCS-F-86-949, Computer Science Dept., University of
             Illinois at Urbana-Champaign, 1986.

s   [417] **Hong, J., and Uhrik, C.,** "The Extension Matrix Approach to
             Attribute-Based Learning," Proceedings of EWSL-87, pp.
             172–182, Bled, Yugoslavia, 1987.

ds   [418] **Hong, J., and Mao, C.,** "THOUGHT/KD1: Theory, Methodology,
             and Implementation of Knowledge Discovery," Proceedings of
             IJCAI-89 Workshop on Knowledge Discovery in Databases, pp.
             147–157, Detroit, MI, 1989.

k   [419] **Hoppe, T.,** "Knowledge Validation in a Multiple-Agent
             Environment: Case Study I," Proceedings of EWSL-89,
             Montpellier, France, 1989.

p   [420] **Hsu, J.Y.J.,** "A Knowledge-Level Analysis of Informing,"
             Proceedings of the 6th International Workshop on Machine
             Learning, pp. 485–488, Ithaca, NY, 1989.

a   [421] **Huhns, M.N., and Acosta, R.D.,** "ARGO: A System for Design
             by Analogy," Proceedings of the 4th IEEE International
             Conference on Artificial Intelligence Applications, pp. 146–151,
             San Diego, CA, 1988.

x   [422] **Huhns, M.N., and Acosta, R.D.,** "Formulating and Retrieving
             Knowledge through Abstraction Extensions to Explanation-Based
             Learning," Proceedings of 1988 Symposium on
             Explanation-Based Learning, pp. 117–121, Stanford, 1988.

dx   [423]   **Hunter, L.,** "Explanation Based Discovery," Proceedings of 1988 Symposium on Explanation-Based Learning, pp. 2–6, Stanford, 1988.

i   [424]   **Hunter, L.,** "Knowledge Acquisition Planning: Results and Prospects," Proceedings of the 6th International Workshop on Machine Learning, pp. 61–65, Ithaca, NY, 1989.

e   [425]   **Hutchinson, A.,** "Building Grammars from Natural Text," Proceedings of EWSL-88, pp. 46–52, Glasgow, Scotland, 1988.

dp   [426]   **Iba, G.A.,** "Learning by Discovering Macros in Puzzle Solving," Proceedings of IJCAI-85, pp. 640–642, 1985.

d   [427]   **Iba, G.A.,** "Learning by Composition," Machine Learning: A Guide to Current Research, Kluwer Academic Publishers, Hingham, MA, T.M. Mitchell, J.G. Carbonell and R.S. Michalski (Eds.), 1986.

d   [428]   **Iba, G.A.,** "A Heuristic Approach to the Discovery of Macro-Operators," Machine Learning, Vol. 3, No. 4, pp. 285–318, 1989.

s   [429]   **Iba, W., Wogulis, J., and Langley, P.W.,** "Trading Off Simplicity and Coverage in Incremental Concept Learning," Proceedings of the 5th International Conference on Machine Learning, pp. 73–79, Ann Arbor, MI, 1988.

st   [430]   **Ibarra, O.H., and Jiang, T.,** "Learning Regular Languages from Counterexamples," Proceedings of the 1988 Workshop on Computational Learning Theory COLT '88, pp. 371–385, MIT, 1988.

t   [431]   **Ishizaka, H.,** "Learning Simple Deterministic Languages," Proceedings of the 1989 Workshop on Computational Learning Theory COLT '89, pp. 162–174, University of California, Santa Cruz, 1989.

n   [432]   **Israel, P., and Koutsougeras, C.,** "Learned from Observation: The CBM Neural Net Model," Proceedings of IEEE International Workshop on Tools for Artificial Intelligence, pp. 456–472, Fairfax, VA, 1989.

t   [433]   **Jain, S., Sharma, A., and Case, J.,** "Convergence to Nearly Minimal Size Grammars by Vacillating Learning Machines," Proceedings of the 1989 Workshop on Computational Learning Theory COLT '89, pp. 189–199, University of California, Santa Cruz, 1989.

d [434] **Jankowski, A., and Zytkow, J.M.,** "A Methodology for Multisearch Systems," Proceedings of the 3rd International Symposium on Methodologies for Intelligent Systems, North-Holland, pp. 343–352, Torino, Italy, 1988.

bm [435] **Johnson-Laird, P.N.,** "Mental Models: Towards a Cognitive Science of Language, Inference, and Consciousness," Harvard University Press, Cambridge, MA, 1983.

dr [436] **Jones, R.,** "Generating Predictions to Aid the Scientific Discovery Process," Proceedings of AAAI-86, pp. 513–517, Philadelphia, PA, 1986.

p [437] **Jones, R.,** "Learning to Retrieve Useful Information for Problem Solving," Proceedings of the 6th International Workshop on Machine Learning, pp. 212–214, Ithaca, NY, 1989.

nt [438] **Judd, S.,** "Learning in Neural Networks," Proceedings of the 1988 Workshop on Computational Learning Theory COLT '88, pp. 2–8, MIT, 1988.

eps [439] **Kadie, C.M.,** "DIFFY-S: Learning Robot Operator Schemata from Examples," Proceedings of the 5th International Conference on Machine Learning, pp. 430–436, Ann Arbor, MI, 1988.

lt [440] **Kaelbling, L.P.,** "A Formal Framework for Learning in Embedded Systems," Proceedings of the 6th International Workshop on Machine Learning, pp. 350–353, Ithaca, NY, 1989.

k [441] **Kahn, G.S., Nowlan, S., and McDermott, J.,** "MORE: An Intelligent Knowledge Acquisition Tool," Proceedings of IJCAI-85, pp. 581–584, Los Angeles, CA, 1985.

k [442] **Kahn, G.S., Nowlan, S., and McDermott, J.,** "Strategies for Knowledge Acquisition," IEEE Transactions on Pattern Analysis and Machine Intelligence, Vol. PAMI-7, No. 5, pp. 511–522, 1985.

k [443] **Kahn, G.S.,** "From Application Shell to Knowledge Acquisition System," Proceedings of IJCAI-87, pp. 355–358, Milan, Italy, 1987.

b [444] **Kahneman, D., Slovic, P., and Tversky, A.,** "Judgement under Uncertainty: Heuristics and Biases," Cambridge University Press, 1982.

x [445] **Kant, E.,** "Approximation and Learning in Mathematical Modeling," Proceedings of 1988 Symposium on Explanation-Based Learning, pp. 112–116, Stanford, 1988.

d   [446]   **Karp, R.,** "Hypothesis Formation as Design," Computational
                Models of Discovery and Theory Formation, J. Shrager and P.W.
                Langley (Eds.), 1989.

x   [447]   **Kass, A., and Owens, C.C.,** "Learning New Explanations by
                Incremental Adaptation," Proceedings of 1988 Symposium on
                Explanation-Based Learning, pp. 180–184, Stanford, 1988.

i   [448]   **Kass, A.,** "Adaptation-Based Explanation: Explanations as
                Cases," Proceedings of the 6th International Workshop on
                Machine Learning, pp. 49–51, Ithaca, NY, 1989.

k   [449]   **Kass, R., and Finin, T.,** "Rules for the Implicit Acquisition of
                Knowledge about the User," Proceedings of AAAI-87, pp.
                295–300, Seattle, WA, 1987.

a   [450]   **Katai, O., Sawaragi, T., and Iwai, S.,** "A Framework for
                Learning and Reasoning via Order Relations," Proceedings of the
                4th International Symposium on Methodologies for Intelligent
                Systems, pp. 297–304, 1989.

in   [451]   **Katz, B.F.,** "Integrating Learning in a Neural Network,"
                Proceedings of the 6th International Workshop on Machine
                Learning, pp. 69–71, Ithaca, NY, 1989.

dk   [452]   **Kaufman, K.A., Michalski, R.S., and Kerschberg, L.,** "Mining
                for Knowledge in Databases: Goals and General Description of
                the INLEN System," Proceedings of IJCAI-89 Workshop on
                Knowledge Discovery in Databases, pp. 158–172, Detroit, MI,
                1989.

cders   [453]   **Kaufman, K.A., Michalski, R.S., and Schultz, A.C.,**
                "EMERALD 1: An Integrated System of Machine Learning and
                Discovery Programs for Education and Research," AI Center,
                George Mason University, User's guide, No. MLI-89–12, 1989.

at   [454]   **Keane, M.,** "Where's the Beef? The Absence of Pragmatic
                Factors in Pragmatic Theories of Analogy," Proceedings of
                ECAI-88, pp. 327–332, Munich, W. Germany, 1988.

a   [455]   **Keane, M., and Brayshaw, M.,** "The Incremental Analogy
                Machine: A Computational Model of Analogy," Proceedings of
                EWSL-88, pp. 53–62, Glasgow, Scotland, 1988.

st   [456]   **Kearns, M., Li, M., Pitt, L., and Valiant, L.G.,** "Recent Results
                on Boolean Concept Learning," Proceedings of the 4th
                International Machine Learning Workshop, pp. 337–352,
                University of California, Irvine, 1987.

t   [457]   **Kearns, M., and Pitt, L.,** "A Polynomial-time Algorithm for Learning k-variable Pattern Languages from Examples," Proceedings of the 1989 Workshop on Computational Learning Theory COLT '89, pp. 57–71, University of California, Santa Cruz, 1989.

a   [458]   **Kedar-Cabelli, S.T.,** "Purpose-Directed Analogy," Proceedings of the 7th Conference of the Cognitive Science Society, Irvine, CA, 1985.

ax   [459]   **Kedar-Cabelli, S.T.,** "Formulating Concepts According to Purpose," Proceedings of AAAI-87, pp. 477–481, Seattle, WA, 1987.

x   [460]   **Kedar-Cabelli, S.T., and McCarty, L.T.,** "Explanation-Based Generalization as Resolution Theorem Proving," Proceedings of the 4th International Machine Learning Workshop, pp. 383–389, University of California, Irvine, 1987.

a   [461]   **Kedar-Cabelli, S.T.,** "Formulating Concepts and Analogies According to Purpose," Thesis, Rutgers University, May, 1988.

x   [462]   **Keller, R.M.,** "Concept Learning in Context," Proceedings of the 4th International Machine Learning Workshop, pp. 91–102, University of California, Irvine, 1987.

x   [463]   **Keller, R.M.,** "Defining Operationality for Explanation-Based Learning," Proceedings of AAAI-87, Seattle, WA, 1987.

x   [464]   **Keller, R.M.,** "The Role of Explicit Contextual Knowledge in Learning Concepts to Improve Performance," Thesis, Computer Science Dept., Rutgers University, 1987.

x   [465]   **Keller, R.M.,** "Operationality and Generality in Explanation-Based Learning: Separate Dimensions or Opposite Endpoints?," Proceedings of 1988 Symposium on Explanation-Based Learning, pp. 153–157, Stanford, 1988.

x   [466]   **Keller, R.M.,** "Compiling Learning Vocabulary from a Performance System Description," Proceedings of the 6th International Workshop on Machine Learning, pp. 492–495, Ithaca, NY, 1989.

k   [467]   **Kellermann, G., and Loevenich, D.,** "Macro Acquisition in a Knowledge Based User Interface," Proceedings of EWSL-89, Montpellier, France, 1989.

dx   [468]   **Kellogg, C.,** "Deductive Power Tools for Knowledge Discovery," Proceedings of IJCAI-89 Workshop on Knowledge Discovery in Databases, pp. 173–180, Detroit, MI, 1989.

dt [469] **Kelly, K.T.,** "Theory Discovery and the Hypothesis Language," Proceedings of the 5th International Conference on Machine Learning, pp. 318–324, Ann Arbor, MI, 1988.

t [470] **Kelly, K.T.,** "Induction from the General to the More General," Proceedings of the 1989 Workshop on Computational Learning Theory COLT '89, pp. 334–348, University of California, Santa Cruz, 1989.

s [471] **Kerber, R.,** "Using a Generalization Hierarchy to Learning from Examples," Proceedings of the 5th International Conference on Machine Learning, pp. 1–7, Ann Arbor, MI, 1988.

a [472] **Kibler, D., and Aha, D.W.,** "Learning Representative Exemplars of Concepts: An Initial Case Study," Proceedings of the 4th International Machine Learning Workshop, pp. 24–30, University of California, Irvine, 1987.

ae [473] **Kibler, D., and Aha, D.W.,** "Comparing Instance-Averaging with Instance-Filtering Learning Algorithms," Proceedings of EWSL-88, pp. 63–80, Glasgow, Scotland, 1988.

b [474] **Kibler, D., and Langley, P.W.,** "Machine Learning as an Experimental Science," Proceedings of EWSL-88, pp. 81–92, Glasgow, Scotland, 1988.

e [475] **Kipps, J.R., and Gajski, D.D.,** "The Role of Learning in Logic Synthesis," Proceedings of IEEE International Workshop on Tools for Artificial Intelligence, pp. 252–258, Fairfax, VA, 1989.

t [476] **Kivinen, J.,** "Reliable and Useful Learning," Proceedings of the 1989 Workshop on Computational Learning Theory COLT '89, pp. 365–382, University of California, Santa Cruz, 1989.

d [477] **Kjellin, H.,** "Discovering a Suitable Event," Proceedings of IJCAI-89 Workshop on Knowledge Discovery in Databases, pp. 181–191, Detroit, MI, 1989.

k [478] **Klinker, G., Boyd, C., Genetet, S., and McDermott, J.,** "A KNACK for Knowledge Acquisition," Proceedings of AAAI-87, pp. 488–493, Seattle, WA, 1987.

k [479] **Klinker, G., Boyd, C., Dong, D., Maiman, J., McDermott, J., and Schnelbach, R.,** "Building Expert Systems with KNACK," An International Journal of Knowledge Acquisition for Knowledge-Based Systems, Vol. 1, No. 3, .

p [480] **Knoblock, C.A.,** "Learning Hierarchies of Abstraction Spaces," Proceedings of the 6th International Workshop on Machine Learning, pp. 241–245, Ithaca, NY, 1989.

ip   [481]   **Ko, H.,** "Toward Integration of Planning and Learning from
             Experience in Robot Assembly," Thesis, University of Illinois at
             Urbana-Champaign, 1988.

i   [482]   **Ko, H., and Michalski, R.S.,** "Types of Explanations and Their
             Role in Constructive Closed-loop Learning," AI Center, George
             Mason University, No. MLI-88–2, 1988.

p   [483]   **Ko, H.,** "Assembly Planning: A Learning Approach," Thesis,
             Computer Science Dept., University of Illinois, Urbana, 1989.

p   [484]   **Kodratoff, Y.,** "Learning Expert Knowledge and Theorem
             Proving," Proceedings of GWAI-86, pp. 164–179,
             Springer-Verlag, 1986.

s   [485]   **Kodratoff, Y., and Ganascia, J.,** "Improving the Generalization
             Step in Learning," Machine Learning: An Artificial Intelligence
             Approach, Volume II, Morgan Kaufmann, San Mateo, CA, R.S.
             Michalski, J.G. Carbonell and T.M. Mitchell (Eds.), pp. 215–244,
             1986.

t   [486]   **Kodratoff, Y.,** "Is AI a Sub-field of Computer Science—or is AI
             the Science of Explanations?," Proceedings of EWSL-87, pp.
             91–106, Bled, Yugoslavia, 1987.

ik   [487]   **Kodratoff, Y., and Tecuci, G.,** "DISCIPLE-1: Interactive
             Apprentice System in Weak Theory Fields," Proceedings of
             IJCAI-87, pp. 271–273, Milan, Italy, 1987.

x   [488]   **Kodratoff, Y., and Tecuci, G.,** "What is an Explanation in
             DISCIPLE?," Proceedings of the 4th International Machine
             Learning Workshop, pp. 160–166, University of California, Irvine,
             1987.

b   [489]   **Kodratoff, Y.,** "Introduction to Machine Learning," Pitman,
             London, (First published in French by Cepadues-Editions, 1986),
             1988. Available in the U.S. from Morgan Kaufmann Publishers.

s   [490]   **Kodratoff, Y., Manago, M., and Blythe, J.,** "Generalization and
             Noise," Knowledge Acquisition for Knowledge-Based Systems,
             Academic Press, London, Gaines B. and Boose J. (Eds.), pp.
             301–324, 1988.

s   [491]   **Kodratoff, Y., and Tecuci, G.,** "Learning Based on Conceptual
             Distance," IEEE Transactions on Pattern Analysis and Machine
             Intelligence, No. 10, pp. 897–909, 1988.

be   [492]   **Kodratoff, Y.,** "Characterizing Machine Learning Programs,"
             Artificial Intelligence: The state-of-the-art, D. Sleeman (Ed.),
             1989.

sxv   [493] **Kodratoff, Y.,** "Symbolic Requirement for the Description of
               Numeric Measures of Explanatory Proofs: Abductive Recovery
               and Analogy," Proceedings of the Conference on Data Analysis,
               Learning Symbolic and Numeric Knowledge, pp. 349–364,
               INRIA, Antibes, 1989.

be   [494] **Kodratoff, Y., and Hutchinson, A.,** "Machine and Human
               Learning, Advance in European Research," Kogan Page, London,
               England, 1989.

i   [495] **Kodratoff, Y.,** "Learning Expert Knowledge by Improving the
               Explanations Provided by the System," Machine Learning: An
               Artificial Intelligence Approach, Volume III, Morgan Kaufmann,
               San Mateo, CA, Kodratoff, Y. and Michalski, R.S. (Eds.), Ch. 16,
               1990.

d   [496] **Koehn, B.W., and Zytkow, J.M.,** "Experimenting and Theorizing
               in Theory Formation," Proceedings of the 1st International
               Symposium on Methodologies for Intelligent Systems, pp.
               296–307, Knoxville, TN, 1986.

d   [497] **Kokar, M.M.,** "Determining Arguments in Invariant Functional
               Descriptions," Machine Learning, Vol. 1, No. 4, pp. 403–422,
               1986.

d   [498] **Kokar, M.M.,** "Coper: A Methodology for Learning Invariant
               Functional Descriptions," Machine Learning: A Guide to Current
               Research, Kluwer Academic Publishers, R.S. Michalski, J.G.
               Carbonell and T.M. Mitchell (Eds.), 1986.

dv   [499] **Kokar, M.M.,** "Discovering Functional Formulas Through
               Changing Representation Base," Proceedings of AAAI-86, pp.
               455–459, Philadelphia, PA, 1986.

l   [500] **Kokar, M.M.,** "Machine Learning in a Dynamic World,"
               Proceedings of IEEE International Symposium on Intelligent
               Control, 1988.

d   [501] **Kokar, M.M.,** "Concept Discovery Through Utilization of
               Invariance Embedded in the Description Language," Proceedings
               of the 6th International Workshop on Machine Learning, pp.
               478–479, Ithaca, NY, 1989.

iv   [502] **Kokar, M.M., and Zadrozny, W.,** "A Logic Structure of a
               Learning Agent," Proceedings of the 4th International Symposium
               on Methodologies for Intelligent Systems, pp. 305–312, 1989.

ap   [503]   **Kolodner, J.L.,** "Extending Problem-Solver Capabilities Through Case-Based Inference," Proceedings of the 4th International Machine Learning Workshop, pp. 167–178, University of California, Irvine, 1987.

s   [504]   **Kononenko, I., Bratko, I., and Roskar, E.,** "ASSISTANT: A System for Inductive Learning," Informatica Journal (in Slovenian), Vol. 10, No. 1, 1986.

ns   [505]   **Kononenko, I.,** "ID3, Sequential Bayes, Naive Bayes and Bayesian Neural Networks," Proceedings of EWSL-89, Montpellier, France, 1989.

a   [506]   **Kopeikina, L., Brandau, R., and Lemmon, A.,** "Case-Based Reasoning for Continuous Control," Proceedings of the Case-Based Reasoning Workshop, pp. 250–259, 1988.

p   [507]   **Korf, R.,** "Learning to Solve Problems by Searching for Macro-Operators," Pitman, London, and Morgan Kaufmann, San Mateo, CA, 1985.

a   [508]   **Koton, P.,** "Reasoning About Evidence in Causal Explanations," Proceedings of the Case-Based Reasoning Workshop, pp. 260–270, 1988.

g   [509]   **Koza, J.R.,** "Hierarchical Genetic Algorithms Operating on Populations of Computer Programs," Proceedings of IJCAI-89, pp. 768–744, Detroit, MI, 1989.

p   [510]   **Krawchuk, B.J., and Witten, I.H.,** "Problem Solvers that Learn," Proceedings of EWSL-88, pp. 93–106, Glasgow, Scotland, 1988.

s   [511]   **Krawchuk, B.J., and Witten, I.H.,** "On Asking the Right Questions," Proceedings of the 5th International Conference on Machine Learning, pp. 15–21, Ann Arbor, MI, 1988.

i   [512]   **Krulwich, B., Collins, G., and Birnbaum, L.,** "Improving Decision-Making on the Basis of Experience," Proceedings of the 6th International Workshop on Machine Learning, pp. 55–57, Ithaca, NY, 1989.

x   [513]   **Kuipers, B.,** "Commonsense Reasoning About Causality: Deriving Behavior from Structure," Qualitative Reasoning About Physical Systems, MIT Press, Cambridge, MA, D.G. Bobrow (Ed.), 1985.

d   [514]   **Kulkarni, D., and Simon, H.A.,** "The Role of Experimentation in Scientific Theory Revision," Proceedings of the 6th International Workshop on Machine Learning, pp. 278–283, Ithaca, NY, 1989.

g   [515] **Kumar, P.R., and Young, G.,** "Distributed Learning of the Global
             Maximum in a Two-Player Stochastic Game with Identical
             Payoffs," IEEE Transactions On Systems, Man, and Cybernetics,
             Vol. SMC-15, No. 6, pp. 743, 1985.

t   [516] **Kurtz, S.A., and Royer, J.S.,** "Prudence in Language Learning,"
             Proceedings of the 1988 Workshop on Computational Learning
             Theory COLT '88, pp. 206–219, MIT, 1988.

t   [517] **Kurtz, S.A., and Smith, C.H.,** "On the Role of Search for
             Learning," Proceedings of the 1989 Workshop on Computational
             Learning Theory COLT '89, pp. 303–311, University of
             California, Santa Cruz, 1989.

p   [518] **Laird, J.E., Rosenbloom, P.S., and Newell A.,** "Chunking in
             SOAR: the Anatomy of a General Learning Mechanism," Machine
             Learning, Vol. 1, No. 1, pp. 11–46, 1986.

px   [519] **Laird, J.E., Rosenbloom, P.S., and Newell, A.,**
             "Overgeneralization During Knowledge Compilation in SOAR,"
             Workshop on Knowledge Compilation, Oregon State University,
             Corvallis, OR, 1986.

m   [520] **Laird, J.E., Newell, A., and Rosenbloom, P.S.,** "SOAR: An
             Architecture for General Intelligence," Artificial Intelligence, Vol.
             33, 1987.

p   [521] **Laird, J.E.,** "Recovery from Incorrect Knowledge in SOAR,"
             Proceedings of AAAI-88, pp. 618–623, Saint Paul, MN, 1988.

px   [522] **Laird, J.E., Yager, E.S., and Tuck, C.M.,** "Learning Control and
             Task Knowledge from Advise in SOAR," Proceedings of Office of
             Naval Research Workshop on Knowledge Acquisition, A.L.
             Meyrowitz (Ed.), Arlington, VA, 1989.

s   [523] **Laird, P.D.,** "Inductive Inference by Refinement," Proceedings of
             AAAI-86, pp. 472–476, Philadelphia, PA, 1986.

dt   [524] **Laird, P.D.,** "Efficient Unsupervised Learning," Proceedings of
             the 1988 Workshop on Computational Learning Theory COLT
             '88, pp. 297–311, MIT, 1988.

n   [525] **Laird, P.D., and Gamble, E.,** "Learning a Probability
             Distribution Using Feature Maps," Proceedings of the 4th
             International Symposium on Methodologies for Intelligent
             Systems, pp. 313–322, 1989.

v   [526] **Lambert, B., Tcheng, D., and Lu, S.C.Y.,** "Generalized
Recursive Splitting Algorithms for Learning Hybrid Concepts,"
Proceedings of the 6th International Workshop on Machine
Learning, pp. 496–498, Ithaca, NY, 1989.

d   [527] **Langley, P.W., Zytkow, J.M., Simon, H.A., and Fisher, D.H.,**
"Discovering Qualitative Empirical Laws," Technical Report
85–18, University of California, Irvine, 1985.

b   [528] **Langley, P.W., and Carbonell, J.G.,** "Language Acquisition and
Machine Learning," Mechanisms for Language Acquisition,
Lawrence Erlbaum Associates, B. MacWhinney (Ed.), 1986.

det [529] **Langley, P.W., and Nordhausen, B.,** "A Framework for
Empirical Discovery," Proceedings of the 1st International
Meeting on Advances in Learning, Les Arcs, France, 1986.

bd [530] **Langley, P.W., Zytkow, J.M., Simon, H.A., and Bradshaw,
G.L.,** "The Search for Regularity: Four Aspects of Scientific
Discovery," Machine Learning: An Artificial Intelligence
Approach, Volume II, Morgan Kaufmann, San Mateo, CA, R.S.
Michalski, J.G. Carbonell and T.M. Mitchell (Eds.), pp. 425–470,
1986.

b   [531] **Langley, P.W., and Carbonell, J.G.,** "Machine Learning:
Techniques and Foundations," Technical Report, University of
California, Irvine, 1987.

st [532] **Langley, P.W., Gennari, J.H., and Iba, W.,** "Hill-Climbing
Theories of Learning," Proceedings of the 4th International
Machine Learning Workshop, pp. 312–323, University of
California, Irvine, 1987.

d   [533] **Langley, P.W., Simon, H.A., and Bradshaw, G.L.,** "Heuristics
for Empirical Discovery," Computational Models of Learning,
Springer-Verlag, Berlin Heidelberg, L. Bolc (Ed.), pp. 21–54,
1987.

bd [534] **Langley, P.W., Simon, H.A., Bradshaw, G.L., and Zytkow,
J.M.,** "Scientific Discovery: Computational Explorations of the
Creative Processes," The MIT Press, Cambridge, MA, 1987.

d   [535] **Langley, P.W., and Zytkow, J.M.,** "Data-Driven Approaches to
Empirical Discovery," Artificial Intelligence , Vol. 40, 1989.

d   [536] **Langley, P.W., and Nordhausen, B.,** "A Framework for
Empirical Discovery," unpublished manuscript.

es   [537] **Lathrop, R.H., and Kirk, R.S.,** "A System which Uses Examples
               to Learn VLSI Structure Manipulations," Proceedings of
               AAAI-86, pp. 1024–1028, Philadelphia, PA, 1986.

ek   [538] **Lavrac, N., and Mozetic, I.,** "Methods for Knowledge
               Acquisition and Refinement in Second Generation Expert
               Systems," ACM SIGART Newsletter, Special issue on Knowledge
               Acquisition, 1989.

is   [539] **Lavrac, N., and Vassilev, H.,** "Meta-Level Architecture of a
               Second Generation Knowledge Acquisition System," Proceedings
               of EWSL-89, Montpellier, France, 1989.

m   [540] **Lawler, R., and Selfridge, O.G.,** "Learning Concrete Strategies
               through Interaction," Proceedings of the 7th Conference of the
               Cognitive Science Society, pp. 670, 1985.

x   [541] **Lawrence, C.,** "A Knowledge-Based System that Supports
               Explanation-Based Learning Applications," Proceedings of the 3rd
               European Workshop on Knowledge Acquisition for
               Knowledge-Based Systems, pp. 327–337, 1989.

x   [542] **Leake, D.B.,** "Using Explainer Needs to Judge Operationality,"
               Proceedings of 1988 Symposium on Explanation-Based Learning,
               pp. 148–152, Stanford, 1988.

c   [543] **Lebbe, J., Lerman, I.C., Nicolas, J., Peter, P. and Vignes, R.,**
               "Conceptual Clustering in Biology: Application and Perspectives,"
               Proceedings of the Conference on Data Analysis, Learning
               Symbolic and Numeric Knowledge, pp. 443–454, INRIA, Antibes,
               1989.

s   [544] **Lebbe, J., Vignes, R., and Darmoni, S.,** "Symbolic Numeric
               Approach for Biological Knowledge Representation: A Medical
               Example with Creation of Identification Graphs," Proceedings of
               the Conference on Data Analysis, Learning Symbolic and
               Numeric Knowledge, pp. 389–398, INRIA, Antibes, 1989.

m   [545] **Lebowitz, M.,** "Categorizing Numeric Information for
               Generalization," Cognitive Science, Vol. 9, pp. 285–308, 1985.

is   [546] **Lebowitz, M.,** "Concept Learning in a Rich Input Domain:
               Generalization-Based Memory," Machine Learning: An Artificial
               Intelligence Approach, Volume II, Morgan Kaufmann, San Mateo,
               CA, R.S. Michalski, J.G. Carbonell and T.M. Mitchell (Eds.),
               1986.

im   [547] **Lebowitz, M.,** "Integrated Learning: Controlling Explanation,"
               Cognitive Science, Vol. 10, No. 2, pp. 219–240, 1986.

s [548] Lebowitz, M., "Not the Path to Perdition: The Utility of Similarity-Based Learning," Proceedings of AAAI-86, pp. 533–537, Philadelphia, PA, 1986.

ci [549] Lebowitz, M., "UNIMEM, a General Learning System: An Overview," Proceedings of ECAI-86, Brighton, England, 1986.

ci [550] Lebowitz, M., "Experiments with Incremental Concept Formulation: UNIMEM," Machine Learning, Vol. 2, No. 2, pp. 103–138, 1987.

s [551] Lebowitz, M., "Deferred Commitment in UNIMEM: Waiting to Learning," Proceedings of the 5th International Conference on Machine Learning, pp. 80–86, Ann Arbor, MI, 1988.

i [552] Lebowitz, M., "The Utility of Similarity-based Learning in a World Needing Explanation," Machine Learning: An Artificial Intelligence Approach, Volume III, Morgan Kaufmann, San Mateo, CA, Kodratoff, Y. and Michalski, R.S. (Eds.), Ch. 15, 1990.

n [553] Lee, H-M., and Hsu, C-C., "Neural Network Processing through Energy Minimization with Learning Ability to the Multiconstraint Zero-One Knapsack Problem," Proceedings of IEEE International Workshop on Tools for Artificial Intelligence, pp. 548–555, Fairfax, VA, 1989.

p [554] Lee, K.F., and Mahajan, S., "A Patter Classification Approach to Evaluation Function Learning," Artificial Intelligence, Vol. 36, pp. 1–25, 1988.

p [555] Lee, S., and Wang, B., "Method Generalization Based on Specialization," Proceedings of the Conference on Data Analysis, Learning Symbolic and Numeric Knowledge, pp. 493–502, INRIA, Antibes, 1989.

s [556] Lee, W.D., and Ray, S.R., "Probabilistic Rule Generator: A New Methodology of Variable-Valued Logic Synthesis," Proceedings of 1986 IEEE International Symposium on Multiple-Valued Logic, Blacksburg, VA, 1986.

s [557] Lee, W.D. and Ray, S.R., "Rule Refinement Using the Probabilistic Rule Generator," Proceedings of AAAI-86, pp. 442–447, Philadelphia, PA, 1986.

ae [558] Lehnert, W.G., "Learning to Integrate Syntax and Semantics," Proceedings of the 4th International Machine Learning Workshop, pp. 179–190, University of California, Irvine, 1987.

ap   [559] Lehnert, W.G., "Cased-Based Problem Solving with a Large
               Knowledge Base of Learned Cases," Proceedings of AAAI-87, pp.
               301–306, Seattle, WA, 1987.

a   [560] Leishman, D., "Analogy as a Constrained Partial Correspondence
               Over Conceptual Graphs," Proceedings of the 1st International
               Conference on Principles of Knowledge Representation and
               Reasoning, pp. 223–234, Toronto, Canada, 1989.

k   [561] Lenat, D.B., Mayank, P., and Shepherd, M., "CYC: Using
               Common Sense Knowledge to Overcome Brittleness and
               Knowledge Acquisition Bottlenecks," AI Magazine, Vol. 6, No. 4,
               1986.

bk   [562] Lenat, D.B., "When Will Machines Learn?," Machine Learning,
               Vol. 4, No. 3/4, 1989.

px   [563] Levi, K.R., Perschbacher, D., and Shalin, V.L., "Learning
               Tactical Plans for Pilot Aiding," Proceedings of the 6th
               International Workshop on Machine Learning, pp. 191–193,
               Ithaca, NY, 1989.

k   [564] Levi, K.R., Shalin, V.L., and Perschbacher, D.L., "Identifying
               Knowledge Base Deficiencies by Observing User Behaviour,"
               Proceedings of the 6th International Workshop on Machine
               Learning, pp. 296–301, Ithaca, NY, 1989.

t   [565] Levin, E., Tishby, N., and Solla, S.A., "A Statistical Approach to
               Learning and Generalization in Layered Neural Networks,"
               Proceedings of the 1989 Workshop on Computational Learning
               Theory COLT '89, pp. 245–260, University of California, Santa
               Cruz, 1989.

t   [566] Li, M., and Vazirani, U., "On the Learnability of Finite
               Automata," Proceedings of the 1988 Workshop on Computational
               Learning Theory COLT '88, pp. 359–370, MIT, 1988.

g   [567] Liepins, G.E., Hillard, M.R., Palmer, M., and Rangarajan, G.,
               "Alternatives for Classifier System Credit Assignment,"
               Proceedings of IJCAI-89, pp. 756–761, Detroit, MI, 1989.

t   [568] Lin, J.-H., and Vitter, J.S., "Complexity Issues in Learning by
               Neural Nets," Proceedings of the 1989 Workshop on
               Computational Learning Theory COLT '89, pp. 118–133,
               University of California, Santa Cruz, 1989.

sv   [569]   **Ling, X.,** "Learning and Invention of Horn Clause Theories—A Constructive Method," Proceedings of the 4th International Symposium on Methodologies for Intelligent Systems, pp. 323–331, 1989.

sv   [570]   **Ling, X., and Ungar, L.,** "Inventing Theoretical Terms in Inductive Learning of Functions—Search and Constructive Methods," Proceedings of the 4th International Symposium on Methodologies for Intelligent Systems, pp. 332–341, 1989.

t   [571]   **Linial, N., Mansour, Y., and Rivest, R.L.,** "Results on Learnability and the Vapnik-Chervonenkis Dimension," Proceedings of the 1988 Workshop on Computational Learning Theory COLT '88, pp. 56–68, MIT, 1988.

s   [572]   **Liquiere, M., and Sallantin, J.,** "INNE: INduction in NEtworks: A Structural Learning Algorithm for Noisy Examples," Proceedings of EWSL-89, Montpellier, France, 1989.

s   [573]   **Liquiere, M., and Sallantin, J.,** "INNE: A Structural Learning Algorithm for Noisy Examples," Proceedings of IEEE International Workshop on Tools for Artificial Intelligence, pp. 70–76, Fairfax, VA, 1989.

t   [574]   **Littlestone, N.,** "Learning Quickly when Irrelevant Attributes Abound: A New Linear-Threshold Algorithm," Machine Learning, Vol. 2, No. 4, 1988.

t   [575]   **Littlestone, N.,** "From On-line to Batch Learning," Proceedings of the 1989 Workshop on Computational Learning Theory COLT '89, pp. 269–284, University of California, Santa Cruz, 1989.

ms   [576]   **Littman, D.,** "Constructing Expert Systems as Building Mental Models," Knowledge Representation and Organization in Machine Learning, Springer Verlag, K. Morik (Ed.), Berlin Heidelberg, 1989.

x   [577]   **Liuh, S., and Huhns, M.N.,** "Using a TMS for EBG," MCC Technical Report AI-445-86, MCC, Austin, TX, 1986.

de   [578]   **Long, J., Irani, E., Slagle, J., and the POSCH group,** "Automating the Discovery of Causal Relationships in a Medical Records Database: The POSCH AI Project," Proceedings of IJCAI-89 Workshop on Knowledge Discovery in Databases, pp. 192–203, Detroit, MI, 1989.

de   [579] **Lubinsky, D.**, "Discovery from Databases: A Review of AI and
             Statistical Techniques," Proceedings of IJCAI-89 Workshop on
             Knowledge Discovery in Databases, pp. 204–218, Detroit, MI,
             1989.

n   [580] **Lynne, K.J.**, "Competitive Reinforcement Learning," Proceedings
             of the 5th International Conference on Machine Learning, pp.
             188–199, Ann Arbor, MI, 1988.

bn   [581] **MacGregor, R.J.**, "Neural and Brain Modeling," Academic Press,
             1987.

vx   [582] **Maclin, R., and Shavlik, J.W.**, "Enriching Vocabularies by
             Generalizing Explanation Structures," Proceedings of the 6th
             International Workshop on Machine Learning, pp. 444–446,
             Ithaca, NY, 1989.

n   [583] **Madala, H.**, "Layered Inductive Learning Algorithms and Their
             Computational Aspects," Proceedings of IEEE International
             Workshop on Tools for Artificial Intelligence, pp. 448–456,
             Fairfax, VA, 1989.

kps   [584] **Mahadevan, S.**, "Verification-Based Learning: A Generalization
             Strategy for Inferring Problem-Decomposition Methods,"
             Proceedings of IJCAI-85, pp. 616–623, Los Angeles, CA, 1985.

px   [585] **Mahadevan, S., Natarajan, B.K., and Tadepalli, P.V.**, "A
             Framework for Learning as Improving Problem-Solving
             Performance," Proceedings of 1988 Symposium on
             Explanation-Based Learning, pp. 215–219, Stanford, 1988.

tx   [586] **Mahadevan, S., and Tadepalli, P.V.**, "On the Tractability of
             Learning from Incomplete Theories," Proceedings of the 5th
             International Conference on Machine Learning, pp. 235–241, Ann
             Arbor, MI, 1988.

x   [587] **Mahadevan, S.**, "Using Determinations in EBL: A Solution to the
             Incomplete Theory Problem," Proceedings of the 6th International
             Workshop on Machine Learning, pp. 320–325, Ithaca, NY, 1989.

es   [588] **Mahood, W.L.**, "Incremental Learning Mechanisms for Speech
             Understanding," Proceedings of IEEE International Workshop on
             Tools for Artificial Intelligence, pp. 237–243, Fairfax, VA, 1989.

s   [589] **Manago, M., and Kodratoff, Y.**, "Model-Driven Learning of
             Disjunctive Concepts," Proceedings of EWSL-87, pp. 183–198,
             Bled, Yugoslavia, 1987.

s   [590] **Manago, M., and Kodratoff, Y.,** "Noise and Knowledge Acquisition," Proceedings of IJCAI-87, pp. 348–354, Milan, Italy, 1987.

s   [591] **Manago, M.,** "Knowledge Intensive Induction," Proceedings of the 6th International Workshop on Machine Learning, pp. 151–155, Ithaca, NY, 1989.

s   [592] **Manago, M., and Kodratoff, Y.,** "Toward a New Generation of ID Algorithm," Proceedings of IJCAI-89 Workshop on Knowledge Discovery in Databases, pp. 219–229, Detroit, MI, 1989.

k   [593] **Marcus, S., McDermott, J., and Wang. T.,** "Knowledge Acquisition for Constructive Systems," Proceedings of IJCAI-85, pp. 637–639, Los Angeles, CA, 1985.

k   [594] **Marcus, S.,** "Understanding Decision Ordering from a Piece-Meal Collection of Knowledge," An International Journal of Knowledge Acquisition for Knowledge-Based Systems, Vol. 1, No. 3, pp. 279–298, .

k   [595] **Marcus, S., and McDermott, J.,** "SALT: A Knowledge Acquisition Language for Propose and Revise Systems," Artificial Intelligence, Vol. 39, pp. 1–37, 1989.

s   [596] **Marie, C.S.,** "Building a Learning Bias from Perceived Dependencies," Proceedings of the 6th International Workshop on Machine Learning, pp. 501–502, Ithaca, NY, 1989.

s   [597] **Marie, X.,** "A Graph Algorithm for Learning Disjunctions," Proceedings of EWSL-89, Montpellier, France, 1989.

m   [598] **Markovitch, S., and Scott, P.D.,** "The Role of Forgetting in Learning," Proceedings of the 5th International Conference on Machine Learning, pp. 459–465, Ann Arbor, MI, 1988.

x   [599] **Markovitch, S. and Scott, P.D.,** "Utilization Filtering: A Method for Reducing the Inherent Harmfulness of Deductively Learned Knowledge," Proceedings of IJCAI-89, pp. 738–743, Detroit, MI, 1989.

i   [600] **Markovitch, S., and Scott, P.D.,** "Information Filters and Their Implementation in the SYLLOG System," Proceedings of the 6th International Workshop on Machine Learning, pp. 404–407, Ithaca, NY, 1989.

s   [601] **Marquis, P.,** "Computing Most Specific Generalizations in Propositional Calculus," Proceedings of EWSL-89, Montpellier, France, 1989.

t   [602] Marron, A., "Learning Pattern Languages from a Single Initial
              Example and from Queries," Proceedings of the 1988 Workshop
              on Computational Learning Theory COLT '88, pp. 345–358, MIT,
              1988.

am   [603] Martin, J.D., "Focusing Attention for Observational Learning:
              The Importance of Context," Proceedings of IJCAI-89, pp.
              562–567, Detroit, MI, 1989.

c   [604] Martin, J.D., "Reducing Redundant Learning," Proceedings of
              the 6th International Workshop on Machine Learning, pp.
              396–399, Ithaca, NY, 1989.

e   [605] Martin, J.H., "The Acquisition of Polysemy," Proceedings of the
              4th International Machine Learning Workshop, pp. 198–204,
              University of California, Irvine, 1987.

s   [606] Mason, M.T., Christiansen, A.D., and Mitchell, T.M.,
              "Experiments in Robot Learning," Proceedings of the 6th
              International Workshop on Machine Learning, pp. 141–145,
              Ithaca, NY, 1989.

m   [607] Matheus, C.J., "Conceptual Purpose: Implications for Concept
              Representation and Learning in Machines and Humans,"
              Technical Report UIUCDCS-87–1370, University of Illinois at
              Urbana-Champaign, 1987.

n   [608] Matheus, C.J., and Hohensee, W.E., "Learning in Artificial
              Neural Systems," Computational Intelligence Journal, Vol. 3, No.
              4, 1987.

tv   [609] Matheus, C.J., "A Constructive Induction Framework,"
              Proceedings of the 6th International Workshop on Machine
              Learning, pp. 474–475, Ithaca, NY, 1989.

v   [610] Matheus, C.J., and Rendell, L., "Constructive Induction on
              Decision Trees," Proceedings of IJCAI-89, pp. 645–650, Detroit,
              MI, 1989.

bm   [611] Maturane, H.R., and Varela, F.J., "The Tree of Knowledge: The
              Biological Roots of Human Understanding," Shambhala
              Publications, New Science Library, 1987.

px   [612] Matwin, S., and Morin, J., "Learning Procedural Knowledge in
              the EBG Context," Proceedings of the 6th International Workshop
              on Machine Learning, pp. 197–199, Ithaca, NY, 1989.

k [613] **Maulsby, D.L., James, G.A., and Witten, J.H.,** "Evaluating Interaction in Knowledge Acquisition: A Case Study," Proceedings of the 3rd European Workshop on Knowledge Acquisition for Knowledge-Based Systems, pp. 406–419, 1989.

bmn [614] **McClelland, J.L., Rumelhart, D.E., and the PDP Research Group,** "Parallel Distributed Processing: Psychological and Biological Models," The MIT Press, Vol. 2, Computational Models of Cognition and Perception, Cambridge. MA, 1986.

p [615] **McCluskey, T.L.,** "The Anatomy of a Weak Learning Method for Use in Goal Directed Search," Proceedings of the 4th International Machine Learning Workshop, pp. 134–140, University of California, Irvine, 1987.

p [616] **McCluskey, T.L.,** "Combining Weak Learning Heuristics in General Problem Solvers," Proceedings of IJCAI-87, pp. 331–333, Milan, Italy, 1987.

i [617] **McCluskey, T.L.,** "Explanation-Based and Similarity-Based Heuristic Acquisition in a General Planner," Proceedings of EWSL-89, Montpellier, France, 1989.

ip [618] **McCluskey, T.L.,** "Heuristic Refinement in a Heuristic Acquiring Planner," Proceedings of the 4th International Symposium on Methodologies for Intelligent Systems, pp. 351–358, 1989.

b [619] **McDermott, J.,** "The World Would Be a Better Place If Non-Programmers Could Program," Machine Learning, Vol. 4, No. 3/4, 1989.

k [620] **McLeish, M., Cecile, M., Garg, M., and Yao, P.,** "An Overview of Methods and Results for Designing Medical Diagnostic Systems from Data," Proceedings of IJCAI-89 Workshop on Knowledge Discovery in Databases, pp. 230–240, Detroit, MI, 1989.

s [621] **Mehler, G., Bentrup, J., and Riedesel, J.,** "INDUCE.4: A Program for Incrementally Learning Structural Descriptions from Examples," Technical Report, Dept. of Computer Science, University of Illinois at Urbana-Champaign, 1986.

v [622] **Mehra, P.,** "Constructing Representations Using Inverted Spaces," Proceedings of the 6th International Workshop on Machine Learning, pp. 472–473, Ithaca, NY, 1989.

v [623] **Mehra, P., Rendell, L., and Benjamin, W.,** "Principled Constructive Induction," Proceedings of IJCAI-89, pp. 651–656, Detroit, MI, 1989.

mn   [624]   Mel, B.W., "Building and Using Mental Models in a
                Sensory-Motor Domain: A Connectionist Approach," Proceedings
                of the 5th International Conference on Machine Learning, pp.
                207–213, Ann Arbor, MI, 1988.

s   [625]   Mennesier, M.O., and Diday, E., "Symbolic Approach of the
                Analysis of Chronological Series in View to Forecasting,"
                Proceedings of the Conference on Data Analysis, Learning
                Symbolic and Numeric Knowledge, pp. 407–416, INRIA, Antibes,
                1989.

b   [626]   Michalski, R.S., Carbonell, J.G., and Mitchell, T.M., "Machine
                Learning: An Artificial Intelligence Approach, Volume I, "
                Morgan Kaufmann, San Mateo, CA, (Japanese translation by Syun
                Ishizaki et al. published by Kyoritsu Schuppan, 1987), 1983.

be   [627]   Michalski, R.S., "Knowledge Repair Mechanisms: Evolution
                versus Revolution," Proceedings of the 3rd International Machine
                Learning Workshop, pp. 116–119, Skytop, PA, 1985.

b   [628]   Michalski, R.S., "Emerging Principles in Machine Learning,"
                Proceedings of the 1st International Symposium on Methodologies
                for Intelligent Systems, pp. 289, Knoxville, TN, 1986.

b   [629]   Michalski, R.S., "Understanding the Nature of Learning: Issues
                and Research Directions," Machine Learning: An Artificial
                Intelligence Approach, Volume II, Morgan Kaufmann, San Mateo,
                CA, R.S. Michalski, J.G. Carbonell and T.M. Mitchell (Eds.), pp.
                3–26, 1986.

b   [630]   Michalski, R.S., Amarel, S., Lenat, D., Michie, D., and,
                Winston, P.H., "Machine Learning: Challenges of the Eighties,"
                Machine Learning: An Artificial Intelligence Approach, Volume II,
                Morgan Kaufmann, San Mateo, CA, R.S. Michalski, J.G.
                Carbonell and T.M. Mitchell (Eds.), pp. 27–42, 1986.

b   [631]   Michalski, R.S., Carbonell, J.G., and Mitchell, T., "Machine
                Learning: An Artificial Intelligence Approach, Volume II, "
                Morgan Kaufmann, San Mateo, CA, (Japanese translation by Syun
                Ishizaki et al. published by Kyouritsu Schppan, 1987), 1986.

s   [632]   Michalski, R.S., Mozetic, I., Hong, J., and Lavrac, N., "The
                Multi-Purpose Incremental Learning System AQ15 and its Testing
                Application to Three Medical Domains," Proceedings of
                AAAI-86, pp. 1041–1045, Philadelphia, PA, 1986.

c   [633] **Michalski, R.S., and Stepp, R.E.,** "Conceptual Clustering of Structured Objects: A Goal-Oriented Approach," Artificial Intelligence, Vol. 28, pp. 43–69, 1986.

b   [634] **Michalski, R.S., and Winston, R.H.,** "Variable Precision Logic," Artificial Intelligence, Vol. 29, pp. 121–146, 1986.

s   [635] **Michalski, R.S.,** "How to Learn Imprecise Concepts: A Method for Employing a Two-Tiered Knowledge Representation in Learning," Proceedings of the 4th International Machine Learning Workshop, pp. 50–58, University of California, Irvine, 1987.

b   [636] **Michalski, R.S.,** "Learning Strategies and Automated Knowledge Acquisition—An Overview," Computational Models of Learning, Springer-Verlag, Berlin Heidelberg, L. Bolc (Ed.), pp. 1–19, 1987.

bs   [637] **Michalski, R.S.,** "Concept Learning," Encyclopedia of Artificial Intelligence, John Wiley & Sons, S.C. Shapiro (Ed.), pp. 185–194, 1987.

bc   [638] **Michalski, R.S., and Stepp, R.E.,** "Clustering," Encyclopedia of Artificial Intelligence, John Wiley & Sons, S.C. Shapiro (Ed.), pp. 103–111, 1987.

ix   [639] **Michalski, R.S., and Ko, H.,** "On the Nature of Explanation or Why Did the Wine Bottle Shatter," Proceedings of 1988 Symposium on Explanation-Based Learning, pp. 12–16, Stanford University, March, 1988.

r   [640] **Michalski, R.S., Ko, H., and Chen, K.,** "Qualitative Prediction: the SPARC/G Methodology for Inductively Describing and Predicting Discrete Processes," Current Issues in Expert Systems, Academic Press Inc., London, Van Lamsweerde and O. Dufour (Eds.), 1988.

i   [641] **Michalski, R.S., and Watanabe, L.M.,** "Constructive Closed-Loop Learning: Fundamental Ideas and Examples," George Mason University, Reports of Machine Learning and Inference Laboratory, No. MLI-88-1, 1988.

s   [642] **Michalski, R.S.,** "Two-Tiered Concept Meaning, Inferential Matching and Conceptual Cohesiveness," Similarity and Analogical Reasoning, Cambridge University Press, S. Vosniadou and A. Ortony (Eds.), 1989.

i   [643] **Michalski, R.S.,** "Multistrategy Constructive Learning," Proceedings of the ONR Workshop on Knowledge Acquisition, Washington, D.C., 1989.

m   [644] **Michalski, R.S., Dontas, K.J., and Boehm-Davis, D.,** "Plausible
              Reasoning: An Outline of Theory and Experiments," Proceedings
              of the 4th International Symposium on Methodologies for
              Intelligent Systems, pp. 260–272, Charlotte, NC, 1989.

b   [645] **Michalski, R.S., and Littman, D.,** "Future Directions of AI in a
              Resource-Limited Environment," George Mason University,
              Reports of Machine Learning and Inference Laboratory, No.
              MLI-89-20, Invited presentation at the panel of Future of AI at the
              IJCAI-89, 1989.

b   [646] **Michalski, R.S., and Kodratoff, Y.,** "Research in Machine
              Learning: Recent Progress, Classification of Methods, and Future
              Directions," Machine Learning: An Artificial Intelligence
              Approach, Volume III, Morgan Kaufmann, San Mateo, Kodratoff,
              Y. and Michalski, R.S. (Eds.), Ch. 1, 1990.

bt   [647] **Michie, D.,** "Machine Learning in the Next Five Years,"
              Proceedings of EWSL-88, pp. 107–122, Glasgow, Scotland, 1988.

t   [648] **Milosavljevic, A., Haussler, D., and Jurka, J.,** "Informed
              Parsimonious Inference of Prototypical Genetic Sequences,"
              Proceedings of the 1989 Workshop on Computational Learning
              Theory COLT '89, pp. 102–118, University of California, Santa
              Cruz, 1989.

es   [649] **Mingers, J.,** "An Empirical Comparison of Selection Measures
              for Decision-Tree Induction," Machine Learning, Vol. 3, No. 4,
              pp. 319–342, 1989.

es   [650] **Mingers, J.,** "An Empirical Comparison of Pruning Methods for
              Decision-Tree Induction," Machine Learning, Vol. 4, No. 2, 1989.

bm   [651] **Minsky, M.,** "The Society of Mind," Simon and Schuster, 1986.

p   [652] **Minton, S.,** "Selectively Generalizing Plans for
              Problem-Solving," Proceedings of IJCAI-85, pp. 596–599, Los
              Angeles, CA, 1985.

x   [653] **Minton, S.,** "Improving the Effectiveness of Explanation-Based
              Learning," Proceedings of the Workshop on Knowledge
              Compilation, Oregon State University, Corvallis, OR, 1986.

x   [654] **Minton, S., Carbonell, J.G., Knoblock, C., Kuokka, and
              Nordin,** "Improving the Effectiveness of Explanation-Based
              Learning," Technical Report, Computer Science Dept.,
              Carnegie-Mellon University, 1986.

px   [655]   Minton, S., and Carbonell, J.G., "Strategies for Learning Search
                Control Rules: An Explanation-Based Approach," Proceedings of
                IJCAI-87, pp. 228–235, Milan, Italy, 1987.

px   [656]   Minton, S., Carbonell, J.G., Etzioni, O., et al., "Acquiring
                Effective Search Control Rules: Explanation-Based Learning in
                the PRODIGY System," Proceedings of the 4th International
                Machine Learning Workshop, pp. 122–133, University of
                California, Irvine, 1987.

xt   [657]   Minton, S., "EBL and Weakest Preconditions," Proceedings of
                1988 Symposium on Explanation-Based Learning, pp. 210–214,
                Stanford, 1988.

x   [658]   Minton, S., "Quantitative Results Concerning the Utility of
                Explanation-Based Learning," Proceedings of AAAI-88, pp.
                564–569, Saint Paul, MN, 1988.

x   [659]   Minton, S., "Learning Search Control Knowledge: An
                Explanation-Based Approach," Kluwer Academic Publishers,
                1988.

px   [660]   Minton, S., Carbonell, J.G., Knoblock, C.A., Kuokka, D.R.,
                Etzioni, O., and Gil, Y., "Explanation-Based Learning: A
                Problems Solving Perspective," Artificial Intelligence, Vol. 40, pp.
                63–118, 1989.

b   [661]   Mitchell, T.M., Carbonell, J.G., and Michalski, R.S., "Machine
                Learning: A Guide to Current Research," Kluwer Academic
                Publishers, 1985.

ek   [662]   Mitchell, T.M., Mahadevan, S., and Steinberg, L.I., "LEAP: A
                Learning Apprentice for VLSI Design," Proceedings of IJCAI-85,
                pp. 573–580, Los Angeles, CA, 1985.

bx   [663]   Mitchell, T.M., Keller, R.M., and Kedar-Cabelli, S.T.,
                "Explanation-Based Generalization: A Unifying View," Machine
                Learning, Vol. 1, No. 1, pp. 47–80, 1986.

b   [664]   Mitchell, T.M., "Can We Build Learning Robots?," Proceedings
                of the Workshop on Representation and Learning in an
                Autonomous Agent, Lagos, Portugal, 1988.

ekx   [665]   Mitchell, T.M., Mahadevan, S., and Steinberg, L.I., "LEAP: A
                Learning Apprentice System for VLSI Design," Machine
                Learning: An Artificial Intelligence Approach, Volume III, Morgan
                Kaufmann, San Mateo, Kodratoff, Y. and Michalski, R.S. (Eds.),
                Ch. 10, 1990.

pv   [666]   **Mohan, S., and Tong, C.,** "Automatic Construction of a Hierarchical Generate-and-Test Algorithm," Proceedings of the 6th International Workshop on Machine Learning, pp. 483–484, Ithaca, NY, 1989.

gn   [667]   **Montana, D.J., and Davis, L.,** "Training Feedforward Neural Networks using Genetic Algorithms," Proceedings of IJCAI-89, pp. 762–767, Detroit, MI, 1989.

x   [668]   **Mooney, R.J.,** "Generalizing Explanations of Narratives into Schemata," Proceedings of the 3rd International Machine Learning Workshop, pp. 126–128, Skytop, PA, 1985.

x   [669]   **Mooney, R.J., and DeJong, G.F.,** "Learning Schemata for Natural Language Processing," Proceedings of IJCAI-85, pp. 681–687, Los Angeles, CA, 1985.

x   [670]   **Mooney, R.J., and Bennett, S.W.,** "A Domain Independent Explanation-Based Generalizer," Proceedings of AAAI-86, pp. 551–555, Philadelphia, PA, 1986.

x   [671]   **Mooney, R.J.,** "A General Explanation-Based Learning Mechanism and its Application to Narrative Understanding," Thesis, University of Illinois at Urbana-Champaign, December, 1987.

px   [672]   **Mooney, R.J.,** "Generalizing the Order of Operators and Its Relation to Generalizing Structure," Proceedings of 1988 Symposium on Explanation-Based Learning, pp. 84–88, Stanford, 1988.

px   [673]   **Mooney, R.J.,** "Generalizing the Order of Operators in Macro-Operators," Proceedings of the 5th International Conference on Machine Learning, pp. 270–283, Ann Arbor, MI, 1988.

x   [674]   **Mooney, R.J.,** "The Effect of Rule Use on the Utility of Explanation-Based Learning," Proceedings of IJCAI-89, pp. 725–730, Detroit, MI, 1989.

i   [675]   **Mooney, R.J., and Ourston, D.,** "Induction Over the Unexplained: Integrated Learning of Concepts with Both Explainable and Conventional Aspects," Proceedings of the 6th International Workshop on Machine Learning, pp. 5–7, Ithaca, NY, 1989.

ens   [676] **Mooney, R.J., Shavlik, J., Towell, G., and Gove, A.,** "An
              Experimental Comparison of Symbolic and Connectionist
              Learning Algorithms," Proceedings of IJCAI-89, pp. 775–780,
              Detroit, MI, 1989.

beks   [677] **Morik, K.,** "Knowledge Representation and Organization in
              Machine Learning," Springer-Verlag, Lecture Notes in Artificial
              Intelligence, Berlin Heidelberg, 1989.

c   [678] **Morik, K., and Kietz, J.U.,** "A Bootstrapping Approach to
              Conceptual Clustering," Proceedings of the 6th International
              Workshop on Machine Learning, pp. 503–504, Ithaca, NY, 1989.

i   [679] **Morris, S.,** "Reducing Search and Learning Goal Preferences,"
              Proceedings of the 6th International Workshop on Machine
              Learning, pp. 46–48, Ithaca, NY, 1989.

bt   [680] **Mortimer, H.,** "The Logic of Induction," Ellis Horwood Limited,
              1988.

ex   [681] **Mostow, J.,** "Searching for Operational Concept Descriptions in
              BAR, MetaLEX and EBG," Proceedings of the 4th International
              Machine Learning Workshop, pp. 376–382, University of
              California, Irvine, 1987.

px   [682] **Mostow, J., and Bhatnager, N.,** "FAILSAFE—A Floor Planner
              that Uses EBG to Learn from its Failures," Proceedings of
              IJCAI-87, pp. 249–255, Milan, Italy, 1987.

p   [683] **Mostow, J.,** "An Object-Oriented Representation for Search
              Algorithms," Proceedings of the 6th International Workshop on
              Machine Learning, pp. 489–491, Ithaca, NY, 1989.

a   [684] **Mostow, J.,** "Design by Derivational Analogy: Issues in the
              Automated Replay of Design Plans," Artificial Intelligence, Vol.
              40, pp. 119–184, 1989.

dp   [685] **Mostow, J., and Prieditis, A.E.,** "Discovering Admissible Search
              Heuristics by Abstracting and Optimizing," Proceedings of the 6th
              International Workshop on Machine Learning, pp. 240, Ithaca,
              NY, 1989.

s   [686] **Mozetic, I.,** "Knowledge Extraction through Learning from
              Examples," Machine Learning: A Guide to Current Research,
              Kluwer Academic Publishers, T.M. Mitchell, J.G. Carbonell, R.S.
              Michalski (Eds.), 1986.

s   [687] **Mozetic, I.,** "Learning of Qualitative Models," Proceedings of
              EWSL-87, pp. 201–217, Bled, Yugoslavia, 1987.

sv   [688] **Mozetic, I.,** "The Role of Abstractions in Learning Qualitative
               Models," Proceedings of the 4th International Machine Learning
               Workshop, pp. 242–255, University of California, Irvine, 1987.

sv   [689] **Mozetic, I.,** "Hierarchical Model-Based Diagnosis," George
               Mason University, Reports of Machine Learning and Inference
               Laboratory, No. MLI-89-1, 1989.

v   [690] **Muggleton, S.,** "Duce, an Oracle Based Approach to Constructive
               Induction," Proceedings of IJCAI-87, pp. 287–292, Milan, Italy,
               1987.

v   [691] **Muggleton, S.,** "A Strategy for Constructing New Predicates in
               First-Order Logic," Proceedings of EWSL-88, pp. 123–130,
               Glasgow, Scotland, 1988.

v   [692] **Muggleton, S., and Buntine, W.,** "Machine Invention of First
               Order Predicates by Inverting Resolution," Proceedings of the 5th
               International Conference on Machine Learning, pp. 339–352, Ann
               Arbor, MI, 1988.

ems   [693] **Muggleton, S., Bain, M., Michie, H.H., and Michie, D.,** "An
               Experimental Comparison of Human and Machine Learning
               Formalisms," Proceedings of the 6th International Workshop on
               Machine Learning, pp. 113–118, Ithaca, NY, 1989.

s   [694] **Murray, K.S.,** "Multiple Convergence: An Approach to
               Disjunctive Concept Acquisition," Proceedings of IJCAI-87, pp.
               297–300, Milan, Italy, 1987.

kp   [695] **Murray, K.S., and Porter, B.W.,** "Controlling Search for the
               Consequences of New Information During Knowledge
               Integration," Proceedings of the 6th International Workshop on
               Machine Learning, pp. 290–295, Ithaca, NY, 1989.

k   [696] **Musen, M.A.,** "Automated Generation of Model-Based
               Knowledge-Acquisition Tools," Pitman, London, and Morgan
               Kaufmann, San Mateo, Research Notes in Artificial Intelligence,
               1988.

k   [697] **Musen, M.A.,** "Automated Support for Building and Extending
               Expert Models," Machine Learning, Vol. 4, No. 3/4, 1989.

b   [698] **Mylopoulos, J., and Brodie, M.L.,** "Readings in Artificial
               Intelligence and Databases," Morgan Kaufmann, 1989.

n   [699] **Namatame, A.,** "A Connectionist Learning with High-order
               Functional Networks and Its Internal Representation," Proceedings
               of IEEE International Workshop on Tools for Artificial
               Intelligence, pp. 542–547, Fairfax, VA, 1989.

t [700] **Natarajan, B.K., and Tadepalli, P.V.,** "Two New Frameworks for Learning," Proceedings of the 5th International Conference on Machine Learning, pp. 402–415, Ann Arbor, MI, 1988.

t [701] **Natarajan, B.K.,** "On Learning from Exercises," Proceedings of the 1989 Workshop on Computational Learning Theory COLT '89, pp. 72–87, University of California, Santa Cruz, 1989.

t [702] **Natarajan, B.K.,** "On Learning Sets and Functions," Machine Learning, Vol. 4, No. 1, 1989.

s [703] **Neves, D.M.,** "Learning Procedures from Examples and by Doing," Proceedings of IJCAI-85, pp. 624–630, Los Angeles, CA, 1985.

el [704] **Nguyen, T.N., and Stephanou, H.E.,** "A Continuous Model of Robot Hand Preshaping," Proceedings of IEEE International Conference on Systems, Man and Cybernetics, 1989.

s [705] **Niblett, T.,** "Constructing Decision Trees in Noisy Domains," Proceedings of EWSL-87, pp. 67–78, Bled, Yugoslavia, 1987.

s [706] **Niblett, T.,** "A Study of Generalization in Logic Programs," Proceedings of EWSL-88, pp. 131–138, Glasgow, Scotland, 1988.

s [707] **Nicolas, J.,** "Consistency and Preference Criterion for Generalization Languages Handling Negation and Disjunction," Proceedings of ECAI-88, pp. 402–407, Munich, W.Germany, 1988.

dl [708] **Nikolic, A.J., and Fu, K.S.,** "An Algorithm for Learning Without External Supervision and Its Application to Learning Control Systems," IEEE Transactions On Pattern Analysis and Machine Intelligence, Vol. PAMI-8, No. 3, pp. 304, 1986.

b [709] **Nilsson, N.J.,** "Probabilistic Logic," Artificial Intelligence, Vol. 28, pp. 71–87, 1986.

c [710] **Nordhausen, B.,** "Conceptual Clustering Using Relational Information," Proceedings of AAAI-86, pp. 508–512, Philadelphia, PA, 1986.

di [711] **Nordhausen, B., and Langley, P.W.,** "Towards an Integrated Discovery System," Proceedings of IJCAI-87, pp. 198–200, Milan, Italy, 1987.

d [712] **Nordhausen, B.,** "Time Measurements in Empirical Discovery," Proceedings of EWSL-89, Montpellier, France, 1989.

d [713] **Nordhausen, B., and Langly, P.W.,** "An Integrated Approach to Empirical Discovery," Proceedings of Office of Naval Research Workshop on Knowledge Acquisition, A.L. Meyrowitz (Ed.), Arlington, VA, 1989.

s   [714] **Norton, S.W.,** "Generating Better Decision Trees," Proceedings of
              IJCAI-89, pp. 639–644, Detroit, MI, 1989.

i   [715] **Numao, M., and Shimura, M.,** "Explanation-Based Acceleration
              of Similarity-Based Learning," Proceedings of the 6th
              International Workshop on Machine Learning, pp. 58–60, Ithaca,
              NY, 1989.

s   [716] **Nunez, G., and Cortes, U.,** "Some Circumscriptional Thoughts
              on SBL," Proceedings of EWSL-89, Montpellier, France, 1989.

t   [717] **Nunez, M.,** "Economic Induction: A Case Study," Proceedings of
              EWSL-88, pp. 139–146, Glasgow, Scotland, 1988.

kt   [718] **O'Leary, D.,** "Knowledge Discovery as a Threat to Database
              Security," Proceedings of IJCAI-89 Workshop on Knowledge
              Discovery in Databases, pp. 241–251, Detroit, MI, 1989.

x   [719] **O'Rorke, P.V.,** "Constraint Posting and Propagation in
              Explanation-Based Learning," Working Paper 70, AI Research
              Group, Coordinated Science Lab., University of Illinois at
              Urbana-Champaign, 1985.

x   [720] **O'Rorke, P.V.,** "Explanation-Based Learning via Constraint
              Posting and Propagation," Thesis, Computer Science Dept.,
              University of Illinois at Urbana-Champaign, 1987.

x   [721] **O'Rorke, P.V.,** "LT Revisited: Experimental Results of Applying
              Explanation-Based Learning to the Logic of Principia
              Mathematica," Proceedings of the 4th International Machine
              Learning Workshop, pp. 148–159, University of California, Irvine,
              1987.

x   [722] **O'Rorke, P.V.,** "Automated Abduction and Machine Learning,"
              Proceedings of 1988 Symposium on Explanation-Based Learning,
              pp. 170–174, Stanford, 1988.

x   [723] **O'Rorke, P.V.,** "LT Revisited: Explanation-Based Learning and
              the Logic of Principia Mathematica," Machine Learning, Vol. 4,
              No. 2, 1989.

px   [724] **O'Rorke, P.V., Cain, T., and Ortony, A.,** "Learning to Recognize
              Plans Involving Affect," Proceedings of the 6th International
              Workshop on Machine Learning, pp. 209–211, Ithaca, NY, 1989.

kx   [725] **O'Rorke, P.V., Morris, S., and Schulenburg, D.,** "Theory
              Formation by Abduction: Initial Results of a Case Study Based on
              the Chemical Revolution," Proceedings of the 6th International
              Workshop on Machine Learning, pp. 266–271, Ithaca, NY, 1989.

p   [726]   **Ohlsson, S.,** "Transfer of Training in Procedural Learning: A Matter of Conjectures and Refutations?," Computational Models of Learning, Springer-Verlag, L.Bolc (Ed.), pp. 55–88, Berlin Heidelberg, 1987.

gn   [727]   **Oosthuizen, G.D.,** "SUPERGRAN: A Connectionist Approach to Learning, Integrating Genetic Algorithms and Graph Induction," Proceedings of the 2nd International Conference on Genetic Algorithms, pp. 132–139, Cambridge, MA., 1987.

ks   [728]   **Oosthuizen, G.D., and McGregor, D.R.,** "Induction Through Knowledge Base Normalization," Proceedings of ECAI-88, pp. 396–401, Munich, W.Germany, 1988.

t   [729]   **Osherson, D.N., Stob, M., and Weinstein, S.,** "On Approximate Truth," Proceedings of the 1989 Workshop on Computational Learning Theory COLT '89, pp. 88–101, University of California, Santa Cruz, 1989.

d   [730]   **Osherson, D.N., and Weinstein, S.,** "Automated Scientific Discovery of First-Order Theories," Proceedings of Office of Naval Research Workshop on Knowledge Acquisition, A.L. Meyrowitz (Ed.), Arlington, VA, 1989.

a   [731]   **Owen, S.G.,** "Heuristics for Analogy Matching," Proceedings of ECAI-86, Brighton, England, 1986.

a   [732]   **Owen, S.G.,** "Finding and Using Analogies to Guide Mathematical Proof," Thesis, Dept. of Artificial Intelligence, Edinburgh, 1987.

e   [733]   **Pachowicz, P.W.,** "Low-level Numerical Characteristics and Inductive Learning Methodology in Texture Recognition," Proceedings of IEEE International Workshop on Tools for Artificial Intelligence, pp. 91–97, Fairfax, VA, 1989.

sv   [734]   **Pagallo, G.,** "Learning DNF by Decision Trees," Proceedings of IJCAI-89, pp. 639–644, Detroit, MI, 1989.

sv   [735]   **Pagallo, G., and Haussler, D.,** "Two Algorithms That Learn DNF by Discovering Relevant Features," Proceedings of the 6th International Workshop on Machine Learning, pp. 119–123, Ithaca, NY, 1989.

s   [736]   **Paredis, J.,** "Learning the Behaviour of Dynamical Systems from Examples," Proceedings of the 6th International Workshop on Machine Learning, pp. 137–140, Ithaca, NY, 1989.

s   [737] **Parodi, A., and Khouas, S.,** "Semantic Network Learning
               through Data Assimilation and Concept Evolution," Proceedings
               of EWSL-89, Montpellier, France, 1989.

ce   [738] **Parsons, T.J.,** "Conceptual Clustering in Relational
               Structures—An Application in the Domain of Vision,"
               Proceedings of EWSL-89, Montpellier, France, 1989.

k   [739] **Patel, J.,** "On the Road to Automatic Knowledge Engineering,"
               Proceedings of IJCAI-89, pp. 628–632, Detroit, MI, 1989.

es   [740] **Patterson, D.W.,** "A Comparison of Some Inductive Learning
               Methodologies," Proceedings of the IEEE International
               Conference on Systems, Man, and Cybernetics, pp. 164–169,
               Atlanta, GA, 1986.

t   [741] **Paturi, R., Rajasekaran, S., and Reif, J.,** "The Light Bulb
               Problem," Proceedings of the 1989 Workshop on Computational
               Learning Theory COLT '89, pp. 261–268, University of
               California, Santa Cruz, 1989.

b   [742] **Pawlak, Z.,** "On Rough Sets," Bulletin of the European
               Association for Theoretical Computer Science, No. 24, pp.
               94–109, 1984.

s   [743] **Pawlak, Z.,** "On Learning—Rough Set Approach," Lecture Notes,
               Springer Verlag, No. 208, pp. 197–227, 1986.

e   [744] **Pawlak, Z., Slowinski, R., and Slowinski, K.,** "Rough
               Classification of Patients after Highly Selective Vagotomy for
               Duodenal Ulcer," International Journal of Man-Machine Studies,
               Vol. 24, pp. 413–433, 1986.

x   [745] **Pazzani, M.J.,** "Explanation and Generalization-Based Memory,"
               Proceedings of the Cognitive Society Conference, Irvine, CA,
               1985.

ix   [746] **Pazzani, M.J.,** "Refining the Knowledge Base of a Diagnostic
               Expert System: An Application of Failure-Driven Learning,"
               Proceedings of AAAI-86, pp. 1029–1035, Philadelphia, PA, 1986.

im   [747] **Pazzani, M.J., Dyer, M., and Flowers, M.,** "The Role of Prior
               Causal Theories in Generalization," Proceedings of AAAI-86, pp.
               545–550, Philadelphia, PA, 1986.

x   [748] **Pazzani, M.J.,** "Explanation-Based Learning for
               Knowledge-Based Systems," International Journal for
               Man-Machine Studies, Vol. 26, 1987.

ix   [749] **Pazzani, M.J.,** "Failure-Driven Learning of Fault Diagnosis Heuristics," IEEE Transactions on Systems, Man, and Cybernetics, Vol. 17, No. 3, 1987.

mx   [750] **Pazzani, M.J.,** "Inducing Causal and Social Theories: A Prerequisite for Explanation-Based Learning," Proceedings of the 4th International Machine Learning Workshop, pp. 230–241, University of California, Irvine, 1987.

mn   [751] **Pazzani, M.J., and Dyer, M.,** "A Comparison of Concept Identification in Human Learning and Network Learning with the Generalized Delta Rule," Proceedings of IJCAI-87, pp. 147–150, Milan, Italy, 1987.

im   [752] **Pazzani, M.J., Dyer, M., and Flowers, M.,** "Using Prior Learning to Facilitate the Learning of New Causal Theories," Proceedings of IJCAI-87, pp. 277–279, Milan, Italy, 1987.

x   [753] **Pazzani, M.J.,** "Selecting the Best Explanation for Explanation-Based Learning," Proceedings of 1988 Symposium on Explanation-Based Learning, pp. 165–169, Stanford, 1988.

isx   [754] **Pazzani, M.J.,** "Integrating Explanation-Based and Empirical Learning Methods in OCCAM," Proceedings of EWSL-88, pp. 147–166, Glasgow, Scotland, 1988.

isx   [755] **Pazzani, M.J.,** "Integrated Learning with Incorrect and Incomplete Theories," Proceedings of the 5th International Conference on Machine Learning, pp. 291–297, Ann Arbor, MI, 1988.

ix   [756] **Pazzani, M.J.,** "Learning Causal Relationships," Thesis, University of California, Los Angeles, May, 1988.

isx   [757] **Pazzani, M.J.,** "Detecting and Correcting Errors of Omission After Explanation-Based Learning," Proceedings of IJCAI-89, pp. 713–718, Detroit, MI, 1989.

d   [758] **Pazzani, M.J.,** "Learning Fault Diagnosis Heuristics from Device Descriptions," Machine Learning: An Artificial Intelligence Approach, Volume III, Morgan Kaufmann, San Mateo, CA, Kodratoff, Y. and Michalski, R.S. (Eds.), Ch. 8, 1990.

b   [759] **Pearl, J.,** "Heuristics: Intelligent Search Strategies for Computer Problem Solving," Addison-Wesley, 1984.

b   [760] **Pearl, J.,** "Probabilistic Reasoning in Intelligent Systems: Networks of Plausible Inference," Morgan Kaufmann, San Mateo, CA, 1988.

t   [761] **Pearl, J., and Dechter, R.,** "Learning Structure from Data: A
                Survey," Proceedings of the 1989 Workshop on Computational
                Learning Theory COLT '89, pp. 230–244, University of
                California, Santa Cruz, 1989.

st   [762] **Pednault, E.P.D.,** "Infering Probabilistic Theories from Data,"
                Proceedings of AAAI-88, pp. 624–628, Saint Paul, MN, 1988.

s   [763] **Pednault, E.P.D.,** "Minimal-length Encoding and Inductive
                Inference," Proceedings of IJCAI-89 Workshop on Knowledge
                Discovery in Databases, pp. 252–263, Detroit, MI, 1989.

es   [764] **Pednault, E.P.D.,** "Some Experiments in Applying Inductive
                Inference Principles to Surface Reconstruction," Proceedings of
                IJCAI-89, pp. 1603–1609, Detroit, MI, 1989.

s   [765] **Perron, M.C.,** "Learning Differential Diagnosis Rules from
                Numerical Knowledge," Proceedings of the Conference on Data
                Analysis, Learning Symbolic and Numeric Knowledge, pp.
                425–434, INRIA, Antibes, 1989.

s   [766] **Pettorossi, A., Ras, Z.W., and Zemankova, M.,** "On Learning
                with Imperfect Teachers," Proceedings of the 2nd International
                Symposium on Methodologies for Intelligent Systems, pp.
                256–263, Charlotte, NC, 1987.

s   [767] **Piatetsky-Shapiro, G.,** "Discovery of Strong Rules in Databases,"
                Proceedings of IJCAI-89 Workshop on Knowledge Discovery in
                Databases, pp. 264–274, Detroit, MI, 1989.

k   [768] **Pingand, P., and Sallantin, J.,** "Knowledge Acquisition by
                Learning: A Full-Scale Experimentation," Proceedings of
                EWSL-89, Montpellier, France, 1989.

st   [769] **Pitt, L., and Valiant, L.G.,** "Computational Limitations on
                Learning from Examples," Technical Report TR-05–86, Aiken
                Computing Lab, Harvard University, 1986.

ct   [770] **Pitt, L., and Reinke, R.E.,** "Criteria for Polynomial-Time
                (Conceptual) Clustering," Machine Learning, Vol. 2, No. 4, pp.
                371–396, 1988.

ak   [771] **Plaza, E., and DeMantaras, L.,** "A Case-Based Apprentice That
                Learns from Fuzzy Examples," Proceedings of EWSL-89,
                Montpellier, France, 1989.

st   [772] **Porat, S., and Feldman, J.A.,** "Learning Automata from Ordered
                Examples," Proceedings of the 1988 Workshop on Computational
                Learning Theory COLT '88, pp. 386–395, MIT, 1988.

ex [773] **Porter, B.W., and Kibler, D.F.,** "A Comparison of Analytic and Experimental Goal Regression for Machine Learning," Proceedings of IJCAI-85, Los Angeles, CA, 1985.

ak [774] **Porter, B.W., and Bareiss, E.R.,** "PROTOS: An Experiment in Knowledge Acquisition for Heuristic Classification Tasks," Proceedings of the 1st International Meeting on Advances in Learning, pp. 159–174, Les Arcs, France, 1986.

p [775] **Porter, B.W., and Kibler, D.F.,** "Experimental Goal Regression: A Method for Learning Problem-Solving Heuristics," Machine Learning, Vol. 1, No. 3, pp. 249–286, 1986.

b [776] **Porter, B.W.,** "A Review of the First International Meeting on Advances in Learning," Machine Learning, Vol. 2, No. 1, pp. 77–83, 1987.

k [777] **Prerau, D.S.,** "Knowledge Acquisition in the Development of a Large Expert System," AI Magazine, Vol. 8, No. 2, pp. 43, 1987.

d [778] **Prieditis, A.E.,** "Discovery of Algorithm from Weak Methods," Proceedings of the 1st International Meeting on Advances in Learning, pp. 37–52, Les Arcs, France, 1986.

px [779] **Prieditis, A.E., and Mostow, J.,** "PROLEARN: A Prolog Interpreter that Learns," Proceedings of AAAI-87, pp. 494–498, Seattle, WA, 1987.

x [780] **Prieditis, A.E.,** "Environment-Guided Program Transformation," Proceedings of 1988 Symposium on Explanation-Based Learning, pp. 201–209, Stanford, 1988.

b [781] Proceedings of the 3rd International Machine Learning Workshops, Mitchell, T.M., Carbonell, J.G., and Michalski, R.S (Eds.), Skytop, PA, 1985.

b [782] Proceedings of the 9th International Joint Conference on Artificial Intelligence, Joshi, A. (Ed.), Los Angeles, CA, 1985.

bg [783] Proceedings of the 1st International Conference on Genetic Algorithms, Pittsburgh, PA, 1985.

b [784] Proceedings of the 5th National Conference on Artificial Intelligence, Kehler, T., and Rosenschein, S. (Eds.), Philadelphia, PA, 1986.

b [785] Proceedings of the European Conference on Artificial Intelligence, Brighton, England, 1986.

b [786] Proceedings of the 4th International Machine Learning Workshops, Langley, P. (Ed.), Irvine, CA, 1987.

b [787] Proceedings of the 10th International Joint Conference on Artificial Intelligence, McDermott, J. (Ed.), Milan, Italy, 1987.

b [788] Proceedings of the 6th National Conference on Artificial Intelligence, Forbus, K., and Shrobe, H. (Eds.), Seattle, WA, 1987.

b [789] Proceedings of the 2nd European Working Session on Learning, Bratko, I, and Lavrac, N. (Eds.), Bled, Yugoslavia, 1987.

bg [790] Proceedings of the 2nd International Conference on Genetic Algorithms: Genetic Algorithms and Their Applications, Grefenstette, J.J. (Ed.), Cambridge, MA, 1987.

b [791] Proceedings of the 5th International Machine Learning Conference, Laird, J. (Ed.), Ann Arbor, MI, 1988.

b [792] Proceedings of the 7th National Conference on Artificial Intelligence, Smith, R.G., and Mitchell, T.M. (Eds.), Saint Paul, MN, 1988.

b [793] Proceedings of the European Conference on Artificial Intelligence, Munich, W. Germany, 1988.

b [794] Proceedings of the 3rd European Working Session on Learning, Sleeman, D., and Richmond, J. (Eds.), Glasgow, Scotland, 1988.

bx [795] Proceedings of the 1988 AAAI Symposium on Explanation-Based Learning, DeJong, G. (Ed.), Stanford, CA, 1988.

bt [796] Proceedings of the Annual Workshop on Computational Learning Theory, Haussler, D., and Pitt, L. (Eds.), Pittsburgh, PA, 1988.

bel [797] Proceedings of the IEEE International Symposium on Intelligent Control, Stephanou, H.E., Meystel, A., and Luh, J.Y.S. (Eds.), 1988.

ab [798] Proceedings of the 1st Workshop on Analogical Reasoning, Prieditis, A.E. (Ed.), Pitman, London, and Morgan Kaufmann, San Mateo, CA, Research Notes in Artificial Intelligence, 1988.

ab [799] Proceedings of the Case-Based Reasoning Workshop, Kolodner, J.L. (Ed.), 1988.

b [800] Proceedings of the 6th International Machine Learning Workshops, Segre, A.M. (Ed.), Ithaca, NY, 1989.

b [801] Proceedings of the 11th International Joint Conference on Artificial Intelligence, Sridharan, N.S. (Ed.), Detroit, MI, 1989.

b [802] Proceedings of the 4th European Working Session on Learning, Morik, K. (Ed.), Montpellier, France, 1989.

bg [803] Proceedings of the 3rd International Conference on Genetic Algorithms, Schaffer, J.D. (Ed.), Fairfax, VA, 1989.

bt   [804]   Proceedings of the Annual Workshop on Computational Learning Theory, Rivest, R., Haussler, D., and Warmuth, M.K. (Eds.), Santa Cruz, CA, 1989.

bcnst   [805]   Proceedings of the Conference on Data Analysis, Learning Symbolic and Numeric Knowledge, Diday, E. (Ed.), 1989.

b   [806]   Proceedings of the Office of Naval Research Workshop on Knowledge Acquisition, Meyrowitz, A.L. (Ed.), Arlington, VA, 1989.

b   [807]   Proceedings of the IEEE International Workshop on Tools for Artificial Intelligence, Bourbakis, N.G. (Ed.), Fairfax, VA, 1989.

px   [808]   **Puget, J.F.,** "Goal Regression with Opponent," Proceedings of EWSL-87, pp. 121–137, Bled, Yugoslavia, 1987.

x   [809]   **Puget J.F.,** "Learning Invariants from Explanations," Proceedings of the 6th International Workshop on Machine Learning, pp. 200–204, Ithaca, NY, 1989.

s   [810]   **Puget, J.F.,** "Learning Concept Negation," Proceedings of EWSL-89, Montpellier, France, 1989.

x   [811]   **Puget, J.F., an Rouveirol, C.,** "A Simple and General Solution for Inverting Resolution," Proceedings of EWSL-89, Montpellier, France, 1989.

s   [812]   **Quinlan, J.R.,** "The Effect of Noise on Concept Learning," Machine Learning: An Artificial Intelligence Approach, Volume II, Morgan Kaufmann, San Mateo, CA, R.S. Michalski, J.G. Carbonell and T.M. Mitchell (Eds.), pp. 149–166, 1986.

s   [813]   **Quinlan, J.R.,** "Induction of Decision Trees," Machine Learning, Vol. 1, No. 1, pp. 81–106, 1986.

s   [814]   **Quinlan, J.R.,** "Decision Trees As Probabilistic Classifiers," Proceedings of the 4th International Machine Learning Workshop, pp. 31–37, University of California, Irvine, 1987.

s   [815]   **Quinlan, J.R.,** "Generating Production Rules from Decision Trees," Proceedings of IJCAI-87, pp. 304–307, Milan, Italy, 1987.

s   [816]   **Quinlan, J.R.,** "Simplifying Decision Trees," International Journal of Man-Machine Studies, Vol. 27, pp. 221–234, 1987.

egs   [817]   **Quinlan, J.R.,** "An Empirical Comparison of Genetic and Decision-Tree Classifiers," Proceedings of the 5th International Conference on Machine Learning, pp. 135–141, Ann Arbor, MI, 1988.

s   [818]   **Quinlan, J.R.,** "Learning Relations: Comparison of a Symbolic and a Connectionist Approach," s [819] **Quinlan, J.R., and Rivest, R.L.,** "Inferring Decision Trees Using the Minimum Description Length Principle," Information and Computation, Vol. 80, No. 3, Basser Dept. of Computer Science, University of Sydney, Australia, 1989.

s [820] **Quinlan, J.R.,** "Probabilistic Decision Trees," Machine Learning: An Artificial Intelligence Approach, Volume III, Morgan Kaufmann, San Mateo, CA, Kodratoff, Y. and Michalski, R.S. (Eds.), Ch. 5, 1990.

nt [821] **Raghavan, P.,** "Learning in Threshold Networks," Proceedings of the 1988 Workshop on Computational Learning Theory COLT '88, pp. 19–27, MIT, 1988.

dk [822] **Rajamoney, S.A., DeJong, G.F., and Faltings, B.,** "Towards a Model of Conceptual Knowledge Acquisition Through Directed Experimentation," Proceedings of IJCAI-85, pp. 688–690, Los Angeles, CA, 1985.

x [823] **Rajamoney, S.A., and DeJong, G.F.,** "The Classification, Detection and Handling of Imperfect Theory Problems," Proceedings of IJCAI-87, pp. 205–207, Milan, Italy, 1987.

x [824] **Rajamoney, S.A.,** "Experimentation-Based Theory Revision," Proceedings of 1988 Symposium on Explanation-Based Learning, pp. 7–11, Stanford, 1988.

x [825] **Rajamoney, S.A.,** "Explanation-Based Theory Revision: An Approach to the Problems of Incomplete and Incorrect Theories," Thesis, University of Illinois at Urbana-Champaign, December, 1988.

x [826] **Rajamoney, S.A., and DeJong, G.F.,** "Active Explanation Reduction: An Approach to the Multiple Explanations Problem," Proceedings of the 5th International Conference on Machine Learning, pp. 242–255, Ann Arbor, MI, 1988.

ak [827] **Rajamoney, S.A.,** "Exemplar-Based Theory Rejection: An Approach to the Experience Consistency Problem," Proceedings of the 6th International Workshop on Machine Learning, pp. 284–289, Ithaca, NY, 1989.

s [828] **Ras, Z.W., and Zemankova, M.,** "Learning in Knowledge-Based Systems: a Possibilistic Approach," Bulletin of the Polish Academy of Sciences—Mathematics, Vol. 34, No. 3–4, pp. 235–247, 1986.

s   [829]   **Ras, Z.W., and Zemankova, M.,** "Imprecise Concept Learning Within a Growing Language," Proceedings of the 6th International Workshop on Machine Learning, pp. 314–319, Ithaca, NY, 1989.

aix   [830]   **Redmond, M.,** "Combining Cased-Based Reasoning, Explanation-Based Learning, and Learning from Instruction," Proceedings of the 6th International Workshop on Machine Learning, pp. 20–22, Ithaca, NY, 1989.

s   [831]   **Reinke, R.E., and Michalski, R.S.,** "Incremental Learning of Concept Descriptions," Machine Intelligence 11, Oxford University Press, J.E. Hayes, D. Mitchie and J. Richards (Eds.), 1988.

gs   [832]   **Rendell, L.,** "Genetic Plans and the Probabilistic Learning System: Synthesis and Results," Proceedings of the 1st International Conference on Genetic Algorithms, pp. 60–73, Pittsburgh, PA, 1985.

stv   [833]   **Rendell, L.,** "Substantial Constructive Induction Using Layered Information Compression: Tractable Feature Formation in Search," Proceedings of IJCAI-85, pp. 650–658, Los Angeles, CA, 1985.

stv   [834]   **Rendell, L.,** "A General Framework for Induction and a Study of Selective Induction," Machine Learning, Vol. 1, No. 2, pp. 177–226, 1986.

s   [835]   **Rendell, L.,** "Conceptual Knowledge Acquisition in Search," Computational Models of Learning, Springer-Verlag, Berlin Heidelberg, L. Bolc (Ed.), pp. 89–159, 1987.

sv   [836]   **Rendell, L., Seshu, R., and Tcheng, D.,** "Layered Concept-Learning and Dynamically-Variable Bias Management," Proceedings of IJCAI-87, pp. 308–314, Milan, Italy, 1987.

sv   [837]   **Rendell, L., Seshu, R., and Tcheng, D.,** "More Robust Concept Learning Using Dynamically-Variable Bias," Proceedings of the 4th International Machine Learning Workshop, pp. 66–78, University of California, Irvine, 1987.

stv   [838]   **Rendell, L.,** "Learning Hard Concepts," Proceedings of EWSL-88, pp. 177–200, Glasgow, Scotland, 1988.

ev   [839]   **Rendell, L.,** "Comparing Systems and Analyzing Functions to Improve Constructive Induction," Proceedings of the 6th International Workshop on Machine Learning, pp. 461–464, Ithaca, NY, 1989.

s   [840] **Rendell, R.,** "A Study of Empirical Learning for an Involved
               Problem," Proceedings of IJCAI-89, pp. 615–620, Detroit, MI,
               1989.

v   [841] **Riddle, P.J.,** "Reformulation from State Space to Reduction
               Space," Proceedings of the 6th International Workshop on
               Machine Learning, pp. 439–440, Ithaca, NY, 1989.

g   [842] **Riolo, R.L.,** "Bucket Brigade Performance: I. Long Sequences of
               Classifiers," Proceedings of the 2nd International Conference on
               Genetic Algorithms, pp. 184–195, Cambridge, MA., 1987.

g   [843] **Riolo, R.L.,** "Bucket Brigade Performance: II. Default
               Hierarchies," Proceedings of the 2nd International Conference on
               Genetic Algorithms, pp. 196–201, Cambridge, MA., 1987.

am   [844] **Rissland, E.L., and Skalak, D.B.,** "Combining Case-Based and
               Rule-Based Reasoning: A Heuristic Approach," Proceedings of
               IJCAI-89, pp. 524–530, Detroit, MI, 1989.

s   [845] **Rivest, R.L.,** "Learning Decision Lists," Machine Learning, Vol.
               2, No. 3, pp. 229–246, 1987.

dt   [846] **Rivest, R.L., and Schapire, R.E.,** "A New Approach to
               Unsupervised Learning in Deterministic Environments,"
               Proceedings of the 4th International Machine Learning Workshop,
               pp. 364–375, University of California, Irvine, 1987.

s   [847] **Rivest, R.L., and Sloan, R.,** "Learning Complicated Concepts
               Reliable and Usefully," Proceedings of AAAI-88, pp. 635–640,
               Saint Paul, MN, 1988.

dt   [848] **Rivest, R.L., and Schapire, R.E.,** "A New Approach to
               Unsupervised Learning in Deterministic Environments," Machine
               Learning: An Artificial Intelligence Approach, Volume III, Morgan
               Kaufmann, San Mateo, CA, Kodratoff, Y. and Michalski, R.S.
               (Eds.), Ch. 23, 1990.

g   [849] **Robertson, G.G.,** "Parallel Implementation of Genetic Algorithms
               in a Classifier System," Proceedings of the 2nd International
               Conference on Genetic Algorithms, pp. 140–147, Cambridge,
               MA., 1987.

g   [850] **Robertson, G.G.,** "Population Size in Classifier Systems,"
               Proceedings of the 5th International Conference on Machine
               Learning, pp. 142–152, Ann Arbor, MI, 1988.

g   [851] **Robertson, G.G., and Riolo, R.L.,** "A Tale of Two Classifier
               Systems," Machine Learning, Vol. 3, No. 2/3, pp. 139–160, 1988.

d   [852]   **Rose, D., and Langley, P.W.,** "STAHLp: Belief Revision in Scientific Discovery," Proceedings of AAAI-86, pp. 528–532, Philadelphia, PA, 1986.

d   [853]   **Rose, D., and Langley, P.W.,** "Chemical Discovery as Belief Revision," Machine Learning, Vol. 1, No. 4, pp. 423–452, 1986.

d   [854]   **Rose, D., and Langley, P.W.,** "A Hill-Climbing Approach to Machine Discovery," Proceedings of the 5th International Conference on Machine Learning, pp. 367–373, Ann Arbor, MI, 1988.

dk   [855]   **Rose, D.,** "Using Domain Knowledge to Aid Scientific Theory Revision," Proceedings of the 6th International Workshop on Machine Learning, pp. 272–277, Ithaca, NY, 1989.

b   [856]   **Rosenbloom, P.S., Laird, J.E., Newell, A., Golding, A., and Unruh,** "Current Research on Learning in SOAR," Proceedings of the 3rd International Machine Learning Workshop, pp. 163–172, Skytop, PA, 1985.

etx   [857]   **Rosenbloom, P.S. and Laird, J.E.,** "Mapping Explanation-Based Generalization onto SOAR," Proceedings of AAAI-86, pp. 561–567, Philadelphia, PA, 1986.

m   [858]   **Rosenbloom, P.S., and Newell, A.,** "The Chunking of Goal Hierarchies: A Generalized Model of Practice," Machine Learning: An Artificial Intelligence Approach, Volume II, Morgan Kaufmann, San Mateo, CA, R.S. Michalski, J.G. Carbonell and T.M. Mitchell (Eds.), pp. 247–288, 1986.

mt   [859]   **Rosenbloom, P.S., Laird, J.E. and Newell, A.,** "Knowledge-Level Learning in SOAR," Proceedings of AAAI-87, pp. 499–504, Seattle, WA, 1987.

x   [860]   **Rosenbloom, P.S.,** "Beyond Generalization as Search, Towards a Unified Framework for the Acquisition of New Knowledge," Proceedings of 1988 Symposium on Explanation-Based Learning, pp. 17–21, Stanford, 1988.

k   [861]   **Roy, S., and Mostow, J.,** "Parsing to Learn Fine Grained Rules," Proceedings of AAAI-88, pp. 547–551, Saint Paul, MN, 1988.

es   [862]   **Royce, R.J., and Herbert, G.,** "ISOLDE: A System for Learning Organic Chemistry through Induction," Proceedings of the 3rd European Workshop on Knowledge Acquisition for Knowledge-Based Systems, pp. 297–310, 1989.

p   [863] **Ruby, D., and Kibler, D.,** "Learning Subgoal Sequences for
               Planning," Proceedings of IJCAI-89, pp. 609–614, Detroit, MI,
               1989.

p   [864] **Ruby, D., and Kibler, D.,** "Learning to Plan in Complex
               Domains," Proceedings of the 6th International Workshop on
               Machine Learning, pp. 180–182, Ithaca, NY, 1989.

s   [865] **Ruff, R.A., and Dietterich, T.G.,** "What Good Are Experiments,"
               Proceedings of the 6th International Workshop on Machine
               Learning, pp. 109–112, Ithaca, NY, 1989.

bmn   [866] **Rumelhart, D.E., McClelland, J.L., and the PDP Research
               Group,** "Parallel Distributed Processing: Foundations," The MIT
               Press, Vol. 1, Computational Models of Cognition and Perception,
               Cambridge. MA, 1986.

st   [867] **Russell, S.J.,** "Preliminary Steps Toward the Automation of
               Induction," Proceedings of AAAI-86, pp. 477–484, Philadelphia,
               PA, 1986.

a   [868] **Russell, S.J.,** "Analogy and Single-Instance Generalization,"
               Proceedings of the 4th International Machine Learning Workshop,
               pp. 390–397, University of California, Irvine, 1987.

st   [869] **Russell, S.J., and Grosof, B.J.,** "A Declarative Approach to Bias
               in Concept Learning," Proceedings of AAAI-87, pp. 505–510,
               Seattle, WA, 1987.

st   [870] **Russell, S.J.,** "Tree-Structured Bias," Proceedings of AAAI-88,
               pp. 641–645, Saint Paul, MN, 1988.

as   [871] **Russell, S.J.,** "The Use of Knowledge in Analogy and Induction,"
               Morgan Kaufmann, 1989.

k   [872] **Rychener, M.,** "Knowledge Acquisition from Formal
               Specifications," Proceedings of IJCAI-89 Workshop on
               Knowledge Discovery in Databases, pp. 275–280, Detroit, MI,
               1989.

t   [873] **Sakakibara, Y.,** "Learning Context-Free Grammars from
               Structural Data in Polynomial Time," Proceedings of the 1988
               Workshop on Computational Learning Theory COLT '88, pp.
               330–344, MIT, 1988.

s   [874] **Salzberg, S.,** "Heuristics for Inductive Learning," Proceedings of
               IJCAI-85, pp. 603–607, Los Angeles, CA, 1985.

ls   [875] **Sammut, C., and Hume, D.,** "Learning Concepts in a Complex
               Robot World," Proceedings of the 3rd International Machine
               Learning Workshop, pp. 173–176, Skytop, PA, 1985.

s   [876] **Sammut, C., and Banerji, R.B.,** "Learning Concepts by Asking
              Questions," Machine Learning: An Artificial Intelligence
              Approach, Volume II, Morgan Kaufmann, San Mateo, CA, R.S.
              Michalski, J.G. Carbonell and T.M. Mitchell (Eds.), pp. 167–192,
              1986.

ls   [877] **Sammut, C., and Hume, D.,** "Observation and Generalisation in
              a Simulated Robot World," Proceedings of the 4th International
              Machine Learning Workshop, pp. 267–273, University of
              California, Irvine, 1987.

el   [878] **Sammut, C.,** "Experimental Results from an Evaluation of
              Algorithms that Learn to Control Dynamic Systems," Proceedings
              of the 5th International Conference on Machine Learning, pp.
              437–443, Ann Arbor, MI, 1988.

g   [879] **Sannier II, A.V., and Goodman, E.D.,** "MIDGARD: A Genetic
              Approach to Adaptive Loan Balancing for Distributed Systems,"
              Proceedings of the 5th International Conference on Machine
              Learning, pp. 174–180, Ann Arbor, MI, 1988.

i   [880] **Sarrett, W.E., and Pazzani, M.J.,** "One-Sided Algorithms for
              Integrating Empirical and Explanation-Based Learning,"
              Proceedings of the 6th International Workshop on Machine
              Learning, pp. 26–28, Ithaca, NY, 1989.

v   [881] **Saxena, S.,** "Evaluating Alternative Instance Representations,"
              Proceedings of the 6th International Workshop on Machine
              Learning, pp. 465–468, Ithaca, NY, 1989.

d   [882] **Schaffer, C.,** "Bacon, Data Analysis and Artificial Intelligence,"
              Proceedings of the 6th International Workshop on Machine
              Learning, pp. 174–178, Ithaca, NY, 1989.

d   [883] **Schaffer, C.,** "An Environment/Classification Scheme for
              Evaluation of Domain-Independent Function-Finding Programs,"
              Proceedings of IJCAI-89 Workshop on Knowledge Discovery in
              Databases, pp. 281–290, Detroit, MI, 1989.

g   [884] **Schaffer, J.D.,** "Learning Multiclass Pattern Discrimination,"
              Proceedings of the 1st International Conference on Genetic
              Algorithms, pp. 74–79, Pittsburgh, PA, 1985.

g   [885] **Schaffer, J.D., and Grefenstette, J.J.,** "Multi-Objective Learning
              via Genetic Algorithms," Proceedings of IJCAI-85, pp. 593–595,
              Los Angeles, CA, 1985.

b   [886]   **Schank, R.C.,** "Explanation Patterns: Understanding Mechanically and Creatively," Lawrence Erlbaum Associates, 1986.

a   [887]   **Schank, R.C., and Leake, D.B.,** "Creativity and Learning in a Case-Based Explainer," Artificial Intelligence, Vol. 40, pp. 353–385, 1989.

b   [888]   **Schank, R.C., and Kass, A.,** "Explanations, Machine Learning, and Creativity," Machine Learning: An Artificial Intelligence Approach, Volume III, Morgan Kaufmann, San Mateo, CA, Kodratoff, Y. and Michalski, R.S. (Eds.), Ch. 2, 1990.

es   [889]   **Schlimmer, J.C., and Fisher, D.H.,** "A Case Study of Incremental Concept Induction," Proceedings of AAAI-86, pp. 496–501, Philadelphia, PA, 1986.

v   [890]   **Schlimmer, J.C., and Granger, R.H.,** "Beyond Incremental Processing: Tracking Concept Drift," Proceedings of AAAI-86, pp. 502–507, Philadelphia, PA, 1986.

sv   [891]   **Schlimmer, J.C., and Granger, R.H.,** "Incremental Learning from Noisy Data," Machine Learning, Vol. 1, No. 3, pp. 317–354, 1986.

sv   [892]   **Schlimmer, J.C.,** "Incremental Adjustment of Representations for Learning," Proceedings of the 4th International Machine Learning Workshop, pp. 79–90, University of California, Irvine, 1987.

sv   [893]   **Schlimmer, J.C.,** "Learning and Representation Change," Proceedings of AAAI-87, pp. 511–515, Seattle, WA, 1987.

sv   [894]   **Schlimmer, J.C.,** "Concept Acquisition through Representational Adjustment," Thesis, University of California, Irvine, July, 1987.

v   [895]   **Schlimmer, J.C.,** "Refining Representations to Improve Problem Solving Quality," Proceedings of the 6th International Workshop on Machine Learning, pp. 457–460, Ithaca, NY, 1989.

kx   [896]   **Schlimmer, J.C., Mitchell, T.M., and McDermott, J.,** "Justification-Based Refinement of Expert Knowledge," Proceedings of IJCAI-89 Workshop on Knowledge Discovery in Databases, pp. 291–300, Detroit, MI, 1989.

d   [897]   **Scott, P.D., and Markovitch, S.,** "Learning Novel Domains through Curiosity and Conjecture," Proceedings of IJCAI-89, pp. 669–675, Detroit, MI, 1989.

s   [898]   **Scott, P.D., and Markovitch, S.,** "Uncertainty Based Selection of Learning Experiences," Proceedings of the 6th International Workshop on Machine Learning, pp. 358–361, Ithaca, NY, 1989.

s   [899]   **Sebag, M., and Schoenauer, M.,** "Iterative Learning and Redundant Generalizations," Proceedings of the Conference on Data Analysis, Learning Symbolic and Numeric Knowledge, pp. 511–518, INRIA, Antibes, 1989.

s   [900]   **Segen, J.,** "Learning Concept Descriptions from Examples with Errors," Proceedings of IJCAI-85, pp. 634–636, Los Angeles, CA, 1985.

s   [901]   **Segen, J.,** "Learning Graph Models of Shape," Proceedings of the 5th International Conference on Machine Learning, pp. 29–35, Ann Arbor, MI, 1988.

c   [902]   **Segen, J.,** "Conceptual Clumping of Binary Vectors with Occam's Razor," Proceedings of the 5th International Conference on Machine Learning, pp. 47–53, Ann Arbor, MI, 1988.

c   [903]   **Segen, J.,** "Incremental Clustering by Minimizing Representation Length," Proceedings of the 6th International Workshop on Machine Learning, pp. 400–403, Ithaca, NY, 1989.

x   [904]   **Segre, A.M.,** "Explanation-Based Manipulator Learning," Proceedings of the 3rd International Machine Learning Workshop, pp. 183–185, Skytop, PA, 1985.

px   [905]   **Segre, A.M., and DeJong, G.F.,** "Explanation-Based Manipulator Learning: Acquisition of Planning Ability Through Observation," Proceedings of the IEEE International Conference on Robotics and Automation, pp. 555–560, St. Louis, MO, 1985.

px   [906]   **Segre, A.M., and DeJong, G.F.,** "From Handware to Hardware: Towards Intelligent Assembly Robots," American Society for Engineering Education NCS-II, pp. 172–185, Dayton, OH, 1985.

px   [907]   **Segre, A.M.,** "Explanation-Based Learning of Generalized Robot Assembly Plans," Thesis, Dept. of Elec. Eng., University of Illinois at Urbana-Champaign, 1987.

kpx   [908]   **Segre, A.M.,** "A Learning Apprentice System for Mechanical Assembly," Proceedings of the 3rd IEEE International Conference on Artificial Intelligence Applications, pp. 112–117, Orlando, FL, 1987.

x   [909]   **Segre, A.M.,** "On the Operationality/Generality Trade-Off in Explanation-Based Learning," Proceedings of IJCAI-87, pp. 242–248, Milan, Italy, 1987.

px   [910]   **Segre, A.M.,** "Machine Learning of Robot Assembly Plans," Kluwer Academic Publishers, Norwell, MA, 1988.

x   [911] **Segre, A.M.,** "Operationality and Real-World Plans," Proceedings of 1988 Symposium on Explanation-Based Learning, pp. 158–163, Stanford, 1988.

x   [912] **Segre, A.M.,** "The Compleat EBLer: A Provably Complete Family of EBL Algorithms," Proceedings of Office of Naval Research Workshop on Knowledge Acquisition, A.L. Meyrowitz (Ed.), Arlington, VA, 1989.

x   [913] **Seifert, C.M.,** "Generating Explanations Using Models of Relationships," Proceedings of 1988 Symposium on Explanation-Based Learning, pp. 190–194, Stanford, 1988.

i   [914] **Seifert, C.M.,** "A Retrieval Model Using Feature Selection," Proceedings of the 6th International Workshop on Machine Learning, pp. 52–54, Ithaca, NY, 1989.

n   [915] **Sejnowski, T.J., and Rosenberg, C.R.,** "Parallel Networks that Learn to Pronounce English Text," Complex Systems, Vol. 1, pp. 145–168, 1987.

m   [916] **Selfridge, M.,** "A Computer Model of Child Language Learning," Artificial Intelligence, Vol. 29, pp. 171–216, 1986.

n   [917] **Selfridge, O.G., Sutton, R.S., and Barto, A.G.,** "Training and Tracking in Robotics," Proceedings of IJCAI-85, pp. 670–672, Los Angeles, CA, 1985.

g   [918] **Selfridge, O.G.,** "Atoms of Learning II: Adaptive Strategies a Study of Two-Person Zero-Sum Competition," Proceedings of the 6th International Workshop on Machine Learning, pp. 412–416, Ithaca, NY, 1989.

p   [919] **Seshu, R.,** "Solving the Parity Problem," Proceedings of EWSL-89, Montpellier, France, 1989.

k   [920] **Shachter, R.D., and Heckerman, D.E.,** "Thinking Backward for Knowledge Acquisition," AI Magazine, Vol. 8, No. 3, pp. 55–61, 1987.

st [921] **Shackelford, G., and Volper, D.,** "Learning k-DNF with Noise in the Attributes," Proceedings of the 1988 Workshop on Computational Learning Theory COLT '88, pp. 97–103, MIT, 1988.

g   [922] **Shaefer, C.G.,** "The ARGOT Strategy: Adaptive Representation Genetic Optimizer Technique," Proceedings of the 2nd International Conference on Genetic Algorithms, pp. 50–58, Cambridge, MA., 1987.

b [923] **Shapiro, S.C. (Ed.),** "Encyclopedia of Artificial Intelligence, Volume I and II," John Wiley & Sons, 1987.

ak [924] **Sharma, S., and Sleeman D.,** "REFINER: A Case-Based Differential Diagnosis Side for Knowledge Acquisition," Proceedings of EWSL-88, pp. 201–210, Glasgow, Scotland, 1988.

x [925] **Shavlik, J.W.,** "Learning about Momentum Conservation," Proceedings of IJCAI-85, pp. 667–669, Los Angeles, CA, 1985.

x [926] **Shavlik, J.W.,** "Generalizing the Structure of Explanations in Explanation-Based Learning," Thesis, University of Illinois at Urbana-Champaign, December, 1987.

x [927] **Shavlik, J.W., and DeJong, G.F.,** "Analyzing Variable Cancellations to Generalize Symbolic Mathematical Calculations," Proceedings of the 3rd IEEE International Conference on Artificial Intelligence Applications, pp. 100–105, Orlando, FL, 1987.

x [928] **Shavlik, J.W., and DeJong, G.F.,** "BAGGER: An EBL System that Extends and Generalizes Explanations," Proceedings of AAAI-87, pp. 516–520, Seattle, WA, 1987.

x [929] **Shavlik, J.W., and DeJong, G.F.,** "An Explanation-Based Approach to Generalizing Number," Proceedings of IJCAI-87, pp. 236–238, Milan, Italy, 1987.

x [930] **Shavlik, J.W.,** "Issues in Generalizing to N in Explanation-Based Learning," Proceedings of 1988 Symposium on Explanation-Based Learning, pp. 78–83, Stanford, 1988.

x [931] **Shavlik, J.W.,** "Acquiring Recursive Concepts with Explanation-Based Learning," Proceedings of IJCAI-89, pp. 688–693, Detroit, MI, 1989.

px [932] **Shavlik, J.W.,** "An Empirical Analysis of EBL Approaches for Learning Plan Schemata," Proceedings of the 6th International Workshop on Machine Learning, pp. 183–187, Ithaca, NY, 1989.

in [933] **Shavlik, J.W., and Towell, G.G.,** "Combining Explanation-Based Learning and Artificial Neural Networks," Proceedings of the 6th International Workshop on Machine Learning, pp. 90–92, Ithaca, NY, 1989.

x [934] **Shavlik, J.W., and DeJong, G.F.,** "Acquiring General Iterative Concepts by Reformulating Explanations of Observed Examples," Machine Learning: An Artificial Intelligence Approach, Volume III, Morgan Kaufmann, San Mateo, CA, Kodratoff, Y. and Michalski, R.S. (Eds.), Ch. 11, 1990.

c   [935] Shekar, B., Narasimha Murty, M., and Krishna, G., "Pattern
               Clustering: An Artificial Intelligence Approach," Proceedings of
               IJCAI-87, pp. 214–216, Milan, Italy, 1987.

ps   [936] Shell, P., and Carbonell, J.G., "Towards a General Framework
               for Composing Disjunctive and Iterative Macro-operators,"
               Proceedings of IJCAI-89, pp. 596–602, Detroit, MI, 1989.

d   [937] Shen, W.M., "Functional Transformation in AI Discovery
               Systems," Proceedings of the 21th Annual Hawaii International
               Conference on System Science, Hawaii, 1988.

d   [938] Shen, W.M., and Simon H.A., "Rule Creation and Rule Learning
               through Environmental Exploration," Proceedings of IJCAI-89,
               pp. 675–680, Detroit, MI, 1989.

p   [939] Shimura, M., and Sakurai, S., "Learning Arithmetic Problem
               Solver," Proceedings of AAAI-86, pp. 1036–1040, Philadelphia,
               PA, 1986.

d   [940] Shrager, J., "Theory Change via View Application in
               Instructionless Learning," Machine Learning, Vol. 2, No. 3, pp.
               247–276, 1987.

dk   [941] Shum, C.D., "Knowledge Discovery and Succinctness of
               Representation," Proceedings of IJCAI-89 Workshop on
               Knowledge Discovery in Databases, pp. 301–311, Detroit, MI,
               1989.

t   [942] Shvaytser, H., "Non-Learnable Classes of Boolean Formulae That
               Are Closed Under Variable Permutation," Proceedings of the 1988
               Workshop on Computational Learning Theory COLT '88, pp.
               155–166, MIT, 1988.

k   [943] Siegel, M., Sciore, E., and Salveter, S., "Rule Discovery for
               Query Optimization," Proceedings of IJCAI-89 Workshop on
               Knowledge Discovery in Databases, pp. 312–326, Detroit, MI,
               1989.

x   [944] Silver, B., "Precondition Analysis: Learning Control Information,"
               Machine Learning: An Artificial Intelligence Approach, Voume. II,
               Morgan Kaufmann, San Mateo, CA, R.S. Michalski, J.G.
               Carbonell and T.M. Mitchell (Eds.), pp. 647–670, 1986.

ix   [945] Silver, B., "A Hybrid Approach in an Imperfect Domain,"
               Proceedings of 1988 Symposium on Explanation-Based Learning,
               pp. 52–56, Stanford, 1988.

k   [946]   **Silverman, B., Hieb, M., Yang, H., Wu, L., Truszkowski, W., and Dominy, R.,** "Investigation of a Simulator-trained Machine Discovery System for Knowledge Base Management Purposes," Proceedings of IJCAI-89 Workshop on Knowledge Discovery in Databases, pp. 327–342, Detroit, MI, 1989.

m   [947]   **Simon, H.A.,** "Prospects for Cognitive Science (invited lecture)," Fifth Generation Computer Systems ICOT Journal, 1989.

ap   [948]   **Simpson, R.L.,** "A Computer Model of Case-Based Reasoning in Problem Solving: An Investigation in the Domain of Dispute Mediation," Thesis, School of Info. and CS, Georgia Institute of Tech., 1985.

di   [949]   **Sims, M.H.,** "Empirical and Analytic Discovery in IL," Proceedings of the 4th International Machine Learning Workshop, pp. 274–280, University of California, Irvine, 1987.

d   [950]   **Sims, M.H., and Bresina, J.L.,** "Discovering Mathematical Operator Definitions," Proceedings of the 6th International Workshop on Machine Learning, pp. 308–313, Ithaca, NY, 1989.

a   [951]   **Skorstad, J., Falkenhainer, B., and Gentner, D.,** "Analogical Processing: A Simulation and Empirical Corroboration," Proceedings of AAAI-87, pp. 322–326, Seattle, WA, 1987.

b   [952]   **Sleeman, D., and Brown, J.S.,** "Intelligent Tutoring Systems," Academic Press, 1982.

kx   [953]   **Smith, R., Winston, H., Mitchell, T., and Buchanan, B.,** "Representation and Use of Explicit Justification for Knowledge Base Refinement," Proceedings of IJCAI-85, pp. 673–680, Los Angeles, CA, 1985.

p   [954]   **Sobek, R.P., and Laumond, J.P.,** "Using Learning to Recover Side-Effects of Operators in Robotics," Proceedings of the 6th International Workshop on Machine Learning, pp. 205–208, Ithaca, NY, 1989.

b   [955]   **Sowa, J.F.,** "Conceptual Structures: Information Processing in Mind and Machine," Addison-Wesley, Reading, MA, 1984.

es   [956]   **Spackman, K.A.,** "Learning Categorical Decision Criteria in Biomedical Domains," Proceedings of the 5th International Conference on Machine Learning, pp. 36–46, Ann Arbor, MI, 1988.

s   [957] **Spackman, K.A.,** "Signal Detection Theory: Valuable Tools for
             Evaluating Inductive Learning," Proceedings of the 6th
             International Workshop on Machine Learning, pp. 160–163,
             Ithaca, NY, 1989.

s   [958] **Spangler, S., Fayyad, U.M., and Uthurusamy, R.,** "Induction of
             Decision Trees from Inconclusive Data," Proceedings of the 6th
             International Workshop on Machine Learning, pp. 146–150,
             Ithaca, NY, 1989.

x   [959] **Star, S.,** "Learning Causal Explanations in an Uncertain World,"
             Proceedings of 1988 Symposium on Explanation-Based Learning,
             pp. 185–189, Stanford, 1988.

de   [960] **Stefanski, P.A., and Zytkow, J.M.,** "A Multisearch Approach to
             Next Event Prediction," Proceedings of the 4th International
             Symposium on Methodologies for Intelligent Systems, pp.
             359–366, Charlotte, NC, 1989.

p   [961] **Steier, D.M.,** "CYPRESS-SOAR: A Case Study in Search and
             Learning in Algorithm Design," Proceedings of IJCAI-87, pp.
             327–330, Milan, Italy, 1987.

mp   [962] **Steier, D.M., Laird, J.E., Newell, A., Rosenbloom, P.S., et al.,**
             "Varieties of Learning in SOAR: 1987," Proceedings of the 4th
             International Machine Learning Workshop, pp. 300–311,
             University of California, Irvine, 1987.

c   [963] **Stepp, R.E., and Michalski, R.S.,** "Conceptual Clustering:
             Inventing Goal-Oriented Classifications of Structured Objects,"
             Machine Learning: An Artificial Intelligence Approach, Volume II,
             Morgan Kaufmann, San Mateo, CA, R.S. Michalski, J.G.
             Carbonell and T.M. Mitchell (Eds.), pp. 471–498, 1986.

c   [964] **Stepp, R.E.,** "Concepts in Conceptual Clustering," Proceedings of
             IJCAI-87, pp. 211–213, Milan, Italy, 1987.

s   [965] **Stepp, R.E.,** "Machine Learning from Structured Objects,"
             Proceedings of the 4th International Machine Learning Workshop,
             pp. 353–363, University of California, Irvine, 1987.

i   [966] **Stepp, R.E., Whitehall, B.L., and Holder, L.B.,** "Towards
             Intelligent Machine Learning Algorithms," Proceedings of
             ECAI-88, pp. 333–338, Munich, W.Germany, 1988.

bm   [967] **Stillings, N.A., Feinstein, M.H., Garfield, J.L., Rissland, E.L.,
             Rosenbaum, D.A., Weisler, S.E., and Baker-Ward, L.,**
             "Cognitive Science: An Introduction," The MIT Press, Cambridge,
             MA, 1987.

tx [968] **Subramanian, D., and Smith, D.,** "Knowledge-Level Learning: An Alternative View," Proceedings of 1988 Symposium on Explanation-Based Learning, pp. 196–200, Stanford, 1988.

b [969] **Subramanian, D.,** "Representational Issues in Machine Learning," Proceedings of the 6th International Workshop on Machine Learning, pp. 426–429, Ithaca, NY, 1989.

n [970] **Sutton, R.S.,** "Learning Distributed Searchable Internal Models," Proceedings of 1985 Distributed AI Workshop, pp. 287, 1985.

n [971] **Sutton, R.S., and Pinette, B.,** "The Learning of World Models by Connectionist Networks," Proceedings of the 7th Conference of the Cognitive Science Society, pp. 54, 1985.

n [972] **Sutton, R.S.,** "Two Problems with Backpropagation and Other Steepest-Descent Learning Procedures from Networks," Proceedings of the 8th Conference of the Cognitive Science Society, pp. 823, 1986.

r [973] **Sutton, R.S.,** "Learning to Predict by the Methods of Temporal Differences," Machine Learning, Vol. 3, No. 1, pp. 9–44, 1988.

ix [974] **Swaminathan, K.,** "Integrated Learning with an Incomplete and Intractable Domain Theory: The Problem of Epidemiological Diagnosis," Proceedings of 1988 Symposium on Explanation-Based Learning, pp. 62–66, Stanford, 1988.

x [975] **Tadepalli, P.V.,** "Learning in Intractable Domains," Proceedings of the 3rd International Machine Learning Workshop, Skytop, PA, 1985.

x [976] **Tadepalli, P.V.,** "Lazy Explanation-Based Learning : A Solution to the Intractable Theory Problem," Proceedings of IJCAI-89, pp. 694–700, Detroit, MI, 1989.

px [977] **Tadepalli, P.V.,** "Planning in Games Using Approximately Learned Macros," Proceedings of the 6th International Workshop on Machine Learning, pp. 221–224, Ithaca, NY, 1989.

s [978] **Tallis, H.,** "Tuning Rule-Based Systems to Their Environments," Proceedings of the 5th International Conference on Machine Learning, pp. 8–14, Ann Arbor, MI, 1988.

m [979] **Tallis, H.,** "Overcoming Feature Space Bias in a Reactive Environment," Proceedings of the 6th International Workshop on Machine Learning, pp. 505–507, Ithaca, NY, 1989.

m [980] **Tambe, M., and Newell, A.,** "Some Chunks Are Expensive," Proceedings of the 5th International Conference on Machine Learning, pp. 451–458, Ann Arbor, MI, 1988.

mpx   [981]   **Tambe, M., and Rosenbloom, P.,** "Eliminating Expensive
               Chunks by Restricting Expressiveness," Proceedings of IJCAI-89,
               pp. 731–737, Detroit, MI, 1989.

ns   [982]   **Tan, M., and Eshelman, L.,** "Using Weighted Networks to
               Represent Classification Knowledge in Noisy Domains,"
               Proceedings of the 5th International Conference on Machine
               Learning, pp. 121–134, Ann Arbor, MI, 1988.

s   [983]   **Tan, M., and Schlimmer, J.C.,** "Cost-Sensitive Concept Learning
               of Sensor Use in Approach and Recognition," Proceedings of the
               6th International Workshop on Machine Learning, pp. 392–395,
               Ithaca, NY, 1989.

px   [984]   **Tanaka, T., and Mitchell, T.M.,** "Embedding Learning in a
               General Frame-Based Architecture," Proceedings of IEEE
               International Workshop on Tools for Artificial Intelligence, pp.
               77–84, Fairfax, VA, 1989.

v   [985]   **Tcheng, D., Lambert, B., Lu, S.C-Y, and Rendell, L.,** "Building
               Robust Learning Systems by Combining Induction and
               Optimization," Proceedings of IJCAI-89, pp. 806–812, Detroit,
               MI, 1989.

ik   [986]   **Tecuci, G., and Kodratoff, Y.,** "Apprenticeship Learning in
               Imperfect Domain Theories," Machine Learning: An Artificial
               Intelligence Approach, Volume III, Morgan Kaufmann, San
               Mateo, CA, Kodratoff, Y. and Michalski, R.S. (Eds.), Ch. 19, 1990.

k   [987]   **Terpstra, P.P, and VanSomeren, M.W.,** "INDE: A System for
               Heuristic Knowledge Refinement," Proceedings of ECAI-88, pp.
               372–374, Munich, W.Germany, 1988.

n   [988]   **Tesauro, G.,** "Connectionist Learning of Expert Backgammon
               Evaluations," Proceedings of the 5th International Conference on
               Machine Learning, pp. 200–206, Ann Arbor, MI, 1988.

n   [989]   **Tesauro, G., and Sejnowski, T.J.,** "A Parallel Network that
               Learns to Play Backgammon," Artificial Intelligence, Vol. 39, pp.
               357–390, 1989.

ps   [990]   **Thagard, P., and Holyoak, K.,** "Discovering the Wave Theory of
               Sound: Inductive Inference in the Context of Problem Solving,"
               Proceedings of IJCAI-85, pp. 610–612, Los Angeles, CA, 1985.

ae   [991]   **Thagard, P., Cohen, D.M., and Holyoak, K.J.,** "Chemical
               Analogies: Two Kinds of Explanation," Proceedings of IJCAI-89,
               pp. 819–824, Detroit, MI, 1989.

kt   [992] Thanassas, D., "A Theory of Knowledge Discovery," Proceedings
             of IJCAI-89 Workshop on Knowledge Discovery in Databases, pp.
             345–357, Detroit, MI, 1989.

ks   [993] Thieme, S., "The Acquisition of Model-Knowledge for a
             Model-Driven Machine Learning Approach," Knowledge
             Representation and Organization in Machine Learning, Springer
             Verlag, K. Morik (Ed.), pp. 177–191, Berlin Heidelberg, 1989.

c   [994] Thompson, K., and Langley, P.W., "Incremental Concept
             Formation with Composite Objects," Proceedings of the 6th
             International Workshop on Machine Learning, pp. 371–372,
             Ithaca, NY, 1989.

et   [995] Thornton, C., "Hypercuboid-Formation Behaviour of Two
             Learning Algorithms," Proceedings of IJCAI-87, pp. 301–303,
             Milan, Italy, 1987.

k   [996] Tong, C., and Franklin, P., "Toward Automated Rational
             Reconstruction: A Case Study," Proceedings of the 6th
             International Workshop on Machine Learning, pp. 302–307,
             Ithaca, NY, 1989.

a   [997] Turner, R.M., "Organizing and Using Semantic Knowledge for
             Medical Diagnosis," Proceedings of the Case-Based Reasoning
             Workshop, pp. 435–446, 1988.

v   [998] Utgoff, P.E., "Machine Learning of Inductive Bias," Kluwer
             Academic, Hingham, MA, 1986.

v   [999] Utgoff, P.E., "Shift of Bias for Inductive Learning," Machine
             Learning: An Artificial Intelligence Approach, Volume II, Morgan
             Kaufmann, San Mateo, CA, R.S. Michalski, J.G. Carbonell and
             T.M. Mitchell (Eds.), pp. 107–148, 1986.

s   [1000] Utgoff, P.E., and Saxena, S., "Learning a Preference Predicate,"
             Proceedings of the 4th International Machine Learning Workshop,
             pp. 115–121, University of California, Irvine, 1987.

sv   [1001] Utgoff, P.E., "Perceptron Trees: A Case Study in Hybrid Concept
             Representations," Proceedings of AAAI-88, pp. 601–606, Saint
             Paul, MN, 1988.

s   [1002] Utgoff, P.E., "ID5: An Incremental ID3," Proceedings of the 5th
             International Conference on Machine Learning, pp. 107–120, Ann
             Arbor, MI, 1988.

x   [1003] Utgoff, P.E., and Saxena, S., "Obtaining Efficient Classifiers
             from Explanations," Proceedings of 1988 Symposium on
             Explanation-Based Learning, pp. 47–51, Stanford, 1988.

s   [1004] **Utgoff, P.E.,** "Improved Training via Incremental Learning," Proceedings of the 6th International Workshop on Machine Learning, pp. 362–365, Ithaca, NY, 1989.

s   [1005] **Utgoff, P.E.,** "Incremental Induction of Decision Trees," Machine Learning, Vol. 4, No. 2, 1989.

st   [1006] **Valiant, L.G.,** "Learning Disjunctions of Conjunctions," Proceedings of IJCAI-85, pp. 560–566, Los Angeles, CA, 1985.

nt   [1007] **Valiant, L.G.,** "Functionality in Neural Nets," Proceedings of AAAI-88, pp. 629–634, Saint Paul, MN, 1988.

nt   [1008] **Valiant, L.G.,** "Observations on Learning and Neural Nets," Proceedings of Office of Naval Research Workshop on Knowledge Acquisition, A.L. Meyrowitz (Ed.), Arlington, VA, 1989.

k   [1009] **Valtorta, M.,** "Automating Rule Strengths in Expert Systems," Proceedings of ECAI-88, pp. 369–371, Munich, W.Germany, 1988.

k   [1010] **Valtorta, M.,** "Some Results on the Complexity of Knowledge-Base Refinement," Proceedings of the 6th International Workshop on Machine Learning, pp. 326–331, Ithaca, NY, 1989.

ks   [1011] **VanDeVelde, W.,** "Explainable Knowledge Production," Proceedings of ECAI-86, pp. 8–22, Brighton, England, 1986.

kx   [1012] **VanDeVelde, W.,** "Learning Through Progressive Refinement," Proceedings of EWSL-88, pp. 211–226, Glasgow, Scotland, 1988.

g   [1013] **VanDeVelde, W.,** "IDL, or Taming the Multiplexer," Proceedings of EWSL-89, Montpellier, France, 1989.

tx   [1014] **VanHarmelen, F., and Bundy, A.,** "Explanation-Based Generalization = Partial Evaluation," Artificial Intelligence, Vol. 36, pp. 401–412, 1988.

ps   [1015] **VanLehn, K.,** "Learning One Subprocedure per Lesson," Artificial Intelligence, Vol. 31, pp. 1–40, 1987.

es   [1016] **VanLehn, K., and Ball, W.,** "A Version Space Approach to Learning Context-Free Grammars," Machine Learning, Vol. 2, No. 1, pp. 39–75, 1987.

d   [1017] **VanLehn, K., and Garlick, S.,** "CIRRUS: An Automated Protocol Analysis Tool," Proceedings of the 4th International Machine Learning Workshop, pp. 205–217, University of California, Irvine, 1987.

p   **[1018] VanLehn, K.,** "Discovering Problem Solving Strategies: What
        Humans Do and Machines Don't (Yet)," Proceedings of the 6th
        International Workshop on Machine Learning, pp. 215–217,
        Ithaca, NY, 1989.

t   **[1019] VanLehn, K.,** "Efficient Specialization of Relational Concepts,"
        Machine Learning, Vol. 4, No. 1, 1989.

ks   **[1020] VanSomeren, M.W.,** "Knowledge-Based Learning: Reducing the
        Description Space for Rule Learning," Proceedings of ECAI-86,
        pp. 1–7, Brighton, England, 1986.

t   **[1021] Vapnik, V.N.,** "Inductive Principles of the Search for Empirical
        Dependences (Method Based on Weak Convergence of Probability
        Measures)," Proceedings of the 1989 Workshop on Computational
        Learning Theory COLT '89, pp. 3–25, University of California,
        Santa Cruz, 1989.

t   **[1022] Velauthapillai, M.,** "Inductive Inference with Bounded Number
        of Mind Changes," Proceedings of the 1989 Workshop on
        Computational Learning Theory COLT '89, pp. 200–213,
        University of California, Santa Cruz, 1989.

t   **[1023] Vitter, J.S., and Lin, J.H.,** "Learning in Parallel," Proceedings of
        the 1988 Workshop on Computational Learning Theory COLT
        '88, pp. 106–124, MIT, 1988.

n   **[1024] Volper, D.J., and Hampson S.E.,** "Connectionistic Models of
        Boolean Category Representation," Biological Cybernetics, Vol.
        54, pp. 393–406, 1986.

as   **[1025] Vosniadou, S., and Ortony, A.,** "Similarity and Analogical
        Reasoning," Cambridge University Press, 1989.

as   **[1026] Vrain, C., and Lu, C.R.,** "An Analogical Method to Do
        Incremental Learning of Concepts," Proceedings of EWSL-88, pp.
        227–236, Glasgow, Scotland, 1988.

as   **[1027] Vrain, C., and Kodratoff, Y.,** "The Use of Analogy in
        Incremental SBL," Knowledge Representation and Organization
        in Machine Learning, Springer Verlag, K. Morik (Ed.), pp.
        231–246, Berlin Heidelberg, 1989.

x   **[1028] Vrain, C.,** "OGUST: A System that Learns Using Domain
        Properties Expressed as Theorems," Machine Learning: An
        Artificial Intelligence Approach, Volume III, Morgan Kaufmann,
        San Mateo, CA, Kodratoff, Y. and Michalski, R.S. (Eds.), Ch. 13,
        1990.

n   [1029] **Wasserman, P.D.,** "Neural Computing: Theory and Practice," Van
         Nostrand Reinhold, 1989.

v   [1030] **Watanabe, L., and Elio, R.,** "Guiding Constructive Induction for
         Incremental Learning from Examples," Proceedings of IJCAI-87,
         pp. 293–296, Milan, Italy, 1987.

n   [1031] **Watrous, R.L., Shastri, L., and Waibel, A.H.,** "Learned Phonetic
         Discrimination Using Connectionist Networks," Technical Report,
         Electrical Engineering Dept., University of Pennsylvania, 1986.

b   [1032] **Webber, B.L., and Nilsson, N.J.,** "Readings in Artificial
         Intelligence," Morgan Kaufmann, San Mateo, CA, 1981.

ps   [1033] **Wefald, E.H., and Russell, S.J.,** "Adaptive Learning of
         Decision-Theoretic Search Control Knowledge," Proceedings of
         the 6th International Workshop on Machine Learning, pp.
         408–411, Ithaca, NY, 1989.

k   [1034] **Weiss, S.M., Galen, R.S., and Tadepalli, P.V.,** "Optimizing the
         Predictive Value of Diagnostic Decision Rules," Proceedings of
         AAAI-87, pp. 521–526, Seattle, WA, 1987.

en   [1035] **Weiss, S.M., and Kapouleas, I.,** "An Empirical Comparison of
         Pattern Recognition, Neural Nets, and Machine Learning
         Classification Methods," Proceedings of IJCAI-89, pp. 781–787,
         Detroit, MI, 1989.

at   [1036] **Wellsch, K., and Jones, M.,** "Computational Analogy,"
         Proceedings of ECAI-86, pp. 153–162, Brighton, England, 1986.

s   [1037] **Werner, M.,** "A General Approach to the Use of Background
         Knowledge in a Numerical Induction Algorithm," Proceedings of
         the 3rd European Workshop on Knowledge Acquisition for
         Knowledge-Based Systems, pp. 420–436, 1989.

d   [1038] **Whitehall, B.L.,** "Substructure Discovery of Macro-Operators,"
         University of Illinois at Urbana-Champaign, Report of
         Coordinated Science Laboratory , No. UILU-ENG-88–2219, May,
         1988.

l   [1039] **Whitehead, S.D., and Ballard, D.H.,** "A Role for Anticipation in
         Reactive Systems that Learn," Proceedings of the 6th International
         Workshop on Machine Learning, pp. 354–357, Ithaca, NY, 1989.

i   [1040] **Widmer, G.,** "An Incremental Version of Bergadano & Giordana's
         Integrated Learning Strategy," Proceedings of EWSL-89,
         Montpellier, France, 1989.

i   [1041] **Widmer, G.,** "A Tight Integration of Deductive and Inductive Learning," Proceedings of the 6th International Workshop on Machine Learning, pp. 11–13, Morgan Kaufmann, 1989.

k   [1042] **Wilkins, D.C., and Buchanan, B.,** "On Debugging Rule Sets When Reasoning Under Uncertainty," Proceedings of AAAI-86, pp. 448–454, Philadelphia, PA, 1986.

k   [1043] **Wilkins, D.C., Clancey, W.J., and Buchanan, B.G.,** "An Overview of the Odysseus Learning Apprentice," Kluwer Academic Press, New York, NY, 1986.

k   [1044] **Wilkins, D.C.,** "Knowledge Base Refinement as Improving an Incorrect and Incomplete Domain Theory," Proceedings of AAAI-88, pp. 646–653, Saint Paul, MN, 1988.

k   [1045] **Wilkins, D.C., and Tan, K.W.,** "Knowledge Base Refinement as Improving an Incorrect, Inconsistent and Incomplete Domain Theory," Proceedings of the 6th International Workshop on Machine Learning, pp. 332–339, Ithaca, NY, 1989.

ik [1046] **Wilkins, D.C.,** "Knowledge Base Refinement Using Apprenticeship Learning," Machine Learning: An Artificial Intelligence Approach, Volume III, Morgan Kaufmann, San Mateo, CA, Kodratoff, Y. and Michalski, R.S. (Eds.), Ch. 18, 1990.

ks [1047] **Wille, R.,** "Knowledge Acquisition by Methods of Formal Concept Analysis," Proceedings of the Conference on Data Analysis, Learning Symbolic and Numeric Knowledge, pp. 365–380, INRIA, Antibes, 1989.

g   [1048] **Wilson, S.W.,** "Knowledge Growth in an Artificial Animal," Proceedings of the 1st International Conference on Genetic Algorithms, pp. 16–23, Pittsburgh, PA, 1985.

g   [1049] **Wilson, S.W,** "Classifier Systems and the Animat Problem," Machine Learning, Vol. 2, No. 3, pp. 199–228, 1987.

g   [1050] **Wilson, S.W.,** "Hierarchical Credit Allocation in a Classifier System," Proceedings of IJCAI-87, pp. 217–220, Milan, Italy, 1987.

g   [1051] **Wilson, S.W.,** "Quasi-Darwinian Learning in a Classifier System," Proceedings of the 4th International Machine Learning Workshop, pp. 59–65, University of California, Irvine, 1987.

b   [1052] **Winston, P.H.,** "Artificial Intelligence," Addison-Wesley, Reading, MA, 2, 1984.

s   [1053] **Winston, P.H.,** "Learning by Augmenting Rules and
         Accumulating Censors," Machine Learning: An Artificial
         Intelligence Approach, Volume II, Morgan Kaufmann, San Mateo,
         CA, R.S. Michalski, J.G. Carbonell and T.M. Mitchell (Eds.), pp.
         45–62, 1986.

e   [1054] **Wirth, J., and Catlett, J.,** "Experiments on the Costs and
         Benefits of Windowing in ID3," Proceedings of the 5th
         International Conference on Machine Learning, pp. 87–99, Ann
         Arbor, MI, 1988.

x   [1055] **Wirth, R.,** "Learning by Failure to Prove," Proceedings of
         EWSL-88, pp. 237–252, Glasgow, Scotland, 1988.

p   [1056] **Wirth, R.,** "Completing Logic Programs by Inverse Resolution,"
         Proceedings of EWSL-89, Montpellier, France, 1989.

n   [1057] **Wisniewski, E.J., and Anderson, J.A.,** "Some Interesting
         Properties of a Connectionist Inductive Learning System,"
         Proceedings of the 5th International Conference on Machine
         Learning, pp. 181–187, Ann Arbor, MI, 1988.

i   [1058] **Wogulis, J.,** "A Framework for Improving Efficiency and
         Accuracy," Proceedings of the 6th International Workshop on
         Machine Learning, pp. 78–80, Morgan Kaufmann, 1989.

v   [1059] **Wogulis, J., and Langley, P.W.,** "Improving Efficiency by
         Learning Intermediate Concepts," Proceedings of IJCAI-89, pp.
         657–662, Detroit, MI, 1989.

m   [1060] **Wolff, J.G.,** "Cognitive Development as Optimization,"
         Computational Models of Learning, Springer-Verlag, Berlin
         Heidelberg, L. Bolc (Ed.), pp. 161–205, 1987.

i   [1061] **Wollowski, M.,** "A Schema for an Integrated Learning System,"
         Proceedings of the 6th International Workshop on Machine
         Learning, pp. 87–89, Morgan Kaufmann, 1989.

s   [1062] **Wong, S.K.M., and Ziarko, W.,** "On Learning and Evaluation of
         Decision Rules in the Context of Rough Sets," Proceedings of the
         1st International Symposium on Methodologies for Intelligent
         Systems, pp. 308–324, Knoxville, TN, 1986.

v   [1063] **Woodfill, J.,** "Labor Saving New Distinctions," Proceedings of
         the 6th International Workshop on Machine Learning, pp.
         430–433, Ithaca, NY, 1989.

t   [1064] **Wright, K.,** "Identification of Unions of Languages Drawn from an Identifiable Class," Proceedings of the 1989 Workshop on Computational Learning Theory COLT '89, pp. 328–333, University of California, Santa Cruz, 1989.

dv   [1065] **Wrobel, S.,** "Automatic Representation Adjustment in an Observational Discovery System," Proceedings of EWSL-88, pp. 253–262, Glasgow, Scotland, 1988.

iksv [1066] **Wrobel, S.,** "Demand-Driven Concept Formation," Knowledge Representation and Organization in Machine Learning, Springer Verlag, K. Morik (Ed.), pp. 289–319, Berlin Heidelberg, 1989.

es   [1067] **Wu, Q., Suetens, P., Oosterline, A., and Cleynenbreugel, J.V.,** "Biomedical Pattern Classification using an Integrated Heuristic and Bayesian Approach," Proceedings of IJCAI–89 Workshop on Knowledge Discovery in Databases, pp. 358–368, Detroit, MI, 1989.

d   [1068] **Wu, Y.H.,** "Reduction: A Practical Mechanism of Searching for Regularity in Data," Proceedings of the 5th International Conference on Machine Learning, pp. 374–380, Ann Arbor, MI, 1988.

d   [1069] **Wu, Y.H., and Wang, S.,** "Discovering Knowledge from Observational Data," Proceedings of IJCAI-89 Workshop on Knowledge Discovery in Databases, pp. 369–377, Detroit, MI, 1989.

d   [1070] **Yager, R.R.,** "On Linguistic Summaries of Data," Proceedings of IJCAI-89 Workshop on Knowledge Discovery in Databases, pp. 378–389, Detroit, MI, 1989.

t   [1071] **Yager, R.R., and Ford, K.M.,** "Participatory Learning: A Constructivist Model," Proceedings of the 6th International Workshop on Machine Learning, pp. 420–423, Ithaca, NY, 1989.

px   [1072] **Yamada, S., and Tsuji, S.,** "Selective Learning Macro-Operators with Perfect Causality," Proceedings of IJCAI-89, pp. 603–608, Detroit, MI, 1989.

cp   [1073] **Yang, H., and Fisher, D.H.,** "Conceptual Clustering of Mean-Ends Plans," Proceedings of the 6th International Workshop on Machine Learning, pp. 232–234, Ithaca, NY, 1989.

es   [1074] **Yokomori, T.,** "Inductive Inference of Context-free Languages—Context-free Expression Method," Proceedings of IJCAI–87, pp. 283–286, Milan, Italy, 1987.

ci   [1075] **Yoo, J.P., and Fisher, D.H.,** "Conceptual Clustering of
        Explanations," Proceedings of the 6th International Workshop on
        Machine Learning, pp. 8–10, Morgan Kaufmann, 1989.

kp   [1076] **Yost, G.R., and Newell, A.,** "A Problem Space Approach to
        Expert System Specification," Proceedings of IJCAI-89, pp.
        621–627, Detroit, MI, 1989.

b   [1077] **Zaremba, J.,** "Overview of Machine Learning," Bulletin of Polish
        Academy of Sciences, 1988.

m   [1078] **Zernik, U.,** "Language Acquisition: Learning a Hierarchy of
        Phrases," Proceedings of IJCAI-87, pp. 125–132, Milan, Italy,
        1987.

m   [1079] **Zernik, U.,** "Learning Idioms-With and Without Explanation,"
        Proceedings of IJCAI-87, pp. 133–136, Milan, Italy, 1987.

m   [1080] **Zernik, U.,** "How Do Machine-Learning Paradigms Fare in
        Language Acquisition?," Proceedings of the 4th International
        Machine Learning Workshop, pp. 191–197, University of
        California, Irvine, 1987.

cr   [1081] **Zernik, U.,** "Lexicon Acquisition: Learning from Corpus by
        Capitalizing on Lexical Categories," Proceedings of IJCAI-89, pp.
        1556–1562, Detroit, MI, 1989.

ln   [1082] **Zhang, B., and Grant, E.,** "A Neural Net Approach to
        Autonomous Machine Learning of Pole Balancing," Proceedings
        of EWSL-89, Montpellier, France, 1989.

i   [1083] **Zhang, J., and Michalski, R.S.,** "A Preference Criterion in
        Constructive Learning: A Discussion of Basic Issues,"
        Proceedings of the 6th International Workshop on Machine
        Learning, pp. 17–19, Ithaca, NY, 1989.

s   [1084] **Zhang, J., and Michalski, R.S.,** "Rule Optimization via
        SG-TRUNC Method," Proceedings of EWSL-89, Montpellier,
        France, 1989.

g   [1085] **Zhou, H.H.,** "Classifier System with Long-term Memory in
        Machine Learning," Proceedings of the 1st International
        Conference on Genetic Algorithms, pp. 178–187, Pittsburgh, PA,
        1985.

g   [1086] **Zhou, H.H., and Grefenstette, J.J.,** "Induction of Finite
        Automata by Genetic Algorithms," Proceedings of the IEEE
        International Conference on Systems, Man, and Cybernetics, pp.
        170–174, Atlanta, GA, 1986.

g   [1087] **Zhou, H.H.,** "CSM: A Genetic Classifier System with Memory for Learning by Analogy," Thesis, Computer Science Dept., Vanderbilt University, 1987.

ag   [1088] **Zhou, H.H., Grefenstette, J.J.,** "Learning by Analogy in Genetic Classifier Systems," Proceedings of the 3rd International Conference on Genetic Algorithms and their Applications, pp. 291– 297, Fairfax, VA, 1989.

d   [1089] **Ziarko, W.,** "A Technique for Discovering and Analysis of Cause-Effect Relationships in Empirical Data," Proceedings of IJCAI-89 Workshop on Knowledge Discovery in Databases, pp. 390–397, Detroit, MI, 1989.

x   [1090] **Zweben, M., and Chase, M.P.,** "Improving Operationality With Approximate Heuristics," Proceedings of 1988 Symposium on Explanation-Based Learning, pp. 100–106, Stanford, 1988.

d   [1091] **Zytkow, J.M., and Simon, H.A.,** "A Theory of Historical Discovery: The Construction of Componential Models," Machine Learning, Vol. 1, No. 1, pp. 107–136, 1986.

d   [1092] **Zytkow, J.M.,** "Combining Many Searches in the FAHRENHEIT Discovery System," Proceedings of the 4th International Machine Learning Workshop, pp. 281–287, University of California, Irvine, 1987.

d   [1093] **Zytkow, J.M., and Simon, H.A.,** "Normative Systems of Discovery and Logic of Search," Synthese, Vol. 74, pp. 65–90, January, 1988.

d   [1094] **Zytkow, J.M.,** "Overcoming FAHRENHEIT's Experimentation Habit: Discovery System Tackles a Database Assignment," Proceedings of IJCAI-89 Workshop on Knowledge Discovery in Databases, pp. 398–406, Detroit, MI, 1989.

dt   [1095] **Zytkow, J.M., and Jankowski, A.,** "Hierarchical Control and Heuristics in Multisearch Systems," Proceedings of the 4th International Symposium on Methodologies for Intelligent Systems, pp. 86–93, Charlotte, NC, 1989.

ABOUT THE AUTHORS

Ray Bareiss is an assistant professor of computer science at Vanderbilt University. He received his PhD from the University of Texas at Austin in 1988. His dissertation research, under the supervision of Dr. Bruce Porter, developed the Protos system for exemplar-based learning and classification. Current research interests include case-based knowledge representations for learning, performing, and teaching diagnostic problem solving. Dr. Bareiss's current address is Computer Science Department, Vanderbilt University, Box 115 Station B, Nashville TN 37235.

Francesco Bergadano obtained his degree in computer science from the University of Torino, Italy. He is currently a PhD candidate at the same university. His research interests are mainly related to machine learning and include inductive inference, logic and induction, explanation-based methods, pattern recognition, and computational learning theory. His current address is Dipartimento di Informatica, Università di Torino, C. Svizzera 185, 10149 Torino, Italy.

Pavel B. Brazdil completed his postgraduate studies at the department of artificial intelligence in Edinburgh in the area of machine learning. He completed the PhD degree in 1981 and afterward moved to Portugal to lecture at the University of Porto. Brazdil is one of the founding members of the Laboratory LIACC (Laboratory for AI and Computer Science) at the University of Porto. His current address is Faculdade de Economia, Rue Dr. R. Frias, 4200 Porto, Portugal.

Jaime G. Carbonell is professor of computer science and director of the Center for machine translation at Carnegie Mellon University. He received Bs degrees in physics and in mathematics from MIT in 1975, and MS and PhD degrees in computer science from Yale University in 1976 and 1978, respectively. Dr. Carbonell has authored about 130 technical papers and has edited or authored several books, four of them in machine learning. He is executive editor of the international journal, *Machine Learning*, and serves on several editorial boards, including that of *Artificial Intelligence*. He has also served as chairman of SIGART (1983–1985) and is a founder and director of Carnegie Group, Inc. Dr. Carbonell's research interests span several areas of AI, including machine learning, natural language processing, planning and problem solving, knowledge-based machine translation, analogical reasoning, knowledge representation, and very large knowledge bases. His current address is Computer Science Department, Carnegie Mellon University, Pittsburgh PA 15213.

Gerald F. DeJong received his PhD in 1979 from Yale University. After postdoctoral work at Yale, he accepted a faculty position at the University of Illinois where he is an associate professor in the computer science department. DeJong's research interests span machine learning, natural language processing, robotics, and problem solving. He is the designer of FRUMP, a robust natural language processing system. Dr. DeJong is also one of the developers of explanation-based learning. His current address is the Beckman Institute, University of Illinois, 405 N. Mathews Dr., Urbana IL 61801.

Kenneth A. De Jong is an associate professor of computer science and associate director of the Center for Artificial Intelligence at George Mason University in Fairfax, Virginia. He received his PhD degree in computer science from the University of Michigan in 1975. Since then he has been a faculty member in the department of computer science at the University of Pittsburgh and a visiting scientist at the Navy Center for Applied Research in Artificial Intelligence. His research interests include adaptive systems, machine learning, expert systems, and knowledge representation. He is an active member of the genetic algorithms research community and is responsible for many of the workshops and conferences on genetic algorithms. He is currently directing a number of research projects involving the use of genetic algorithms on NP-hard problems and to learn task programs in domains such as robotics, diagnosis, navigation, and game playing. Dr. de Jong is also interested in experience-based learning in which systems must improve their performance while actually performing the desired tasks in enivironments not directly under their control or the control of a benevolent teacher. His current address is Center for Artificial Intelligence, George Mason University, Fairfax VA 22030.

Brian C. Falkenhainer is a member of the research staff at Xerox Palo Alto Research Center. He received his BS in engineering physics from Santa Clara University (1982) and his MS (1985) and PhD (1988) in computer science from the University of Illinois, Urbana-Champaign. His dissertation explored an analogical approach to explanation in PHINEAS, a program that proposes causal explanations for observed physical phenomena. His current research focuses on computational models of analogy, learning, and automated modeling of physical systems. Dr. Falkenhainer has authored or coauthored several publications in the areas of scientific discovery, analogical reasoning, compositional modeling, and probabilistic truth maintenance. His current address is Xerox PARC, Palo Alto CA 94304.

Jean-Gabriel Ganascia is professor of computer science at Paris VI University. He received is MA in computer science at Paris VI University (1980). He then moved to LRI, Paris-Sud University, where he received a *Doctorat d'Ingénieur* (1983) and a *Doctorat d'Etat* (1987). His research interests include modeling expert knowledge in domains with uncertain data and inexact reasoning, generalization applied to machine learning, and automatic construction of knowledge bases from sets of examples. His current address is LAFORIA, Université Pierre-et-Marie-Curie, Tour 45-46, 4 Pl. Jussieu, F-75230 Paris Cedex 05, France.

Yolanda Gil is a doctoral candidate in the department of computer science at Carnegie Mellon University. She graduated from the Computer Science School at the Polytechnical University of Madrid (Spain) in 1985, where she presented a thesis on the concurrent simulation of logic circuits. After teaching in the University for a year, she joined Carnegie Mellon University. Since then, she has worked with Dr. Jaime Carbonell. Her research interests include learning in the context of problem solving and learning in reactive environments. Her current address is School of Computer Science, Carnegie Mellon University, Pittsburgh PA 15213.

Attilio Giordana obtained his doctoral degree in electrical engineering and is currently a professor at the computer science department of the University of Torino, Italy. He initially worked in the domain of computer architecture and pattern recognition, moving later to AI. He is currently interested in machine learning and is involved in the development of systems integrating explanation-based learning and similarity-based learning in domain with imperfect theory. His current address is Dipartimento di Informatica, Università di Torino, C. Svizzera 185, 10149 Torino, Italy.

Stephen José Hanson is group leader of the Learning and Knowledge Acquisition research group, Siemens Research Center, and a visiting scientist in the Cognitive Science Laboratory at Princeton University. He received his PhD in experimental and quantitative psychology from Arizona State University, Tempe. He spent two years at Indiana University, Bloomington as an assistant professor and then joined Bell Laboratories as a member of the technical staff in 1982. In 1984, he joined Bellcore in the AI and Information Science research group. In 1989, he joined Siemens Corporate Research in Princeton, New Jersey. He has done modeling and research in human-computer interaction, programming productivity, and learning complex skills. He has specialized in learning theory and studied and published papers on earning in humans, animals, and machines. His interests include conceptual clustering, connectionist models, and general adaptive processes. His current address is Siemens Corporate Research, 55 College Rd. E., Princeton NJ 08542.

David Haussler is assistant professor of computer and information sciences at the University of California at Santa Cruz. He received his MS in applied mathematics from California Polytechnic State University, San Luis Obispo in 1979 and his PhD from the University of Colorado, Boulder in 1982. His research interests are in theoretical foundations of machine learning and in developing and analyzing empirical learning algorithms. His current address is Department of Computer Science and Information Sciences, University of California, Santa Cruz CA 95064.

Geoffrey Hinton is professor of computer science and psychology at the University of Toronto and a fellow of the Canadian Institute for Advanced Research. He received his BA in psychology from the University of Edinburgh in 1978. He is interested in ways of using connectionist networks for learning, memory, perception, symbol processing, and motor control. He coedited *Parallel Models of Associative Memory* and was a major contributor to *Parallel Distributed Processing: Explorations in the Microstructure of Cognition*. His current address is Department of Computer Science, University of Toronto, 10 Kings College Road, Toronto M5S 1A4 Canada.

Haym Hirsh is assistant professor of computer science at Rutgers University. He received his BS degree (1983) in mathematics/computer science from UCLA, and his MS (1985) and PhD (1989) degrees in computer science from Stanford University. His current machine learning research interests include combining empirical and explanation-based approaches to concept learning and learning from inconsistent data. His current address is Department of Computer Science, Rutgers University, New Brunswick NJ 08903.

Robert C. Holte is Assistant Professor in the computer science department of the University of Ottawa. He received degrees in computer science (BSc, 1977; MSc, 1980) from the University of Manitoba, Canada, and a PhD (1988) from Brunel University, U.K. His work investigates representation issues in machine learning. He was a co-organizer of the workshop on Change of Representation and Inductive Bias held at Philips Laboratories (Briarcliff, New York) in June 1988. From January 1988 through April 1989 he was a visiting scholar in the computer sciences department of the University of Texas, Austin. His current address is Computer Science Department, University of Ottawa, Ottawa, Ontario K1N 6N5 Canada.

Alex Kass studied AI at Yale University under the direction of Professor Roger Schank. He received an AB from Brown University in 1983 and a MS from Yale in 1985. He expects to receive his PhD from Yale in 1990. His PhD dissertation is on the process of adapting stored explanations to new situations. His research interests include machine learning, case-based reasoning, story understanding, hypothesis formation, creativity, and computer-based teaching. Kass is currently working with Professor Schank at the Institute for the Learning Sciences at Northwestern University. His current address is Institute for Learning Sciences, Northwestern University, 1890 Maple St., Evanston IL 60208.

Yves Kodratoff is director of research at the French *Centre National de la Recherche Scientifique* at Paris-Sud University and an adjunct professor at the Center for Artificial Intelligence, George Mason University. He has played an important role in the organization of the European machine learning scientific community by participating very actively in three ESPRIT projects: ALPES on logic programming environments, in which some place has been found for inductive inference; INSTIL, which integrates his group's results on the use of theorem provers in machine learning; Michalski's star methodology and Quinlan's techniques of inductive construction of decision tree; and the Machine Learning Toolbox, a $7000-funded machine learning project, which began in March 1989. He has been the coordinator of the European project COST-13, and he started several European meetings, such as the International Meeting on Advances in Learning (Les Arcs, July 1986), the first European Working Session on Learning (EWSL 86, Orsay), and the European Summer School on Machine Learning (ES2ML, Les Arcs July 1988). He recently authored *Introduction to Machine Learning*, published by Pitman, and he is starting a new series published by Pitman, *Advanced Tutorials in AI*. His research interests cover all kinds of inductive inference systems, including program synthesis from specifications. His address in France is Equipe Inference et Apprentissage, UA 410 of the CNRS, Laboratoire de Recherche en Informatique, Université de Paris-Sud, Bldg. 490, F-91405 Orsay, France.

Michael Lebowitz is a vice president in the Analytical Proprietary Unit of Morgan Stanley and Company. The work described in his chapter was carried out while he was an associate professor at the department of computer science at Columbia University. He received his SB (1975) from the Massachusetts Institute of Technology and his MS (1978) and PhD (1980) from Yale University. His research at Columbia involved a variety of areas in natural language processing and machine learning. His UNIMEM learning program has been applied to a wide range of domains including census data, software evaluations, and congressional voting records. His current address is Morgan Stanley and Company, 1251 Avenue of the Americas, 19th floor, New York NY 10020.

Sridhar Mahadevan is a doctoral candidate in the department of computer science at Rutgers University. He received his MTech in electrical engineering (1983) from the Indian Institute of Technology, Kanpur. He is research assistant in the LEAP learning apprentice project at Rutgers University. He was a visiting student in the department of computer science at Carnegie Mellon University from 1986 to 1988. His dissertation research is concerned with theoretical and empirical studies of explanation-based learning methods in the presence of incomplete domain theories. He is also interested in applying formal models of learnability to study knowledge-intensive learning methods. He has written several papers on these topics. His current address is Department of Computer Science, Rutgers University, New Brunswick NJ 08903.

Ryszard S. Michalski is Planning Research Corporation Professor of Computer Science, and director of the Center for Artificial Intelligence at George Mason University in Fairfax, Virginia. He studied at the Cracow and Warsaw Technical Universities in Poland, received his MS from the Leningrad Polytechnical Institute in the USSR, and his PhD from the University of Silesia in Poland in 1969. He was a professor of computer science and, more recently, director of the AI Laboratory at the University of Illinois, Urbana-Champaign from 1970 until 1988, when he moved to George Mason University and established there the Center for Artificial Intelligence. Dr. Michalski has made numerous contributions to artificial intelligence and cognitive science, among them: the algorithm AQ, which is the basis of many inductive learning programs; the variable-valued logic; a theory of inductive inference; the initiation of research on conceptual clustering and constructive induction; the development of variable precision logic (with P.H. Winston); a theory of human plausible reasoning (with A. Collins); and the idea of two-tiered representation of imprecise concepts. He coedited *Machine Learning: An Artificial Intelligence Approach, Volume I* and *Volume II*, cofounded the *Machine Learning* journal, and co-organized several international machine learning workshops/conferences. He held visiting appointments at MIT, CMU, University of Wisconsin, University of London, University of Paris, University of Torino, and University of Mons. He has lectured worldwide and authored or coauthored over 150 papers in areas of his interest. His current research areas include methods of learning, inference and discovery, cognitive models of learning and reasoning, knowlege acqusition for expert systems, intelligent autonomous robots, and various AI applications. His current address is Center for Artificial Intelligence, George Mason University, Fairfax VA 22030. E-mail: michalski@gmuvax2.gmu.edu.

Tom M. Mitchell is professor of computer science at Carnegie Mellon University. He earned his BS degree (1973) from MIT and his MS (1975) and PhD (1978) degrees from Stanford University. He taught in the computer science department at Rutgers University from 1978 until moving to Carnegie Mellon in 1986. He is the recipient of the 1983 IJCAI Computers and Thought Award in recognition of his research in machine learning, and of a 1984 NSF Presidential Young Investigator Award. Mitchell is coeditor of *Machine Learning: An Artificial Intelligence Approach, Volume I* and *Volume II*. His current research focuses on developing robots that learn and on general architectures for problem solving and learning. His current address is Department of Computer Science, Carnegie Mellon University, Pittsburgh PA 15213.

Michael J. Pazzani is assistant professor of computer science at the University of California, Irvine. His research has focused on acquiring efficient diagnostic heuristics through failure-driven, explanation-based learning and on integrating empirical and explanation-based learning methods. He is the author of OCCAM, a system that uses empirical methods to acquire the background knowledge needed for explanation-based learning. He received the BS and MS degrees in computer science from the University of Connecticut. In 1988, he received a PhD degree in computer science from the University of California, Los Angeles. Prior to joining the faculty at the University of California, Irvine, Dr. Pazzani was a member of the technical staff at the Aerospace Corporation and a group leader at the Mitre Corporation. His current address is Department of Information and Computer Science, University of California, Irvine CA 92717.

Bruce Porter is an assistant professor of computer science at the University of Texas, Austin. He received his PhD from the University of California, Irvine (1984). His dissertation research with Dr. Dennis Kibler developed the PET system for learning operator semantics and control heuristics. His research with Ray Bareiss at the University of Texas includes exemplar-based learning and classification in Protos. His current research is on knowledge integration: "learning at the fringes" of a structured knowledge base. Other research activities include studying explanation structures, and their use, in legal reasoning and tutoring. Dr. Porter's current address is Computer Sciences Department, University of Texas, Austin, Austin TX 78712.

Armand Prieditis is a doctoral candidate in the department of computer science at Rutgers University. He received his BA (1983) from the University of Minnesota and his MS (1987) from Rutgers University. He is currently finishing his thesis on discovering effective admissable heuristics by abstraction and speedup. His other research interests include machine learning applications in software development, logic programming, and AI applications in molecular biology. He has published several papers in machine learning and is the editor of *Analogica* (Pitman, 1988). His current address is Department of Computer Science, Rutgers University, New Brunswick NJ 08903.

J. Ross Quinlan is professor of computer science and head of the Basser Department of Computer Science in the University of Sydney. He obtained his BSc from the University of Sydney in 1965 and his PhD from the newly formed computer science group at the University of Washington in 1968. Professor Quinlan has held appointments at Carnegie Mellon University, the University of Sydney, the Rand Corporation, the New South Wales Institute of Technology, and the Massachusetts Institute of Technology. His research in AI dates back to 1965; current interests include empirical learning techniques, plausible reasoning, and expert systems. His current address is Basser Department of Computer Science, University of Sydney, Sydney, Australia 2006.

Larry A. Rendell, after completing his BSc in physics at the University of Toronto and his PhD in computer science at the University of Waterloo, spent three years as assistant professor of computing and information science at the University of Guelph. He moved to the U.S. in 1984. Currently at the University of Illinois, Rendell is associate professor of computer science and electrical and computer engineering, at the Beckman Institute for Advanced Science and Technology. Working primarily in machine learning, he has published over 40 papers in books, conference proceedings, and journals. Rendell's early work developed empirical techniques to learn evaluation functions, and integrated pattern recognition methods with artificial intelligence approaches. His recent research focuses on feature extraction and contructive induction, particularly ways to merge knowledge with evidence. He serves as an editor for *Computational Intelligence*. His current address is University of Illinois, Beckman Institute, 405 N. Mathews Ave., Urbana IL 61801.

Ronald L. Rivest is professor of computer science and associate director of MIT's Laboratory for Computer Science, and head of that laboratory's Theory Group. He received a BA in mathematics from Yale University in 1969 and a PhD in computer science from Stanford University in 1974. He joined the faculty of MIT in 1974. He has worked in the areas of algorithms, combinatorics, cryptography, machine learning, and VLSI design automation. He is a member of ACM, a director of the International Association of Cryptologic Research, and a founder of RSA Data Security. His current address is MIT Laboratory for Computer Science, 545 Technology Square, Cambridge MA 02139.

Roger Schank directs the Institute for Learning at Northwestern University, where he is also the John Evans Professor of electrical engineering and computer science, psychology, and education. Previously he was chairman of the computer science department at Yale University and director of the Yale Artificial Intelligence Project. In addition, he was assistant professor of linguistics and computer science at Stanford University. Schank holds a PhD in linguistics from the University of Texas, Austin. He is the founder of several businesses, including Compu-Teach, Inc., an educational software company, and Cognitive Systems, Inc., a company specializing in natural language processing. Schank also founded the Cognitive Science Society and serves on the board of editors of several publications. His current address is Institute for Learning Sciences, Northwestern University, 1890 Maple St., Evanston IL 60208.

Robert E. Schapire is currently pursuing his PhD at MIT's Laboratory for Computer Science. He received his ScB in mathematics and computer science from Brown University in 1986, and his SM in electrical engineering and computer science from MIT in 1988. His primary research interests focus on the theoretical aspects of machine learning. His current address is MIT Laboratory for Computer Science, 545 Technology Square, Cambridge MA 02139.

Jude Shavlik is assistant professor in computer sciences at the University of Wisconsin, Madison. He received BS degrees in electrical engineering and in biology from the Massachusetts Institute of Technology in 1979. In 1980 he received an MS in biophysics from Yale University. After working for the Mitre Corporation for several years, he received his PhD in computer science from the University of Illinois in 1988. His research interests include learning iterative and recursive concepts, combining symbolical and connectionist learning, and applying machine learning to problems in molecular biology. His current address is Computer Sciences Department, University of Wisconsin, 1210 W. Dayton Street, Madison WI 53706.

Pawel A. Stefanski is a doctoral candidate in the department of computer science and a research assistant in the Center for Artificial Intelligence at George Mason University. He received his MS in Computer Science in 1985 from Warsaw University, Poland. His interests include machine learning, knowledge representation, and automated reasoning. His dissertation deals with the development of multistrategy, constructive learning systems and their applications. His current address is 4400 University Drive, Department of Computer Science, George Mason University, Fairfax VA 22030. E-mail: stefan@gmuvax2.gmu.edu.

Louis Steinberg is associate professor of computer science at Rutgers University. He earned his BS degree (1972) from the University of Illinois, Urbana-Champaign and his PhD (1980) from Stanford University. He is the principal investigator of the Rutgers AI/Design Group. His current research focuses on AI approaches to the design of useful artifacts and on learning in the context of design. His current address is Department of Computer Science, Rutgers University, New Brunswick NJ 08903.

Robert E. Stepp received his AB (1970) and MS (1971) degrees from the University of Nebraska, Lincoln and his PhD (1984) degree in computer science at the University of Illinois. Dr. Stepp has authored or coauthored many publications in the areas of conceptual clustering and machine learning with structured objects. His interests include machine learning, conceptual data analysis, knowledge acquisition and discovery, and knowledge-based systems for learning. His current address is University of Illinois, Beckman Institute for Advanced Science and Technology, 405 N. Mathews St., Urbana IL 61801.

Gheorghe Tecuci is researcher at the Research Institute for Computers and Informatics in Bucharest. He received his MS degree in computer science from the Polytechnic Institute of Bucharest in 1979, and his PhD degree in computer science from the Université de Paris-Sud and from the Polytechnic Institute of Bucharest in 1988. His current research focuses on machine learning, integrated learning paradigms, analogy, expert systems with learning capabilities, domain modeling, and scientific discovery. His address is Research Institute for Computers and Informatics, 71316, Bd. Miciurin 8-10, Sector 1, Bucharest, Rumania. As of the fall of 1990, he will be visiting professor at the Center for Artificial Intelligence, George Mason University, Fairfax VA 22030.

Christel Vrain is assistant professor (*Maître de Conférences*) in computer science at the University of Orléans. She studied mathematics at the *Ecole Normale Supérieure* where she obtained an *Agrégation* in mathematics. She has a *Doctorat de 3ème Cycle* (1987), from Paris-Sud University, Orsay. Her research focuses on the use of background knowledge for concepts learning and involves the development of a generalization tool, called OGUST. She is currently studying the use of analogy in order to allow such a system to become incremental. Her current address is LIFO, Dep. Math et Info., Rue de Chartres, BP6759 F-45067 Orléans Cedex 2, France.

Craig C. Wier is currently program manager in the Advanced Product Division at Mentor Graphics Corp. He received his PhD in psychology from Washington University in St. Louis. The research reported in this book was done while he was an associate professor of communication disorders, University of Texas, Austin, and on research leave in the Artificial Intelligence Laboratory, Department of Computer Sciences also at the University of Texas, Austin. His research interests are in hardware and software components of the computer–user interface, and in knowledge engineering to support both human- and machine-based decision making. His current address is Advanced Products Division, Mentor Graphics Corporation, 8500 Creekside Pl., Beaverton OR 97005.

David Wilkins is assistant professor of computer science at the University of Illinois. He received his PhD from the University of Michigan in 1987. His dissertation research, carried out at the Knowledge Systems Lab at Stanford University, developed the ODYSSEUS apprenticeship learning program. His current research focuses on how different methods of organization, representation, and inference for large knowledge-based systems faciliate machine learning and automatic program debugging. He is currently coediting a book, *Readings in Knowledge Acquisition and Learning*, with Bruce Buchanan. His current address is University of Illinois, Department of Computer Science, 405 N. Mathews Ave., Urbana IL 61801.

Janusz Wnek is a doctoral candidate in the department of computer science and a research assistant in the Center for Artificial Intelligence at George Mason University. He received his MS in Computer Science in 1983 from Jagiellonian University, Cracow, Poland. His interests include machine learning and robotics. His dissertation explores methods for applying machine learning to robot navigation. His current address is 4400 University Drive, Department of Computer Science, George Mason University, Fairfax VA 22030.

Jianping Zhang is a doctoral candidate in the department of computer science at University of Illinois, Urbana-Champaign and a research assistant in Artificial Intelligence Center at George Mason University. He received his BS in Computer Science in 1982 from Wuhan University, China. His interests include machine learning and plausible reasoning. His dissertation explores methods for learning flexible concepts. His current address is 4400 University Drive, Department of Computer Science, George Mason University, Fairfax VA 22030.

AUTHOR INDEX

SUBJECT INDEX